REGULATORY LAW AND POLICY

CASES AND MATERIALS
Third Edition

SIDNEY A. SHAPIRO

Rounds Professor of Law
University of Kansas

JOSEPH P. TOMAIN

Dean and Nippert Professor of Law
University of Cincinnati

™ LexisNexis™
Matthew Bender®

Library of Congress Cataloging-in-Publication Data

Shapiro, Sidney A., 1947-
    Regulatory law and policy : cases and materials / Sidney A. Shapiro,
    Joseph P. Tomain.--3rd ed.
        p.   cm. —
    Includes bibliographical references and index.
    ISBN 0–8205–5758–7
        1. Administrative procedure--United States--Cases. 2. Delegated legislation--United
    States--Cases. 3. Administrative agencies--United States--Decidion making--Case
    studies. I. Tomain, Joseph P., 1948-II. Title.
    KF5411.S53 2003
    342.73'066--dc21   2003047742

ISBN#: 0820557587

This publication is designed to provide accurate and authoritative information in regard to the subject matter covered. It is sold with the understanding that the publisher is not engaged in rendering legal, accounting, or other professional services. If legal advice or other expert assistance is required, the services of a competent professional should be sought.

LexisNexis, the knowledge burst logo, and Michie are trademarks of Reed Elsevier Properties Inc, used under license. Matthew Bender is a registered trademark of Matthew Bender Properties Inc.

Editorial Offices
744 Broad Street, Newark, NJ 07102 (973) 820-2000
201 Mission St., San Francisco, CA 94105-1831 (415) 908-3200
701 East Water Street, Charlottesville, VA 22902-7587 (804) 972-7600
www.lexis.com

(Pub.03098)

Dedicated to
Justice Stephen Breyer
whose scholarship on administrative law
and government regulation inspired this book.

PREFACE TO THE THIRD EDITION

Regulatory Law and Policy explores regulatory decision making, but unlike the traditional course in administrative law, it focuses on the substance of government regulation. The focus has two parts. You will study the justifications for regulation and the methods or "tools" that are used to implement the regulation. When you are finished, your understanding of the basic concepts that underlie regulatory law and policy should enable you to pursue specific areas of regulation more effectively.

Regulatory law and practice involves special lawyering skills, and those skills are addressed in this book. Like lawyers that practice in other disciplines, regulatory lawyers must be able to read and understand statutes and cases. These establish the authority of an agency to regulate and specify the limits of its authority. But those who are involved in a regulatory practice must also have an understanding of the policy and political aspects of administrative regulation. Moreover, this need does not differ when a lawyer's focus is a state or local agency instead of a federal one.

Although policy, politics, and law are three elements of administrative regulation, only the third element—the legal limits of regulation—is covered in most other law school courses. Our aim is to permit you to consider the missing elements—how policy and politics affect regulatory decisions—and how these elements are related to the legal authority of agencies. For this reason, although we do not neglect the study of the legal limits of regulation, we emphasize policy analysis and politics. Because of this emphasis, this course is a complement to other courses about regulation, such as environmental law, securities law, and labor law that you might take or have taken.

Our goal is to teach you "regulatory analysis," which functions similarly to case analysis, uncovers the principles and arguments behind the justifications for government intervention in markets, and reveals the strengths and weaknesses of the regulatory tools employed to correct market defects. Regulatory analysis is a way of understanding government regulation by identifying and analyzing patterns of regulatory activity that cut across industries and markets, just as case analysis cuts across various areas of private law. Regulatory analysis also helps explain the limits and benefits of regulatory tools. Finally, in the situation of deregulation and regulatory reform, regulatory analysis can explicate the limits of regulation itself.

The 3rd edition explores these themes relying on the prior edition but with updated material to reflect important developments, including the fate of the Telecommunications Act of 1996, the collapse of the airline industry, new farm subsidy legislation, the fate of the 1996 welfare reform legislation, and the 2001 No Child Left Behind Act, reforming federal educational support. We also track the significant new Supreme Court cases, especially involving takings law and commercial free speech.

Part I of the casebook explores these ideas by providing different perspectives on government regulation. Chapter 1 presents a short history of government regulation and a case study to illustrate the entire regulatory process. Chapter 2 introduces the topics of market analysis and policy analysis by introducing you to the reasons and justifications for government regulation. Chapter 3 explores the politics of regulation, particularly as it relates to public participation before regulatory agencies. In summary, Part I examines the contextual background of the regulatory state.

Parts II and III are organized according to the various justifications for government regulation. In each chapter, we examine a specific justification for government regulation and one or more regulatory programs that were enacted in response to that justification. For each regulatory program, the materials address two policy issues: Is the justification for regulation defensible, and is the government utilizing the appropriate regulatory method or tool? The materials also raise legal and political issues, although the extent of this coverage varies depending on the regulatory program being studied.

We have considered the writing of this casebook as a conversation about the nature of government and its potential to improve or hinder the development of society. We hope that our efforts will not only educate you about the practice of regulatory law, but that it will also challenge you to contemplate the role of government in making this a better society.

Dean Joseph Tomain would like to thank his research assistants, Dan Dodd, Joshua Nolan, and Emily Shults for their invaluable help in the preparation of this edition.

Sidney A. Shapiro
Joseph P. Tomain

Lawrence, Kansas
Cincinnati, Ohio
March 1, 2003

SUMMARY TABLE OF CONTENTS

TABLE OF CONTENTS

PART II
ECONOMIC REGULATION

PART III
SOCIAL REGULATION

Part I
Introduction

Chapter 1

THE REGULATORY PROCESS

Regulatory Law and Policy is about why and how the government engages in regulation. The making of regulatory policy in American government is influenced by politics, policy considerations and legal constraints. In this chapter, we will introduce you to these concepts and suggest how they interrelate. We start the chapter by explaining the different perspectives that can be used to explain and understand regulation. We then examine the history of regulation in this country, in which you will see the interplay of these factors. We conclude the chapter with a problem that asks you about the interrelated roles of politics, policy and law in influencing government regulation.

A. REGULATORY PERSPECTIVES

Regulation can be studied from at least four perspectives: policy, politics, institutional and historical.[1] The first three perspectives are not mutually exclusive. All of them may help us to understand and explain regulatory outcomes, although the insight that one gains from each perspective may be different and even contradictory to another perspective. For the student of regulation, these perspectives are like viewing the Grand Canyon from different locations. Depending on where the observer is standing, the canyon may appear different. One's perception of the canyon may vary depending on whether the viewer is on one rim or the other of the canyon or is viewing the canyon from the bottom or on the way down.

A "policy" perspective explains regulation as the outcome of policy arguments which explain and justify the regulation that occurred. This perspective assumes legislators and regulators weigh the justifications for and against regulatory intervention and determine whether there are objective reasons for the government to act. These decisionmakers then choose the method of implementing regulatory policy that they judge to be the most effective. In short, this perspective seeks to understand regulatory government as the product of policy deliberation and judgment.

As noted earlier, regulatory lawyers are generally involved with this perspective. Attorneys representing private clients make policy arguments to agencies and legislatures why the public interest requires some specific action or non-action. Lawyers who work for agencies and in legislatures must evaluate these arguments and advise their clients about the best way to proceed. One of the goals of this book is to equip you to make these types of arguments. Although the lawyer's job is to make policy arguments, he or she must also be aware of the political and institutional settings in which

---

[1] *See* R. BALDWIN & M. CAVE, UNDERSTANDING REGULATION: THEORY, STRATEGY & PRACTICE ch. 3 (1999) (explaining the policy, politics and institutional perspectives).

mandatory penalty statute
NJDEP v. NJDEC example?

*citizen concern***

regulation occurs in order to give his or her client strategic advice and to tailor policy arguments to the political and institutional settings in which the lawyer is operating.

A political perspective explains regulation as the outcome of political considerations. It focuses on what groups seek the adoption of new regulatory programs and how such programs might benefit those groups. If there are groups which both support and oppose regulation, this perspective seeks to understand which group prevailed and why, or if there is a compromise, what political factors produced the compromise. In short, this perspective seeks to understand regulatory government as the product of political power and influence.[2]

An institutional perspective seeks to understand how governmental institutions influence regulatory outcomes. This perspective considers how legal rules impact regulatory outcomes, and the role of lawyers in producing those outcomes. Regulatory lawyers, of course, must be aware of the legal authority of a regulator. This perspective, however, is also interested in how the institutional makeup of regulatory agencies affects policy. For example, does it matter whether a regulator is elected or appointed? Does it matter whether government officials have tenure or can be fired by the president or a governor?[3] In short, this perspective explains regulatory outcomes as the product of legal norms and bureaucratic behavior.

B. A HISTORY OF REGULATION

The history of regulation reveals the influence of politics, policy and institutions in regulation and how these influences have changed over time. There are time periods in our history in which there has been a significant expansion of regulatory activity and periods in which there has been a retrenchment or reform of regulation. In the following brief history of regulation, we identify five periods of regulatory expansion, which we describe as the Mecantilist, Populist, Progressive, New Deal and the Great Society/Public Interest eras. We also identify two periods of regulatory retrenchment and reform, which we describe as the Laissez-faire and Regulatory Reform eras.

What the reader will notice about the history of regulation is its ebb and flow. There are periods of regulatory expansion, typically followed by periods in which regulatory expansion slows or stops, or there is a reduction in the amount of regulation. At the end of this section, we will consider the role of politics, policy and institutions in promoting this pattern. We will consider some possible explanations for these regulatory cycles.

1. THE MERCANTILIST ERA

Government intervention in economic affairs was the custom in the American colonies and in the early years of the country. The historian Arthur

---

[2] *See* A. OGUS, REGULATION: LEGAL FORM AND ECONOMIC THEORY ch 3–4 (1994) (contrasting the policy and political perspectives of regulation).

[3] *See* J. MARCH & J. OLSEN, REDISCOVERING INSTITUTIONS: THE ORGANIZATIONAL BASIS OF POLITICS (1989) (proposing that organizational behavior, including laws and bureaucracy, has an essential impact on policy and policy decisionmaking).

Schlesinger, Jr. explains, "In the seventeenth century, such intervention was essential to survival in a society of limited resources. In the eighteenth century colonial resentments of British Mercantilist restrictions led to the American revolution; but independence tempted the revolutionaries in part because it promised them the opportunity of establishing a mercantilist regime of their own."[4] The government was called "mercantilist" because it assumed the responsibility for moving the country from a primarily agrarian society to a commercial and industrial state. The states and, to a lesser extent, the federal government financed badly needed internal improvements, such as canals, roads, railroads, and bridges, and used the power of eminent domain to secure rights-of-way, and even materials, for the previous projects. Later, the federal government opened up the West by first offering grants-in-aid in the form of free land to the railroads, and then free land to settlers who agreed to homestead the land.

Although the government played a central role in the development of the early American economy, its role was not as large or encompassing as it is today. Lawrence Friedman explains, "A century before Adam Smith, the proprietors, squires, and magistrates of America certainly did not believe that government was best that governed the least. But the desire to rule, and rule broadly, was tempered by modest means, in taxes and in staff, that rulers had at their command."[5]

The limited government that did exist was organized like it was in England, which meant that local courts, country and city, had most of the power to run the economy. These courts performed all three functions of government, writing laws, administering and enforcing them. There was no systematic relationship between different levels of government and regulatory matters were assigned to some institution as the need arose.[6] Until the revolution, local government was subject to English control, but there was little direct supervision of local regulation.

While the government supported economic expansion, the role of the government was subject to considerable debate and dispute, particularly at the federal level. Alexander Hamilton and his followers saw the national government as a "grand instrument by which to transform a pastoral economy into a booming industrial nation."[7] By comparison, Thomas Jefferson "saw America as a paradise of small farms, a rural Arcadia with every freeholder secure under his own vine and fig tree."[8] As an adherent to the classical "liberal" political philosophy associated with John Locke, Jefferson feared that the national government could be dominated by a few groups who would promote their own self-interest, and therefore favored a more limited national government.

---

[4] A. SCHLESINGER, JR., THE CYCLES OF AMERICAN HISTORY 220 (1986).

[5] L. FRIEDMAN, A HISTORY OF AMERICAN LAW 77 (2d ed. 1985).

[6] Id. at 77–78.

[7] SCHLESINGER, supra note 4, at 220.

[8] Id. at 221.

2. THE LAISSEZ-FAIRE ERA

In the nineteenth century, the country slowly repudiated the mercantilist state on the basis of a laissez-faire political philosophy. The changeover reflected two developments. The economy had entered a period of self-sustaining growth. At the same time, popular faith in government intervention was discredited by the ineffectual policies of the Jackson administration and general graft and corruption in government. Supporters of a laissez-faire approach cited the writings of Thomas Jefferson, who, as stated earlier, saw America as a nation of small property owners free of governmental interference, of Adam Smith, who suggested that unfettered individualism produced the greatest economic good, and of Charles Darwin and Herbert Spenser, whose writings encouraged the belief that survival of the fittest through economic competition was necessary for civilization to progress.

Although nineteenth century opponents of government regulation were quick to embrace a laissez-faire political philosophy, they also did not hesitate to accept governmental assistance when it was helpful. Schlesinger notes:

> Most of the worshipers at the shrine of undefined private enterprise found the new cult entirely compatible with governmental assistance to business. The protective tariff flourished. The courts favored capitalists over trade unions, creditors over debtors, railroads over farmers and consumers. . . . The American version of laissez-faire meant aid from the state without interference from the state.[9]

Lawrence Friedman concurs. While "[g]overnment, by habit and design, kept its heavy hands off the economy," there is a more "complex reality." It is "certainly true that, for much of the century, opinion leaders and policy were both strongly supportive of business, productivity and growth," but government "reflecting its powerful constituencies, did what it could to help the economy grow; where this required subsidy or intervention, no overriding theory held government back."[10]

The policy rationale for this activity was that government assistance and support was necessary to stimulate economic growth in a fledgling economy. For example, government investment in roads, canals and even corporations was considered necessary because of a lack of capital in the country, which prevented or inhibited private development. As Friedman explains, "Policy aimed—in William Hurst's phrase—at the release of creative energy; and that meant economic energy, enterprise energy."[11]

Most of the governmental activity that assisted business development was located in the states. The states aided economic development by granting permission for business to operate, which often gave the business exclusive rights to engage in particular activities, contributed money to business activities, and used their "lawmaking power to make rules and give instructions to legal institutions, in ways that would help the entrepreneur."[12] Most

---

[9] SCHLESINGER, *supra* note 4, at 234.

[10] FRIEDMAN, *supra* note 5, at 177.

[11] *Id.* at 177.

[12] *Id.* at 182.

of this activity took place in transportation and finance, but other areas of the economy were promoted, depending on a state's individual situation.

Although the focus of governmental activity was on economic development, states continued earlier regulatory policies aimed at protecting consumers, such as laws to regulate weights and measures and to prescribe standards used to grade commodities and laws intended to protect the public health. As earlier, however, these efforts were constrained by the lack of financial resources and staff. Friedman elaborates, "Two pillars of the modern state were missing: a strong tax base and a trained civil service. Without these two, and perhaps without a firmer grip on economic information, the state could not hope to master and control behavior in markets."[13] Thus, typically administrative tasks were given to existing office holders, rather than create new positions. Moreover, the "law let private citizens enforce what regulation there was. If no one brought a law suit, or complained to the district attorney about some violation, nothing was done."[14]

The administration of regulation changed with the adoption of the federal and state constitutions when government took on the familiar tripartite form that we still see today with a legislature, executive and court system. The federal and state constitutions were intended to be limitations on the powers of the government and, after *Marbury v. Madison*, 5 U.S. 137 (1803), the courts assumed the role of determining the scope of these limitations. Most of these decisions reflected the tenor of the times. For example, the United States Supreme Court gave a broad interpretation of the contract clause,[15] which forbids states from impairing the obligation of contract, which supported a laissez-faire philosophy:

> The state was duty-bound to support a broad, free market; to do so, business had to rely on the stability of arrangements legally made, at least in the short and middle run. The contract clause guaranteed precisely that kind of stability, or tried to. . . . There would be no *ex post facto* tampering with bargains, for whatever reason.[16]

3. THE POPULIST ERA

As the United States moved from an agrarian society to an industrial one, it entered a period of labor and small business unrest associated with the accumulation and concentration of wealth. The first prominent manifestation of these problems was the Populist movement in the 1870s, which sought state regulation of arbitrary and unreasonable rate practices by the railroads. Robert Rabin explains:

> . . . [V]irtually every group affected by the railroads favored government regulation in one form or another. . . . Even in the heyday of free enterprise, no substantial economic interest involved in the railroad controversy showed any particular ideological commitment to

---

[13] *Id*. at 185.

[14] *Id*. at 187.

[15] U.S. Const. art. I, § 10.

[16] FRIEDMAN, *supra* note 5, at 276.

unrestricted private commercial activity. Indeed, if there was a consensus among the groups, it was that an unregulated market constituted an invitation to chaos. What each group sought first and foremost was freedom from perceived discriminatory practices. Farmers, merchants, grain buyers, railroad magnates, and all the others, desired above everything else a form of government intervention that would eliminate 'arbitrary' rate practices.[17]

Regulatory activity started in the states and took different forms. "Controls ran the gamut from a 'weak' commission system featuring a single elected commissioner with limited investigatory powers to a 'strong' system headed by a multimember commission, appointed for a term and vested with ratemaking authority backed by substantial penalties."[18]

In *Munn v. Illinois*, 94 U.S. 113 (1876), the Supreme Court upheld the constitutionality of an Illinois statute fixing the rate charged by grain elevators and warehouses under the state's police power. Referring to English law, which had upheld the regulation of private property that is "affected with the public interest," the Court interpreted the Constitution as likewise permitting regulation because when "one devotes his property to a use in which the public has an interest, he, in effect, grants to the public an interest in that use, and must submit to be controlled by the public for the common good, to the extent of the interest that he has created." *Munn* was addressed to the power of the states to regulate business, but it provided the rationale for the Court's support of regulation by the federal government under the Commerce Clause of the Constitution,[19] which authorizes Congress to regulate "Commerce. . . among the several States."[20] The Court, however, became an impetus for Congress' creation of the Interstate Commerce Commission (ICC), created in 1887, to regulate the railroads. In *Wabash, St. Louis & Pacific Railroad v. Illinois*, 118 U.S. 557 (1886), it invalidated a state statute on the ground that a state could not regulate shipping that was part of interstate commerce, which meant that no state could regulate local traffic that eventually ended up outside of its borders.

The ICC had limited success in carrying out its mission to hear complaints about railroad practices and to undertake investigations on its own initiative. President Grover Cleveland appointed Thomas M. Cooley, as the ICC's first chairman, who was a former judge of the Michigan Supreme Court and an influential advocate of a laissez-faire political philosophy. The Commission also suffered from the legislative compromises responsible for its creation, which limited its authority, and from adverse court decisions, which limited its power.[21] Professor Rabin explains how the Supreme Court hobbled the ICC:

> If the first political impulse to create a federal regulatory system was weak and ambivalent, the initial response of the Court was strong and

---

[17] Rabin, *Federal Regulation In Historical Perspective*, 38 STAN. L. REV. 1189, 1199 (1986).

[18] *Id.* at 1203.

[19] *See* Nebbia v. New York, 219 U.S. 502 (1934).

[20] U.S. Const. art. I, § 8.

[21] K. HALL, THE MAGIC MIRROR: LAW IN AMERICAN HISTORY 205 (1989).

hostile. The Court did not doubt the legislative power to prescribe rates, but it did seriously mistrust the administrative capacity to adjudge rates fairly . . . and as a consequence [it reviewed] rate determinations de novo while denying the ICC authority to establish rates itself. Similarly, . . . [t]he notion that a regulatory commission might stitch together the ambiguities scattered throughout the statute into a coherent (competition-restraining) pattern was entirely foreign to Populist era judicial thought. Through the vehicle of statutory interpretation, the Court was able to limit the plenary authority of the ICC to regulate private activity without questioning its right to exist. Agencies might police the market, but only so long as the final authority remained the courts. . . .[22]

The Commission became more effective in the Progressive Era, when Congress enhanced its oversight and enforcement powers.

Despite its initial lackluster record, the ICC is significant because, as Kermit Hall notes, it "provided the building block upon which the administrative state of the twentieth century subsequently rose."[23] For one thing, it constituted a shift in the location of regulation from the states to the federal government that would accelerate over time. For another, it constituted a shift from the previous focus of government, which was the promotion of business activity. In Professor Rabin's terminology, the government shifted from "promotional" regulation to "policing model of regulation."[24] Kermit Hall, explains:

> The Populist party, which began as social and mutual-aid societies known as the Grange, by the late 1880s and 1890s had a distinctly political form and a platform that aimed to assist farmers (black and white), laborers, and in some places people with small business. . . .
>
> Populists urged government to switch its role from distribution to regulation and administration. Government was encouraged to pursue an active public policy of improving the conditions under which citizens lived.[25]

4. THE PROGRESSIVE ERA

After the ICC was established, public agitation shifted to labor unrest and industrial concentration, provoking new government efforts to control the industrial economy. The transformation of the country from an agrarian society to an industrial one generated the support for a greater role for government. Lawrence Friedman explains:

> In a society of mass markets, mass production and giant enterprises, the individual shrinks into relative insignificance. What she eats and wears is made in some distant factory; there is no *personal* control over safety, over quality. . . . Moreover, the great aggregations–in

---

[22] RABIN, *supra* note 17, at 1215.

[23] HALL, *supra* note 21, at 205–06.

[24] RABIN, *supra* note 17, at 1192.

[25] HALL, *supra* note 21, at 195.

business, for example—themselves exercise more and more power, and visibly so. To the general public, it seems as if the only source of control is that system called law.[26]

The battle for additional regulation was led by a group of religious and social reformers, known as the Progressives, who directed their efforts at more effective policing of business trusts, unscrupulous industries, and corrupt politicians. The Progressives saw science and technology, and ultimately bureaucracy, as the answer to the rampant excesses of the marketplace. In the manner of science, they sought to categorize the problems of public policy and sought to create regulatory agencies as role-specific, problem-solving institutions. They believed that "if problems were investigated only neutrally and empirically, rather than from an a priori perspective, the factual knowledge gained might well suggest desirable public policies."[27] In other words, the Progressives looked to expertise as a solution to restrain politics and the market conditions that politics had produced. They "hoped that administratively organized 'communities' of highly trained, objective professionals could stand in to restrain the politics of interest."[28]

The Progressives were aided in the battle to control industrial activity by muckraking journalists and regulatory crusaders who had a knack of calling public attention to the dangers posed by unregulated business. In 1905, for example, Upton Sinclair published his famous novel, *The Jungle*, which exposed in nauseating detail the unsavory conditions in the meat packing industry. After reading the book, Theodore Roosevelt appointed his own team of investigators, who supported Sinclair's "thinly disguised" fictional account of the risks posed by the packing houses to employees and consumers.[29] Harvey Wiley, head of the Bureau of Chemistry in the Department of Agriculture, "galvanized trade groups, testified before congressional committees, published monographs, organized publicity efforts, and generally devoted himself unstintingly to the passage of legislation aimed at providing accurate information about the ingredients and risks of food additives and drugs.[30]

In response to Progressive agitation, Congress passed the Sherman Antitrust Act in 1890, the Food and Drug Act, the Meat Inspection Act, and Hepburn Act, which strengthened the ICC, in 1906; the Federal Trade Commission Act in 1917; the Federal Power Act and the Radio Act in 1920, and the Air Commerce Act in 1926. This legislation shared two important traits. First, this legislation accelerated the transfer of regulatory authority from the states to the federal government. Second, the responsibility for policing business passed from the courts to the administrative agencies. Professor Friedman regards these trends as politically inevitable. The courts

---

[26] FRIEDMAN, *supra* note 5, at 440.

[27] W. NELSON, THE ROOTS OF AMERICAN BUREAUCRACY (1830-1900) 111 (1982);

[28] Schwartz, *Book Review*, 97 HARV. L. REV. 815, 820 (1984); *see* T. MCGRAW, PROPHETS OF REGULATION: CHARLES FRANCIS ADAMS, LOUIS D. BRANDEIS, JAMES M. LANDIS AND ALFRED E. KAHN 80–142 (1984); R. CRUNDEN, MINISTERS OF REFORM: THE PROGRESSIVES ACHIEVEMENT IN AMERICAN CIVILIZATION (1889-1920) 163–66 (1982); HALL, *supra* note 21, at 203; Rabin, *supra* note 17, at 1218.

[29] Rabin, *supra* note 17, at 1226.

[30] *Id.* at 1226–27.

"were simply not good regulators. They were passive and untrained . . . and not geared to the task of overseeing enterprise." Moreover, "in an age of steel rails and telegraphs, town and county authorities were equally futile and ineffective." The "cure was at first, statewide controls," but when "the states could not meet the demands of their constituents, these constituents embarked on federal adventure."[31]

Although state and federal legislators reacted positively to the public's demand for more effective regulation than the courts could, or would, provide, the judiciary was generally hostile to the federal regulation during the Progressive era, but not unrelentingly so. Robert Rabin explains the attitude of the United States Supreme Court:

> While the Court may have been out of touch with the temper of the times, it appears to have been realistic about the limits of its own power. As in the Populist era, the Court evidenced a greater attachment to the sanctity of property rights than did the popular branches of government. But, as the same time, it recognized that the propriety of regulating competitive trade practices that were generally perceived to be "excessive" was beyond question. The ICC was an established institution. Antitrust legislation was an accepted fact. . . . Given this backdrop, the Court could hardly question the legitimacy of economic legislation per se.[32]

Thus, while the Court significantly limited the regulatory powers of the Food and Drug Administration (FDA) and the Federal Trade Commission (FTC), the "ICC was treated in quite a different fashion," which Rabin attributes to the fact that, after two decades of legislation that reacted to hostile court decisions, "Congress had finally gotten across the message that the agency was to have plenary power in policing unfair competitive practices within its bailiwick."[33] Professor Rabin concludes, "In sum, it is surely inaccurate to characterize the Supreme Court of the Progressive era as a steadfast advocate of *laissez-faire*. . . . The justices pressed their predilections for limited controls on the market as far as seemed rhetorically defensible in dealing with a particular regulatory agency or state regulatory scheme, and no further."[34] Kermit Hall offers a similar assessment:

> The industrial world was a reality, and judges gave far broader discretion to legislatures than historians have usually recognized. . . . But the judiciary clung to the notion that they had a special responsibility to protect traditional economic rights and, with the help of counsel and law writers such as Cooley and Tiedeman, they fashioned doctrines substantive due process and freedom of contract. These doctrines were judicial expressions of the laissez-faire mentality that pervaded, but never completely controlled, American social and economic thought between the Civil War and World War I. The judiciary before the Great Depression of the 1930s only gradually and

---

[31] FRIEDMAN, *supra* note 5, at 441.

[32] Rabin, *supra* note 17, at 1235.

[33] *Id.*

[34] *Id.* at 1236.

incompletely recognized the breadth of social and economic change that swirled about it.[35]

As the previous paragraph indicates, the courts employed two approaches to limiting the power of the government to regulate business practices. One strategy was to interpret statutes in as narrow a manner as possible. This was the strategy that the Supreme Court employed regarding the FDA and the FTC. In *United States v. Johnson*, 221 U.S. 488 (1911), for example, the Court construed FDA's authority as limited to regulating only statements concerning the ingredients of a drug and not statements concerning a drug's curative properties, despite statutory language strongly suggesting that FDA had authority to regulate both types of statements. Similarly, in *FTC v. Gratz*, 253 U.S. 421 (1920), the Court limited the FTC to policing trade practices that were recognized as illegal under common law, even though Congress created the FTC because of dissatisfaction with the scope of the court's regulatory authority under the common law.

The other strategy was to strike down legislation as being unconstitutional. In *Hammer v. Dagenhardt*, 247 U.S. 251 (1918), for example, the Court struck down federal legislation that prohibited interstate commerce in products made by workers under 14 years of age, finding that manufacturing was a purely local activity beyond Congress' authority to control as interstate commerce. Similarly, the Court struck down a state statute limiting the maximum number of hours that a baker could work to sixty per week (and ten per day) in *Lochner v. New York*, 198 U.S. 45 (1905), holding that a state's interference with the freedom to contract violated the Fourteenth Amendment. *Lochner* is the most famous (or infamous) of a number of decisions employing substantive due process to strike down regulatory legislation. Prior to the Civil War, the courts construed the Fifth Amendment of the Constitution, which guarantees that no person can be "deprived of life, liberty or property, without due process of law,"[36] and similar provisions of state constitutions as providing procedural protections guaranteeing that a person was entitled to a hearing before adverse government action. After the Civil War, the courts added a substantive component finding that there "existed an irreducible sum of rights that vested with the individual and with which the government could not arbitrarily interfere."[37] Using this doctrine, *Lochner* reserved the power to determine whether legislation was "fair, reasonable, and appropriate exercise of the police power of the State," and "not an unreasonable, unnecessary and arbitrary interference with the right of the individual to his personal liberty. . . ."

As mentioned earlier, the courts followed the lead of legal theorists, such as Thomas Cooley, who "insisted that government should not use its power to improve the condition of one social group at the expense of another."[38] They objected to such legislation because it restricted liberty and threatened the property of the rich and middle classes, thereby undermining their wealth and

---

[35] HALL, *supra* note 21, at 246.

[36] U.S. Const. amend. 5.

[37] HALL, *supra* note 21, at 232.

[38] *Id.* at 226.

the nation's economic prosperity. In *Lochner*, however, Justice Holmes famously objected that no particular economic philosophy was written into the Constitution, and that it was up to the legislature, not the courts, to determine public policy. "The Fourteenth Amendment," he observed, "does not enact Mr. Hebert's Social Statics"; it "is not intended to employ a particular economic theory, whether paternalism and the organic relation of the citizen to the State or *laissez-faire*."

5. THE NEW DEAL ERA

The New Deal expanded the policing functions of the federal government started in the Populist and Progressive Eras, but it also returned the government to promotional forms of regulation that assisted in economic development. Some of these initiatives, like the creation of the National Labor Relations Board, the Securities and Exchange Commission, and bank regulatory agencies, addressed business practices that contributed to the country's economic troubles. Others, like the National Industrial Recovery Act (NIRA) and the Agricultural Adjustment Act (AAA), created an infrastructure for economic recovery. Still others, like the Social Security Act, the Civilian Conservation Corps and the Works Progress Administration, protected individuals from the unemployment and poverty that sapped consumer demand and contributed to the continuation of the depression.

The different types of programs adopted in the New Deal reflected a policy disagreement in the Roosevelt administration concerning how best to address the deep depression in which the nation found itself.[39] The expansion of policing activity reflected a distrust of large businesses that emerged in the Populist and Progressive eras. Those favoring this approach believed that the cause of the Depression was rigid prices that were set and maintained by business monopolies. The return to government promotion of the economy reflected a belief that economic prosperity required government planning, which would replace the destructive competition that had caused the depression with coordination of business production and pricing. Those favoring this approach cited government planning during World War I as a model for what needed to be done. During World War I, the government fostered cooperative agreements among businesses in order to facilitate war production and control domestic prices. The NIRA and the AAA, mentioned above, were based on this approach. Both acts sought to address the depression by rationalizing production and marketing through trade associations, standardization boards, and loose cartels. Legislation creating the Social Security Act, the Civilian Conservation Corps and the Works Progress Administration reflected a third approach towards ending the depression. These programs sought to rescue the economy through direct stimulation of demand rather than government planning which coordinated economic activity.

From the perspective of today's highly regulated society, it is difficult to understand the social and constitutional threat the New Deal posed for many people. First, although there had been regulation of private markets since

---

[39] *See* J. HURTGEN, THE DIVIDED MIND OF AMERICAN LIBERALISM ch. 2 (2002) (describing the difference in viewpoints); Rabin, *supra* note 17, at 1243–53 (same).

before the American Revolution, the New Deal constituted an unprecedented increase in governmental activity. Second, the New Deal was premised on the belief that the capitalistic market system was fundamentally flawed, which was a dramatic change from earlier times. Prior to the New Deal, administrative law and government regulation were dominated by what has been referred to as a "common-law baseline." The common law of property, torts, and contracts provided the government with its substantive regulatory principles. The regulatory principles that emerged were wedded to laissez-faire thinking, individual autonomy, private arrangements, market transactions, and judge-made rights. In other words, government was a passive actor in the market and existed to let individuals transact as freely as possible without government interference.[40] Franklin Roosevelt's New Deal dramatically transformed this common law thinking. No longer were private market arrangements the *sine qua non* of government. Rather, government itself, politics and all, was recognized as the architect of markets. To correct the economic dislocation of the Great Depression, and the severe ills of rapid industrialization before it, government became the dominant active player in the market. The New Deal hope was that, through an expert, specialized bureaucratic machinery, government could bring about economic stability and increase social welfare by promoting economic efficiency, redistributing resources, reducing or eliminating socioeconomic subordination, and protecting future generations.

The New Deal was also a significant departure from the Progressive and Populist eras. Professor Rabin explains:

> In historical perspective, the New Deal appears as a distinct break from the past. The regulatory initiatives of the Populist and Progressive eras were largely discrete and limited measures . . . aimed largely at particularized fields of activity in which vigorous competition led to sharp market practices. Pre-New Deal regulatory initiatives rested upon the common assumption that minor government policing could ensure a smoothly functioning market. But the Depression put to rest this constrained view of national power. Even the more traditional regulatory aspects of the New Deal conceived of government activity as a permanent bulwark against deep-rooted structural shortcomings in the market economy.[41]

Further, New Deal agencies violated such cherished constitutional concepts as separation of powers (because of the combination of functions), due process (because administrative adjudication was more informal than its judicial counterpart), and political accountability (because the President was prohibited by legislation from removing many of the administrators in the new agencies).[42] New Dealers responded that traditional concepts of administrative procedure and law were counterproductive and outmoded. As "Progressives," they believed that science and expertise, and ultimately bureaucracy,

---

[40] C. SUNSTEIN, AFTER THE RIGHTS REVOLUTION: RECONCEIVING THE REGULATORY STATE 1–24, 230 (1990).

[41] Rabin, *supra* note 17, at 1252–53.

[42] The analysis in this and the next paragraph is drawn from Shapiro, *A Delegation Theory of the APA*, 10 ADMIN. L.J. 89,97–98 (1996).

was necessary to address the country's economic woes. They argued that traditional procedures would not only slow the government's capacity to act, but that such limitations were less necessary if government was composed of highly trained objective professionals.

The fusillade of substantive criticisms launched by New Deal critics made little impression on voters still reeling from the worst depression in the history of the country. But, as economic conditions slowly improved, the momentum for procedural reform picked up steam. In 1939, Congress passed the Walter-Logan Bill, which was based on an American Bar Association (ABA) proposal. Denounced by opponents as so rigid to cause a crippling of the administrative process, the bill was vetoed by President Roosevelt. In 1947, Congress passed the Administrative Procedure Act, which has been in effect ever since without substantial amendment of its terms. The Act was a compromise in the sense that Congress rejected both the procedural straight jacket favored by the New Deal's critics and the level of procedural informality favored by its supporters. Moreover, while Congress required judicial review of agency policy decisions, it also instructed the courts to review the merits of an agency's policy decision under a scope of review of whether the decision is "arbitrary and capricious."[43] In other legislation, Congress has sometimes required that an agency have "substantial evidence" for a policy decision. Under either standard, however, the Supreme Court has recognized that the judiciary is not to substitute its own policy views for those of the agency. Agency policy decisions are to be confirmed as long as they are "reasonable."[44]

Initially, the Supreme Court resisted the New Deal, in particular by declaring unconstitutional the NIRA[45] and AAA,[46] which as noted earlier, were suppose to create an infrastructure for economic recovery. The former act was declared unconstitutional because Congress failed to provide sufficient limitations on the power of the President to act, as required by the Constitution,[47] and the latter because Congress lacked the power under the interstate commerce clause to regulate agricultural production. The Court also sought to reign in state responses to the depression by reasserting substantive due process checks on state regulatory efforts. Suddenly, however the Court reversed course.[48] The Court upheld state legislation establishing a minimum wage for women,[49] although it had declared unconstitutional a similar law just one year earlier.[50] It then upheld the National Labor Relations Act, adopting a broad definition of the commerce clause, which was as expansive as the Court's early interpretation was restrictive.[51] In a series of cases that

---

[43] 5 U.S.C. § 706(2) (1988).

[44] *See* PIERCE, SHAPIRO, & VERKUIL, ADMINISTRATIVE LAW AND PROCESS § 7.3 (3d ed. 1999).

[45] Schechter Poulty Company v. United States, 295 U.S. 495 (1935).

[46] United States v. Butler, 297 U.S. 1 (1936).

[47] The Constitution requires that all "legislative powers shall be vested in a Congress," U.S. Const. art. I, § 1, which the Court determined was violated because Congress failed to establish sufficient limitations on the President's power to act under the Act.

[48] These events are recounted in Rabin, *supra* note 17, at 1259–62.

[49] West Coast Hotel Co. v. Parrish, 300 U.S. 379 (1937).

[50] *See* Morehead v. Tipaldo, 298 U.S. 587 (1936).

[51] *See* NLRB v. Jones & Laughlin, 301 U.S. 1 (1937).

followed, the Court "systematically rejected every tenant of the conservative majority that had so recently provoked a constitutional crisis in its challenge to the New Deal conception of regulatory power."[52]

In hindsight, the Supreme Court's invalidation of the NIRA and the AAA turned out to be beneficial to the Roosevelt administration. The NIRA turned about to be a "dismal failure," because it encouraged corporations to establish business cartels which did little to benefit consumers or the economy, AAA "proved to be most beneficial to the relatively prosperous farmers who needed it the least."[53] At the time, however, it promoted a constitutional crisis because it appeared that the Court was prepared to consign the rest of the New Deal to the same unconstitutional fate. Faced with this potential fate, President Roosevelt proposed to increase the number of justices on the Supreme Court, which would have enabled him to create a pro-New Deal majority. When Congress held hearings on the plan, even ardent New Dealers were aghast at the President's audacious plan to remake the judiciary for political reasons. Whether it was this threat or some other influence, "the two swing votes on the Court (Justices Roberts and Hughes), joined the liberals, providing the basis for the derisive contemporary comment that . . . their actions were a 'switch in time that saved nine.'"[54]

To the extent that *Lochner* and substantive due process epitomized the pre-New Deal era of constitutional law, *United States v. Carolene Products Co.*, 304 U.S. 144 (1938), illustrates the Court's new deference to legislative decisions about regulation. In upholding legislation that prohibited the shipment in interstate commerce of milk compounded with any fat or oil so as to resemble milk or cream, the Court announced a new test for the constitutionality of regulation under the due process clause. According to the Court, "regulatory legislation affecting ordinary commercial transactions is not be pronounced unconstitutional unless in light of the facts made known or generally assumed it is of such a character as to preclude the assumption that it rests on some rational basis within the knowledge and experience of the legislators." In other words, "where the legislative judgment is drawn into question," a courts inquiry "must be restricted to the issue whether any state of facts either known or which could reasonable be assumed affords support for it." Since it was at least "debatable whether commerce in filled milk should be left unregulated, or in some measure restricted, or wholly prohibited, the Court declared that the "decision was for Congress," and "neither the finding of a court arrived at by weighing the evidence, nor the verdict of a jury, can be substituted for it."

6. THE GREAT SOCIETY AND PUBLIC INTEREST ERAS

The next wave of regulation extended governmental assistance to the poor and addressed racial discrimination. Building on the efforts of President Kennedy, Lyndon Johnson's "Great Society" program—and its central thrust, the "War on Poverty"—recognized that minorities and the poor were the

[52] Rabin, *supra* note 17, at 1260.

[53] *Id.* at 1248.

[54] HALL, *supra* note 21, at 282.

subject of continuing educational, employment, and other types of discrimination and that, despite sustained national prosperity, many citizens (minority
and non-minority) lived under conditions of poverty. Regulatory schemes were
established to channel additional resources to the poor, and eliminate discrimination in housing, education, voting, public accommodations, and the workplace.[55]

In the 1970s, reformers turned their attention to environmental degradation, unsafe products and dangerous workplaces.[56] The problem, as the
reformers defined it, was the government's inability to prevent corporations
and others from despoiling the environment, injuring consumers and workers,
discriminating against racial minorities, and committing other social ills.
These claims were buttressed, as in the Progressive Era, by books and news
stories indicating the social harm that had occurred. In the early 1960s, for
example, Rachel Carson's book, *Silent Spring*, called attention to the environmental destruction caused by the widespread use of pesticides, while Barry
Commoner's book, *The Closing Circle*, warned that, unchecked, the use of
"counter-ecological technologies" could result in environmental ruin. At about
the same time, the public learned that modern medicines could injure, as well
as heal, after it was revealed that Frances Kelsey, an employee of the Food
and Drug Administration (FDA), almost single-handedly kept thalidomide
from being sold in the United States. The issue of automobile safety came to
the public's attention after General Motors admitted in a congressional
hearing that it had hired private investigators to follow Ralph Nader in order
to discredit his book *Unsafe at Any Speed*. Frequent mining catastrophes, such
as the death of eighty-eight miners in Farmington, West Virginia, and the
discovery of new occupational diseases, such as "brown lung," focused the
public on occupational safety and health risks.

For the reformers, the "solution" for the failure to protect the public and
the environment followed from their definition of the cause. First, it was
necessary to shift responsibility from the "lax authority of market mechanisms
and common law to . . . federal government regulation."[57] Legislators heeded
this call and Congress engaged in a frenzy of legislation unmatched since the
New Deal. By one count, Congress passed 25 laws regulating business between
1967 and 1973 alone,[58] and by another, it passed 42 laws regulating business
between 1962 and 1978.[59] Congress enacting comprehensive changes to air,
water, and pesticide regulation, and President Nixon, using his powers of
reorganization, created the Environmental Protection Agency (EPA). Congress
created the Consumer Product Safety Commission (CPSC) to administer new
and existing statutes to protect children and the general public from hazardous products, the Occupational Safety and Health Administration (OSHA) to

---

[55] For a description of these events, see Rabin, *supra* note 17, at 1272–78.

[56] The following description of the public interest era is drawn from Shapiro, *Administrative
Law After the Counter-Reformation: Restoring Faith in Pragmatic Government*, 48 U. KAN. L. REV.
689, 692–696 (2000).

[57] M. MCCANN, TAKING REFORM SERIOUSLY: PERSPECTIVES ON PUBLIC INTEREST LIBERALISM
82 (1986).

[58] M. PERTSCHUK, REVOLT AGAINST REGULATION: THE RISE AND PAUSE OF THE CONSUMER MOVE-
MENT 5 (1982).

[59] M. WEIDENBAUM, BUSINESS, GOVERNMENT AND THE PUBLIC 7–10 (2d ed. 1981).

protect workers from workplace accidents and toxic chemicals, and the National Highway Traffic Safety Administration (NTSA) to create safer automobiles and trucks. In addition, Congress authorized the Federal Trade Commission to write regulations in support of its mandate.

Reformers, however, were also concerned about how the government would use this new regulatory authority. This concern arose from their perception that the business community had undue influence over the regulatory programs that predated the public interest era. Numerous studies by Ralph Nader, which documented corporate abuses that had gone unregulated by the government, convinced reformers that agencies routinely ignored and subverted "the rule of law itself—whether it be antitrust law, environmental regulations, freedom-of-information procedures, or OSHA standards."[60] They concluded that the administrative discretion granted to agency officials in most regulatory matters only invited corporate capture.

In light of this agency capture, reformers sought changes in administrative procedures that held agencies accountable for their failure to protect the public and the environment. In a series of decisions, federal judges responded by interpreting the APA to facilitate challenges by statutory beneficiaries to the failure of government to act or to act sufficiently.[61] In retrospect, these changes had two significant ramifications. Agencies could no longer ignore the policy input of interest groups representing statutory beneficiaries, such as the Environmental Defense Fund, the National Resources Defense Council, or Ralph Nader's organization, Public Citizen, because courts would refuse to enforce agency decisions that appeared to have ignored such input. Moreover, because such groups could sue agencies and seek this relief, the groups had bargaining leverage when they negotiated with agencies concerning policy outcomes.

Congress also reacted to the reformer's agenda. It passed open government laws, such as the Freedom of Information Act (FOIA) and the Federal Advisory Committee Act (FACA), which made it more difficult for agencies to adopt industry-friendly policies behind closed doors that would then be difficult to dislodge. Congress also passed the National Environmental Policy Act of 1969 (NEPA), which required agencies to analyze and disclose to the public the potential environmental impacts of agency actions, and it subjected agency compliance with these requirements to judicial review. NEPA, like the open government laws, made it easier for environmentalists and other public interest groups to monitor agencies, like the Department of Agriculture, that were perceived by them to be excessively friendly to corporate and business interests. Congress also passed legislation to permit persons who sued the government to collect legal fees, which reduced the transaction costs of collective action by statutory beneficiaries.

As compared to policing regulation in the New Deal, the regulatory goals of the Great Society and the Public Interest eras were fundamentally different. This new regulation is usually described as "social regulation," to distinguish it from the older "economic" regulation. This designation calls attention to the

---

[60] MCCANN, *supra* note 57, at 44.

[61] For a description of these developments, see Stewart, *The Reformation of American Administrative Law*, 88 HARV. L. REV. 1669 (1975).

fact that most of the previous regulation was intended to assist business development, protect individuals from economic deprivation, or ensure that business did not abuse its monopoly power, manipulate prices, or deceive consumers. The new regulation, by comparison, focused on social ills directed at specifically disenfranchised groups, the poor, and the public in general.

The reformers who sought this increase in policing regulation shared one trait with their Progressive predecessors, but they also differed from them in an important way. The activists, like the Progressive reformers, believed that the best antidote for big business was big government, but as "civic skeptics"[62] they were not prepared to trust regulators to protect citizens and the environment. Whereas the Progressives put their faith in "neutral" experts to choose the most appropriate decisions, the reformers distrusted the bureaucratic elites in whom the Progressives placed their faith. Michael McCann explains, "Indeed, it is against the very ideal of government by scientists, experts, and bureaucrats understood to be above politics that the new reformers have pitted themselves."[63] They understood that regulatory decisions were inherently political, and they sought to use the legal process to ensure that the view of regulatory beneficiaries could not be ignored because agencies were captured by the very corporations that they were suppose to regulate.

David Vogel has attempted to explain why the business community, which often wields considerable political power, was unable to stem the outpouring of regulation during this period.[64] Vogel contends that the environmental and consumer groups caught industry and producer groups unaware, the business community was surprised by the environmental and consumer movements and was initially unprepared to contest these developments. Because there was little federal health and safety regulation prior to this period, most businesses were not well organized in Washington to oppose the environmental and consumer forces. The business community quickly recovered, however, and it built a considerable presence in Washington. The focus on regulatory reform in the next period no doubt reflects this recovery.[65]

7. THE REGULATORY REFORM ERA

When President Ronald Reagan took office, declaring that the "government is not the solution to the problem," it "is the problem," the previous era of regulatory expansion had come to an end. Since the 1970s, there has been a reassessment of regulation in this country. Some forms of economic regulation have been deregulated, but public opposition has blunted efforts to eliminate or drastically curtail social regulation. Efforts to reform economic and social regulation have, however, met with some success. Unlike deregulation, these reforms continue regulation but change the method of regulation to yield better results.

---

[62] MCCANN, *supra* note 57, at 90 (attributing the description of the reformers as "civic skeptics" to Andrew McFarland).

[63] *Id.* at 99–100.

[64] D. VOGEL, FLUCTUATING FORTUNES: THE POLITICAL POWER OF BUSINESS IN AMERICA (1989).

[65] D. RICCI, THE TRANSFORMATION OF AMERICAN POLITICS: THE NEW WASHINGTON AND THE RISE OF THE THINK TANKS (1993).

The idea that government regulation required reform started with academic critics and was picked up by the business community and political leaders. The failure of government regulation, for example, received an early and prominent endorsement in *Regulation and Its Reform*,[66] written by Justice Stephen Breyer while he was an academic. Breyer proposed that regulatory failure occurs because of "mismatches" or the failure "to correctly match the [regulatory method or] tool [used] to the problem at hand." A mismatch can occur because government can misdiagnose the problem that it is attempting to solve and apply the wrong regulatory approach as a result, or even if a problem is correctly identified, government chooses a regulatory tool that is less effective and more expensive than other options. While the first mistake justifies deregulation, the more usual problem is the second mistake. The government fails not because government regulation is unnecessary, but because it does not take advantage of the most rational way to implement regulation.

Today, the idea that government programs fail because of poor design and the failure to rationalize policy has many proponents. Cass Sunstein's explanation of "how regulation fails" is typical:

> The regulatory state has not been a failure. On the contrary, regulatory statutes have brought about significant improvements in a variety of areas, including the environment, energy conservation, automobile safety, endangered species, and discrimination on the basis of race and sex. At the same time, however, some statutes have produced benefits that are dwarfed by the costs, had unanticipated side effects, or have in any case been far less successful than their advocates had hoped. Moreover, the entire area is pervaded by what we might call paradoxes of regulation: regulatory strategies that are self-defeating in the sense that they bring about results precisely the opposite to those that are intended.

Thus, according to Professor Sunstein, "even when it is possible to identify a good reason for statutory intervention, governmental regulation may not be successful." Rather, the "statutory solution might be poorly designed, producing a 'government failure' parallel to or more costly than the market failure that gave rise to regulation in the first instance."[67]

The first idea—that government sometimes misdiagnoses the problem—was influential in the deregulation of transportation and energy markets. Reformers argued that government regulation in these markets was premised on competitive conditions or problems that no longer existed, if they ever did. According to the critics, regulation was premised on policy arguments that were no longer valid because of economic and technological developments, and in some cases the critics doubted that regulation was valid even at the time it was adopted. This initiative actually started in the Carter administration, when President Carter appointed Professor Alfred Kahn as chair of the Civil Aeronautics Board (CAB) with the mandate to abolish price controls for airline services. In 1978, Congress agreed with this recommendation after hearings

---

[66] S. Breyer, Regulation and its Reform (1982).

[67] Sunstein, *supra* note 41, at 74, 83.

chaired by Senator Kennedy established that price controls disadvantaged consumers by artificially raising prices. In the following decade, Congress also abolished price controls for interstate railroad, truck and bus services, and the states abolished regulation of the same intrastate services. Congress also ended price controls for natural gas producers after it became clear that regulation was unnecessary and counterproductive. Some states and federal regulators also deregulated the business of generating electrical energy on the ground that the industry was competitive and price regulation was unnecessary.

Congress also made changes in the regulation of telecommunications, passing the Telecommunications Reform Act of 1996. The bill dissolved a 1982 federal court decree ordering the breakup of AT&T and creating the Regional Bell Operating Companies (RBOCs), and installed in its place a regulatory scheme that permits the RBOCS to offer long-distance telephone service if they meet certain regulatory conditions. The Act also permits the RBOCs to offer cable television service, eliminates some prior forms of cable television regulation, and establishes some new regulatory requirements. Finally, the Act eliminates some prior regulatory restrictions on television and radio broadcasters, but it also establishes some additional restrictions.

Another major reform effort that reflected the misdiagnosis idea concerned welfare. During the Clinton Administration, Congress eliminated a previous welfare program, Aid to Dependent Children (ADC), which dated back to the New Deal, and replaced it with the *Personal Responsibility and Work Opportunity Reconciliation Act.* The legislation was premised on the idea that the previous structure of the program promoted a cycle of dependency by encouraging women to stay on welfare. The new legislation authorized states to condition eligibility for government assistance on working or attending school, and it limited the total number of years that people were entitled to benefits.

Finally, President Bush signed legislation that restructured the relationship between the federal government and the states regarding federal aid to education. When Congress reauthorized the *Elementary and Secondary Education Act* in 2001, renaming it the "No Child Left Behind" Act, it included new testing and accountability measures that significantly increase federal supervision of primary and secondary education. Among its numerous requirements, the legislation requires states to establish a baseline or starting point they will use to measure their progress over the next 12 years in ensuring that all students are performing at a "proficient" level or above on state reading and math assessments by 2013–14.

The second idea–that government has chosen a regulatory solution that is less effective and more expensive than other options–has also been influential. This critique accepts the idea that regulation is necessary, but it contends that society would be better off with smarter regulation that is more rationally addressed to the problems it is suppose to solve. All three branches of government have reacted to this critique. The President and Congress have imposed new obligations on agencies to study the impacts of regulation before rules are promulgated, and legislation is pending in Congress to expand these requirements. For their part, the courts have used aggressive statutory interpretation to require agencies to use risk assessment and other techniques of policy analysis before they act.

Reformers initially chose presidential oversight as the principal vehicle for reform, and the Reagan and Bush Administrations put these plans into effect.[68] Oversight of regulation during the Reagan and Bush Administrations occurred under a series of executive orders that established reporting requirements monitored by the Office of Information and Regulatory Affairs (OIRA) in the White House Office of Management and Budget (OMB). Beginning with Executive Order 12,291, which required executive agencies to assess the benefits and costs of proposed rules, President Reagan also required assessment of family, federalism, and property impacts. The Bush Administration extended these analytical requirements in several ways, and in January 1992, he instituted a ninety-day regulatory moratorium on all new regulations and renewed it for another ninety days in April 1992, during which time agencies were ordered to reassess previous regulations and report the results to the White House. Finally, both presidents established highly visible task forces to reform particular regulations: the Task Force on Regulatory Relief, headed by Vice-President Bush, in the Reagan Administration and the Competitiveness Council, headed by Vice-President Quayle, in the Bush Administration.

These forms of oversight have been continued in the last two administrations. President Clinton issued Executive Order 12,866, which requires agencies to assess the costs and benefits of proposed and final rules and establishes a review process similar to that of his predecessors. Also like its predecessors, the Clinton administration established a highly visible White House regulatory reform effort, although it was oriented towards process changes, rather than specific regulatory relief. Under the guidance of Vice-President Gore, the National Performance Review set out to create a "government that works better and costs less," including, as one of the key steps, "eliminating regulatory overkill." President Bush has continued to require agencies to comply with the impact requirements issued by the Clinton administration, and he has appointed well-known academic critic of government regulation, John Graham, to head up OIRA, the office that oversees agency compliance with the regulatory impact requirements.

The Republican presidents during the regulatory reform era have also generally appointed administrators of regulator agencies that were skeptical of the value of regulation, if not sometimes downright hostile to it. President Clinton's appointees were generally more favorable to government regulation, although his administrators did reflect his commitment that regulation required more rational analysis.

Congress has also supported the effort to make regulation more rational. The Regulatory Flexibility Act, originally passed in 1980, requires agencies to prepare a regulatory flexibility analysis whenever they propose a rule that may have a significant economic impact on a substantial number of small businesses, organizations, or governments. The Act was significantly amended in 1996. The Paperwork Reduction Act, also passed in 1980 and reauthorized in 1995, requires agencies to analyze the necessity of imposing paperwork requirements and gain the approval of OMB to do so. Title II of the Unfunded

---

[68] For an account of procedural reform by the White House, see Shapiro, *supra* note 56, at 707–09.

Mandate Reform Act, entitled "Regulatory Accountability and Reform," requires federal agencies, before promulgating either a proposed or final regulation that would include a "mandate" resulting in costs over $100 million annually on state, local, or tribal governments or the private sector, to prepare a statement assessing the effect of the regulation.

Congress considered, but ultimately rejected, even more sweeping regulatory reform, after the Republicans took control of Congress after the 1994 elections. In the 104th Congress, the Republicans sought a sweeping set of revisions to the nation's environmental, natural resources, and occupational safety and health laws as part of their "Contract for America." Professor Glicksman explains:

> The focal point of national press coverage of the campaign by Republicans running for election to the House of Representatives was the Contract with America devised and announced by soon-to-be Speaker of the House Newt Gingrich. The Contract, which served as a policy blueprint for the first 100 days of the Republican-controlled House of Representatives of the 104th Congress, concentrated on three "core principles" increased government accountability to the electorate, restoration of personal responsibility, and restoration of opportunity through regulatory and tax relief.
>
> The common theme behind these three principles was the notion that the federal government was too big and that its regulatory apparatus was too intrusive. As the measure introduced to implement the Contract later made clear, the supporters of the contract believed that the federal environmental regulation in particular was creating a drag on the national economy, that the costs of this regulation often outweighed its benefits, that biased, overly conservative, and inaccurate information about risks posed by regulated activities often resulted in overregulation, that the commitment of environmental policy decisions to federal bureaucrats interfered with governmental accountability, and that environmental regulation caused unjustified if not unconstitutional invasions of private property rights. . . .[69]

The Contract's supporters had similar criticisms of occupational safety and health regulation.

Despite the high priority that the Republicans gave to this effort, they were able to achieve only limited reform. The House passed a global regulatory reform bill in February 1995, but the Senate failed to support cloture on a similar bill. Congress was able to amend laws concerning safe drinking water and pipeline safety to require regulators to compare the costs and benefits of regulation in some limited circumstances.

Several factors appear to explain the Republican's failure to adopt more significant reforms. First, although the regulatory reform effort was linked to prior criticisms of environmental and health and safety regulation and to previous regulatory reform proposals, some of the proposed changes were radical departures from previous reform proposals. Second, newspaper stories

---

[69] Glicksman, *Regulatory Reform and (Breach of) the Contract with America: Improving Environmental Policy or Destroying Environmental Protection?*, 5 KAN. J. L. & PUB. POL. 9, 16 (1996).

disclosed that many of the provisions for regulatory reform introduced by House Republicans were written by business lobbyists and that these lobbyists helped plan the hearings and other efforts to gain passage of the legislation. Finally, public approval of Newt Gingrich and other House Republicans fell dramatically after they forced the federal government to shut down on two occasions because President Clinton would not accede to their demands concerning how the budget was to be written.

During this period, the Supreme Court has sent mixed signals about regulatory reform, although in general the Court has supported increased judicial scrutiny of agencies. In 1983, the Court decided *Motor Vehicle Mfgs. Ass'n. v. State Farm ins. Co.*, 463 U.S. 29 (1983), which required an agency to "examine the relevant data and articulate a satisfactory explanation for its action including a 'rational connection between the facts found and the choice made.'" The Court said that judges were to be reasonably deferential to agencies, but the justices also engaged in a searching and detailed review of the agency's evidence, which undercut the previous message. The Court's opinion therefore appeared to endorse so-called "hard look" review in which a court carefully examines an agency's reasons for regulating. This approach decreases the deference that the APA requires for judicial review because, although the APA obligates courts to affirm an agency's policy decisions unless they are "arbitrary and capricious," courts can remand a decision for a better explanation before they ultimately apply that standard. The Court's endorsement of hard look review has led some appellate judges to consider, frequently in painstaking detail, an agency's factual predicate, analytical methodology, and its chain of reasoning concerning new regulations. In *Chevron v. Natural Resources Defense Council, Inc.*, 467 U.S. 837 (1984), the Court established a test of statutory interpretation that requires courts to defer to agency interpretations of statutes when "Congress has not directly addressed the precise question in issue." The Court explained, "If Congress has explicitly left a gap for the agency to fill, there is an express delegation of authority to the agency to elucidate a specific provision of the statute, by regulation." In some subsequent cases, however, the Court has been reluctant to find that Congress left a gap in a statute, despite Congress' use of ambiguous terms, which has decreased its deference to agency statutory interpretations in those cases.

NOTES AND QUESTIONS

1. What does this history teach us about the interplay of law and regulation? The Constitution places limitations on the legislature and administrative agencies concerning the types of powers they can possess and the methods by which those powers can be exercised. How significant are these limitations? Does your answer change before and after 1937? Today most regulation is constitutional based on the Court's jurisprudence since 1937. A number of constitutional requirements apply to most types of regulation, but Congress and state legislatures normally write laws that comply with these requirements. In other words, constitutional commands establish the boundaries of regulation, but these boundaries are generous enough to accommodate most of the regulatory objectives of Congress and state legislatures.

This does not mean, of course, that constitutional requirements are irrelevant. The alert lawyer may be able to mount a constitutional challenge to some legislation. Nevertheless, because successful challenges are relatively uncommon, we devote only a limited amount of the book to studying constitutional law and regulation. We do not ignore this subject, however, because the regulatory lawyer should understand the constitutional boundaries and when they might apply.

2. Legal limitations established by Congress are another limitation on regulation. Congress can, and does, delegate decisionmaking discretion to agencies under applicable legal standards. What does the previous history teach us about Congress' propensity to delegate administrative discretion?

Congress is capable of narrowing an agency's regulatory discretion, but it has tended to do so only when it has lost faith in the agency's commitment to its regulatory mission, its own staff has substantial expertise in the area, and there is broad public support for the specific regulatory solution Congress has chosen.[70] Thus, unless the Supreme Court requires Congress to delegate more specifically as a matter of constitutional interpretation, agency discretion will continue to be a regulatory fact of life in the administrative state. As you read, the Supreme Court struck down two New Deal statutes because Congress failed to establish sufficient limitations on the President's authority to act, but the Court has struck down no statute since these cases on these grounds. Why do you think the Supreme Court has chosen not to require Congress to make legislation more specific?

3. How an agency exercises its freedom to choose one of several regulatory options is influenced by policy arguments and political influences. Policy and politics have an impact specifically because an agency can normally defend any one of several choices as being consistent with its statutory mandate. The fact that regulatory decisions are the product of both political and policy influences has important practical significance for the practicing lawyer. As the next chapters discuss, persuading an agency to favor your client's position requires policy advocacy skills and an understanding of the political environment in which an agency operates.

Can you think of examples from the previous history where policy arguments appear to have been important to the outcome of the regulatory debate? What was the role of politics in the development of regulation? How do the two influences interact? We will have more to say about the answer to this question in Chapter 3.

4. Recent historical efforts have been skeptical of accounts that attribute the dominance of business at the turn of the century solely to its political power. These authors conclude that business success at blocking regulatory initiatives was aided by existing economic theory and political values that favored the business position.[71] If this perception is accurate, it suggests that producer and industry groups will be most successful when they can associate

[70] Shapiro & Glicksman, *Congress, the Supreme Court, and the Quiet Revolution in Administrative Law*, 1988 DUKE L.J. 1, 841–43.

[71] *See* H. HOVENKAMP, ENTERPRISE AND AMERICAN LAW (1836-1937) (1991); M. KELLER, REGULATING A NEW ECONOMY: PUBLIC POLICY AND ECONOMIC CHANGE IN AMERICA (1900-1933) (1990).

their opposition to regulation with policy ideas that are held by a large number of citizens. Conversely, the same interests can stumble despite their political power when they are defending unpopular policy ideas and values. Does the history of regulation comport with this observation? Has business succeeded when its policy goals were popular and has it failed when they were not?

C. EXPLAINING REGULATORY CYCLES

The public's enthusiasm for regulation has waxed and waned since the beginning of the country. This ambivalence appears to be related to public attachment to incompatible ideas concerning the scope of government and to the imperfection of government itself.

1. INCOMPATIBLE TRADITIONS

Samuel Huntington defines the elements of our political culture, which he calls the "American Creed," as "constitutionalist, individualism, democracy, and egalitarianism."[72] Two of these values—individualism and democracy—are often in conflict because individualism is so closely linked to capitalism. As the history of regulation indicates, both "individualism" and "capitalism" have been understood since the end of the nineteenth century to emphasize private achievement, maximum individual freedom, and unregulated private markets. By comparison, democracy upholds the rights of popular majorities to replace the decisions made in private markets when necessary to alleviate social and economic stress.

Despite this conflict, public opinion polls indicate that Americans generally support both sets of values. As Robert McCloskey has noted, it is "characteristic of the American mind . . . to hold contradictory ideas simultaneously without bothering to resolve the potential conflict between them."[73] But McCloskey and John Zaller, in a review of opinion polling data, find that "people who are most attached to democracy values tend to exhibit the least support for capitalism" and "[t]hose who ardently support the values of capitalism display the least overall support for democratic values." They conclude that conflict between those who adhere most strongly to one or the other set of values "manifests itself mainly in the form of disagreements over incremental adjustments in existing practices" such as "greater or lesser regulation of business."[74]

2. IMPERFECTION OF GOVERNMENT

Arthur Schlesinger offers another theory of regulatory cycles. He asks, "[if] the citizenry has steadily approved a larger role for government, and if affirmative government has on balance served the republic well, why the periodic revulsion against it?" His answer:

---

[72] S. HUNTINGTON, THE PROMISE OF DISHARMONY 151–56 (1981).

[73] McCloskey, *The American Ideology, in* CONTINUING CRISIS IN AMERICAN POLITICS 14 (M. Irish ed. 1963).

[74] H. MCCLOSKEY & J. ZALLER, THE AMERICAN ETHOS: PUBLIC ATTITUDES TOWARDS CAPITALISM AND DEMOCRACY 162, 185–86 (1984).

The underlying cause is that elemental human experience in which enthusiasm gives way to fatigue and disenchantment—the experience that characterizes the ebb and flow of the political cycle. There are more specific reasons in the case of affirmative government. The national government, like all tools, is liable to misuse and to abuse. . . . Sometimes government intervenes too much. Its regulations become pointless. Its programs fail. After a time, exasperations accumulate and produce indictments.[75]

We offer a related theory for regulatory cycles. The process of government regulation can be seen as a "life cycle,"[76] which falls into six more or less identifiable stages as depicted in Figure 1-1.

Figure 1-1: Life Cycle of Government Regulation

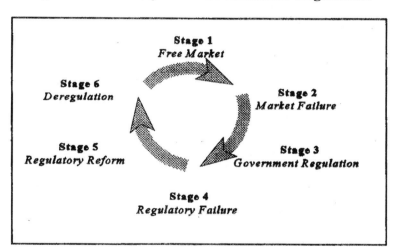

Stage one, the free market, is the period when government intervention is absent from a particular industry or market. This stage adopts a version of laissez-faire or of limited government. If the market is functioning properly or reasonably well or, in other words, if the market is efficient and fair, government intrusion cannot improve the situation. Simply, in the face of a well-working (efficient and fair) market, government regulation will at least add unnecessary administrative costs, thus reducing allocative efficiency, and may cause inequitable distributions.

Achieving or maintaining a free market, however, is rare and difficult. Instead, the frequent situation is of a market in disequilibrium because of the existence of a market failure, as described in Chapter 2 and throughout the book. In stage two, once a failure, such as a pollution externality, is identified, a regulatory response from government is suggested. In other words, the existence and the identification of the market failure becomes the justification

---

[75] SCHLESINGER, *supra* note 4, at 245.

[76] *See* M. BERNSTEIN, REGULATING BUSINESS BY INDEPENDENT COMMISSION (1955).

for government intervention into private enterprise, thus moving regulation into the next stage.

Stage three is government regulation. In order to reach this stage, a justification for government intervention must be given. As Chapter 2 will discuss, two justifications exist. Government intervenes to promote economic efficiency or to promote a noneconomic value, such as distributional equity. More often than not, these two justifications are mixed.

Such a justification for government intervention is a necessary but insufficient condition for government regulation, because the government must respond to the perceived market failure with the correct regulatory tool. The particular form of regulation must be the appropriate corrective for the identified market failure. The consequence of using the wrong regulatory tool—using price supports to correct inadequate information, for example—may worsen a situation rather than improve it.

The wrong tool may make regulation more costly or impose the costs more unfairly than the market defect. The use of an inadequate or incorrect regulation thus creates regulatory failure, or stage four. As a crude test of regulatory failure, if the costs outweigh the benefits of regulation, government regulation has failed.

There are two reactions to regulatory failure. In the last two stages of the life cycle, government can either respond by fixing the failure through regulatory reform at stage five, such as modifying existing regulations, or government can extract itself from the market all together by complete deregulation at stage six, *i.e.*, by eliminating regulations, thus reverting back to stage one, the free market. Although the cycle ends at stage five or six, government regulation of a particular market or industry might be located at any stage of the cycle at any given time.

NOTES AND QUESTIONS

1. The McCloskey and Zaller findings raise several fundamental questions about regulation in this country. They suggest that everyone in America believes in government regulation, but that we differ concerning how much regulation is necessary. Do you think this is an accurate description of citizen beliefs? But if citizens both support and oppose government regulation, what determines which set of attitudes will prevail? Will citizens oppose regulation when the country is free of any economic or social crisis, but support it when such a crisis occurs?

2. If citizens both support and oppose government regulation, how do you explain the fact that the total amount of regulation has increased since the founding of the country? Theodore Lowi has suggested that citizens support those aspects of regulation that benefit themselves, and decline to oppose regulation that benefits others. He argues that each group nevertheless agrees not to oppose regulation for others, if those groups support the regulation it favors. According to Lowi, this creates a policy gridlock that makes it impossible to alter the status quo.[77] Would you agree with this assessment?

---

[77] T. Lowi, the End of Liberalism: the Second Republic of the United States (2d ed. 1979).

3. Do you agree that there have been cycles of regulation and regulatory reform/deregulation? What causes such cycles? Do you agree with Huntington's thesis that regulation is built on incompatible values, with Schlesinger's theory of government imperfection, or do you have a theory of your own?

4. Although the principal focus of the regulatory reform era was the reform of existing governmental programs, Congress passed the *Sarbanes-Oxley Act* as a response to the Enron debacle. The legislation aims to establish greater corporate responsibility by, among other measures, creating a new oversight and regulatory regime for the public accounting industry, requiring reforms in public company governance and disclosure requirements, and increasing criminal penalties for fraud and the destruction of documents. Do you think that this legislation signals a new era in which the political pendulum swings back in favor of new regulation of private markets and away from regulatory reform of existing systems of regulation?

D.   THE AIR BAG CONTROVERSY

The following story is about how it came to pass your automobile has airbags and seatbelts. At the end of this story, we will ask you to consider the roles of law, policy and politics in the resolution of this controversy.

In the morning of April 21, 1981, Mrs. Lawana Hansen was driving her eighty-one-year-old mother-in-law from her home in Sandy, Utah, to Twin Falls, Idaho, when her 1975 Oldsmobile was suddenly sideswiped by another car. Although Mrs. Hansen's car was sent careening across the median into a loaded gasoline tanker, both she and her mother survived the crash, which totally demolished her car and seriously injured both of them. They survived because, totally unknown to them, their car was equipped with air bags which had inflated in 1/25 of a second upon impact, cushioning the women from the full force of the crash. The Hansens had purchased the Oldsmobile as a used car, unaware that it was one of about ten thousand vehicles with air bags built by General Motors during the 1970s. After seeing the mangled car, Mr. Hansen stated, "It's a miracle that my wife and mother lived. The steering wheel was pushed back to within inches of the back seat."[78]

Mrs. Hansen's experience was both typical and unique. It was typical because automobiles are involved in twenty million accidents each year within the United States. Of the roughly five million persons injured in these accidents, several hundred thousand suffer severe injuries, and over forty thousand are killed. In monetary terms, the total yearly cost of the accidents is somewhere between $60 and $100 billion, including the costs associated with property damage, bodily injury, and premature death.[79] Her experience was unique because her car was one of the small fraction of automobiles manufactured in the 1970s with air bags.

Whether the federal government should require car manufacturers to install air bags in cars is a regulatory controversy that dates back to the 1960s. In 1966, Congress passed the National Traffic and Motor Vehicle Safety Act,

---

[78] J. CLAYBROOK, RETREAT FROM SAFETY: REAGAN'S ATTACK ON AMERICA'S HEALTH 165 (1984).

[79] Thompson, *Regulating Motor Vehicle Safety Maintenance: Can We Make It Cost-Effective?*, 9 J. HEALTH POL. & L. 695, 695 (1985).

which directed the Department of Transportation (DOT) to "reduce traffic accidents and deaths and injuries to persons resulting from traffic accidents" by promulgating regulations that "shall be practical, shall meet the need for motor vehicle safety, and shall be stated in objective terms."[80] DOT delegated its general authority to promulgate safety standards to the National Highway Traffic Safety Administration (NHTSA), an agency within DOT.

Efforts to reduce the number and severity of automobile accidents prior to the Act rested on the tort system. The staggering number of persons killed and injured each year indicated the failure of this approach, but Congress did not act until the publication of Ralph Nader's book, *Unsafe At Any Speed,* which exposed the design hazards of General Motors' Corvair automobile. Shortly after Nader published the book, it was revealed that General Motors had hired detectives to spy on him in an attempt to find some "dirt" that could be used to besmirch his reputation. Wounded by these revelations, the company was unable to exert its political influence to stop the automobile safety legislation.

One of NHTSA's first efforts was a 1967 regulation that required all new automobiles to have seat belts.[81] By 1972, however, the agency found that the level of seat belt usage was too low to reduce traffic injuries significantly. It therefore promulgated a new regulation that required all automobiles manufactured after 1975 to have either automatic seat belts, which would deploy without any effort by passengers to buckle them, or air bags, which would automatically inflate if an automobile were in an accident.[82] It also required that all automobiles built between 1973 and 1975 be equipped either with passive restraints or with an "ignition interlock" that would not allow them to be started unless the car's seat belts were buckled.

The Sixth Circuit affirmed the regulation,[83] but it was short-lived nevertheless. The automobile manufacturers chose to comply with these regulations by installing ignition interlocks. Congress was then flooded with complaints from motorists who objected to being unable to start their cars without buckling up, and thousands of car owners disconnected the interlock system. In response, Congress passed the Motor Vehicle and Schoolbus Safety Act Amendments of 1974, which prohibited DOT from requiring interlocks and required all future regulations to be submitted to Congress for a possible legislative veto.[84]

At this point, air bags became a political ping-pong ball. William Coleman, President Ford's Secretary of Transportation, rescinded the existing regulations. In their place Coleman obtained the agreement of several manufacturers to supply at least forty thousand (and up to four hundred thousand) air bag-equipped cars to demonstrate the feasibility of the technology. A few

---

[80] Pub. L. No. 89-563, 80 Stat. 718, §§ 1, 103(a) (codified as 15 U.S.C. §§ 1381, 1392(a)).

[81] 52 Fed. Reg. 2408, 2415 (1967).

[82] 37 Fed. Reg. 3911, 3912 (1972).

[83] *Chrysler Corp. v. Dep't of Transp.,* 472 F.2d 659, 675 (6th Cir. 1972).

[84] Pub. L. No. 93-492, 88 Stat. 1482, § 109 (codified as 15 U.S.C. § 1410b). The legislation was passed prior to the Supreme Court's decision that the legislative veto was unconstitutional. *See* Immigration & Nat'l Serv. v. Chadha, 462 U.S. 919 (1983) (legislative veto declared unconstitutional).

months later, after President Carter appointed Brock Adams as Secretary, DOT promulgated a revised standard. It required new automobiles to have passive restraints (either air bags or automatic seat belts) by 1982.[85] Congress did not veto the regulation, and it was upheld by the D.C. Circuit in 1979.[86] This regulation, however, did not survive even as long as the previous one.

The Reagan administration took office with considerable deregulatory zeal. As you read in the previous history, Vice President Bush was put in charge of a "Task Force on Regulatory Relief," which, after consultations with the auto industry, issued a report calling for a thirty-four point agenda of "Actions to Help the U.S. Auto Industry." Among the items listed was a proposal to delay the passive restraints standard. Drew Lewis, President Reagan's Secretary of Transportation, told the National Automobile Dealers Association, "If I could do it, there would be a four year moratorium [on new regulations]. I know four years is unrealistic, but my point is that this administration opposes regulations."[87] In October 1981, Lewis took one action he could accomplish—he revoked the existing regulation. He explained that because manufacturers would likely choose to install detachable automatic seat belts, rather than air bags, so many car occupants would detach the belts that DOT could not justify their cost.[88]

In *Motor Vehicle Mfrs. Ass'n v. State Farm Ins. Co.*, 463 U.S. 29 (1983), the Supreme Court heard a challenge to the rescission brought by several insurance companies, which believed that passive restraints would lower insurance costs, and by several public interest groups. The suit was defended by DOT and the automobile manufacturers. When the dust of the legal battle cleared, the Court gave a clear victory to those who challenged the rescission. As noted, DOT justified the rescission of the rule on the basis that because car manufacturers were likely to install detachable automatic seat belts instead of air bags, so many persons would detach the belts that they would not be worth their cost. The Court unanimously rejected this reasoning, because DOT did not consider the obvious alternative of modifying the rule to eliminate the automatic seat belt option and to keep the air bag requirement.[89]

In February 1983, four months before the *State Farm* decision, President Reagan appointed Elizabeth Dole to succeed Drew Lewis as Secretary of Transportation. Secretary Dole had been a commissioner at the Federal Trade Commission (FTC) in the 1970s and had served in a behind-the-scenes position in the Reagan White House before her appointment. She came to DOT with a reputation as a moderate Republican who had supported tough consumer

---

[85] 42 Fed. Reg. 34,289, 34,297 (1977).

[86] *Pacific Legal Found. v. Department of Transp.*, 593 F.2d 1338, 1349 (D.C. Cir.), *cert. denied*, 444 U.S. 830 (1979).

[87] CLAYBROOK, *supra* note 78, at 180.

[88] 46 Fed. Reg. 21,205–08 (1981).

[89] The Court admitted that DOT might have good reasons for not requiring an air bag-only regulation. The reversal was based on DOT's failure to consider this option at all. 463 U.S. at 46. By a five to four vote, the Court also reversed as arbitrary and capricious the agency's subsidiary finding that automatic seat belts would be ineffective because car occupants would be likely to detach them. The majority based its reversal on NHTSA's own studies, which showed a doubling of seat belt usage when automatic seat belts replaced manual belts. *Id.* at 51–57.

protection rules while at the FTC. Although the White House still remained opposed to a passive restraint regulation, Secretary Dole found support for a new regulation in Congress, including that of several prominent Republican Senators including John Danforth, Orrin Hatch, and John Warner.[90]

Dole managed to walk a tightrope between the anti-regulation and pro-regulation forces by devising an ingenious political compromise. In 1984, DOT promulgated a regulation that required automobile manufacturers to install either air bags or automatic seat belts by 1989. The regulation provided, however, that it would not go into effect if two-thirds of the nation's population were covered by state laws requiring the use of manual seat belts before April 1, 1989, and if those laws met the minimum criteria set out in the regulation. These criteria included a penalty for violating a state's seat belt law of not less than twenty-five dollars, an educational program to increase compliance, and a provision specifying that the violation of the belt usage requirement may be used to mitigate damages with respect to any person who is involved in a passenger car accident and who seeks in any subsequent litigation to recover damages for the injury.[91]

After the regulation was promulgated, lobbyists from the automobile manufacturers swooped down on state legislatures in a $15 million campaign for the adoption of laws requiring the use of seat belts.[92] The lobbying campaign failed. Although most states did enact seat belt laws, most of these did not meet the minimum criteria in the regulation. As a result, the regulation requiring passive restraints quietly went into effect on April 1, 1989. There was no press coverage and no more outside interest than a handful of telephone calls to NHTSA from automobile manufacturers.

By 1997, air bags were well on their way to becoming a standard technology. Of the 100 million cars and trucks on the roads, about 55 million had driver-side air bags, and some 28 million also had passenger-side air bags. This growth is remarkable. As late as 1988, only two percent of new cars were equipped with air bags. Since the widespread adoption of air bags exceeds regulatory requirements, the car manufacturers are apparently responding to consumer demand. As consumers learned about air bags through the media and friends, car buyers were willing to pay the higher price for automobiles equipped with air bags.

The government mandate continues to be controversial despite the widespread use of air bags. NHTSA estimates that air bags have saved nearly 1,700 lives since the mid-1980s, but it also attributes the deaths of 55 persons, including 35 children, to air bags.[93] Air bags deploy with such explosive force that they can injure or kill children, because of their small size, or short adults, particularly women who are five feet, two inches tall or shorter, who sit less than 15 inches from the bag compartments.

Critics claimed that NHTSA knew about the danger of air bags and failed to require safer, less powerful air bags. The agency responded that the more

---

[90] Graham, Secretary Dole and the Future of Automobile Air bags, BROOKINGS REV. 10, 12 (Summer 1985).

[91] 49 Fed. Reg. 28,962 (1984) (codified at 49 C.F.R. § 517.208.4.1.5).

[92] Pressley, *Public in Middle of U.S. Seat Belt Debate,* N.Y. TIMES, March 11, 1985, at C1

[93] Widavsky, *Deflating Air Bags,* NAT'L J., Feb. 15, 1997, 322.

powerful air bags were necessary to protect persons who did not wear seat belts because only about 15 percent of occupants wore seat belts at the time that the regulation was promulgated. Seat belt usage, however, has now gone up to about 67 percent. This statistic prompted a NHTSA critic, Representative Dirk Kempthorne, to sponsor legislation to require the agency to promulgate a regulation to de-power air bags on the assumption that they only need to be powerful enough to protect persons wearing seat belts. Instead of less powerful air bags, NHTSA was considering requiring car manufacturers to install a switch which would shut off air bags.

Joan Claybrook, who was NHTSA's administrator in the Carter Administration, proposed a third option. Claybrook favored "dual-inflation" air bags that deploy with less force in low-speed accidents and greater force in high speed crashes. Claybrook opposed doing away with powerful air bags because approximately 50 percent of those persons who are killed in crashes are unbelted.

NOTES AND QUESTIONS

1. Like most regulation, this story involves law as well as policy and politics. Regulatory decisionmaking was influenced not only by what safety engineers, economists, and other policy analysts believed was the best way to reduce automobile accidents and injuries, but also by the reaction of the political system to their policy proposals. Who were the key actors in this story, and what roles did they play? What legal and political institutions are involved in this story and what are their purposes?

2. What is NHTSA's statutory authority to require automobile manufacturers to install safety devices? How did Congress limit NHTSA's authority to act? How much discretion did the agency have to choose one device over another?

3. Clearly, there is a significant public consensus in favor of highway safety. Further, that goal can be fairly easily embodied in a statute. However, the means to achieving that goal can stimulate controversy. Regarding the tension between legal goals and legal means, Professor Cass Sunstein defines an *incompletely specified agreement* as one to which there is agreement to a general principle or abstraction but not as to specific outcomes. Thus:

> Abstract provisions protect "freedom of speech," "religious liberty," and "equality under the law," and citizens agree on those abstractions in the midst of sharp dispute about what these provisions really entail. Much lawmaking becomes possible only because of this phenomenon. Consider the fact that the creation of large regulatory agencies has often been feasible only because of incompletely specified agreements. In dealing with air and water pollution, occupational safety and health, or regulation of broadcasting, legislators converge on general, incompletely specified requirements—that regulation be "reasonable," or that it provide "a margin of safety." If the legislature attempted to specify these requirements—to decide what counts as reasonable regulation—there would be a predictably high level of dispute and conflict, and perhaps the relevant laws could not be enacted at all.[94]

---

[94] C. Sunstein, Legal Reasoning & Political Conflict 36 (1996).

4. In *Chrysler Corp. v. Department of Transportation,* 472 F.2d 659, 674 (6th Cir. 1972), which upheld the first passive restraint rule, the court stressed that the choice of whether to rely on air bags or seat belts was a policy choice that Congress delegated to the agency:

> The [automobile companies] contend that Standard 208 does not meet the need for automobile safety because belts offer better protection to occupants than do air bags. The Agency defends the standard by contending that air bags offer better protection to occupants than do belts. The record supports the conclusion that each type of occupant restraint offers protection in a slightly different form for different impact situations. Neither is clearly superior to the other in every respect. Consequently, we conclude that the Agency's decision to abandon active restraints in favor of passive restraints was a proper exercise of its administrative discretion.

The court therefore refused to reverse the standard because the agency's judgment was reasonable in light of the evidence it had compiled. *Pacific Legal Found. v. Department of Transportation,* 593 F.2d 1338, 1347 (D.C. Cir. 1979), which upheld the passive restraint rule promulgated during the Carter administration, stressed that in light of the evidence, the court could not "conclude that the Secretary abused his discretion in assessing the tradeoffs between the expected benefits and the potential dangers of air bags."

5. The fact that courts defer to an agency's policy decisions does not mean, however, that the agency is free to ignore its mandate. In *State Farm,* where the Supreme Court refused to enforce DOT's rescission of the Carter administration regulation, the Court required agencies to have "adequate reasons" for their policy choices. 436 U.S. at 43. The Court remanded NHTSA's decision to withdraw the Carter rule because it failed to give any reason why it eliminated the requirement of air bags. The impact of the *State Farm* case is discussed in more detail in Chapter 4.

6. What policy arguments do you think the automobile companies employed to convince NHTSA not to require air bags? What arguments did the insurance companies likely employ to convince the agency to require air bags?

7. Even if worn, lap and shoulder belts provide less protection to car occupants than using the same protection in conjunction with an air bag. Manual lap and shoulder belts prevent about forty percent of fatal injuries and about fifty percent of moderate to critical injuries. When air bags and lap and shoulder bags are combined, they reduce the risk of fatalities by fifty percent and injury risk by fifty-five percent. Moreover, air bags alone are crucial in those cases where occupants failed to buckle their belts. Even if every state passes a law requiring the use of belts, compliance will probably be in the forty to fifty percent range. Compliance among high risk groups, such as teenagers and drivers who drink and drive, will be even lower.

These facts raise questions such as these: Can you justify a regulation requiring the installation of air bags to add to the protection already provided by state laws which require the use of belts? Should the answer to this question depend on a comparison of costs and benefits of the regulation? Consider the following analysis:

Since 1985, more than 650,000 air bag "deployments" have occurred and, by NHTSA's count, 1,136 lives have been saved. But at what price? The industry puts the cost of an air bag installment at about $500, not including "engineering spillovers," such as dashboard and steering wheel redesign. At $500 a car, the total cost (to the consumer—not the car companies, who pass the cost along) of installing even one air bag in each of the 35 million-plus cars now so equipped is about $18 billion, to date, and the cost per life saved is close to $16 million.[95]

Is it reasonable for DOT to take into account the costs of such a regulation as compared to its benefits (in terms of the reduction in fatalities and injuries)? Would you favor a regulation even if it could not be demonstrated that the benefits exceeded the costs? How should society resolve questions such as these? Chapter 9 will take up this question when it considers the relationship of benefit-cost analysis and health and safety regulation.

8. How did politics influence NHTSA's various decisions concerning what safety requirements to impose? Which options were blocked by the politics of the situation and why? How do you suppose the proponents and opponents of the various regulatory options used their political contacts?

9. Why do you think most states failed to enact laws that met the minimum criteria set out by NHTSA? Recall that one requirement was that state laws provide that the failure to use a seat belt could be taken into account as a mitigating factor when a jury calculated the damages to which a person was entitled? Do you think Secretary Dole inserted this provision in anticipation that most states would not accept it? Why did states reject this provision?

10. The United States is the only country in the world that has considered passive restraints to protect automobile occupants. Most developed countries—including Australia, Canada, England, France, Germany, Israel, and Sweden—have long had laws that simply require motorists to wear manual (not automatic) seat belts. Compliance varies greatly—seat belts are used by forty to ninety percent of car occupants.[96] As the previous account indicates, the United States did not seriously consider mandating the use of seat belts for adults until Secretary Dole came up with her ingenious political compromise.

Is there something different about politics in the United States which would explain this delay? For example, Stephen Kelman argues that there are cultural differences between Sweden and the United States which make it easier to establish regulations in Sweden than in this country.[97] Can you identify any of these differences?

11. What explains the reluctance of some persons to wear seat belts? As noted above, compliance with seat belt laws varies widely. Compare the debate about helmet laws for motorcycle drivers. Opponents of helmet laws argue that, as an individual, lifestyle decision, motorcycle drivers should be able to decide for themselves whether to wear helmets—the government should not

---

[95] Allen, *Killer Air Bags: More Misadventures in the Quest for Perfect Safety*, SLATE, www.slate.com., Nov. 7, 1996.

[96] Graham, *supra* note 90, at 12.

[97] S. KELMAN, REGULATING SWEDEN, REGULATING THE UNITED STATES (1981).

have the power to force motorcycle drivers to wear helmets. Do you agree with this argument? What argument do helmet law proponents make? Is air bag regulation a similar lifestyle issue? When polled, students most often say that they either have purchased or would purchase a car with air bags. Where did this preference come from? Was this preference innate? Was it shaped by the market? Was it shaped by government?

12. In their study of automobile safety, Mashaw & Harfst note the interplay of law, policy, and politics with a six-lesson "message for would-be regulators."[98]

> *Lesson One.* Statute and regulatory policies are the beginning of a "political" process and reliance on "rational-technocratic regulation" is an illusion.
>
> *Lesson Two.* Legislative history is rarely decisive. Rather, such history helps identify influential political actors, forces, and institutions.
>
> *Lesson Three.* Regulators must regard private and public interest groups and the information they provide with suspicion. These groups, understandably, seek to further their own agendas rather than further the agency's mission particularly as political winds shift.
>
> *Lesson Four.* Even though courts have "proceduralized" their review of agency activity, they have been actively involved in scrutinizing agency decisionmaking.
>
> *Lesson Five.* Public support for social legislation, e.g., health and safety, is broad but not deep. People do not want government regulation to affect their lifestyle.
>
> *Lesson Six.* "[I]f a regulatory agency like NHTSA wants to be more successful in promoting safety design, it must attempt to accommodate, if not co-opt its adversaries." In other words, the agency must gather political and public support.

How do these rules demonstrate the interaction of policy, politics?

E. A DYNAMIC RELATIONSHIP

The materials that follow relate to the dynamic explanation of regulation suggested by the history of regulation and the air bags story. They will indicate the boundaries established by an agency's mandate and applicable constitutional restrictions. Besides understanding these limitations, you will be asked to consider what insights are revealed by policy analysis, such as what are the regulatory solutions to a particular problem. Often you will also be asked to consider what impact politics has on the decisionmaking process. Finally, from time to time the materials will address how politics and policy analysis can cause changes in the legal rules themselves.

Before you are presented these materials about regulation, we offer two additional introductory chapters. As this chapter indicates, policy analysis is a central element of the book. To prepare you for this coverage, Chapter 2

---

[98] J. Mashaw & D. Harfst, The Struggle for Auto Safety 247–50 (1990).

discusses the policy basis for the regulatory state. These materials indicate how the many and varied programs of government regulation have generally been justified as useful to society. Chapter 3 discusses politics and regulation. It describes how politics influence regulatory decisionmaking, discusses the interrelationship of politics and policy, and presents a short history of regulation in the United States.

Chapter 2

REGULATION AND PUBLIC POLICY

The United States has hundreds of regulatory agencies, enforcing thousands of laws and regulations. Despite the bewildering array of statutes, regulations, and agencies, it is possible to study regulation as a generic or unitary subject. The basic goal of this book is to demonstrate the fundamental principles of government regulation that can be applied to any form of domestic or international, local or national regulation. Indeed, as a lawyer you cannot avoid encountering regulation in some form.

The key to understanding the regulatory state is to recognize that government intervenes in markets for a limited number of reasons or justifications. In other words, when government intervenes in markets it has a limited number of goals. Further, when government does intervene it uses a similar number of regulatory tools or methods. Understanding those goals and those methods is to understand the policies underlying most regulatory programs.

Indeed, as this chapter explains, learning the methods and goals is analogous to learning how to read and analyze cases in the first year of law school. Once you learn the basic building blocks of reading cases, you are able to interpret cases in any legal field. Likewise, once you are familiar with certain key concepts concerning regulation, you can use these concepts as the starting point to understanding any area of regulation.

The next section introduces you to the regulatory goals that are used to justify government regulatory programs and the section following addresses the methods used to implement this regulation. A summary listing of these goals and methods is shown in Table 2-1. We would remind you that this chapter is introductory—the remainder of the book will elaborate these concepts.

Regulatory critics object that regulation does not always serve the public interest in one of these ways. A more specific objection is that government regulation is inefficient by harming consumers, producers, or both. Another objection, a variation of the inefficiency claim, is that government regulation is unfair because an industry or group of citizens may be successful in obtaining a regulatory program (or series of regulatory decisions) that favor the industry or group and disfavor the majority of citizens. This possibility exists because regulatory decisions are often subject to political influence and the political system may produce arrangements that favor an industry or group over the majority of citizens.

Table 2-1

GOALS AND METHODS OF REGULATION	
Regulatory Goals	*Regulatory Methods*
Address Market Failure due to: • Competitive Conditions • Restricted Entry or Exit • External Costs • Inadequate or Inaccurate Information • Public Goods	• Price Controls • Entry and Exit Controls • Standard Setting • Allocation • Taxes and Other Economic Incentives
Achieve Social Goals: • Prohibit Objectionable Exchanges • Eliminate Price As The Basis of Exchange • Remedy Distribution of Wealth • Subject Exchanges To Collective Values	

Those favoring regulations, or at least not heavily critical, argue that imperfect markets justify government intervention. In short, government regulations can make markets more efficient. Could the Enron/Arthur Anderson financial debacle have been avoided with better oversight, by way of example? Or is all regulation the outcome of the give-and-take of politics as usual? Another argument is that the distribution of wealth and resources is unfair and regulation can promote equity.

We argue that regulation is the product of the interaction of policy, politics, and law, that regulation can be based on either fairness or efficiency grounds. Further when a regulatory program makes policy sense, there is a strong inference that it is the product of a deliberative process rather than the result of untoward political influences. Alternatively, a weak policy rationale supports the conclusion that a program is the result of self-interested political behavior. But observers may reasonably differ concerning whether a program makes policy sense because it can be difficult to determine whether regulation is justifiable. When an industry or group supports a regulatory program or decision, it normally offers one of the regulatory justifications that are identified in this chapter. The proponent argues that the regulation serves a public purpose as well as being for its own benefit. Opponents make the opposite argument. They contend that the regulation will not serve a public purpose and thus will benefit only the proponents. Thus, a determination whether a program is justifiable will turn on the observer's conclusions about the merits of the policy arguments offered for it.

A. REGULATORY GOALS

Thus, a good first question for students of government regulation is: *Why regulate at all?* This question is often followed by the comment that more regulation is unnecessary because *the market can take care of things; the government is too intrusive.* The question is a fair one and implicates issues that we cover throughout this book. It presents an excellent starting point and uncovers basic attitudes about the relationship of government and markets.

Often, when persons discuss government regulation, the debating sides take positions supporting either government or markets.[1] We believe that such a dichotomy is simply false. Think about a rule of torts, property, or contracts, for example. A tort rule which provides compensation for injury is intended both to make the injured person whole and to deter wrongful conduct which is wasteful. A property rule that allows for the alienability of property is intended to promote wealth. And contracts rules which enforce bargains are intended to allow people to achieve their gains. In other words, the common law rules of property, torts, and contracts promote public policies of efficiency and fairness.

The rules of property, tort, and contract, which define, protect, and allow the transfer of wealth, are all enforced by the government. Without government and its legal rules, there would be no markets.[2] Thus, the choice is not between free market and government regulations. Rather, the choice is about the *degree of involvement of* government in markets.

Nevertheless, the question first posed—*Why regulate at all ?*—suggests a preference for more markets and less government as a way of social ordering. This preference is not unreasonable. Those who extol the market because it places the burden of justification on those proffering a regulation as a form of social ordering can point to many of the market's virtues. When markets work, the proper quantities of goods are put on the market at the proper prices. In such cases, consumer choice is maximized as is producer profit. Moreover, as producers and consumers bargain, innovation is encouraged. All of these virtues can be explained in technical economic terms, which you will learn in this course. Below we will discuss the perfectly competitive market and the attributes it needs to work its magic.

The market has other virtues as well. From the standpoint of social justice, free markets maximize liberty and equality. Liberty is maximized as government constraints are at their minimum. Equality is maximized insofar as every "vote" in the marketplace is counted equally. People buy and sell at will without constraint and without discrimination.

Thus, the virtues of efficiency, liberty, and equality are promoted by competitive markets. No wonder that markets are seen to be a desirable form of social ordering. Therefore, one goal of public policy is to maintain and support competitive markets in order to promote and maintain these virtues. The first reason for government regulation is to make market corrections when market failures are noted. When markets are not competitive and do not have the characteristics they need in order to function properly, then government can step in to address the imperfection.

---

[1] *See e.g.* R. Kuttner, Everything for Sale: The Virtues and Limits of Markets (1997).

[2] C. Sunstein, Free Markets and Social Justice 3–9 (1997); R.Epstein, Simple Rules for a Complex World (1995).

A second reason for government regulation is related to the idea of equality. While it is true that every "vote" counts in the market equally, it is not true that people start with an equal number of votes. In other words, inequality and mal-distribution of wealth give some people many more votes than others regardless of merit or achievement.[3] Regulation is the response to the citizens' wish to ensure that society is also fair and equitable in its social arrangement.

Taken together, these economic and noneconomic policy reasons have been used to justify government regulation in a wide variety of circumstances. This section briefly describes the economic and noneconomic policies that are used to justify government intervention in markets.

1. ECONOMIC GOALS

Economists start with the premise that government regulation is usually socially undesirable because the competitive market system is the best way for a society to organize itself. The advantage of a market system is that it best guarantees that the goods and services which society produces are the ones that the citizens want. In economic terminology, a private market is a place where the unfettered forces of supply and demand operate to maximize consumer welfare. The system also maximizes producer welfare by rewarding the most efficient and eliminating the inefficient. When a market delivers the exact mix of goods and services that consumers desire, it operates in an "efficient" manner.

Regulation is justified on the ground of "market failure" or the absence of one or more of the factors necessary for an efficient market. A market will operate inefficiently if there is inadequate information about goods or services, insufficient competition, externalities or spillover costs, or where public goods exist. These terms will be defined shortly. For now, our point is that the purpose of regulation is to address these "market failures" and thereby make markets operate more efficiently. Or, to put it another way, the purpose of regulation is to make it possible for the market to do a better job of matching supply and demand.

a. THE PERFECTLY COMPETITIVE MARKET

An understanding of the perfectly competitive market will aid an understanding of the justifications for government regulation. This explanation will also introduce you to some economic terms and concepts that will be used in the remainder of the book. After explaining the operations of the "perfectly competitive market," we will describe how markets can be defective and how regulation can mitigate these defects.

According to economic theory, a perfectly competitive market can be attained if the market has the following attributes:

    1. Numerous buyers and sellers;

---

[3] *See e.g.* K. PHILIPS, THE POLITICS OF RICH AND POOR: WEALTH AND THE AMERICAN ELECTORATE IN THE REAGAN AFTERMATH (1990); P. KRUGMAN, THE AGE OF DIMINISHED EXPECTATIONS: U.S. ECONOMIC POLICY IN THE 1990s (1990).

2. Large enough quantity of goods so that no single buyer or seller perceives that he or she can affect price by varying either the quantity demanded or supplied;

3. Product homogeneity so that buyers and sellers can trade with numerous other buyers and sellers;

4. Accurate and complete product information for buyers and sellers; and

5. Freedom of entry into and exit from the marketplace.

Under these strict conditions, a market attains its virtues by moving toward equilibrium, where the proper amount of goods are placed on the market at the proper prices. If any one of these five conditions is missing, the market is imperfect, a market failure exists, and government regulation may be needed to address that failure. A market with only one seller, for example in violation of the first condition, is a monopoly which distorts markets as will be explained in more detail below. Similarly, if consumers do not receive accurate information (for the condition) about the safety of a product, tobacco perhaps, then the product will be inefficiently over-consumed. Regulations are used to correct these defects.

In the absence of failure, a perfectly competitive market works toward equilibrium through the following market operations:

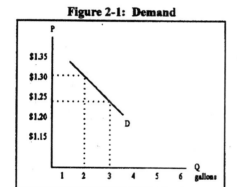

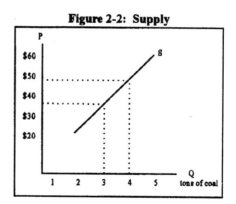

(1) DEMAND

The law of demand is a fundamental economic principle driving the equilibrium market model. The law holds that consumers are less willing to pay for another unit of a good if the price rises. It also means that people will pay less for an additional unit of a good. In other words, there is an inverse ratio between price and quantity. If gasoline could be purchased for $1.25 per gallon, and if it rose to $1.30 per gallon, the law of demand says that less gasoline would be purchased. The law is graphically shown by a downward sloping demand curve (D) in Figure 2-1. Quite simply, as prices increase, demand decreases.

Can you think of any good for which you would rather pay more than less? Why does someone buy brand name goods rather than non-brand name? Assuming that the quality is identical, then people are literally paying for the name, the cachet that comes with prestige goods. Why do some students choose a more expensive private law school over a less expensive public law school if the quality of education is the same?

(2) SUPPLY

The law of supply is a corollary to the law of demand. As prices increase, producers are encouraged to place more goods on the market. The classic supply curve (S in Figure 2-2) is upward-sloping. The higher the price of a ton of coal, the more coal will be produced for the market. Figure 2-2 demonstrates that four tons of coal will be placed on the market at $50 per ton, whereas only three tons of coal will be placed on the market at $40 per ton. When the world price of oil increases, the domestic oil companies spend more money on drilling and exploration.

These simple, perhaps obvious, economic laws of supply and demand are significant. They determine which goods are produced and, in turn, which resources are used in production. When the price of oil is higher than the price of natural gas, producers, following the supply curve, are encouraged to produce oil, just as consumers, following the demand curve, are encouraged to purchase natural gas. It would seem that producers' desire for higher prices and consumers' desire for lower prices produce an unresolvable conflict. Not so. Rather, the give and take of producers and consumers push the market toward equilibrium as consumers' increased demand for a particular good has an upward effect on prices, and as producers' increased supply has a downward effect on prices. Thus, the give and take of the laws of supply and demand move the market toward equilibrium.

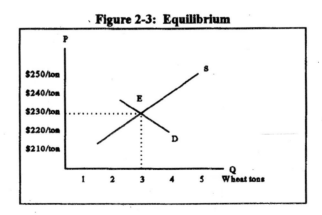

. **Figure 2-3: Equilibrium**

(3) EQUILIBRIUM

Imagine a market for wheat in which the equilibrium price (E) is $230 per ton. The graphic depiction of that market would have the demand and the supply curves intersect at $230 per ton, as shown in Figure 2-3.

At the equilibrium point (E), three tons of wheat will be sold at $230. Given a competitive market, i.e., buyers and sellers so numerous that no single buyer or seller can affect price, no producer will supply wheat at $240 per ton, because there will be no buyers, because consumers can purchase all of the wheat that they want at $230. Likewise, no consumer can purchase wheat at $220, because no producer can afford to supply at that price; otherwise, they will go broke, as explained below in the discussion of costs.

Regulation can distort this price equilibrium. If, for example, a government imposes a price control on wheat and reduces the price of wheat below the equilibrium point to $220 per ton, there will be a "shortage" of wheat, because consumer demand will be greater than producer supply. Can you see why? Simply, as the graph shows, there are consumers willing to pay more than $220 per ton but because the equilibrium point is $230 per ton some producers will find it unprofitable to sell at the $220 control price.

Similarly, if the government imposes a price support on wheat and the price is raised above the equilibrium point to $240 per ton, there will be a "surplus" of wheat, as producers place more wheat on the market than consumers would want to purchase at the higher price. We will examine such farm programs later in the book. In both situations, shortage and surplus, the market is in disequilibrium. Note also that the shortage and surplus were created by government. This governmental intervention may or may not be justified as a matter of policy. Any policy decision, however, must take into account economic impacts.

(4) COSTS

Producers place goods on the market when it is profitable for them to do so. Profit is revenue minus costs. When the costs of drilling for oil exceed the revenue to be gained, it is no longer profitable to drill, and no oil will be produced.

Costs follow a pattern. In the beginning of the production cycle, costs start high. But costs decline as more units are produced. The initial costs including exploration, drilling and construction of producing the first barrel of oil are extremely high, but fall for the next several thousand barrels. Costs will decline until there are diminishing returns, i.e., until it becomes necessary to drill deeper, or to use enhanced recovery techniques, or to drill another well. Each of these events adds costs. In other words, as output increases, costs for the production of a single unit will decline, until they reach the point of diminishing returns; then, costs will rise if production is increased.

It is also important to distinguish between marginal and average costs. Average costs are determined by dividing all costs by the number of units produced, as the U-shaped cost curve in Figure 2-4 demonstrates.

Figure 2-4: Average Cost

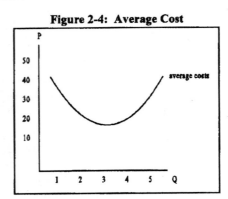

Figure 2-5: Marginal Cost

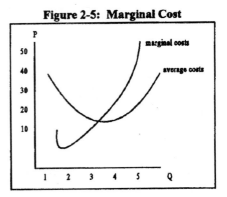

Costs may also be defined as marginal costs—the costs associated with the production of an additional unit. The marginal cost curve is more J-shaped, as costs decline and then continue to rise over a range of output. The marginal cost curve, as shown in Figure 2-5, resembles the traditional supply curve.

The distinction between average cost and marginal cost is important. If a single oil well produces 1,000 barrels of oil for a total cost of $20,000, the average cost is $20 per barrel ($20,000 divided by 1,000 barrels). If the next barrel of oil costs $25 to produce because of higher drilling costs, the average cost is approximately $20.005 ($20,025 divided by 1,001 barrels), even though the marginal cost is $25 (the cost of producing the unit number 1,001). A producer should charge $25 for barrel 1,001, rather than $20.005, because $25 accurately represents production costs. If the producer charges $20.005 for the barrel 1,001, the producer is losing money on the sale of that barrel. The marginal cost curve is also the individual firm's supply curve, because the seller will supply goods or commodities as long as marginal revenue is greater than marginal cost. We now turn to marginal revenue.

(5) MARGINAL REVENUE

A discussion of marginal revenue demonstrates why the marginal cost of producing the next unit is the more accurate indicator of cost (and profit). Producers want to maximize profits. However, profit maximization does not depend on selling the most units. Rather, profit is maximized when marginal cost equals marginal revenue. Table 2-2 shows the relationship between revenue and profits.

Table 2-2

Quantity Q	Price P	Total Revenue TR	Total Cost TC	Total Profit TP	Marginal Cost MC	Marginal Revenue MR
PROFIT MAXIMIZATION						
1	10	10	8	2		
2	9	18	10	8	2	8
3	8	24	14	10	4	6
4	7	28	16	12	2	4
5	6	30	18	12	2	2
6	5	30	20	10	2	0
7	4	28	22	6	2	− 2
8	3	24	24	0	2	− 4
9	2	18	26	− 8	2	− 6
10	1	10	28	− 18	2	− 8

Notice that total revenue (TR) is maximized at 30, when either 5 or 6 units (Q) are sold. Contrast this level of revenue with the TR of 10, when 10 (Q) is the maximum level of units sold. Notice that as more units are sold the price declines. As Q increases, P declines because, in a competitive market, where the laws of supply and demand determine price, prices will fall when the supply of a good (Q) increases. This result occurs because to sell a greater quantity of a good or service, the producer must lower its price, thus running the risk of reducing total revenue. Notice, then, how this seller can increase its TR until it sells 6 units and after that point TR decreases, despite the fact that the seller has increased the quantity of the good or service sold. Thus at some point in the production cycle, increasing the number of units sold does not increase total revenue.

From a total revenue standpoint, it makes no difference if 5 or 6 units are sold, because TR is the same at 30. However, if one considers total profitability (TP), at 5 units TP is 12, and at 6 units TP is 10. Total profit is the result of deducting total cost (TC) from total revenue (TR). Therefore, a greater profit is made by selling 5 units than by selling 6 or more units. Notice that profit is maximized when marginal cost (MC of 2) is equal to marginal revenue (MR of 2).

(6) INDUSTRY PRICE AND FIRM PRICE

In competitive markets, individual firms are called price takers, and they sell their products at the price set by the industry. Recall the first condition of a competitive market is that a market must have numerous buyers and sellers no one of which can affect supply or price. Consequently, in a competitive market all firms must sell at the price set by "the market" (actually by the laws of supply and demand) and so single firm can set its own price. Instead, the firm "takes" its price from the market.

Cost lies behind a firm's supply curve, and cost helps set the market price for a good in an industry. An industry's supply curve is simply the sum of the supply curves of all the individual firms in the industry. An industry then competes for resources with other industries. The price a firm in a competitive industry charges for its product is related to the industry's cost curve, as shown in Figures 2-6(A) and 2-6(B).

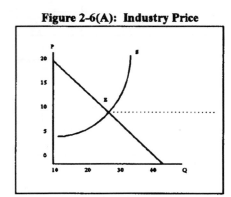

Figure 2-6(A): Industry Price

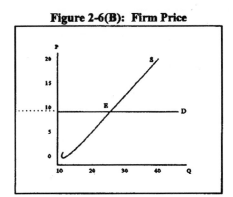

Figure 2-6(B): Firm Price

Figure 2-6(A) depicts an industry's supply (S) and demand (D) curves and the industry's equilibrium point (E). The industry's equilibrium point sets the individual firm's price (Figure 2-6(B)) as indicated by the dotted line. Notice, further, that the individual firm's price line (D) in Figure 2-6(B) is horizontal. This is because in a perfectly competitive market one firm among many cannot change the industry's market price. Thus, the firm's price line is set by the industry, and it fixes the individual firm's demand as well as its level of marginal revenue. For an individual firm in a competitive industry, therefore, $P = D = MR$. The individual firm cannot raise its prices in the hope of greater profitability, because the firm will lose all of its customers to other firms in the industry. A firm in such a perfectly competitive industry cannot lower price without losing money, because the firm's costs are just below its price. Further, it would be irrational for a firm to lower price, even if there were a margin of profit, because in a perfectly competitive market, the individual firm can sell all of its product at the prevailing market price. There is simply no need to lower price in the hope of gaining a larger market share.

The demand curve for the industry does not have this horizontal characteristic, because if the prices in the industry change, consumers will respond by buying more of the goods when the price declines or less of the goods when the price increases. In other words, consumers will move their resources to other industries in response to price rises and will move their resources from other industries in response to declining prices. Manufacturing plants, for example, may switch to natural gas rather than burn coal to generate electricity when the price of coal is greater than the price of natural gas. Thus, money is moved from the coal industry to the natural gas industry when the price of coal increases or the price of natural gas decreases beyond the other's equilibrium point.

(7) PRICE ELASTICITY OF DEMAND

The law of demand requires that for every change in price there will be a change in demand. For every price rise, there will be a decline in demand. And, for every decrease in price there will be increase in demand. The more refined question is: What is the rate of change? If, for every 1% price rise, there is a 1% decrease in demand, the price elasticity is said to be unitary. For ordinary goods in a competitive market, elasticity will be unitary. Elastic prices are those that respond with a greater percentage decrease in demand for every percentage increase in price. In a highly competitive market, a firm that sets prices higher than the market price risks losing all consumers. Likewise, a firm that can sell below the market price will capture customers.

Some goods, however, are highly valued, so that there will be less of a decline in demand for every corresponding price rise. Such a situation is said to be inelastic. When prices are inelastic, producers can raise prices without an exact corresponding decrease in demand. Inelastic demand has the effect of increasing producers' revenues and affecting a greater transfer of resources from consumers to producers. For many years, electricity prices were thought to be so inelastic that electric utilities could raise prices indefinitely to increase profits (absent close public utility commission oversight). However, in the 1970s, as electricity (and all energy) prices escalated at a rate greater than inflation, consumers did respond to rising electricity prices by reducing consumption. This reduction in demand had the result of forcing electricity prices down.

b. THE BENEFITS OF EFFICIENT MARKETS

When a market performs according to the previous description, society obtains a number of important benefits. Because markets match supply and demand (at the equilibrium price), they are efficient in the sense that they minimize mismatches between the supply and demand. In other words, consumers buy the goods they most want and value, because producers place those goods on the market. In this way resource use is maximized, not wasted. Markets conserve scarce resources by reducing the surpluses and shortages of goods and services. Markets also stimulate firms to lower costs and engage in technological innovation. In a perfectly competitive market, no consumer will pay more money for a product or service when the same product or service is being sold at a lower price. A firm, however, can gain additional business if it can charge less than its competitors. By reducing costs, a firm has this opportunity. Moreover, if a firm can produce a new product, or improve a product, it has the opportunity to increase its sales. Consumers will be willing to pay more for the new or improved product because it is not identical to other similar products.

Another advantage is that a perfectly competitive market maximizes social wealth. The market is able to accomplish this feat because it produces a "consumer surplus." Consider Figure 2-7. At the equilibrium price (P), many consumers are able to purchase a product for less money than they are willing to pay for it. Consumers have different preferences for a product, and some persons will pay more than others for it. The demand curve in Figure 2-7 (which is pictured as a straight line) reflects this reality. Consumers are willing to pay prices all along this curve including prices higher than the equilibrium price at point P. However, at higher prices, fewer persons are willing to buy the product than at lower prices. This means that all of those persons who are willing to pay more than P get a benefit. They can spend or invest the money that they would have paid for the product if it had cost more than P. Thus, competition generates a consumer surplus by lowering the price that many consumers have to pay to less than the maximum price that they are willing to pay. In Figure 2-7, this "consumer surplus" is represented by the shaded triangle (A-E-P).

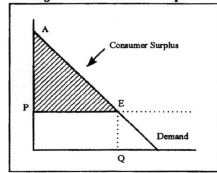

Figure 2-7: Consumer Surplus

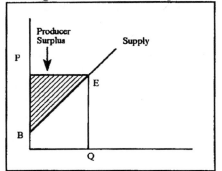

Figure 2-8: Producer Surplus

Similarly, producer surplus is created when there are producers willing to supply goods in a market below the equilibrium point. Just as there is a range of consumers willing to pay more than the equilibrium price, there is a range of producers willing to put goods on the market below the equilibrium price. There are producers along the line B-E willing to supply goods below the equilibrium price. The total surplus from these goods is represented in Figure 2-8 by the shaded triangle (B-E-P).

The trick of the competitive market is to maximize both producer and consumer surplus. Similarly, it is the economic goal of government regulation to maximize such surpluses when markets fail to do so.

c. MARKET DEFECTS

Perfectly competitive markets achieve the previously noted virtues. The operative phrase here, of course, is "perfectly competitive." Perfect competition, however, is an idealized version of microeconomic theory. Few, if any, markets are perfectly competitive. Can you explain why?

Actually, the answer is quite simple—no firm wants to follow the rules of the perfectly competitive market. Go back to the five conditions of the perfectly competitive market. In effect, all firms want to cheat the market. Every firm would like to violate the first condition by being a monopolist (Microsoft?); violate the second condition by cornering a market in goods (Major League Baseball?); violate the third condition through product specializations (every firm?); violate the fourth condition by not disclosing information (doctors?); and, violate the fifth condition by imposing high entry barriers (pharmaceutical companies?).

We do not want our comments about "cheating the market" to be taken too far or misconstrued. Firms legitimately attempt to violate competitive market conditions because that is the nature of business and public companies have fiduciary obligations to their shareholders. Even the Mom and Pop Pizza Shop wants to product differentiate and price local competitors out of their market. Also, information is costly to obtain and firms do not rush to give information away for free for fear of hurting their own competitive advantage. These behaviors are a far cry from the business practices of several firms in the energy, telecommunications, and investment banking businesses as reported in 2002.

Regardless of the legitimacy of firm behavior, when perfectly competitive conditions are not obtained, market defects can be identified. When a defect is identified, government can step in to address the defect and make the market either more competitive, more fair or both.[4] In this section, we examine regulatory justifications that relate to such market failures.

(1) COMPETITIVE CONDITIONS

The perfectly competitive market model requires that there be numerous buyers and sellers who react to the forces of supply and demand in the manner described above. Buyers and sellers, however, may not behave according to the model for several reasons.

Monopoly: Some industries, such as public utilities and railroads, are so structured that only one firm or only a small number of firms can operate efficiently in a market.[5] These firms enjoy large economies of scale, and entry costs are high. For example, the cost of adding additional customers is very low for an existing telephone company—the company only has to connect the new customer to existing lines. By comparison, a new competitor must acquire the right to and build the lines in the first place. Moreover, it would be wasteful to install a duplicate set of lines in a neighborhood to add competing telephone service. If, however, telephone service does not require using landlines, this problem is avoided. Thus, cellular service offers the opportunity for new companies to compete with the existing telephone company. If a sufficient number of customers treat cellular service as a substitute for traditional

---

[4] *See generally* C. SUNSTEIN, *supra* note 2; R. EPSTEIN, *supra* note 2; A. OGUS, REGULATION: LEGAL FORM AND ECONOMIC THEORY (1994); J. STEVENS, THE ECONOMICS OF COLLECTIVE CHOICE (1993); D. SPULBER, REGULATION AND MARKETS (1989); S. BREYER, REGULATION AND ITS REFORM (1982); A. STONE, REGULATION AND ITS ALTERNATIVES (1982).

[5] *See* A. KAHN, I THE ECONOMICS OF REGULATION: PRINCIPLES & INSTITUTIONS PART I (1988).

telephone service, the telephone company would not be able to maintain its monopoly.

Monopolies have market power. Because such firms have no competitors, they need not set prices according to the laws of supply and demand or according to their costs. Rather, firms in a monopoly position can restrict output, increase profits, and consequently impose a social welfare loss by charging higher than competitive prices. Government regulation is used in such cases to set prices at competitive levels or to establish entry conditions for competitors that mitigate the power of a monopolist to set monopoly prices.

Excessive competition: Excessive competition occurs when a firm sets its prices so low that rival companies are driven out of business. When enough companies leave the market, the remaining companies can then engage in noncompetitive (oligopolistic) pricing. (At the extreme, the market ends up with one firm only.) Airlines, trucks, and other forms of passenger transportation were regulated at one time in order to prevent excessive competition. Later, we will explain that all of these forms of transportation have been deregulated on the theory that the excessive competition rationale is no longer viewed as valid for those industries. This rational is still used, however, to justify some types of price controls and government subsidies in the agriculture industry to be discussed later in the book. Moreover, in light of the financial chaos in the airline industry, some analysts argue the excessive competition rationale does have merit.

Unequal bargaining: If persons in contract negotiations do not have equal bargaining power, fully voluntary exchange transactions cannot take place. For example, producers with superior bargaining power can take advantage of consumers, or employers with superior bargaining power can take advantage of employees. Government will protect the weak consumer or employee through regulation. For example, states regulate the contract terms under which insurance companies sell insurance; otherwise, consumers would be at the mercy of sellers of a product that many consumers demand but few can bargain about.

Moral hazard: A moral hazard is a situation in which the probability of a loss, as well as the size of the loss, may be increased because a person has less of an incentive to take precautions.[6] Most simply, moral hazard, is a situation in which someone else pays. Expense accounts, insurance, and medical benefits have the effect of encouraging consumers to consume more than they would if the expenses were paid directly (internalized) by the consumer, as the economic model assumes. The economic difficulty with a moral hazard is that costs can be inflated over what they otherwise would be if someone else were not paying.

Rationalization: A market is more efficient when goods, such as light bulbs, are standardized, even when they are made by different manufacturers. If one firm, or a small group of firms, control a particular market, they may lack an adequate incentive to standardize products. One example of a need for rationalization is a computer's digital operating system such as Microsoft's DOS. Computers need to talk with each other. The market will be more

---

[6] M. POLINSKY, AN INTRODUCTION TO LAW AND ECONOMICS 54 (1983).

efficient if the operating systems are standardized so that information can move smoothly and easily. Another example is that of music CDs. They all need to be a standard size so that they can be played on any CD player. Such standardization is also known as rationalization. Thus, government regulation can facilitate uniformity by regulation.

(2) RESTRICTED ENTRY OR EXIT

A perfectly competitive market also requires that buyers and sellers have freedom of entry and exit from the market. For example, if existing sellers raise their prices, new sellers must be free to enter the market attracted by the prospect of making additional revenue. Eventually the additional supply will force the price down to the benefit of consumers. In some markets, however, existing sellers may be able to block the entry of competitors, or force new competitors to pay higher costs that will make them less competitive. When this occurs, there is a "bottleneck" in the market. Regulation concerning natural gas distribution and cable television has the function of addressing such bottlenecks. Bottlenecks can also occur in airline markets as discussed in a later chapter.

(3) EXTERNAL COSTS

The price that consumers pay for a product in an efficient market reflects the full value of the resources that are used in the production of that product. A market flaw exists when the producer of a product avoids paying for some of these production costs. For example, if the owner of a factory that emits pollution does not pay the medical expenses of persons who become ill from the pollution, the price of the product will not reflect such medical costs. The market will be inefficient because there will be more demand for the product than if the factory owner had paid for the damages caused by the pollution. If the factory owner had made such payments, the price of the firm's products would have been higher, and fewer products would have been sold.

The costs associated with the production of a product which are not paid by the producer of the product are called "spillover costs," because they spill over as a result of the production process and are borne by someone other than the producer. These costs are also called "externalities," because they are paid by persons outside of—or "external" to—the producer. As noted, unregulated markets with spillover costs will generally be inefficient, because firms in the position of the previous factory owner have no incentive to pay for the medical expenses of those who become ill.

There are three potential remedies for spillover costs.[7] Under some circumstances, a company may adjust the price of a product, because persons who are adversely affected by its production will bargain for that result. Such a situation may occur between an employee union and management for example. In most markets, however, the costs of reaching a bargain between a producer and persons harmed by the production process are prohibitive, because of the large number of persons who are injured. The tort system

---

[7] *See* N. Komesar, Imperfect Alternatives: Choosing Institutions in Law, Economics & Public Policy (1994).

compensates for the lack of such a bargain by forcing manufacturers to pay for the harmful consequences of many of their actions. Nevertheless, Congress has reached the judgment in many circumstances that agency regulation is necessary to avoid additional injuries. Agencies such as the Environmental Protection Agency (EPA) and the Occupational Health and Safety Administration (OSHA) have the authority to order manufacturers to reduce pollutants (see the discussion of environmental regulation) or to remedy dangerous working conditions.

(4) INADEQUATE AND INACCURATE INFORMATION

The economic model of efficient markets is predicated on the assumption that buyers and sellers have accurate and complete information about products. When product information is inadequate, the government can make a market more efficient by providing the missing information or by requiring the seller to provide it. Government regulation might also be justified if a consumer might misinterpret market information. (The capacity of consumers to act on information is sometimes limited by psychological factors, sophistication, etc.)

Inadequate information: When consumers lack adequate product information, they can purchase goods and services that will fail to perform adequately, or that will harm them or their property. A market without adequate information is inefficient because consumers with better information would have purchased other products. Market flaws of various types are responsible for inadequate information. For example, some types of sellers, like itinerant roofers, are free to mislead consumers because they do not depend significantly on repeat sales. Regulation by agencies such as the Federal Trade Commission (FTC) addresses this problem by prohibiting sellers from "false or deceptive acts or practices" in the sale of their products or services.[8] In other markets, information about the performance of products is too expensive for consumers to obtain. For example, time-consuming and costly scientific testing is necessary to develop data concerning the safety of pharmaceutical drugs or pesticides. Because consumers are unlikely to undertake the testing on their own, sellers can exploit the consumer's lack of knowledge in selling dangerous drugs or pesticides. In response to this danger, the Environmental Protection Agency (EPA) and the Food and Drug Administration (FDA) require the testing of pesticides and drugs before they can be sold to consumers.[9]

Psychological factors: The economic paradigm assumes that markets are composed of rational individuals who act in their own self-interest. For this to be true, individuals must be able to process available information accurately concerning alternative decisions, rank those decisions in order of their expected utility, and choose the best decision. Psychologists maintain, however, that the economist's assumption of rationality exaggerates human cognitive capacities.[10] For example, individuals may underestimate the

---

[8] 15 U.S.C. §§ 45, 52 (1982).

[9] *See* 21 U.S.C. §§ 351–360ee (drug and device regulation); 7 U.S.C. §§ 136–136y (pesticide regulation).

[10] *See* C. SUNSTEIN, *supra* note 2, chs. 1–4; Ellickson, *Bringing Culture and Human Frailty to Rational Actors: A Critique of Classical Law and Economics,* 65 CHI.-KENT L. REV. 23, 40–43 (1989).

riskiness of their own behavior because of their fear of death. In this and similar circumstances, a society may decide that regulation is justified to protect consumers from their cognitive inability to understand the consequences of their actions. Thus, a law requiring automobile occupants to wear seat belts can be justified, in part, on the ground that some people will undervalue the benefit of seat belts because they erroneously judge themselves as unlikely to be hurt. For this reason, teenagers and drunk drivers are the least likely to wear seat belts. Some economists have embraced the idea that psychological factors may be a form of market failure,[11] but others tend to ignore this possibility when they make policy recommendations.

(5) PUBLIC GOODS

Some products and services, like the armed forces which defend this country, will not be produced in private markets because of what economists call the "free rider" problem.[12] These services, called "public goods," have the unique characteristic that consumption of them by one consumer does not diminish the possibility of consumption by another consumer. As a result, they must be purchased by the government, if they are to be purchased at all. Otherwise, every consumer will attempt to become a free rider by waiting for someone else to purchase the product or service so that it can be used for free. For example, the government uses tax revenues to pay for the national defense because citizens cannot be denied the benefit of these services and if payment were voluntary it is quite likely that many, if not most, people would not pay. Taxes, historically, have been used exactly for such purposes.

Other public goods will be produced in private markets, but there will be an inefficient amount of them. Education is an example of this latter type of public good. When a society has an educated citizenry, there is an increase in economic productivity and a decrease in crime, juvenile delinquency, and welfare payments. If there were no public education, parents would send their children to private schools which would be created to meet the demand for educational services. In a private market, however, efforts to maximize the social benefits of education will be stymied for two reasons. First, citizens without children would have no incentive to contribute to the cost of education. They would instead attempt to become free riders. Second, the cost of private education would be prohibitive to many citizens thus imposing further costs on society.

Welfare programs can also be identified as a response to the failure of private markets to produce an appropriate amount of "public goods." Although private charity exists, some people fail to contribute, because they can be "free riders" on the efforts of others. To the extent that helping the poor to escape poverty generates social benefits (in the form of increased economic productivity, decreased crime, etc.), all citizens will be the recipients of these benefits, regardless of whether they make a contribution.

---

[11] Ellickson, *supra* note 10, at 40–43; Posner, *The Future of Law and Economics: A Comment on Ellickson,* 65 CHI.-KENT. L. REV. 57–60; *see* Hirschleifer, *The Expanding Domain of Economics,* 75 AM. ECON. REV., Dec. 1985, at 53.

[12] *See* N. BARR, THE ECONOMICS OF THE WELFARE STATE (2d ed. 1993).

Two forms of regulation address the problem of public goods. First, regulation of the method of taxation and the collection of revenues ensures that each citizen pays a share of the cost of governmental purchases of public goods. Second, regulation is used to guarantee that those who provide public goods do so in a manner that maximizes their benefit and minimizes their cost. For example, the federal, state, and local governments all have administrative agencies which monitor how local school districts spend tax money they collect. Similarly, welfare regulation ensures that benefits go only to those persons who are entitled to them.

NOTES AND QUESTIONS

1. We will return to most of these concepts of market failure in the second and third parts of this book. If the concepts are vague to you at this time, you will become more familiar with them as we address them in more detail.

2. Economics can be classified as a behavioral science that studies how humans satisfy unlimited wants with limited resources. The initial rules of supply and demand are rules about human behavior. Thus, the economic study of scarcity contains other assumptions about human behavior. *Homo economicus* is said to be a rational maximizer of individual self-interest. Is this a congenial description of human behavior? Are these assumptions acceptable to you? Can we build on economic theory based on these assumptions? Should social policies be based on a theory so built? Do counter examples disprove the assumptions about individual, rational, wealth-maximizing behavior? Can you think of counter examples of when you have acted jointly or irrationally, or traded for a loss? Regarding the assumption of rationality, a theory built on irrational behavior seems impossible. Moreover, regarding wealth maximization, it seems reasonable to say that more is better than less. Still, these assumptions may well be questioned and may not hold for some transactions.[13]

3. Robert Kuttner writes that health care offers an instructive example of a market that "violates several conditions" of the textbook perfectly competitive market.[14] Review the previous list of market defects and consider which operate in health care markets.

Unlike perfectly competitive markets, there is no free entry to health care. He explains, "you cannot simply open a hospital, or hang out your shingle as a doctor. This gives health-care providers a degree of market power that compromises the competitive model—and raises prices." Of course, physicians are seldom monopolists, but to what extent do such barriers to entry permit physicians to charge more than they could if entry were easier? Are there instances where physicians have a monopoly, such as in small communities? How about hospitals? If a community has only one hospital, does it have a

---

[13] For a critique of some of the behavioral assumptions used in economics, see A.O. HIRSCHMAN, RIVAL VIEWS OF MARKET SOCIETY AND OTHER RECENT ESSAYS (1986); Sen, *Rational Fools: A Critique of the Behavioral Foundations of Economic Theory,* 6 PHIL. & PUB. AFFAIRS 317 (1977). *Compare* West, *Authority, Autonomy, and Choice: The Role of Consent in the Moral and Political Visions of Franz Kafka and Richard Posner,* 99 HARV. L. REV. 384 (1985) *with* Posner, *The Ethical Significance of Free Choice: A Reply to Professor West,* 99 HARV. L. REV. 1431 (1986).

[14] R. KUTTNER, *supra* note 1, at 17–18.

monopoly? How much competition is there between multiple hospitals in a community?

Health care markets are also subject to "moral hazard" because most Americans have some form of health insurance. Is this problem responsible for rising costs in health care markets? Is health care over consumed because people do not pay as they go out of their own pockets? What happens in the health care market? Kuttner explains:

> In ordinary markets, sellers maximize profits by minimizing costs. But in health care, the profit maximizer's object is to maximize insurance reimbursement. The more complex the procedure and the more inflated the cost base, the more money can be billed to the insurance company. In recent years, private and government insurers have tried to crack down—by intensively reviewing what doctors and hospitals do, publishing book-length schedules of permissible procedures and reimbursements. Providers have fought back, by further complicating their own billing. All this inflates the cost of the whole system.

Thus, in reality, consumers do not purchase the services of a physician or other health care provider. They purchase insurance which in turns buys such services on behalf of the consumer.

The health care insurance market presents problems of its own. How competitive is this market? How much bargaining power for health insurance do consumers have? As Kuttner notes, "Increasingly, . . . insurance companies seek to minimize costs simply be refusing to insure people likely to become sick." What market recourse do consumers have?

The situation is further complicated by the fact that consumers are not the actual purchasers of medical insurance in many cases. For many, medical insurance is obtained from the person's employer. Do employers and consumers have the same incentives when it comes to purchasing insurance? Is there a problem with equal bargaining power between employees and employers concerning the purchase of insurance?

4. Is the lack of health insurance also a flaw in health care markets? The failure of an employer to purchase insurance spills over to others because the cost of treating uninsured persons is borne by the other consumers of health care providers. This occurs when physicians and hospitals treat some patients who cannot pay. In order to recoup such costs, they raise their prices for consumers that can pay. In the first Clinton term, the President proposed to Congress a requirement that all employers provide health insurance. The President recognized that employers would raise prices for their products and services in order to pay for the cost of such insurance, but he argued that citizens were already paying for such care. The President also argued that requiring employers to purchase insurance for every employee could decrease the cost of medical care. If employees had insurance, they would be more likely to seek preventive care or to seek earlier intervention once they became ill.

5. There are also public goods problems in health care markets. Kuttner offers the example of vaccinations for diseases like polio: "The value to society of mass vaccinations far exceeds the profits that can be captured by the doctor or drug company. If vaccinations and other public health measures were left to private supply-and-demand, society would seriously under-invest." Why? How do persons other than those who take the vaccine benefit? What is the free rider problem?

2. NONECONOMIC GOALS

Justifying regulation on the basis of noneconomic values is the mirror image of the economist's approach to regulation. The noneconomic analyst starts with the premise that society uses its political system to establish a set of values that defines how it wishes to be organized. In short, society should promote fairness or equity as examples of values. Once these values are established, the government accepts the operation of the market system to the extent that it does not conflict with society's value choices. If there is a conflict, government acts to eliminate the conflict between the market and social values.[15] "In this conceptual framework," Richard Andrews explains, "government is not simply a corrective instrument at the margins of economic markets, but [a] . . . central arena in which the members of society choose and legitimate their collective values. The principal purposes of legislative action are to weigh and affirm social values and to define and enforce the rights and duties of the society, through representative democracy."[16]

From the noneconomic perspective, the moral problem with relying on markets to organize social relationships is that the operation of markets reflects only "commodity" values. Professor Anderson has identified four such norms:

> First, in determining the product and distribution of goods, the market does not recognize any distinction between wants, principles or needs. Second, the parties to market exchange have no precontractual obligations to provide the goods being exchanged. Third, the power of an individual to promote her interests in a market is a function of her financial resources and competitive position. Finally, the market provides an avenue for expression of discontent through exit, not voice.[17]

Because markets reflect only commodity values, they can produce results that society will consider inappropriate in terms of other inconsistent values. Society intervenes in the following contexts to conform markets to these noneconomic values.

a. PROHIBIT OBJECTIONABLE EXCHANGES

In an unfettered market economy, everything would be for sale and no activity would be forbidden. Yet, a society might object that certain market exchanges are morally objectionable and should for that reason be forbidden.

---

[15] *See* Schroeder, Book Review, 88 MICH. L. REV. 1483, 1500–01 (1990) (reviewing FRANK CROSS, ENVIRONMENTALLY INDUCED CANCER AND THE LAW (1989)); Stewart, *Regulation in a Liberal State: The Role of Noncommodity Values,* 92 YALE L.J. 1537 (1983).

[16] Andrews, *Cost-Benefit Analysis As Regulatory Reform,* in COST-BENEFIT ANALYSIS AND ENVIRONMENTAL REGULATIONS: POLITICS, ETHICS, AND METHODS 107, 112 (D. Swartzman, R. Liroff & K. Croke eds. 1982).

[17] Anderson, *Values, Risks, and Market Norms,* 17 PHIL. & PUB. AFF. 54 (1988).

For example, a market system permits the buying and selling of slaves, as long as there are willing buyers and sellers with the means to subjugate the slaves. The influence of individuals opposed to slavery depends on their financial resources and competitive positions. Persons with sufficient resources can buy slaves for the purpose of setting them free, but for those without resources, the only avenue for their discontent is not to participate in the market, which is "exit" in Anderson's description of market norms.[18]

If slavery is to be prohibited as a matter of principle, the political system must act to limit the operation of markets. In the political system, where opponents of slavery can "voice" their objections, opponents of slavery can ban it—and thereby conform the market to social principles. In other words, society uses regulation to prohibit some exchanges because of their morally objectionable nature.[19]

b. ELIMINATE PRICE AS THE BASIS OF EXCHANGE

The distribution of wealth in a society determines which persons will acquire scarce goods and services. When goods or services are in scarce supply, many people are unable to buy them because of their high price. Society may regard this result as inequitable when certain goods or services are involved. Some regulatory programs involve replacing the allocation of scarce goods or services by markets with government allocation. While we may all be content living in a society in which only the few own two hundred foot yachts, should only the wealthy have access to life-saving health care? The government, for example, prohibits a market in which organs for transplantation would be bought and sold, and relies instead on health care providers to determine who is to receive such organs. Should price, as determined by willingness (and ability) to pay determine who gets what?

c. REMEDY DISTRIBUTION OF WEALTH

The previous reason for regulation objects to market allocation because it is unfair or inappropriate to allocate a good or service on the basis of price in light of the distribution of wealth. Other regulatory programs seek to remedy the distribution of wealth produced by the operation of markets.

Some persons will prosper in a market economy, but others will not. A person may "need" food to survive, but if he or she lacks resources, he or she will go hungry. The market system will not "recognize" a person's needs without resources. By comparison, a rich person may "want" a third automobile. Even though that person can only drive one car at a time, the market will recognize the person's wants, because the person has the money to purchase the automobile. Thus, even an efficient market system can produce a distribution of wealth that a majority of citizens find unsatisfactory because some people are too poor to live a humane existence. Welfare and related programs reflect a collective judgment that a just society does not relegate the poorest of its citizens to conditions of degradation and despair.

---

[18] *See also* A. HIRSCHMAN, EXIT, VOICE, AND LOYALTY (1970).

[19] P. BROWN, RESTORING THE PUBLIC TRUST: A FRESH VISION FOR PROGRESSIVE GOVERNMENT IN AMERICA 57–58 (1994).

d. SUBJECT EXCHANGES TO COLLECTIVE VALUES

Some forms of regulation seek to promote collective values which a society wishes to protect and cultivate. Cass Sunstein explains:

> Some statutes should be understood as an embodiment not of privately held preferences, but of what might be described as collective desires, including aspirations, . . . or considered judgments on the part of significant segments of society. Laws of this sort are a product of deliberative processes on the part of citizens and representatives. They cannot be understood as an attempt to aggregate or trade off private preferences. . . .
>
>   . . . Some people may, for example, want nonentertainment broadcasting on television, even though their own consumption patterns favor situation comedies; they may seek stringent environmental laws even though they do not use the public parks; they may approve of laws calling for social security and welfare even though they do not save or give to the poor; they may support antidiscrimination laws even though their own behavior is hardly race-or gender-neutral. The choices people make as political participants are different from those that they make as consumers. . . .[20]

By comparison, an economist assumes that the aggregation of individual market decisions by consumers results in the best use of resources for the community. If no market defects are present, the economist would permit markets to determine the use and distribution of basic and valuable resources, such as air, water, and mineral rights.[21] Are all prices determined in markets without government involvement? Notice that liquor, gasoline, and tobacco are taxed. Note also that milk, sugar and wheat are often subsidized. How do free market economists react to the treatment of these goods?

Many who object to relying on markets to define resource use believe that some "natural entities and/or states of affairs are intrinsically valuable, and thus deserve to be the object of our moral concern, irrespective of whether they are useful or valuable to us in meeting *our* needs."[22] For example, some laws seek to protect natural resources because market exchanges only reflect the preferences of today's consumers. The protection of endangered species reflects this commitment. So do laws protecting natural areas from environmental degradation that is impossible or extraordinarily expensive to repair. Laws protecting cultural artifacts have the same motive.

NOTES AND QUESTIONS

1. Persons who promote noneconomic values such as fairness over efficiency must confront a basic question: Does fairness exist independently of efficiency? Harvard Law School Professors Louis Kaplow and Steven Shavell argue that fairness is chimerical and, instead, legal policies should only be established

---

[20] C. SUNSTEIN, *supra* note 2, at 57–58.

[21] Malloy, *The Limits of Science in Legal Discourse — A Reply To Posner,* 24 VAL. U.L. REV. 175, 179–80 (1990).

[22] Thompson, *A Refutation of Environmental Ethics,* 12 ENVT'L ETHICS 147, 148 (1990).

if they increase an individual's well-being. Kaplow and Shavell define well-being in terms of welfare economics: "It incorporates in a positive way everything that an individual can consume, social and environmental amenities, personally held notions of fulfillment, sympathetic feelings and so forth." Kaplow & Shavell, Fairness Versus Welfare, 114 Harv. L. Rev. 961, 980 (2001). The notion of fairness as a basis of social policy, they argue, leaves people worse off and has no independent weight for policy analysis. *Id.* at 96. Do you agree?

2. Professor Sunstein discusses why citizens will support noneconomic values through political actions. He explains that a person's role as a consumer is different than the person's role as a "citizen" in a democracy:

> First, citizens may seek to fulfill individual and collective aspirations in political behavior, not in consumption. As citizens, people may seek the aid of the law to bring about a social state in some sense higher than what emerges from a market ordering. Second, people may, in their capacity as political actors, attempt to satisfy altruistic or other-regarding desires, which diverge from the self-interested preferences characteristic of other markets. Third, political decisions might vindicate what might be called meta-preferences or second-order preferences. A law protecting environmental diversity and opposing consuming behavior is an example. People have wishes about their wishes; and sometimes they try to vindicate these second-order preferences, or considered judgments about what is best, through law. Fourth, people may precommit themselves with regulation, to a course of action they consider to be in the general interest;. . . . The adoption of a Constitution is itself an example of a precommitment strategy.[23]

Do you agree? Would you refuse to endorse a regulatory decision unless its economic benefits exceeded its economic costs?

3. You should recall that redistributive programs can also be justified on economic grounds as public goods. Such programs are public goods because they benefit society in terms of increased economic productivity, reduced crime, less infant mortality, and so on. Under the economic rationale, however, spending on welfare would be subject to a cost-benefit test. In economic terms, it is useful to spend money on welfare as long as the benefits from this investment (in terms of greater economic productivity, reduced crime, etc.) are greater than the cost of the welfare programs. By comparison, analyzing welfare in terms of noncommodity values may justify spending more money on welfare than would be indicated under a cost-benefit test. This would be true even if the level of spending did not eliminate all of the effects of poverty.

4. Professor Richard Epstein argues that the government should not forbid employers from making employment decisions on any grounds whatsoever, including discrimination based on race, sex, age, or religion.[24] Epstein believes that the attempt to use regulation to end discrimination costs more money than the benefits that can be derived and he would repeal laws which ban employment discrimination on the grounds mentioned. He believes that

---

[23] C. SUNSTEIN, *supra* note 2, at 57–58.

[24] R. EPSTEIN, FORBIDDEN GROUNDS: THE CASE AGAINST EMPLOYMENT DISCRIMINATION (1991).

employers are unlikely to discriminate because firms which turn away good employees will not be competitive with other firms who hire the best employees that they can find. Epstein acknowledges that the market may not end all discrimination, but he claims that most victims of discrimination will be able to find employment with employers who will not discriminate against them.

In a perfectly competitive market, why would employers find it unprofitable to engage in discrimination? Are employment markets perfectly competitive? Would any of the market flaws described earlier prevent an employment market from operating in the manner Epstein claims?

Are Epstein's arguments relevant? Are laws against discrimination intended to remedy some market flaw, or are they intended to achieve some other social value. Does this situation fit any of the categories of regulation that promote social values?[25]

5. Health care also raises equity concerns. Many persons lack health insurance because it is not offered by their employer and they cannot afford to purchase it on their own. If health care were left entirely to private markets, such persons would not receive care, except as provided by private charity. If private charity is insufficient, should the government intervene? Does a society have an ethical obligation to help those persons who cannot afford health care obtain it? How great is this obligation? To what extent should society seek to remedy the distribution of wealth in light of its impact on access to medical services?

As mentioned earlier, the government also intervenes in health care markets to prohibit the sale of organs for transplant. This prohibition constitutes a decision to eliminate price as the basis of exchange. Chapter 12 discusses whether this is an appropriate policy.

Society also uses regulation to prohibit objectionable exchanges. For example, a terminally ill person who desired to commit suicide could purchase the necessary drugs and assistance in an unregulated market—assuming that a willing seller could be found. In the United States, however, there are laws prohibiting such transactions, because they are considered to be morally objectionable.

3. ECONOMIC VERSUS NONECONOMIC JUSTIFICATIONS

The choice whether to adopt a policy based on an economic or noneconomic justification is a political issue. Economic concepts are useful in informing the public and decisionmakers about which choices and alternatives are available. Economists can also describe the likely economic consequences of those choices and alternatives. However, economists have no special expertise regarding which choices society should make. This insight becomes clear if one distinguishes between "positive" and "normative" uses of economics.

---

[25] *See Symposium: Epstein / Title VII Symposium*, 31 SAN DIEGO L. REV. 1 (1994).

a. POSITIVE AND NORMATIVE ECONOMICS

It is important to distinguish two senses in which the discipline of economics is used. In a formal and traditional sense, economics is a positive social science. Economics describes or models human behavior. For example, an economist who relies on the microeconomic model can say with a fair degree of certitude that as price rises, people will consume less. This is purely a descriptive statement. It is also a positive statement as contrasted with a normative one. People also talk about economics in a normative sense. Instead of simply describing the way markets work, they will use economics to make pronouncements about how markets ought to work. This "ought" statement then becomes evaluative and prescriptive for how public policy should be shaped. An economist, for example, can talk about the effects of a rise in the minimum wage (however, not too accurately as it turns out) but they cannot advise whether a rise is good for society any more than a lawyer or politician can so advise.

Positive economics helps us identify when the function of markets can be improved and the costs and benefits of various policy alternatives to make such improvements. What economics cannot do is to tell us how to weigh or balance these economic impacts. That is, an economist true to the discipline can provide predictions about the impact of proposed policies on price, quality, and market behavior, but the person has no special expertise concerning whether citizens should adopt or reject a policy because of these economic impacts.

A similar limitation exists concerning the distribution of wealth. As a positive matter, an economist can tell us what the distribution of wealth is, or given certain changes, what the distribution will become. No economist, *qua* economist, can tell us what the best, most valuable distribution is or ought to be. Regarding these political questions, public policymakers have as much expertise in setting goals as do economists.

b. ECONOMIC AND NONECONOMIC TRADEOFFS

The choice between economic and noneconomic goals is also inherently political because the two types of goals can be in conflict. That is, the adoption of a noneconomic goal can often cause a market to operate less efficiently. Thus, citizens must decide what degree of tradeoff between economic efficiency and noneconomic considerations to accept.[26] The nature of this conflict will become clearer as you move through the book. As noted earlier, Congress often chooses to avoid such fundamental value conflicts by delegating authority to agencies in a broad and ambiguous manner. In this situation, the conflict over values moves to an agency, where it reoccurs in the context of specific regulatory choices the agency must make. This makes regulatory decisionmaking inherently contentious.

Those who prefer an economic orientation towards policy analysis usually acknowledge that society may wish to take noneconomic considerations into account, but they generally downplay the importance of these other values. Economists concede that human behavior may not always be self-interested,

---

[26] *See* THE MORAL DIMENSIONS OF PUBLIC POLICY CHOICES (J. Gillroy & M. Wade eds. 1992); A. OKUN, EQUALITY AND EFFICIENCY: THE BIG TRADEOFF (1975).

or that it is motivated by commodity values, but they contend that such economic assumption offers a more accurate picture of human behavior than any other available theory. They point out that any theory simplifies the world in order to create testable hypotheses and that if a theory is predictive as an empirical matter, the accuracy of its assumptions are sufficiently established.[27]

The economist's claim to predictive accuracy is an empirical question. Nevertheless, in areas where there is only weak proof of the accuracy of economic theory, some economists are prone to make public policy judgments on the basis that the theory has been proven, or confuse predictive accuracy with normative attractiveness. When this occurs, these judgments constitute a normative judgment about how people should behave, rather than an empirical statement concerning how they do behave. Moreover, while some economists have attempted to reconcile economic theory with inconsistent evidence from other disciplines,[28] other economists simply ignore the contrary evidence.[29]

Viewing economics as a positive discipline deflects normative criticisms of economic theory by disclaiming any normative judgments implicit in economic theory. Nonetheless, as noted, most proponents of economic theory make normative judgments based on their understanding of that theory.[30] In particular, they are generally critical of regulatory actions related to the distribution of wealth or in support of other noneconomic values when actions constrain the market's capacity to maximize society's wealth.[31]

NOTES AND QUESTIONS

1. Regulatory lawyers must be conversant with how economics is used in policy analysis, even if they might disagree that such use is appropriate, because those who are involved in the regulatory decisionmaking process rely heavily on market-failure arguments when they engage in policy analysis. As Professor Mashaw points out, the economic theory of regulation "provides the substantive criteria for the application of law, describes its underlying rationale or defines parameters for the evaluation of the law's success or failure."[32]

2. Some students react negatively to the topic of economics in law school courses. Sometimes this reaction is simply a form of math phobia. After all, what do numbers have to do with law? Other times, the negative reaction to economics is more ideological. Persons may be critical of *homo economicus* for example, for being too selfish or materialistic or inherently conservative.

---

[27] M. Friedman, *The Methodology of Positive Economics, in* ESSAYS IN POSITIVE ECONOMICS 3 (1953).

[28] *E.g.,* R. FRANK, THE STRATEGIC USE OF REASON (1988).

[29] R. RHODES, THE ECONOMIST'S VIEW OF THE WORLD: GOVERNMENT, MARKETS AND PUBLIC POLICY 214 (1985).

[30] Leff, *Economic Analysis of Law: Some Realism About Nominalism,* 60 VA. L. REV. 451, 478–81 (1974).

[31] RHODES, *supra* note 29, at 192.

[32] Mashaw, *The Economics of Politics and the Understanding of Public Law,* 65 CHI.-KENT L. REV. 123, 123 (1989).

These criticisms are valid normative issues concerning whether economics should guide public policy decisionmaking. As noted, the student of regulatory law and policy cannot afford to ignore economic concepts because of their strong influence on public policy deliberations; however, the student can object to the use of economic arguments when she or he believes such arguments are inappropriate.

B. REGULATORY METHODS

Government intervenes to remedy market failures or to promote additional social values. Although these reasons may justify regulation in a wide variety of circumstances, there are only a few categories of regulatory and nonregulatory goals. Likewise, there are only a small number of methods used to implement regulation for either purpose. This fact aids the ability to study and analyze regulation. As Lester Salamon has observed, "A crucial starting point for [understanding regulation] must be the concept of a tool or instrument of public action itself. Underlying this concept is the notion that the multitude of individual government programs actually embody a limited array of mechanisms or arrangements that define how the programs work."[33] Earlier we discussed the limited number of reasons used to justify government intervention into markets. When government does intervene, it relies on a limited number of regulatory tools that are applied to myriad situations. The basic regulatory tools follow.

1. PRICE CONTROLS

The government in some circumstances will regulate the price charged for products or services. The most common use of price controls is in the regulation of utilities, such as electrical and natural gas distribution companies and local telephone companies. "Cost of service ratemaking" is the specific form of price control used in utility regulation, and it will be discussed in detail. Price controls are also used to control the high profits (called "rents" in economics) earned by firms who control goods or services in short supply. "Historical price controls," or "price ceilings," are typically used in response to rents, and this form of regulation will also be discussed. The government also utilizes price controls in agricultural markets, primarily through "subsidies" to farmers as will be seen.

2. ENTRY AND EXIT CONTROLS

The government also regulates the conditions of entry into or exit from a market. In utility regulation, entry and exit controls are applied to entire firms. State regulators determine when utilities can enter new markets and when they can exit old ones. In other types of regulation, entry and exit controls are applied to individual products or services. For example, pharmaceutical drugs are licensed by the federal Food and Drug Administration (FDA).

---

[33] Salamon, *The Changing Tools of Government Action: An Overview, in* BEYOND PRIVATIZATION: THE TOOLS OF GOVERNMENT ACTION 4 (L. Salamon & M. Lund eds. 1989); *see also* Tomain, *Simple Rules for the Regulatory State*, 36 JURIMETRICS J. 409 (1996) (book review of R. EPSTEIN, SIMPLE RULES FOR A COMPLEX WORLD (1995)).

A drug cannot be marketed until it is approved by FDA; FDA also has the authority to order drugs removed from the market if they pose an unreasonable risk to consumers. Occupational licensing is another example of exit and entry control. Individuals cannot practice law in a state unless they are licensed to do so by a licensing board, and such boards have the authority to order an individual to stop practicing law if he or she is unfit to do so.

The control over entry and exit by government licensing has been a fertile area for deregulation, primarily in the area of transportation. Later we discuss deregulation of the airline industry, and cover the rationale for the transportation deregulation that has occurred. At the same time, deregulation has created the need for additional entry controls to address bottleneck problems such as electricity transmission and natural gas transportation.

3. STANDARD SETTING

A third regulatory tool is standard setting. It consists of the government's promulgation of a "standard" or a "rule" that has the same legal status as legislation passed by Congress or by a state legislature. Persons or firms subject to the standard have a legal duty to comply with it; they will be subject to fines, or even imprisonment, for failure to obey.

Standard setting is used in a variety of regulatory contexts. NHTSA has used standards to specify safety precautions automobile manufacturers are required to take. Other health and safety agencies also rely on standard setting. (For example, we will describe standard setting in environmental protection.) Standard setting is also used by agencies to define further a vague statutory mandate. For example, the Federal Communications Commission (FCC) uses standard setting to define the obligations of television and radio broadcasters to operate in the "public interest."

4. ALLOCATION

Allocation refers to the distribution by the government of some benefit or entitlement. Later in the book we discuss the allocation of welfare benefits and public education. Other commodities such as radio signals, farm products, energy products, and health care are allocated by government sometimes directly by allocation orders, sometimes indirectly by price or entry and exit controls.

5. TAXES AND OTHER ECONOMIC INCENTIVES

Instead of using standards to compel persons or firms to take certain actions, the government can sometimes obtain the same result by relying on taxes or other economic incentives. For example, the government could forbid a firm from emitting more than a certain amount of a pollutant. Alternatively, the government could tax the firm for emitting pollution above some minimum amount. Because taxes and other economic incentives are often discussed as potential alternatives for other forms of regulation, the possible use of this tool as part of regulatory reform is discussed in several chapters.

C. REGULATORY ANALYSIS

Regulatory analysis is built on an understanding of the regulatory justifications and methods described in the previous sections. This section explains the nature of regulatory analysis that is employed in the remainder of this book. The goal is to develop an understanding of regulatory principles similar to the understanding of legal principles that law students (and lawyers) employ in reading cases. Just as case analysis reveals the basic legal principles and structures of private law, regulatory analysis reveals the principles and structures of public law. In addition, regulatory analysis yields an understanding of the types of policy justifications and techniques used by government to intervene in private markets. From these justifications and techniques, the analyst can begin to describe the substantive values and norms of the regulatory state.

Ever since the New Deal, the regulatory state has expanded to the point where it has largely displaced the common law. Today, the ordinary tools of the regulatory lawyer are statutes and regulations more so than cases. Case analysis, which proceeded by identifying relevant facts, pertinent issues of law, the holding of the court, and the court's rationale for its holding, is a legal skill necessary for the practice of law. The great strength of the common law method is that it provides lawyers with a way to read cases in any discipline and to derive from those cases the essential arguments, fundamental principles, and justifications that drive the common law. Case analysis works less well in explaining regulatory decisions involving statutory and regulatory rules. For that, we must turn to regulatory analysis.

Regulatory analysis functions similarly to case analysis and uncovers the principles and arguments behind the justifications for government intervention in markets and reveals the strengths and weaknesses of the regulatory tools employed to correct market defects. Regulatory analysis is a way of understanding government regulation by identifying and analyzing patterns of regulatory activity that cut across industries and markets, just as case analysis cuts across various areas of private law. Regulatory analysis also helps explain the limits and benefits of regulatory tools. Finally, in the situations of deregulation and regulatory reform, regulatory analysis can explicate the limits of regulation itself.

Table 2-3

CASE AND REGULATORY ANALYSIS	
Case Analysis	*Regulatory Analysis*
Fact Analysis: Which factors are relevant?	Market Analysis: Does a market produce results inconsistent with economic or social values?
Legal Issue: Which legal issues apply to the factual predicate?	Policy Issue: Which regulatory methods (institutions and tools) will produce more consistent market or social results?
Holding: Which rule of law disposes of the dispute?	Resolution: Which regulatory method is being used or proposed?
Ratio: Assess whether the holding addresses the identified problem and furthers justice.	Ratio: Assess the efficacy and political feasibility of it and alternative methods.

Table 2-3 indicates how regulatory analysis proceeds along a logical path similar to case analysis.[34] The first issue addresses the reason for government regulation. Simply, does government have an economic or noneconomic justification to intervene in a private market? As discussed earlier, an economic justification exists when a market fails to perform in an efficient manner and government intervention is intended to address this "market failure." A noneconomic justification exists when a market produces results which are unfair, inequitable or inconsistent with other social values.

The second issue considers the options available to the government to obtain the economic or noneconomic result sought, while the third issue considers which approach is being used or proposed. As you have read, the government has at its disposal a relatively limited arsenal of regulatory approaches and more than one of these approaches may be relevant to the regulatory problem it is attempting to solve.

The final issue is whether the government has chosen the most effective method of regulation. If not, then, in Justice Breyer's phrase, a "mismatch" has occurred because government has failed "to correctly match the regulatory method or tool used to the problem at hand."[35] As noted, the problem that the government is trying to resolve might be economic or noneconomic. A mismatch can occur for two reasons. First, the government can misdiagnose the problem it is attempting to solve and can apply the wrong regulatory approach as a result. A similar mismatch can occur if there is a change in the political climate and political leaders no longer support the previous goal. Second, even if the problem is correctly identified, regulatory tools will vary

---

[34] This analysis is suggested by S. BREYER, *supra* note 2, but the structure and conclusions of the table are those of the authors.

[35] *Id.* at 191.

in terms of their effectiveness and cost. In other words, another regulatory response may generate lower costs or more benefits.

The pedagogical value of regulatory analysis should now be clear. Students can become familiar with the patterns of regulatory justification and response. It is less necessary to know intimate details of multiple industries, which will come with experience and on a need-to-know basis, than it is to understand the uses and limits of particular regulatory tools. In other words, it is more important for you to know how licensing works for nuclear power plants, magnetic resonance indicators, new drugs, and beauticians than it is to know about the specific details of regulating the electricity, health care, pharmaceutical, and cosmetology industries. Armed with this background knowledge, you can appreciate and utilize policy arguments that are appropriate to their field of practice or service.

Regulatory analysis also gives scholars a common denominator from which advanced arguments can be built. The ideas of "match" and "mismatch" focus scholarly analysis on the justifications for a regulatory program and the suitability of the regulatory tools used to carry it out. These insights enable scholars to consider both the substantive and procedural issues that arise from a regulatory program, and to contribute to the resolution of both.

NOTES AND QUESTIONS

1. Since administrative lawyers are engaged in making policy arguments of the type described in this chapter, their practice before agencies is different than courtroom practice. As Patricia Bailey, a former commissioner of the Federal Trade Commission (FTC), notes, "[Y]ou have to remember . . . when you go forward to do battle with the government agency . . . that an agency is not a courtroom."[36] "[T]he principles of legal advocacy," adds James DeLong, a Washington lawyer, "are only partially applicable to policy advocacy, and in places where they are not applicable they can be misleading and downright harmful."[37]

Cornish Hitchcock, who is an attorney at the Public Citizen Litigation group founded by Ralph Nader, explains:

> Agency practice is much more like congressional practice. Your focus really has to be to persuade the agency, whoever may be reading it, why the world would be a better place if your proposal is enacted. And that is a different exercise than trying to persuade an appellate court that case A is really distinguishable from case B, or that the court is compelled to rule in your favor on the basis of case C. That is what litigation is about.[38]

DeLong elaborates:

> In a lawsuit, a judge personally hears the evidence and argument and reaches a decision with the help of, at most, a clerk. Decisions . . .

---

[36] Bailey, *Initiating Agency Action*, 5 AD. L.J. 23, 25 (1991).

[37] DeLong, *How to Convince an Agency: A Handbook for Policy Advocates*, REGULATION, Sept./Oct., 1982, at 27.

[38] Hitchcock, *Influencing The Substance Of Agency Action*, 5 AD. L.J. 51, 61 (1991).

are all influenced by the fact that everything is ultimately funneled through one intelligence. In contrast, government policy processes are fragmented both horizontally and vertically and decisions on different aspects of a problem may all be made by different people. It would not be unusual, for example, for a policy to be made through the combined efforts of units for operations (program knowledge), policy analysis (economics), technical review (scientific issues), and general counsel (law), with only cursory review by higher levels. Even when an issue is important enough to receive serious attention higher up, the decision will be based primarily on material prepared by these specialized units rather than on raw data and arguments submitted by outsiders.

These facts of life are important in a number of ways. . . . There is little point in arguing law to the economists, economics to the scientists and so on. The recipient of the argument is not likely to be interested, and even if he is he usually cannot respond. A characteristic of internal division of labor is that within its area of expertise each office gets to make decisions that are binding on its peer units, and these decisions will rarely be reversed, even by hierarchical superiors. [39]

2. Another difference between legal advocacy and policy advocacy is that the regulatory lawyer must find ways to argue that the policies favored by the client are consistent with the agency's policy mandate. Bailey explains:

Let's say that you are dealing with an agency where a decision is going to be made and a proposal has already been made about it. I think that there is no need to come whining to the agency that some policy or decision that they made is going to harm your client or harm consumers or do harm to someone. Because almost any decision that an agency makes is going to harm someone. Allegation without more does not surprise them and does not cause them to change course.

You have to know what the agency's mission is, what its purpose is, what its causes are. And that may enable you to argue that whatever action it is that they are proposing to take will damage their own interests. This is often a good tactic to take, because, hopefully, you can get them to see that whatever it is you want them to do is in their own best interest, based on your understanding of what they have been told to do and what they are trying to do. And at the same time, don't even try to conceal your own self-interest, because your reasons from the outside are inherently suspect.

If you understand an agency's position, you may discover that what is primary for the agency is really secondary or even unimportant to you. But what may be crucial to you is only secondary for the agency. If you can look at it that way, you may be able to get something that is very important to you eliminated or added, whatever your interest is, in a way that will enable the agency to deal with the problem without compromising its own cause. . . . [40]

---

[39] DeLong, *supra* note 35, at 28–29.
[40] Bailey, *supra* note 34, at 25–26.

3. Why is administrative law practice different than law practice in the federal or state courts? Why do administrative lawyers need to know something about how economists and policy analysts make policy arguments?

Chapter 3

REGULATION AND POLITICS

There are two explanations for the creation and survival of regulatory programs: either they serve a useful social purpose or they are the result of the political power of regulatory interests. In Chapter 2 we discussed the policy reasons for regulation. Looking at regulation through the lens of public policy, regulatory agencies act to correct market defects or to achieve a degree of social fairness. This chapter tests that assumption by examining the politics of regulation.

Common sense and observation tells us that politics affect the policies that emanate from government. Unfortunately, there is no social science model that can predict political behavior to the same degree that the microeconomic model can predict economic behavior. Nevertheless, *Regulatory Law and Policy* is based on the assumption that a descriptive model of regulatory behavior does exist of which students of regulation must be aware. The model posits that a successful regulatory proposal is one that satisfies the requirements of law, policy, and politics. This model cannot predict which policy proposals will emerge from the legislature. It can only describe which ones are likely to fail. This chapter analyzes the political variable of that model.

A further complication of building a model of political behavior is the fact that there are two competing ideas about the nature of politics in our country. One idea is that politics exists for the public good. The other is that politics satisfies the interests of private groups. Throughout our history, these competing ideas have had many iterations and in this chapter we will suggest examples of both.

Our discussion of regulation and politics proceeds in four parts. We consider first how democratic theorists legitimize political choices. These theorists seek to justify political outcomes as serving the public interest. The next section looks at the most popular current explanation of political behavior known as "public choice." The public choice model attempts to analyze politics as a marketplace much as an economist would use the microeconomic model to look at a market. This approach explains political outcomes as serving the narrow self-interest of participants and decisionmakers, rather than the general public interest. Public choice explanations highlight the fact that not all interests are equally represented in the political process, which can have the effect of skewing the results to favor those who do participate. The relationship of politics and policy is the subject of the fourth section. This section considers the extent to which regulatory decisions are the outcome of politics versus policy.

A. DEMOCRATIC THEORY

Whatever the goal of regulation, the consequence is to effectuate a wealth transfer from one group to another. After all, any regulatory decision produces winners and losers. Thus, politics has been defined as "who gets what, when and how."[1] As students of regulation, we can properly ask, "Why are such government-caused wealth transfers legitimate?" Democratic theory offers three answers: the *pluralist* defense, the *republican* thesis, and the theory of *democratic deliberation*.

1. PLURALIST DEFENSE

The pluralist defense of the legitimacy of government-sanctioned wealth transfers is that the transfers are the product of bargaining between the representatives of numerous interested parties. (This bargaining process is also known as the "deals" thesis of legislation.) Through pluralistic conflict and compromise among private groups or individuals over scarce resources, public policies are established. If a majority of persons (by their representatives) favor a policy, it is legitimate, because in a democratic system, there is rule by majority. In the long run, continual bargaining will lead to a fair and equitable division of the benefits and burdens of government. Since democratic practices are thus devices for resolving conflicts, the symbol of this thesis is the "market."[2]

In this model, administrators will make the decision that satisfies the largest number of people possible and minimizes the displeasure of others. The decisionmaking process is an "interactive" or bargaining process, in which the administrator will attempt to reconcile competing claims with the agreement of those who assert the claims.

2. REPUBLICAN THESIS

The republican thesis argues that wealth transfers from one group to another are legitimate only if the transfers are related to some public value.[3] According to the republican conception, public values are discovered through deliberation.[4] Thus, democratic practices provide a setting in which citizens or their representatives can seek the common principles that underlie their disagreements. These common principles justify the decisions that transfer wealth from one group to another. For this reason, the republican thesis could be symbolized by the "town meeting."

The republican thesis links two concepts in the ideal of self-government: deliberation and civic virtue. As Professor Michael Sandel puts it: "[T]o deliberate well about the common good requires more than the capacity to

---

[1] H. LASSWELL, POLITICS: WHO GETS WHAT, WHEN, HOW (1936); *see also* R. LEONE, WHO PROFITS: WINNERS, LOSERS, AND GOVERNMENT REGULATION (1966).

[2] Sunstein, *Interest Groups in American Public Law*, 38 STAN. L. REV. 29 (1985).

[3] J. APPLEBY, LIBERALISM AND REPUBLICANISM (1992); T. ANGLE, THE SPIRIT OF MODERN REPUBLICANISM (1988); Frank Michelman, *Law's Republic*, 97 YALE L.J. 1493 (1988); Michelman, *Forward: Traces of Self Government* 100 HARVARD L. REV. 4 (1986); Sunstein, *Naked Preferences and the Constitution*, 84 COLUM. L. REV. 1689 (1984).

[4] C. SUNSTEIN, THE PARTIAL CONSTITUTION (1993); J. DRYZEK, DISCURSIVE DEMOCRACY (1990); J. FISHKIN, DEMOCRACY AND DELIBERATION (1971); Seidenfeld, *A Civic Republication Justification for the Bureaucratic State*, 105 HARV. L. REV. 1512 (1992); Estlund, *Who's Afraid of Deliberative Democracy? On the Strategic/Deliberative Dichotomy and Recent Constitutional Jurisprudence*, 71 TEX. L. REV. 1437 (1993).

choose one's ends and respect other's rights to do the same. It requires a knowledge of public affairs and also a sense of belonging, a concern for the whole, a moral bond with the community whose fate is at stake. To share in self-rule therefore requires that citizens possess, or come to acquire, certain qualities of character, or civic virtues."[5] Those citizens so informed then can debate about the means and ends of the public good.

The republican theory has the appeal of defining the public interest in other-regarding, instead of self-interested, terms. As Professor Sunstein explains in the following excerpt, participants in the political process are expected to reason together to find the public interest, rather than merely asserting their own self-interest.

CASS R. SUNSTEIN, THE PARTIAL CONSTITUTION 27–28 (1993) *

We might distinguish between two bases for treating one group or person differently from another. The first is a naked preference. For example, state A may treat its own citizens better than those of state B—say, by requiring people of state B to pay for the use of the public parks in state A—simply because its own citizens have the political power and want better treatment. Or a city may treat blacks worse than whites—say, by denying them necessary police and fire protection—because whites have the power to restrict government benefits to themselves. In these examples, the political process is a mechanism by which self-interested individuals or groups seek to obtain wealth or opportunities at the expense of others. The task of the legislator is to respond to the pressures imposed by those interests.

Contrast with this a political process in which outcomes are justified by reference not to raw political power, but to some public value that they can be said to serve. For the moment we can define a public value extremely broadly, as any justification for government action that goes beyond the exercise of raw political power. . . . For example, a state may relieve a group of people from a contractual obligation because the contract called for an act—say, the sale of heroin—that violated a public policy. Or state A may treat its own citizens better than those of state B—say, by limiting welfare payments to its own citizens—because it wants to restrict social spending to those who in the past have made, or in the future might make, a contribution to state revenues. In these examples, the role of the representative is to deliberate rather than to respond mechanically to constituent pressures. If an individual or group is to be treated differently from others, it must be for a reason that can be stated in public-regarding terms.

These competing portraits of the political process are of course caricatures of a complex reality. It is rare that government action is based purely on raw political power. Losers in the political process may have lost for a very good reason that has little to do with the power of their adversaries. Belief that

---

[5] M. SANDEL, DEMOCRACY'S DISCONTENT: AMERICA IN SEARCH OF A PUBLIC PHILOSOPHY 6 (1996).

an action will promote at least some conception of the public good almost always plays at least some role in government decisions. Sometimes people motivated to vote for certain legislation cannot easily disentangle the private and public factors that underlie the decision.

It is also rare for government action to be based on a disembodied effort to discern and implement public values, entirely apart from consideration of private pressure. Representatives are almost always aware of the fact that their vote will have electoral consequences. What emerges is therefore a continuum of government decisions, ranging from those that are motivated primarily by interest-group pressures to those in which such pressures play a very minor role. In any particular case, it may well be difficult to see which of these is dominant. But the occasional or even frequent difficulty should not be taken to obscure the existence of a real distinction. There is all the difference in the world between a system in which representatives try to offer some justification for their decisions, and a system in which political power is the only thing that is at work.

If naked preferences are a legitimate basis for government action, it is sufficient that a particular group has been able to assume the political power to obtain what it seeks. Might makes right. If naked preferences are forbidden, however, and the state is forced to invoke some public value to justify its conduct, government behavior becomes constrained. . . .

3.   DELIBERATIVE DEMOCRACY

The republican thesis seeks to legitimize government by validating decisions according to their outcome. When such decisions can be defended according to some public value, they are legitimate. But when such decisions are naked preferences—*i.e.*, without such a justification—they are not legitimate.

This concept rests on the belief that a common good can be discovered. Yet, discovering that shared consensus or common good, while it may seem plausible in a homogenous community, seems increasingly difficult to find in an increasingly pluralistic nation.[6] In the next excerpt, Professors Gutmann and Thompson offer the concept of "deliberative democracy" as the resolution to this problem. They argue that the legitimacy of decisionmaking in a democracy depends on the "moral" quality of the decisionmaking process in addition to the values by which the decisions are reached.

AMY GUTMANN & DENNIS THOMPSON, DEMOCRACY AND DISAGREEMENT 1–4 (1996) *

Of the challenges that American democracy faces today, none is more formidable than the problem of moral disagreement. Neither the theory nor the practice of democratic politics has so far found an adequate way to cope

---

[6] Ferejohn & Weingast, *Limitations of Statutes: Strategic Statutory Interpretation*, 80 GEO. L.J. 565, 569–70 (1992).

* Reprinted by permission of the publisher from DEMOCRACY AND DISAGREEMENT by Amy Gutmann and Dennis Thompson, Cambridge, Mass.: Harvard University Press, Copyright © 1996 by the President and Fellows of Harvard College.

with conflicts about fundamental values. We address the challenge of moral disagreement here by developing a conception of democracy that secures a central place for moral discussion in political life.

Along with a growing number of other political theorists, we call this conception deliberative democracy. The core idea is simple: when citizens or their representatives disagree morally, they should continue to reason together to reach mutually acceptable decisions. . . .

Deliberative democracy involves reasoning about politics, and nothing has been more controversial in political philosophy than the nature of reason in politics. We do not believe that these controversies have to be settled before deliberative principles can guide the practice of democracy. Since on occasion citizens and their representatives already engage in the kind of reasoning that those principles recommend, deliberative democracy simply asks that they do so more consistently and comprehensively. . . .

The aim of the moral reasoning that our deliberative democracy prescribes falls between impartiality, which requires something like altruism, and prudence, which demands no more than enlightened self-interest. Its first principle is reciprocity. . . . When citizens reason reciprocally, they seek fair terms of social cooperation for their own sake; they try to find mutually acceptable ways of resolving moral disagreements.

The precise content of reciprocity is difficult to determine in theory, but its general countenance is familiar enough to practice. It can be seen in the difference between acting in one's self-interest (say, taking advantage of a legal loophole or a lucky break) and acting fairly (following rules in the spirit that one expects others to adopt). . . . [T]he possibility of any morally acceptable resolution depends on citizens' reasoning beyond their narrow self-interest and considering what can be justified to people who reasonably disagree with them. Even though the quality of deliberation and the conditions under which it is conducted are far from ideal in the controversies we consider, the fact that in each case some citizens and some officials make arguments consistent with reciprocity suggests that a deliberative perspective is not utopian.

To classify what reciprocity might demand under non-ideal conditions, we develop a distinction between deliberative and nondeliberative disagreement. Citizens who reason reciprocally can recognize that a position is worthy of moral respect even when they think it morally wrong. . . . The presence of deliberative disagreement has important implications for how citizens treat one another and for what policies they should adopt. When a disagreement is not deliberative (for example, about a policy to legalize discrimination against blacks and women), citizens do not have any obligations of mutual respect toward their opponents. In deliberative disagreement (for example, about legalizing abortion), citizens should try to accommodate the moral convictions of their opponents to the greatest extent possible, without compromising their own moral convictions. . . .

Some readers may still wonder why deliberation should have such a prominent place in democracy. Surely, they may say, citizens should care more about the justice of public policies than the process by which they are adopted, at least so long as the process is basically fair and at least minimally democratic. One of our main aims in this book is to cast doubt on the dichotomy between policies and process that this concern assumes. Having good reason as individuals to believe that a policy is just does not mean that collectively as citizens we have sufficient justification to legislate on the basis of those reasons. The moral authority of collective judgments about policy depends in part on the moral quality of the process by which citizens collectively reach those judgments. Deliberation is the most appropriate way for citizens collectively to resolve their moral disagreement not only about policies but also about the process by which policies should be adopted. Deliberation is not only a means to an end, but also a means for deciding what means are morally required to pursue our common ends.

NOTES AND QUESTIONS

1. According to the pluralist defense of democracy, why should you as a citizen accept the results of the democratic process? What assumption does the pluralist defense make about the outcome of the distribution of costs and benefits of regulatory and other legislative decisions?

2. According to the republican thesis, when are the results of governmental decisionmaking valid or legitimate? According to Professor Sunstein, what is a "naked preference?" Why is a naked preference illegitimate under the republican thesis of democratic decisionmaking?

3. What problem do Professors Gutmann and Thompson see with the republican thesis? What solution do they offer to this conundrum? How does deliberative democracy legitimize decisionmaking in situations where citizens cannot agree about the fundamental values used to validate decisions?

4. Which of these theories of democracy do you find most persuasive? Why?

B. PUBLIC CHOICE

The public interest model of politics is based on the hope that through active citizen participation and discussion acceptable compromises about public policies can be reached on the basis of policy analysis and moral deliberation. But can the political system be trusted to deliberate in this manner? James Madison, in Federalist No. 10, concluded that self-interested groups, which he called factions, will always be with us and that their drive should be harnessed in some positive way. Madison's solution, which favored formation of a national government, was to multiply factions, and allow their self-interests to cancel each other out. Madison went on to extend this idea in Federalist No. 51 by noting that just as interest groups work in their self-interest, so do departments of government. For this reason, through multiple departments of government, "ambition must be made to counteract ambition."

In the 1960s and 1970s, political theorists began to question the efficacy of such interest group politics noting that excessive pluralism may enable some organized interest groups to "capture" benefits of government to their advantage and to the disadvantage of the public interest.[7] Professor Levine explains the intellectual foundations for this conclusion in the next excerpt.

MICHAEL LEVINE, REVISIONISM REVISED: AIRLINE DEREGULATION AND THE PUBLIC INTEREST, 44 LAW AND CONTEMPORARY PROBLEMS 179, 180–85 (1981)[*]

[As scholars began to examine the results of government regulation in fields like transportation and agriculture, a consensus started to emerge that regulation was] a device used by relatively small subgroups of the general population, either private corporations or geographic or occupational groups, to produce results favorable to them which would not be produced by the market. The regulatory services provided were variously described as organization of a cartel, wealth transfers as a form of "taxation," enshrinement of capitalistic class interests, or preservation of congressional and bureaucratic power. Of course, all gains, whether from regulation or the market, are in a sense realized by private human beings. The operational significance of this view is that government processes are used by organized subgroups of the population to enforce inefficient arrangements which transfer wealth or power to them.

. . . The central notion underlying virtually all revisionist theory comes from Downs.[11] In effect, he asks us to view public officials not as officials primarily concerned with public matters, but rather as private individuals trying to maximize their own utility much in the way a firm maximizes profits. Just as businessmen compete with other businessmen to accumulate consumer dollars which will bring them wealth, politicians compete with each other for electoral support which keeps them in office (their "wealth") and bureaucrats deal with the public and the legislature to accumulate power, prestige, tenure, et cetera. From this, it follows that public officials will try to assemble coalitions of support. Individuals and groups support public officials whose actions make those individuals or groups better off, either financially or by satisfying their "tastes" for public policies.

But supporting an official—even if only by voting—entails costs which will be borne willingly only if the payoff from a public policy to an individual or group exceeds the cost of supporting the public official who will implement it. Accordingly, those willing to put the most effort into supporting public officials are those whose gains from a particular policy most exceed the cost of implementing it, and public officials can gain support best by inventing or supporting policies which provide disproportionate benefits to groups who are in a position to affect political outcomes by delivering votes (or money to attract votes) or by supporting the activities of an agency.

Using this central notion, one can proceed to derive the central themes of the revisionist view of regulation. Policies which generate economic profits (rents) are likely to gain support from the groups in whose favor the profits

---

[7] *See, e.g.*, T. Lowi, The End of Liberalism: The Second Republic of the United States (2d ed. 1979).

[*] Copyright © 1981 Duke University School of Law. Reprinted by permission.

[11] A. Downs, [An Economic Theory of Government (1957).]

will be distributed. One method of generating rents is to limit entry into an industry and to facilitate price coordination. According to Stigler, groups which can benefit from this kind of intervention use the political process to persuade legislators to create regulatory agencies to accomplish it.[12] These groups are ordinarily private firms. If a group of users or a geographic area has low enough organization costs compared to potential benefits from intervention, it too will influence the political process to intervene in markets for the group's benefit. Generally, this intervention will take the form of what Posner has called "taxation by regulation," namely, use of the regulatory process to generate monopoly profits from users who are not specially organized in order to finance excess service (compared to revenues) for the favored group or geographic area.[13]

Kolko[14] has developed a revisionist account of the origins of regulation which is essentially Marxist in its use of class concepts, but which produces results strikingly similar to the Downsian line of development. He posits capitalists who find market competition unprofitable and consumer sovereignty unattractive and who seize control of the apparatus of the state in order to establish and preserve monopoly positions. In order to succeed politically in doing so, they exploit populist sentiment which favors controlling monopolies through regulation. Thus, regulatory mechanisms are created, supposedly to satisfy popular demand, but actually to permit capitalists to use the government to eliminate market forces which operate to reduce their profits.

Revisionist accounts of the legislative origin of regulation are integrated with revisionist accounts of agency-created regulation by Fiorina and Noll.[15] They describe a process in which legislators who want to be reelected discover that individual service to constituents (and particularly help to constituents having difficulty with government agencies) is a particularly effective form of vote-getting, not least because it cuts across party lines and issue positions. At the same time, bureaucrats who wish to continue in their jobs and who favor their own continued intervention into the economy discover that it is in *their* interest to be responsive to inquiries from legislators on behalf of their constituents. And, of course, potential beneficiaries continue to be interested in interventions which will transfer wealth to them. The result, as seen by Fiorina and Noll, is a powerful conjunction of forces in favor of establishing and continuing regulation. Legislators, bureaucrats, and favored constituents unite to create complex programs which transfer wealth. The legislator gets credit every time he helps a constituent deal with bureaucratic complexity independently of the position he or the constituent take on the desirability of the underlying program. The bureaucrat gets to run a bigger program, organized in ways that increase his discretion. Any constituent benefitted by the program, of course, remains in favor of it. Any constituents who oppose a program in general but who can benefit from assistance in dealing with it ignore those general views in favor of supporting legislators whose help is

---

[12] Stigler, [*The Theory of Economic Regulation*, 2 BELL J. ECON. & MGMT. SCI. 3 (1971).]

[13] Posner, [*Taxation by Regulation*, 2 BELL J. ECON. & MGMT. SCI. 22 (1971).]

[14] G. KOLKO, RAILROADS AND REGULATION (1965); G. KOLKO, THE TRIUMPH OF CONSERVATISM (1963).

[15] Fiorina & Noll, *Majority Rule Models and Legislative Elections*, 41 J. POL. 1031, 1099 (1976).

financially more salient to them—incumbents who know their way around the bureaucracy. So powerful is this combination that Fiorina and Noll predict that rational legislators will choose voluntarily to make a program of intervention more complicated, discretionary, administrative, and "regulatory" than it need be to accomplish its purpose, because doing so maximizes the political advantage to be gained from it.

In summary, examining revisionist theories of regulation, reveals a great many common threads; revisionist theories owe a great deal to Downs. They posit groups with relatively low organization costs relative to their possible gains from political intervention who become disproportionately influential in the political process. These groups persuade Congress to set up a framework which will transfer wealth to them through the regulatory process. If the group is a private firm or firms, the government service may take the form of a cartel run at public expense. If the groups are user or geographic in nature, the regulation often will take the form of what Posner has called "taxation," generating monopoly profits from some disfavored sector of the public and transferring them as excess services for the benefit of the favored sector. A Marxist such as Kolko may describe all this in class terms rather than the more general Downsian analysis, but the end result is largely the same. And, finally, Fiorina and Noll describe an elaborate interaction of legislators, bureaucrats, and favored groups joining hands to achieve wealth transfers through the regulatory process which will redound to the credit of the legislators and to vocational benefit of the bureaucrats.

These theories of regulatory genesis are closely related to theories of regulatory behavior. The cartel theory of origin generates a corresponding view of agency behavior which has a counterpart in the "capture" theory.[16] The capture theory seems implicitly to accept the possibility of public interest view of agency origin but postulates that, whatever the reasons that may have created a regulatory agency, it becomes captured by the industry it regulates and acts as a protector and cartel manager for that industry. A refinement of this view has the agency operating to continually shift resources in *somebody's* favor, thus maximizing its political power. The beneficiary of the wealth shift will change from producers to consumers to subgroups of consumers, depending on demand shifts and technical changes, but the wealth shifts will be undertaken without regard to efficiency.

---

[16] M. BERNSTEIN, REGULATING BUSINESS BY INDEPENDENT COMMISSION (1955). One anonymous regulator described the operation of the capture process as follows:

> It all begins when a fellow out in Indianapolis is designated to be a member of a regulatory commission. First he gets into the going-away period. There are banquets in his honor, and the women say to his wife, "For goodness sake, be sure to tell us what Pat [Nixon] is really like." She demurely replies, "I am sure I won't see her often," believing, of course, that she will. After the goodbyes, the fellow comes to Washington and assumes his role as a member of a commission, believing that he is really a pretty important guy. After all, he almost got elected to Congress back home in Indiana. He is used to public attention. But after a few weeks in Washington, he realizes that nobody ever heard of him or cares much what he does — except one group of very personable, reasonable, knowledgeable, delightful human beings, who recognize his true worth. Obviously, they might turn his head just a bit.

R. NOLL, REFORMING REGULATION 100 (1971).

This view, in turn, is buttressed by Fiorina's[18] general theory of the interaction between Congress and bureaucrats. Fiorina postulates that legislators win reelection by influencing governmental processes which affect wealth to operate in their constituents' favor. For such influence to be possible, government intervention in the form of regulation needs to exist and the regulators need to be cooperative in the way they carry out their mandate. . . .

NOTES AND QUESTIONS

1. The description of regulatory politics as a market system is known as "public choice" theory because it describes how governmental or public choices are made. Public choice theory predicts that regulatory outcomes depend on which group or groups offer the greatest rewards to the legislators and administrators. The medium of exchange is the repayment of past favors or the creation of a stock of credits for obtaining future favors. In the case of elected officials, the favors concern activities that will assist the person's reelection. In the case of unelected administrators, the favors concern activities that will improve the person's professional advancement (a better job outside of the agency), bureaucratic advancement (a bigger budget and more prestige for the agency), or political advancement (increased opportunity for elected office).

2. The public choice model of politics is not unattractive. First, it is based upon reasonable observations that people do act in their own self-interest. Recall Madison's Federalist No. 10 and its observation about factions. Second, it purports to use a heuristic of the microeconomic model, which has been a very successful method in the social sciences. Third, it has certain explanatory power for the "deals" that are cut in legislatures all of the time. Finally, proponents of public choice theory admit that individuals may not always be motivated by their "self-interest" when they engage in politics, but they contend that relying on self-interest to explain (or predict) public choices will be more accurate than competing explanations.[8]

3. Public choice, however, is not without its critics.[9] Some critics react to what they believe to be the inherent conservative ideology of the discipline, which puts private market interest over politics and public interest. Other critics argue that empirical efforts to establish the validity of the theory have largely failed. A recent study of public choice empirical research, for example, that "successful empirical applications of rational choice models have been few and far between."[10] More broadly, the public choice perspective does not explain significant elements of the regulatory state. Industry and producer groups were unable to stop the passage of many environmental, health and

[18] M. FIORINA, CONGRESS, KEYSTONE OF THE WASHINGTON ESTABLISHMENT (1977).

[8] Brennan & Buchanan, *Is Public Choice Immoral? The Case for the "Nobel" Lie*, 74 VAL. L. REV. 179 (1988).

[9] *See, e.g.*, J. MASHAW, GREED, CHAOS & GOVERNANCE: USING PUBLIC CHOICE TO IMPROVE PUBLIC LAW (1997); D. GREEN & I. SHAPIRO, PATHOLOGIES OF RATIONAL CHOICE THEORY: A CRITIQUE OF APPLICATIONS IN POLITICAL SCIENCE (1994); D. FARBER & P. FRICKEY, LAW AND PUBLIC CHOICE: A CRITICAL INTRODUCTION (1991).

[10] D. GREEN & I. SHAPIRO, *supra* note 8, at ix.

safety, and consumer protection laws, and they have been unable to secure the repeal of these laws. They have also been unable to stop deregulation efforts in the airline, trucking, banking, and telecommunications industries that disfavored them, or to prevent some unfavorable tax legislation. Indeed, the public choice theory "has been confounded by much of the major legislative product of the Congress during the past thirty years."[11]

4. There are other legal scholars and theorists who try to break out of the dichotomy between private interest politics and public interest politics. Some argue that civic virtue and public good can be achieved outside of highly formal legal processes, such as federal or state legislatures and courts, through intermediate institutions. In a provocative book, *Bowling Alone,*[12] Professor Robert Putnam argues that there is a decline in American participation in civic life in such groups as parent/teacher associations, church groups, and even sports leagues. The significance of Putnam's work, however, is recognizing these institutions as important parts of the fabric of democracy.[13] Closely linked to these proponents of intermediate civic institutions are a group of scholars forming the "communitarian movement" which argue that individual responsibility has been weakened through an excess of rights and that politics needs an infusion of such responsibility which can best be delivered through the communitarian spirit.[14]

C. THE PROBLEM OF COLLECTIVE ACTION

The key insight of the public choice theory of regulation is that government can be captured by political interests for their own self-interest. This capture is possible because industry associations and similar special interest groups are more likely to lobby legislatures or appear before administrative agencies than representatives of the majority of citizens affected by such decisions. There are two general reasons for this imbalance. First, the members of special interest groups have more money (or revenue, etc.) at stake in potential decisions than most citizens. This means that group members can afford to invest more time and effort in attempting to affect the government's decision. Second, it is difficult and expensive to organize interest groups that will represent large numbers of citizens. In short, it is easier and cheaper for interest groups to organize and lobby than it is for the general public.

Although private groups participate more than public groups in policy formation, public interest legislation does get passed. In the following excerpt, Professor Wilson explains that the distribution of regulatory costs and benefits can explain various results. He also explains why regulatory programs that benefit large numbers of persons are sometimes passed over the stiff

---

[11] Shapiro, *Of Interest and Values: The New Politics and the New Political Science*, in THE NEW POLITICS OF PUBLIC POLICY 5 (M. Landy & M. Levin eds. 1995).

[12] R. PUTNAM, BOWLING ALONE: THE COLLAPSE AND REVIVAL OF AMERICAN COMMUNITY (2000).

[13] R. PUTNAM, MAKING DEMOCRACY WORK: CIVIC TRADITIONS IN MODERN ITALY (1993); Putnam, *The Strange Disappearance of Civil America* 24 AMERICAN PROSPECT 34 (1996); *see also* D. MATHEWS, POLITICS FOR PEOPLE: FINDING A RESPONSIBLE PUBLIC VOICE (1994).

[14] *See* M. GLENDON, RIGHTS TALK: THE IMPOVERISHMENT OF POLITICAL DISCOURSE (1991); A. ETZIONI, THE NEW GOLDEN RULE: COMMUNITY AND MORALITY IN A DEMOCRATIC SOCIETY (1996).

opposition of manufacturers and producers despite the citizen's lack of representation in the political process.

JAMES Q. WILSON, THE POLITICS OF REGULATION, IN THE POLITICS OF REGULATION 367–72 (J. WILSON ED. 1980) *

When both costs and benefits are widely distributed, we expect to find *majoritarian* politics. All or most of society expects to gain; all or most of society expects to pay. Interest groups have little incentive to form around such issues because no small, definable segment of society (an industry, an occupation, a locality) can expect to capture a disproportionate share of the burdens. Not all measures that seem to offer a net gain to popular majorities are passed: proposals must first get onto the political agenda, people must agree that it is legitimate for the government to take action, and ideological objections to the propriety or feasibility of the measures must be overcome. All these issues had to be dealt with in the case of such conspicuously majoritarian policies as the Social Security Act of 1935 and the proposal to maintain a large standing army just before and just after World War II.

The passage of the Sherman Antitrust Act, and perhaps also of the Federal Trade Commission Act, arose out of circumstances that approximate those of majoritarian politics. No single industry was to be regulated; the nature and scope of the proposed regulations were left quite vague; any given firm could imagine ways in which these laws might help them (in dealing with an "unscrupulous" competitor, for example). But though there was no determined industry opposition, neither was there strong business support. The measures could not be passed until popular sentiment supported them (Grangers and muckrakers had first to persuade people that a problem existed and that there was a gain to be had) and elite opinion was convinced that it was legitimate for the federal government to pass such laws. . . .

When both costs and benefits are narrowly concentrated, conditions are ripe for *interest-group politics*. A subsidy or regulation will often benefit a relatively small group at the expense of another comparable small group. Each side has a strong incentive to organize and exercise political influence. The public does not believe it will be much affected one way or another; though it may sympathize more with one side than the other, its voice is likely to be heard in only weak or general terms. The passage of the Commerce Act in 1886 resulted from interest-group politics as each affected party—long-haul and short-haul railroads, farm groups, oil companies, and businessmen representing various port cities—contended over how, if at all, railroad rates should be regulated. Much labor legislation—the Wagner Act, the Taft-Hartley Act, the Landrum-Griffin Act, the proposed labor law reform act of 1978—is also a product of interest-group politics . . . .

When the benefits of a prospective policy are concentrated but the costs widely distributed, *client politics* is likely to result. Some small, easily organized group will benefit and thus has a powerful incentive to organize and lobby; the costs of the benefit are distributed at a low per capita rate over a large number of people, and hence they have little incentive to organize in opposition—if, indeed, they even hear of the policy. As we shall see, however, an important organizational change has occurred that has altered the normal advantage enjoyed by the client group in these circumstances—the emergence of "watchdog" or "public interest" associations that have devised ways of maintaining themselves without having to recruit and organize the people who will be affected by a policy. Absent such watchdog organizations, however, client politics produces regulatory legislation that most nearly approximates the producer-dominance model. Countless industries and occupations have come to enjoy subsidies and regulations that, in effect, spare them the full rigors of economic competition.

Finally, a policy may be proposed that will confer general (though perhaps small) benefits at a cost to be borne chiefly by a small segment of society. When this is attempted, we are witnessing *entrepreneurial politics.* Antipollution and auto-safety bills were proposed to make air cleaner or cars safer for everyone at an expense that was imposed, at least initially, on particular segments of industry. Since the incentive to organize is strong for opponents of the policy but weak for the beneficiaries, and since the political system provides many points at which opposition can be registered, it may seem astonishing that regulatory legislation of this sort is ever passed. It is, and with growing frequency in recent years—but it requires the efforts of a skilled entrepreneur who can mobilize latent public sentiment (by revealing a scandal or capitalizing on a crisis), put the opponents of the plan publicly on the defensive (by accusing them of deforming babies or killing motorists), and associate the legislation with widely shared values (clean air, pure water, health, and safety). The entrepreneur serves as the vicarious representative of groups not directly part of the legislative process. Ralph Nader was such an entrepreneur, and the Auto Safety Act of 1966 was one result. Policy entrepreneurs are found not only in the politics of business regulation. Howard Jarvis was an entrepreneur who helped pass Proposition 13 in California; Joseph R. McCarthy was an entrepreneur when he galvanized large parts of the public into an anticommunism crusade. . . .

Entrepreneurial politics depends heavily on the attitudes of third parties. The reaction of the regulated industry is predictably hostile . . .; the reaction of the public that is to benefit may be hard to discern or evident only in general terms ("do something about this problem"). Third parties are those members of various political elites—the media, influential writers, congressional committee staff members, the heads of voluntary associations, political activists— not affected by the policy whose political response to the entrepreneur's campaign is important. Reverend Martin Luther King, Jr. was such an entrepreneur when he led his small but dedicated band of civil rights followers into confrontations with the police in Selma and Birmingham. The vivid scenes of police violence that followed had a galvanic effect on key third parties, and, to a degree, on the public at large. The 1965 Civil Rights Act was the result.

In sum, the politics of regulation follows different patterns, mobilizes different actors, and has different consequences depending, among other things, on the perceived distribution of costs and benefits of the proposed policy. In some of these political patterns, the economic interests of the key actors are both plain and decisive—for example, in most forms of client and interest-group politics. In others, economic interests are either not apparent (at least among the proponents) or are not of decisive importance—for example, in many instances of entrepreneurial politics. In still other cases, such as certain examples of majoritarian politics, the material interests of affected parties may be plain but not decisive or too dependent on future events to be known at all. Any theory that fails to account for these and other variations in regulatory policies is defective.

———

In order to understand the constraints that limit collective action by large numbers of persons, it is necessary first to understand the concept of "public goods," and second to perceive government regulation as a public good. A public good has been defined as follows: "A commodity whose benefits may be provided to all people (in a nation or town) at no more cost than that required to provide it for one person. The benefits of the good are indivisible and people cannot be excluded."[15] Police and military protection, and public facilities such as streets and services such as water and sewer service, are examples of public goods, because multiple persons can consume these services. Indeed, the central problem with public goods is that private markets will not supply, or will under-supply, these goods because there is little incentive for private actors to provide them. Private actors lack sufficient incentive because they cannot exclude (or can only partially exclude) non-payers from the consumption of public goods. As a result, private actors cannot capture all of the benefits of producing such goods.

Government regulation can be seen as just such a public good. Whether government acts to stabilize the economy, distribute welfare, protect the environment, or prevent the exercise of market power, the advantages of regulation are available to everyone within that government's jurisdiction who benefits. Yet, every time the government regulates, there usually will be economic winners and losers. It follows, then, that it is in the best interest of some groups to organize and either capture the benefits of regulation or avoid its burdens.

Organizing collectively, however, has real problems. First, organizing involves transaction costs, such as identifying and contacting like-minded actors. Second, even assuming that the appropriate actors can be identified, some of those actors, known as "free riders," will not contribute to the transaction costs, thus raising the cost to other participants. An environmentally sensitive individual, for example, may find it more compelling to join a neighborhood grassroots organization to protest an adjacent development than join a Save-the-Seals-in-Newfoundland campaign. Yet, that individual may also derive some benefit from the Save-the-Seals campaign.

One consequence of the existence of transaction costs and free riders is that small, focused interest groups are more likely to form than are large, diffuse

---

15 P. SAMUELSON & W. NORDHAUS, ECONOMICS 913 (12th ed. 1985).

interest groups. In the sense that we use the term here, collective action presents a challenge to a realization of the democratic ideal. We might assume "at least where economic objectives are involved, that groups of individuals with common interests usually attempt to further those common interests."[16] This proposition about self-interested group behavior would seem to follow logically from the assumption that individuals act in their own self-interest.

If the assumption about the self-interest of groups is true, the democratic ideal might become a reality, insofar as consumers, employees, and small businesses can act collectively to advance their interests and serve as sources of countervailing power against producers, employers, and large integrated firms, respectively. Yet, the prior analysis exposes the falsity of the proposition that groups can act effectively in their self-interest to attain the democratic ideal. "Indeed, unless the number of individuals in a group is quite small, or unless there is coercion or some other special device to make individuals act in their common interest, *rational, self-interested individuals will not act to achieve their common or group interests.*"[17]

But why is this so? Simply, the costs and incentives for some groups to organize are such as to preclude effective action. Take government regulation of the television, utility, or airline industries as examples. In a world of no transaction costs, thousands of viewers, ratepayers, or passengers could either advocate for themselves or organize and participate in agency proceedings. Incentives to organize are skewed, however, because the cost of getting together can be prohibitive. Even if a group were formed, it must incur participation costs for lawyers, experts, discovery, etc. The transaction costs for an individual or for a large, diffuse group are proportionately greater than the benefits to be derived from organizing and participating. Thus, the cost of regulation to an individual viewer, ratepayer, or passenger can make participation at an agency hearing prohibitively expensive.

NOTES AND QUESTIONS

1. Recall the saga of air bag regulation described in Chapter 1. The automobile industry was able to stymie and delay an air bag requirement although the proponents of this safety device ultimately prevailed. Do Wilson's models help explain what occurred during the air bag story? Which type of politics was involved according to Wilson's categories? Can you give an example for each of Wilson's categories?

2. You should now be able to see the relationship between collective action incentives and disincentives and the problem of regulatory capture discussed in the Levine excerpt. Public choice analysts model public decisionmaking as a market where regulators exchange favorable decisions for support of bigger budgets, promotion, and other resources that will help them obtain their own self-interest. Agency capture occurs, according to this theory, because the regulated industry is in a better position to offer these quasi-payments than the beneficiaries of the regulation.

---

[16] M. OLSON, THE LOGIC OF COLLECTIVE ACTION: PUBLIC GOODS AND THE THEORY OF GROUPS 1 (1965).

[17] *Id.* at 2.

3. Political scientists offer two additional reasons for agency capture. First, frequently agencies are in an inherently weak position, because the effectiveness of regulation is often linked to the industry's willingness to cooperate, and because agencies have limited fact-finding resources and therefore depend on the industry for information, which sometimes forces a compromise. Second, regulated industries are intensely familiar with the workings of agencies and work well within that "regulatory culture."[18] Aside from creating an advantage for the industry over members of the public, this familiarity may create an alignment between the agency and the industry.

D. RELATIONSHIP OF POLITICS AND POLICY

This book recognizes that both policy arguments and political influence impact regulatory decisions. Politics can have a powerful influence on regulatory choices. As discussed earlier in Chapter 2, when the policy rationale for a regulatory action is substantially weak, the lack of a rationale supports the conclusion that a program is the result of self-interested behavior. However, when a regulatory program makes strong policy sense, there is a powerful inference that it is not the product of public choice politics. Many programs fall somewhere in between these extremes. Outcomes are determined by the efficacy of the policy evidence and the political feasibility of the supporting arguments. To further complicate matters the weights accorded the variables of policy and politics vary over time. In other words, the value and styles of policy analysis change.[19]

1. INFLUENCE OF POLICY

Observation reveals that "[p]olitical participants, the electorate, the legislature, the executive, the courts, the media, interest groups, and independent experts all engage in a continuous process of debate and reciprocal persuasion."[20] According to William Grieder, "As lobbyists will tirelessly explain, their basic function in politics is to provide information, fact-filled arguments that provide a . . . public rationale for the governing decisions."[21] Or, as a longtime Washington lobbyist, Tommy Boggs, comments, "In the old days, if you wanted a levee in Louisiana, you voted for a price support program for potatoes in Maine. Nobody knew what was going on. Now, all of the sudden, there's this tremendous need for a public rationale for every action that these guys take."[22]

Unless one is prepared to ignore the constant policy debates in regulatory deliberations, the student of regulation must account for the influence of both policy and politics. This is no easy task. The linkages between policy arguments and regulatory outcomes are not easily observed, because often the

---

[18] Meidinger, *Regulatory Culture: A Theoretical Outline,* 9 Law & Pol'y 355 (1987).

[19] M. Howlett & M. Ramesh, Studying Public Policy: Policy Cycles and Policy Subsystems (1995).

[20] G. Majone, Evidence, Argument & Persuasion in the Policy Process 1 (1989).

[21] W. Grieder, Who Will Tell The People? The Betrayal of American Democracy 45 (1992).

[22] *Id.*

motivating factor—an idea—is difficult to track and its influence is difficult to measure.[23] Yet, the process by which politics and policy come together can be described. Moreover, this description verifies the central role of policy arguments in regulatory decisionmaking.

Once Congress decides to act, interest groups and political actors then compete to influence solutions to be adopted by advocating policies that serve their interests.[24] An interest group normally must have at least some political power to be successful. As a former chairman of the Federal Trade Commission has observed, "Reports to Congress suggesting Congressional action, unaccompanied by political momentum, ordinarily move through Congress with all the force of a bulldozer with an empty gas tank."[25] But even powerful groups do not depend on political influence alone. Rather, they spend considerable time and money developing policy rationales for their proposals, and their lobbyists stress the importance of making good policy arguments.[26] Which alternative policy the legislature will adopt depends on the relative merits of competing proposals, the political influence of the competing parties, and the institutional arrangements in Congress.[27] Thus, political intensity can fuel the passage of policies with marginal policy justifications, and good ideas can prevail even in the face of intense political opposition.

Several reasons account for the impact of policy on regulatory decisionmaking.[28] Building coalitions among groups with different conceptions of self-interest and of the public interest requires finding general ideas in common. Moreover, political success is more likely if persons defend their initiatives as consistent with existing policies, institutions, and implementation capacities, and, more generally, with social norms concerning the appropriate role of the state in society, or with society's normative and emotional commitments. In particular, ideas are necessary to defend initiatives as consistent with general public purposes in light of public distrust of special interest pleading. Ideas, according to Peter Schuck, also "give eloquent voice to a previously inarticulate sense among members of the public that social values and ways of thought are changing and that policies need to be brought into harmony with these new practices. By engendering a kind of cognitive dissonance, ideas can underscore tensions in our political life, stimulating the search of new modes of behavior or governance."[29]

When a regulatory decision has been delegated to an administrative agency, ideas are important for additional reasons. First, agency decisionmakers have

---

[23] Schuck, *The Politics of Rapid Legal Change: Immigration Policy in the 1980s,* in THE NEW POLITICS OF PUBLIC POLICY 51 (M. Landy & M. Levin eds., 1995).

[24] J. KINGDON, AGENDAS, ALTERNATIVES AND PUBLIC POLICIES 52 (1st ed. 1984); F. BAUMGARTNER & B. JONES, AGENDAS & INSTABILITY IN AMERICAN POLITICS 29 (1993).

[25] M. PERTSCHUK, GIANT KILLERS 45 (1986).

[26] D. RICCI, THE TRANSFORMATION OF AMERICAN POLITICS: THE NEW WASHINGTON AND THE RISE OF THINK TANKS 165–66 (1993); J. HEINZ, ET AL., THE HOLLOW CORE: PRIVATE INTERESTS IN NATIONAL POLICY MAKING ch. 2 (1993); B. WOLPE, LOBBYING CONGRESS: HOW THE SYSTEM WORKS 24 (1990).

[27] KINGDON, *supra* note 24, at 170–72, 209–10, G. MUCCIARONI, REVERSALS OF FORTUNE: PUBLIC POLICY & PRIVATE INTERESTS 9 (1995).

[28] This analysis follows Schuck, *supra* note 23, at 77–85.

[29] *Id.* at 80.

usually been trained to approach problem solving in a rational manner. As lawyers, scientists, engineers, public administrators, or economists, they will feel compelled to justify their views according to the logical problem solving methods they were taught. They will therefore justify regulatory options by using their training to explain the relationship of those options to the agency's goals and purpose.[30]

Second, the agency's organizational culture also creates expectations that agency employees will seek rational policy solutions. Sociologists explain that organizations are structured so that decisionmakers consider whether various options open to the organization serve its goals or purposes. Because organizations exist for a purpose, members will establish "norms" or mutual expectations of what constitutes acceptable behavior. These can be indefinite and general, such as unwritten purposes or values, or specific and detailed, such as written guidelines. Since members are expected to justify their actions in terms of these norms, the acceptability of actions proposed by one person to others will depend on the strength of the logical connection between the reasons given for the action and the principles, values, or guidelines to which it relates.[31]

This culture is reinforced by analytical obligations that the President and Congress have imposed on agencies. For example, recent presidents have imposed several analytical requirements that agencies must study the policy impacts of significant rules by comparing their costs and benefits and by identifying other regulatory impacts.[32] Congress has also imposed such obligations, including the Unfunded Mandates and Regulatory Accountability Reform Act,[33] National Environmental Policy Act,[34] and the Paperwork Reduction Act.[35]

Third, administrators are spurred to act rationally because there is judicial review in which neutral decisionmakers determine whether the agency applied its expertise to technical problems in a bona fide way and responded to significant objections from affected persons. An agency's legislative mandate establishes an affirmative obligation to achieve a set of policy goals. As was the case in *State Farm,* discussed in Chapter 1, the courts will review an agency's decision for its consistency with those goals. Thus, even if an agency's motives are purely political, it must still defend its actions as being consistent with the general policy goals of its mandate.

2. INFLUENCE OF POLITICS

Which factor—policy or politics—might have a greater influence will vary from situation to situation. Nevertheless, some generalizations can be made.

---

[30] For an excellent account of the role of both organization and professional influences in bureaucratic decisionmaking, see J. MASHAW, BUREAUCRATIC JUSTICE (1983).

[31] Nonet, *The Legitimization of Purposive Decision,* 68 CAL. L. REV. 263 (1980); *see also* Frug, *The Ideology of Bureaucracy in American Law,* 97 HARV. L. REV. 1277 (1984).

[32] *E.g.,* Exec. Order 12,866, 58 Fed. Reg. 51,735 (1993) (issued by President Clinton).

[33] Pub. L. No. 104-4, 109 Stat. 48 (1995).

[34] 42 U.S.C. §§ 4321–4344.

[35] 44 U.S.C. § 3501 et seq.

First, as you read in Chapter 1, Congress usually delegates broad discretion to administrative agencies because of the political and policy difficulties of resolving specific regulatory issues. Second, an agency's response to political influences will depend in part on the relationship between those influences and the agency's mandate. In some cases, because the agency's mandate is clear and precise, it will be illegal for the agency to choose some options proposed by the White House, legislators, or interest groups. Even in cases where the agency's mandate is general, the agency must be able to reconcile any choice made in response to "political" input with its mandate. This was DOT's downfall when it rescinded the Carter administration's passive restraint rule. As the Supreme Court explained in *State Farm,* the agency had not come up with a "logical" explanation to justify doing nothing. In other words, an agency's decision cannot be "pure" politics—it must have a policy component that indicates how the decision is serving the goals established for the agency by Congress.[36]

Third, the agency's response to political forces will also depend on what its policy analysis reveals. If the expectations produced by organizational and professional pressures are sufficiently general and abstract, administrators will feel free to respond to the interest group process to a considerable degree. For example, recall the question earlier about whether a rule requiring air bags would be justified even if the states have adopted laws requiring the use of seat belts. Regulatory analysis reveals that such a requirement would cost from $500 thousand to $5.0 million per life saved. Since there is no objective or neutral answer concerning what a life is worth, the decision whether to promulgate such a regulation will depend on the administrator's own political views and on the impact of the political views of elected officials.

Fourth, the agency's response to political influences will depend on the makeup of the interest groups and elected officials attempting to influence the agency. If there are powerful political forces for and against an option, the most "political" response is for a regulator to attempt to find a compromise. As you read in Chapter 1, this was Elizabeth Dole's response when she adopted her ingenious solution to the air bag controversy. But you should note that the fact that there were strong political forces in favor of regulation permitted Secretary Dole to stand up to those in the White House who did not want any regulation. If political pressure is united in favor of one regulatory option, an administrator may find it difficult to choose another, even if policy analysis indicates it may be a better approach.

Finally, the agency's response to political pressure can also depend on who the President appoints to head an agency and how easily that person can be removed by the President. Recall from Chapter 1 that President Reagan appointed an administrator hostile to regulation as Secretary of Transportation. Such appointments suggest that the White House, aware of professional and organizational influences, sought to appoint ideologically committed administrators who would resist such influences.

Presidential appointments can have the opposite effect as well. President Carter sought to solidify his standing with environmentalists and consumers

---

[36] Shapiro & Levy, *Heightened Scrutiny of the Fourth Branch: Separation of Powers and the Requirement of Adequate Reasons for Agency Decisions,* 1987 DUKE L.J. 387, 428 (1987).

by appointing as administrators of health and safety agencies such as NHTSA and the Environmental Protection Agency (EPA) persons who had formerly worked for environmental and other public interest groups. These persons resisted White House pressure later in Carter's term to weaken planned regulatory initiatives on grounds they cost too much.[37]

The agency's response to political influences can depend on the terms of administrators' tenure. Some administrators are appointed under statutes that prohibit their removal by the President except for "cause," which is usually defined as "inefficiency, neglect of duty, or malfeasance in office."[38] These terms are traditionally understood to preclude the President from removing an administrator over a policy disagreement.[39] Other administrators serve at the President's discretion and can be removed for any reason, including policy disagreements. If the President, for example, believes the EPA Administrator is issuing unwise regulations, the President can fire the administrator, but the President cannot dismiss an FTC Commissioner for the same reason because this official has protected tenure. Agencies headed by administrators with protected tenure are called "independent agencies," based on the idea that administrators who can be dismissed only for cause are freer to ignore White House policy preferences.[40] Administrators at agencies are entitled to remain in office in a succeeding administration if their term of office has not expired.

3. IMPACT OF LEGAL PROCEDURES

To the extent that public choice theory holds true and that it is easier for small, narrowly focused interest groups to organize and, as a corollary, it is difficult for amorphous public interest groups to form, then there is an imbalance of participation in the political process. To what extent is it possible to rely on legal mechanisms to correct the imbalance? Is this a proper function of government? Do such procedures produce better policies? In fact, Congress and the states have used several strategies to open the processes of government to public participation.

The Alternative Dispute Resolution Act directs agencies to adopt procedures addressing the use of ADR in such agency activities as adjudications, rulemakings, enforcement actions, licensing procedures, and other agency actions.[41] Agencies are further directed to appoint and train ADR specialists in the theory and practice of negotiation, mediation, arbitration, and related techniques. In addition to these techniques, agencies are authorized to use conciliation, facilitation, fact-finding, mini trials, or any combination of ADR methods. Thus, ADR facilitates public participation in agency decisionmaking

---

[37] *See, e.g., Sierra Club v. Costle,* 657 F.2d 298 (D.C. Cir. 1981) (White House officials, including President Carter, pressed EPA to adopt less costly regulations).

[38] *E.g.,* 15 U.S.C. § 41 (1982) (limitation on President's authority to fire Federal Trade Commissioners).

[39] *See Humphrey's Ex'r v. United States,* 295 U.S. 602 (1935) (declaring President Roosevelt's attempt to fire FTC Commissioner for policy disagreement invalid under statute which limited removal except for "cause").

[40] PIERCE, SHAPIRO, & VERKUIL, ADMINISTRATIVE LAW & PROCESS § 4.4 (2d ed. 1992).

[41] Pub. L. No. 101-552, 104 Stat. 2738 (1990) (codified at 5 U.S.C. §§ 571–83).

by reducing the cost of such participation and by attempting to facilitate decisions acceptable to all interested parties.

The Regulatory Negotiation Act authorizes agencies to utilize ADR procedures for rulemaking.[42] Because rulemaking is forward-looking and often involves several parties with various interests, structured negotiation is a method than can reduce the time and expense of a rulemaking proceeding. Through negotiated rulemaking (or "reg-neg"),[43] the affected parties can participate in the development of the rule, share information and technical knowledge, and increase the acceptability of the outcome.

Occasionally, state governments have realized that the disparity in representation is so great that a government agency is necessary to adequately represent the public interest before a regulatory agency. During the energy crisis of the 1970s, for example, several states adopted agencies to represent consumers in rate hearings. The Office of Consumers Counsel in Ohio is just such an example. In New Jersey, there is a Department of Public Advocate which has six divisions, including the Office of Public Defender, Office of Inmate Advocacy, Division of Rate Counsel, Division of Mental Health Advocacy, the Division of Citizen Complaint and Dispute Settlement, and the Division of Public Interest.[44] Lawyers who represent the public interest in this manner reduce the need for citizens to pay for lawyers to represent them in agency proceedings.

The "American rule" regarding attorney's fees is that the "prevailing litigant is ordinarily not entitled to collect a reasonable attorney's fee from the loser,"[45] but Congress has abrogated this rule in several regulatory contexts. Among statutes designed to provide attorneys' fees to prevailing parties when persons may not have the resources to fund litigation themselves are the Equal Access to Justice Act,[46] and the Civil Rights Attorney's Fees Awards Act of 1976,[47] both of which are intended to reduce the transaction costs of access to the legal system. In addition, at least sixteen federal statutes provide for attorney's fees in regulated areas or before administrative agencies, "whenever [the court] determines that such award is appropriate."[48]

Even with representation, citizens need access to information to make their participation meaningful. The government has taken steps to make general information available to the public through such measures as the Freedom of Information Act,[49] which provides that each federal agency, upon request for reasonable identifiable records, shall make the records promptly available

---

[42] Pub. L. No. 101-648, 104 Stat. 4969 (1990) (codified at 5 U.S.C. §§ 561–70).

[43] See, e.g., Perritt, *Negotiated Rulemaking Before Federal Agencies: Evaluation of Recommendations by the Administrative Conference of the United States*, 74 GEO. L.J. 1625 (1986); Harter, *Negotiating Regulations: A Cure of Malaise*, 71 GEO. L.J. 1 (1982).

[44] *Mt. Laurel Twp. v. Public Advocate of New Jersey*, 83 N.J. 522, 416 A.2d 886 (1980).

[45] *Alyeska Pipeline Co. Serv. v. Wilderness Soc'y*, 421 U.S. 240, 247 (1975).

[46] 28 U.S.C. § 2412 (1988).

[47] 42 U.S.C. § 1988 (1988).

[48] See, e.g., Toxic Substances Control Act, 15 U.S.C. § 2618(d); Surface Mining Control and Reclamation Act, 30 U.S.C. § 1270(d); Clean Water Act, 33 U.S.C. § 1365(d).

[49] 5 U.S.C. § 552.

(with limited exceptions), and the Sunshine Act,[50] which provides for open meetings.

Still, these statutes alone may not provide sufficient technical information for adequate representation. The government can also require the collection and dissemination of more specific and technical information, as it does with consumer products.[51] When such information is available to the public, lawyers and others who represent the public can use it in agency proceedings.

Finally, some legal scholars associated with Civic Republicanism have urged the courts to promote public deliberation and good policy outcomes by vigorously enforcing the requirement that agencies fully and completely explain the nature of their reasoning process.[52] As discussed in Chapter 1, some courts have required courts to give a "hard look," or a high degree of scrutiny to whether a proposed action will serve the public interest. Other scholars object on pluralist-related grounds that activist review delays agencies from meeting their statutory mandates and invites federal judges to meddle in the resolution of political and policy issues.[53]

NOTES AND QUESTIONS

1. The professional training of administrative personnel will affect their reaction to policy arguments. Some of the choices concerning the structure of the government are made to strengthen organizational and professional norms. The Civil Service System, for example, was created in the belief that persons hired, trained, and retained on the basis of expertise and job performance are better decisionmakers than persons whose only qualifications are their political contacts and experience.[54] Does the existence of a nonpolitical civil service system assume that regulatory questions are capable of resolution by the application of neutral, impartial expertise? Is this necessarily true? While the vast majority of federal employees have civil service protection, the persons who occupy the top administrative positions in government agencies and departments are political appointees. Is this appropriate?

2. Because regulation is the product of law, policy, and politics, Michael Reagan describes the study of regulation as a "political economy." He explains:

> [R]egulation, as a governmental activity, always depends on political circumstances for its inception and operation, it is not legislated as a deduction from microeconomic analysis of markets . . .; and its purposes are as diverse as its political origins. While the functions that regulation may serve sometimes include the strengthening of resource allocation on market principles, alliances forged to create a regulatory

---

[50] 5 U.S.C. § 552b.

[51] 15 U.S.C. § 2054 (1988).

[52] Seidenfeld, *Hard-Look in a World of Techno-Bureaucratic Rationality: A Reply to Professor McGarity*, 75 TEX L. REV. 559 (1997); Sunstein, *Interest Groups in American Public Law*, 38 STAN. L. REV. 29 (1985).

[53] McGarity, *The Courts and the Ossification of Rulemaking: A Response to Professor Seidenfeld*, 75 TEX. L. REV. 525 (1997)

[54] Kaufman, *Emerging Conflicts in the Doctrines of Public Administration, in* THE POLITICS OF THE FEDERAL BUREAUCRACY 75 (A. Altshuler ed. 1968).

program are more likely to be unified by a perception of consumer protection, or abuse of corporate power, than by economic principles. . . . [This means] that regulation cannot adequately be described, analyzed, or evaluated by any single academic discipline. The three that have each had periods of explanatory supremacy—law, political science, and economics—are all necessary tools of the regulatory observer's trade. . . .

[This also means] that regulatory issues turn at least as much on questions of values imbedded in competing criteria for action as on any "scientific" analysis, whether by the social or physical or biological sciences. All policy formation, it has been argued, arrays values and facts against posited goals. While values can be analyzed for internal consistency (conflicts with the value assumptions of other programs, and so forth), they are peculiarly the public's province in a democracy, not the expert's. And the public's realm is the realm of politics.[55]

3. Should lawyers practice "politics"? The fact that agencies operate in a political environment affects the nature of a regulatory lawyer's practice. A lawyer's advocacy role is not limited to talking with agency personnel. The lawyer will also seek the assistance of elected officials in various ways. Tom Susman, a former chair of the Administrative Law and Regulatory Practice section of the American Bar Association, has noted that such contacts are a regular part of agency practice, and he defends the use of political influence:

Politics defines relationships among people—and among institutions—especially governmental institutions. Politics is thus irrelevant or peripheral, only in the most focused, structured, and formalized proceeding—like a hearing room without a jury . . . .

Joseph Goulden, in The Superlawyers, saw this as the dark side of Washington law practice and characterized the exercise of the lawyer's art of influencing government decisionmaking a violation of the public interest. Goulden sold a lot of books but missed the point. Our system of checks and balances and counterbalances—which includes in Washington many cross-checks and counterbalances—works on many levels, and in many ways.

Politics provide both the board and the rules for the game of government, the game that many Washington Lawyers play for their livelihood. Whether personal or partisan, issue-development or fundraising, endorsements or referrals, grass-roots or national or international, politics touches . . . most aspects of Washington lawyering. Politics have become an integral part of the regular practice of law for the Washington Lawyer.[56]

Do you agree with Susman that the presence of political influence in regulatory decisionmaking is defensible, or would you conclude that Joseph Goulden was correct that this is the "dark side" of Washington law practice?

---

[55] M. REAGAN, REGULATION: THE POLITICS OF POLICY 208 (1987).

[56] Susman, *A Perspective on the Washington Lawyer Today and Charles Horsky's Washington Lawyer of 1952*, 44 ADMIN. L. REV. 1, 6–7 (1992).

Is the exercise of the lawyer's art of influencing government decisionmaking a violation of the public interest, or is it merely democracy at work?

4. Why is it the responsibility of the courts or the legislature to foster greater participation by groups or persons who are underrepresented in the regulatory process? Is this role for government supported by any of the versions of democratic theory studied earlier? Is it unfair for government to assist some parties, such as consumers or regulatory beneficiaries, and not others, such as regulated entities?

Part II
Economic Regulation

The United States prides itself on the vigor and virtue of its market economy. The market, in which numerous buyers and sellers bargain voluntarily and in which the laws of supply and demand operate, is the heart of the system. The direct consequence of a multiplicity of market transactions is to reach an equilibrium, in which producers provide the proper amount and variety of goods, and consumers have extensive choices to maximize their economic welfare. Further, through the market, principles of democracy and capitalism reinforce each other, to the end of promoting voluntary exchange transactions for the purpose of enhancing efficiency, maximizing wealth, and encouraging individual liberty.

Producers are attracted to the market because, through their integrity and their entrepreneurial ability, they can make a profit. If a producer can sell more goods less expensively, or sell better goods at about the same price, it can maximize its profits. This freedom to set one's own price in pursuit of profit is attractive because it encourages innovation. A producer innovates by producing goods more cheaply or by improving the product. Similarly, through advertising and marketing, producers can search for buyers, and thus decide to whom they will sell their goods. Actually, according to microeconomic theory, "the market" sets the price and allocates the goods. Still, producers have the freedom to experiment with the pricing and allocation of goods for profit maximization.

Consumers are attracted to the market, because a variety of goods, in terms of both price and quality, are available. Further, consumers have the freedom and power to tell producers what goods to produce through their purchasing choices. Individual liberty and equality are promoted because, through market choices, consumers exercise their voting power, where one dollar equals one vote. Thus, the market is free of bias and prejudice, because all votes are equal.

The virtues of the market, then, are several: resources are used efficiently; wealth is created; consumer satisfaction and producer profit are maximized; goods are properly priced and allocated; innovation and variety are encouraged; and liberty and equality are valued.

Viewed from another perspective, in a laissez-faire market economy, no central government authority tells a producer what goods to produce, at what prices to sell, or to whom these goods should be allocated, nor does government limit the choice of goods or prices available to consumers. Many countries in the post-Cold War era now face the problem of moving societies from centralized, planned economies, where governments make pricing and allocation decisions, to laissez-faire market economies, where the bargainers make those decisions.

The government of the United States is often referred to as the prime example of democratic capitalism. In this society, policymakers and analysts, whether they are legislators, bureaucrats, lawyers, or judges, start with the premise that a market economy is preferable to government regulation.

If a market economy is the preference, and if government regulation is the reality, how are preference and reality reconciled? The short answer is that markets do not follow microeconomic theory. It should come as no surprise to anyone in a modern law school, let alone students in a course on government regulation, to read that competitive markets (and their virtues) are not infrequently absent. There are technical, positive reasons for a market imperfection; *e.g.*, a market has only one or a few producers who exercise pricing power, thus constricting choices. There are also theoretical, normative criticisms of the market that contest basic behavioral assumptions, such as the notion that transactions are voluntary, or that individuals behave rationally from an economic sense, or that people consent to participating in a market.

Market failures or imperfections occur for a variety of reasons, many of which will be examined in detail throughout this book. Market failures play a dual role in government regulation. First, the identification of a market failure is descriptive, in that it indicates the specific technical breakdown in the market. Second, the identified market failure is prescriptive, in that is serves as a justification for government regulation and suggests the proper government response. If the improper response is chosen, the cure may be worse (more costly) than the malady. The regulation may increase costs, thus reducing efficiency, or may aggravate inequitable distributions.

As the following table indicates, Part II identifies four failures of the competitive market (natural monopoly, bottlenecks, economic rents, and excessive competition) which have been used to justify regulation. We also discuss three tools (rate setting, entry and exit controls, and subsidies) used to address these failures. In addition, we indicate that some industries (airlines), or a portion of some industries (natural gas), have been deregulated. This decision represents a rejection of the original rationale for regulation. Thus, in the case of natural gas, the decision was reached that the natural monopoly rationale was inaccurate. Likewise, Congress determined that the excessive competition rationale did not justify regulation in the case of airline transportation.

If the market is attractive to producers because of the freedom to set prices, make profits, allocate goods, and compete, government regulation of these activities is antithetical to the market preference. It follows, then, that the government must offer a strong justification for intervening in these activities.

In the chapters that follow, the same justification is offered–market failure. In Chapter 4, we explore the market failure caused by natural monopolies. Chapters 5 and 6 examine the bottleneck problem (*i.e.*, the capacity of a firm to block entry into a market by its competitors). Chapter 7 questions whether regulation is an appropriate response to capture economic rents through price controls in rental housing. Finally, Chapter 8 examines the problem of excess capacity in the airline and agriculture industries and why the government has chosen to deregulate the airline industry but not agriculture.

Many of these terms and concepts will not be clear until you finish Section II. You may wish to return to this introduction at that time as a form of review and to help you organize your notes.

ECONOMIC REGULATION				
MARKET FAILURES	*REGULATORY TOOLS*			
	Rate Setting	*Entry and Exit Controls*	*Subsidies*	*Deregulation*
Natural Monopoly	Electricity (Chapter 4)			Natural Gas (Chapter 5)
Bottlenecks		Natural Gas (Chapter 5) Telecommunications (Chapter 6)		
Economic Rents	Housing Rentals (Chapter 7)			
Excessive Competition			Agriculture (Chapter 8)	Airlines (Chapter 8)

Chapter 4

NATURAL MONOPOLY: PRICE CONTROLS AND ELECTRICITY REGULATION

A. THE RATIONALE FOR REGULATION

A perfectly competitive market requires numerous buyers and sellers. This chapter addresses: how utility markets can become dominated by only one seller, a so-called "natural monopolist;" what regulatory responses are available; and, why these responses are constitutional. The chapter ends by discussing how regulatory reform has changed the traditional approach to the regulation of natural monopolies.

1. NATURAL MONOPOLY

A natural monopoly is defined as follows: "A firm or industry whose average cost per unit of production falls sharply over the entire range of its output. Thus a single firm, a monopoly, can supply the industry output more efficiently than can multiple firms."[1] Public utilities are the best example of a natural monopoly.

Utilities are natural monopolies, especially, if not exclusively, along their transmission segment, because they depend on a system of grids—interconnecting pipes or wires—to deliver service. Because of the grids, utilities have the characteristics identified in the definition. These industries are large and capital intensive; have high entry costs (i.e., initial capital investment is significant); and, have fixed costs which decrease over the range of output. In other words, the natural monopolist realizes significant economies of scale. Further, because of the high front-end capital costs, competitors are discouraged. Once a transmission or telephone line is installed, the cost of a unit of electricity or of a telephone call is relatively low. A single firm will have lower average costs than two firms, each of which will have to incur higher fixed costs.

In economic terms, the barriers to entry (for a competitor) are high, thus entrenching the monopolist. The competitor would have to install an entirely new grid system to sign up its first customer. By comparison, the existing utility would only need to extend service from its existing grid of pipes or wires. As a result, the existing utility can offer service to new customers at

---

[1] P. SAMUELSON & W. NORDHAUS, ECONOMICS 911 (12th ed. 1985). In addition to the Samuelson and Nordhaus definition of monopoly, more technical definitions and extended discussion can be found in M. ARMSTRONG, S. COWAN, & J. VICKERS, REGULATORY REFORM: ECONOMIC ANALYSIS & BRITISH EXPERIENCE (1994); S. BERG & J. T. SCHIRHART, NATURAL MONOPOLY REGULATION: PRINCIPLES AND PRACTICE (1988); J. BONBRIGHT, A. DANIELSEN & D. KAMERSCHEN, PRINCIPLES OF PUBLIC UTILITY RATES 17–24, 33–36 (2d ed. 1988); M. CREW & P. KLEINDORFER, THE ECONOMICS OF PUBLIC UTILITY REGULATION (1986); Posner, *Natural Monopoly and Its Regulation*, 21 STAN. L. REV. 548 (1969).

far lower prices than the new entrant. Given this advantage, it is unlikely that a new entrant would be willing to spend millions of dollars to establish a competitive grid system. In addition, consumers expect immediate service, and this means that capital must be invested to satisfy peak demand. Thus, a new entrant must not only establish a grid, but the grid must be large enough to handle peak demand.

The direct consequence of these characteristics is that it makes little economic sense—in fact, it is wasteful—to duplicate large front-end capital costs. In other words, having only one grid lowers the cost of service for consumers. Consumers, however, may be unable to reap the rewards of such efficiency because the utility, as a monopolist, will be able to price its services to maximize its own profits.

2. IMPACT ON CONSUMERS

The problem with a single firm supplying a market is that it can cause a change in price by withholding supply. In fact, a monopolist can charge a supracompetitive price that is unrelated to production costs. In this sense, then, a monopoly has none of the desirable attributes of perfect competition. The monopolist is in a position simultaneously to raise prices, reduce output, and impose a welfare loss on society.

A producer in a competitive market maximizes profits when it sets its prices at the intersection of its marginal revenue and marginal cost curves. Figure 4-1 indicates how a monopolist sets its prices. A monopolist's marginal revenue curve (MR_m) is downward-sloping and is always below its demand curve (D), because a monopolist, by definition, cannot engage in price discrimination by selling its product to different customers at different prices. If a monopolist sold goods to Consumer A at a price lower than to Consumer B, Consumer A would purchase more from the monopolist and sell to Consumer B, capturing the monopolist's profit. Therefore, if a monopolist lowers its price to one consumer, it is forced to lower prices on its entire output, thus reducing total revenue.

Figure 4-1: Natural Monopoly

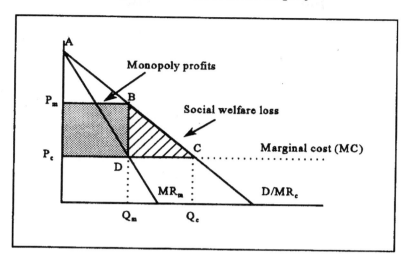

Notice that the monopolist's marginal revenue curve intersects the marginal cost curve in a different place than it intersects the demand (D) curve. In a competitive market, goods are priced at P_c, and quantity Q_c is produced because P_c and Q_c are derived from the intersection of the MC and D/MR$_c$ curves. Here, the MC curve is flat, assuming a competitive firm in an industry.

The monopolist, however, derives its price and quantity from the intersection of the MC curve and the monopolist's marginal revenue curve MR$_m$. Thus, the monopolist prices at P_m and produces at Q_m. Notice that the result of the monopoly pricing is a price *increase* from P_c to P_m and a quantity *decrease* from Q_c to Q_m.

This lower output and higher price results in monopoly profits represented by the darkened rectangle (P_c-P_m-B-D). The shaded triangle (B-C-D) indicates a loss of consumer surplus or social welfare loss. This loss occurs because, to raise prices, the monopolist cuts production below the level that would have occurred in a competitive market, and consumers are forced to forego consumption of the monopolized good for which their marginal benefit, represented by their willingness to pay, exceeds the marginal cost of production. In other words, there are consumers that would have been willing to buy goods along a price range from P_c to P_m. However, these consumers are denied this opportunity, because output has been reduced and those goods are not available for consumption. Thus, in a monopoly market, consumers pay higher prices than a competitive market would dictate, and they must forego some consumption opportunities.

Another way of graphically demonstrating this loss is to compare the consumer surplus in a competitive market, represented by the large triangle (A-C-P_c), with the consumer surplus in the monopoly market, represented by the small triangle (A-B-P $_m$). The difference in consumer surplus between these two triangles is allocated to the monopolist's profits and to a social, or deadweight, loss.

NOTES AND QUESTIONS

1. When a firm can profit by raising its price significantly above the competitive level for a considerable period of time, the firm has what economists describe as "market power." Why does a natural monopolist have market power? What prevents new firms from becoming competitors of the monopolist attracted by the high prices that the monopolist is charging?

2. A firm may have market power without being a natural monopolist. For example, firms may cooperate, or even collude, to raise prices and restrict entry. "Economists would say that such firms have market power, indicating that even though these firms are not pure monopolists, they do possess some monopoly power."[2] Some of this activity may run afoul of the antitrust laws, which are enforced by both public authorities and private litigants in federal and state courts. Because antitrust enforcement is implemented by judges on a case-by-case basis, it is not within the scope of the coverage of this book.

3. Reliance on a grid system to deliver utility services is not inevitable. Technological improvements may make it possible to bypass the grid. For example, increasing numbers of people use cellular telephones which transmit their signals by radio wave. At the present time, however, cellular telephone service is more expensive than traditional service (and therefore does not significantly limit the ability of the local telephone company to raise its prices). Cellular service is more expensive because the government has allotted only limited space on the radio spectrum for use by cellular telephone companies. This means that cellular companies are unable to carry the same volume of messages that companies which rely on a grid system of wires can carry. Cellular service will become more competitive with traditional service if the government makes more of the spectrum available, or if technological improvements make it possible to transmit more telephone messages in the currently available spectrum.

4. Technological change also explains why the long-distance telephone market is now competitive. At one time, American Telephone and Telegraph (AT&T) was the only long-distance company, with a nationwide grid system of wires to transmit calls. Microwave and later satellite transmission technology permitted a host of competitors to enter the market. These firms were competitive with AT&T because several firms can use microwave or satellite technology to transmit calls on many routes without significantly increasing unit costs. These developments led to the deregulation of the long-distance telephone market.

5. Is government regulation of natural monopolies necessary? Some scholars, like Harold Demsetz, argue that the market, rather than government regulation, can control natural monopolies.[3] His thesis is that, even if a firm

---

[2] J. Gwartney & R. Stroup, Economics: Private and Public Choice 294 (7th ed 1995).

[3] Demsetz, *Why Regulate Utilities?,* 11 J. L. & Econ. 55 (1968).

realizes economies of scale, it does not follow that prices will be set at monopoly levels, because rival sellers can contract with some buyers and there can be competition for those contracts that will bring prices below the monopoly level. "The existence of scale economies in the production of the service is irrelevant to a determination of the number of rival bidders." In other words, Demsetz is not convinced that the rivals would avoid entering utility markets because of the cost of building a rival grid system. He notes that competition was common, particularly in the delivery of electrical services, at the turn of the century.[4]

Is there a difference between competitive conditions when utility industries were just beginning to develop and now? Does Demsetz's argument have more validity when applied to new markets than existing markets?

6. Demsetz admits that it may be desirable to employ some sort of regulation because competition among utilities might be disruptive to the public if it resulted in continual construction of grid systems. Still, he proposes that regulation is still unnecessary. For example:

> An alternative arrangement would be public ownership of the distribution system. This would involve the collection of competing bids for installing the distribution system. This system could then be installed by the bidder offering to do the specified job at the lowest price. This is the same process used by communities to build highways and it employs rival bidding and not commissions to determine that price. The community would then allow its distribution system to be used by that utility company offering to provide specified utility services at lowest cost to residents. Again, the market is substituted for the regulatory commission. . . .

Why is it that most states and cities rely on regulation of a utility's prices rather than the type of bidding system that Demsetz recommends?

B. REGULATORY OPTIONS

The government traditionally has responded to the problem of natural monopoly by relying on a "regulatory compact" which defines the terms and conditions under which a utility can sell its services. Recently, however, regulators have begun to blend traditional regulation with a new approach, which we call *regulatory markets*. This section briefly describes these two options.

1. REGULATORY COMPACT

Government's answer to the problem of natural monopoly may seem counterintuitive, but its response is a government-protected monopoly! The government permits the utility to maintain its monopoly status, but it regulates the utility in an effort to set the price and quantity of service at what would be a competitive level. For this purpose, the government and the utility enter into what is usually described as a "regulatory compact." As the

---

[4] For the contrary view to Demsetz, see W. TROESKEN, WHY REGULATE UTILITIES?: THE NEW DISTRIBUTIONAL ECONOMICS AND THE CHICAGO GAS INDUSTRY, 1849–1924 (1996).

following description elaborates, this compact benefits both the utility and the ratepayers:

> The utility business represents a compact of sorts; a monopoly on service in a particular geographical area (coupled with state-conferred rights of eminent domain or condemnation) is granted to the utility in exchange for a regime of intensive regulation, including price regulation, quite alien to the free market. . . . Each party to the compact gets something in the bargain. As a general rule, utility investors are provided a level of stability in earnings and value less likely to be attained in the unregulated or moderately regulated sector; in turn, ratepayers are afforded universal, non-discriminatory service and protection from monopolistic profits through political control over an economic enterprise. [5]

The regulatory compact imposes significant obligations on both the government and the regulated firm (which most often is a public utility). In exchange for a government-protected monopoly, the public utility lets government set its prices. The utility is frequently given the power of eminent domain, is given a franchise or a service area, and is the only firm authorized to sell its product in that area. In fact, the utility acquires an obligation to serve. The government, through ratemaking, sets the price of the service. Generally, rates will be set so that a prudently managed utility will cover its operating expenses and earn a reasonable return on its capital investment, thus enabling the utility to earn a profit. The regulatory control of natural monopoly, then, occurs by: (1) limiting entry; (2) setting prices; (3) controlling profits; and (4) imposing a service obligation. Section C of this chapter will examine government price controls for regulated firms concentrating on ratemaking.

2. REGULATORY MARKETS

Cost-of-service ratemaking has been the traditional method of regulating natural monopolies. Recently, however, regulators have been turning to a new approach. This approach gives consumers a choice of the firm from which they purchase gas, electricity, or long-distance telephone service.

As explained earlier, competition is unlikely, and it may be counterproductive, in the transmission of utility services. This market defect exists because utility services are delivered by a grid of pipes or wires. Markets which do not rely on grids are not subject to this defect. For example, the generation of power can be competitive, although it has not been for reasons you will study. Unlike the delivery of power, the generation of power is not an enterprise where the cost per unit of production falls sharply over the entire range of output. Instead, the behavior of generation costs follows the description of a competitive market that you read about in Chapter 2. Costs decline as more units are produced until there are diminishing returns; then costs will rise if production is increased. As a result, a number of firms can compete to sell electricity to a local buyer.

---

[5] *Jersey Cent. Power & Light Co. v. FERC,* 810 F.2d 1168, 1189 (D.C. Cir. 1987) (*Jersey Central III*).

Regulators are seeking to restructure electricity markets in light of the competitive nature of the generation portion of the industry. In a restructured market, the local buyer picks the generation firm from which electricity is purchased. The buyer does this on the basis of price: the buyer will buy the lowest cost electricity available. The buyer then pays the distribution company—the natural monopolist—a fee to transmit the electricity the buyer has purchased. In this manner, the distribution company becomes a common carrier. The government requires it to carry the electricity produced by any generator which makes a local sale.

We describe these new arrangements as "regulatory markets" in recognition that regulators are establishing the terms and conditions by which the generation of electricity is delivered. This is not an easy task. Regulators will need to continue some form of price control over distribution services because they will continue to be a natural monopoly. Moreover, regulators will need to protect those local buyers who will not have the opportunity to choose their generator. In addition, the government will need to ensure that the distribution company treats all generators on a fair and equal basis. Regulators should be cautious if the distribution company is also in the business of generating electricity since it will be tempted to try to gain a competitive advantage by making it more expensive for competing generators to obtain local delivery. Finally, regulators must manage the transition from the old method of regulation to a regulatory market. This task involves a particularly challenging issue known as "stranded costs." When one regulated market is altered by another regulation, the firm in that market may have invested capital in reliance on the first regulatory scheme. The question then arises: Should those "stranded costs" due to the new regulation be recouped by the relying firm?

C.   COST-OF-SERVICE RATEMAKING

The traditional form of price control for utilities has been cost-of-service ratemaking or rate setting. In the traditional market, the regulator determines the price that a natural monopoly can charge consumers for electricity or natural gas which the distributor has generated or produced, or which it has purchased from some other generator or producer. In a regulatory market, a government agency determines the price that the natural monopoly can charge consumers for delivering electricity, natural gas, or long-distance telephone service that the consumer has purchased directly from the generator or producer.

Government price setting through ratemaking is an attempt to set a price that mimics the market. Another way of saying this is that, through ratemaking, profits are controlled and, hopefully, profits are closer to the competitive market level than they are to the monopoly level.

As a matter of practical experience, however this goal is impossible to achieve. Sometimes, the regulators are too generous, sometimes too miserly. When rates are set too high, consumers suffer, because they are paying more than the "real" price (cost) of the service. When rates are too low, shareholders suffer, because the return on investment is inadequate (i.e., the return is not as high as in the competitive market).

Rate setting can be seen as the paradigm of economic regulation, because it involves a mathematical-looking formula, reams of financial data, and even special accounting rules. Yet, these trappings of quantitative analysis cannot obscure the role played by politics. Government regulation, for all of its technical sophistication, its talk of economic efficiency, even its aspirations for social justice, cannot remain unaffected by politics. It is imperative, then, that the student of government regulation be sensitive to and aware of the political choices (the policy preferences) being made through all regulation including ratemaking.

1.　RATEMAKING GOALS

Public utility scholars agree that there are both economic and noneconomic reasons for ratemaking. A leading treatise on ratemaking[6] lists four goals:

a.　PRODUCTION MOTIVATION OR CAPITAL ATTRACTION

This ratemaking goal is to make the utility business attractive to producers, which, in turn, means that the enterprise must attract investors. Although heavily regulated, most utilities are privately owned, and regulation should not be a disincentive for private interests to invest in and produce utility services. If investors can find either more remunerative or less risky investments elsewhere, their capital will be directed away from public utilities. Rates should be set at a level high enough to encourage sufficient investment.

b.　EFFICIENCY INCENTIVE

The rate formula should be designed so that resources are priced in such a way that waste is reduced and consumer surplus is not lost. In other words, the price of natural gas or electricity should allocate resources to their most valued uses. This ratemaking goal is difficult to achieve. Rates have been set at levels that both encourage waste and over-reward producers. At times electricity or natural gas is either underpriced or overpriced through ratemaking. To maximize the use of resources, prices should reflect their "true cost."

c.　DEMAND CONTROL OR CONSUMER RATIONING

Sometimes regulators intend to create the allocatively inefficient effects of overpricing or underpricing just described. In a market with abundant and relatively cheap resources, rates can be set low to promote consumption. In a market of declining resources, rates can be set high to promote conservation. In both cases, demand is controlled by overpricing or underpricing the utility service. Thus, ratemaking can be used to control demand, which is to say that ratemaking can perform a rationing function.

d.　INCOME DISTRIBUTION

Rates can be set in such a way that some consumer classes subsidize others. Through ratemaking, large industrial users can help offset residential rates, or all customer classes can help subsidize the poor, or the utility (i.e., its

---

[6] BONBRIGHT, DANIELSEN & KAMERSCHEN, *supra* note 1, at 48–62.

shareholders) can provide discounts to some customers. In this way, wealth is redistributed either from producers to consumers, or among customer classes.

It should be noted that these four ratemaking goals may conflict with one another. Setting rates to reduce demand, for example, may discourage capital attraction or may reduce consumption by desired classes of consumers. The choice of which ratemaking goals are to be served at any specific point in time depends on economic, political, and legal circumstances. The primary vehicle with which regulators attempt to achieve these goals is the rate formula.

2. THE RATE FORMULA

The objective of ratemaking is to set prices for utility services comparable to the prices set in a competitive market. Regulators use a formula for making this comparison which can be simply stated as:

$$R = O + (V - d)r$$

The variables of this formula are:

R	firm's **revenue requirement** or the total amount of money that the regulatory authority decides that the firm is entitled to earn
O	firm's **operating expenses**
V	gross value of the firm's **capital investment**
d	firm's accrued **depreciation**
(V - d)	firm's **rate base**
r	**rate of return** the utility is allowed by the regulatory authority to earn on its capital investment or rate base

This simple formula and the corresponding simple definitions obscure the often delicate and difficult applications and consequences of the formula. A description of some of these difficulties follows.

a. OPERATING EXPENSES

Generally, operating expenses are the least controversial variable. A utility must recoup its expenses if it is going to stay in business. These expenses typically constitute 75 to 80 percent of a utility's revenue requirement. They are comprised of such items as wages, salaries, maintenance, fuel, taxes, advertising, research and development, and depreciation.

Operating expenses can be summarized as: $O = (c + d + t)$. In this formulation, c stands for all operating expenses except depreciation (d) and taxes (t). Note that depreciation is included as an operating expense, and it is deducted from V (capital investment) to determine the rate base.

In ascertaining operating expenses, the regulatory authority must confront two issues. First, should a particular item be included as an operating expense recoverable from the ratepayers? Second, is the amount of the expense reasonable? A public utility commission (PUC), for example, may exclude excessive wages, advertising costs, or charitable contributions from the operating expense category. If an item is excluded, shareholders, rather than ratepayers, absorb the cost. If, for example, a PUC determines that a portion of wages is excessive, it may exclude that portion from being recovered through rates.[7]

Occasionally, the amount of the operating expenses will be questioned. The problem that regulators face in examining the amount of expenses is similar to the problem that courts face when asked to examine the management of a private corporation. Neither courts nor PUCs are willing to get involved, too closely, with the day-to-day management of a firm. Instead, the general legal principle is one of regulatory deference to utility managers and a presumption of managerial competency.[8] This general standard of deference works as long as the utility is prudently operated. If, however, consumers prove that utility management was imprudent—for example, if management engaged in unnecessary litigation—the litigation expenses will be excluded from this component of the ratemaking formula.

A current problem surrounding operating expenses involves a utility's health costs. Utilities are applying for rate increases to finance the medical benefits promised to present and future retirees. It is estimated that medical expenses could add more than $4 billion each year to the nation's electric, gas, and telephone rates. Medical costs for present retirees are already included in rates, and the controversy surrounds whether to include in present rates the costs predicted for future retirees. Medical benefits for utility employees are far more generous than in other industries, not infrequently paying 100 percent of medical costs for retirees and their dependents. Should present ratepayers finance the medical costs of future retirees?[9]

b. RATE BASE

Rate base represents the utility's capital investment. Just as a utility must recoup its operating expenses to stay in business, it must also maintain its capital investment in order to attract investors. The rate formula performs a capital attraction function by calculating the value of capital investment and by allowing the utility to earn a return on that valuation.

Regulators must decide two broad issues. First, should a particular item be included in the rate base? Rate base items include such things as physical plant and equipment and may include cash working capital, deductions for accumulated depreciation, deferred taxes, or deferred investment tax credits. Second, once an item is included in the rate base, a regulator must decide how the item should be valued.

Rate base issues are more complicated than operating expenses. One scholar has written: "Determination of the rate base—the value of a utility's property used and useful in the public service minus accrued depreciation—is one of the most important and most difficult problems confronting both the commissions and the utilities. No other conflict in the history of regulation has

---

[7] *See, e.g., Southwestern Bell Tel. Co. v. Arkansas Pub. Serv. Comm'n,* 18 Ark. App. 260, 715 S.W.2d 451 (1986); *Southern Cal. Edison Co. v. Public Util. Comm'n,* 20 Cal. 3d 813, 144 Cal. Rptr. 905, 576 P.2d 945, *appeal dismissed,* 439 U.S. 905 (1978).

[8] *Missouri ex rel. Southwestern Bell Tel. Co. v. Public Serv. Comm'n,* 262 U.S. 276 (1923).

[9] *See* Freudenheim, *Utilities Want Rates to Cover,* N.Y. Times, Jan. 7, 1992, at D1, col. 5.

received so much attention or been the subject of so much litigation."[10] There are two major reasons for the difficulty. First, large expenditures that threaten rate increases attract public attention and bring pressure on utility commissions to closely scrutinize the utility. Second, rate base is more difficult to value, and several valuation methods exist.

There are two general accounting methods of evaluating rate base—the original cost and the reproduction cost methods—with subparts, as follows:[11]

Original Cost	(1) *"First" Original Cost:* The amount actually paid for the original plant and equipment and additions.
	(2) *Book Cost:* The amount actually paid as shown in the investment accounts of the company's books.
	(3) *Prudent Investment:* Original cost minus imprudent investments.
	(4) *Capitalized Cost:* Capital invested as measured by outstanding stocks, bonds, and other securities.
Reproduction Costs	(5) *Current Reproduction Cost:* Cost of construction at time of valuation.
	(6) *Taxation Value:* Value of property as assessed for tax purposes.
	(7) *Market Value:* The probable earnings capacity of the firm.
	(8) *Exchange Value:* Price of utility as determined by what another party will pay to buy it.

Most federal and state ratemaking authorities use some form of original cost valuation, but inflation makes each of the two general methods problematic. If inflation is low or construction costs are declining, the utility will favor original cost rather than reproduction cost. The opposite is true if inflation is high and construction costs are increasing—then, utilities favor reproduction cost and reject original cost.

The subparts are also problematic. Methods (4), (7), and, to some extent, (8) depend on revenue and, therefore, involve circular reasoning, because the purpose of the rate formula is to determine revenue. Methods (1), (2), (3), and (5) depend on the accuracy of data and, taken alone, treat inflation unevenly. Method (6) is perhaps the least accurate, because tax valuation usually underestimates true market value.

c.   RATE OF RETURN

Rate of return is "the amount of money earned by a public utility, over and above operating costs, expressed as a percentage of the rate base."[12] In the

---

[10] C. PHILLIPS, THE REGULATION OF PUBLIC UTILITIES: THEORY AND PRACTICE 301 (2d ed. 1988). *See also* J. BONBRIGHT, DANIELSEN, & KAMERSCHEN, *supra* note 1, at chs. 10–13.

[11] This table is adapted from PHILLIPS, *supra* note 10, at 304–05.

[12] *Id.* at 358.

ratemaking formula, rate base is multiplied by rate of return; then the product is added to operating expenses to yield a rate level or revenue requirement. The rate of return, expressed as a percentage, is analogous to the interest rate payable by a bank on a savings account. The rate of return reflects the utility's cost of capital, and it must be set at a rate attractive enough for investors and not so high that it imposes an unreasonable rate on ratepayers.

Investors will invest in a regulated utility when they perceive the financial risks and returns worth their investment as compared to other investment opportunities. Historically, utility investments were seen as less risky than investments in other industries, because utilities had a government-backed opportunity to earn a return. Therefore, the return on those investments would be lower and still attract investors. After the experience with commercial nuclear power in which regulators disallowed returns on certain investments, utilities are experiencing more risk than they have been used to, and the current higher rates of return on a utility's common stock, preferred stock, and bonds reflect that increased risk.

The rate of return is a composite figure of the rates on the proportionate amount of debt (bonds and preferred stock) and equity (common stock) of the utility. In determining rate of return, regulators calculate the percentages of common stocks and preferred stocks and bonds which comprise the financial structure of the utility, and then determine the rate of return for each class of investment. This second calculation is not susceptible to precise measurement. In their attempt to find the cost of capital for debt and equity, PUCs examine the interest rates for stocks and bonds in comparable industries or firms. A comparable industry or firm would be one that presents similar investment risks.

Regulatory statutes require that the rate of return must be fair and reasonable, and this standard has been interpreted to include a return on investment and a return for risk.[13] As discussed in Section D, these statutory requirements have a constitutional origin. Courts prefer to defer to regulatory authorities in establishing the rate of return.[14]

d. REVENUE REQUIREMENT

The revenue requirement reveals what the utility is allowed to earn. It does not indicate which class of customers pays what amount for the goods and services. A utility regulator must therefore determine a rate structure which will produce enough revenue to equal the revenue requirement. The function of the rate structure is to apportion the rate level among customer classes. The three most general customer classes consist of industrial, commercial, and residential customers. While rate level is judged in terms of reasonableness, rate structure is judged by whether it discriminates among customer classes. A rate structure will be upheld as long as it does not impose an undue discrimination by unfairly imposing costs on one customer class at the expense of another customer class.

[13] *Wilcox v. Consolidated Gas Co.,* 212 U.S. 19 (1909); *Bluefield Water Works & Improvement Co. v. Public Serv. Comm'n of W. Va.,* 262 U.S. 679 (1923).

[14] *Northwestern Pub. Serv. Co. v. City of Chamberlin,* 265 N.W.2d 867 (S.D. 1978).

Traditionally, ratemaking has been based on a cost-of-service theory; that is, a ratepayer's rates are based on the utility's historic cost of providing the service. Generally, the utility's costs are divided into three components:

(1) Demand Costs

These costs vary with a customer's demand. Demand costs are roughly the equivalent of a utility's fixed costs. An electric utility invests in generating plants, transmission lines, and distribution systems. A customer with a demand of 100 kilowatts (kw) is responsible for less of a utility's fixed investment in plant and equipment than a customer with a demand of 2000 kw, and customers will be charged accordingly.

(2) Energy Costs

This charge is largely comprised of fuel and labor expenses and is roughly the equivalent of a utility's variable costs. A customer's energy costs vary with the amount of energy the customer consumes.

(3) Customer Costs

The utility's costs for billing, metering, maintenance, and the like change with the number of users. For example, it costs less for a utility to meter one industrial user which consumes 10,000 kw than it does to meter 100 residences each using 100 kw, thus totaling 10,000 kw.

Because these three costs vary among customer classes, rates that are purely cost-based will vary. It is cheaper on a per kilowatt basis for a utility to sell electricity to a large industrial user than to several residential users who consume as much as the single industrial user, because both demand costs and customer costs are lower for industrial users. Consequently, cost-based ratemaking can result in discrimination, and it remains for the regulatory agency to determine whether the discrimination is undue. Undue rate discrimination does occur when a utility charges different rates to two customers who are similarly situated.

Rate structure or design, then, has the intent and effect of apportioning costs among various classes of customers. It can also encourage efficiency or discourage consumption, promote particular social policies such as environmentalism, conservation, or energy efficiency, or redistribute wealth. Prior to the mid-1970s, for example, utility rates were set according to a declining block design. In a declining block design, the cost of electricity or natural gas stays constant over a range (a block) of consumption and is then lowered over the next range (or block) of consumption. Naturally, this design encouraged consumption, because the more electricity or natural gas a user consumed, the less expensive was the next block. Inverted block rates discourage consumption. Under this design, the cost of electricity or natural gas stays constant over a range of consumption, and then the cost increases over the next range of consumption. Consequently, conservation is promoted, because as costs rise, users consume less.

Another issue in rate design is whether some buyers should subsidize the amount that other buyers pay for utility services. Flat rates—that is, charging the same rate to all customers—have the effect of having larger users subsidize smaller users, because larger users are paying a larger portion of customer costs. Another example of subsidization is a lifeline rate design. The objective of lifeline rates is to provide a minimum amount of utility service for low income users and have other customers pick up this charge.

These rate design issues are mentioned to emphasize the point that once a revenue requirement is determined, other important matters remain to be decided. Further, rate design is not a purely economic matter. Instead, PUCs, if they are so inclined, can engage in social policymaking through the rate structure, as a lifeline rate design indicates.

3.   RATE FORMULA CONSEQUENCES

The traditional formula encourages capital expansion, which means that a utility tries to put as many capital investment items at a high value into the rate base as possible under this formula. Put simply, the more a utility builds, the more it earns. This can result in excess capital investment and an overcharge to customers.[15]

This incentive system works well in an expanding economy and for an industry with stable or declining costs. If the economy grows with increased energy use, and if energy is cheaper to buy, plant expansions make economic, social, and political sense. When the economy shrinks, when production costs increase, when there is skepticism about a direct energy-GNP link, and when the industry experiences a greater demand elasticity than it anticipated, as the electric industry did in the 1970s, capital expansion does not make economic, social, or political sense. Put simply, the rising cost of electricity to consumers did not go unnoticed by regulators.[16] As you will read later in the chapter, regulators sought to exclude from the rate base excess capital investment.

Other consequences follow from the application of the traditional formula. The decision to include or exclude a canceled nuclear plant from the rate base, for example, has a dramatic impact on either shareholders or ratepayers, as will be demonstrated later in this chapter. Investment in a failed project is a cost that must be borne by someone. If the regulatory agency includes the plant in the rate base, thus allowing a return to investors, the ratepayers pay and receive no electricity for that investment. If it excludes the plant from

---

[15] *See* Averch & Johnson, *Behavior of the Firm Under Regulatory Constraint,* 52 Am. Econ. Rev. 1052 (1962).

[16] *See* P. Navarro, the Dimming of America: the Real Costs of Electric Utility Regulatory Failure (1985).

the rate base, the utility still has a service obligation (i.e., ratepayers receive electricity), and the shareholders' return declines. Thus, rate base decisions affect wealth distribution. The rate formula can also be used to effectuate social policy, such as conservation, research, and development or energy efficiency. By including or disallowing certain investments in rate base, these social policies can be encouraged or discouraged.

NOTES AND QUESTIONS

1. Given the formulaic expression of the rate formula, it might well appear that ratemaking is the quintessential example of economic regulation. You should now understand that there are social as well as political dimensions involved with the application of the ratemaking formula. What are these social and political consequences of ratemaking?

2. The following analogy may be useful in describing the difficulty that regulators have in using the rate formula to obtain the appropriate level of prices:

> Suppose that the government is commissioning a new project—say, a rail link—from a firm. This project will cost an uncertain amount, but the cost can be affected by the firm exerting effort. The government has a choice: it can offer a contract to carry out the project in return for a particular fixed price that depends in some way upon the final cost of the project, an offer the firm either accepts or refuses, or it can offer to pay a price that depends in some way on the final cost of the project. In the former case the government bears no risk in the price it will pay, the firm has every incentive to minimize total cost, but it may turn out that the government pays significantly more than the cost of the project. At the other extreme, the government could simply contract to pay whatever the project eventually costs. In this case, the government is uncertain what the price will eventually be, price is in line with cost, the firm makes no abnormal profits, but the firm has no incentive to undertake any cost-reducing measures. Intermediate contracts, which pay the firm more than some reference price if cost turns out to be particularly high or allow government to claw back some of the offered price if the cost is low, have incentive and efficiency effects that lie between these extremes. Exactly the same dilemma exists when regulating utilities. . . .[17]

Why do regulators have the same dilemma as described in the hypothetical? How does the rate formula create this dilemma?

D. LEGAL BASES FOR REGULATION

As noted, state and federal regulators operate under statutory mandates that guarantee to a utility a "fair and reasonable" rate of return. In this section, you will learn why this statutory mandate has a constitutional origin.

The Supreme Court vacillated concerning the constitutionality of rate regulation in the early years of such regulation. After the 1930s, the picture

---

[17] Armstrong, Cowan, & Vickers, *supra* note 1, at 39.

became clearer. Under substantive due process, the Court defers to legislative judgments concerning the scope and nature of rate regulation. Under the Takings Clause, regulators must permit utilities to earn a "fair" or "reasonable" rate of return. Despite this restraint, regulators have considerable discretion concerning the regulation of utility prices.

The Court was initially favorable to rate regulation. In *Munn v. Illinois,* 94 U.S. 113, 126 (1876), it upheld the constitutionality of an Illinois statute fixing the rates charged by grain elevators and warehouses under the state's police power. The majority rejected the elevators' argument that the regulation violated the Takings Clause by reducing the value of their property. The Court indicated that the government could regulate private business, despite the adverse impact on property values, as long as the activity of a business was "affected with the public interest." As the Court put it, "When, therefore, one devotes his property to a use in which the public has an interest, he, in effect, grants to the public an interest in that use, and must submit to be controlled by the public for the common good, to the extent of the interest he has thus created." This "in the public interest" language is explicitly incorporated in many regulatory statutes.[18]

The majority found that the elevators were exercising monopoly power. Rate regulation of electricity and natural gas prices lends itself to a public interest justification, because natural gas and electricity are necessities of modern life, and these industries are susceptible to monopolization.

Some language in *Munn* suggested that rate regulation was the province of the legislature which was answerable to the voters and not to the courts. Consequently, rates were originally set by legislatures. Legislators, however, soon consigned rate regulation to administrative agencies. Fourteen years after *Munn,* the Court held that judicial review was available. In *Chicago, Milwaukee & St. Paul Ry. Co. v. Minnesota ex rel. R.R. & Warehouse Commission,* 134 U.S. 418 (1890), the Court reviewed a Minnesota statute which denied courts the power to review railroad haulage rates set by a Minnesota railroad commissioner, even if the rates set for transporting property were discriminatory or unreasonable. The Court found that by denying judicial review, the statute violated the due process and equal protection provisions of the United States Constitution.

1. SUBSTANTIVE DUE PROCESS

During the *Lochner* era of substantive due process, when the Supreme Court applied strict judicial scrutiny to rate regulation, it struck down a number of rate regulation statutes. The Court's switch to deferential review occurred in *Nebbia v. New York*, 291 U.S. 502 (1934), where the Court held that a state could regulate prices as part of its police power as long as such laws have a "reasonable relation to a proper legislative purpose, and are neither arbitrary nor discriminatory." In *Nebbia*, retailers challenged a New York state statute setting the price of milk at nine cents a quart. A basic part of

---

[18] *See, e.g.,* Federal Power Act, 16 U.S.C. § 824a; Natural Gas Act, 15 U.S.C. § 717(a); *see also* Atomic Energy Act, 42 U.S.C. § 2012(d); Surface Mining Control and Reclamation Act, 30 U.S.C. § 1201(b) ("in the national interest").

the challenge was that the state lacked authority to regulate a private business that was neither a public utility nor a business affected with a public interest. The Court rejected this challenge, holding that under its sovereign police power, a state can regulate for the general welfare. Regarding price setting, the Court opined:

> A state is free to adopt whatever economic policy may reasonably be deemed to promote public welfare, and to enforce that policy by legislation adapted to its purpose. The courts are without authority either to declare such policy, or, when it is declared by the legislature, to override it. If the laws passed are seen to have a reasonable relation to a proper legislative purpose, and are neither arbitrary nor discriminatory, the requirements of due process are satisfied, and judicial determination to that effect renders a court *functus officio.* "Whether the free operation of the normal laws of competition is a wise and wholesome rule for trade and commerce is an economic question which this court need not consider or determine." And it is equally clear that if the legislative policy be to curb unrestrained and harmful competition by measures which are not arbitrary or discriminatory it does not lie with the courts to determine that the rule is unwise. With the wisdom of the policy adopted, with the adequacy or practicability of the law enacted to forward it, the courts are both incompetent and unauthorized to deal. The course of decision in this court exhibits a firm adherence to these principles. Times without number we have said that the legislature is primarily the judge of the necessity of such an enactment, that every possible presumption is in favor of its validity, and that though the court may hold views inconsistent with the wisdom of the law, it may not be annulled unless palpably in excess of legislative power.

The law-making bodies have in the past endeavored to promote free competition by laws aimed at trusts and monopolies. The consequent interference with private property and freedom of contract has not availed with the courts to set these enactments aside as denying due process. Where the public interest was deemed to require the fixing of minimum prices, that expedient has been sustained. If the law-making body within its sphere of government concludes that the conditions or practices in an industry make unrestricted competition an inadequate safeguard of the consumer's interests, produce waste harmful to the public, threaten ultimately to cut off the supply of a commodity needed by the public, or portend the destruction of the industry itself, appropriate statutes passed in an honest effort to correct the threatened consequences may not be set aside because the regulation adopted fixes prices reasonably deemed by the legislature to be fair to those engaged in the industry and to the consuming public. And this is especially so where, as here, the economic maladjustment is one of price, which threatens harm to the producer at one end of the series and the consumer at the other. The Constitution does not secure to anyone liberty to conduct his business in such fashion as to inflict injury upon the public at large, or upon any substantial group of the people. Price control, like any other form of regulation, is unconstitutional only if arbitrary, discriminatory, or demonstrably irrelevant to the policy the legislature is free to adopt, and hence an unnecessary and unwarranted interference with individual liberty.

––––

2. TAKINGS CLAUSE

Once the Court abandoned substantive due process as a constraint on rate regulation, the Takings Clause became the primary constitutional limitation on the power of regulators to set utility prices. In its early cases, the Court evaluated two aspects of rate regulation for compliance with the Fifth Amendment: the calculation of the rate base and the size of the rate of return.

a. RATE BASE

The Court's method of reviewing the rate base for compliance with the Takings Clause has evolved. The Court originally established a "fair value" test, which required it to review the methodology used by a regulator to calculate the rate base. It eventually abandoned this approach and replaced it with another, more deferential test. Today the Court asks whether the method chosen by the regulator to calculate the rate base has produced a "fair" or "reasonable" result.

In the beginning of ratemaking, at the end of the nineteenth century, the Court was asked to review whether the rates set by regulators were so low as to be confiscatory. In the early case of *Smyth v. Ames,* 169 U.S. 466 (1898), the Court defined the "fail value" test as follows:

> We hold, however, that the basis of all calculations as to the reasonableness of rates . . . must be the fair value of the property being used by it for the convenience of the public. And in order to ascertain that value, the original cost of construction, the amount expended in permanent improvements, the amount and market value of its bonds and stock, the present as compared with the original cost of construction, the probable earning capacity of the property under particular rates prescribed by statute, and the sum required to meet operating expenses, are all matters for consideration, and are to be given such weight as may be just and right in each case. We do not say that there may not be other matters to be regarded in estimating the value of the property. What the company is entitled to ask is a fair return upon the value of that which it employs for the public convenience. On the other hand, what the public is entitled to demand is that no more be exacted from it for the use of a public highway than the services rendered by it are reasonably worth.

The fair value test was a legal conclusion, not a valuation method. An examination of the elements enumerated in *Smyth v. Ames* indicates that some are contradictory and others are circular. Justice Brandeis, who was a critic of *Smyth v. Ames,* announced another formula in his dissent in *Missouri ex rel. Southwestern Bell Tel. Co. v. Missouri Pub. Serv. Commission*, 262 U.S. 276, 289 (1923):

. . . The Court, adhering to the so-called rule of *Smyth v. Ames*, and further defining it, declares that what is termed value must be ascertained by giving weight, among other things, to estimates of what it would cost to reproduce the property at the time of the rate hearing.

The so-called rule of *Smyth v. Ames* is, in my opinion, legally and economically unsound. The thing devoted by the investor to the public use is not specific property, tangible and intangible, but capital embarked in the enterprise. Upon the capital so invested the Federal Constitution guarantees to the utility the opportunity to earn a fair return. Thus, it sets the limit to the power of the State to regulate rates. . . .

The investor agrees, by embarking capital in a utility, that its charges to the public shall be reasonable. His company is the substitute for the State in the performance of the public service; thus becoming a public servant. The compensation for which the Constitution guarantees an opportunity to earn is the reasonable cost of conducting the business. Cost includes not only operating expenses, but also capital charges. Capital charges cover the allowance, by way of interest, for the use of the capital, whatever the nature of the security issued therefore; the allowance for risk incurred; and enough more to attract capital. The reasonable rate to be prescribed by a commission may allow an efficiently managed utility much more. But a rate is constitutionally compensatory, if it allows to the utility the opportunity to earn the cost of the service as thus defined. . . .

The adoption of the amount prudently invested as the rate base and the amount of the capital charge as the measure of the rate of return would give definiteness to these two factors involved in rate controversies which are now shifting and treacherous, and which render the proceedings peculiarly burdensome and largely futile. Such measures offer a basis for decision which is certain and stable. The rate base would be ascertained as a fact, not determined as matter of opinion. It would not fluctuate with the market price of labor, or materials, or money. It would not change with hard times or shifting populations. It would not be distorted by the fickle and varying judgments of appraisers, commissions, or courts. It would, when once made in respect to any utility, be fixed, for all time, subject only to increases to represent additions to plant, after allowance for the depreciation included in the manual operating charges.

The Brandeis formulation did not extract the courts from valuation determinations. Rather, it shifted the courts' focus to a choice between prudent investment and reproduction cost.

In a seminal, and lasting, opinion, Justice Douglas, in *Federal Power Commission v. Hope Natural Gas Co.,* 320 U.S. 591 (1944), took the Court out of the valuation business and established the "end result" test, which is a constitutional standard to determine when rates are confiscatory. *Hope* began an era of court deference to decisions of federal and state public utility commissions. In *Hope,* the Court established the principle that the judiciary should defer to the rate determinations of federal commissions as long as the "end result" was "fair" or "reasonable." After *Hope,* the generally accepted test for the rate base is prudently invested original cost less depreciation. The *Hope* decision and its current progeny are discussed in more detail below.

b. RATE OF RETURN

Under *Hope*, utility regulators may calculate the rate base by any method they choose as long as the method produces a rate of return which is "fair" or "reasonable." The Court's test for whether a rate of return is confiscatory dates back to *Bluefield Water Works Improvement Co. v. Public Service Commission,* 262 U.S. 679, 692–93 (1923):

> A public utility is entitled to such rates as will permit it to earn a return on the value of the property which it employs for the convenience of the public equal to that generally being made at the same time and in the same general part of the country on investments in other business undertakings which are attended by corresponding risks and uncertainties; but it has no constitutional right to profits such as are realized or anticipated in highly profitable enterprises or speculative ventures. The return should be reasonably sufficient to assure confidence in the financial soundness of the utility and should be adequate, under efficient and economical management, to maintain and support its credit and enable it to raise the money necessary for the proper discharge of its public duties. A rate of return may be reasonable at one time and become too high or too low by changes affecting opportunities for investment, the money market and business conditions generally.

In other words, rates will pass constitutional muster—that is, they will be deemed "just and reasonable" and not confiscatory—if they fall into a zone of reasonableness.[19] According to *Permian Basin*, a court must therefore

> determine whether the order may reasonably be expected to maintain financial integrity, attract necessary capital, and fairly compensate investors for the risks they have assumed, and yet provide appropriate protection to the relevant public interests, both existing and foreseeable. The court's responsibility is not to supplant the Commission's balance of these interests with one more nearly to its liking, but instead to assure itself that the Commission has given reasoned consideration to each of the pertinent factors.[20]

Among the "relevant public interests" to be considered are consumer protection for high rates, industry stability, and reliable supply. As you will see shortly, balancing these interests is deeply complicated by the fact that a regulated business has no real or obvious parallel in the competitive market.

3. THE *HOPE* CASE

Federal Power Commission v. Hope Natural Gas Co., 320 U.S. 591 (1944), which is the seminal case for modern public utility regulation, stands for two

---

[19] *Federal Power Comm'n v. Natural Gas Pipeline Co.,* 315 U.S. 575, 585 (1942).

[20] *In re Permian Basin Area Rate Cases,* 390 U.S. 747, 791–92 (1968).

important propositions. First, the judiciary will not embroil itself in assessing valuation methodology as long as the "end result" of the ratemaking process is reasonable. Second, and related, the judiciary will largely defer to the regulator, rather than set rates itself. *Hope* remains a vital opinion, and it has recently become the focus of no small amount of judicial and scholarly attention as discussed below. The focal point of *Hope* has been the respective weight to be accorded to the conflicting interests of owners (shareholders) and consumers (ratepayers).

Hope Natural Gas Company sold gas in interstate commerce, and thus came under the jurisdiction of the Federal Power Commission. Upon customers' complaints that rates were excessive, the FPC conducted a hearing to determine the reasonableness of the rates. The FPC ordered a reduction in future rates and established "just and reasonable" rates. The utility challenged the rates as confiscatory. As you read the case, pay attention to how the Commission valued the rate base ("actual legitimate cost"—a form of original cost) and how the utility valued the rate base (reproduction cost). What formulation did the Court choose?

FEDERAL POWER COMMISSION v. HOPE NATURAL GAS CO.
320 U.S. 591 (1944)

Mr. Justice Douglas delivered the opinion of the Court.

The Commission established an interstate rate base of $33,712,526 which, it found, represented the "actual legitimate cost" of the company's interstate property less depletion and depreciation and plus unoperated acreage, working capital and future net capital additions. The Commission, beginning with book cost, made certain adjustments not necessary to relate here and found the "actual legitimate cost" of the plant in interstate service to be $51,957,416, as of December 21, 1940. It deducted accrued depletion and depreciation, which it found to be $22,328,016 on an "economic-service-life" basis. And it added $1,392,021 for future net capital additions, $566,105 for useful unoperated acreage, and $2,125,000 for working capital. It used 1940 as a test year to estimate future revenues and expenses. It allowed over $16,000,000 as annual operating expenses—about $1,300,000 for taxes, $1,460,000 for depletion and depreciation, $600,000 for exploration and development costs, $8,500,000 for gas purchased. The Commission allowed a net increase of $421,160 over 1940 operating expenses, which amount was to take care of future increase in wages, in West Virginia property taxes, and in exploration and development costs. The total amount of deductions allowed from interstate revenues was $13,495,584.

Hope introduced evidence from which it estimated reproduction cost of the property at $97,000,000. It also presented a so-called trended "original cost" estimate which exceeded $105,000,000. The latter was designed "to indicate what the original cost of the property would have been if 1938 material and labor prices had prevailed throughout the whole period of the piecemeal construction of the company's property since 1898." Hope estimated by the "per cent condition" method accrued depreciation at about 35% of reproduction cost new. On that basis Hope contended for a rate base of $66,000,000. The Commission refused to place any reliance on reproduction cost new, saying that it was "not predicated upon facts" and was "too conjectural and illusory to be given any weight in these proceedings." It likewise refused to give any "probative value" to trended "original cost" since it was "not founded in fact" but was "basically erroneous" and produced "irrational results."

Hope's estimate of original cost was about $69,735,000—approximately $17,000,000 more than the amount found by the Commission. The item of $17,000,000 was made up largely of expenditures which prior to December 31, 1938, were charged to operating expenses. Chief among those expenditures was some $12,600,000 expended in well-drilling prior to 1923. Most of that sum was expended by Hope for labor, use of drilling-rigs, hauling, and similar costs of well-drilling. Prior to 1923 Hope followed the general practice of the natural gas industry and charged the cost of drilling wells to operating expenses. Hope continued that practice until the Public Service Commission of West Virginia in 1923 required it to capitalize such expenditures, as does the Commission under its present Uniform System of Accounts. . . .

Hope contended that it should be allowed a return of not less that 8%. The Commission found that an 8% return would be unreasonable but that 6½% was a fair rate of return. That rate of return, applied to the rate base of $33,712,526, would produce $2,191,314 annually, as compared with the present income of not less that $5,801,171.

The Circuit Court of Appeals set aside the order of the Commission for the following reasons. (1) It held that the rate base should reflect the "present fair value" of the property, that the Commission in determining the "value" should have considered reproduction cost and trended original cost, and that "actual legitimate cost" (prudent investment) was not the proper measure of "fair value" where price levels had changed since the investment. (2) It concluded that the well-drilling costs and overhead items in the amount of some $17,000,000 should have been included in the rate base. (3) It held that accrued depletion and depreciation and the annual allowance for that expense should be computed on the basis of "present fair value" of the property, not on the basis of "actual legitimate cost." . . .

Order Reducing Rates. Congress has provided in § 4(a) of the Natural Gas Act that all natural gas rates subject to the jurisdiction of the Commission "shall be just and reasonable, and any such rate or charge that is not just and reasonable is hereby declared to be unlawful." Sec. 5(a) gives the Commission the power, after hearing, to determine the "just and reasonable rate" to be thereafter observed and to fix the rate by order. Section 5(a) also empowers the Commission to order a "decrease where existing rates are unjust, . . . unlawful, or are not the lowest reasonable rates." And Congress has provided in § 19(b) that on review of these rate orders the "finding of the Commission as to the facts, if supported by substantial evidence, shall be conclusive." Congress, however, has provided no formula by which the "just and reasonable" rate is to be determined. It has not filled in the details of the general prescription of § 4(a) and § 5(a). It has not expressed in a specific rule the fixed principle of "just and reasonable."

When we sustained the constitutionality of the Natural Gas Act in the *Natural Gas Pipeline Co.* case, we stated that the "authority of Congress to regulate the prices of commodities in interstate commerce is at least as great under the Fifth Amendment as is that of the States under the Fourteenth to regulate the prices of commodities in intrastate commerce." Rate-making is indeed but one species of price-fixing. The fixing of prices, like other applications of the police power, may reduce the value of the property which is being regulated. But the fact that the value is reduced does not mean that the regulation is invalid. It does, however, indicate that "fair value" is the end product of the process of rate-making not the starting point as the Circuit Court of Appeals held. The heart of the matter is that rates cannot be made to depend upon "fair value" when the value of the going enterprise depends on earnings under whatever rates may be anticipated.

We held in *Federal Power Commission v. Natural Gas Pipeline Co.* that the Commission was not bound to the use of any single formula or combination of formulae in determining rates. Its rate-making function, moreover, involves the making of "pragmatic adjustments." And when the Commission's order is challenged in the courts, the question is whether that order "viewed in its entirety" meets the requirements of the Act. Under the statutory standard of "just and reasonable" it is the result reached not the method employed which is controlling. It is not theory but the impact of the rate order which counts. If the total effect of the rate order cannot be said to be unjust and unreasonable, judicial inquiry under the Act is at an end. The fact that the method employed to reach that result may contain infirmities is not then important. Moreover, the Commission's order does not become suspect by reason of the fact that it is challenged. It is the product of expert judgment which carries a presumption of validity. And he who would upset the rate order under the Act carries the heavy burden of making a convincing showing that it is invalid because it is unjust and unreasonable in its consequences.

The rate-making process under the Act, i.e., the fixing of "just and reasonable" rates, involves a balancing of the investor and the consumer interests. Thus we stated in the *Natural Gas Pipeline Co.* case that "regulation does not insure that the business shall produce net revenues." But such considerations aside, the investor interest has a legitimate concern with the financial integrity of the company whose rates are being regulated. From the investor or company point of view it is important that there be enough revenue not only for operating expenses but also for the capital costs of the business. These include service on the debt and dividends on the stock. By that standard the return to the equity owner should be commensurate with returns on investments in other enterprises having corresponding risks. That return, moreover, should be sufficient to assure confidence in the financial integrity of the enterprise, so as to maintain its credit and to attract capital. The conditions under which more or less might be allowed are not important here. Nor is it important to this case to determine the various permissible ways in which any rate base on which the return is computed might be arrived at. For we are of the view that the end result in this case cannot be condemned under the Act as unjust and unreasonable from the investor or company viewpoint. . . .

In view of these various considerations we cannot say that an annual return of $2,191,314 is not "just and reasonable" within the meaning of the Act. Rates which enable the company to operate successfully, to maintain its financial integrity, to attract capital, and to compensate its investors for the risks assumed certainly cannot be condemned as invalid, even though they might produce only a meager return on the so-called "fair value" rate base. . . .

In view of this disposition of the controversy we need not stop to inquire whether the failure of the Commission to add the $17,000,000 of well-drilling and other costs to the rate base was consistent with the prudent investment theory as developed and applied in particular cases. . . .

It is suggested that the Commission has failed to perform its duty under the Act in that it has not allowed a return for gas production that will be enough to induce private enterprise to perform completely and efficiently its functions for the public. The Commission, however, was not oblivious of those matters. It considered them. It allowed, for example, delay rentals and exploration and development costs in operating expenses. No serious attempt has been made here to show that they are inadequate. We certainly cannot say that they are, unless we are to substitute our opinions for the expert judgment of the administrators to whom Congress entrusted the decision. Moreover, if in light of experience they turn out to be inadequate for development of new sources of supply, the doors of the Commission are open for increased allowances. This is not an order for all time. The Act contains machinery for obtaining rate adjustments.

But it is said that the Commission placed too low a rate on gas for industrial purposes as compared with gas for domestic purposes and that industrial uses should be discouraged. It should be noted in the first place that the rates which the Commission has fixed are Hope's interstate wholesale rates to distributors, not interstate rates to industrial users and domestic consumers. We hardly can assume, in view of the history of the Act and its provisions, that the resales intrastate by the customer companies which distribute the gas to ultimate consumers in Ohio and Pennsylvania are subject to the rate-making powers of the Commission. . . .

NOTES AND QUESTIONS

1. As a matter of constitutional law, a statute is susceptible to a Fifth Amendment takings challenge in two ways. First, the statute *on its face* must not destroy a property interest. Second, the statute *as applied* in a specific instance may be a taking of private property for public use without just compensation. Why do challenges to utility rates fall into the second category? Recall that rate regulation statutes guarantee to utilities a "just and reasonable" rate of return.

2. In *Duquesne Light Co. v. Barasch*, 488 U.S. 299 (1989), the Court observed that in theory the "*Smyth v. Ames* fair value standard mimics the operation of the competitive market" and that the "fair value rule gives utilities strong incentive to manage their affairs well and to provide efficient service to the public." Why? If the investment by a utility in a plant is a good one, how is the utility rewarded under the "fair value" test with the opportunity to earn an "above-cost" return? If the investment turns out to be a poor one, if construction of a plant is canceled or if the plant is never used, how does the utility suffer under the "fair value" test?

3. In *Hope*, Justice Douglas noted:

> The fixing of prices, like other applications of the police power, may reduce the value of the property which is being regulated. But the fact that the value is reduced does not mean that the regulation is invalid. It does, however, indicate that "fair value" is the end product of the process of rate-making not the starting point as the Circuit Court of Appeals held. The heart of the matter is that rates cannot be made to depend upon "fair value" when the value of the going enterprise depends on earnings under whatever rates may be anticipated.

Why does the "value of the going enterprise depend on earnings under whatever rates may be anticipated"? How does this relationship hinder the fair value approach?

4. Applying the rate formula to the facts of *Hope*: What was the Federal Power Commission's rate base, and how was it calculated? What was the FPC's rate of return? What was the company's rate base and rate of return? The FPC disallowed a $17,000,000 item; why was it disallowed? What was the difference between the company's and the FPC's rate base? What legal argument for the difference did the company make? How did the Court decide?

5. Did the Court in *Hope*: (1) simply authorize other rate base valuation methods; (2) take the judiciary out of the ratemaking process; (3) abandon the takings test for rate base valuation; (4) abandon the takings test for the end result of the ratemaking process? Following is an argument that *Hope* abandoned judicial valuation:

> *Hope* abandoned the judicial preoccupation with valuation as the measure of whether the due process provisions of the fifth and fourteenth Amendments had been satisfied. Henceforth, the test of the constitutionality of commission ratemaking was not to be determined by whether the valuation of rate base provided "just compensation," but by whether the end result was "reasonable." Investors were no longer "entitled" to "just compensation" because *Hope* abandoned the taking analogy that underlay *Smyth*. Under *Hope* a "reasonable end result" was framed in terms of the procedural standards of due process laid down by the Court in *Nebbia v. New York,* and not in terms of substantive economic rights in law. Any reasonable end result was constitutionally defensible regardless of the rate base employed, or even if no rate base was employed at all, as long as it was based upon substantial evidence, did not constitute an abuse of discretion, and the means employed were reasonably related to a legitimate public purpose which the agency was empowered to obtain.[21]

6. How should a PUC treat a canceled plant? Kolbe and Tye distinguish four methods of calculating the rate base as shown in the following table.[22]

The most frequently used rule is the "used and useful" rule, under which a plant (or an investment) is not included in the rate base until that plant

---

[21] Copeland & Nixon, *Procedural Versus Substantive Economic Due Process for Public Utilities,* 12 ENERGY L.J. 81, 89 (1991).

[22] Kolbe & Tye, *The Duquesne Opinion: How Much "Hope" is There for Investors in Regulated Firms?,* 8 YALE J. REG. 113, 121–22 (1991).

is on-line and is producing electricity. The second, less used, rule is a prudent investment standard, under which an investment that is prudent when made can be included in the rate base, even if the plant is canceled. Four methods are likely.

(1) Pure prudent investment	All prudent investments are included in the rate base whether or not they are used or useful. Investors thus receive a return *of* investment and a return *on* investment.
(2) Modified prudent investment	Unused and unuseful investments are amortized as expenses but do not go into the rate base. Thus, investors receive a return *of* but not *on* unused or unuseful investment.
(3) Used and useful	Only used and useful investment goes into rate base. Investors receive neither a return *of* nor a return *on* the unused or unuseful portion of investment.
(4) Fair value	Rate of return is calculated on the "market value" of the plant. Investors have an opportunity to earn an "above-cost" return.

Which rule was applied in *Hope*? Which in the following cases?

a. *HOPE* DEBATED

From the end of World War II until the "energy crisis" of the mid-1970s, the natural gas and electricity industries were relatively secure. Both industries enjoyed capital expansion and economies of scale which kept prices low and stable. For different reasons, both industries began to experience economic dislocations in the mid-1960s, which contributed to the energy crisis.

The electric industry grew steadily and strongly from the end of the war until about 1965.[23] From 1945 to 1965, electricity production and sales expanded, prices were stable and were decreasing (utilities even sought rate reductions), and stock prices peaked. After 1965, production costs increased, and so did rates.

When an industry has predictable growth, continued economies of scale, and a rate formula that rewards capital investment, both shareholders and ratepayers enjoy the fruits of plant expansion as rates stay low and returns increase. Add to these factors the promise of great technological innovation in the form of commercial nuclear power, which would generate electricity "too cheap to meter," and industry managers had a clear signal—construct nuclear plants.

---

[23] L. Hyman, America's Electric Utilities: Past, Present and Future chs. 13, 14 (6th ed. 1997).

Beginning in the 1960s, however, the situation changed for many electrical utilities. Production costs, including fuel costs, rose because of higher inflation, as did construction costs. Utilities which had decided to build nuclear power plants were particularly hard hit. Few of these utilities were able to construct nuclear plants on time or on budget, with cost overruns on a single project running into the billions of dollars. Besides inflation, construction costs were increased because utilities mismanaged the construction process and were subject to stricter regulatory scrutiny than they anticipated when they decided to build these plants. The accident at Three Mile Island in 1979 virtually stopped nuclear construction. All plants ordered since 1974 were canceled, and no new plants were ordered after 1978. Instead of a healthy industry, public utilities with nuclear construction projects were faced with problems involving poor cash flow,[24] excess capacity,[25] canceled plant construction projects,[26] and imprudent investment.[27]

As a result of these developments, federal and state regulatory agencies had to address the question: Who pays? Should shareholders or ratepayers pay for the problems just listed? It should come as no great surprise that agencies (and, in turn, reviewing courts) adopted a number of strategies, sometimes allocating costs to shareholders and other times to ratepayers, and, not infrequently, apportioning costs between both groups.

Ultimately, the issue of who was to pay for nuclear plant cancellations worked its way up to the Supreme Court in the case of *Duquesne Light Co. v. Barasch*,[28] which presented the Court with the opportunity to review the *Hope* doctrine. Before *Duquesne,* the United States Circuit Court of Appeals for the District of Columbia, in three lengthy opinions, raised serious questions about the continued vitality of the *Hope* "end result" test and the "used and useful" principle.[29] The majority and dissenting opinions in *Jersey Central Power & Light Co. v. FERC (Jersey Central III),* an excerpt of which follows, disagreed about the application of the *Hope* test. Although both sides recognized the need to balance investor and consumer interests, the majority tended toward protecting the financial integrity of the utility, while the dissent tended toward protecting consumers by disallowing certain costs from the rate base. In questioning the *Hope* test, the majority and dissenting opinions also differed about the degree of deference courts should accord agency ratemaking.

At issue in *Jersey Central III* was an investment of $397 million in the canceled Forked River nuclear power plant. The Federal Energy Regulatory Commission (FERC) allowed Jersey Central Power and Light Company to

---

[24] *Mid-Tex Elec. Coop. v. FERC,* 773 F.2d 327 (D.C. Cir. 1985).

[25] *Gulf Power Co. v. Florida Pub. Serv. Comm'n,* 453 So. 2d 799 (Fla. 1984).

[26] *Citizens Action Coalition of Ind., Inc. v. Northern Ind. Pub. Serv. Co.,* 485 N.E.2d 610 (Ind. 1985).

[27] *In re Long Island Lighting Co.,* Util. L. Rep. State (CCH) ¶ 24,922 (N.Y. Pub. Serv. Comm'n, Dec. 16, 1985). *See also* J. TOMAIN, NUCLEAR POWER TRANSFORMATION (1987); Pierce, *The Regulatory Treatment of Mistakes in Retrospect: Canceled Plants and Excess Capacity,* 132 U. PA. L. REV. 497 (1984).

[28] 488 U.S. 299 (1989).

[29] *See Jersey Cent. Power & Light Co. v. FERC,* 730 F.2d 816 (D.C. Cir. 1984) (*Jersey Central I*); 768 F.2d 1500 (D.C. Cir. 1985) (*Jersey Central II*); and 810 F.2d 1168 (D.C. Cir. 1987) (*Jersey Central III*).

amortize its $397 million investment over a fifteen-year period. However, Jersey Central was not allowed to put the unamortized balance in the rate base, because the plant was not "used and useful." The effect of this treatment means that the interest costs are charged to shareholders while the principal costs are charged to ratepayers over a fifteen-year period.

An understanding of rate amortization may aid the reading of *Jersey Central III*. Assume that an investment in a canceled nuclear plant was $397 million. Under a fifteen-year amortization scheme, a public utility commission would allow the utility to charge its customers approximately $26.5 million per year ($397 million ÷ 15) as an operating expense for fifteen years, thus recouping its entire principal of $397 million after fifteen years. But what about the time value of money (interest)? After the first year, the utility receives its first $26.5 million amortization payment from the ratepayers and has $370.5 million yet to recover. Therefore, the utility is losing the use of $370.5 million in the first year. By comparison, if the regulator had put the entire $370.5 million into the rate base, the utility would have been earning a return on the entire investment. FERC, and other state commissions, chose to split the costs of the canceled plant by letting the shareholders recover their principal investment over the amortization period, but not the use of the money, by disallowing the unamortized portion from being included in the rate base.

Jersey Central argued that such a cost allocation threatened its financial integrity. FERC responded that this approach was its usual practice and it did not give the utility a hearing on whether or not the amortization treatment constituted a Fifth Amendment taking. Judge Bork, writing for a majority of the D.C. Circuit, sitting en banc, held that FERC must hold an evidentiary hearing concerning whether the failure to include a prudent investment in the rate base produced an unreasonable rate of return. Judge Starr concurred and Judge Mikva dissented, joined by four other judges.

JERSEY CENTRAL POWER & LIGHT CO. v. FERC
(JERSEY CENTRAL III)
810 F.2d 1168 (D.C. Cir. 1987)

BORK, CIRCUIT JUDGE:

Jersey Central Power and Light Company petitions for review of Federal Energy Regulatory Commission orders modifying the electric utility's proposed rate schedules and requiring the company to file reduced rates. Jersey Central charges that it alleged facts which, if proven, show that the reduced rates are confiscatory and violate its statutory and constitutional right as defined by the Supreme Court in *FPC v. Hope Natural Gas Co.* Though it is probable that the facts alleged, if true, would establish an invasion of the company's rights, the Commission refused the company a hearing and reduced its rates summarily. . . .

The decision of the Commission is vacated and the case remanded for a hearing at which Jersey Central may finally have its claim addressed. . . .

[After reviewing *Hope* and *Permian Basin* among other cases, Judge Bork continued:] The teaching of these cases is straightforward. In reviewing a rate order courts must determine whether or not the end result of that order constitutes a reasonable balancing, based on factual findings, of the investor interest in maintaining financial integrity and access to capital markets and the consumer interest in being charged non-exploitative rates. Moreover, an order cannot be justified simply by a showing that each of the choices underlying it was reasonable; those choices must still add up to a reasonable result. . . .

The allegations made by Jersey Central and the testimony it offered track the standards of *Hope* and *Permian Basin* exactly. The *Hope* Court stated that the return ought to be "sufficient to ensure confidence in the financial integrity of the enterprise, so as to maintain its credit and to attract capital," and that "it is important that there be enough revenue not only for operating expenses but also for the capital costs of the business. These include service on the debt and dividends on the stock." *Permian Basin* reaffirmed that the reviewing court "must determine" whether the Commission's rate order may reasonably be expected to "maintain financial integrity" and "attract necessary capital."

[Jersey Central alleged that it was having difficulty raising money through the sale of stock or by seeking loans because of its precarious financial position, and that the rate increase it requested was the minimum necessary to permit it to pay for new capital which was necessary to maintain the past high quality of service.]

The Commission maintains that because excluding the unamortized portion of a canceled plant investment from the rate base had previously been upheld as *permissible,* any rate order that rests on such a decision is unimpeachable. But that would turn our focus from the end result to the methodology, and evade the question whether the component decisions together produce just and reasonable consequences. . . . The fact that a particular ratemaking standard is generally permissible does not *per se* legitimate the end result of the rate orders it produces. . . .

. . . At oral argument before the *en banc* court, counsel for the Commission indicated that the "end result" test *did* allow a court to set aside a rate order when the company would otherwise go bankrupt and the Commission had refused to take that into account. The source of this constricted standard is elusive, not to say invisible. *Hope Natural Gas* talks not of an interest in avoiding bankruptcy, but an interest in maintaining access to capital markets, the ability to pay dividends, and general financial integrity. While companies about to go bankrupt would certainly see such interest threatened, companies less imminently imperiled will sometimes be able to make that claim as well. Jersey Central alleges that it is such a company. The contention that no company that is not clearly headed for bankruptcy has a judicially enforceable right to have its financial status considered when its rates are determined must be rejected. . . .

In addition to prohibiting rates so low as to be confiscatory, the holding of *Hope Natural Gas* makes clear that exploitative rates are illegal as well. If the inclusion of property not currently used and useful in the rate base automatically constituted exploitation of consumers, as one of the *amici* maintains, then the Commission would be justified in excluding such property summarily even in cases where the utility pleads acute financial distress. A regulated utility has no constitutional right to a profit, and a company that is unable to survive without charging exploitative rates has no entitlement to such rates. *Market Street Ry. v. Railroad Comm'n of Cal.,* 324 U.S. 548 (1945). But we have already held that including prudent investments in the rate base is not in and of itself exploitative, and no party has denied that the Forked River investment was prudent. Indeed, when the regulated company is permitted to earn a return not on the market value of the property used by the public, but rather on the original cost of the investment, placing prudent investments in the rate base would seem a more sensible policy than a strict application of "used and useful," for under this approach it is the investment, and not the property used, which is viewed as having been taken by the public. The investor interest described in *Hope,* after all, is an interest in return on *investment.*

The central point, however, is this: it is impossible for us to say at this juncture whether including the unamortized portion of Forked River in the rate base would exploit consumers *in this case,* or whether its exclusion, *on the facts of this case,* constitutes confiscation, for no findings of fact have been made concerning the consequences of the rate order. Nor, for the same reason, can we make a judgment about the higher rate of return the utility sought as an alternative to inclusion in the rate base of its unamortized investment. Jersey Central has presented allegations which, if true, suggest that the rate order almost certainly does not meet the requirements of *Hope Natural Gas,* for the company has been shut off from long-term capital, is wholly dependent for short-term capital on a revolving credit arrangement that can be canceled at any time, and has been unable to pay dividends for four years. In addition, Jersey Central points out that the rates proposed in its filing would remain lower than those of neighboring utilities, which at least suggests, though it does not demonstrate, that the proposed rates would not exploit consumers. The Commission treated those allegations as irrelevant and hence has presented us with no basis on which to affirm its rate order. The necessary findings are simply not there for us to review. When the Commission conducts the requisite balancing of consumer and investor interests, based upon factual findings, that balancing will be judicially reviewable and will be affirmed if supported by substantial evidence. That is the point at which deference to agency expertise will be appropriate and necessary. But where, as here, the Commission has reached its determination by flatly refusing to consider a factor to which it is undeniably required to give some weight, its decision cannot stand. The case should therefore be remanded to the Commission for a hearing at which the Commission can determine whether the rate order it issued constituted a reasonable balancing of the interests the Supreme Court has designated as relevant to the setting of a just and reasonable rate. . . .

STARR, CIRCUIT JUDGE, concurring: . . .

The Commission's stated justification for summarily dismissing these allegations was the weight of its prior "used and useful" precedent. But as the court's opinion shows, that body of precedent did not constitute as ironclad a rule as the Commission would have us believe. It is certainly not evident from those precedents that the rule could be summarily applied in the face of the financial demise of the regulated entity.

Indeed, the Commission as a matter of policy has departed over the years from the strictures of the "used and useful" rule. This is illustrated by its treatment of "construction work in progress" (CWIP),* part of which, the Commission recently determined, can be included in a utility's rate base. In that proceeding, the Commission recognized that its own practice admits of "widely recognized exceptions and departures" from the "used and useful" rule, "particularly when there are countervailing public interest considerations." In that setting, financial difficulties in the electric utility industry played a significant role in the Commission's decision to bend the rule.

This policy of flexibility, it seems to me, reflects the practical reality of the electric utility industry, namely that investments in plant and equipment are enormously costly. Rigid adherence to "used and useful" doctrines would doubtless imperil the viability of some utilities; thus, while not articulating its result in *Hope* or "takings" terms, the Commission—whether as a matter of policy or perceived constitutional obligation—has in the past taken these realities into account and provided relief for utilities in various forms.

. . . Requiring an investment to be prudent when made is one safeguard imposed by regulatory authorities upon the regulated business for benefit of ratepayers. As I see it, the "used and useful" rule is but another such safeguard. The prudence rule looks to the time of investment, whereas the "used and useful" rule looks to the later time. The two principles are designed to assure that the ratepayers, whose property might otherwise of course be "taken" by regulatory authorities, will not necessarily be saddled with the results of management's defalcations or mistakes, or as a matter of simple justice, be required to pay for that which provides the ratepayers with no discernible benefit.[1] . . .

For me, the prudent investment rule is, taken alone, too weighted for constitutional analysis in favor of the utility. It lacks balance. But so too, the "used and useful" rule, taken alone, is skewed heavily in favor of ratepayers. It also lacks balance. In the modern setting, neither regime, mechanically applied with full rigor, will likely achieve justice among the competing interests of investors and ratepayers so as to avoid confiscation of the utility's property or a taking of the property of ratepayers through unjustifiably exorbitant rates. Each approach, however, provides important insights about the ultimate object of the regulatory process, which is to achieve a just result in rate regulation. And that is the mission commanded by the Fifth Amendment. . . .

---

* Editor's note: "Construction work in progress" (CWIP) is the amount of money that a utility is spending on construction prior to the plant becoming operational. This amount of money can either be included in the rate base and recouped from current ratepayers or accumulate as a specific accounting entry on the utility's books in which case it is called an "allowance for funds used during construction" (AFUDC). AFUDC would be included in the rate base once the plant is put into operation. If CWIP is used, then the utility receives cash flow but current ratepayers are paying for a plant to be used in the future. If AFUDC is used, then future ratepayers will pay for the plant, but do so at the risk of "rate shock" *i.e.* large increase in rates. FERC used a 50% CWIP rule in *Jersey Central*.

[1] The obvious danger in not examining both ends of the continuum—both the prudence of the investment and whether the end result of the investment was used and useful—is to build in pressures for building excess generating capacity. The "used and useful" rule operates as a restraining principle, reminding utility managers that they must assume the risk of economic forces working against an investment which is prudent at the time it is made.

Thus it is that a taking occurs not when an investment is made (even one under legal obligation), but when the balance between investor and ratepayer interests—the very function of utility regulation—is struck unjustly. Although the agency has broad latitude in striking the balance, the Constitution nonetheless requires that the end result reflect a reasonable balancing of the interests of investors and ratepayers. As we have seen, both investors and ratepayers were the intended beneficiaries of the Forked River investment; both should presumptively have to share in the loss. Filling in the gaps, the making of the specific judgments that constitutes the difficult part of this enterprise, belongs in the first instance to the politically accountable branches, specifically to the experts in the agency, not to generalist judges. . . .

MIKVA, CIRCUIT JUDGE, with whom CHIEF JUDGE WALD, and CIRCUIT JUDGES SPOTTSWOOD W. ROBINSON, III and HARRY T. EDWARDS join, dissenting: . . .

The real mischief of today's decision lies not in the majority's belief that the utility has raised an issue of fact necessitating a hearing, but in its determination that Jersey Central has actually made out a case of constitutional confiscation. . . . In our view, it is beyond cavil that Jersey Central has not presented allegations which, if true, would establish that the Commission's orders result in unjust and unreasonable rates. . . .

Permian Basin teaches that if the Commission reasonably balances consumer and investor interests, then the resulting rate is *not* confiscatory. The separate opinion ably translates this into a working definition of a confiscatory rate: it exists when "an unreasonable balance has been struck in the regulation process so as unreasonably to favor ratepayer interests at the substantial expense of investor interests." The majority appears to agree with the teaching of *Permian Basin*. The lesson it gleans, however, is incongruous. According to the majority, balancing competing interests is not enough; a rate is confiscatory if it does not *satisfy* the "legitimate investor interest" outlined by the Court in *Hope*. This interpretation of *Hope* and *Permian Basin* is implausible.

. . . The *Hope* Court did not define "unjust or unreasonable"; nor did it articulate when a rate would be confiscatory. It certainly did not hold that the end result could be condemned if the investor criteria defined in the case were not fulfilled. Indeed, it expressly noted that its holding made no suggestion that more or less might not be allowed.

This understanding of *Hope* is the only way to reconcile the Court's recitation of investor interests with its avowal that "regulation does not insure that the business shall produce net revenues." Investor interests are only one factor in the assessment of constitutionally reasonable, therefore non-confiscatory, rates. In any instance, the rate must also "provide appropriate protection to the relevant public interests, both existing and foreseeable." A just and reasonable rate which results from balancing these conflicting interests might not provide "enough revenue not only for operating expenses but also for the capital costs of the business . . . includ[ing] service on the debt and dividends on the stock."

The Court made this abundantly clear in *Market Street*. . . . Neither the regulatory process nor the fifth amendment shelter a utility from market forces. Thus, contrary to the majority's intimations, rates do not fall outside the zone of reasonableness merely because they do not enable the company to operate at a profit or do not permit investors to recover all their losses. . . .

Application of this principle is readily apparent in the Commission's current treatment of electric utility plants, investments prudent when made but sometimes frustrated in fruition. If the investment is successful, the customer benefits from controlled rates for the service provided. But the ratepayer also shares the costs if the investment fails; he must pay for the expenditure made on an unproductive facility from which he obtains no service. From the investor's viewpoint, price regulation cabins both his upside and downside risk. He cannot collect the windfall benefits if the project is a boon; he does not bear all costs if the project is a bust. Electric utility stockholders do not lose equity in the non-serviceable facility, as they might in the marketplace. They simply do not procure a return on the investment.

The majority quibbles with this risk allocation; it would prefer a world in which the investor is guaranteed a return on his investment, if prudent when made. Its resultant holding today is directly at odds with fundamental principle laid out in *Hope* and its progeny. Adherence to the majority's insistence on the inclusion of prudent investments in the rate base would virtually insulate investors in public utilities from the risks involved in free market business. This would drastically diminish protection of the public interest by thrusting the entire risk of a failed investment onto the ratepayers. . . .

NOTES AND QUESTIONS

1. The majority and dissenting opinions cite *Market Street Ry. v. Railroad Comm'n of Cal.,* 324 U.S. 548 (1945). In *Market St. Ry.,* the state regulatory commission reduced streetcar passenger fares from seven cents to six cents, believing that a rate reduction might stimulate passenger traffic. The streetcar company complained that the rate reduction was confiscatory. The Supreme Court examined the takings claims of an "ailing unit of a generally sick industry":

> . . . It was noted in the *Hope Natural Gas* case that regulation does not assure that the regulated business make a profit. All that was held was that a company could not complain if the return which was allowed made it possible for the company to operate successfully. . . .

Without analyzing rate cases in detail, it may be safely generalized that the due process clause never has been held by this Court to require a commission to fix rates on the present reproduction value of something no one would presently want to reproduce, or on the historical valuation of a property whose history and current financial statements showed the value no longer to exist, or on an investment after it has vanished, even if once prudently made, or to maintain the credit of a concern whose securities already are impaired. The due process clause has been applied to prevent governmental destruction of existing economic values. It has not and cannot be applied to insure values or to restore values that have been lost by the operation of economic forces.

The owners of a property dedicated to the public service cannot be said to suffer injury if a rate is fixed for an experimental period, which probably will produce a fair return on the present fair value of their property. If it has lost all value except salvage, they suffer no loss if they earn a return on salvage value. . . .

Under these circumstances we do not find that anything has been taken from the appellant by the impact of public regulation. If the expectations of the Commission as to traffic increase were well founded, it would earn under this rate on the salvage value of its property, which is the only value it is shown to have. If expectations of increased traffic were unfounded, it could probably not earn a return from any rate that could be devised. We are unable to find that the order in this case is in violation of constitutional prohibitions, however unfortunate the plight of the appellant.

2. Judge Bork's opinion in *Jersey Central III* was controversial because he appeared to suggest that the Takings Clause might bar the used and useful rule. As you read, he observes:

But we have already held that including prudent investments in the rate base is not in and of itself exploitative, and no party has denied that the Forked River investment was prudent. Indeed, when the regulated company is permitted to earn a return not on the market value of the property used by the public, but rather on the original cost of the investment, placing prudent investments in the rate base would seem a more sensible policy than a strict application of "used and useful," for under this approach it is the investment, and not the property used, which is viewed as having been taken by the public. The investor interest described in *Hope,* after all, is an interest in return on *investment.*

Judge Bork did not regard *Market St. Ry.* as precluding the inclusion of prudent investment in the rate base. He interpreted the case as establishing that a regulated utility has no constitutional right to a profit, and a company that is unable to survive without charging exploitative rates has no entitlement to such rates. In Judge Bork's view, a company *is* entitled to the inclusion of prudent investments in the rate base *unless* inclusion produces exploitive rates for consumers.

Is Judge Bork's suggestion that the Takings Clause might bar the used and useful rule inconsistent with *Hope* which held that utility regulators could calculate the rate base by any method as long as a utility was entitled to earn a reasonable rate of return? As a matter of constitutional law, should the owners of a utility be permitted to earn a rate of return on any investment if it was prudent at the time it was made? Why or why not?

3. Judge Starr suggests that the Takings Clause might preclude reliance on either the prudent investment rule or the used and useful rule. If an investment was prudent at the time it was made, he argues that the constitution requires that investors and ratepayers must share in the loss: "As we have seen, both investors and ratepayers were the intended beneficiaries of the Forked River investment; both should presumptively have to share in the loss." At the same time, he acknowledges that judicial review should be limited. Thus, he would defer to how the regulator apportioned the costs between ratepayers and investors: "Filling in the gaps, the making of the specific judgments that constitute the difficult part of this enterprise, belongs in the first instance to the politically accountable branches, specifically to the experts in the agency, not to generalist judges."

As a matter of constitutional law, should investors and ratepayers be required to share any losses when a prudent investment turns out not to be used and useful? FERC relied on the modified prudent investment rule, which does allocate the loss to both investors and ratepayers. As you read, Judge Mikva defended this approach:

> . . . If the investment is successful, the customer benefits from controlled rates for the service provided. But the ratepayer also shares the costs if the investment fails; he must pay for the expenditure made on an unproductive facility from which he obtains no service. From the investor's viewpoint, price regulation cabins both his upside and downside risk. He cannot collect the windfall benefits if the project is a boon; he does not bear all costs if the project is a bust. Electric utility stockholders do not lose equity in the non-serviceable facility, as they might in the marketplace. They simply do not procure a return on the investment.

Was Judge Starr suggesting that this "compromise" was not sufficient?

4. On rehearing, FERC sustained the amortization scheme after holding a hearing. *Jersey Cent. Power & Light,* 49 FERC ¶ 63,004 (1989). The Commission adopted the findings and conclusions of the Administrative Law Judge.

5. One of Judge Bork's concerns was that Jersey Central's access to long-term capital markets was impaired, thus threatening the financial integrity of the utility. What is the difference between borrowing long-term and short-term capital? Regarding access to long-term capital markets, Professor Richard Pierce poses the following problem:

> Consider, for instance, the situation of a utility that has already invested $500 million in a plant when it concludes that any further investment would be wasteful. It has managed the rest of its activities so well that a loss of $500 million would not impair its access to long-term capital markets, but a loss of $1 billion would. The utility's CEO, with guidance from her lawyers, might well conclude that the plant should not be canceled until the utility has sunk another $500 million into the ill-fated project, thereby paying its price of admission to the constitutional courts. [30]

What course of action should the CEO take?

---

[30] Pierce, *Public Utility Regulatory Takings: Should the Judiciary Attempt to Police the Political Institutions?,* 77 Geo. L.J. 2031, 2062 (1989); *see also* Hoecker, *"Used and Useful": Autopsy of a Ratemaking Policy,* 8 Energy L.J. 303 (1987).

b. *HOPE* REDUX

After *Jersey Central III*, it appeared that the stage was set for Supreme Court review of the *Hope* test, particularly as it applies to canceled nuclear plants. The Court seemed poised to do so after having accepted two such cases.

In *Kansas Gas and Electric Company v. State Corporation Commission*, 239 Kan. 483, 720 P.2d 1063 (1986), *prob. juris. noted*, 479 U.S. 1082, *appeal dismissed*, 481 U.S. 1044 (1987), the utility challenged the state commission's disallowances of (1) $183 million as an imprudent investment; (2) a return on $944 million because of excess capacity; and (3) a return of $266 million on excess economic capacity. The appeal to the Supreme Court was withdrawn as part of a settlement between the state and the utility. The Court then accepted another plant cancellation case, *Duquesne Light Co. v. Barasch*, which you will read next.

At issue in *Duquesne* was the inclusion of an approximately $35 million investment in a canceled nuclear power project in Duquesne Light Company's rate base. The Pennsylvania Public Utility Commission found that the investment was prudent when made and authorized an amortization of the expenditure over a ten-year period. The Pennsylvania Office of Consumer Advocate challenged the amortization in the state supreme court, based on a state statute that adopted the "used and useful" test. The court reasoned that, since no electricity was generated by the project, the ratepayers should not be required to absorb the loss and reversed the PUC. The utility appealed to the Supreme Court.

DUQUESNE LIGHT CO. v. BARASCH
488 U.S. 299 (1989)

The CHIEF JUSTICE delivered the opinion of the Court.

Pennsylvania law required that rates for electricity be fixed without consideration of a utility's expenditures for electrical generating facilities which were planned but never built, even though the expenditures were prudent and reasonable when made. The Supreme Court of Pennsylvania held that such a law did not take the utilities' property in violation of the Fifth Amendment to the United States Constitution. We agree with that conclusion, and hold that a state scheme of utility regulation does not "take" property simply because it disallows recovery of capital investments that are not "used and useful in service to the public."

In response to predictions of increased demand for electricity, Duquesne Light Company (Duquesne) and Pennsylvania Power Company (Penn Power) joined a venture in 1967 to build more generating capacity. The project, known as the Central Area Power Coordination Group (CAPCO), involved three other electric utilities and had as its objective the construction of seven large nuclear generating units. In 1980 the participants canceled plans for construction of four of the plants. Intervening events, including the Arab oil embargo and the accident at Three Mile Island, had radically changed the outlook both for growth in the demand for electricity and for nuclear energy as a desirable way of meeting that demand. At the time of the cancellation, Duquesne's share of the preliminary construction costs associated with the four halted plants was $34,697,389. Penn Power had invested $9,569,665. . . .

In 1982, Duquesne again came before the PUC to obtain a rate increase. Again, it sought to amortize its expenditures on the canceled plants over 10 years. In January 1983, the PUC issued a final order which granted Duquesne the authority to increase its revenues $105.8 million to a total yearly revenue in excess of $800 million. The rate increase included $3.5 million in revenue representing the first payment of the 10-year amortization of Duquesne's $35 million loss in the CAPCO plants.

The Pennsylvania Office of the Consumer Advocate (Consumer Advocate) moved the PUC for reconsideration in light of a state law enacted about a month before the close of the 1982 Duquesne rate proceeding. The Act . . . provided that "the cost of construction or expansion of a facility undertaken by a public utility producing . . . electricity shall not be made a part of the rate base nor otherwise included in the rates charged by the electric utility until such time as the facility is used and useful in service to the public." . . .

. . . The Consumer Advocate then appealed to the Supreme Court of Pennsylvania, and that court reversed. That court held that the controlling language of the Act prohibited recovery of the costs in question either by inclusion in the rate base or by amortization. The Supreme Court rejected appellants' constitutional challenge to the statute thus interpreted, observing that "[t]he 'just compensation' safeguarded to a utility by the fourteenth amendment of the federal constitution is a reasonable return on the fair value of its property at the time it is being used for public service." Since the instant CAPCO investment was not serving the public and did not constitute an operating expense, no constitutional rights to recovery attached to it. . . . Duquesne and Penn Power appealed to this Court arguing that the effect of [Pennsylvania law] excluding their prudently incurred costs from the rate violated the Takings Clause of the Fifth Amendment, applicable to the States under the Fourteenth Amendment. . . .

Forty-five years ago in the landmark case of *FPC v. Hope Natural Gas Co.*, this Court abandoned the rule of *Smyth v. Ames*, and held that the "fair value" rule is not the only constitutionally acceptable method of fixing utility rates. In *Hope* we ruled that historical cost was a valid basis on which to calculate utility compensation. . . . We also acknowledged in that case that all of the subsidiary aspects of valuation for ratemaking purposes could not properly be characterized as having a constitutional dimension, despite the fact that they might affect property rights to some degree. Today we reaffirm these teachings of *Hope Natural Gas:* "[I]t is not theory but the impact of the rate order which counts. If the total effect of the rate order cannot be said to be unreasonable, judicial inquiry . . . is at an end. The fact that the method employed to reach that result may contain infirmities is not then important." This language, of course, does not dispense with all of the constitutional difficulties when a utility raises a claim that the rate which it is permitted to charge is so low as to be confiscatory: whether a particular rate is "unjust" or "unreasonable" will depend to some extent on what is a fair rate of return given the risks under a particular rate-setting system, and on the amount of capital upon which the investors are entitled to earn that return. At the margins, these questions have constitutional overtones.

Pennsylvania determines rates under a slightly modified form of the historical cost/prudent investment system. Neither Duquesne nor Penn Power alleges that the total effect of the rate order arrived at within this system is unjust or unreasonable. In fact the overall effect is well within the bounds of *Hope,* even with total exclusion of the CAPCO costs. Duquesne was authorized to earn a 16.14% return on common equity and an 11.64% overall return on a rate base of nearly $1.8 billion. Its $35 million investment in the canceled plants comprises roughly 1.9% of its total base. The denial of plant amortization will reduce its annual allowance by .4%. Similarly, Penn Power was allowed a charge of 15.72% return on common equity and a 12.02% overall return. Its investment in the CAPCO plants comprises only 2.4% of its $401.8 million rate base. The denial of amortized recovery of its $9.6 million investment in CAPCO will reduce its annual revenue allowance by only .5%.

Given these numbers, it appears that the PUC would have acted within the constitutional range of reasonableness if it had allowed amortization of the CAPCO costs but set a lower rate of return on equity with the result that Duquesne and Penn Power received the same revenue they will under the instant orders on remand. The overall impact of the rate orders, then, is not constitutionally objectionable. No argument has been made that these slightly reduced rates jeopardize the financial integrity of the companies, either by leaving them insufficient operating capital or by impeding their ability to raise future capital. Nor has it been demonstrated that these rates are inadequate to compensate current equity holders for the risk associated with their investments under a modified prudent investment scheme. . . .

Finally we address the suggestion of the Pennsylvania Electric Association as *amicus* that the prudent investment rule should be adopted as the constitutional standard. We think that the adoption of any such rule would signal a retreat from 45 years of decisional law in this area which would be as unwarranted as it would be unsettling. . . .

The adoption of a single theory of valuation as a constitutional requirement would be inconsistent with the view of the Constitution this Court has taken since *Hope Natural Gas.* . . . The designation of a single theory of ratemaking as a constitutional requirement would unnecessarily foreclose alternatives which could benefit both consumers and investors. The Constitution within broad limits leaves the States free to decide what Rate setting methodology best meets their needs in balancing the interest of the utility and the public.

NOTES AND QUESTIONS

1. What do you think the Court would have done if the disallowance was $350 million, rather than $35 million? A $350 million disallowance would significantly raise the risk of investment in Duquesne Light Company, or even threaten bankruptcy. Does *Duquesne* settle the controversy enunciated in *Jersey Central III*? Although *Duquesne* reaffirms *Hope,* did the Court leave the door open to second-guess a regulator's choice of how to measure the rate base? In *Duquesne,* the Court observed:

Today we reaffirm these teachings of *Hope Natural Gas:* "[I]t is not theory but the impact of the rate order which counts. If the total effect of the rate order cannot be said to be unreasonable, judicial inquiry . . . is at an end. The fact that the method employed to reach that result may contain infirmities is not then important." This language, of course, does not dispense with all of the constitutional difficulties when a utility raises a claim that the rate which it is permitted to charge is so low as to be confiscatory: whether a particular rate is "unjust" or "unreasonable" will depend to some extent on what is a fair rate of return given the risks under a particular rate-setting system, and on the amount of capital upon which the investors are entitled to earn that return. At the margins, these questions have constitutional overtones.

Copeland and Nixon read this language with alarm: "a wolf in sheep's clothing, the *Duquesne* decision has resurrected the language of substantive economic due process, and has the potential for undoing everything for which *Hope* stood."[31] By comparison, Professor Pierce maintains that *Hope* and *Duquesne* effectively take the judiciary out of the constitutional review of rulemaking, and he views this development with approval.[32] He explains:

> Detailed judicial review of ratemaking has little, if any, effect in constraining the political process. Moreover, the judicial review process impose[s] high error costs and high judicial resource costs. Thus, the "end result" test announced in *Hope* can be seen as a decision to allocate to the political institutions of government near total power to protect the constitutional values underlying the takings clause in the ratemaking context. This is required by the severe institutional limitations of the judiciary as a potential source of protection for those values.

How do you interpret *Duquesne* ? Do you agree with Copeland and Nixon or with Pierce?

2. The application of the used and useful rule makes it more likely that a utility will earn less money. How should this investment risk be taken into account by a reviewing court? Can a higher rate of return reflect such an increased risk? Kolbe and Tye argue that the rate of return must be higher than the cost of capital in order to compensate investors for such high risks.[33] Is the Kolbe and Tye hypothesis good law as well as good economics?

E. ELECTRICITY REGULATION

In Chapter 1 we noted that we are in a period of regulatory reform and the electricity industry has been undergoing a major restructuring at both the federal and state levels. Federally, open access in interstate commerce for wholesale sales of electricity is ongoing. For open access to work well the entire grid must participate and that means that state regulation, which affects retail sales, must also be coordinated with federal efforts. This section describes the rationale for the regulation of the electricity industry and its history of regulation.

---

[31] For an affirmative response, see Copeland & Nixon, *supra,* note 21.
[32] Pierce, *supra,* note 30.
[33] Kolbe & Tye, *supra* note 29.

JOSPEH P. TOMAIN, THE PAST AND FUTURE OF ELECTRICITY REGULATION, 32 ENVIRONMENTAL LAW 435, 443–450 (2002)[*]

The electricity industry provides an excellent case study of government regulation. Like other network industries such as natural gas, telephone, and railroad, the regulation of electricity was based on the central political economic idea that the industry had natural monopoly characteristics *and* that electricity served the public interest. As a fundamental matter of political economy, markets and the property exchanged and valued in them exist only because of government protection. Still, it is the degree of protection that distinguishes government treatment of some industries from the treatment of others. It is also the case that the degree of government intervention changes over time.

In its beginning at the end of the nineteenth century, electricity was an unregulated competitive industry. The industry, for the most part, consisted of investor owned utilities (IOUs) that owned and operated generation, transmission, and distribution. Later, as the industry consolidated, government regulation was justified as a way to stem the abuses of market power exercised by these vertically integrated utilities. The particular market imperfection in the electric industry was natural monopoly and government responded with command-and-control regulations setting the prices that could be charged by utilities and limiting the profits that utilities could earn. Price and profit controls are a form of heavy-handed economic regulation that comes with costs of its own. Starting in the mid-1960s, traditional utility regulation appeared to have run its course as market distortions arose and as policymakers began to look at regulatory reform and deregulation. While it is true that the heavy hand of command-and-control price regulation is being lifted and market-based price mechanisms are preferred, government still has a large and continuing regulatory role to play. . . .

D. Precursors to Electric Industry Restructuring

For most of the twentieth century, producers, consumers, and regulators believed in the wisdom of the traditional regulation of the utility industry based on the natural monopoly assumptions. There were good reasons for that belief, as it was supported by the economy and by the effects on shareholders' and ratepayers' pocketbooks.

The U.S. economy was expanding throughout most of the century with of course, the exception of the Great Depression. The political-economic response to the Great Depression, in the form of the New Deal, was quite favorable to the electric industry. As part of the New Deal program to stabilize the economy, the government pushed forward a plan to stabilize the country's energy infrastructure, particularly in the electric and natural gas industries. These legislative schemes proved particularly fruitful after the Second World War, as both the economy and energy production expanded at predictable rates. As a consequence of traditional rate regulation and a friendly economy,

---

[*] Reprinted by permission.

shareholders were happy because producers expanded plants at little or no financial risk, thus earning reliable returns and receiving reliable service. Ratepayers were happy because neither producers nor consumers were complaining, rate hearings were relatively uncomplicated, and public utility commissions were largely nonpolitical agencies.

Understandably, traditional utility regulation could not last forever. Just as there are natural business cycles for industry, so there are cycles of regulation. A business, for example, may start competitively then consolidate to reduce competition, resulting in competitive market failure. In such a case, government regulation can attempt to correct that failure until regulation experiences failure itself. The regulation of the electric industry has gone through that cycle, from an unregulated competitive market, to market failure and attendant regulation, then to regulatory failure. Now politicians, regulators, and other interested actors are responding to the regulatory failure in the electric industry for political and economic reasons.

1. Economic and Political Justification

Starting roughly in 1965, the industry reached technological and financial plateaus at which industry expansion slowed considerably; economies of scale were not being realized, costs were increasing, generation was overbuilt, and alternative providers were coming into the market. Economic indicators were such that utilities could no longer rely on the annual seven percent growth rate they had enjoyed since the end of World War II. The traditional rate formula which encouraged capital expansion put utilities in the position of continuing to dump money into the rate base, thus increasing costs. Inflation and other economic indicators caused marginal costs to exceed average costs as utilities ran into trouble with cost overruns, plant cancellations, and the like. In short, competition was peeking from behind regulatory blankets.

Politically, things also changed dramatically in the mid-1960s. Production costs began to increase and rates began to rise for a number of reasons. General economic inflation, increased concern about the environment and an attendant increase in regulatory costs, Vietnam War expenditures, an unstable world economy, the 1965 Northeast blackout, and the failure of nuclear power all contributed to unsettling the electric industry and its customers. The Organization of Petroleum Exporting Countries (OPEC) added to this state of affairs by flexing its cartel muscles and closing the oil spigot, which pushed inflation to double digits, and increased energy prices generally. Also, the price elasticity of demand for electricity was more elastic than anticipated, and consumers both reduced their electricity consumption and sought energy from alternative sources, further reducing their dependence on traditional utilities. Large consumers, for example, became self-generators, and small consumers installed solar panels. The reduction in consumption also caused rates to increase for remaining customers. All of these events made the formerly staid public utility commissions politically charged agencies, as critics attacked the basis of traditional rate regulation from both sides. Producers wanted rates to be more market sensitive and ratepayers wanted to avoid rate shock.

2. PURPA's Surprise: Increased Competition

The combined effects of the political and economic events in the late 1960s and early 1970s raised public concern about the country's energy future and raised particular concern in the Carter White House, which viewed the Energy Crisis as the "moral equivalent of war." Jimmy Carter addressed the Energy Crisis through two major legislative initiatives. The first was the massive and ambitious National Energy Act, which addressed conventional fuels. . . . Carter's second initiative, the Energy Security Act of 1980, addressed conservation and alternative fuels from biomass, wind and solar to tar sands and oil shale. The surprising part of the National Energy Act was the Public Utility Regulatory Policies Act (PURPA), which was aimed at securing reasonably priced energy for the nation through conservation, increasing use of alternative sources, and moving toward market-based rates.

PURPA encouraged . . . independent power production through cogeneration and small power generation as energy source alternatives to large public utilities. What surprised everyone was how much new nonutility generated electricity was available and how eager independent power producers (IPPs) were to enter the [electricity] market. The success of PURPA revealed that traditional regulation had run its course. . . . In microeconomic terms, the traditional, regulated electric industry had reached the end of its scale economies. In other words, unregulated producers existed that were willing to supply the market with electricity priced lower than the electricity being supplied by incumbent regulated utilities, and the new entrants profited by doing so with a little help from government. . . .

PURPA stimulated a deeper rethinking of the concept of natural monopoly. Under the traditional regulatory scheme, investor owned utilities (IOUs) owned and operated generation, transmission, and distribution as state-protected monopolies. However, cheaper electricity was available because the generation segment of IOUs became too big and costly to maintain. In microeconomic terms, marginal cost exceeded average cost signaling the failure of traditional rate regulation because the traditional formula set rates on average, historic costs rather than market sensitive marginal costs. In other words, traditional utilities found it more costly to do business because they could not charge market rates and had overbuilt. As a result, smaller units and newer technologies became increasingly attractive.

PURPA thus caused a rethinking of regulation at both ends of the fuel cycle. At the generation end, the existence of the NUGs indicated that the market was competitive. At the buyers' end, consumers wanted to purchase the cheaper electricity. . . .

E. The Current Status of Electricity Regulation

1. The Energy Policy Act of 1992

By the early 1990s, PURPA made two things clear. First, alternative power producers wanted to get into the market. Second, the market was not as robust as it could be because transmission access was not open due to two limiting factors. Nonutility generators, other than QFs, found it difficult to enter the market because they had to follow the PUHCA. These generators were particularly desirable because they could provide new generation at a lower cost. The second constraint was FERC's lack of authority to mandate wheeling over transmission lines.

In 1992, Congress passed the Energy Policy Act (EPAct) and partially eliminated both constraints. EPAct advanced restructuring by authorizing firms exclusively in the business of selling electric energy at wholesale (exempt wholesale generators (EWGs)) to be exempt from PUHCA's ownership restrictions. This exemption set the stage for the development of a more competitive and unregulated wholesale market. Second, EPAct authorized FERC to order utilities that owned transmission facilities to transmit wholesale power over their systems. The Act gave FERC broad authority, subject to a public interest standard, to order "virtually any transmission owning entity in the U.S. to wheel power for wholesale transactions at the request of a broad range of potential applicants involved in wholesale power transactions." However, EPAct prohibited FERC from ordering access to transmission for retail power. EPAct advanced the restructuring ball by promoting EWGs and by opening transmission access. All that remained was for FERC to implement the Act.

———

In short, the supply of electricity increased because there were new entrants to the market who could produce electricity cheaper than that provided by traditional regulated utilities. Additionally, consumers wanted the cheaper electricity but there was no easy way for consumers to buy that electricity because the transmission lines were owned by vertically integrated utilities that had little or no interest in selling low priced electricity let alone someone else's low priced electricity. The electricity transmission system constituted a classic bottleneck that had to be opened for the free flow of cheaper electricity. To this end federal and state government engaged in massive and widescale restructuring.

JOSEPH P. TOMAIN, THE PERSISTENCE OF NATURAL MONOPOLY, 16 NATURAL RESOURCES & ENVIRONMENT 242, 244–246 (SPRING, 2002).

. . . [The Public Utility Regulatory Policy Act of 1978] accelerated the movement into the market of unregulated producers. PURPA's surprise was that new generation was available and these new producers were willing to supply the market with electricity priced lower than the electricity being supplied by incumbent regulated utilities. . . .

At this point in the regulatory story, transmission becomes more important as regulators begin to rethink regulation. While new producers could sell power to the local utility, they did not have access to the utility's transmission lines to "wheel" their power to any other utility or end user. Consequently, the existence of new producers meant the formal introduction of competition into generation and increased production began to force open the access door.

New generators needed access to transmission owned and controlled by utilities to expand their market and to compete effectively. However, the Federal Energy Regulatory Commission (FERC) did not have explicit authority under the Federal Power Act to order utilities to wheel power for the new generators and, therefore, sought to get the utilities to provide transmission access "voluntarily.". . .

In 1992, Congress passed the Energy Policy Act (EPAct) furthering competition. EPAct exempted nonutility generators from certain regulations and authorized FERC to mandate wholesale wheeling. EPAct, however, prohibited FERC from ordering access to transmission for retail power sales. As general legislation, EPAct advanced the restructuring ball by authorizing new producers and opening transmission access. It remained for FERC to implement the Act for wholesale deregulation and for the states to engage in retail deregulation.

There are certain physical attributes of electricity that directly affect its regulation, however. First, electrons travel through the network virtually instantaneously. At the speed of light one might say. Second, electricity cannot be stored effectively in large quantities.

The first principle of physics is a good thing for consumers, but a headache for regulators. As long as the network is open, consumers can draw down electricity. The regulatory headache is that within a grid no one knows the point of origin of any electricity. They simply know how much is in the system and how much generators are willing to charge. The second principle of physics is good for producers and a headache for consumers and regulators. Producers have a steady demand and a need for their supply. Consumers and regulators must worry about reliability and cost.

What all this means for transmission can be summarized in one word—bottleneck. Consumers want the product, producers want to supply it, and transmission owners want to make a profit by controlling access. Thus, controlled access constitutes a competitive bottleneck for the delivery of electricity from producers to consumers. Because the privately owned transmission segment has both monopolistic and monopsonistic attributes, profits at both ends of the line can be excessive. In other words, without some form of price regulation the transmission owner can set the price it is willing to pay producers either for the product or for the transportation and can set the price it is willing to charge consumers. Consequently, for full competition in the utility industry, the transmission segment must have adequate *capacity*, maintain *reliability*, avoid *congestion*, and do so at *reasonable* prices with *no discrimination* among customers.

FERC Order No. 888 is a major access initiative implementing EPAct, requiring utilities transmitting in interstate commerce to file open access nondiscriminatory tariffs. Order 888 also requires utilities to "functionally unbundled," as distinct from divest, their transmission service from their generation and power marketing functions. The unbundling was intended to reduce or eliminate self-dealing and discrimination and involves separating transmission charges into one charge for the electricity and one charge for its transportation. FERC estimated that open access would save U.S. electric consumers between $3.8 billion and $5.4 billion a year, and encourage more technical innovation in the industry. Companion Order No. 889 established an electronic information system, called OASIS (pen access same-time information system), to further competition and make information more transparent. Although Orders 888 and 889 had a dramatic impact on the wholesale industry, retail wheeling was untouched and left to the states. So too, was the appropriate form for a transmission entity. FERC partially addressed this issue in Order 2000.

FERC Order 2000—Regional Transmission Organizations

While a regulatory bright line can be drawn between interstate wholesale sales of electricity and retail sales, that bright line is one largely of political convenience rather than physical reality. Regulatory restructuring has continued to follow this neat division between state and federal regulation. This continued allegiance to dual regulation may make political sense. It does not make good economic sense. While restructuring prefers competition to heavier-handed price controls believing that the market can generate lower prices, increase consumer choice, and produce reliably, it also recognizes that transmission poses the potential for the abuse of market power. FERC found that the market was still insufficiently competitive because of engineering and economic inefficiencies, including concerns over reliability, transmission capacity, congestion management, transmission maintenance and expansion, and price discrimination.

The challenge is to move from a vertically integrated, privately owned utility in which generation and transmission are linked to an open and nondiscriminatory transportation system. The private ownership of transmission facilities presents difficulties. Private owners have a fiduciary duty to their shareholders to maximize value and because of this fiduciary responsibility there is little incentive to give up either transmission ownership or operation. Nor is there any reason to favor competitors. Nevertheless, the consensus is that some form of independent operation is necessary to avoid uncompetitive behavior.

To this point, regional coordination has occurred through voluntary power tools. Interconnections have extended throughout the country to form three power pools east and west of the Rocky Mountains and in Texas. These three pools together with the Hydro-Quebec System form the North American Electric Reliability Council (NERC), another voluntary organization, to coordinate operations, planning, and transmission.

FERC found that the voluntary coordination is no longer effective and responded with Order 2000 requiring transmission-owning utilities to file a regional transmission organization (RTO) proposal with FERC by October 15, 2000, or file an extension as to why they could not.

RTOs are transmission entities that are independent of the owners of generation facilities. FERC requires utilities to "functionally unbundled" the transmission function of the utility from its generation and power marketing functions rather than divest its assets. A utility can own transmission assets but must operate them independently from the generation assets. There are two fundamental approaches to organizing an RTO: the nonprofit independent system operator (ISO) and the for-profit independent transmission company (transco). Regardless of form, however, transcos and ISOs must achieve five goals. Every RTO must have sufficient capacity, provide reliable service, manage congestion, not discriminate, and offer reasonable prices.

———

FERC Order No. 888 was the first major open access initiative and was upheld by the United States Supreme Court in the following case:

NEW YORK v. FERC
535 U.S. 1 (2002)

JUSTICE STEVENS delivered the opinion of the Court.

These cases raise two important questions concerning the jurisdiction of the Federal Energy Regulatory Commission (FERC or Commission) over the transmission of electricity. First, if a public utility "unbundles"—*i.e.*, separates—the cost of transmission from the cost of electrical energy when billing its retail customers, may FERC require the utility to transmit competitors' electricity over its lines on the same terms that the utility applies to its own energy transmissions? Second, must FERC impose that requirement on utilities that continue to offer only "bundled" retail sales?

In Order No. 888, issues in 1996 with the stated purpose of "Promoting Wholesale Competition Through Open Access Non-Discriminatory Transmission Services by Public Utilities," FERC answered yes to the first question and no to the second.

I

In 1935, when the FPA became law, most electricity was sold by vertically integrated utilities that had constructed their own power plants, transmission lines, and local delivery systems. Although there were some interconnections among utilities, most operated as separate, local monopolies subject to state or local regulation. Their sales were "bundled," meaning that consumers paid a single charge that included both the cost of the electric energy and the cost of its delivery. Competition among utilities was not prevalent.

Prior to 1935, the States possessed broad authority to regulate public utilities, but this power was limited by our cases holding that the negative impact of the Commerce Clause prohibits state regulation that directly burdens interstate commerce. When confronted with an attempt by Rhode Island to regulate the rates charged by a Rhode Island plant selling electricity to a Massachusetts company, which resold the electricity to the city of Attleboro, Massachusetts, we invalidated the regulation because it imposed a "direct burden upon interstate commerce." Creating what has become known as the "*Attleboro* gap," we held that this interstate transaction was not subject to regulation by either Rhode Island or Massachusetts, but only "by the exercise of the power vested in Congress."

When it enacted the FPA in 1935, Congress authorized federal regulation of electricity in areas beyond the reach of state power, such as the gap identified in *Attleboro*, but it also extended federal coverage to some areas that previously had been state regulated. . . .

Since 1935, and especially beginning in the 1970's and 1980's, the number of electricity suppliers has increased dramatically. Technological advances have made it possible to generate electricity efficiently in different ways and in smaller plants. In addition, unlike the local power networks of the past, electricity is now delivered over three major networks to "grids" in the continental United States. . . . It is only in Hawaii and Alaska and on the "Texas Interconnect"—which covers most of that State—that electricity is distributed entirely within a single State. In the rest of the country, any electricity that enters the grid immediately becomes a part of a vast pool of energy that is constantly moving in interstate commerce. As a result, it is now possible for power companies to transmit electric energy over long distances at a low cost. . . .

Thus, in 1995, FERC initiated the rulemaking proceeding that led to the adoption of the order presently under review. FERC proposed a rule that would "require that public utilities owning and/or controlling facilities used for the transmission of electric energy in interstate commerce have on the file tariffs providing for nondiscriminatory open-access transmission services." . . . The stated purpose of the proposed rule was "to encourage lower electricity rates by structuring an orderly transition to competitive bulk power markets.". . .

In 1996, . . . FERC issued Order No. 888. It found that electric utilities were discriminating in the "bulk power markets," in violation of § 205 of the FPA, by providing either inferior access to their transmission networks or no access at all to third-party wholesalers of power. Invoking its authority under § 206, it prescribed a remedy containing three parts that are presently relevant.

First, FERC ordered "functional unbundling" of wholesale generation and transmission services. FERC defined "functional unbundling" as requiring each utility to state separate rules for its wholesale generation, transmission and ancillary services, and to take transmission of its own wholesale sales and purchases under a single general tariff applicable equally to itself and to others.

Second, FERC imposed a similar open access requirement on unbundled *retail* transmissions in interstate commerce. . . .

Third, FERC rejected a proposal that the open access requirement should apply to "the transmission component of bundled retail sales.". . .

Because of the importance of the proceeding, we granted both the petition of the State of New York et al. (collectively New York) questioning FERC's assertion of jurisdiction over unbundled retail transmissions and the petition of Enron Power Marketing, Inc. (Enron), questioning FERC's refusal to assert jurisdiction over bundled retail transmissions. We address these two questions separately. At the outset, however, we note that no petitioner questions the validity of the order insofar as it applies to wholesale transactions: The parties dispute only the proper scope of FERC's jurisdiction over *retail* transmissions. Furthermore, we are not confronted with any factual issues. Finally, we agree with FERC that transmissions on the interconnected national grids constitute transmissions in interstate commerce.

III

The first question is whether FERC exceeded its jurisdiction by including unbundled retail transmissions within the scope of its open access requirements in Order No. 888. New York argues that FERC overstepped in this regard, and that such transmissions—because they are part of retail transactions—are properly the subject of state regulation. New York insists that the jurisdictional line between the States and FERC falls between the wholesale and retail markets.

As the Court of Appeals explained, however, the landscape of the electric industry has changed since the enactment of the FPA, when the electricity universe was "neatly divided into spheres of retail versus wholesale sales." As the Court of Appeals also explained, the plain language of the FPA readily supports FERC's claim of jurisdiction. Section 201(b) of the FPA states that FERC's jurisdiction includes "the transmission of electric energy in interstate commerce" and "the sale of electric energy at wholesale in interstate commerce." The unbundled retail transmissions targeted by FERC are indeed transmissions of "electric energy in interstate commerce," because of the nature of the national grid. There is no language in the statute limiting FERC's *transmission* jurisdiction to the wholesale market, although the statute does limit FERC's *sale* jurisdiction to that at wholesale.

In the face of this clear statutory language, New York advances three arguments in support of its submission that the statute draws a bright jurisdictional line between wholesale transactions and retail transactions. First, New York contends that the Court of Appeals applied an erroneous standard of review because it ignored the presumption against federal pre-emption of state law; second, New York claims that other statutory language and legislative history shows a congressional intent to safeguard preexisting state regulation of the delivery of electricity to retail customers; and third, New York argues that FERC jurisdiction over retail transmissions would impede sound energy policy. These arguments are unpersuasive. [Discussion of the first two issues is omitted.]

Sound Energy Policy

New York argues that FERC jurisdiction over unbundled retail transmission will impede sound energy policy. Specifically, New York cites the States' interest in overseeing the maintenance of transmission lines and the siting of new lines. It is difficult for us to evaluate the force of these arguments because New York has not separately analyzed the impact of the loss of control over unbundled retail transmissions, as opposed to the loss of control over retail transmissions generally, and FERC has only regulated unbundled transactions. Moreover, FERC has recognized that the States retain significant control over local matters even when retail transmissions are unbundled. ("This Final Rule will not affect or encroach upon state authority in such traditional areas as the authority over local service issues, including reliability of local service; administration of integrated resource planning and utility buy-side and demand-side decisions, including DSM [demand-side management]; authority over utility generation and resource portfolios; and authority to impose non-bypassable distribution or retail stranded cost charges"). We do note that the Edison Electric Institute, which is a part to these cases, and which represents that its members own approximately 70% of the transmission facilities in the country, does not endorse New York's objections to Order No. 888. And, regardless of their persuasiveness, the sort of policy arguments forwarded by New York are properly addressed to the Commission or to the Congress, not to this Court.

IV

Objecting to FERC's order from the opposite direction, Enron argues that the FPA gives FERC the power to apply its open access remedy to *bundled* retail transmissions of electricity, and, given FERC's findings of undue discrimination, that FERC had a duty to do so. In making this argument, Enron persistently claims that FERC held that it had no jurisdiction to grant the relief that Enron seeks. That assumption is incorrect: FERC chose not to assert such jurisdiction, but it did not hold itself powerless to claim jurisdiction. Indeed, FERC explicitly reserved decision on the jurisdictional issue that Enron claims FERC decided. . . . Absent Enron's flawed assumption, FERC's ruling is clearly acceptable.

As noted above, in both Order No. 888 and rehearing Order No. 888-A, FERC gave two reasons for refusing to extend its open-access remedy to bundled retail transmissions. First, FERC explained that such relief was not "necessary." Second, FERC noted that the regulation of bundled retail transmissions "raises numerous difficult jurisdictional issues" that did not need to be resolved in the present context. Both of these reasons provide valid support for FERC's decision not to regulate bundled retail transmissions. . . .

Accordingly, the judgment of the Court of Appeals is affirmed.

NOTES AND QUESTIONS

1. We have omitted the dissent by Justice Thomas in *New York v. FERC*. Justice Thomas would have sided with Enron's position that FERC should have extended and exercised its jurisdiction over bundled retail sales. Justice Thomas would have rejected FERC's reasons for not extending its jurisdiction. FERC stated that such an extension was unnecessary and raised complicated jurisdictional issues. Justice Thomas responded:

> Because the statute unambiguously grants FERC jurisdiction over all interstate transmission and § 824e mandates that FERC remedy undue discrimination with respect to all transmission within its jurisdiction, at a minimum the statute required FERC to consider whether there was discrimination in the marketplace warranting application of either the OATT or some other remedy.

> I would not, as petitioner Enron requests, compel FERC to apply the OATT to bundled retail transmission. I would vacate the Court of

Appeals' judgment and require FERC on remand to engage in reasoned decisionmaking to determine whether there is undue discrimination with respect to transmission associated with retail bundled sales, and if so, what remedy is appropriate.

For all of these reasons, I respectfully dissent.

122 S.Ct. at 1034. Why would Enron be interested in having FERC exercise more jurisdiction over state electricity transmission issues?

2. To date FERC has reviewed several RTO applications and has given full approval to two.[34] While FERC, in discussions with various utilities and state regulators, has gone back and forth about the number of RTOs needed throughout the country, it has been committed to the idea and is moving forward. In March, 2002, FERC released a cost-benefit study showing savings in wholesale power costs of approximately $40.9 billion over the next 20 years.[35] This study has not been without critics.[36]

———

1. MARKET STANDARDIZATION

Electrical industry restructuring confronts a continuing problem—natural monopoly in transmission. FERC Orders 888, 889, and 2000 have gone a long way to open access. In the summer of 2002, FERC issued a list of proposed rulemakings entitled Remedying Undo Discrimination Through Open Access Transmission Service and Standard Electricity Market Design, Docket No. RMO1-12-000.[37] The Notice of Proposed Rulemaking, known as the SMD NOPR, is intended to elicit responses regarding the further development of electricity restructuring. Building upon Order No. 888 and Order No. 2000, FERC proposed to standardize the structure and operation of competitive wholesale power markets throughout the country for the purpose of avoiding the type of dysfunction found in the California experience. The rulemaking proposes that FERC will actively monitor market abuses, organize a central spot power market to complement a contract for these markets for long-term power supplies, create transparency in market prices, all for the purpose of avoiding new discrimination.

As this book goes to press and through late September 2004, FERC will collect data, comments, as well as require jurisdiction on utilities to implement the rule and file open-access transmission tariffs in accordance with final regulations. The central idea behind the SMD NOPR is that unless markets are standardized nationally, there will continue to be unjust, unreasonable, or unduly discriminatory service. If the rule is promulgated as initially written all FERC-regulated transmission providers will be required to come under the

---

[34] *Midwest Indep. Transmission Sys. Operator, Inc.*, 97 F.E.R.C. ¶ 61,326 (Dec. 20, 2001); *PJM Interconnective LLC*, Docket RT01-2 (Dec. 19, 2002).

[35] Economic Assessment of RTO Policy, ICF Consulting (2002); available at: www.ferc.gov/electric/rto/mrkt-strct-comments-rtostudy_final_0226.pdf.

[36] See Clapp & McGrath, *Studying Apples and Oranges: RTO Studies are Difficult to Reconcile*, PUBLIC UTILITIES FORT. 32 (Sept. 25, 2002).

[37] 67 Fed. Reg. 55,451 (Aug. 29, 2002); FERC Stats. & Regs.¶ 32,563 (2002).

control of an independent transmission provider (ITP) that would provide a single, flexible transmission service called Network Access Service with the purpose of rationalizing service throughout the country.

Standard market design is not free from discussion or debate. At this point, it seems as if those states that have actively been involved in forming and joining RTO's look favorably upon the standard market design whereas those that are not, have questions. Most particularly, the questions concern who will be the winners and losers of standard market design. Will customers be affected in low cost states? How will retail customers fare against large customers? What will be the role of the state regulatory authorities? What will be the effects on independent power producers versus traditional vertical utilities?[38]

2. ENERGY TRADING

The central concept behind electric industry restructuring is to move the industry away from the command-and-control price and profit regulation into a more competitive environment. Because, however, electricity is a vital product, a reliable supply is needed. Under the traditional command-and-control scheme, reliability was provided by a public utility's "reserve margin," that is, an excess of supply over and above average daily requirements. The utility was able to recapture those costs through the rate formula.

The major attraction for restructuring is competition. Consumers should benefit by price competition and more choice; producers should benefit by higher profits through more efficient service. The competitive environment requires trading either on the spot market or in the future. Unfortunately, restructuring was dealt two severe blows both of which demonstrated that trading markets were manipulated rather than competitive.

In a non-regulated world, products are traded in open markets as supply satisfies demand. Products can be purchased in spot markets for use now or in the immediate future or they can be stored for future use. With sensitive commodities such as food stuffs and currencies, futures contracts allow sellers and buyers to anticipate supply and demand. Because electricity cannot be stored efficiently, it can be traded on either spot or future markets. Thus, electricity futures contracts can, theoretically, take the place of reserve margins. We emphasize the theoretical nature of electricity futures contracts because the first significant foray into energy trading resulted in the California electricity crisis, the collapse of Enron, market manipulation, and criminal investigations, all of which are interrelated. Still, the idea of viable energy trading markets is sound and necessary for a developed restructuring. Unfortunately, the first large experiment in California was a failure.

---

[38] Burkhart, *The Fight Over Market Design*, PUBLIC UTILITIES FORTNIGHTLY, 18 (Nov. 15, 2002).

JOSEPH P. TOMAIN, THE PAST AND FUTURE OF ELECTRICITY REGULATION, 32 ENVIRONMENTAL LAW 435, 438–443 (2002) *

. . . It is at this point in the developing history of the electricity industry and its regulation that two new words enter our vocabulary—California and Enron. For the last year and one-half, the California electricity crisis and the Enron debacle appear to demonstrate the failure of electricity restructuring. That appearance is false even though the restructuring movement has been slowed. As of January 2002, seven states have delayed restructuring activities, California has suspended action, and 25 states are listed as not active. Both the California restructuring effort and Enron's energy trading *modus operandi* were the products of design failure, not faulty theoretical assumptions. Indeed, although both were failed attempts, California's electricity restructuring and Enron's energy trading point to the future of a restructured electric industry.

A. CALIFORNIA

There is no shortage of analyses of the California electricity crisis. Fundamentally, the crisis was a matter of supply and demand resulting in prices beyond any previously recognized level and in a bankruptcy filing by Pacific Gas & Electric, one of California's Big Three utilities. The market distortions were created by poor predictions about demand, a hot summer, a dry Northwest, high natural gas prices, miscalculations about supply, no new generation, and most significantly, a poor regulatory design.

Although the crisis has passed, and prices have lowered and blackouts, rolling or otherwise, are not on the horizon, there are lessons to be learned from the California experience. Chief among these lessons involves regulatory design, the crux of which was an inflexible market for buying, selling, and pricing electricity. There are three notable aspects to this design, one of which was fatal. First, the major public utilities in California divested their generating units while maintaining an obligation to serve their customers. As long as costs are passed through to consumers, the obligation to serve does not present a severe problem because the utilities earn money to pay their bills. Second, two new regulatory entities were established, the California Power Exchange (PX) which set prices, and the California Independent System Operator (ISO) which directed the movement of electricity through the system. The PX was the market mechanism intended to make the industry competitive. The PX and the ISO are perfectly appropriate entities, again if properly designed.

The fatal flaw was the price restrictions. They were the medicine intended to help the consumers but killed the restructuring. Utilities had to buy wholesale energy at market price from the PX in no more than day-ahead or hour-ahead markets which meant that they could not enter long-term contracts. These spot-market purchases were subject to a great deal of volatility and the highest bid set the price. At the same time, retail prices to consumers were capped until the utility recovered its stranded costs. The problem was

---

* Reprinted with permission.

that the utilities bought in the spot-market at extraordinarily high prices and sold in a capped retail market, thus putting themselves in a credit crunch with high profits for other producers, high prices to some consumers, and a political crisis for the Governor.

The market distortion was aggravated by the fact that the retail cap sent consumers the wrong price signals. They had little incentive to conserve and, to aggravate matters, California had stopped bringing power plants on-line. Indeed, demand had risen 25% in the past eight years while in-state power generation only rose six percent.

There are several culprits to blame for the California energy crisis of 2000. Governor Gray Davis blames the owners of power production as "out-of-state profiteers" for allegedly withholding power from California companies in an attempt to drive up prices. Consumer groups blame the same energy companies as well as California politicians willing to bail out the California power retailers, such as SoCal Edison, Pacific Gas and Electric (PG&E), and San Diego Gas and Electric (SDG&E). The out-of-state owners of energy production, Dynegy, Duke Energy, and Enron criticize the California politicians and bureaucrats that crafted a system that allowed them to capitalize on the circumstances that led to the problems in California. . . .

B. ENRON

Enron's role as power marketer and energy trader is exactly what a deregulated electricity market needs. Unfortunately, its bankruptcy and ensuing civil and criminal investigations prevent Enron from fulfilling that role. Because demand requires instantaneous supply (i.e., reliability), there must be some mechanism to assure that supply. In the traditional regulated environment, the local utility maintained adequate reserves to satisfy demand. In unregulated or deregulated markets, consumers protect themselves either with contracts for futures or with back-up power. Enron bought and sold futures contracts and helped make a market in electricity, among other commodities. Enron was the industry leader in taking advantage of deregulation and restructuring. It was estimated that Enron controlled about one-quarter of the country's energy trading.

Enron was a small traditional natural gas pipeline firm that went on to become a huge company with market capitalization of about $60-70 billion. It also transformed its business from a stodgy enterprise to a high flying trader which traded in electricity futures, bandwidth, advertising space, and even weather features. In the end, Enron became less an energy company than it did a hedge fund. It had a difficult enough time explaining its business even to its CEO, ultimately collapsing into bankruptcy. Nevertheless, energy futures can be an effective way to provide reliable sources of electricity, supplement the reserve margins helped by traditional utilities, and control price uncertainty. Futures, then, can work with either power exchanges or ISOs to stabilize electricity markets.

The collapse, however, has little to say about energy markets in general or even hedge funds in particular. Nor should its collapse have anything to do with change in direction for energy deregulation. As Congress, the Justice

Department, and the Securities Exchange Commission continue investigation into Enron, the deregulation of the deregulation of the energy industry continues as Enron sells off assets and settles lawsuits and other companies take up futures trading where Enron left off.

———

The major design flaw in California's restructuring legislation was the provision that froze retail price rates while allowing wholesale rates to rise freely without limit which opened the door to market manipulation. The deregulation law required utilities to provide energy at all times thus forcing them to purchase power even at inflated rates. If a firm is obligated to buy and they are restricted from buying under a long-term contract, then a supplier can raise prices simply by withholding supply. In fact, investigations indicate that this was the case together with a number of other market manipulation practices neatly set out in internal Enron documents.[39]

The most frequent market abuse was the practice of "round-tripping" of energy, also known as "wash trades." FERC defined wash trades as the sale of electricity "to another company together with a simultaneous purchase of the same product at the same price."[40] The round-trip starts with one energy-trading company selling electricity to another. Simultaneously, the second firm sells the same electricity, at the same price, back to the first company.[41]

Although the Securities and Exchange Commission (SEC) has been prosecuting brokers using wash trades in securities,[42] the practice is apparently not illegal in the unregulated market.[43] Such trading activity involves two sins. First, the trader is perceived as a bigger market actor than it actually is. Second, and more serious, is that prices are inflated as demand appears to increase.[44] According to one energy company, CMS Energy, the round-trip trades were done solely to boost trading volumes for marketing to try and attract new business.[45] If there is a determination by FERC that prices were driven up as the result of round-tripping, the likely lawsuits would lead to situations similar to that of Enron.

Enron used four main schemes in order to capitalize on the inadequacies of the California deregulation laws. The first strategy, known as "Death Star,"

---

[39] *See* FERC, Initial Report on Company-Specific Separate Proceedings and Generic Reevaluations; Published Natural Gas Price Data; and Enron Trading Strategies: Fact-Finding Investigation of Potential Manipulation of Electric and Natural Gas Prices, Docket No-PA02-2-000 (Aug. 2002). *See also* William Powers, Report of Investigation by the Special Investigation Committee of the Board of Directors of Enron Corp., (Feb. 1, 2002), available at: news.findlaw.com/wp/docs/enron/specinv020102 rpt1.pdf; www.ferc.gov/Electric/bulkpower/PA02-2/pa02-2.htm.

[40] *FERC Expands Probe As Firms Deny Deception.* GAS DAILY, May 22, 2002, at 1.

[41] *Prepare to Be Shocked,* THE ECONOMIST, May 18, 2002.

[42] Mitchell, Cummins, and Sapsford, *Trade Disclosures Shake Faith in Damaged Energy Market,* WALL ST. J., May 13, 2002, at A1.

[43] Cummins and Friedland, *CMS Energy Admits Questionable Trades Inflated Its Volume,* WALL ST. J., May 16, 2002, at A1.

[44] *Prepare to Be Shocked, supra* note 41.

[45] Bredemeier, *Power Trading's High Toll,* WASH. POST, May 29, 2002, at E01; Schwartz, *Is Energy Trading a Big Scam?,* FORTUNE, June 10, 2002, at 126, 130.

involved Enron receiving payments for relieving congestion in areas with too much electricity by transporting energy away from congested areas to out-of-state locations.[46] When the transmission paths became too congested in certain areas of California, Enron would be paid to send power in another direction.[47] Enron, however, imported the power back into the state and back into the congested areas, with the effect being that Enron was paid for relieving congestion without actually moving any energy or relieving congestion.

The next strategy was known to Enron officials as "Fat Boy." In the day-ahead ISO market, Enron would schedule an artificially high number of megawatts to be delivered to one of its subsidiaries. The subsidiary would receive the energy, but only use a fraction. However, under the California rules, Enron had to be paid a percentage of the contract price relating to the total amount of electricity that it transferred. Thus, Enron was paid for power it did not need to produce.

A third strategy used by Enron was known as "Get Shorty." Enron agreed to provide ancillary services in the day-ahead market and then provided these services through buying them at a lower price in the hour-ahead market. At no time, however, did Enron actually have the services to sell on the day-ahead market, so Enron provided falsified information to identify ancillary services sources.

The final strategy used by Enron negatively affected people inside California and in other Western power markets as well. Dubbed "Ricochet," Enron would buy wholesale power on the California market at $250/MWh, which was the capped rate. Enron would then sell the power in other deregulated power markets that were also suffering from shortages, such as Washington. Since rates were not capped in other states, Enron was able to sell the power purchased in California at a higher rate, sometimes reaching $1,200/MWh. By exporting the power out of California, Enron was also contributing to the power shortages in California by decreasing the amount of power available on the market.[48]

While much of the publicity regarding market manipulation focused on Enron, that company was not alone in its fraudulent trading. Dynegy paid a $3 million fine to the SEC and a $5 million fine to the Commodity Futures Trading Commission, and the Williams Cos. settled a suit with California for $150 million.[49] All in all what appeared to be a $300 billion industry collapsed with investors losing billions of dollars. Further, deregulatory efforts have slowed as questions arise not so much about whether to have energy trading but how to do so. Trading will be necessary for reliable supplies in a competitive market. The difficult question is how much regulation of energy trading will be necessary.

---

[46] Foster Natural Gas Report. *Questionable Trading Practices Prompt Further Inquiry By FERC, Claims of Vindication by California, and Concern Among Other Power Supplies and Shareholders,* Report No. 2386 (May 9, 2002), at 2.

[47] Banerjee. *New Questions on Handling Of Power Prices in California,* N.Y TIMES, June 8, 2002, at C1.

[48] See Foster Report, *supra* note 46.

[49] Beckett, Sapsford & Arrionuevo, *Power Outage: How Energy Trades Turned Bonaza Into an Epic Bust,* WALL ST. J., Dec. 31, 2002, at A1.

The effect of the revelations about trading abuse has been nothing less than disastrous to energy companies in the investment sector. Investors have been avoiding investing in electricity-generating companies, which then hampers efforts to develop generation and transmission.[50] In Congressional hearings, FERC commissioners explained how the effect of the Enron disclosures, as well as admissions of unethical and possibly illegal trading practices from other energy companies, has kept people away from contributing capital to energy industries for the development of transmission and generation infra-structure.[51]

Fortunately, there is little evidence to indicate that the problems encoun-tered by California in its attempt at deregulation will affect other states that are also trying to deregulate electricity.[52] The main reason why California differs from other states can be found in California's heavy dependence on hydroelectric energy. Fossil-fuel shortages can cause brief spikes in prices, but when a region dependent on water for power faces a drought, the region will be susceptible to price spikes for a prolonged period. However, with the controversy that surrounded California's problems, the move towards de-regulation has been slowed, if not completely stopped, and will continue to be stagnant in the near future.[53]

F. RATE REFORM

As noted electric industry restructuring is active and dynamic involving several deep seated and difficult political and economic principles such as continued regulation v. competitive markets, federalism and pre-emption and the roles of incumbent firms and regulators.

While there is a large consensus that competitive electric markets make good policy sense, more precise designs are lacking. In this section we briefly present rate concepts alternative to the traditional rate formula. Briefly, the traditional formula is cost-based. If a firm acts prudently, then they can recoup their costs and earn profits. This method does not provide an incentive to economize, i.e. behave efficiently. Instead, it provides an incentive to spend.

Rates can be designed to provide incentives to firms to behave efficiently and earn greater profits than they did under the traditional formula. Below we describe different incentive rates.

1. MARGINAL COST PRICING

Recall the discussion in Chapter 2 that compares average and marginal costs. When a utility bases its prices on average costs, it may put itself in the position of losing money. In Chapter 2, we demonstrated that there are points during the life of a firm where production costs rise and the cost of

---

[50] Oppel, *U.S. Regulators Are Requiring Full Details of Energy Sales,* N.Y. TIMES, May 15, 2002, at C1.

[51] Sullivan, *FERC Fires Back at "Sham" Traders,* GREENWIRE, May 16, 2002, at v. 10, n. 9.

[52] Hieronymus, Henderson, and Berry, *Market Power Analysis of the Electricity Generation Sector,* 23 ENERGY L.J. 1 (2002).

[53] Id.

producing the next unit will be greater than the average cost of producing that unit. In this circumstance, a firm will lose money if it bases its prices on average costs.

At least since the end of World War II through the mid-1960s, average costs (AC) have exceeded marginal costs (MC) for the electric industry. Thus, a rate formula based on AC favored utilities. Happily, utilities were continuing to achieve economies of scale which kept rates relatively flat for consumers. The cost picture for electric utilities, however, changed in the mid-1960s and early 1970s with the consequence that MC>AC. Thus, utilities whose rates were based on average costs found themselves in a profitability squeeze. Not surprisingly, utilities and economists favorable to them argued that rates should be set on marginal costs as part of the regulatory compact.

Marginal cost pricing has two effects. First, because the rate will be set at the cost of the next unit, consumers will receive price signals that are more accurate than average cost pricing. This fact implicates the second effect. Electricity prices can then be set based on time of use. Another way of understanding marginal cost pricing, also referred to as *incremental cost pricing*, is to realize that at different times of the day or on different days of the year, the cost of producing electricity is higher. You can well imagine that on the hottest day of the summer more people turn on their air conditioners and greater demand is put on the electric utility to provide service. Utilities run some generators constantly (baseload generators) and have other generators in reserve (peak load generators). When demand increases, reserve or peak load generators are brought online at an added cost to the utility. It makes economic sense, then, that consumers pay the true cost of the service that they are using. Naturally, if MC>AC, then consumers will pay more under marginal cost pricing. However, the consumption (demand) will be more aligned with cost and they will not overconsume electricity.

NOTES AND QUESTIONS

1. What is wrong in economic terms with setting prices based on average cost? Why is such pricing inefficient? What hinders a regulatory agency from setting prices based on the utility's marginal cost? How do information asymmetries impact this approach?

2. Marginal cost pricing, however, is not without its problems, including the following difficulties:[54] (1) incremental costs are difficult to measure; (2) it is expensive to install meters to measure usage in a way that is useful for incremental costs analysis; (3) certain classes of customers would be disadvantaged by incremental cost pricing; and (4) marginal pricing of a product in an imperfect economy in which many other products are not priced at the margin does not bring about efficient allocation of resources.

2. PRICE LEVEL REGULATION

Marginal cost pricing may be difficult because of information asymmetries. The regulatory agency may lack good methods to verify marginal cost data

---

[54] L. HYMAN, *supra* note 23, at 233; *see also*, R. PIERCE, ECONOMIC REGULATION: CASES AND MATERIALS 129 (1994).

presented by utilities. Reformers have therefore proposed that regulation should create financial incentives which align the interests of the regulatory agency and utilities.

Regulators have been experimenting in the last decade with price level regulation as a replacement for cost-of-service ratemaking or "profit" regulation. In this approach, regulators set a maximum price that a utility can charge, as compared to establishing the rate of profit that the utility can earn using cost-of-service ratemaking. Because the utility's profits are not controlled, it has an incentive to become more productive. If the utility is able to lower its costs, it can keep some (or sometimes all) the additional revenue it generates. The next two excerpts explain how price level regulation would work. They also debate whether it will be effective.

RICHARD J. PIERCE, PRICE LEVEL REGULATION BASED ON INFLATION IS NOT AN ATTRACTIVE ALTERNATIVE TO PROFIT LEVEL REGULATION, 84 NORTHWESTERN LAW REVIEW 665, 665–679 (1990) *

I. THE PROMISE OF PRICE LEVEL REGULATION

Hillman and Braeutigam have performed a major service by evaluating the potential advantages and disadvantages of substituting price level regulation for traditional profit level regulation. Properly designed and implemented, price level regulation has the potential to eliminate the many significant productive and allocative inefficiencies that invariably accompany profit level regulation. Changing the incentives given to regulated firms encourages greater efficiency. By allowing regulated firms to retain the benefits of cost reduction, and by forcing them to suffer the consequences of inflated costs, price level regulation can provide incentives for productive efficiency equivalent to the effects of a competitive market. This is in sharp contrast to the effects of profit level regulation, which provides weak incentives to minimize costs and, in some important contexts, even perverse incentives to inflate costs. . . .

Price level regulation can create incentives for firms to set prices based on marginal cost and to establish price relationships reflective of economically efficient price discrimination. . . .

Efficiencies concerning the regulatory process also accrue from price level regulation. Price level regulation can reduce the direct costs of regulation by eliminating the need for frequent protracted hearings to answer questions that have no answer, cannot be answered because of a paucity of data, or are economically irrelevant. This alone would be a nontrivial contribution to enhanced social welfare. Price level regulation also promises to eliminate, or at least to reduce, the present tendency to base regulated prices on economically irrelevant embedded costs and arbitrarily determined or politically manipulated allocations of common costs.

---

* Reprinted by special permission of Northwestern University School of Law, *Northwestern University Law Review*, Volume 84, Issue 2, pp. 665, 665–679 (1990).

Given the demonstrated high costs of profit level regulation, some forms of price level regulation actually may fulfill these promises. Unfortunately, the CPI -3 formula adopted by the British Department of Trade and Industry, the FCC, and at least two states is likely to yield results less appealing than unconstrained monopoly or profit level regulation. The reason for this pessimistic outlook is that conditions for successful implementation of this form of price level regulation cannot be attained. Consequently, although Hillman and Braeutigam make a good case for price level regulation, their proposal ultimately must be rejected.

II. THE CONDITIONS FOR EFFECTIVE PRICE LEVEL REGULATION

[Hillman and Braeutigam identify several conditions that are necessary for price level regulation to meet its potential. Among these conditions are:] (a) an initial price level somewhere near the economically efficient price; (b) initial price relationships somewhere near efficient price relationships; (c) a price adjustment mechanism that provides a tolerably accurate surrogate for uncontrollable changes in firm costs; . . . (e) a price adjustment mechanism that includes a tolerably accurate surrogate for the firm's ability to enhance its productive efficiency and that divides expected productivity increases equitably between the firm and consumers; . . . and (g) avoidance of use or threatened use of profit data for any regulatory purposes. . . .

A. Initial Price Level

The starting point in designing a price level regulation regime is to select an initial ceiling price. Consistent with political reality and experience to date, Hillman and Braeutigam suggest that the present regulated price should be used as a presumptive initial price level. They also identify the problem with this approach. Present regulated prices were determined through the process of profit level regulation. They reflect all of the sources of inefficiency that inhere in profit level regulation. There is every reason to expect that they are wrong, often by a wide margin. . . .

Hillman and Braeutigam note that this problem can be remedied in theory by making a one-time adjustment to the present regulated price to eliminate any significant disparities between that price and the economically efficient price. They also appear to recognize the existence of political constraints on this theoretically available corrective. I differ with them only with respect to the magnitude of this political constraint and the likelihood that it can be overcome by meritocratic arguments based on appeals to economic efficiency. I am not sure which seems less likely—convincing a utility with a new plant to accept a fifty percent reduction in its rates or convincing consumers of electricity supplied by a utility with an old plant to accept a one hundred percent rate increase. It is hard to imagine any political body—legislature or agency—undertaking this combination of daunting tasks.

JORDAN J. HILLMAN AND RONALD R. BRAEUTIGAM, THE POTENTIAL BENEFITS AND PROBLEMS OF PRICE LEVEL REGULATION: A MORE HOPEFUL PERSPECTIVE, 84 NORTHWESTERN LAW REVIEW 695, 695–96, 699–708 (1990) *

Our sympathetic approach to price level regulation falls short of unqualified advocacy. As Pierce states, we "urge [its] serious consideration . . . as a substitute for profit level regulation." Our position can be described more fully as follows: Given the serious deficiencies of profit level regulation and the potential efficiency benefits of price level regulation, especially in the case of diversified public utilities serving both natural monopolies and other markets with varying price elasticities, we should continue efforts to minimize certain impediments to the success of price level regulation in the natural monopoly markets.

Pierce initially seems to agree with us about the serious deficiencies of profit level regulation and the substantial potential benefits of price level regulation. In the end, however, his views and ours on the potential comparative efficacy of the two systems diverge in two major respects: (1) we attach greater weight to the identified deficiencies of profit level regulation, and (2) we are more hopeful that credible economic standards and decisional processes important to the success of a price level regime can be established. . . .

III. PROBLEMS IN IMPLEMENTING A WORKABLE PRICE LEVEL REGIME: SOME COMPARATIVE VIEWS

As noted at the outset, the major points of difference between us and Pierce do not involve the potential benefits theoretically available under price level regulation or the deficiencies of profit level regulation. They go instead to the likelihood of realizing the theoretical benefits of price level regulation through the operation of a workable regulatory regime and to the importance attached to current regulatory failings in assessing the potential comparative efficacy of the two regimes. In subsection III(a) we consider the first major area of disagreement.

A. Initial Price Levels and Relationships

Pierce contends that among "the conditions . . . required for price level regulation to meet its potential are: (a) an initial price level somewhere near the economically efficient price; [and] (b) initial price relationships somewhere near efficient price relationships." While we agree on the desirability of meeting this standard from the outset, we do not regard it as necessary. First, even if prices were such that total revenues equaled actual total costs, the costs themselves would likely exceed efficient levels. Second, price relation-ships are likely to reflect the impact of arbitrary cost allocations rather than current marginal costs and differential demand conditions.

On these points we all may agree. Unlike Pierce, however, we look more favorably on longer-range solutions to these problems. It may not be feasible

---

* Reprinted by special permission of Northwestern University School of Law, *Northwestern University Law Review*, Volume 84, Issue 2, pp. 695, 695–96, 699–708 (1990).

to adjust prices to efficient cost levels or market conditions immediately. The firm's revenues should not be forced down until it has had a reasonable opportunity to lower its costs. Over the long-term, though, the price adjustments needed to reflect these gradual cost reductions might be achieved through the productivity factor in the price adjustment formula. New incentives and the resulting potential for affecting cost reductions could be a valid factor in estimating likely future productivity. . . .

Similarly, as regards initial price relationships, Pierce correctly attributes to us the belief that the immediate elimination of inefficient price relationships is not in the cards. Once again, however, the answer lies in more gradual adjustments over time, under circumstances in which cost allocations and their resulting nonmarket influence on price relationships will have been eliminated. . . .

C. The Inflation Index

Pierce's first concern regarding the operation of the inflation index is "that surrogates based on the general level of inflation will not perform well." He has greater hopes, however, that a more complex index "tailored to a particular industry or firm" could serve "tolerably well" as a cost surrogate. We agree that the use of readily available inflation indices such as the Consumer Price Index, the Producer Price Index, or the Gross National Price Index may offer little more than the virtue of simplicity. We also agree that, within limits, precision should not be sacrificed to simplicity. As we have emphasized in the book, the "central aim" of the index is not to reflect "changes in the purchasing power of money," but "the impact of inflation on the firm's costs."

Having stated the desired character of an inflation index, Pierce suggests that politicians and regulators will opt for the simplicity and safety of established measures of inflation rather than use industry or firm-specific indices. In general, the problem of political manipulation under price level regulation can be taken no more lightly than under profit level regulation. However, as a practical matter, it will be difficult at best to predict whether a general or specific index is more likely to prove politically palatable. To opt a priori for greater precision in the inflation index is to start with the advantage of greater logic. Moreover, if the overall price adjustment formula should generate excessive political heat, regulators will likely find the productivity factor more manipulable to their purposes. (This possibility gives rise to concerns addressed below.) . . .

D. The Productivity Factor

Pierce attributes excessive pessimism to us in suggesting that we seem to recognize as "impossible" the inclusion of a term in the price adjustment formula "that allocates to consumers some portion of anticipated productivity gains." Our book does set out the difficulties in any quest for precision in resolving the essentially technical problem (i.e., the likely productivity rate) and the largely political problem (i.e., how the projected productivity gains should be allocated between the firm and its consumers). We also recognize that political opportunism can corrupt the technical decision and that all of these difficulties must be considered in assessing the potential efficacy of a price level regime. But at no point do we declare, or mean to imply, that the undertaking is "impossible."

For one thing, we question whether exactitude in determining the productivity rate and in allocating the productivity gains is essential to a reasonable degree of success. To operate successfully the inflation deflator (consisting of the portion of the productivity rate allocated to consumers) cannot be so high as to impair the financial integrity of the firm. But it should be high enough to give promise that the productivity adjustment will operate to keep overall price levels below what might otherwise be justified by cost inflation alone. The productivity adjustment should work tolerably well if it satisfies these goals and provides some rewards for managerial efficiency. Even for these relatively modest objectives, the initial effort may require adjustment in the light of experience. That is why even "final" decisions must be viewed as tentative. . . .

G. *Minimizing the Use of Profits as a Regulatory Standard*

Again, we all agree that threatened recourse to the traditional cost standards of profit level regulation could erode the firm's efficiency incentives under price level regulation. The erosion will vary with the strength of the threat and the imminence of the recourse. The main pressure points for applying these standards will be found in adjustments to the productivity factor and in special procedures to reflect nonprogrammed exogenous changes in cost or demand.

As for the productivity factor, the quest for a suitable slice of the productivity pie will be viewed widely as an issue of equity. As such, it invites a political solution that may well center on the question, "How is the company doing?" Indeed, that question may be asked in respect to the firm's total earnings as well as its earnings in the relevant regulated market. Focusing on regulated operations, however, if profits are higher than some anticipated level, the cause may be external or internal to the firm's operations. Higher profits may result from an inflation rate below the index rate (i.e., external) or from greater than expected internal efficiency improvements. However distinctive the economic causes, a common political denominator may be sought in the firm's earnings. . . .

It is with regard to the proper role of profits in determining price levels that Pierce seems to disagree most fundamentally with us in assessing the potential efficacy of price level regulation. We understand him to counsel reliance on profit levels rather than price levels in assessing the welfare consequences of a regulatory system. In our view, the most serious failings of profit level regulation arise from this mistaken contention.

The profits of regulated firms are neither the prime measure of general welfare nor of the welfare of the regulated firm's consumers. A principal measure of general welfare under any regulatory system is whether the desired output is produced at the lowest feasible costs. The economy is not well served by the fact that the regulated firm's revenues do not exceed its total allowed costs if, in fact, those costs are significantly higher than those which would prevail under a proper incentive system. In turn, comparative consumer welfare under alternative regulatory regimes does not revolve around whether the firm's revenues exceed its costs. From the consumer's viewpoint, the question is whether the desired services are available at higher or lower prices.

The first task in measuring consumer welfare under price level regulation is to develop a credible surrogate for the illusory profit level standard, the hallmark of cost based regulation. To this end our book suggests an econometric methodology for comparing actual current prices under price level regulation with projections of those that might be expected had profit level regulation continued. The process would involve a regression model that relates price movements under the former profit level regime to a set of economic factors exogenous to the firm. The regression relationships could then be applied to current exogenous variables to project prices which would be in effect under a continuing profit level regime. In addition, as long as an appreciable sample of comparable firms remains under profit level regulation, "yardstick" comparisons can be made of changes in the prices of firms and sectors under the separate regimes.

Nevertheless, the reality must be recognized that the profit level standard for regulated firms is likely to persist as a politically significant measure of welfare. The second task, therefore, is to retain its use in a manner that minimizes its impairment of the firm's efficiency incentives. In general, this might be achieved by limited regulatory recourse to earnings in the firm's regulated sector, as determined by Generally Accepted Accounting Principles. . . .

I. The Problem of Service Quality

Pierce correctly observes that the managerial quest for cost reduction under price level regulation also "has the potential to create incentives for regulated firms to reduce service quality to large classes of customers." While we recognize the problem, we do not share his pessimism regarding the inability of regulators to deal with it. First, there exists a market-type constraint to which any regulated firm is subject. That is, any incentive to cut costs through reduced service quality "will operate only to the point that the financial and psychic costs of dealing with complaints of consumers and regulators are less than the added profits." Beyond such informal limits, we see no serious impediments to the development by regulators of service standards governing reliability, technical quality, and responsiveness to complaints. Such standards currently are used as a measure of service quality in British Telecom's regulated markets. If necessary, compliance with similar standards can be enforced through fines or other financial penalties. . . .

NOTES AND QUESTIONS

1. As noted earlier, analysts criticize cost-of-service ratemaking because prices are based on average cost, rather than marginal cost. Proponents of price ceilings claim that their approach is preferable to the profit level approach in part because a utility will set prices based on its marginal costs, as long as the prices are not higher than the price ceiling. Why will utilities base prices on marginal costs under this approach? Professor Pierce objects that the initial price set under this approach is unlikely to reflect a utility's marginal cost, and that the prices that a utility sets for different types of customers (price relationships) are likewise unlikely to reflect the company's marginal costs. What is the basis of Pierce's objection? What is Hillman's and Braeutigam's response?

2. According to the formula used by British Telecommunications, the present price equals the initial price, plus inflation, minus a 3 percent productivity adjustment factor (CPI -3). What is the function of the productivity adjustment? Why is it necessary? Professor Pierce also has doubts about how the adjustments for productivity and inflation would function. What does he allege is the problem with the inflation and productivity adjustments, and what responses do Hillman and Braeutigam give? Pierce and Hillman and Braeutigam also differ concerning the extent to which, if any, a regulator should consider a utility's profits in adjusting the price ceiling. What is the basis of this disagreement?

3. Price ceilings have been adopted in a number of regulatory areas. As Professor Pierce mentions, the Federal Communications Commission (FCC) adopted price ceilings for AT&T's long distance service.[55] Pierce also notes that the FCC had under consideration a similar system for local exchange carriers (LEC), and it subsequently adopted this proposal.[56] The Federal Energy Regulatory Commission (FERC) uses a price ceiling known as "trended original cost" for controlling the prices charged by interstate natural gas pipelines. This method "applie[s a] 'real' rate of return (that is, one that *removes* the effects of inflation) to a net original cost rate base that itself is adjusted to reflect the impact of inflation."[57] Congress established ceiling prices for gas producers in the Natural Gas Policy Act.[58] State utility regulators have also turned to price ceilings, particularly for the regulation of intrastate telephone service.[59]

Please note, however, that regardless of how attractive a particular rate theory may be, the regulatory agency must follow its enabling legislation. In *Farmers Union Central Exchange, Inc. v. FERC*, 734 F. 2d 1486 (D.C. Cir. 1984), for example, the price ceiling was set so high that the court invalidated it because it was not connected to the "just and reasonable" rate requirement of the statute.

---

[55] Policy and Rules Concerning Rates for Dominant Carriers, Report and Order and Second Further Notice of Proposed Rulemaking, 4 FCC Rcd. 2873 (1989); *rev'd in part, American Tel. & Tel. v. FCC*, 974 F.2d 1351 (D.C. Cir. 1992). The policy was reconsidered in 1991. Memorandum Opinion and Order on Reconsideration, 6 FCC Rcd. 665 (1991). *See generally* Ghosh, *The Future of FCC Dominant Carrier Rate Regulation, The Price Caps Scheme*, 41 Fed. Comm. L. 401 (1989).

[56] 5 FCC Rcd 2176 (1990); Second Report and Order, 5 FCC Rcd 6786 (1990); Order on Reconsideration, 6 FCC Rcd 2637 (1991); *aff'd sub. nom. National Rural Telecom. Ass'n v. FCC*, 988 F.2d 174 (D.C. Cir. 1993).

[57] Brose, *Oil Pipelines*, 3 Energy L. & Transactions 85-42 (D. Muchow & W. Mogel eds. 1991).

[58] 15 U.S.C. §§ 3301-3432 (1988). *See also South Dakota Pub. Util. Comm'n v. FERC*, 934 F.2d 346 (D.C. Cir. 1991).

[59] *See* Meitzen, *Recent State Legislation for Telecommunications: Brave New World, or Bad Public Utility Law?*, 4 Geo. Mason U. L. Rev. 99 (1993).

4. The Public Utility Regulatory Policies Act of 1978 authorized another form of price ceiling.[60] The Act requires state utility commissions to require electric utilities to purchase power from small power producers and qualified cogenerators at a price that represents each utility's "full avoided cost" of generating electricity. A utility's "full avoided cost" is the cost to the utility of producing the next increment of electricity or the cost to the utility of purchasing replacement power.[61] How does this price ceiling protect consumers; *i.e*, why are consumers no worse off under this approach than cost-of-service ratemaking?

5. Chapter 2 discussed how policy ideas become enmeshed in the political system as they are wielded by interest groups and regulators who are seeking reform. In addition to the previous excerpts, reformers can consult a robust literature on price level regulation. For further study, the reader can consult a number of reports,[62] monographs,[63] and articles.[64]

3. MARKET BASED RATES

In the 1980s, FERC began a series of experiments with market-based ratemaking, particularly at the point of bulk power sales. In essence, FERC would not set rates under the traditional cost-of-service basis and would allow utilities to negotiate to purchase bulk power or purchase through a bidding process under particular circumstances, such as: "[W]here there is no affiliation between the seller and the purchaser (and any utility interconnected with the purchaser), where the seller does not own or control transmissions that reaches the buyer, and where the capacity being offered is new capacity."[65] As will be explained in more detail below, FERC's central concerns with this method are that the seller lacks market power and that market-based pricing can open up transmission.

Now FERC entertains requests for market-based rates on an ad hoc basis.[66] The excerpt below is from FERC Opinion No. 349, authorizing a market-based rate for the Public Service Company of Indiana (PSI) for the sale of up to 450 megawatts of power. PSI's request for a market-based rate, which is referred in the case as "FS-1 power," was opposed by another utility, UtilCo Group,

---

[60] Pub. L. 95-617, 92 Stat. 3117 (1978) (codified at 16 U.S.C. § 2601 et seq.).

[61] *See American Paper Inst. v. American Elec. Power Serv. Corp.*, 461 U.S. 402 (1983).

[62] *E.g.*, NATIONAL TELECOMMUNICATIONS AND INFORMATION ADMINISTRATION, U.S. DEPT. OF COMMERCE, REGULATORY ALTERNATIVES REPORT (1989).

[63] *E.g.*, J. HILLMAN & R. BRAEUTIGAM, PRICE LEVEL REGULATION FOR DIVERSIFIED PUBLIC UTILITIES (1989).

[64] *See, e.g., Symposium: Harvard Electricity Policy Group: Regulatory Decisionmaking Reform*, 8 ADMIN. L.J. AM. U. 789 (1995); Liston, *Price-Cap Versus Rate-of-Regulation*, 5 J. REG. ECON. 25 (1993); Kovacic, *Commitment in Regulation: Defense Contracting and Extensions to Price Caps*, 3 J. REG. ECON. 219 (1991); Isaac, *Price Cap Regulation: a Case Study of Some Pitfalls of Implementation*, 3 J. REG. ECON. 193 (1991).

[65] Stafford, *Electric Wholesale Power Sales at Market-Based Rates,* 12 ENERGY L.J. 291, 292 (1991) (suggested proposal by FERC Commissioner Trabandt).

[66] Market-based rates are permitted under FERC Order No. 888. Regarding these rates see Lock & Stein, *Electricity Transmission*, 4 ENERGY L. & TRANSACTIONS ¶ 81.03[4] (D. Muchow & W. Mogel eds. 1991); Norton & Camet, *Electricity: Open Access, Transmission & Comparability*, 4 ENERGY L. & TRANSACTIONS ¶ 82.05[2][B] (D. Muchow & W. Mogel eds. 2001).

Inc. (UtilCo). In its opinion, FERC explains its authority to adopt market-based rates and why such rates will benefit consumers.

PUBLIC SERVICE COMMISSION OF INDIANA
51 FERC ¶ 61,367 (1990)

. . . . In its request for rehearing of our hearing order, UtilCo Group, Inc. (UtilCo) argues that the Commission erred in concluding that it could accept for filing a wholesale rate by a regulated public utility capped exclusively at the buyer's avoided costs. UtilCo claims that PSI's proposal is tantamount to deregulation of wholesale sales of electricity and may, therefore, exceed the Commission's authority to approve just and reasonable rates under sections 205 and 206 of the FPA. According to UtilCo, a public utility's rates are just and reasonable only if they are based on a variant of sellers' costs. . . .

The rehearing request and comments thus raise several interrelated issues regarding the approval as just and reasonable of PSI's market-based pricing. These issues, which will be addressed in turn, are: (1) What is the Commission's authority under the FPA to approve rates which are not based on the seller's embedded costs? (2) Why is PSI an appropriate case to deviate from traditional cost-based ratemaking? (3) Is non-traditional pricing just and reasonable in this particular case, and should the buyer's certification of avoided cost be retained? . . .

1. Commission Authority to Accept Non-Cost-Based Rates

Under section 205 of the FPA the Commission must ensure that all rates for the transmission or sale of electric energy at wholesale in interstate commerce are "just and reasonable." Section 206 of the FPA authorizes the Commission, after a hearing, to fix by order a rate determined to be unjust or unreasonable. However, neither the FPA nor its legislative history defines "just and reasonable."

While UtilCo is correct that the Commission historically has accepted rates under section 205 of the FPA based on the supplier's cost of service, the FPA does not require the Commission to use any particular methodology in determining whether a proposed rate satisfies the statutory standards of section 205. Rather, the courts have deferred to the Commission's reasoned choice of ratemaking methods. The Supreme Court, in discussing the "just and reasonable" standard of the Natural Gas Act (NGA) in *FPC v. Hope Natural Gas Co.,* stated that:

> Under the statutory standard of "just and reasonable" it is the result reached and not the method employed which is controlling. . . . It is not the theory but the impact of the rate order which counts. If the total effect of the rate order cannot be said to be unjust and unreasonable, judicial inquiry . . . is at an end. The fact that the method employed to reach that result may contain infirmities is not then important.

The Supreme Court reaffirmed these fundamental principles in *Duquesne Light Co. v. Barasch.* The Commission thus has the discretion to consider a variety of factors to determine whether a rate is just and reasonable.

Another fundamental premise articulated by the courts is that, under the FPA, the ratemaking methodology employed by the Commission must serve a legitimate statutory objective and produce a rate that is within a "zone of reasonableness." This zone is "bounded at one end by the investor interest against confiscation and at the other end by the consumer interest against exorbitant rates." In addition, when the Commission adopts a ratemaking methodology that differs from historical practice, the Commission must explain why this departure meets these statutory objectives. . . .

As discussed below, we disagree with UtilCo that our approval of market-based rates under the circumstances of this case is inconsistent . . . with any of the case law cited above.

2. Non-Traditional Pricing Is Appropriate for PSI . . .

The electric utility industry is moving from a period of excess supply into a period of new supply needs. It is estimated that the Nation will need to build or conserve over 100 gigawatts of capacity over the next decade, in order to meet supply needs. Unlike PSI, many utilities and regions of the country are short on supply, and the Nation faces the need to more efficiently use existing supply and encourage new supply. In recent years, there has been a substantial increase in competitive activity within the industry. . . .

The industry has also developed in ways that make traditional cost-of-service rate regulation inappropriate in some circumstances. . . . The outcome has been that coordination trade has grown to the point where about a third of the electricity sold by IOUs [independent operating units] to end users is purchased from other sources, often under highly competitive conditions in the coordination market. Utilities thus have had expanded options to buy lower cost electricity from neighboring utilities to replace higher cost electricity that would be self-generated. End-use customers have benefitted from this bulk power trade. . . .

. . . We conclude that the PSI proposal is consistent with the Commission's public interest "responsibility to further the maintenance of an adequate and efficient electric utility industry."

PSI's proposal will help to fulfill the Commission's statutory objectives in three ways:

(1) It will allow existing base-load generating assets to be more fully utilized. It is not efficient to build new generating plants if existing ones can do the job at lower cost. . . .

(2) It will provide PSI's neighboring utilities with new power supply options from PSI and its competitors because of PSI's commitment to provide firm transmission service. These options are likely to cost less than those built under traditional cost-of-service regulation. . . .

(3) It will create more incentives for productivity-enhancing innovation by placing greater competitive pressure on potential suppliers in the region. The experience with nontraditional technologies under the Public Utility Regulatory Policies Act of 1978 demonstrates that innovative activity is encouraged under relaxed regulation. . . .

In sum, we believe nontraditional pricing is appropriate for PSI in light of recent events occurring in the electric utility industry, and because PSI's proposal will create incentives for the efficient use of resources, to the benefit of all parties: PSI will be better off by marketing its underutilized capacity, the buyers will be better off for being able to purchase needed capacity at prices and on terms more competitive than those offered by their alternative suppliers, and the ultimate customers of both PSI and the buying utilities will benefit from rate reductions resulting from the passthrough of the savings.

3. Non-Traditional Pricing Will Result in Just and Reasonable Rates for PSI

There are several non-cost factors that we have considered in determining that nontraditional pricing in this case will result in rates that are within the legally mandated zone of reasonableness.

First, as has been demonstrated above, PSI lacks market power over generation in the relevant region and it has mitigated its market power over transmission by offering long-term transmission access at cost-based rates. Thus, it is unable to increase price by restricting supply or by denying to the customer access to alternative sellers. . . .

Second, PSI must offer trades that reduce the buyer's cost if it is to succeed in selling FS-1 power. If the buyer determines that a better trade could be made with another seller, it will not trade with PSI. The benefit of the market process that allows PSI to provide a service at or below the cost of the buyer's alternatives is important from the standpoint of the buyer, its customers, and the Commission. If the buyer makes a more efficient trade as a result of PSI's program, i.e., one which results in lower overall costs, it should be able to pass these savings along to the ultimate consumer. Thus, the trade benefits the seller, the buyer, and the ultimate consumer.

Third, we have provided means of monitoring the market in which PSI's sales will take place, as well as the individual customers who purchase FS-1 power, and we will not hesitate to reimpose cost-of-service regulation if competition among generating utilities fails to improve overall efficiency as expected or if PSI gains market power with respect to FS-1 sales. . . .

As noted above, UtilCo has made much of the fact that under PSI's proposal, rates would not be tied to PSI's own costs, but rather to the costs of the purchaser. . . . UtilCo also argues that the Commission cannot rely on competition alone to keep rates within a zone of reasonableness. In response to these arguments, a few points of clarification are warranted.

Contrary to UtilCo's implication, the Commission is not in this case relying on competition alone to set rates, nor is it simply transferring the PURPA avoided cost concept to the FPA. Essential to our approval of PSI's nontraditional rates is not only the avoided cost cap, but also the record evidence as to lack of market power on the part of the seller, our examination of the market in which the FS-1 sales will take place, and the monitoring mechanism which will allow us to readily re-impose cost-based rates on PSI. It is true that any market process should reveal to a purchaser its alternative supply options (including self-generation and purchase options), and that a rational purchaser will not purchase power at a price higher than that of its alternatives (i.e., higher than its avoided cost). The difference is that here we have concluded that a market process will be at work wherein the seller receiving market-based rates will not be able to exercise market power in the relevant market, and wherein all potential purchasers have a number of meaningful supply alternatives, in addition to self-generation. Therefore, we are not simply equating avoided cost to a just and reasonable rate.

We will retain PSI's proposed avoided cost certification. PSI voluntarily has proposed that FS-1 purchasers must certify to us that the price they pay PSI is at or below their expected alternative cost of similar electric power. The certification will ensure against the possibility of excessive rates, i.e., that the buyer is no worse off than if PSI were not an entrant in the market. Under the circumstances presented, PSI will have to be the more efficient supplier if it is to beat potential buyers' existing alternatives. The written certification will provide the buyers' customers, state commissions, and this Commission a verification under oath that the buyer has evaluated alternative supply options, and that PSI is not charging the buyer any more than the cost of the buyer's alternatives.

We conclude that PSI's proposed rates will fall within the zone of reasonableness articulated in *Hope, Duquesne,* and *Jersey Central.* At one end of the zone, the rates will not be excessive to the buyers and their customers because: the buyers will certify that the rate will not exceed their expected alternative cost of similar electric power, based on our market findings and the conditions imposed herein, market forces will serve to constrain the rates within a zone of reasonableness; and we will be able to monitor the market and to reimpose cost-based rates should circumstances warrant. At the other end of the zone, the rates will not be confiscatory to PSI because sales under FS-1 will be strictly voluntary on PSI's part. Therefore, PSI's proposed rates will be just and reasonable under the FPA.

NOTES AND QUESTIONS

1. How do market-based rates reduce the information that FERC must obtain in order to control the wholesale price of electricity? How do market based rates produce a rate of return that is within the zone of reasonableness? What protection do investors have? Would PSI be willing to enter into a contract that was financially disadvantageous for its owners? What protection do ratepayers have? How does this requirement that PSI cannot charge more than the buyer's "avoided cost" guarantee that ratepayers will be no worse off than if the buyer had generated the electricity itself, or bought it from another source besides PSI?

2. FERC sought to protect buyers in two others ways besides requiring that PSI could charge no more than the purchaser's avoided cost. First, PSI had to establish that it lacked market power over generation in the relevant region. As discussed earlier in this chapter, the term "market power" refers to the ability of a seller to raise its price significantly above the competitive level for a considerable period of time. In other words, if PSI attempted to charge more for its electricity than other generators, there is no reason why the purchasers could not turn to other sellers. How does this finding protect consumers?

Second, PSI had to agree to offer long-distance transmission rates to other generators which sought to sell power to PSI's buyers. Thus, there was a *quid pro quo* in the experiment—the utility could experiment with market-based, rather than government-set rates, in exchange for open access on its transmission system, in the name of both competition and efficiency. How does open access protect consumers?

3. In the foregoing discussion of the changes in the electric industry there lurks an awareness of consumer power. The traditional rate formula encouraged capital expansion and construction into the 1970s. At that time, costs escalated and the price elasticity of demand for electricity proved to be more elastic than economists once thought. In other words, consumers began making smarter energy choices by consuming proportionately less electricity in response to price increases. Utilities, then, found themselves in an awkward position. They committed capital to expansion projects and needed to recover that capital from consumers. Unfortunately, consumers were looking for cheaper sources of electricity other than their local public utility.

4. Congress unwittingly discovered that there was a dynamic market in electricity through the Public Utility Regulatory Policies Act (PURPA).[67] PURPA was signed into law for the purpose of lessening dependence on foreign oil and promoting conservation of fossil fuels, including those used to produce electricity. Under PURPA, small generating facilities known as qualifying facilities (QFs) were encouraged to generate electricity either for self consumption or for resale. To the extent that the QFs were unable to consume or sell all of the electricity that they generated, the local public utility was obligated by law to purchase the excess electricity that was generated for "avoided cost." Avoided cost was defined as the cost the utility would have incurred had it generated the electricity itself or purchased the electricity from another source. *American Paper Inst. v. American Electric Power Service Corp.*, 416 U.S. 402, 404 (1983). What was surprising about this statute was how successful it was in bringing non-traditional generators online. In short, the electricity market was competitive, consumers were demanding cheaper electricity and producers were available to generate it.

---

[67] 16 U.S.C. § 2601 et seq. (1994).

Chapter 5

BOTTLENECKS I: ENTRY AND EXIT CONTROLS AND THE NATURAL GAS INDUSTRY

In the previous chapter, we examined the regulation of natural monopolies through price controls. Price controls alone, however, do not correct the market failures caused by natural monopoly. Recall that monopolies can raise prices, reduce output, and create social losses simultaneously. Price controls can limit the profit levels of natural monopolies and they can set reasonable prices for consumers but they do not effectively assure the adequacy or the reliability of service. Instead, entry and exit controls address service problems.

In cases of natural monopoly, entry and exit restrictions limit, in some circumstances to only one, the number of actors who may participate in a given and identified market. This limitation of the number of actors as a regulatory control of monopoly power may seem counterintuitive. If the market imperfection is insufficient competition, then the seemingly obvious response should be to encourage, not limit, competition by increasing the number of firms in a market. As it turns out, the obvious response is not necessarily efficient. As you have already seen, natural monopolies enjoy economies of scale such that they can reduce their variable costs over the entire range of output. The additional fixed costs (capital investment) by a competitor is wasteful and inefficient. Instead, the proper response to insure efficiency and reliability of service is to restrict entry and impose an obligation to serve. Once entry is restricted, regulation makes exit costly. Thus, costly exit is a condition of the regulatory compact in which government sets prices in exchange for the utility undertaking an obligation to provide service within a franchise or service area. The integrity of the exclusive service area and of the service obligation is maintained through entry and exit controls.

Restricting a market to one producer, even to promote efficiencies derived from a natural monopoly's economies of scale, brings problems of its own. Specifically, a firm may control monopoly assets which hinder the development of more competitive markets. In the case of the electricity industry, regulating the industry as a monopoly led to the transmission bottleneck described at the end of the last chapter. This same transportation bottleneck occurs in the natural gas industry and can be seen as a regulatory failure.

The story of the development and regulation of both the electric power and the natural gas industries is illustrative of the life cycle of government regulation described earlier. This chapter will illustrate the stages of competition, market failure, regulation, regulatory failure and the regulatory reform and deregulation experienced by the natural gas industry. The chapter will focus on how the "nonprice" controls of entry and exit regulations can create (and later distort) a market. Here we look at the success and then failure of regulations aimed at protecting the one firm in a regulated market and at attempting to assure service reliability for consumers.

In a recent book about natural gas regulation, Yale economist Paul MacAvoy writes: "The natural gas industry over the past sixty years has provided a natural experiment in regulation's effects on the performance of suppliers in wholesale and retail markets."[1] MacAvoy should know because he has long studied the federal regulations of the natural gas industry starting with his doctoral dissertation published in 1962. In addition, together with now Justice Stephen Breyer, MacAvoy co-authored two seminal papers on the need for deregulating the natural gas industry.[2] Not surprisingly, MacAvoy is critical of government interventions into natural gas markets, arguing that price regulations caused shortages, then large surpluses known as a "gas bubble" because of inconsistent federal and state regulations causing a dual market. He also concludes that regarding 60 years of regulation that "Nothing has 'worked,' in that there were no gains to consumers, nor were there gains to producers or pipelines."[3]

This chapter tells that story through the lens of entry and exit controls. Simply, by controlling the firms that can act in a market, the supply and price of a product can be affected. For the last two or more decades, the federal government has been "deregulating" the natural gas market in the hope of moving gas from suppliers to customers or end users more efficiently. Deregulation, however, is not complete, controls remain in place and the efficiency of the market is questioned. The reasons for the partial deregulation, and resultant continuing regulations, are also the subject of this chapter.

A. IMPOSING ENTRY CONTROLS

Licensing is a regulatory tool that has been applied to a wide variety of industries—from hydroelectricity to hospitals and from natural gas to radio and television. It is tailored to monitor different aspects of any given industry. Among other things, licensing permits the government (by controlling entry) to assess the financial qualifications of a regulated entity before it enters a market, to approve before construction the plans and designs of a nuclear power plant, to consider the environmental consequences of a regulatee's actions before it acts, or to analyze the market effects of a utility merger before it occurs among many other licensing conditions. Licensing is used to establish

---

[1] P. MACAVOY, THE NATURAL GAS MARKET: SIXTY YEARS OF REGULATION AND DEREGULATION xiii (2000).

[2] Breyer & MacAvoy, *The Natural Gas Shortage and Regulation of Natural Gas Producers*, 86 HARV. L. REV. 941 (1973); S. BREYER & A. MACAVOY, ENERGY REGULATION BY THE FEDERAL POWER COMMISSION (1974).

[3] MACAVOY, *supra* note 1 at xiv.

a market by limiting entry and/or exit as a form of economic regulation. This chapter studies licensing as a form of entry and exit control in the context of the natural gas industry.

1. THE NATURAL GAS INDUSTRY[4]

Today, natural gas accounts for approximately 25% of the energy consumed in the United States (and most of that gas is produced domestically). Natural gas consumption is divided among residential, industrial, and commercial end users. Residential users consume natural gas for heating, cooling, and cooking. Industrial users consume this resource for heating, direct fuel use, and for the generation of electricity. (Importantly, many industrial end users adapt systems to allow quick conversions from natural gas to alternate energy sources such as fuel oil and coal during periods when those competing fuels can be obtained at lower costs.) Commercial users consume natural gas for heating their buildings and for producing the energy needed for internal operations.

The natural gas fuel cycle consists of exploration, production, transmission, and distribution. Exploration involves the search for both oil and natural gas by oil companies. Less than 15% of all exploratory wells drilled encounter economically recoverable reserves. Most exploration—approximately 85% of all wells drilled—is performed by independent oil companies instead of the major, integrated companies.

Production companies are often sister companies to the exploration companies; in some instances, a firm operates as both an exploration and production company. Sometimes, but not often, producers are affiliated with pipeline companies. Producers develop, exploit, and produce the natural gas (and oil) that is discovered in the field. This cycle involves drilling and completion of new wells, recovery of natural gas, and the processing of the gas for sale to natural gas pipeline and gathering companies.

Once there are producing wells, the production company, or another entity called a gatherer, will build a pipeline to gather natural gas from the individual wells and sell it to any one of several potential buyers. The gas may be purchased by a nearby natural gas processing plant or local industrial users. Intrastate or interstate pipelines may buy the gas for resale in another location. Or independent marketers will buy it to aggregate a supply of gas for eventual sale to intrastate or interstate pipelines.

Pipeline companies ("pipelines") usually wear two hats. As merchants of natural gas, pipelines purchase gas from producers and transmit the gas from the wellhead to purchasers—either the wholesale local distribution company (LDC) or the industrial customer. This transportation and sale of gas owned by the pipelines is known as a bundled transaction, and the fee to consumers includes the cost of the natural gas and the cost of its transportation. Pipelines also act solely as transporters of natural gas. In this situation, pipelines do not buy the gas from the producer but only transmit the gas for a transportation fee, thus acting as common carrier between the producer or marketer and the direct industrial or LDC buyers. The distribution of natural gas to

---

[4] See J. TOMAIN AND J. HICKEY, ENERGY LAW AND POLICY ch.7 (1989).

residential, commercial, and other industrial customers is accomplished by LDCs which are often privately owned local public utilities who charge the end-user a rate for the gas used at the burnertip. These rates are set by state public utility commissions.

2. EARLY REGULATION

Initially, gas was produced from coal (and later cabureted water) by unregulated private companies which also distributed it to nearby customers. Its primary use was lighting and was increasingly popular through the last half of the 19th century. Gas companies soon found it profitable to divide service territories among themselves and agree not to engage in price competition. This collusion grew and evolved into gas trusts which curtailed competition over a greater area. These trusts eventually captured the attention of municipal and state regulators in the first decades of the 20th century.[5]

About this time large oil and natural gas fields were discovered in the southwestern United States. At first, producers considered natural gas to be a nuisance by-product of oil exploration and production and they "flared" or burned it in the fields or permitted it to escape into the atmosphere. The practices were eventually eliminated as a market for natural gas developed over time. In the 1920s and 1930s, there was more natural gas (and oil) being produced than the market could absorb because the Great Depression drove down prices. As the price of natural gas (and oil) fell precipitously, natural energy producing states passed gas (and oil) conservation legislation to support these industries.[6] As the economy recovered, large pipelines were constructed to transport natural gas from the fields to refineries in other parts of the country.

3. TRADITIONAL FEDERAL REGULATION

Prior to 1938, the federal government did not regulate natural gas production or transportation. In 1924, the United States Supreme Court, in *Missouri v. Kansas Natural Gas Co.*,[7] ruled that the Commerce Clause prohibited the states from regulating the wholesale sales and transportation of natural gas sold across state lines. While states could regulate intrastate sales, there was no federal regulation of interstate sales and transportation.

This ruling strengthened the monopoly position of the few major interstate pipeline companies that owned much of the physical facilities used to transport natural gas throughout the country. These pipeline companies had substantial monopoly and monopsony power. These pipelines had monopoly power because they were the only source of natural gas in many local areas. This meant the pipelines could set their own sales price to LDCs and other direct consumers without state regulatory oversight. At the same time, the pipelines were the only buyer of natural gas in many areas, which gave them monopsony

---

[5] W. TROESKEN, WHY REGULATE UTILITIES?: THE NEW INSTITUTIONAL ECONOMICS AND THE CHICAGO GAS INDUSTRY, 1849–1924 (1996); McManus, *Natural Gas* in D. MUCHOW & W. MOGEL, 2 ENERGY LAW & TRANSACTIONS ch. 50 (1997).

[6] *See* N. ELY, THE OIL AND GAS CONSERVATION STATUTES (ANNOTATED) (1933).

[7] 265 U.S. 298 (1924).

power. A buyer has monopsony power when it is the only purchaser for a particular good or service. As the only purchaser, the buyer is in a position to dictate the purchase price to sellers, and because the sellers cannot sell their output to another buyer, the sellers must accept this price. Thus, a firm with monopsony power is in a position to pay less than a competitive price for the good or service it purchases. A pipeline with monopsony and monopoly power paid less than competitive wholesale prices for the natural gas it purchased, and it resold the gas for more than competitive retail prices. This absence of regulation by either the state or federal government created what was called the "Attleboro gap."[8]

Because of their market power, interstate natural gas pipelines were able to raise prices or threaten curtailment to distribution companies until they received their demanded price. In response to complaints, the Federal Trade Commission investigated the situation of pipelines and in 1935 issued a report which found that interstate natural gas pipelines had monopoly and monopsony power which the pipelines were exercising to the economic disadvantage of consumers. As a result of the FTC report, Congress passed the Natural Gas Act of 1938 (NGA).[9]

The key provisions of the NGA are its ratemaking and licensing procedures. Regarding licenses, the Act holds:

> No natural-gas company or person which will be a natural-gas company upon completion of any proposed construction or extension shall engage in the transportation or sale of natural gas, subject to the jurisdiction of the Commission, or undertake the construction or extension of any facilities therefor, or acquire or operate any such facilities or extensions thereof, unless there is in force with respect to such natural-gas company a certificate of public convenience and necessity issued by the Commission authorizing such acts or operations. . . .[10]

Section 7(e) of the NGA states that the certificate of public convenience and necessity (i.e., the license) will be granted when the Commission finds that the applicant is able and willing to perform the proposed service and that the certificate is required by the public convenience and necessity.

The D.C. Circuit discussed Section 7 in *Northern Natural Gas Company v. FERC* as follows:

> [S]ections 4, 5, and 7 of the Act reveal a single and coherent design. Under sections 4 and 5, the Commission determines the allowable price of natural gas services, holding price (i.e., rate) to a "just and reasonable" standard. Under section 7, the Commission determines what services may be provided (as well as through what facilities), reviewing them under a "public convenience and necessity" standard. Congress' concern in regulating the provision of services and facilities under section 7 was to avoid "the possibilities of waste, uneconomic

---

[8] *Public Utilities Comm'n v. Attleboro Steam & Elec. Co.*, 273 U.S. 83 (1927).

[9] 15 U.S.C. § 717 et seq. (1994).

[10] 15 U.S.C. § 717f(c) (1994).

and uncontrolled extensions," thereby "conserving one of the country's valuable but exhaustible energy resources" as well as ensuring "the lowest possible reasonable rate consistent with the maintenance of adequate service in the public interest."[11]

Certification under Section 7 of the Natural Gas Act is thus an integral part of the regulatory scheme creating an interstate natural gas market. Through licensing, the government authorizes specific firms to enter the interstate market. Licensing regulations established under the authority of the Act require applicants to disclose financial and marketing data, the location of facilities, design capacity, gas supply, and environmental compliance among other information.[12] Through ratemaking, the government sets the prices that can be charged in that market. And, as we will show below, through exit controls, the government attempts to maintain reliable service in the interstate market.

In *FPC v. Transcontinental Gas Corporation*, below, the Supreme Court was asked to review the FPC's denial of a certificate of public convenience and necessity. The FPC based its denial on the grounds of the public interest. The Transcontinental Gas Company (Transco) sought the certificate to sell natural gas to a private utility company in New York, Consolidated Edison (Con Ed), for use as a boiler fuel. Among other arguments, FPC staff argued on "policy" grounds that boiler use was inferior to other uses such as residential and commercial heating, and that the direct sale would raise prices to other consumers. Con Ed asserted as its "policy" argument that the burning of natural gas was preferable environmentally to burning coal. As you read the case, notice the factors that the FPC considered in the licensing process and notice how the Court handles the policy arguments offered by the parties.

FEDERAL POWER COMMISSION v. TRANSCONTINENTAL GAS CO.
365 U.S. 1 (1961)

MR. CHIEF JUSTICE WARREN delivered the opinion of the Court.

The question in these cases is whether the Federal Power Commission has gone beyond the scope of its delegated authority in denying a certificate of public convenience and necessity under § 7(e) of the Natural Gas Act of 1938. The principal respondents are Transcontinental Gas Pipe Line Corp. (Transco), a pipeline company engaged in transporting natural gas in interstate commerce, and Consolidated Edison Co. (Con. Ed.), a public utility in New York City which uses gas under its boilers and also sells gas to domestic consumers. . . .

Before the hearing examiner, Transco's application was opposed by the FPC staff and groups representing the coal industry. Con. Ed. intervened in favor of Transco's proposal. Transco offered proof that its application met all the conventional tests—adequate gas reserves, pipeline facilities and market for the gas—and this showing, with one immaterial exception, has never been challenged. However, the FPC's staff argued vigorously that the public

---

[11] 827 F.2d 779, 787 (D.C. Cir. 1987).

[12] 18 C.F.R. § 157.

interest would suffer were Transco's petition granted. Among the grounds advanced were that the gas was to be transported for use under industrial boilers, this disposition being an "inferior" use from the standpoint of conserving a valuable natural resource; that authorization of this and similar direct sales to major industrial users would result in preemption of pipeline capacity and gas reserves to the detriment of domestic consumers competing for gas supply; and that the effect of this sale, as well as the resulting increase in direct sales, would effect a general rise in field prices. These contentions were presented as "policy" arguments and no testimony was taken in support. Con. Ed. contended in return that certification was in the public interest, principally because a firm supply of natural gas under the Waterside boilers would reduce the air pollution problem then being aggravated by fly-ash and sulphur dioxide emissions from these boilers. . . .

On review before the full FPC, the Commission held that the broad considerations advanced by its staff were cognizable in a § 7 proceeding. The Commission agreed with respondents that the "idea of ameliorating a smoke condition found unpleasant and annoying . . . is an attractive one" but concluded that "more weighty considerations compel the denial of the grant." . . . The Court of Appeals reinstated the conclusion of the hearing examiner that the policy considerations advanced by the FPC were outside the scope of a § 7 proceeding. . . .

The principal question before this Court, then, is whether Congress intended to preclude the Commission from denying certification on the basis of the policy considerations advanced by its staff. For purposes of analysis, the litigants have grouped these factors into two broad categories. The first has been labeled the "end use" factor and reflects the Commission's concern that Con. Ed.'s proposed "inferior" use of gas under its industrial boilers would be wasteful of gas committed to the Commission's jurisdiction and, by the same token, would pre-empt space in pipelines that might otherwise be used for transportation of gas for superior uses. The second may be called the "price" consideration and involves the Commission's fear that this sale—which was executed at a price higher than the maximum filed by the Commission in the producing districts here involved—would increase the price of natural gas in the field, thus triggering a rise in the price provisions in other contracts. . . .

End use. No one disputes that natural gas is a wasting resource and that the necessity for conserving it is paramount. As we see it, the question in this case is whether the Commission, through its certification power, may prevent the waste of gas committed to its jurisdiction. One apparent method of preventing waste of gas is to limit the uses to which it may be put, uses for which another, more abundant fuel may serve equally well. Thus the Commission in this case, as it often has in the past, has declared that the use of gas under industrial boilers is an "inferior" use, the assumption being that other fuels, particularly coal, are an adequate substitute in areas where such other fuels abound. However, respondents, while conceding the premise that gas may be wasted where coal is readily available, argue that Congress has not awarded the Commission *any* powers over conservation; rather, this authority has been reserved to the States. This contention is based on the legislative history of the Natural Gas Act.

When Congress initially enacted the Natural Gas Act in 1938, all the indications were that Congress intended the States to be the primary arbiters of conservation problems. The 1938 Act was based on a 1936 report rendered by the Federal Trade Commission and the section in that report devoted to conservation stresses the powers of state bodies to adopt corrective measures. The final recommendation of the Federal Trade Commission in regard to conservation contemplated primary state authority, with federal agencies being relegated to a reporting function. This recommendation formed the basis of § 11 of the Act as ultimately passed and the section reveals a secondary role for the Commission in this regard.

However, in 1940, the Commission reported its dissatisfaction with the limited scope of § 7. The 1938 version of § 7 restricted the Commission's jurisdiction to certification of transportation into areas where the market was already being served by another natural gas company; if a pipeline wished to extend service into virgin territory, the Commission had no power to act. The Commission felt that this limitation barred it from considering "the broad social and economic effect of the use of various fuels" in a § 7 proceeding, and, in its 1940 Annual Report, the Commission urged that the restriction be deleted in order that conservation considerations might be weighed. The language used by the Commission is particularly relevant to this case:

"The Natural Gas Act as presently drafted does not enable the Commission to treat fully the serious implications of such a problem. The question should be raised as to whether the proposed use of natural gas would not result in displacing a less valuable fuel and create hardships in the industry already supplying the market, while at the same time rapidly depleting the country's natural-gas reserves. Although, for a period of perhaps 20 years, the natural gas could be so priced as to appear to offer an apparent saving in fuel costs, this would mean simply that social costs which must eventually be paid had been ignored.

"Careful study of the entire problem may lead to the conclusion that use of natural gas should be restricted by functions rather than by areas. Thus, it is especially adapted to space and water heating in urban homes and other buildings and to the various industrial heat processes which require concentration of heat, flexibility of control, and uniformity of results. Industrial uses to which it appears particularly adapted include the treating and annulling of metals, the operation of kilns in the ceramic, cement, and lime industries, the manufacture of glass in its various forms, and use as a raw material in the chemical industry. General use of natural gas under boilers for the production of steam is, however, under most circumstances of very questionable social economy."

The Commission implemented its recommendation by submitting to Congress a proposed amendment to § 7 with the restrictive language eliminated, and an amendment substantially similar to the one drafted by the Commission was enacted in 1942. . . .

. . . [W]e think it plain the Congress acquiesced in the Commission's position. . . .

Price. As we read the opinion, the Commission's second objection to certification was based on its forecast that this and similar direct sales of gas at unregulated prices higher than those allowed in sales for resale would attract gas to the high-bidding direct purchasers and thus lever upwards field prices both in direct sales and sales for resale. . . .

The question for consideration in this section, therefore, is whether in a § 7 proceeding the Commission may consider sales price or, more accurately, the effect the inflated price charged in one sale will have on future field prices. We have recently answered this question in favor of the Commission's jurisdiction. . . .

In the present case, the Commission was concerned with the effects this certification might have in the future on field prices generally. The Commission was attempting to consider not only the interests of consumers in New York but those in all States. To be compared with the problem before the Commission are the determinations that a consuming state commission may properly make in exercising authority over a direct sale. Certainly, the consuming State can regulate retail rates at which gas can be sold within the State. . . . The point is, as we have stated, that Congress did not desire an "attractive gap" in its regulatory scheme; rather, Congress intended to impose a comprehensive regulatory system on the transportation, production, and sale of this valuable natural resource. Therefore, when we are presented with an attempt by the federal authority to control a problem that is not, by its very nature, one with which state regulatory commissions can be expected to deal, the conclusion is irresistible that Congress desired regulation by federal authority rather than nonregulation. . . .

Neither this Court nor the Commission holds in this case that sales to pipelines are generally more in accord with the public interest than other sales; nor do we authorize the elimination of direct sales of gas under appropriate circumstances nor the denial of a certificate to any arbitrarily chosen group of purchasers. All we hold is that the Commission did not abuse its discretion in considering, among other factors, those of end use, preemption of pipeline facilities and price in deciding that the public convenience and necessity did not require the issuance of the certificate requested. . . .

NOTES AND QUESTIONS

1. Why did Congress require companies like Transcontinental Gas Corporation to obtain a license from the Federal Power Commission? What types of information should the regulatory agency require the utility to disclose?

2. Why did Con Ed support Transco's request for a license? What do you make of its environmental claims?

3. In its opinion, the Court noted that "natural gas is a wasting resource and that the necessity for conserving it is paramount." Also, the FPC's decision was premised on a supply shortage and on a concern about increased prices. What in all likelihood neither the Court nor the Commission knew at the time was that the natural gas "shortage" was the result of federal price regulation.[13] You will read about this regulatory failure shortly. Today, there is a

---

[13] *See* Breyer & MacAvoy, *supra* note 2.

relative abundance of this "wasting" resource. There is also an abundance of coal. Both natural gas and coal are used to generate electricity. Given contemporary sensitivity to global warming and acid rain, do you suppose that today FERC would reach the same conclusion and deny the certificate? Has FERC's statutory mandate changed?

4. *Transcontinental* examines the "end use" and "price" factors that the Commission uses in determining whether to grant a certificate of public convenience and necessity. In general, FERC considers antitrust policy,[14] conservation,[15] public interest,[16] price,[17] and size of facilities.[18] Note also that the Commission is authorized to set conditions when granting certificates.[19]

5. One of the purposes of the Natural Gas Act is to regulate the interstate sales of natural gas in the public interest. What constitutes the public interest in interstate sales of natural gas? To what extent are the market criteria examined by FERC for certification? Does the public interest differ from market-based variables? Does the public interest change over time? You will note in the next section that the market changes over time and, not surprisingly, pressure is put on regulators to change government regulation accordingly.

4.   THE BEGINNING OF REGULATORY FAILURE

Section 7 licensing proceedings required a hearing and the examination of a great deal of technical information. The theory behind this administrative process was that if the regulation of the natural gas industry is being done "in the public interest" then a careful monitoring of market entrants makes sense. After all, there is a public interest in financially stable firms providing reliable supplies of this good. Strong incumbents may complain outwardly about such administrative burdens, yet close, individual hearings tend to protect incumbents because regulator and regulatee are familiar with each other. As the industry matures, however, must the hearings be as detailed and lengthy as initial hearings? Or should the certification process be expedited? We examine these questions in this section.

The NGA explicitly regulates wholesale sales and the transportation of gas in interstate commerce by "natural gas companies." From 1938 until 1954, the FPC construed its certification authority under the NGA to reach only interstate *pipelines*; the Commission avoided regulating *producers*, believing this limitation to be its mandate from Congress. However, in *Interstate Natural Gas Co. v. FPC*,[20] federal regulation was extended to producers "affiliated" with interstate pipelines. Because the FPC was authorized to set just and

---

[14] *Northern Natural Gas Co. v. FPC*, 399 F.2d 953 (D.C. Cir. 1968).

[15] *Public Serv. Comm'n of Kentucky v. FERC*, 610 F.2d 439 (6th Cir. 1979).

[16] *Office of Consumer's Council v. FERC*, 655 F.2d 1132 (D.C. 1980).

[17] *Public Serv. Comm'n of New York v. FPC*, 534 F.2d 757 (D.C. Cir. 1974).

[18] *Tennessee Gas Pipeline Co. v. FERC*, 689 F.2d 212 (D.C. Cir. 1982).

[19] *Transcontinental Gas Pipe Line Corp. v. FERC*, 589 F.2d 186 (5th Cir. 1979), *cert. denied*, 445 U.S. 915 (1980).

[20] 331 U.S. 682 (1947).

reasonable rates, the Court determined that it also should assess the reasonableness of pipeline-affiliated producer prices reasoning that if producer prices are automatically passed through to consumers, then the affiliated producer's rate became a component of the overall interstate pipeline's rates. If the affiliated producer prices were unreasonable, then the pipeline rates to distributors would be unreasonable as well. Certification was thus extended to affiliates.

With this reasoning, it was only a short step to the regulation of producers generally. In *Phillips Petroleum Co. v. Wisconsin,*[21] the Court subjected independent producers who sold natural gas to interstate pipelines to FPC jurisdiction. Again, the reasoning was that if pipelines simply passed through producer prices without regulatory oversight, then consumers could well be paying unnecessarily high rates.

Phillips created a major administrative problem for the FPC because now thousands of producers, in addition to interstate pipelines, were entitled to individual, adjudicative hearings. The Landis Report to president-elect Kennedy noted that even if the FPC tripled its staff, it would take until the year 2043 to complete the producer-rate docket that existed in 1960.[22] No wonder Landis cited the FPC as the "outstanding example of the breakdown of the administrative process."[23]

Gross delay in administrative hearings, however, scratches only the surface of the regulatory failure concerning the scheme of natural gas regulations. Because of its crowded docket, the FPC changed the way it did business. Instead of individual adjudications for producer rates, the FPC held rulemaking proceedings[24] to first set area rates[25] and then national rates.[26] Thus, in the late 1960s and early 1970s the natural gas industry went through a national market design process similar to what FERC now contemplates for the electricity industry. Moreover, natural gas prices in the *interstate* market were kept low because of the traditional cost-based rate formula, while *intrastate* rates were allowed to move to world market prices which escalated in the 1970s. As a result, as you will read next, there was a regulatory failure.

5. REGULATORY FAILURE

Federal regulators caused a shortage of natural gas in the interstate market in the 1970s, which led to additional problems in the 1980s. The reasons for this regulatory failure are complicated and can only be briefly related here.

---

[21] 347 U.S. 672 (1954).

[22] Senate Comm. on the Judiciary 86th Cong., Report on Regulatory Agencies to the President-Elect 6 (Comm. Print 1960).

[23] *Id.* at 54.

[24] Shapiro, *The Choice of Rulemaking and Adjudication in the Development of Administrative Policy,* 78 HARV. L. REV. 921 (1965).

[25] *Wisconsin v. FPC,* 373 U.S. 294 (1963); Permian Basin Area Rate Cases, 390 U.S. 747 (1968).

[26] *Shell Oil Co. v. FPC,* 520 F.2d 1061, *reh. denied,* 525 F.2d 1261 (5th Cir.); *cert. denied,* 426 U.S. 941 (1971).

This account is based on several good books which explain in detail what went wrong.[27]

The shortages developed when producers failed to increase the supply of natural gas in the interstate market despite an increase in demand caused by a world-wide energy crisis. The crisis was precipitated by events in the Middle East which reduced the supply of oil from that area of the world. Since some consumers can switch from oil to natural gas as a source of energy, the shortage of oil led to an increase in the demand for natural gas. Despite these developments, producers preferred to sell their gas in the more lucrative intrastate market. As noted above, regulators permitted intrastate prices for natural gas to move to world market prices, but interstate prices were kept low because regulators relied on cost-of-service ratemaking. Under the traditional cost-based formula, the increase in world energy prices was not a reason to increase consumer prices. As you studied previously, prices are based on a utility's revenue requirements, which are based on its costs.

Although producers preferred to sell their gas in the intrastate market, they were blocked from reducing the supply of gas to the interstate market. According to federal regulation, once producers had "dedicated" the gas in a well to the interstate market, they could not "abandon" that market without the approval of federal regulators.[28] Because of the interstate shortage, federal regulators were not inclined to let natural gas companies leave the interstate market.

Nevertheless, federal regulation contributed to the interstate shortage. The interstate price structure discouraged producers from searching for new sources of natural gas for two reasons. First, if producers found additional supplies, they could not charge more for the gas than would be justified based on their exploration and production costs. Thus, producers knew that they could not earn as much money selling new found gas in the interstate market as in the intrastate market where prices reflected the higher world energy prices. Second, those producers who did sell new found gas in the interstate market found their customers were reluctant to buy this gas. The customers resisted because the "new" gas, *i.e.*, the newly found gas, sold for a higher price than "old" gas, *i.e.*, gas that had been discovered before the energy crisis. The "new" gas had a higher price because it was more expensive to find and develop. The fact that the "old" gas was less expensive caused a shortage of "old" gas. To address this problem, regulators based the price of gas on an average of the old and new prices. This solution, however, discouraged producers from finding new sources of supply for the interstate market because it reduced the price of the new gas.

The interstate pipelines, which needed reliable sources of supply, reacted to the shortage of natural gas by creating an incentive for producers to supply more natural gas to the interstate market. The pipelines entered into long-term contracts with producers in which they promised either to "take-or-pay"

---

[27] *See* A. TUSSING & C. BARLOW, THE NATURAL GAS INDUSTRY; EVOLUTION, STRUCTURE & ECONOMICS (1984); M. SANDERS, THE REGULATION OF NATURAL GAS: POLICY AND POLITICS, 1938–1978 (1981); BREYER & MACAVOY, *supra* note 2.

[28] The terms "dedicate" and "abandon" are terms of art which will be explained below in Section B.

for a certain amount of gas at a certain price. In other words, the pipelines promised to pay for a certain amount of gas at a certain price regardless of whether they actually took delivery of the gas.

This strategy was successful in encouraging producers to provide additional supplies of natural gas to the interstate pipelines in the 1970s, but it backfired in the 1980s, when the energy crisis subsided and the demand for natural gas declined.[29] Despite the decline in demand, the pipelines had to purchase, or at least pay for, natural gas which they could not resell because of the reduced demand. The pipelines then applied to federal regulators for reimbursement of this expense. This raised the issue covered in the last chapter: should ratepayers be responsible for costs that are not associated with the production and transportation of energy which they actually use? When regulators balked at approving these costs, the pipelines sought relief in the courts where they tried to have the take-or-pay contracts declared void, or at least modified to their advantage. The courts, however, were reluctant to annul or modify these contracts. Judges noted that the contracts were signed by sophisticated parties and they were content to let the risk fall according to where the parties contractually assigned it.[30]

Thus, traditional federal regulation resulted in a dual market, a natural gas shortage, and awkward contractual arrangements. One regulatory response came with the Natural Gas Policy Act of 1978 (NGPA)[31] which was a central element of President Carter's National Energy Act legislation. The key purposes of NGPA were to unify the dual market and to deregulate prices. To take advantage of the emerging market, pipelines, producers, and consumers all petitioned FERC for relief. In response to these requests and to changing market conditions, FERC attempted to loosen price, entry, and exit controls for the purpose of letting gas flow more smoothly through the distribution system from producer to end-user or, in industry jargon, from wellhead to burnertip. Pipelines were the target of FERC's deregulatory efforts.[32]

B. EASING ENTRY CONTROLS

During the last two decades, the markets for natural gas and electricity experienced severe economic dislocations. In part, the dislocations were caused by the volatile world energy economy. The notorious "energy crisis" of the mid-1970s disrupted these markets with gross price and supply distortions. However, the regulated structure of these industries was another reason for the dislocations in these two markets. One antidote was to ease entry and

---

[29] Pierce, *Reconstituting the Natural Gas Industry from Wellhead to Burnertip*, 9 ENERGY L.J. 1 (1988).

[30] *See, e.g., Wagner & Brown v. ANR Pipeline, Inc.*, 837 F.2d 199 (5th Cir. 1988) (upholding district courts' dismissal of take-or-pay action deferring to primary jurisdiction of FERC); *Golsen v. Ong Western, Inc.*, 756 P.2d 1209 (Oka. 1988) (take-or-pay liability not extinguished by *force majeure* clause).

[31] 15 U.S.C. § 3301 et seq. (1994).

[32] Pierce, *Reconsidering the Roles of Regulation and Competition in the Natural Gas Industry*, 97 HARV. L. REV. 345 (1983) (questioning need for pipeline regulation in today's market); Note, *Is Natural Gas Pipeline Regulation Worth the Fuss?*, 40 STAN. L. REV. 753 (1988) (same).

exit controls in order to make the markets more flexible and competitive. FERC has been active trying to make both markets more competitive and more market-driven.

In order to take advantage of available supplies and to alleviate shortages, FERC encouraged pipelines to sell gas to high priority users (commercial and industrial customers) in danger of curtailment.[33] Then, under § 3311 of the Natural Gas Policy Act, FERC allowed some forms of transportation without NGA certification. Under the Natural Gas Act, certificates of public convenience and necessity are granted after individual evidentiary public hearings which specify duration, price, customers, and other terms and conditions. The jurisdictional pipeline, with the exception of emergencies, cannot sell or transport natural gas outside of these restrictions. This procedure is costly, time consuming, and inflexible. In 1979, FERC said that no certificates would issue under § 7(c) of the Natural Gas Act unless there were extraordinary reasons a pipeline was unable to comply under § 3311 of the NGPA, thus encouraging the self-executing provisions of the NGPA rather than the more formal licensing requirements of the NGA.

Next, FERC began a "blanket certificate" program:

> A blanket certificate enables an interstate natural gas pipeline company to engage in transportation arrangements without first applying for and obtaining for each specific transaction a Section 7 certificate of public convenience and necessity from FERC. A blanket certificate eliminates the delay of an interstate pipeline obtaining a certificate for each of many similar projects or transactions.[34]

Under such programs, the holder of a blanket certificate could transport gas, or sell new or uncommitted gas, to high priority users such as schools and hospitals without going through a formal licensing procedure.

Another notable response by FERC was the "special marketing" program (SMP) which it adopted to address a problem created by the "take-or-pay" contracts. As you read, many pipelines were locked into such contracts with producers, which meant that these utilities were forced to pay for specified quantities of natural gas at an agreed upon price. Because of these arrangements, the pipelines charged higher prices than they would have if they had not been subject to the contracts. As a result, the pipelines' customers who could switch to other less expensive fuels (*i.e.*, fuel switchable end-users) did so. The SMP plan addressed this problem by permitting a pipeline in this situation to amend its take-or-pay contract with a producer. The producer was permitted to sell the gas committed to a take-or-pay contract to a fuel switchable end-user and to credit the volume of such sales against the pipeline's take-or-pay purchase obligations. The pipeline agreed to carry the fuel to the end-user for a transportation fee. This arrangement had two benefits. First, it relieved the pipeline of its obligation to purchase gas under the unfavorable take-or-pay contracts. Second, it permitted fuel switchable end-users to buy natural gas at lower prices. The SMP plan, however, was

---

[33] *See American Public Gas Ass'n v. FERC*, 587 F.2d 1089 (D.C. Cir. 1978).

[34] Mogel, *Natural Gas Transportation*, in Energy Law and Transactions 83-23 (D. Muchow & W. Mogel eds. 1991).

challenged by customers of the pipeline, such as LDCs (local distribution companies), who were not eligible to purchase gas under the plan because FERC had restricted participation to fuel switchable end-users. The ineligible customers objected that they were stuck with higher priced natural gas prices. They also argued that they were forced to pick up the additional fixed costs that were not covered by the money that the pipelines earned from transporting the gas sold under the SMP plan. The D.C. Court of Appeals invalidated the SMP plan for precisely this reason. The court found that FERC's mandate did not permit it to discriminate against some pipeline customers in this manner. [35]

FERC had the right idea with blanket certification and with the SMPs, but it failed to execute it in a nondiscriminatory way. Both programs favored large consumers and disfavored small consumers. Following the lead of the SMP, new FERC regulations attempted a better utilization of the transportation portion of the industry and a move toward open access of (i.e. easier entry to) pipelines.

Recall that pipelines serve two functions: (1) They buy gas from producers and then market the gas to customers; and/or (2) they transport gas that the producer's customers have purchased from producers. Prior to the natural gas shortage in the 1970s, pipelines served the former "merchant" function by buying, transporting, and selling natural gas in a "bundled" transaction. As a result of the shortage, the latter separate (unbundled) transportation services gained attention. Large industrial customers and LDCs wanted to purchase the cheaper natural gas in the field and to purchase transportation services from the pipelines with which they were connected to avoid the high priced take-or-pay contract gas and to enjoy reliable supplies.

With Order No. 436, [36] FERC proposed to open access for captive customers and others who found it difficult to switch fuels by making it possible for such customers to deal directly with producers. In other words, FERC sought to separate pipelines' merchant and transportation roles by allowing customers to buy directly from producers and pay pipelines for transportation. The open access provisions of Order No. 436 were conditioned on non-discriminatory carriage. Pipelines who obtained blanket certification did so conditioned on nondiscrimination, i.e., they would charge just and reasonable rates for natural gas transportation for all users.

Every element of the natural gas industry challenged Order No. 436. In *Associated Gas Distributors v. FERC*, the D.C. Circuit remanded Order No. 436 to FERC for FERC's failure to address adequately the take-or-pay issues. The court, however, did hold that the FERC had authority to promote open-access transportation as a legitimate regulatory end.

---

[35] *Maryland People's Counsel v. Federal Energy Regulatory Comm'n*, 761 F.2d 768 (D.C. Cir. 1985) (MPC I) (SMP declared unlawful); 761 F.2d 780 (D.C. Cir. 1985) (MPC II) (blanket certificate declared unlawful).

[36] 50 Fed. Reg. 42,408 (1985) (Order No. 436), *modified*, 50 Fed. Reg. 52,217 (1985) (Order No. 436-A) *modified*, 51 Fed. Reg. 6398 (1986) (Order No. 436-B).

ASSOCIATED GAS DISTRIBUTORS v. FERC
824 F.2d 981 (D.C. Cir. 1987), *cert. denied,*
485 U.S. 1006 (1988)

WILLIAMS, CIRCUIT JUDGE.

I. Introduction . . .

The Order's regulatory package includes these elements: (1) If a pipeline seeks to take advantage of "blanket certification" of transportation (*i.e.*, a certificate authorizing transportation services generically and thus obviating the need for unwieldy individual certification), it must commit itself to provide transportation on a nondiscriminatory basis (and thus become an "open-access" pipeline). (2) When demand outruns capacity for open-access transportation, the open-access pipeline shall allocate capacity on a "first-come, first-served" basis. (3) Rate regulation for open-access transportation will take the form of ceilings and floors, with the pipeline free to adjust rates within that band. (4) Any open-access pipeline, by applying for certification, agrees to allow its LDC customers to convert their "contract demand" ("CD") (*i.e.*, contract commitment to purchase gas) from an obligation to purchase gas to an obligation to use (or pay for) transportation services. The point of the option is to make open access a reality for the pipelines' LDC customers despite long-term contractual service arrangements previously certificated by the Commission. The Order also requires an open-access pipeline to give its LDC customers the option to reduce contract demand. (5) The Commission will issue "Optional, Expedited Certificates" for new facilities, services and operations where the pipeline undertakes the entire economic risk of the project. The Commission declined to include in the package any special provision to relieve pipelines from the burden of take-or-pay contracts providing for prices well above current competitive levels. . . .

II. Open-Access Requirements

. . . Here the Commission has found (a) that pipelines continue to possess substantial market power; (b) that they have exercised that power to deny their own sales customers, and others without fuel-switching capability, access to competitively priced gas; and (c) that this practice has denied consumers access to gas at the lowest reasonable rates. Thus, despite the removal of regulation over the price and non-price aspects of wellhead transactions, and the evolution of an interconnected nationwide pipeline grid, discrimination in transportation has denied gas users, and the economy generally, the benefits of a competitive wellhead market.

Despite a sweeping suggestion that the Order is "unsupported," the pipelines do not in fact challenge these factual findings. Their objection is rather on matters of policy, grounded on beliefs that the kind of discrimination here prohibited is not "undue" within the meaning of the NGA. Indeed, the burden of their attack on the Order is precisely that it may disable them from passing on to customers gas purchase costs that they incur under contracts entered into years ago under premises now obsolete. In other words, enforcement of Order No. 436 will expose them to competition that their discriminatory practices enable them to avoid. Their claim thus tends to substantiate the Commission's views (1) that in the absence of Order No. 436 competition will be thwarted and (2) that the practices controlled by Order No. 436 are indeed anticompetitive and discriminatory.

. . . [O]ur decision in *Maryland People's Counsel v. FERC*, 761 F.2d 780 (D.C.Cir.1985) ("MPC II"), came about as close to endorsing the Commission's approach as Article III permits. There we vacated orders of the Commission that had established "blanket certificate" transportation without any specific effort to prevent pipelines from offering such transportation on a discriminatory basis. . . . We ended by saying:

> We vacate the challenged orders to the extent that they allow transportation of direct-sale gas to fuel-switchable, non-"high-priority" end users without requiring pipelines to furnish the same service to LDCs and captive consumers on nondiscriminatory terms.

Our holding in *MPC II* obviously did not require the Commission to make the findings that it has. It surely carried the implication, however, that if it did make supportable findings of undue discrimination in pipeline use of the old blanket certificates, it would have the authority to employ suitable remedies. And it carried the further implication that among them might be a requirement that any pipeline offering blanket-certificate transportation agree to serve "LDCs and captive consumers on non-discriminatory terms."

The interstate pipelines appear to suggest that Order No. 436's impact on their financial integrity is so grave as to be equivalent to a rule denying them the legal right to pass on costs, and invalid as such a rule would be. It is true that the Commission has only very limited power to deny the pipelines the legal right to pass gas purchase costs through to customers. But petitioners have called our attention to nothing that bars the Commission from devising rules that remedy a lack of competition by exposing pipelines to competition and its normal consequences. . . . [N]othing in the NGA protects the pipelines from the market forces to which Order No. 436 subjects their gas marketing business, even though those forces are derived in part from a restriction on their discrimination in transportation.

It is finally argued that the Commission's not having imposed any requirements like those of Order No. 436 in the period from enactment in 1938 until the present demonstrates the lack of any power to do so. But as our introductory review of the economic background sought to illustrate, the Commission here deals with conditions that are altogether new. Thus no inference may be drawn from prior non-use. While the Supreme Court's decision in *Chevron U.S.A. Inc. v. Natural Resources Defense Council, Inc.*, 467 U.S. 837 (1984), is not a wand by which courts can turn an unlawful frog into a legitimate prince, the case bolsters our conclusion. Congress has given the Commission in § 5 of the NGA a broad power to stamp out undue discrimination; in § 7 the power to approve certificates of service subject to "such reasonable terms and conditions as the public convenience and necessity may require"; and in § 16 the power to "perform any and all acts, and to prescribe . . . such orders, rules, and regulations as it may find necessary or appropriate to carry out the [NGA's] provisions." The alleged negative restriction on this power is at best ambiguous, if indeed it exists at all. Under these circumstances, *Chevron* binds us to defer to Congress's decision to grant the agency, not the courts, the primary authority and responsibility to administer the statute. The Commission's view represents "a reasonable interpretation" of the Act, for which we may not substitute our view.

Conclusion

As a general matter we uphold the substance of Order No. 436 and the procedures the Commission employed in adopting it. However, we have found problems in a few of the Order's components and must remand the matter to FERC for further proceedings. We now summarize these defects briefly.

The CD adjustment conditions suffer from a want of both legal authority and reasoned decisionmaking. The problem with legal authority stems from the Commission's misplaced reliance on § 7(e); the lack of reasoned decisionmaking lies in its failure to trace the path that led it from the statutory authority and the facts to its adoption of the CD reduction option. On remand, FERC is free to attempt to remedy these problems. If, however, it elects to go forward with the Order without CD conversion, it must, of course, explain why it feels that such a condition is no longer necessary.

The Commission's decision not to take any affirmative action to solve the problems posed by the uneconomic producer-pipeline contracts also fails to meet the standards of reasoned decisionmaking. On remand, FERC must more convincingly address the magnitude of the problem and the adverse consequences likely to result from the nondiscriminatory access and CD adjustment conditions. It is not our place to say whether FERC should have measures to shift these losses from where they now lie; we ask only that it explain its course.

Finally, FERC has failed to adequately explain some of its grandfathering decisions. Even though a certain amount of arbitrariness goes with this territory, the Commission must reveal a reasoned basis for its decisions.

The parts of Order No. 436 are interdependent. The nondiscriminatory access and CD adjustment provisions aggravate the pipelines' jeopardy from take-or-pay liability. When coupled with take-or-pay liability, those provisions may bring about a wasteful imbalance between pipeline sales and unbundled transportation service. Thus the Commission's apparent insouciance on take-or-pay taints the package. And CD adjustment, which the Commission has identified as essential to remedying problems deriving from the pipelines' market power, suffers from independent vulnerabilities. Accordingly, we vacate Order No. 436 and remand for further proceedings consistent with this opinion.

———

Associated Gas Distributors is a landmark decision for natural gas regulation. Although the case did result in a remand, the opinion largely accepted

FERC's regulatory efforts. The D.C. Circuit upheld FERC's jurisdiction to promulgate open access provisions as long as the provisions were nondiscriminatory. FERC responded with Order No. 500,[37] which largely adopted the transportation regulations of Order No. 436 with the following significant revisions:

(1) Procedures must credit certain volumes transported by a pipeline against take-or-pay liability;

(2) the order provides for mechanisms for equitable sharing between pipeline and its customers of costs of settling accrued take-or-pay obligations; and

(3) principles were adopted regarding future gas supply charges with intent of avoiding future take-or-pay problems.[38]

Although Order No. 500 was remanded to FERC to comply with *Associated Gas Distributors*, especially the take-or-pay issue, the nondiscriminatory open access provisions were accepted by the reviewing court.[39] In response, FERC adopted Order No. 500-H[40] which modified some of the Commission's take-or-pay rules. Order No. 500-H was largely affirmed in *AGA II*.[41]

With Order No. 436, FERC began its efforts to make pipelines into common carriers. The Commission would authorize blanket certificates for transportation with the condition on the pipeline's acceptance of non-discrimination requirements guaranteeing equal access for all customers to the new service.

The producer sales market was completely deregulated by Congress with the Natural Gas Wellhead Decontrol Act of 1989.[42] Decontrol of wellhead prices and open access thus go hand in hand with the intent of moving cheaper gas to market more easily and more quickly, without discrimination.

In promulgating Order No. 636,[43] the Commission found that, despite the legislation and its prior actions, the market still had impediments to full competition and that transactions were not as unbundled as a free market would indicate. Among other provisions, Order No. 636 contained the following:

(1) [M]andatory unbundling of pipeline sales and transportation; (2) blanket certificates authorizing pipelines to make unbundled sales at market-based rates; . . . (4) requirement that open access transportation services be provided "equal in quality" regardless of seller; (5) definition of transportation to include storage so as to subject storage to all open access regulations; . . . (9) pregranted abandonment authorizing pipelines to abandon sales, interruptible transportation and short-term (one year or less) firm transportation services upon

---

[37] 52 Fed. Reg. 30,334 (1987).

[38] McManus, *supra* note 5, at 50–81 to 50–82.

[39] *See American Gas Association v. FERC*, 888 F.2d 136 (D.C. Cir. 1989).

[40] Order No. 500-H, 54 Fed. Reg. 52,344 (1989) (final rule with modifications).

[41] *American Gas Ass'n v. FERC*, 912 F.2d 1496 (D.C. Cir. 1990).

[42] Pub. L. No. 101-60, 103 Stat. 157 (codified in scattered sections of 15 U.S.C.).

[43] F.E.R.C. Stats. & Regs. (CCH) ¶ 30, 939 (1992).

expiration or termination of a contract, and with long-term firm transportation contracts subject to existing customer's right of first refusal in response to an alternative offer; and (10) policies permitting full recovery of "transition costs" incurred by pipelines in complying with the Restructuring Rule. [44]

If, pursuant to federal regulations, an industry followed a certain course of action, what happens to physical property when the rules change? The natural gas industry for years had been regulated under a traditional ratemaking formula which rewarded capital investment. Once the industry was restructured, pipeline investment in storage facilities, for example, contributed to its fixed costs with no customers on whom to offload those investments based upon reliance on a regulatory scheme. Both in the electric and natural gas industries, these investments, in reliance on regulation, are known as stranded costs, discussed next in *United Distribution Cos. v. FERC*.

UNITED DISTRIBUTION COS. v. FERC
88 F.3d 1105 (D.C. Cir. 1996)

B. Stranded Costs and the "Used and Useful" Doctrine

A separate class of Order No. 636 transition costs are "stranded costs," which are those "incurred by pipelines in connection with their bundled sales services that cannot be directly allocated to customers of the unbundled services." To be denominated "stranded," an investment (1) must have been prudently made, but (2) must be no longer "used and useful." Examples include upstream pipeline capacity for which a downstream pipeline cannot find a buyer, and storage capacity that a pipeline no longer needs when the volume of its sales service shrinks. . . .

The PUCs' challenge the Commission's ruling that pipelines may recover 100% of their stranded costs. Their presentation is straightforward: items that are not currently "used and useful" may not be included in a utility's rates. . . .

In its brief, the Commission replies along two fronts. First, it contends that the PUCs' objection is premature, given that in Order No. 636, the Commission stated that, in subsequent restructuring proceedings, it would "consider arguments about whether particular facilities are used and useful, or whether that costs should be recoverable as transition costs" in § 4 rate proceedings. Second, the Commission contends that the "used and useful" principle invoked by the PUCs, while generally sound, does not apply to facilities that have been stranded only because of the Commission's own action. In other words, the pipelines should recover on their investments as they would have had Order No. 636 never been promulgated.

While we ultimately affirm the position taken by the Commission in the administrative proceedings, we believe that both the PUCs and the Commission itself may have overlooked a relevant distinction on appeal: the difference

---

[44] McManus, *supra* note 5, at 50–88.3; *see also* Schneider, Lorenzo & Beh, *Natural Gas Transportation* in 3 D. Muchow & W. Mogel, Energy Law & Transactions ch. 83 (1997).

between a utility's *rates* and its *rate base*. "The rate allowed a utility is the sum of (1) its cost of service, and (2) its rate base multiplied by its rate of return." "Generally, the rate base is comprised of total capital invested in facilities minus depreciation plus cash working capital. The rate of return, on the other hand, is a weighted average of different rates applied to debt, preferred stock and common stock." "Calculation of rate base is a critical step in establishing maximum rates, since the product of rate base multiplied by allowed rate of return is the total sum of money the agency allows to investors in the firm."

The cases cited by the PUCs, and not challenged by the Commission, stand for the proposition that the items in a utility's *rate base* generally should currently be used and useful to consumers. As a result, investors generally profit only from those investments that presently benefit consumers. However, that principle does not answer the question whether investments that are not used and useful may nonetheless be included in the utility's *rates*, *i.e.*, still treated as part of the utility's cost of service.

Viewed in this light, the general statement in Order No. 636 that pipelines will recover 100% of their stranded costs still leaves the Commission with a number of options in the § 4 rate proceedings. For example, the Commission could decide that stranded costs should merely be included in the pipeline's cost of service, recoverable through amortization over time. In such an instance, "FERC has already moved somewhat in the direction of balancing competing interests by permitting recovery of the costs of building the plant in the cost of service. Investor interests have not, therefore, been entirely ignored." *Jersey Central*, 810 F.2d at 1192 (Starr, J., concurring). The Commission might also allow the pipeline to recover not only the amortization, but also interest, *i.e.*, the "cost" of the unamortized portion of the investment. The Commission could further decide to include stranded investments in the utility's rate base and thereby generate a profit for investors.

In the administrative proceedings, the Commission assiduously avoided announcing a general standard that would control the manner in which stranded costs may be recovered. Thus, Order No. 636 states that while "most of the costs of *new facilities* would be includable in rate base, . . . there is no way of anticipating the nature and amount of the *stranded costs*, and thus no way at this time of devising an appropriate billing mechanism on a generic basis."
. . .

The PUCs' objection therefore is ripe for review only to the extent that they contend that pipelines should not recover 100% of their Order No. 636 stranded costs *in any fashion*. We cannot at this point address the specific question of whether pipelines should be permitted to include stranded costs in their rate base, and thereby receive a profit on the investment, because Order No. 636 adopted no such rule. . . .

We reject the PUCs' claim (now properly limited to the argument that the "used and useful" principle *per se* prohibits pipeline recovery of stranded costs even when merely amortized as part of the cost of service), because it was previously rejected in *NEPCO Municipal Rate Committee v. FERC*. . . . In *NEPCO*, we considered "whether FERC's refusal to include project expenditures in the rate base, while allowing their recovery as costs over time, is a valid approach to allocating the risks of project cancellation." We found such an approach acceptable because, in that case, the Commission's decision was based on substantial evidence and had adequately balanced the interests of investors and ratepayers. So long as the Commission's decisionmaking in the individual § 4 proceedings satisfies that standard, it will survive any subsequent challenge brought on "used and useful" grounds.

———

FERC has been actively involved with natural gas industry restructuring since 1978 with NGPA. The difficulty with moving to a completely free and deregulated market has been transportation. Historically, the Natural Gas Act of 1938 was based on the assumptions that pipelines exercised market power and behaved like monopolies. This position has been criticized and again we can cite Paul MacAvoy: "There is no analytical foundation for the argument that transportation has to continue to be regulated because it is noncompetitive."[45] Be that as it may, federal and state regulations have focused their efforts on opening access to the transmissions segment of the industry and have done so by requiring pipelines to separate ownership from transportation and requiring non-discriminating access to all purchasers. The major regulatory initiative is FERC Order No. 636 as refined by Order No. 637.[46] The thrust of the new order has been to remove certain rate ceilings and to permit a more flexible rate formula for the purpose of developing more competitive markets for gas and its transportation.[47] As noted, this Order has largely been upheld. Most recently, FERC issued a notice of proposed rulemaking to revise standards of conduct regulations that would apply uniformly to electric transmission providers and natural gas pipelines.[48] Clearly, FERC sees electricity and gas transmission in a similar light and desires to treat them uniformly. The key difference, of course, remains storage. While both products need to be available on demand natural gas can be more readily and reliably stored than electricity.

NOTES AND QUESTIONS

1. Should regulated firms receive compensation for stranded costs? What is the legal basis of the utility's argument? What is the effect on consumer rates?[49]

2. Does open access transportation make sense? How do you imagine that it will work? Who "owns" the pipeline? What rates should be charged for the transportation? Who should set the rate?

---

[45] MACAVOY, *supra* note 1 at 119–20.

[46] FERC & Stats. & Reg. ¶ 31,091 (Feb. 9, 2000).

[47] Interstate Natural Gas Ass'n v. FERC, 285 F.3d 18 (D.C. Cir. 2002).

[48] Standards of Conduct for Transmissions Providers, 96 FERC ¶ 61,334, 66 Fed. Reg. 50,919 (Sept. 27, 2002).

[49] *See generally* J. SIDAK & D. SPULBER, DEREGULATORY TAKINGS AND THE REGULATORY CONTRACT (1997).

3. Does open access cure the transportation bottleneck problem? Are there downsides to open access? Will natural gas service be reliable? Will the market work?

4. As noted, licensing is used to shore up sagging markets or create new ones for the purpose of economic efficiency. By limiting or expanding entry, government can avoid waste, control supply and prices, and monitor service quality and reliability by choosing financially responsible firms. In this vein, licensing as an entry control performs an essentially economic function.

C. EXIT CONTROLS

Once a regulatory market is created, a firm in that market incurs some obligations. In exchange for an exclusive service territory, the public utility allows regulators to set its rates and obligates itself to provide reliable service within that territory. Customers within that territory then rely on the service. Therefore, once the service area is established, exit from the service area may cause economic hardship because of inadequate or unreliable supplies. To prevent the rapid exit of a firm from a market, government regulators impose exit restrictions.

The central reason for the federal regulation of natural gas "in the public interest" was to sustain a competitive interstate natural gas market. One mechanism used to maintain that market was the rule of law that once natural gas was "dedicated" to interstate commerce it could not be removed without Commission approval. This dedication requirement was broadly interpreted to keep as much natural gas in the interstate market as possible.[50] Equally stringent were FERC rules on abandonment.

1. IMPOSING EXIT CONTROLS

In the interstate natural gas market, the Natural Gas Act requires FERC approval before a natural gas company leaves, or "abandons," the interstate market:

> No natural gas company shall abandon all or any portion of its facilities subject to the jurisdiction of the Commission, or any service rendered by means of such facilities, without the permission of the Commission first had and obtained, after due hearing, and a finding by the Commission that the available supply of natural gas is depleted to the extent that the continuance of service is unwarranted, or that the present or future public convenience or necessity permit such abandonment.[51]

The rationale for restricting exit is simple—keep the market working. However, exit restrictions may impose economic hardship on particular firms within that market as the following cases show.

In *California v. Southland Royalty Co.*, which follows, landowners entered into a 50-year oil and gas lease in 1925 with Gulf Oil Corporation under which

---

[50] *See Sunray Mid-Continent Oil Co. v. FPC*, 364 U.S. 137 (1960).

[51] 15 U.S.C. § 717f(b) (1982).

Gulf Oil sold gas in interstate commerce. The owners received royalties from Gulf and in 1926 sold one-half of their mineral fee interest to Southland Royalty Co., the respondents in the case below. When the lease expired in 1975, the rights to the oil and gas reserves reverted to Southland Royalty who wished to sell gas in the more lucrative intrastate market. An interstate pipeline purchaser of that gas, El Paso Natural Gas Co., filed a petition with the Federal Power Commission, opposing the removal of Southland's gas from the interstate market without abandonment authorization. Southland was prohibited from selling gas in the intrastate market without the required certificate of abandonment which the FPC was unwilling to issue.

CALIFORNIA v. SOUTHLAND ROYALTY CO.
436 U.S. 519 (1978)

MR. JUSTICE WHITE delivered the opinion of the Court.

. . . This issuance of a certificate of unlimited duration covering the gas at issue here created a federal obligation to serve the interstate market until abandonment authorization had been obtained. The Commission reasonably concluded that under the statue the obligation to continue service attached to the gas, not as a matter of contract but as a matter of law, and bound all those with dominion and power of sale over the gas, including the lessors to whom it reverted. Just as in *Sunray* [*Mid-Continent Oil Co. v. FERC*, 364 U.S. 137 (1960)], the service obligation imposed by the Commission survived the expiration of the private agreement which gave rise to the Commission's jurisdiction.

. . . Just as the federal obligation to continue service was held paramount to private arrangements in *Sunray*, that obligation must be recognized here. Once the gas commenced to flow into interstate commerce from the facilities used by the lessees, § 7(b) required that the Commission's permission be obtained prior to the discontinuance of "any service rendered by means of such facilities." Private contractual arrangements might shift control of the facilities and thereby determine who is obligated to provide that service, but the parties may not simply agree to terminate the service obligation without the Commission's approval.

Respondents contend that the gas at issue here was never impressed with an obligation to serve the interstate market because it was never "dedicated" to an interstate sale. The core of their argument is that "no man can dedicate what he does not own." This maxim has an appealing resonance, but only because it takes unfair advantage of an ambiguity in the term "dedicate." For most lawyers, as well as laymen, to "dedicate" is to "give, present, or surrender to public use." But gas which is "dedicated" pursuant to the Natural Gas Act is not surrendered to the public; it is simply placed within the jurisdiction of the Commission, so that it may be sold to the public at the "just and reasonable" rates specified by § 4(a) of the Act. Judicial review insures that those rates will not be confiscatory. Thus, by "dedicating" gas to the interstate market, a producer does not effect a gift or even a sale of that gas, but only changes its regulatory status. Here the lessee dedicated the gas by seeking and receiving a certificate of unlimited duration from the Commission.

Respondents apparently had no objection, for they could have intervened in those proceedings but did not do so. . . .

In *Sunray*, the Court discussed the "practical consequences" for the consumer if the term of the sales contract limited the term of the certificate. The Court reasoned:

> "If petitioner's contentions . . . were . . . sustained, the way would be clear for every independent producer of natural gas to seek certification only for the limited period of its initial contract with the transmission company, and thus automatically be free at a future date, untrammeled by Commission regulation, to reassess whether it desired to continue serving the interstate market."

A "local economy which had grown dependent on natural gas as a fuel" might experience disruption or significantly higher prices. These observations are equally pertinent to private arrangements by way of leases. If the expiration of a lease to mineral rights terminated all obligation to provide interstate service, producers would be free to structure their leasing arrangements to frustrate the aims and goals of the Natural Gas Act. . . .

We conclude that the Commission acted within its statutory powers in requiring that respondents obtain permission to abandon interstate service. "A regulatory statute such as the Natural Gas Act would be hamstrung if it were tied down to technical concepts of local law." By tying the concept of dedication to local property law, respondents would cripple the authority of the Commission at a time when the need for decisive action is greatest. Guided by *Sunray*, we believe that the structure and purposes of the Natural Gas Act require a broader view of the Commission's authority.

————

In the next case, the Court upheld a decision of FERC also finding dedication to interstate commerce—a critical factor in assuring continuing supply to the interstate market. In *United Gas Pipe Line Co. v. McCombs*, the owner of land executed an oil and gas lease with Quinn in 1948. In 1953, Quinn's widow contracted to sell to United Gas Pipe Line Company (United) all "merchantable" gas for a 10-year period. Because United was an interstate pipeline company, Quinn and United applied for and received a certificate of public convenience and necessity authorizing the sale in interstate commerce. The certificate from the FPC contained neither a limitation on the duration of the certificate nor any designation concerning the depth from which the gas was to be produced.

United began producing gas from 2,960 feet deep. The lease was assigned several times, eventually to Pagenkopf. Pagenkopf agreed to extend United's gas purchase contract through February 7, 1981. In 1963, upon Pagenkopf's application, the FPC issued a new certificate under the same terms as the original certificate relating to the Quinn sale. Pagenkopf then assigned the lease to Haring.

McCombs purchased an interest in a portion of the tract between the depths of 6,500 feet and 8,653 feet. New gas reserves were discovered at these deeper levels and McCombs wanted to sell this newly discovered gas in the higher priced intrastate market. In order to retain supply for its interstate customers, United asserted rights under its original lease and asked the FERC to determine that McCombs could not sell in intrastate commerce. FERC agreed with United. The Tenth Circuit reversed the FERC's decision. The Supreme Court reversed the Tenth Circuit and upheld FERC's authority to forbid such intrastate sales from acreage that had been dedicated to interstate commerce under an unlimited certificate of public convenience and necessity.

UNITED GAS PIPE LINE CO. v. McCOMBS
442 U.S. 529 (1979)

MR. JUSTICE MARSHALL delivered the opinion. . . .

Thus, we have consistently recognized that the Commission's "legal control over the continuation of service" is a fundamental component of the regulatory scheme. To deprive the Commission of this authority, even in limited circumstances, would conflict with basic policies underlying the Act.

Requiring Commission approval, "after due hearing," permits all interested parties to be heard and therefore facilitates full presentation of the facts necessary to determine whether § 7(b)'s criteria have been met. Contrary to respondents' assumption, the Commission does not automatically approve abandonments whenever production has ceased. Indeed, the agency recently refused to grant an application where the producer had not adequately tested for new gas reserves. Had the lessees in the instant case filed an application for abandonment between 1966 and 1971, United might well have demonstrated that exploration of the leasehold had been insufficient to justify finding "the available supply of natural gas . . . depleted to the extent that the continuance of service [was] unwarranted." And the Commission might have concluded that production from deeper reserves or other measures to restore service were feasible. Permitting natural gas companies to bypass abandonment proceedings simply because known reserves appear depleted would obviously foreclose these factual inquiries. Consequently, the abandonment determination would rest, as a practical matter, in the producer's control, a result clearly at odds with Congress' purpose to regulate the supply and price of natural gas.

Moreover, the obligation to obtain Commission approval promotes certainty and reliability in the regulatory scheme. Knowledge that termination of service is lawful only if authorized by the Commission enables producers, prospective assignees, and other interested parties to determine with assurance whether a particular tract remains dedicated to interstate commerce. In contrast, the Court of Appeals' test for *de facto* abandonment would invite speculation regarding the extent of the Commission's jurisdiction. The confusion that would inevitably result from the lack of clear standards as to when producers must seek Commission approval fortifies our conclusion that Congress intended agency supervision of all abandonments. . . .

Finally, respondents defend the judgment below on the ground that only the depleted shallow reserves underlying Butler B, as opposed to the newly discovered gas, were subject to the approval requirements of § 7(b). In their view, the deliveries actually made in interstate commerce, rather than the certificates of public convenience and necessity, define the "service" that may not be abandoned without Commission approval. Although deliveries were once made from a reservoir approximately 2,900 feet deep, the "separate and distinct" gas from the deeper reservoirs was never delivered into interstate commerce. Thus, according to respondents, the current production is not subject to the requirements of § 7(b), even though the certificates of public convenience and necessity cover all reservoirs located on Butler B.

Our prior decisions compel rejection of this narrow statutory interpretation. In *California v. Southland Royalty Co.*, we expressly agreed with the Commission that the "initiation of interstate service pursuant to the certificate *dedicated all fields subject to that certificate*." And as the Court emphasized in *Sunray Mid-Continental Oil Co. v. FPC*, "once so dedicated there can be no withdrawal of that supply from continued interstate movement without Commission approval."

NOTES AND QUESTIONS

1. In both *McCombs* and *Southland Royalty*, the Court upheld FPC determinations that natural gas once dedicated to the interstate market cannot be removed from that market without a certificate of abandonment. While both Supreme Court opinions are sound and based on statutory language, the effect of strict abandonment proceedings was harsh and the rulings of both cases were reversed by statute. What are the direct consequences of tight exit restrictions? Do such restrictions help or hurt the interstate market? Did FERC's refusal to permit abandonment contribute to the natural gas shortage discussed earlier?

2. *Southland Royalty* and *McCombs* both restrict exit and such restrictions make some sense in the face of a market shortage by keeping gas in that market. In the face of a surplus, however, limiting abandonment makes less sense. Instead, less restrictive entry and exit regulations can stimulate competition, as you read about next.

2. EASING EXIT CONTROLS

FERC's policy had been that exit controls were necessary and the Supreme Court concurred that the agency had the legal authority to impose such restrictions. What happened when FERC sought to ease such controls? In *Transcontinental Gas Pipeline Corp. v. Federal Power Commission*, the court reviews the laws of abandonment in light of the difficult market conditions in the mid-1970s.

TRANSCONTINENTAL GAS PIPELINE CORP. v. FEDERAL POWER COMMISSION
488 F.2d 1325 (D.C. Cir. 1973)

Per Curium:

This case involves petitions to review orders of the Federal Power Commission (the Commission) granting abandonment of natural gas supplies in the context of a critical nationwide fuel shortage. As such, it raises important issues relating to the proper standard to be applied in natural gas abandonment proceedings for the foreseeable future. All parties to this controversy agree that an early determination of the issues is necessary and this court has acted accordingly.

I

The facts of this case are fully stated in the Presiding Examiner's Initial Decision; we only summarize here those necessary to understand the precise issues decided. Petitioner, Transcontinental Gas Pipe Line Corporation (Transco), and intervenor, Natural Gas Pipeline Company of America (Natural), are natural gas pipelines engaged in the transportation and sale of natural gas in interstate commerce. Transco and Natural have purchased natural gas production from the La Gloria field area in Texas since the late 1940's and early 1950's respectively. In the middle 1950's, the La Gloria producers contended they could not continue to meet the requirements of both companies and still have adequate gas for other needs. For this reason the producers attempted to discontinue service to Natural by invoking certain "escape clauses" in their contracts. Pending court review of a Commission decision disallowing the proposed discontinuance, the producers and Natural agreed upon a settlement of the controversy. The settlement agreement, as approved by the Commission, provided for a substantial reduction in deliveries to Natural and the continued delivery of 81,000 Mcf per day to Transco until its contract with the producers expired in 1971. The quid pro quo for acceptance by Natural of the reduced deliveries was a contract with the producers that dedicated all the natural gas reserves in the La Gloria Field to Natural and required the producers to seek abandonment of deliveries of the 81,000 Mcf per day to Transco when its contract expired. Although Transco was not a party to the settlement agreement, it had intervened in the original proceeding before the Commission.

In early 1971 after Transco's contract expired, the La Gloria producers filed applications with the Commission to abandon sales to Transco. These applications were consolidated and hearings were held in the fall of 1971. The Commission, reversing the decision of the Presiding Examiner, granted the applications for abandonment and certificated the sale of the abandoned gas to Natural. Thus Natural presently is receiving the 81,000 Mcf per day formerly delivered to Transco. Upon denial of its request for a rehearing before the Commission, Transco filed the instant petitions for review with this court. We vacate the orders of the Commission, restore the parties to the status quo ante, and remand the case to the Commission.

II

Based upon an extensive and careful review of the evidence, the Presiding Examiner found, *inter alia*, that Transco had greater need for the La Gloria field gas than Natural. Accordingly, he denied the application for abandonment pursuant to the comparative need standard enunciated by this court in *Michigan Consolidated Gas Co. v. FPC*, 283 F.2d 204 (D.C. Cir. 1960). On review, the Commission reversed the Examiner's decision, ordered abandonment and certificated sale of the gas to Natural. In its decision the Commission stated that the comparative need standard was not appropriate in the context of this case, which involves: (1) a critical natural gas shortage in all areas of the country, (2) the expiration of Transco's contract with the La Gloria producers, and (3) Natural's contract rights to the gas under the 1958 Commission approved settlement agreement. For these reasons the Commission formulated a new standard that would give controlling weight to the settlement agreement absent "compelling proof" of countervailing "unequivocal public necessity."

III

Section 7(b) of the Natural Gas Act provides that abandonment of natural gas facilities or services subject to the Commission's jurisdiction can be granted only "after due hearing, and a finding by the Commission . . . that the present or future public convenience or necessity permit such abandonment." In *Michigan Consolidated*, this court, in considering the criteria for abandonment under § 7(b), recognized two important principles: (1) a pipeline which has obtained a certificate of public convenience and necessity to serve a particular market has "an obligation, deeply embedded in the law, to continue service," and (2) the burden of proof is on the applicant for abandonment to show that the "public convenience and necessity" permits abandonment, that is, that the public interest "will in no way be disserved" by abandonment.

The fundamental tenets established by *Michigan Consolidated* are that the public interest is the ultimate criterion under § 7(b) and that all factors relevant to the determination of which course of action best promotes the overall public interest must be fully considered. The Commission there proposed, and this court accepted, a comparative needs test which balanced the relative needs of the competing pipelines and their ultimate consumers as the principal index of the public interest.

Against these principles of statutory and case law, it is clear that the Commission's orders cannot stand. At bottom, the Commission's decision stands for the simple proposition that where all parties need contested gas supplies the party having the contractual right to such gas will prevail. This proposition possesses the alluring qualities of simplicity and precision; indeed, it seems to have so mesmerized the Commission that it abdicated its statutory responsibility to guarantee that the overall public interest "will in no way be disserved" by abandonment. Simply stated, the Commission apparently failed to perceive that the fact that all need gas does not mean that all need it equally. The approach thus taken failed to consider adequately and fully all the factors relevant to an intelligent determination of the overall public interest.

The Commission also erred in according dispositive weight to private, albeit Commission approved, contractual arrangements absent a showing of countervailing "unequivocal public necessity." The Commission essentially argues that failure to honor long term gas acquisition contracts would be "disastrous since no pipeline would be able to plan for the future." Clearly there are advantages to insuring as great certainty in gas acquisition plans as is possible. Moreover, if such plans and contracts are not given significant weight, then a pipeline in Transco's position might not be inclined, or at least would not have as great an incentive, to seek new sources of supply to replace those lost upon expiration of its contracts. Thus it is conceded that private, long term contracts, at least where they are part of a Commission approved settlement agreement, must be accorded significant weight in the determination of the overall public interest. But to argue that anything less than controlling weight would be "disastrous" grossly overstates the case. Rigid deferral to contractual arrangements without a searching inquiry into other factors relevant to the public interest as required by § 7(b) simply is an inadequate means to assure vindication of the transcendent interests of the public.

IV

It is appropriate to reiterate here the principle that guides our review of abandonment orders as stated in *Michigan Consolidated*:

> Where, as here, a regulatory agency has ignored factors which are relevant to the public interest, the scope of judicial review is sufficiently broad to order their consideration. These limits are not to be confused with the narrower ones governing review of an agency's conclusions reached upon proper consideration of the relevant factors.

We contemplate on remand, therefore, a searching and comprehensive inquiry by the Commission into all factors relevant to determining the overall public interest in this abandonment proceeding. For this purpose it will doubtless be necessary to supplement the record with additional evidence with respect to these factors. Primary importance must be given to a broadly conceived comparison of the needs of the two natural gas systems and the public markets they serve. Additionally, the Commission should consider the environmental effects of its decision, the economic effect on the pipelines and their consumers, the presumption in favor of continued service and the relative diligence of the respective pipelines in providing for adequate natural gas for adequate natural gas supplies. As discussed previously, the Commission should also accord significant weight to Natural's contract rights that resulted from the 1958 Commission approved settlement agreement. For the purpose of judicial review it is, of course, essential that the Commission's findings with respect to the factors it considered in determining the public interest be apparent from its opinion.

We recognize that the balancing process we impose upon the Commission is a complex one, but we perceive no acceptable alternative that would guarantee that the public interest "will in no way be disserved" in abandonment proceedings. Accordingly, the orders of the Commission are vacated, the parties are restored to the status quo ante, and the case is remanded to the Commission for further proceedings not inconsistent with this opinion.

The natural gas shortage in the 1970s stimulated the complex contractual/ regulatory scheme that gave rise to the FERC orders, and judicial review of these orders, discussed earlier. The thrust of all of these activities was to encourage competition through easing entry restrictions and, concomitantly, in easing exit restrictions. Easing exit restrictions for pipelines was accomplished through pre-granted abandonment regulations that allowed the pipelines to discontinue service without the necessity of formal administrative hearings.

In 1985, FERC set new standards for abandonment by focusing on the natural gas market in *Felmont Oil Corp.*[52] On review in *Consolidated Edison Co. of New York v. FERC*, the Court of Appeals, in the excerpt below, agreed that FERC could change abandonment standards according to market changes but remanded the order concerning the take-or-pay issue.

CONSOLIDATED EDISON CO. OF NEW YORK v. FERC
823 F.2d 630 (D.C. Cir. 1987)

WALD, CHIEF JUDGE:

Under the Natural Gas Act of 1938, a natural gas producer whose facilities are subject to Federal Energy Regulatory Commission (Commission of FERC) jurisdiction may not "abandon" those facilities — *i.e.*, "permanently reduce[] a significant portion of a particular service," *Reynolds Metals Co. v. FPC*, — unless the Commission first finds, after a hearing, either "that the available supply of natural gas is depleted to the extent that the continuance of service is unwarranted, or that the present or future public convenience or necessity permits[s] such abandonment."

Until recently, the Commission employed a "comparative needs test" to determine whether "the present or future public convenience or necessity permit[s] . . . abandonment." Under this test, the Commissioner would weigh the needs of the current consumers of the gas against the needs of the proposed new consumer, with the "burden of proof . . . on the applicant for abandonment to show that the . . . public interest 'will in no way be deserved' by abandonment."

In a 1985 opinion granting a natural gas producer's abandonment petition, the FERC changed its abandonment policy. Instead of companying the needs of the current consumers with the needs of identified specific new consumers, the Commission announced that it would now compare the needs of current consumers against the benefit that would accrue to the natural gas market as a whole were the facilities in question released from Commission jurisdiction. Consolidated Edison Company of New York (Con Ed), a local distribution company (LDC) that formerly purchased some of the gas at issue here, petitioned the court to review FERC's new abandonment test.

---

[52] 33 F.E.R.C. ¶ 61,333, *rev'd and remanded sub. nom. Consolidated Edison Co. v. FERC*, 823 F.2d 630 (D.C. Cir. 1987), *on remand Felmont Oil Corp.*, 42 F.E.R.C. ¶ 61,172 (1988).

Although we agree with the FERC that the statutory "public convenience or necessity" language frees it to develop new policies to accommodate a shifting energy marketplace, we nonetheless reverse and remand to the Commission because of its reliance upon an erroneous factual premise as a critical justification for its new policy.

I. Background

During the depression, the few pipelines that existed exerted double-edged control over the natural gas market. As both monopsonist and monopolists, the pipelines could buy and sell natural gas according to their own whims, with producer and consumer caught in the resultant squeeze, both as to price and supply.

The Natural Gas Act of 1938 changed all that. For the first time, the Federal Power Commission (FPC or Commission) was authorized to regulate the rates at which natural gas could be bought and sold. The FPC's jurisdiction extended only to the interstate market, but since gas that traveled interstate at any point was included in the Commission's jurisdiction, its authority covered a broad span.

The abandonment provision was one aspect of Congress' scheme to protect natural gas consumers from exploitation:

> No natural-gas company shall abandon all or any portion of its facilities subject to the jurisdiction of the Commission, or any service rendered by means of such facilities, without the permission and approval of the Commission first had and obtained, after due hearing, and a finding by the Commission that the available supply of natural gas is depleted to the extent that continuance of service is unwarranted, or that the present or future public convenience or necessity permit such abandonment.

Under this provision, before a natural gas producer can sell gas outside the Commission's jurisdiction after its interstate contract expires, it must seek the Commission's approval. In an energy market in which natural gas supplies were problematic and in which the unregulated intrastate markets threatened to swallow up large portions of those supplies, the abandonment provision served as a brake on the movement of gas out of the interstate stream.

The Commission, of course, had the responsibility to formulate a more precise abandonment test than "public convenience or necessity." In [two prior cases], this court approved the FPC's comparative needs test:

> . . . [T]he public interest is the ultimate criterion under § 717f(b) and . . . all factors relevant to the determination of which course of action best promotes the overall public interest must be fully considered. The Commission [has] proposed, and this court accepted, a comparative needs test which balanced the relative needs of the competing pipelines and their ultimate consumer as the principal index of the public interest.

In the late 1970's, the Natural Gas Policy Act (NPGA) reshaped the landscape of natural gas regulation. The Act was the product of two forces, an energy shortage, caused in large part by the Organization of Petroleum Exporting Countries' control over foreign imports, and an emerging view on Capitol Hill that deregulation of many heavily controlled national economic markets was needed to stimulate the nation's growth and development.

The NPGA itself reflected a compromise between widely divergent views on how best to protect consumers: some legislators believed that moderate price controls were still necessary to ward off residual oligopolistic tendencies in the natural gas industry, while others were convinced that only sweeping deregulation could produce a booming agora of new supplies and lower prices. The lengthy debates that preceded the NGPA's passage in 1978 focused almost exclusively on what degree of deregulation of "new" gas was appropriate. All of the legislators agreed that the regulatory structure of the NGA would continue to govern pre-NPGA "old" gas; since production-investment decisions with regard to that gas had already been made, there was no need to calibrate the price of that gas to the costliness of its production. Thus, although the NGPA ushered in a deregulated natural gas market for new gas, it explicitly left gas that was already "committed or dedicated to interstate commerce," under the watchful eye of the Commission (now dubbed the Federal Energy Regulatory Commission, or the FERC). . . .

II. Decision

At the outset, we agree with the FERC that the NGA itself does not mandate a comparative needs test but only a determination that present or future public convenience and necessity permits the abandonment at issue. In other words, by delegating abandonment power in such broad terms, Congress expected that the Commission would develop an appropriate test to fit the regulatory climate. . . .

As the Commission acknowledges, though, it is the reviewing court's duty to ensure "that the agency has . . . really taken a "hard look" at salient problems, and has . . . genuinely engaged in reasoned decisionmaking." *Greater Boston Television Corp. v. FCC*, 444 F.2d 841, 851 (D.C. Cir. 1970), *cert. denied*, 403 U.S. 923 (1971). The issue before us, accordingly, is not *whether* the FERC may change its abandonment policy, but whether its reasons for doing so in its chosen manner are permissible ones. In its critical discussion of the economic factors favoring a liberalized abandonment policy, the FERC relied heavily upon the "several salutary effects" resulting from the release of shut-in gas to the spot market:

1) "It will give other purchasers an opportunity to lower their gas costs by displacing high-cost gas or other fuels with this cheap gas."

2) "[T]o the extent this cheap gas creates more competition in the marketplace of suppliers, it will exert a pressure on all sellers of gas, be it high or low priced gas, to reduce prices or risk being shut-in."

3) "If the gas dedicated to an interstate pipeline is likely to be subject to a request for abandonment, that pipeline would be more likely to take this gas, thus lowering its overall cost of gas, or risk losing it forever."

4) "[I]f cheap gas displaces more expensive gas on a pipeline's system, both the pipeline and high-cost gas producer have an incentive to renegotiate their contracts to reduce take or pay requirements and lower the price of gas, so that it will make economic sense for the pipeline to continue to buy that gas."

We review these reasons seriatim:

1) On a theoretical level, the FERC's first reason is sound: an increase in supply of a product will normally lower the cost of that product to consumers. We do not doubt that if the natural gas spot market were an ideal free market, the release of shut-in cheap gas to that market would permit gas purchasers to switch from higher priced gas. Even in the present imperfect natural gas market, there are some fuel-switchable end-users—such as power plants and large industrial companies—that can go with the flow, as it were, and adjust their purchasing portfolios to take advantage of this influx of cheaper gas to the spot market. But at the same time the FERC has not explained how other, captive consumers in the natural gas market will be able to benefit from the new abandonment policy. These less mobile consumers are geographically bound to pipelines that are in turn contractually bound by take-or-pay contracts that make it uneconomical for them to switch to a new market for natural gas, since the pipelines must still pay for the higher priced contractual gas whether or not they take delivery.

In short, the natural gas market is not a classic free market, where the laws of supply and demand operate ineluctably for all participants. The FERC's apparent assumption that such standard laws apply across-the-board—or at least its failure to acknowledge the substantial obstacles to free-flowing gas exchange—is troubling. Nonetheless, at least the FERC's first reason for its new policy is valid with regard to some consumers, the fuel-switchable end-users, who will be able to lower their gas costs by virtue of the increased supply of cheap gas.

2) The Commission's second reason that the competition of the new gas will pressure all sellers to lower their prices or risk being shut-in—appears to be merely a corollary of the first, assuming that all the FERC means by a "risk [of] being shut-in" is the risk of not being able to sell one's gas if purchasers can buy the cheaper gas on the spot market. As with the first reason, the implication is that an increase in supply of cheaper gas will lower costs in the end throughout the marketplace. But also as with the first reason, only those consumers who can actually switch to spot market purchases will apply any pressure on producer-sellers. Additionally, as we discuss below with regard to the fourth reason, producer-sellers who benefit from the safety of long-term or take-or-pay contracts will feel little pressure from a dip in the spot market price.

3) We have serious doubts about the validity of the FERC's third reason—that pipelines threatened with abandonment under a more liberal policy will purchase more gas. The FERC's assumption that a pipeline that has hitherto taken only a small percentage of deliverable gas will decide to take most or all of the gas in order to avoid losing it forever makes sense if demand increases to accommodate such takes, a scenario that seems likely to occur only if enough fuel-switchable energy buyers move from non-gas supplies to

the gas market in response to the influx of previously shut-in gas. However, if demand does not increase to cover the volume of abandoned gas that the FERC assumes the affected pipelines will purchase, then those pipelines would be taking low-cost abandoned gas in lieu of high-cost take-or-pay gas while still incurring take-or-pay liability, thus raising, not lowering, their cost of gas. As we discuss in response to the FERC's fourth reason, below, this apparent Commission confusion regarding the effect of its new policy on the take-or-pay problem is a fundamental and pervasive flaw that infects the major part of its reasoning on abandonment.

4) As we have indicated at the end of our discussions of the FERC's second and third reasons, the FERC's assumption that the take-or-pay problem will be alleviated by the new policy is highly problematic. The Commission's fourth reason lies at the center of our apprehension in this regard. In both its initial and rehearing opinions, the FERC relied heavily . . . on the argument that the existence of more cheap gas on the spot market (which is where the abandoned gas will go) will provide an incentive both to the pipelines and the producers to renegotiate take-or-pay contracts. The Commission's logic seems to be that the newly released, cheaper gas will entice the pipelines away from the more expensive take-or-pay contract gas, and that, as a result, the producers will be willing to renegotiate those contracts to keep their customers.

This reasoning is difficult to understand. A take-or-pay contract is the product of a deal between a producer and a pipeline whereby the pipeline gains the security of a long-term supply contract in exchange for guaranteeing its supplier that it will pay for a minimum volume of gas whether or not it takes delivery of that gas. One of the major problems facing the natural gas industry today is the burden of such expensive take-or-pay contracts on the pipelines in a market with cheap alternative energy supplies. We sympathize with the Commission's desire to alleviate this problem, but it will not be wished away. It seems counterintuitive to argue that pipelines will stop taking gas that they have to pay for anyway and that as a result producers will have an incentive to renegotiate contracts in which they are guaranteed high payments whether or not the customer takes the gas. On the contrary: The whole purpose of take-or-pay contracts is to give producers the same benefit whether or not the gas in question actually leaves the ground. . . .

In this case, the FERC's fourth reason for its new abandonment policy—and implications arising from its second and third reasons as well—indicate that the Commission is still confusing "the pipelines' *incentives* to renegotiate contracts"—admittedly great—"with their *ability* to do so"—increasingly slim. In both cases, the FERC has embarked on an essentially deregulatory path to bring the natural gas marketplace into line with 1987 economic reality. In both cases, however, the increased power given to producers and consumers appears at least on first glance to give them *fewer* incentives to help out pipelines with their take-or-pay worries. [The court noted that a prior case had remanded an order, most elements of which it would otherwise have upheld, because of an unexplained take-or-pay rationale. Likewise, the court was remanding] this case for the same pervasive defect, although given proper bases we might well uphold it. Similarly, like the [prior case], we acknowledge that FERC may reach the same result if it explains adequately how it intends to deal with the take-or-pay problem.

Of course, it may be argued that the predicted mitigation of the take-or-pay problem is but one reason given for the new policy, and that therefore we may affirm on the basis of other, legitimate grounds. The general rule in this area is clear: "an administrative order cannot be upheld unless the grounds upon which the agency acted in exercising its powers were those upon which its action can be sustained." This black-letter statement of the law, however, does not resolve the familiar dilemma of what to do when an agency has given multiple reasons for a new policy, some of which are acceptable, some of which are not. Here the FERC provided what amounts to one acceptable reason and one unacceptable one for its new policy: Because more gas will flow to the spot market, producers of the abandoned gas will make more sales and those consumers able to purchase this newly available gas will benefit from the price dip. However, precisely because producers will benefit from selling the previously shut-in gas, it seems that there will be less, not more, pressure on them to renegotiate take-or-pay contracts. The critical question is how to tell whether the FERC would have made the same policy shift given a more thorough consideration of the effect on take-or-pay contracts.

Ultimately, we decide to remand the policy for reconsideration because of the nature and implications of the "bad" reason given by the Commission. It is not some minor misstatement of law or fact that can be passed over as an unfortunate lapse. Rather, it reflects a pervasive frame of mind of the Commission about a crucial problem in the natural gas industry, repeated in Order No. 436, i.e., a refusal to face the fact that the burdensome take-or-pay contracts will not go away through deregulatory actions that, while aiding much of the industry, actually appear to place more pressure on the pipelines. Because of the FERC's insistence that freeing up cheap gas will alleviate the problems associated with these contracts, we can not be at all sure that the FERC would have adopted its new abandonment policy absent its unexplained take-or-pay reasoning; this justification appears to be infusing much of the Commission's work these days. In the circumstances, we think the wiser course is to remand for the Commission to take a new, and we hope, harder look at the purported benefits of the looser abandonment policy. Ultimately, of course, the difficult questions of distributional equity that are necessarily implicated in a resolution of the take-or-pay problem are for the FERC, and not the courts, to answer. . . .

Conclusion

We agree with the FERC that the "public convenience or necessity" language of the NGA's abandonment provision, 15 U.S.C. § 717f(b), envisions agency policymaking to fit the regulatory climate. Indeed, the FERC's new abandonment policy may yet prove to be well justified. However, in articulating the reasons for this new policy the FERC relied heavily upon an unexplained notion of how the shift would affect the take-or-pay contracts problem. Because this cryptic view of the take-or-pay problem appears to infect many aspects of the FERC's natural gas decisionmaking, we remand for the Commission to address forthrightly the issue of whether a more liberal abandonment policy can stand given honest and full consideration of its effect on the take-or-pay problem. . . .

————

NOTES AND QUESTIONS

1. State the "comparative needs" test. How does it relate to the public interest? What is the rationale for looser abandonment standards? Is the comparative needs test a statutory requirement? Is it in the public interest? What are the efficiency consequences of the proposed abandonment policy? What are the distributional consequences?

2. Does a lessening of exit requirements, alone, stimulate competition? Are other regulations (or deregulations) needed to achieve more competitive markets? May FERC accomplish this on its own or does it need statutory (Congressional) authorization? What circumstances changed to move abandonment regulation to looser standards? What were FERC's reasons for a more liberal policy? What was the court's analysis of FERC's policy?

————

As FERC encouraged easier exit and more competition, it utilized looser abandonment standards as a form of deregulation. Thus, Order No. 490 further eased exit regulations so that buyers and sellers of natural gas could respond more quickly to market changes.[53]

A loosening of the abandonment policy makes sense for some categories of natural gas and for some markets. Recall that one of the purposes of the NGPA was to eliminate the dual natural gas market and to create a united national market. Recall also that producers attempted to move from the lower priced interstate market to the higher priced intrastate market and requested abandonment authorization to do so. The FERC resisted these requests precisely to fulfill the mandate of the NGA to maintain adequate supplies to the interstate market in furtherance of the public interest.

Consequently, to the extent that the NGPA created a national market and eliminated the dual market, that act correspondingly eliminated the need to move from one market to the other and it created a more competitive environment. In response to this new environment, FERC issued Order No. 490, which permits automatic abandonment for NGPA "first sales," when the underlying contract expires or is terminated at the request of either the purchasers or suppliers. The FERC's background discussion of the final version of Order No. 490 follows.

———

[53] 18 C.F.R. Part 157.

ORDER NO. 490-A
ABANDONMENT OF SALES AND PURCHASES OF NATURAL GAS
UNDER EXPIRED, TERMINATED, OR MODIFIED CONTRACTS
53 Fed. Reg. 29,002 (1988)

. . . The rule authorizes abandonment by both sellers and purchasers where the underlying contract term has expired, or where the sales and purchase obligations have been terminated or by mutual agreement of the parties. Similarly, where the sales or purchase obligation has been unilaterally reduced, suspended or terminated by the exercise of a contractual provision, abandonment is authorized to the extent of the contractually authorized adjustment of takes or deliveries. When a contract has expired or been terminated, either party to the contract may, upon thirty [30] days written notice, abandon its service obligation to sell or purchase the gas. The abandonment is automatically effective in accordance with the notice given. If the parties agree to terminate the contract or to modify their sales and purchase obligations under the contract, the abandonment is effective in accordance with the parties' agreement. Where there is unilateral abandonment, the abandoning party must notify the Commission of the abandonment within thirty [30] days of the effective date of the abandonment. When abandonment occurs by mutual agreement, the former purchaser must notify the Commission within thirty [30] days of the effective date of abandonment. . . .

III. THE RATIONALE FOR THE RULE

The Commission concluded that under the conditions created by the Natural Gas Policy Act of 1978 (NPGA), the Commission's former approach to abandonment required modification. The Commission found that continuation of the service obligation after the contract has expired is no longer reburied by the public convenience and necessity because it prevents market forces from operating efficiently. When either a producer or a purchaser concludes that it is no longer economically efficient to continue sales or purchases under an expired contract, Congress' NPGA policies are thwarted by policies that prevent that gas from entering the marketplace.

The rule must be viewed in the context of the Congressional and Commission policy of permitting market forces to determine the allocation of the nation's gas reserves to the greatest extent possible. By encouraging open access on the pipelines in other proceedings, and thereby more competitive markets, the Commission is seeking to permit the market itself to determine where the gas should flow and at what price. This rule is an integral part of that overall strategy. It allows gas to move where it is needed, rather than tying it indefinitely to the dedicated purchaser who may have no current need for the gas.

At the same time the Commission seeks to ensure that the rule is consistent with other important policy considerations. The constituent elements of the rule reflect these factors.

In light of the court's concerns with respect to the potential for aggravating a pipeline's take-or-pay problems, . . . the Commission has not imposed a transportation requirement upon the pipeline when the producer unilaterally abandons sales. Thus, where a pipeline does not provide open-access transportation, a producer that abandons sales will be required to negotiate with the pipeline for the transportation of the gas. The rule is not intended to enhance the pipeline's bargaining position, nor does it grant the pipeline any rights it did not have previously, but merely continues the status quo except for the abandonment right.

The Commission recognizes that in the event a carrier elects to take advantage of the regulations promulgated under Order No. 500 to become an open-access carrier, it would be required to transport the gas that a producer abandons under the rule. This follows not from the rule, but because of the pipeline's status as a Part 284 carrier. The Order No. 500 series constitutes a comprehensive treatment to date of the take-or-pay problem, where the Commission, after making a thorough examination of all aspects of that problem, carefully balanced the various competing interests in light of the public interest. Under these orders no take-or-pay credits are required for transportation of gas that the producer formerly sold to the transporting pipeline under a terminated take-or-pay contract and that is not currently subject to a gas purchase contract between the parties. The Commission concluded in Order No. 490 that it would not modify the provisions of Order No. 500 when a producer terminates its sales obligations under this rule because it could upset the delicate balance crafted in Order No. 500.

———

Although FERC eased exit restrictions, regulatory problems remained. In *Mobil Oil Exploration & Production v. FERC*, the Fifth Circuit considered free abandonment as problematic. It held that the Commission lacked statutory authority for this policy. The decision usefully illustrates how FERC's efforts to ease exit controls constituted almost a complete reversal of its prior policies.

MOBIL OIL EXPLORATION & PRODUCTION v. FERC
885 F.2d 209, 221–23 (5th Cir. 1989)

JOHNSON, CIRCUIT JUDGE: . . .

When Congress enacted the NGPA, it retained, for most "committed or dedicated" natural gas, the abandonment requirements of Section 7(b) of the NGA. Under the Commission's Order No. 451, a producer may, in the event of unsuccessful good faith negotiation, receive automatic abandonment by executing a new sales agreement with a new purchaser and by providing the former pipeline purchaser with at least thirty days notice of contract termination. Thus, the Commission essentially has authorized "pre-granted" abandonment. The controlling regulation, found at 18 C.F.R. § 157.301(b), is captioned "Pre-granted abandonment" and provides that "[a]ny first seller who sells natural gas under the blanket certificate authority of paragraph (a) of this section is authorized to abandon the sale upon termination of the contract under which the sale is made."

The petitioners argue that the automatic abandonment procedures promulgated by the Commission amount to a flagrant and unacceptable evasion by the Commission of its regulatory responsibilities under Section 7(b) of the NGA. Further, the petitioners argue that by allowing abandonment determinations to "turn on producer discretion" and by precluding pipeline challenge to producer abandonment and subsequent fact-specific Commission review, the Commission has exceeded its authority under the NGA. The petitioners contend that through the blanket abandonment provisions adopted in Order No. 451, the "Commission withdrew its regulatory presence and allowed abandonment [to turn on] virtually absolute unilateral producer discretion, as guided by economic self-interest." The Commission [argues] that there is "no procedural objection to the Commission's identification of circumstances, in an otherwise valid rulemaking, which automatically trigger its approval of abandonment. . . ."

The petitioners point to the "after due hearing" language of section 7(b) as support for their argument that the Commission is obligated by the plain language of the statute to conduct a case specific review regarding abandonment. The Commission on the other hand contends that pre-granted abandonment in the context of Order No. 451 serves the overall public interest by ensuring that old gas is kept flowing to a willing purchaser. . . . The Commission argues that the abandonment provisions of Order No. 451 represents Commission policy that the propriety of abandonment is governed by a balancing of the needs of current gas consumers being served by the gas reserves with the benefits that would be conferred on the natural gas market as a whole if these reserves were released from dedication.

The pre-grant of abandonment runs contrary to the instruction of the Supreme Court in *United Gas Pipe Line Co. v. McCombs*, 442 U.S. 529 (1979). In *McCombs*, the Supreme Court reversed a court of appeals' decision which held that, upon depletion of reserves, a producer may abandon sales without obtaining prior Commission approval. The Supreme Court concluded that such abandonment, without prior Commission approval, would, in effect, allow producers to determine when abandonment would be appropriate. This result, the Court reasoned, was inconsistent with congressional intent. The Commission distinguishes the *McCombs* case by noting that in the instant case, prior abandonment approval has, in fact, been granted by the Commission. We are persuaded, however, that such a distinction is not helpful to the Commission's argument. Rather, it appears that the pre-grant of abandonment contemplated by Order No. 451 would, as in the *McCombs* case, allow a producer, for all practical purposes, to control abandonment through the largely one sided GFN [good faith negotiation] procedure.

In *Public Serv. Comm'n of the State of New York v. FPC*, 511 F.2d 338 (D.C. Cir. 1975), the D.C. Circuit emphasized that "[t]here may be reason for the legislature to enact a deregulation for the natural gas industry, but so long as it prescribes a system of regulation by an agency subject to court review the courts may not abandon their responsibility by acquiescing in a charade or a rubber stamping of nonregulation in agency trappings." Accordingly, we are constrained to conclude that, in the instant case, the Commission has abdicated its responsibility under Section 7(b) of the NGA by providing for an across the board, preauthorized abandonment provision. Surely such abandonment procedure, being altogether in the producer's control and which may be implemented only at the behest of the producer, would be used only when such utilization would serve the producer's economic interest. As the Supreme Court noted in *United Gas Pipeline Corp. v. McCombs*, the absence of provisions for factual inquiry into the circumstances of an abandonment allows for the "abandonment determination [to] rest, as a practical matter, in the producer's control, a result clearly at odds with Congress' purpose to regulate the supply and price of natural gas."

———

In *Mobil Oil Exploration & Producing Southeast. Inc. v. United Distribution Co.*, the Supreme Court rejected the Fifth Circuit's analysis and ruled that the FERC's abandonment procedures under Order No. 451 comport with the NGA. The Court's interpretation requires FERC to: (1) grant "permission and approval" of the abandonment; (2) make a "finding" that "present and future public convenience or necessity permit such abandonment;" and, (3) hold a hearing that is "due." The Court found that all three factors were satisfied in the case.

———

MOBIL OIL EXPLORATION & PRODUCTION v. UNITED DISTRIBUTION CO.
498 U.S. 211, 226–29 (1991)

We further hold that Order No. 451's abandonment procedures fully comport with the requirements set forth in § 7(b) of the NGA. In particularly, we reject the suggestion that this provision mandates individualized proceedings involving interested parties before a specific abandonment can take place.

Section 7(b), which Congress retained when enacting the NGPA, states:

> "No natural-gas company shall abandon all or any portion of its facilities subject to the jurisdiction of the Commission, or any service rendered by means of such facilities, without the permission and approval of the Commission first had and obtained, after due hearing, and a finding by the Commission that the available supply of natural gas is depleted to the extent that the continuance of service is unwarranted, or that the present or future public convenience or necessity permit such abandonment." 15 U.S.C. § 717f(b).

As applied to this case § 7(b) prohibits a producer from abandoning its contractual service obligations to the purchaser unless the Commission has, first, granted its "permission and approval" of the abandonment; second, made a "finding" that "present or future public convenience or necessity permit such abandonment"; and, third, held a "hearing" that is "due." The Commission has taken each of these steps.

First, Order No. 451 permits and approves the abandonment at issue. That approval is not specific to any single abandonment but is instead general, prospective, and conditional. These conditions include: failure by the purchaser and producer to agree to a revised price under the GFN procedures;

execution of a new contract between the producer and a new purchaser; and 30-day's notice to the previous purchaser of contract termination. Neither respondents nor the Court of Appeals holding directly questions the Commission's orders for failing to satisfy this initial requirement. As we have previously held, nothing in § 7(b) prevents the Commission from giving advance approval of abandonment.

Second, the Commission also made the necessary findings that "present or future public interest or necessity" allowed the conditional abandonment that it prescribed. Reviewing "all relevant factors involved in determining the over-all public interest," the Commission found that preauthorized abandonment under the GFN regime would generally protect purchasers by allowing them to buy at market rates elsewhere if contracting producers insisted on the new ceiling price; safeguard producers by allowing them to abandon service if the contracting purchaser fails to come to terms; and serve the market by releasing previously unused reserves of old gas. At bottom these findings demonstrate the agency's determination that the GFN conditions make certain matters common to all abandonments. Contrary to respondents' theory, § 7(b) does not compel the agency to make "specific findings" with regard to every abandonment when the issues involved are general. As we have held in the context of disability proceedings under the Social Security Act, "general factual issue[s] may be resolved as fairly through rulemaking" as by considering specific evidence when the questions under consideration are "not unique" to the particular case.

Finally, it follows from the foregoing that the Commission discharged its § 7(b) duty to hold a "due hearing." Before promulgating Order No. 451, the agency held both a notice and comment hearing and an oral hearing. As it correctly concluded, § 7(b) required no more. Time and again, "[t]he Court has recognized that even where a agency's enabling statute expressly requires it to hold a hearing, the agency may rely on its rulemaking authority to determine issues that do not require case-by-case consideration." The Commission's approval conditions establish, and its findings confirm, that the abandonment at issue here is precisely the type of issue in which "[a] contrary holding would require the agency continually to relitigate issues that may be established fairly and efficiently in a single rulemaking proceeding."

Neither the Court of Appeals nor respondents have uncovered a convincing rationale for holding otherwise. Relying on *United Gas Pipe Line Co. v. McCombs*, the panel majority held that Order No. 541's prospective approval of abandonment was impermissible given the "practical" control the GFN process afforded producers. *McCombs*, however, is inapposite since that case dealt with a producer who attempted to abandon with no Commission approval, finding, or hearing whatsoever. Nor can respondents object that the Commission made no provision for individual determinations under its abandonment procedures where appropriate. Under Order No. 451, a purchaser who objects to a given abandonment on the grounds that the conditions the agency has set forth have not been met may file a complaint with the Commission.

____

NOTES AND QUESTIONS

1. It should be noted that Order No. 490 responds to the national market situation of NGPA, rather than NGA, categories of gas. However, an issue not addressed in the order is the issue of withholding natural gas from the market altogether. Should the FERC retain jurisdiction to prevent abandonment in order to maintain supply when a producer attempts to keep gas off the market because the producer is holding out for a higher price? How does FERC's order relate to the regulatory attitudes of the Reagan and Bush administrations? In other words, what is the relationship between presidential politics and agency policy? What role does law play here?

2. FERC further refined its pre-grant abandonment rules in Order No. 636. The order was closely reviewed by the D.C. Circuit Court of Appeals in *United Distribution Cos. v. FERC*, 88 F.3d 1105, 1138–42 (D.C. Cir. 1996). The court upheld most aspects of the rules, but it did remand certain aspects to FERC for more explanation.

D. ALLOCATION CONTROLS

FERC undertook to address the shortage of natural gas in the interstate market by adopting less restrictive entry and exit regulations, but the shortages persisted for a considerable period of time despite its efforts. FERC was therefore confronted with the following issue: to whom should natural gas owners (producers and pipelines) sell their supplies? This issue would not arise in an unregulated market where allocation is accomplished by price. When demand exceeds supply, the price of a good or service will rise and scarce goods or services are purchased by those persons who are willing to pay the most for them. The interstate natural gas market, however, was regulated and producers and pipelines sold natural gas at a price fixed by regulation. At the regulated price, the quantity demanded exceeded the quantity supplied. Thus, FERC had to decide how the scarce supplies of gas were to be allocated.

The need for allocation controls arose because of a regulatory scheme that prevented prices from fluctuating in response to demand. There is also another justification for allocation controls during periods when natural gas is in short supply. If allocation is left to an unregulated market, those end-users who can pay the most will end up with the available natural gas. More likely than not, this market response would cause severe hardship because large industrial users would outbid schools, hospitals, and agricultural users, and large manufacturing firms would outbid their smaller competitors.

There are two basic alternatives for curtailment plans—"pro rata" plans in which each customer is curtailed the same percentage, and "end use" plans where customers are provided with gas according to a list of priorities on an historical basis.

The FPC opted for end use plans for which they promulgated a series of regulations later codified in the NGPA. According to the NGPA the highest priority was to residential users, small commercial users, schools, and hospitals. The second category was agricultural users. The lowest priority was interruptible customers, that is, those users who had viable fuel alternatives.

In *Consolidated Edison Co. v. FERC*, a utility sought judicial review of FERC's end use curtailment plan. In an opinion by Judge Wald, the Commission plan was explained and upheld.

CONSOLIDATED EDISON CO. v. FERC
676 F.2d 763 (D.C. Cir. 1982)

WALD, CIRCUIT JUDGE.

Petitioner, Consolidated Edison ("Con Ed") challenges the Federal Energy Regulatory Commission's ("FERC" or "Commission") approval of an end use curtailment plan for natural gas that does not require customers who undergo below average curtailment to compensate those who are curtailed more than the average customer. Con Ed argues that FERC's action constitutes a taking of property without just compensation, and is thus a violation of the fifth amendment. It also argues that FERC's rejection of a compensation scheme was not a product of reasoned decisionmaking and was arbitrary and capricious. For the reasons set forth below, we affirm the Commission.

I. BACKGROUND

Following natural gas shortages on a number of pipelines in 1970, the Commission issued Order No. 431, directing each interstate pipeline company to report to the Commission stating whether it expected to experience natural gas shortages. Those companies that anticipated shortages were required to submit a revised tariff outlining their plans for allocating short supplies. Pipeline companies filed two types of curtailment plans: "pro-rata" plans and "end use" plans. Under a pro-rata plan, all customers would receive the same proportion of the natural gas they contracted for. The worse the shortage, the smaller that proportion would be; but no customer would receive a greater percentage of his contract than any other customer. In contrast, an end use plan would allocate gas according to the use to which that gas would ultimately be put. Under an end use plan, the contracts providing gas to the highest priority end users must be performed before any gas is allocated to the next highest user.

Two years after it first solicited curtailment plans, the Commission issued a policy statement stating its preference for end use curtailment plans. As modified by a subsequent order, this policy statement established nine priority rankings for end users. [The Court's explanation of priorities is omitted.]

The Commission explained its priority scheme both on efficiency grounds and on an assessment of the comparative hardship suffered by different end users should they be required to reduce their consumption of natural gas. Generally, the Commission found an end use scheme preferable to a pro-rata scheme "because contracts do not necessarily serve the public interest requirement of efficient allocation of this wasting resource." By employing an end use plan, natural gas could be directed to those who could burn it most efficiently or for whom it would be most expensive to convert to other fuels. . . .

. . . [I]n *North Carolina v. FERC*, 584 F.2d 1003 (D.C. Cir. 1978), we . . . explain[ed] that discriminatory treatment of distributors is only justified to the extent that a curtailment plan reasonably reflects the actual impact that plan will have on ultimate consumers. Thus, we suggested that an end use plan based on a fixed-base period must be justified in terms of its current effects on preferred end users.

One issue that arose repeatedly in prior proceedings is whether an end use curtailment plan should be accompanied by a compensation scheme. Over-curtailed customers argued that it was unfair to require them to shoulder the full cost of purchasing supplemental fuel supplies while other customers continued to receive the natural gas they needed at low regulated prices. They suggested that even if an end use plan is necessary to allocate gas to those who could not readily convert to alternative fuels, all customers should share in the costs incurred by overcurtailed customers when they purchased supplemental supplies. As Judge Leventhal explained in *Elizabethtown Gas Co v FERC (Elizabethtown I)*, 572 F.2d 885 (D.C. Cir. 1978), a compensation scheme would "[balance] the benefit accorded a high-priority purchaser with a charge that offsets, at least in part, the added expense imposed by a curtailment plan upon a lower-priority purchaser."

The Commission originally opposed compensation plans on the ground that it lacked jurisdiction to order such payments. We disagreed, and in *Elizabethtown I* and *North Carolina* remanded curtailment plans to the Commission for further consideration of the propriety of a compensation scheme. We now face squarely for the first time the question whether the Commission's *policy* justifications for refusing to order compensation are adequate. . . .

[Concerning its refusal to order compensation, the] Commission began its analysis by distinguishing between two types of compensation claimants—low priority end users making direct purchases form Texas Eastern and distribution companies which buy from Texas Eastern and sell natural gas to low priority end users. In discussing the first group, the Commission referred to its past practices in certifying natural gas transportation for low priority end users. Under section 7 of the Natural Gas Act, certificates of public convenience and necessity are issued when they are "necessary or desirable in the public interest." The Commission explained that when supplies were adequate, service to large low priority users met this standard because it benefitted the entire pipeline. The low priority end user received cheap fuel and costs to the rest of the pipeline's customers were reduced as a result of the increased load factor. But in times of natural gas shortages other customers no longer benefitted from continued service to low priority users. Thus, the Commission's decision to cut off or curtail low priority users mirrored its earlier policy of authorizing low priority gas usage only when doing so would benefit higher priority users. In addition, the Commission suggested that shifting the low priority customers' cost of obtaining alternate fuels to high priority users would interfere with the goals of an end use curtailment plan. Compensation payments, it explained, would unduly burden high priority users and might undermine efforts on the part of low priority customers to minimize their costs in alternative energy markets.

With regard to the distribution companies, the Commission found that compensation would unduly reward those companies that had successfully played the "load factor game" in the past by providing service to low priority end users. A distribution company's "load factor" reflects the ratio of average demand to peak demand. The higher the load factor, or the more demand is pushed from peak to off-peak periods, the lower the distributor's unit costs. Thus, distributors typically sought to raise their load factor: some by providing offpeak service to low priority industrial customers; and others by building storage facilities to hold gas purchased during off-peak periods for resale in periods of peak demand. Not all distributors, however, were able to employ either method for increasing their load factor. These distributors, who generally served small towns in rural areas, simply paid higher prices for natural gas supplies.

The Commission recognized that a consequence of these different methods for increasing load factor is that some residential end users are more severely affected by an end use curtailment plan than others. The heaviest curtailment-related costs fall on customers of distribution companies that had relied on low-priority industrials to increase their load factor. Due to their above average curtailment, these distribution companies must either purchase above average amounts of expensive alternative fuels—which would lead to higher retail prices—or else they must discontinue service to some customers—which would lead to higher unit costs for the remaining customers. In contrast, distribution companies that had invested in storage facilities to increase their load factor or had not played the "load factor game," receive proportionately more natural gas during curtailment because proportionately more of their retail customers are residential users. As a result, these latter distribution companies are under less pressure to increase their retail prices during periods of curtailment.

The Commission found that these disparate effects of curtailment fairly reflect the past load factor strategy of distributors. It reasoned that customers of distributors without industrial loads had paid increased prices in the past due to low load factor of the distributor's costs of constructing and maintaining storage facilities. It concluded "[n]o one earlier suggested during times of plentiful supplies that the benefits obtained from service to industrials should be shared by one distributor with another distributor who did not have an industrial load; and we find no cause to now engage in the reverse process."

. . .

The Commission then proceeded to consider the implications of the Natural Gas Policy Act of 1978. It noted that Title IV of the NGPA ratified the Commission's end use approach to curtailment plans. Although the NGPA did not specifically address the issue of compensation, the Commission suggested that a compensation scheme would be inconsistent with the conference committee's concern with preventing sharp price increases on goods produced by preferred end users. The Commission also considered the implications of the Powerplant and Industrial Fuel Use Act of 1978. It found that while the Fuel Use Act places more severe restrictions on natural gas usage than a curtailment plan, it only provides for compensation in narrow circumstances. Although the Commission conceded that the Fuel Use Act does not prohibit compensation in the context of end use curtailment plans, it concluded that nothing in that statute suggests that regulation of boiler fuel uses under the Natural Gas Act should be accompanied by compensation.

Turning finally to the particular compensation schemes offered by Elizabethtown and Con Ed, the Commission found that neither scheme would equitably allocate the economic hardship of a natural gas shortage. The Commission first noted that both plans sought to reallocate costs so as to require high and low priority customers to share equally in the economic hardship attending natural gas shortages—an objective the Commission had earlier rejected in its policy discussion. But even assuming that compensation would be appropriate in some circumstances, the Commission found the two proposed schemes to be defective. Elizabethtown's plan, which would compensate curtailed customers for their most expensive supplemental supplies, placed no cap on costs that could be charged to the pipeline. The Commission explained that this plan contained a potential for abuse since customers curtailed at above average rates would have little incentive to minimize their most expensive supplemental supplies—costs which would be passed along to other pipeline customers. The Commission concluded that approving Elizabethtown's plan would be a violation of its duty to avoid exploitation of the ultimate consumer.

Unlike Elizabethtown's plan, Con Ed's compensation scheme would not skew incentives to minimize costs. Con Ed's plan would employ an index of substitute fuel costs—the price of No. 6 residual fuel oil—to determine the excess cost incurred by those customers undergoing above average curtailment. Regardless of the costs they actually incurred, curtailed customers would receive compensation computed by multiplying the difference between the price of fuel oil and the regulated natural gas price times the difference between the company's pro-rata share of natural gas and the amount it actually receives. Thus, each individual pipeline customer would have an interest in minimizing the cost of alternative fuels. Nonetheless, the Commission found that Con Ed's plan also suffered from serious deficiencies. First, it measured compensation by reference to a single alternative fuel, and could therefore distort the actual average costs of conversion. Second, it did not deduct for customers of distribution companies who actually converted to other fuels or otherwise left the distributor's system. Unless state commissions required distributors to direct compensation payments to these customers, who would no longer receive natural gas, the payments would end up in the hands of the distributors' residential customers. In essence, the plan could simply transfer payments from one set of residential customers to another even though the main impact of end use curtailment is on low priority end users. Finally, the Commission compared the actual rates borne by Con Ed's customers and the retail customers of a neighboring utility—Brooklyn Union—whose distributor had not been heavily curtailed. Although it recognized that such comparisons of retail rates are imperfect, the Commission found it noteworthy that this rough comparison did not bear out Con Ed's contention that its customers had been subject to greater rate increases as a result of above average curtailment. The Commission concluded that there was "no basis for awarding either Con Edison or its gas customers compensation.". . .

II. ANALYSIS

. . . If the Natural Gas Act requires that curtailment plans distribute the economic hardship of a natural gas shortage equally among customers of a pipeline, then the Commission abused its authority by approving Texas Eastern's plan without a compensation component. If, however, there is no statutory mandate for such an allocation, the Commission's order must be sustained absent some showing that its grounds for denying compensation were arbitrary and capricious.

The Supreme Court first filed on the Commission's curtailment powers in *FPC v. Louisiana Power & Light Co.*, [T]he Court ruled that such regulations are within the Commission's power. Turning to the scope of that power, the Court first stated that the Commission, as an "[agency] created to protect the public interest, must be free, 'within the ambit of [its] statutory authority to make practical adjustments which may be called for by particular circumstances.'" The Court then referred to section 4(b) of the Natural Gas Act as the substantive standard which governs the Commission's evaluation of curtailment plans. Section 4(b) provides:

> No natural-gas company shall, with respect to any transportation or sale of natural gas subject to the jurisdiction of the Commission, (1) make or grant any undue preference or advantage to any person or subject any person to any undue prejudice or disadvantage, or (2) maintain any unreasonable difference in rates, charges, service, facilities, or in any other respect, either as between localities or as between classes of service.

Con Ed urges there that Texas Eastern's curtailment plan created "undue" or "unreasonable" discrimination because it fails to treat all customers' contracts equally. It argues that "[r]egulation of the natural gas industry was founded upon contracts between natural gas companies and their customers."
. . .

We do not view section 4's mandate against "undue" preferences and "unreasonable" discrimination so strictly. The mere fact that Texas Eastern's plan treats different kinds of contracts for natural gas differently does not mean that the plan is "undu[ly]" preferential or "unreasonabl[y]" discriminatory as to those whose contract rights are affected. As the Commission explained in its original policy statement endorsing end use curtailment plans, contractual commitments do not necessarily serve the public interest in efficiently allocating scarce natural gas supplies. Through its approval of end use curtailment plans, the Commission has sought to protect the public interest by funneling natural gas supplies to those who face the highest conversion costs or for whom curtailment represents the greatest hardship. . . . The fundamental premise of end use curtailment is that different classes of end users are *not* similarly situated simply because they have equivalent contractual rights. Thus, even though the Commission was empowered to order compensation, . . . "compensation . . . is not required by the Natural Gas Act in order to avoid discrimination. . . ." . . .

Con Ed also disputes the Commission's reliance on the NGPA and the Fuel Use Act to support its denial of compensation. Con Ed argues that neither Act directly addressed the compensation issue, although the propriety of compensation provisions was at the time being vigorously contested before the Commission and in the courts. We agree with Con Ed that these Acts do not point clearly in favor or against compensation plans. We do believe, however, that these Acts generally support our conclusion that the decision whether to employ end use or pro rata concepts in allocating the economic hardship of a natural gas shortage is a matter of policy for the Commission.

The Commission sought support for its rejection of compensation schemes in the conference report accompanying the NGPA. It noted that in establishing agricultural uses of natural gas as a matter of relatively high priority, the conference committee expressed its concern that, absent such a provision, food prices would rise sharply in times of shortage. . . .

We find this argument unpersuasive. Although compensation payments would no doubt lead to increased prices for food, and similarly would burden high priority residential users, compensation payments would not begin to duplicate the dramatic economic dislocations and price consequences stemming from the gas curtailments themselves that led Congress to raise the priority status of agricultural users. In establishing a high priority status for agricultural end users, Congress recognized that many agricultural processes are not readily adaptable to alternative fuels. . . . Past cutoffs of natural gas supplies to these users had resulted in wasted food supplies. . . . Cutoffs had also severely limited the production of agricultural supplies, thereby causing the price of such supplies to increase sharply. . . . By allocating natural gas to agricultural users on a priority basis, the NGPA works to prevent these price consequences of natural gas shortages as well as the price effects that would follow from requiring those agricultural users who can convert to alternative fuels to bear the full brunt of paying for high cost alternatives. Thus, while Congress sought to avoid the type of price shocks caused by past curtailment priorities, we find it a bit farfetched to read into the NGPA a Congressional policy which precludes compensation altogether in curtailment plans.

The Commission also seeks support for its refusal to require compensation in the Fuel Use Act's provisions prohibiting powerplants from using natural gas as a primary energy source after 1990. . . . The Fuel Use Act says nothing about whether curtailed customers should receive compensation payments; it only says that those who do not have a right to the physical receipt of natural gas during periods of curtailment cannot create such a right in those to whom they sell their natural gas contracts. If we were to rule that curtailed customers had a right to receive compensation payments during periods of curtailment, they could no doubt pass the right along to those who purchase their natural gas contracts.

[NGPA and the Full Use Act] support our conclusion that the provision of compensation is a matter of policy properly left to the Commission. Read as a whole, the Energy Acts indicate Congressional concern both with protecting high priority end users from cost increases, and with providing compensation, measured by reasonable replacement costs, to lower priority end users when their "contractual interests" in receiving natural gas are transferred in accordance with certain statutory provisions. But the Energy Acts are conspicuously ambiguous on the question of how curtailment plans affect contractual interests to receive natural gas — that is, whether a curtailment plan (1) suspends the rights and responsibilities of the parties to natural gas contracts or (2) leaves those pipeline customers who do not receive natural gas with a right to damages (or compensation). Indeed, the compensation provisions of the Acts specifically provide that they only govern contractual interests *as they are affected* by curtailment plans. Congress thus appears to have left the question of how curtailment plans affect contractual interests to the Commission to be resolved in accordance with the general policies of the Natural Gas Act and the Energy Acts. . . .

If a compensation plan were necessary to render a curtailment plan just and reasonable, we do not doubt that the burden of establishing a workable plan would rest on the proponent of the plan. But we have previously held that curtailment plans may be reasonable without any compensation features. Since compensation schemes are not a required part of a curtailment plan, we conclude that the Commission did not err by placing the burden of developing a workable plan on those parties requesting compensation.

Turning to the specific plan proposed by Con Ed, we find that the Commission did not err by concluding that the plan was seriously defective. First, the plan was based on the unrealistic and rigid assumption that curtailed customers would convert to oil. Should oil prices rise by more than alternative fuels, Con Ed's plan would provide windfalls to curtailed customers at the expense of higher priority end users. Indeed, the Commission found that Con Ed's own experience in adjusting to natural gas curtailment indicated that this hypothesis was grounded in experience. Second, Con Ed's plan provided no assurance that compensation paid to distributors would be directed to curtailed end users. Absent such assurance, the plan allowed for payments from one group of residential customers to another which would be disproportionate to any economic burdens associated with end use curtailment. The Commission properly found that these deficiencies demonstrated that Con Ed's plan would not assure an equitable distribution of the economic burden of the natural gas shortage. . . .

CONCLUSION

In conclusion, we find that the Commission has adequately justified its refusal to require Texas Eastern to provide compensation measured by replacement costs to customers curtailed more than the system average. We therefore affirm the Commission's rulings in this case.

NOTES AND QUESTIONS

1. How do end use plans and pro rata plans operate? How are they different? What are the market effects of each? FERC reasoned that end use plans were preferable to pro-rata plans because "contracts do not necessarily serve the public interest requirement of efficient allocation of this wasting resource." What does this mean?

2. What is the purpose of a curtailment plan? What is the purpose of a compensation scheme as part of a curtailment plan? Who benefits from a compensation scheme? Who is hurt by one? Did the plans meet their objectives according to the Commission?

3. What policy reasons does FERC offer for rejecting a compensation requirement for direct customers and for distribution companies? What is the "load factor game"?

4. Did the court defer to the Commission? How was the deference character-ized or justified? What is the market effect of deference? In *Consolidated Edison*, the petitioners argued that the curtailment plan was confiscatory and that FERC's reasoning was arbitrary, capricious, and violative of the APA. What was the court's response to these challenges?

5. *Consolidated Edison* remains a major case regarding curtailment plans. Other important cases are *North Carolina v. FERC*, 584 F.2d 1003 (D.C. Cir. 1978); *City of Mesa v. FERC*, 993 F.2d 888 (D.C. Cir. 1993). Both Order No. 436 and Order No. 636 incorporate curtailment provisions which employ both end use and pro-rata curtailments for different sorts of transactions. See *United Distribution Cos. v. FERC*, 88 F.3d 1105, 1142–48 (D.C. Cir. 1996).

Chapter 6

BOTTLENECKS II: ENTRY CONTROLS AND TELECOMMUNICATIONS

Price controls are the classic form of economic regulation, especially regarding the regulation of natural monopolies. Theoretically, at least, the regulation of natural monopolies promises lower cost because of the avoidance of duplication and waste. Still, price controls are complex, heavy-handed, and imperfect, never quite mimicking a competitive market.

Traditional utilities like natural gas and electricity have been price regulated for over a century, but these industries are currently undergoing significant price deregulation for two reasons. First, the imperfections of price regulation have distorted these markets and have actually kept customers away from less expensive gas and electricity. Second, policy analysts now believe that both industries can be more competitive than natural monopoly theory would allow. Consequently, state and federal regulators have begun to reduce price regulations and have attempted to increase competition through nonprice controls. We can call this approach a "regulatory market" to recognize that regulators have taken an active role in structuring the market to promote more competition.

The previous two chapters examined the traditional utilities of electricity and natural gas. This chapter is about the telecommunications industry, although it is more accurate to say telecommunications industries. One way of focusing on telecommunications is to pose two questions. First, was your last telephone communication on a wired or wireless device? In other words, did you use a cell phone or one attached to wires leading to telephone lines?

The second question is: Was the last television show that you watched from a broadcast network (ABC, CBS, NBC), a local affiliate or from a cable channel (ESPN, HBO or the like)? If we had to guess, we would say that the majority of you would answer cell phone and cable television. When we wrote the first edition of this casebook in 1993 the answers would be quite the opposite because neither technology was as prevalent then as they are today. It is also the case that in 1993 we were yet to reach the heights of the technological revolution that occurred. Nor would we reach the lows of a market collapse.

How does regulatory law and policy handle financial, economic, political and economic changes as rapidly occurring as it did in telecommunications over the last decade? Our answer to that question is less evaluative than it is descriptive. Evaluatively, the jury is justly out as to whether regulatory law and policy did well or poorly. Advocates and critics can be found on both sides of the issue. Descriptively, however, we can say that regulatory transformations in the telecommunications industries occurred over recognizable paths. Indeed, it is the fundamental premise of our book that regulatory law and policies are limited in number but myriad in application.

In this chapter we will concentrate on two telecommunications issues; one in the cable television industry and one in the telephone industry. You will also see familiar regulatory concepts such as unbundling, rate setting, and allocation.

The electricity, natural gas and telecommunications industries have "bottleneck problems" and those problems are addressed through different forms of regulation. In the electricity and natural gas industries, we concentrated on price regulation. In this chapter, we will concentrate on entry controls, although the bottleneck problems in all three industries have been addressed by both sorts of regulation.

A. HISTORY OF TELECOMMUNICATIONS REGULATION

The telecommunications industry is experiencing the most rapid change in its history.[1] Historically, telephone service, like gas and electricity, was seen as a traditional utility, treated like a natural monopoly, and was price regulated. Radio, television, and cable also have natural monopoly characteristics and were heavily regulated. Today, because of technological change, policy makers regard traditional telecommunications regulation as outdated and they seek to introduce more competition.

Telecommunications is an enormous industry. According to the Council for Economic Advisors, telecommunications accounts for a full one-sixth of the U.S. economy. But what exactly comprises the "telecommunications" industry?

For decades, government treated the telephone, radio, and television industries as separate, each constituting a distinct technology and a different product and each governed by a separate regulatory structure. However, technological innovation is removing the physical limitations that once separated these industries. For example, fiber optic technology enables the telephone industry to function as a television programming distributor and the television industry to function as a telephone service provider. The term "telecommunications" has been traditionally restricted to the telephone, telegraph, and related industries such as cellular communications, with television and radio broadcasting falling under the designation "mass media." Now, however, it is more appropriate to view all of these industries as part and parcel of the new age of "telecommunications."

By 1996, our national telecommunications policy was no longer able to deal with the technological changes of the telecommunications industry. On February 8, 1996, however, President Clinton signed into law the long-awaited Telecommunications Act of 1996 passed by Congress seven days earlier.[2] The Act is the culmination of nearly fourteen years of congressional debate on telecommunications reform, and represents a bipartisan mandate for increased private competition in the telecommunications industry. It is the first

---

[1] *See* R. HORWITZ, THE IRONY OF REGULATORY REFORM: THE DEREGULATION OF AMERICAN TELECOMMUNICATIONS (1989).

[2] The Telecommunications Act of 1996 §§ 301-305, 110 Stat. 56, 114-127 (1996) (to be codified at 47 U.S.C. §§ 522-613 (1996)). In the technologically-advanced spirit of the Act, President Clinton signed the bill using a device that immediately posted the Act on the World Wide Web. Thyfault, *Presidential Pen Starts Telecom Race*, Information Week, Feb. 12, 1996, at 26.

complete overhaul of telecommunications law since the Communications Act of 1934, and requires a new set of Federal Communications Commission (FCC) rules and regulations to implement the new congressional policy. Although bipartisan, the Act did not please everyone. Years in the making, numerous actors, complexity and private deal making all contribute to a less than coordinated piece of legislation.[3]

In the new Act, Congress had to update national telecommunications policy from the days when the primary communications problem facing the country was the static caused by the surplus of radio stations on the airwaves. Prior to the new legislation, the communications landscape had been framed largely by FCC regulations and court decisions interpreting the 1934 Act, several intermittent congressional statutes, a 1982 federal court decree which ordered the breakup of American Telephone and Telegraph (AT&T) (and which created the Regional Bell Operating Companies (RBOCs)),[4] and the regulations of state and local public utilities commissions (PUCs). The remainder of this section describes these forms of telecommunications law and then indicates how the new legislation reflects changes in the market structure of telecommunications.

1. TELEPHONY

The history of telephony can be viewed as divided into three eras: the first 100 years, which were dominated by AT&T, also known as the Bell System; the post-1982 decree era, which introduced meaningful competition into at least one arena of telephony, the long-distance market; and the post-1996 Act era, which promises to unleash almost all telecommunications industries—not just telephony—in competition with one another to various degrees. These three eras were largely defined by separate regulatory schemes, each introduced by separate entities, respectively: the FCC and the Department of Justice; a single federal district court judge; and the Congress.

a. THE FIRST 100 YEARS

The early history of telephone communications is dominated by the history of a single company, the Bell Company, later renamed American Telephone & Telegraph.[5] From the acquisition of the original patent for the telephone in 1876 to the breakup of the company in 1982 into a long-distance company and the RBOCs, the Bell System had developed into one of the most successful monopolies in any industry.

After Bell's early patents expired, there was nothing to prevent competitors from building their own telephone wire system. At the turn of the century, the telephone industry was competitive with a substantial part of local phone service provided by smaller companies in individual cities. In the meantime,

---

[3] For an inside look at the Act from a former FCC Chair see R. HUNDT, YOU SAY YOU WANT A REVOLUTION: A STORY OF INFORMATION AGE POLITICS (2000). For a recent critique of the Act see J. EISENACH & R. MAY, COMMUNICATIONS DEREGULATION AND FCC REFORM (2001).

[4] United States v. AT&T, 552 F. Supp. 131 (D.D.C. 1982).

[5] See R. K. VIETOR, CONTRIVED COMPETITION: REGULATION AND DEREGULATION IN AMERICA ch. 4 (1994).

Bell had concentrated on the long-distance market, developing technology and service that the local phone companies were unable to provide. Thus, the telephone industry, much like the electricity and natural gas industries, moved from local markets and local regulation to national markets and federal regulation.

Early regulatory efforts took place exclusively on the local level, as cities granted local users of early telephone systems permission to run their lines over public rights-of-way. An important feature of these early efforts was the treatment of telephone companies as "common carriers," a regulatory approach that remains today. The law of common carriers essentially requires that an industry so designated holds itself out to serve the general public. Under federal regulation, an entity so designated must provide adequate service at reasonable and nondiscriminatory rates and accept all customers on the same terms. In return, the industry receives a guaranteed service area.[6]

An important question during this early period was whether telephone companies had to offer their services to would-be competitors on terms equivalent to those offered to the general public. In other words, did telephone common carriers have to interconnect with other common carriers? Cases involving telephone companies concluded that interconnection could not be mandated. This development of common carrier law allowed the Bell System to use its position in the long-distance market to acquire most of the local telephone industry. By refusing these companies access to its own long-distance lines, the Bell System was able to force the smaller companies to either fold or merge into the growing Bell empire. This pattern of dominance continued largely uninterrupted until 1982.

In 1910, Congress passed the Mann-Elkins Act, which brought regulation of interstate telephone communications within the jurisdiction of the Interstate Commerce Commission (ICC).[7] It specifically denominated telephone companies as "common carriers," but did not specify their obligations toward other carriers. By the time of the Communications Act of 1934, by which time the Bell System had grown into a communications giant, monopoly regulation of telephone services was inevitable. The 1934 Act required Bell to provide "just and reasonable" prices, and allowed competition only if the FCC determined that the "public convenience and necessity" required it. A major objective of the 1934 Act was the realization of universal service—telephone service for every home, whether or not it would be profitable in a truly "open" market. In addition, because the size of the Bell System constituted a possible threat to related industries, the 1934 Act codified earlier commitments by Bell not to use the technology developed by Bell Labs, one of the major sources of technological innovation in the 20th century, to enter related industries, such as broadcasting. Thus, Congress and the FCC helped to both entrench Bell as the monopoly provider of telephone services and curtail technological innovation.

---

[6] *See* generally, M. KELLOGG, J. THORNE & P. HUBER, FEDERAL TELECOMMUNICATIONS LAW § 212 (1992); D. GINSBURG, M. BOTEIN & M. DIRECTOR, REGULATION OF THE ELECTRONIC MASS MEDIA 65-68 (1991).

[7] *See* Mann-Elkins Act of 1910, ch. 309, 36 Stat. 539 (1910).

The regulatory scheme of the first 100 years utilized three primary tools. First, telephone companies were protected franchises; potential competition was stifled because telephone companies were not required to interconnect with other telephone companies. Second, telephone companies were quarantined; Bell was not permitted to enter competitive markets other than telephony. Third, telephone companies were subject to extensive, "cradle-to-grave" regulation; all pricing and terms of service were subject to regulatory approval.

b. THE POST-1982 DECREE ERA

From 1934 to 1982, technological advances in telecommunications allowed the Bell System to expand into limited adjacent markets without violating the dictates of the 1934 Act. Microwave communications, coaxial cable development, telephony equipment, large business communications structures known as customer premises equipment (CPE), and enhanced communications services such as data processing through telephone lines all became part of the Bell empire.

The enormous growth of Bell during the first half of this century eventually became worrisome to the FCC and the Department of Justice, who began to allow competitors of Bell to enter certain niche markets. Antitrust law became the favored weapon of the Department of Justice and Bell competitors in the 1960s and 1970s, and these efforts eventually met with success. Faced with increasing pressure from all fronts, Bell finally gave in, and the resulting 1982 decree by Judge Harold Greene implementing a settlement agreement between Bell and the federal government.[8]

The decree was divided into four major parts. First, it required Bell-AT&T to divest itself of all of the RBOCs, nearly two-thirds of the company's capitalization. Second, it required the newly-formed RBOCs to interconnect to any long-distance carrier on an equal basis. Third, the decree prohibited the RBOCs from entering the long-distance market and placed severe limitations on the RBOCs ability to compete in any industry aside from local telephone service, including prohibitions on manufacturing its own consumer telephone equipment. Finally, the decree freed AT&T, now only a long-distance carrier, from any limitations on adjacent markets it wished to enter.

The decree thus had two opposite effects. On the one hand, it reinforced the regulatory scheme in the local telephone service industry. Considered natural monopolies because they operated using a grid of wires, the RBOCs were guaranteed a fair rate of return, but they were strictly limited in how they could enter other businesses. They were also now subject to the obligation to provide interconnection to other carriers on nondiscriminatory terms, except, of course, when that carrier sought to compete with the RBOC directly for its local telephone service market.

On the other hand, the decree virtually declared the long-distance service industry a "competitive" market, and opened it to rivals of AT&T such as MCI and Sprint.

---

[8] See United States v. AT&T, 552 F. Supp. 131 (D.D.C. 1982). GTE, another provider of local phone service, was similarly prohibited from offering long-distance and related services under the terms of a separate decree, United States v. GTE Corp., 603 F. Supp. 730 (D.D.C. 1984).

c. THE POST-1996 ACT ERA

With the passage of the Telecommunications Act of 1996, Congress ushered in a new era of telecommunications. Although the ramifications of the Act will not be fully revealed for decades, it is safe to say that the traditional regulatory paradigms for telephone services are now a part of history.

The 1996 Act abolishes the two-tiered framework for wire-based telephone companies created by the 1982 antitrust consent decree. The 1996 Act preempts any state regulation that prohibits entry to, or limits competition within, either the local or long-distance telephone market. It also contains provisions ensuring "universal service" of telecommunications services to educational institutions, public libraries, and other public institutions at discounted rates.

Local exchange carriers (LECs), which include the RBOCs, are permitted to enter the long-distance market once they satisfy a "competitive checklist" of reforms designed to ensure that LECs will not engage in anticompetitive behavior within its traditional service area. Among the requirements, LECs must provide:

- "interconnectivity" which allows competitors to tap into the network at any technically feasible point;

- facilities and services on an "unbundled" basis which makes it possible for carriers to purchase transmission and switching services "a la carte";

- "number portability" or the retention of an existing phone number by a customer who switches carriers; and,

- telephone pole access and emergency and directory assistance.

This entry regulation is intended to prevent RBOCs from using their control of existing telephone grids to block competitors from entering local telephone service markets.

2. RADIO AND TELEVISION BROADCASTING

While the 1996 Telecommunications Act also makes important changes in the regulation of radio and television broadcasting, government regulation of radio began in 1910 with the Wireless Ship Act and two years later with the Radio Act of 1912.[9] These two acts primarily regulated maritime communications and did not authorize the regulation of the nascent radio broadcasting industry over land. Radio broadcasters, however, soon began to lobby for regulation. As the number of stations increased, the amount of interference also increased. The growing number of radio stations during that time caused the problem of overlapping radio signals, which produced unintelligible reception. "With everybody on the air, nobody could be heard."[10] Unable to work out an acceptable system of self-regulation, radio industry executives cried out to the government for assistance. In 1924, President Hoover commented,

---

[9] Radio Act of 1912, 37 Stat. 302 (1912).

[10] *National Broadcasting Co. v. United States*, 319 U.S. 190, 212 (1943).

"[T]his is probably the only industry of the United States that is unanimously in favor of having itself regulated."[11]

After early attempts by President Hoover to control broadcasters' use of radio frequencies were struck down in 1926 by the Supreme Court,[12] Congress passed the Radio Act of 1927.[13] This act created the Federal Radio Commission (FRC) and gave it the authority to classify radio stations, assign frequencies to each class and to each individual station within a class, and to determine the power, hours of operation, and geographical service area of the stations. Congress gave the FRC broad authority to determine "whether the public interest, convenience, and necessity will be served" by the award of a radio broadcast license to an applicant.[14]

The FRC was reconstituted in 1934 as the Federal Communications Commission (FCC).[15] Although the FCC was given expanded powers with regard to the telephone and telegraph industries, Title III of the 1934 Act, which dealt with radio, was essentially unchanged from the 1927 Act. Despite the dramatic increases in the number of radio stations that obtained FCC licenses to operate a radio station, the basic structure of the FCC and the criteria used to determine whether a license will be awarded remained the same.

Before World War II and viable television transmitting and reception technology, radio dominated the broadcasting industry. Since the late 1940s, though, the medium of television has become one of the primary, and arguably one of the most important, sources of entertainment and information in the United States. Government regulation of television broadcasting closely mirrors that of radio broadcasting. Although the frequencies on which television signals are carried are different from those of radio, the problems of interfering signals are the same.

Government regulation of the broadcasting industry was necessitated by the problem of interfering signals or "electromagnetic incompatibility."[16] Once the government began to allocate spaces along the radio spectrum and to license companies to broadcast, however, the rationale for regulation became "scarcity." Because the FCC allocated fewer radio and television licenses than it had applicants, there had to be some method to choose which applications to grant. Rather than rely on a market, where licenses would be sold to those entities that paid the most for them, Congress assigned the responsibility for allocation to the FCC. The FCC was required to choose the applicants that would best serve the "public interest, convenience, and necessity." In Chapter 11, we will discuss Congress' decision when we consider the general issue of when should the government block market transactions to allocate scarce goods and services.

---

[11] S. Head, Broadcasting in America: A Survey of Television and Radio 126 (3rd ed. 1976).

[12] E. Krasnow & L. Longley, the Politics of Broadcast Regulations 9-10 (2d ed. 1978); see also Hoover v. Intercity Radio, 286 F. 1003 (D.C. Cir. 1923).

[13] Radio Act of 1927, 44 Stat. 1162 (1927).

[14] 47 U.S.C. § 154.

[15] Communications Act of 1934, ch. 652, 48 Stat. 1064 (1934).

[16] E. Diamond et al., Telecommunications in Crisis: the First Amendment, Technology, and Deregulation 67 (1983).

Under the 1934 Communications Act, Congress authorized the Commission to condition the grant of a license, or its renewal, on the licensee's compliance with FCC regulations. The FCC used the authority to establish service obligations which broadcasters had to meet concerning programming, advertising, and public service.

The FCC also used its authority to award licenses to structure competition in the broadcast industry. Again, the FCC based its actions on its authority to regulate broadcasting in the "public interest, convenience, and necessity." These requirements for licensing and renewal are of relevance to the topic of this chapter because they are a form of entry control. For example, through a policy known as "localism," the FCC stated an objective to provide a local radio station for every community capable of supporting one. This would help ensure that radio stations were responsive to the needs of the individual communities. Another objective was the guarantee of radio service to rural areas not capable of supporting a station—an objective closely analogous to the "universal service" policy pursued by the FCC in the telephone industry. In the television arena, the "localism" policy meant that low-power local stations were preferred to high-power national ones, so that "universal service" of television broadcasting was feasible. The FCC also interpreted the 1934 Act as prohibiting the entry of AT&T into television broadcasting. The Commission believed that AT&T had both the capital and technology necessary for dominating virtually any mass media or communications industry it wished.

The 1996 Telecommunications Act makes some adjustments in the regulation of broadcasting, but leaves in tact the basic structure of the 1934 Act. These changes affect both the FCC's efforts to establish service obligations and its efforts to use the system of licensing to structure competition in broadcasting.

In terms of the obligations of licensees to serve the public, the 1996 Act addresses the problem of protecting children from inappropriate programming. It mandates that all televisions manufactured after 1996 be installed with the controversial "V-chip," which would allow parents to control more effectively the television programs their children watch. Although the Act does not implement a rating system for television programs, it permits the FCC to promulgate regulations for such implementation if television broadcasters fail to implement their own ratings system within one year.

Congress also made changes that structure competition in broadcasting. Congress relaxed the Commission's previous "media concentration limits," restrictions on the number of television stations that any single company may own that reach a certain percentage of the national television market, increasing that percentage from 25% to 35%. Broadcast networks are allowed to own cable system operators, but the prohibition on networks owning other networks is maintained. Networks are permitted to use a new broadcast spectrum that will allow the transmission of "high-definition television" (HDTV), but the FCC is prohibited from awarding a portion of the spectrum until Congress has an opportunity to hold hearings on the desirability of holding an auction for these frequencies. Similarly, the Act addresses competition conditions in radio broadcasting. It repeals all national restrictions on ownership of radio stations, but maintains radio station ownership concentration limits in local markets. Companies are now prohibited from owning or operating more than a certain number of commercial radio stations in any market that has forty-five or more stations.

3. INTERNET

Congress not only addressed the problem of children's access to inappropriate broadcast programming; it attempted to deal with the same problem on the Internet. The Communications Decency Act of 1996, a subpart of the 1996 Telecommunications Act, has made it a crime to engage in the "knowing" transmission of material considered "indecent to minors" over the Internet and its provisions seem to ban all discussion and dissemination of information of abortion-related activities.[17] The Clinton administration announced that it would not enforce the abortion-related provisions of the Act because of doubts over its constitutionality.[18] An amendment to the Act that would have prohibited the FCC from regulating services on the Internet failed, although the FCC has stated that it currently has no plans or intentions to do so.

In *Reno v. American Civil Liberties Union*, 521 U.S. 844 (1997), those provisions of the 1996 Communications Decency Act which prohibited the knowing, transmission, or displaying to minors over the Internet of any "communication that, in context, depicts or describes, in terms patently offensive as measured by contemporary community standards, sexual or excretory activities or organs" was held unconstitutional. The Court ruled that the statute was content-based, facially overbroad, and constituted vague speech restrictions that violated the First Amendment. The Court also upheld § 505 of the Act, which requires cable television operators to scramble or block channels "primarily dedicated to sexually oriented programming" from children's viewing times. See, *United States v. Playboy Entertainment Group*, 529 U.S. 803 (2000).

4. CABLE TELEVISION

A final aspect of the 1996 Telecommunications Act is to recognize and regulate the cable television industry. Cable television is a prime example of a technological development that did not fit neatly into the regulatory structure created by the 1934 Communications Act. The hybrid nature of cable television and its resemblance to different forms of telecommunications make it an ideal subject to consider regulation in telecommunications and so we devote the last part of this chapter to the subject.

B. REGULATION OF LOCAL TELEPHONE MARKETS

The Telecommunications Act of 1996 is a massive piece of "deregulatory" legislation that cannot be covered in one book, let alone one chapter. The story

---

[17] *See* Shea v. Reno, 930 F. Supp. 916 (S.D.N.Y. 1996); ACLU v. Reno, 929 F. Supp. 824 (E.D. Pa. 1996).

[18] *Abortion Is OK Topic on Internet; Clinton Insists U.S. Won't Enforce Legal Curb*, THE BUFFALO NEWS, Feb. 9, 1996.

of the telecommunications industry restructuring has been complicated by the complete financial turnaround experienced in the market and highlighted by the WorldCom bankruptcy in 2002. The fallout from the financial meltdown of dot.com and telecommunications markets will not be clearly assessed for several years. Nevertheless, the deregulation process is well underway.

The first significant test of the Telecommunications Act of 1996 to promote competition in local telephone markets came in the case of *AT&T v. Iowa Utilities Board*, which is excerpted below. The parties to the suit read like a Who's Who of the telephone industry, including AT&T, MCI, GTE and Ameritech. Several provisions of the Act were challenged that imposed upon incumbents the obligation to share their network with competitors. The FCC's regulations addressed which network elements were to be shared; set out rules for negotiations and dispute resolution about the sharing arrangement; and, established a rate setting mechanism. Needless to say, incumbents were less than thrilled with having such obligations imposed upon them and thus challenged the FCC's regulations and the FCC's jurisdiction. The jurisdictional challenge was based on the traditional regulatory scheme, which meant that telephone rates were regulated by the states not by the federal government. Why, do you suppose, an incumbent telephone company would prefer state regulation?

We have greatly edited the opinion below. The jurisdictional challenge was resolved in favor of the FCC although not without a vigorous dissent particularly by Justice Breyer who wrote that the FCC did not have the authority to "promulgate the pricing and unbundling rules" before the Court.

We have omitted the jurisdictional discussion of the majority and most of the dissenting opinions. We have left the introduction of the majority opinion and the discussion regarding unbundling. As you read this except identify the regulatory justifications for this federal legislation intended to promote competition in local telephone markets.

AT&T V. IOWA UTILITIES BOARD
525 U.S. 366 (1999)

JUSTICE SCALIA delivered the opinion of the Court.

. . . Until the 1990s, local phone service was thought to be a natural monopoly. States typically granted an exclusive franchise in each local service area to a local exchange carrier (LEC), which owned, among other things, the local loops (wires connecting telephones to switches), the switches (equipment directing calls to their destinations), and the transport trunks (wires carrying calls between switches) that constitute a local exchange network. Technological advances, however, have made competition among multiple providers of local service seem possible, and Congress recently ended the longstanding regime of state-sanctioned monopolies.

The Telecommunications Act of 1996 fundamentally restructures local telephone markets. States may no longer enforce laws that impede competition, and incumbent LECs are subject to a host of duties intended to facilitate market entry. Foremost among these duties is the LEC's obligation to share its network with competitors. Under this provision, a requesting carrier can obtain access to an incumbent's network in three ways: It can purchase local telephone services at wholesale rates for resale to end users; it can lease elements of the incumbent's network "on an unbundled basis"; and it can interconnect its own facilities with the incumbent's network.[1] When an entrant seeks access through any of these routes, the incumbent can negotiate an agreement without regard to the duties it would otherwise have. . . . But if private negotiation fails, either party can petition the state commission that regulates local phone service to arbitrate open issues, which arbitration is subject to § 251 and the FCC regulations promulgated thereunder.

Six months after the 1996 Act was passed, the FCC issued its First Report and Order implementing the local-competition provisions. . . .

III

A

We turn next to the unbundling rules, and come first to the incumbent LECs' complaint that the FCC included within the features and services that must be provided to competitors under Rule 319 items that do not (as they must) meet the statutory definition of "network element"—namely, operator services and directory assistance, operational support systems (OSS), and vertical switching functions such as called I.D., call forwarding, and call waiting. The statute defines "network element" as

> "a facility or equipment used in the provision of a telecommunications service. Such term also includes features, functions, and capabilities that are provided by means of such facility or equipment, including subscriber numbers, databases, signaling systems, and information sufficient for billing and collection or used in the transmission, routing, or other provision of a telecommunications service."

Given the breadth of this definition, it is impossible to credit the incumbents' argument that a "network element" must be part of the physical facilities and equipment used to provide local phone service. Operator services and directory assistance, whether they involve live operators or automation, are "features, functions, and capabilities . . . provided by means of" the network equipment. OSS, the incumbent's background software system, contains essential network information as well as programs to manage billing, repair ordering, and other functions. Section 153(29)'s reference to "databases . . . and information sufficient for billing and collection or used in the transmission, routing, or other provision of a telecommunications service" provides ample basis for

---

[1] 47 U.S.C. § 251(c) (1994 ed., Supp. II) provides [in part] as follows: . . .

　　"(3) Unbundled Access

　　"The duty to provide, to any requesting telecommunications carrier for the provision of a telecommunications service, nondiscriminatory access to network elements on an unbundled basis at any technically feasible point on rates, terms, and conditions that are just, reasonable, and nondiscriminatory in accordance of this section and section 252 of this title. An incumbent local exchange carrier shall provide such unbundled network elements in a manner that allows a requesting carriers to combine such elements in order to provide each telecommunications service." . . .

treating this system as a "network element." And vertical switching features, such as caller I.D., are "functions . . . provided by means of" the switch, and thus fall squarely within the statutory definition. We agree with the Eighth Circuit that the Commission's application of the "network element" definition is eminently reasonable.

B.

We are of the view, however, that the FCC did not adequately consider the "necessary and impair" standards when it gave blanket access to these network elements, and others, in Rule 319. That rule requires an incumbent to provide requesting carriers with access to a minimum of seven network elements: the local loop, the network interface device, switching capability, interoffice transmission facilities, signaling networks and call-related databases, operations support systems functions, and operator services and directory assistance. If a requesting carrier wants access to additional elements, it may petition the state commission, which can make other elements available on a case-by-case basis.

Section 251(d)(2) of the Act provides:

> "In determining what network elements should be made available for purposes of subsection (c)(3) of this section, the Commission shall consider, at a minimum, whether—
>
> "(A) access to such network elements as are proprietary in nature is necessary; and
>
> "(B) the failure to provide access to such network elements would impair the ability of the telecommunications carrier seeking access to provide the services that it seeks to offer."

The incumbents argue that § 251(d)(2) codifies something akin to the "essential facilities" doctrine of antitrust theory opening up only those "bottleneck" elements unavailable elsewhere in the marketplace. We need not decide whether, as a matter of law, the 1996 Act requires the FCC to apply *that* standard; it may be that some other standard would provide an equivalent or better criterion for the limitation upon network-element availability that the statute has in mind. But we do agree with the incumbents that the Act requires the FCC to apply *some* limiting standard, rationally related to the goals of the Act, which it has simply failed to do. In the general statement of its methodology set forth in the First Report and Order, the Commission announced that it would regard the "necessary" standard as having been met regardless of whether "requesting carriers can obtain the requested proprietary element from a source other than the incumbent," since "[r]equiring new entrants to duplicate unnecessarily even a part of the incumbent's network could generate delay and higher costs for new entrants, and thereby impede entry by competing local providers and delay competition, contrary to the goals of the 1996 Act." And it announced that it would regard the "impairment" standard as having been met if "the failure of an incumbent to provide access to a network element would decrease the quality, or increase the financial or administrative cost of the service a requesting carrier seeks to offer, compared with providing that service *over other unbundled elements in the incumbent LEC's network,"* (emphasis added)—which means that comparison with self-provision, or with purchasing from another provider, is excluded. Since any entrant will request the most efficient network element that the incumbent has to offer, it is hard to imagine when the incumbent's failure to give access to the element would not constitute an "impairment" under this standard. The Commission asserts that it deliberately limited its inquiry to the incumbent's own network because no rational entrant would seek access to network elements from an incumbent if it could get better service or prices elsewhere. That may be. But the judgment allows entrants, rather than the Commission, to determine whether access to proprietary elements is necessary, and whether the failure to obtain access to nonproprietary elements would impair the ability to provide services. The Commission cannot, consistent with the statute, blind itself to the availability of elements outside the incumbent's network. That failing alone would require the Commission's rule to be set aside. In addition, however, the Commission's assumption that *any* increase in cost (or decrease in quality) imposed by denial of a network element renders access to that element to "impair" the entrant's ability to furnish its desired services is simply not in accord with the ordinary and fair meaning of those terms. An entrants whose anticipated annual profits from the proposed service are reduced from 100% of investment to 99% of investment has perhaps been "impaired" in its ability to amass earnings, but has not *ipso facto* been "impair[ed] . . . in its ability to provide the services it seeks to offer"; and it cannot realistically be said that the network element enabling it to raise its profits to 100% is "necessary." In a world of perfect competition, in which all carriers are providing their service at marginal cost, the Commission's total equating of increased cost (or decreased quality) with "necessity" and "impairment" might be reasonable; but it has not established the existence of such an ideal world. We cannot avoid the conclusion that, if Congress had wanted to give blanket access to incumbents' networks on a basis as unrestricted as the scheme the Commission has come up with, it would not have included § 251(d)(2) in the statute at all. It would simply have said (as the Commission in effect has) that whatever requested element can be provided must be provided.

When the full record of these proceedings is examined, it appears that that is precisely what the Commission *thought* Congress had said. The FCC was content with its expansive methodology because of its misunderstanding of § 251(c)(3), which directs an incumbent to allow a requesting carrier access to its network elements "at any technically feasible point." The Commission interpreted this to "impos[e] on an incumbent LEC *the duty to provide all network elements for which it is technically feasible to provide access,"* and went on to "conclude that we have authority to establish regulations that are coextensive" with this duty. As the Eighth Circuit held, that was undoubtedly wrong: Section 25(c)(3) indicates "*where* unbundled access must occur, not *which* [network] elements must be unbundled." The Commission does not seek review of the Eighth Circuit's holding on this point, and we bring it into our discussion only because the Commission's application of § 251(d)(2) was colored by this error. The Commission began with the premise that an incumbent was obliged to turn over as much of its network as was "technically feasible," and viewed (d)(2) as merely permitting it to soften that obligation by regulatory grace:

"To give effect to both sections 25(c)(3) and 251(d)(2), we conclude that the proprietary and impairment standards in section 251(d)(2) grant us the authority to refrain from requiring incumbent LECs to provide all network elements for which it is technically feasible to provide access on an unbundled basis."

The Commission's premise was wrong. Section 25(d)(2) does not authorize the Commission to create isolated exemptions from some underlying duty to make all network elements available. It requires the Commission to determine on a rational basis *which* network elements must be made available, taking into account the objectives of the Act and giving some substance to the "necessary" and "impair" requirements. The latter is not achieved by disregarding entirely the availability of elements outside the network, and by regarding *any* "increased cost or decreased service quality" as establishing a "necessity" and an "impair[ment]' ' " of the ability to "provide . . . services." . . .

. . . Because the Commission has not interpreted the terms of the statute in a reasonable fashion, we must vacate 47 CFR § 51.319 (1997).

C

The incumbent LECs also renew their challenge to the "all elements" rule, which allows competitors to provide local phone service relying solely on the elements in an incumbent's network. This issue may be largely academic in light of our disposition of Rule 319. If the FCC on remand makes fewer network elements unconditionally available through the unbundling requirement, an entrant will no longer be able to lease every component of the network. But whether a requesting carrier can access the incumbent's network in whole or in part, we think that the Commission reasonably omitted a facilities-ownership requirement. The 1996 Act imposes no such limitation; if anything, it suggests the opposite, by requiring in § 251(c)(3) that incumbents provide access to "any" requesting carrier. We agree with the Court of Appeals that the Commission's refusal to impose a facilities-ownership requirement was proper.

D

Rule 315(b) forbids an incumbent to separate already-combined network elements before leasing them to a competitor. As they did in the Court of Appeals, the incumbents object to the effect of this rule when it is combined with others before us today. TELRIC[19] allows an entrant to lease network elements based on forward-looking costs, Rule 319 subjects virtually all network elements to the unbundling requirement, and the all-elements rule allows requesting carriers to rely only on the incumbent's network in providing service. When Rule 315(b) is added to these, a competitor can lease a complete, preassembled network at (allegedly very low) cost-based rates.

The incumbents argue that this result is totally inconsistent with the 1996 Act. They say that it not only eviscerates the distinction between resale and

---

19 [Editor's note:] TELRIC pricing is based upon the cost of operating a hypothetical network built with the most efficient technology available.

unbundled access, but that it also amounts to Government-sanctioned regulatory arbitrage. Currently, state laws require local phone rates to include a "universal service" subsidy. Business customers, for whom the cost of service is relatively low, are charged significantly above cost to subsidize service to rural and residential customers, for whom the cost of service is relatively high. Because this universal-service subsidy is built into retail rates, it is passed on to carriers who enter the market through the resale provision. Carriers who purchase network elements at cost, however, avoid the subsidy altogether and can lure business customers away from incumbents by offering rates closer to cost. This, of course, would leave the incumbents holding the bag for universal service.

As was the case for the all-elements rule, our remand of Rule 319 may render the incumbents' concern on this score academic. Moreover, § 254 requires that universal-service subsidies be phased out, so whatever possibility of arbitrage remains will be only temporary. In any event, we cannot say that Rule 315(b) unreasonably interprets the statute.

Section 251(c)(3) establishes:

> "The duty to provide, to any requesting telecommunications carrier for the provision of a telecommunications service, nondiscriminatory access to network elements on an unbundled basis at any technically feasible points on rates, terms, and conditions that are just, reasonable, and nondiscriminatory in accordance with the terms and conditions of the agreement and the requirements of this section and section 252. . . . An incumbent local exchange carrier shall provide such unbundled network elements in a manner that allows requesting carriers to combine such elements in order to provide such telecommunications service."

Because this provision requires elements to be provided in a manner that "allows requesting carriers to combine" them, incumbents say that it contemplates the leasing of network elements in discrete pieces. It was entirely reasonable for the Commission to find that the text does not command this conclusion. It forbids incumbents to sabotage network elements that *are* provided in discrete pieces, and thus assuredly contemplates that elements *may* be requested and provided in this form (which the Commission's rules do not prohibit). But it does not say, or even remotely imply, that elements *must* be provided only in this fashion an never in combined form. Nor are we persuaded by the incumbents' insistence that the phrase "on an unbundled basis" in § 251(c)(3) means "physically separated." The dictionary definition of "unbundled" (and the only definition given, we might add) matches the FCC's interpretation of the word: "to give separate prices for equipment and supporting services."

The reality is that § 251(c)(3) is ambiguous on whether leased network elements may or must be separated, and the rule the Commission has prescribed is entirely rational, finding its basis in § 251(c)(3)'s nondiscrimination requirement. As the Commission explains, it is aimed at preventing incumbent LECs from "disconnect[ing] previously connected elements, over the objection of the requesting carrier, not for any productive reason, but just to impose wasteful reconnection costs on new entrants." It is true that Rule

315(b) could allow entrants access to an entire preassembled network. In the absence of Rule 315(b), however, incumbents could impose wasteful costs on even those carriers who requested less than the whole network. It is well within the bounds of the reasonable for the Commission to opt in favor of ensuring against an anticompetitive practice.

IV

The FCC's "pick and choose" rule provides, in relevant part:

> "An incumbent LEC shall make available without unreasonable delay to any requesting telecommunications carrier any individual interconnection, service, or network element arrangement contained in any agreement to which it is a party that is approved by a state commission pursuant to section 252 of the Act, upon the same rates, terms, and conditions as those provided in the agreement."

Respondents argue that this rule threatens the give-and-take of negotiations, because every concession as to an "interconnection, service, or network element arrangement" made (in exchange for some other benefit) by an incumbent LEC will automatically become available to every potential entrant into the market. A carrier who wants one term from an existing agreement, they say, should be required to accept *all* the terms in the agreement.

Although the latter position seems eminently fair, it is hard to declare the FCC's rule unlawful when it tracks the pertinent statutory language almost exactly. Section 252(i) provides:

> "A local exchange carrier shall make available any interconnection, service, or network element provided under an agreement approved under this section to which it is a party to any other requesting telecommunications carrier upon the same terms and conditions as those provided in the agreement."

The FCC's interpretation is not only reasonable, it is the most readily apparent. Moreover, in some respects the rule is more generous to incumbent LECs than § 252(i) itself. It exempts incumbents who can prove to the state commission that providing a particular interconnection service or network element to a requesting carrier is either (1) more costly than providing it to the original carrier, or (2) technically infeasible. And it limits the amount of time during which negotiated agreements are open to requests under this section. The Commission has said that an incumbent LEC can require a requesting carrier to accept all terms that it can prove as "legitimately related" to the desired term. Section 252(i) certainly demands no more than that. And whether the Commission's approach will significantly impede negotiations (by making it impossible for favorable interconnection-service or network-element terms to be traded off against unrelated provisions) is a matter eminently within the expertise of the Commission and eminently beyond our ken. We reverse the Eighth Circuit and reinstate the rule.

It would be gross understatment to say that the Telecommunications Act of 1996 is not a model of clarity. It is in many important respects a model of ambiguity or indeed even self-contradiction. That is most unfortunate for a piece of legislation that profoundly affects a crucial segment of the economy worth tens of billions of dollars. The 1996 Act can be read to grant (borrowing a phrase from incumbent GTE) "most promiscuous rights" to the FCC vis-à-vis the state commissions and to competing carriers vis-à-vis the incumbents—and the Commission has chosen in some instances to read it that way. But Congress is well aware that the ambiguities it chooses to produce in a statute will be resolved by the implementing agency. We can only enforce the clear limits that the 1996 Act contains, which in the present case invalidate only Rule 319.

For the reasons stated, the July 18, 1997 judgment of the Court of Appeals, is reversed in part and affirmed in part; the August 22, 1997 judgment of the Court of Appeals, is reversed in part; and the cases are remanded for proceedings consistent with this opinion.

———

Iowa Utilities Board established two fundamental principles in the effort to promote local telephone competition. First, the FCC had jurisdiction to regulate the more competitive environment. Second, new entrants could use incumbent facilities through a process of negotiation. But what if negotiation fails? Then what? Pursuant to the provisions of the act the FCC was authorized to prescribe methods for state commissions to use in setting rates when negotiations failed.

This form of ratesetting, not unlike traditional ratemaking, is intended to mimic the competitive market. However, ratesetting in the new telecommunications market is based on future costs, as compared to traditional ratemaking which, as we have seen, is based on historic costs. The next case examines the ratesetting under the Telecommunications Act of 1996. Justice Souter wrote the majority opinion in *Verizon* and nicely sets out a brief history of the telephone industry and of traditional ratemaking in that industry that is worth reading. The excerpt below addresses the contemporary scheme of ratesetting.

VERIZON COMMUNICATION, INC. V. FCC
122 S.Ct 1646 (2002)

JUSTICE SOUTER delivered the opinion of the Court.

. . . The 1996 Act both prohibits state and local regulation that impedes the provision of "telecommunications service," § 253(a), and obligates incumbent carriers to allow competitors to enter their local markets, § 251(c). Section 251(c) addresses the practical difficulties of fostering local competition by recognizing three strategies that a potential competitor may pursue. First, a competitor entering the market (a "requesting" carrier, § 251(c)(2)), may decide to engage in pure facilities-based competition, that is, to build its own network to replace or supplement the network of the incumbent. If an entrant takes this course, the Act obligates the incumbent to "interconnect" the competitor's facilities to its own network to whatever extent is necessary to allow the competitor's facilities to operate. At the other end of the spectrum, the statute permits an entrant to skip construction and instead simply to buy and resell "telecommunications service," which the incumbent has a duty to sell at wholesale. Between these extremes, an entering competitor may choose to lease certain of an incumbent's "network elements," which the incumbent has a duty to provide "on an unbundled basis" at terms that are "just, reasonable, and nondiscriminatory."

Since wholesale markets for companies engaged in resale, leasing, or interconnection of facilities cannot be created without addressing rates, Congress provided for rates to be set either by contracts between carriers or by state utility commission rate orders. Like other federal utility statutes that authorize contracts approved by a regulatory agency in setting rates between businesses, *e.g.,* (Federal Power Act); (Natural Gas Act), the Act permits incumbent and entering carriers to negotiate private rate agreements. State utility commissions are required to accept any such agreement unless it discriminates against a carrier not a party to the contract, or is otherwise shown to be contrary to the public interest. Carriers, of course, might well not agree, in which case an entering carrier has a statutory option to request mediation by a state commission. But the option comes with strings, for mediation subjects the parties to the duties specified in § 251 and the pricing standards set forth in § 252(d), as interpreted by the FCC's regulations. These regulations are at issue here.

As to pricing, the Act provides that when incumbent and requesting carriers fail to agree, state commissions will set a "just and reasonable" and "nondiscriminatory" rate for interconnection or the lease of network elements based on "the cost of providing the . . . network element," which "may include a reasonable profit." In setting these rates, the state commissions are, however, subject to that important limitation previously unknown to utility regulation: the rate must be "determined without reference to a rate-of-return or other rate-based proceeding." In *AT & T Corp. v. Iowa Utilities Bd.,* this Court upheld the FCC's jurisdiction to impose a new methodology on the States when setting these rates. The attack today is on the legality and logic of the particular methodology the Commission chose. . . .

. . . [T]he Eighth Circuit held that the FCC had no authority to control the methodology of state commissions setting the rates incumbent local-exchange carriers could charge entrants for network elements. . . .

. . . We reversed in upholding the FCC's jurisdiction to "design a pricing methodology" to bind state ratemaking commissions. . . .

With the FCC's general authority to establish a pricing methodology secure, the incumbent carriers' primary challenge on remand went to the method that the Commission chose. . . .

. . . Within the discretion left to it after eliminating any dependence on a "rate-of-return or other rate-based proceeding," the Commission chose a way of treating "cost" as "forward-looking economic cost," something distinct from the kind of historically based cost generally relied upon in valuing a rate base after *Hope Natural Gas.* In Rule 505, the FCC defined the "forward-looking economic cost of an element [as] the sum of (1) the total element long-run incremental cost of the element [TELRIC]; [and] (2) a reasonable allocation of forward-looking common costs," common costs being "costs incurred in providing a group of elements that "cannot be attributed directly to individual elements." Most important of all, the FCC decided that the TELRIC "should be measured based on the use of the most efficient telecommunications technology currently available and the lowest cost network configuration, given the existing location of the incumbent['s] wire centers."

"The TELRIC of an element has three components, the operating expenses, the depreciation cost, and the appropriate risk-adjusted cost of capital." A concrete example may help. Assume that it would cost $1 a year to operate a most-efficient loop element; that it would take $10 for interest payments on the capital a carrier would have to invest to build the lowest cost loop centered upon an incumbent carrier's existing wire centers (say $100, at 10 percent per annum); and that $9 would be reasonable for depreciation on that loop (an 11-year useful life); then the annual TELRIC for the loop element would be $20. . . .

Before us, the incumbent local-exchange carriers claim error in the Eighth Circuit's holding that a "forward-looking cost" methodology (as opposed to the use of "historical" cost) is consistent with § 252(d)(1), and its conclusion that the use of the TELRIC forward-looking cost methodology presents no "ripe" takings claim. The FCC and the entrants, on the other side, seek review of the Eighth Circuit's invalidation of the TELRIC methodology and the additional combination rules. We granted certiorari and now affirm on the issues raised by the incumbents, and reverse on those raised by the FCC and the entrants.

III

A

The incumbent carriers' first attack charges the FCC with ignoring the plain meaning of the word "cost". . . . The argument boils down to the proposition that "the cost of providing the network element" can only mean, in plain language and in this particular technical context, the past cost to an incumbent of furnishing the specific network element actually, physically, to be provided.

The incumbents have picked an uphill battle. At the most basic level of common usage, "cost" has no such clear implication. A merchant who is asked about "the cost of providing the goods" he sells may reasonably quote their current wholesale market price, not the cost of the particular items he happens to have on his shelves, which may have been bought at higher or lower prices.

When the reference shifts from common speech into the technical realm, the incumbents still have to attack uphill. To begin with, even when we have dealt with historical costs as a ratesetting basis, the cases have never assumed a sense of "cost" as generous as the incumbents seem to claim. . . .It would also be a mistake to forget that "cost" was a term in value-based ratemaking and has figured in contemporary state and federal ratemaking untethered to historical valuation.

What is equally important is that the incumbents' plain-meaning argument ignores the statutory setting in which the mandate to use "cost" in valuing network elements occurs. First, the Act uses "cost" as an intermediate term in the calculation of "just and reasonable rates," and it was the very point of *Hope Natural Gas* that regulatory bodies required to set rates expressed in these terms have ample discretion to choose methodology. Second, it would have been passing strange to think Congress tied "cost" to historical cost without a more specific indication, when the very same sentence that requires "cost" pricing also prohibits any reference to a "rate-of-return or other rate-based proceeding," each of which has been identified with historical cost ever since *Hope Natural Gas* was decided.

The fact is that without any better indication of meaning than the unadorned term, the word "cost" in § 252(d)(1), as in accounting generally, is "a chameleon," a "virtually meaningless" term, R. Estes, Dictionary of Accounting 32 (2d ed.1985). As Justice BREYER put it in *Iowa Utilities Bd.*, words like "cost" "give ratesetting commissions broad methodological leeway; they say little about the 'method employed' to determine a particular rate." We accordingly reach the conclusion adopted by the Court of Appeals, that nothing in § 252(d)(1) plainly requires reference to historical investment when pegging rates to forward-looking "cost."

B

The incumbents' alternative argument is that even without a stern anchor in calculating "the cost . . . of providing the . . . network element," the particular forward-looking methodology the FCC chose is neither consistent with the plain language of § 252(d)(1) nor within the zone of reasonable interpretation subject to deference under *Chevron U.S.A. Inc. v. Natural Resources Defense Council, Inc.* This is so, they say, because TELRIC calculates the forward-looking cost by reference to a hypothetical, most efficient element at existing wire-centers, not the actual network element being provided. . . .

Similarly, the claim that TELRIC exceeds reasonable interpretative leeway is open to the objection already noted, that responsibility for "just and reasonable" rates leaves methodology largely subject to discretion. . . .

The incumbents' (and Justice BREYER's) basic critique of TELRIC is that by setting rates for leased network elements on the assumption of perfect competition, TELRIC perversely creates incentives against competition in fact. The incumbents say that in purporting to set incumbents' wholesale prices at the level that would exist in a perfectly competitive market (in order to make retail prices similarly competitive), TELRIC sets rates so low that entrants will always lease and never build network elements. And even if an entrant would otherwise consider building a network element more efficient than the best one then on the market (the one assumed in setting the TELRIC rate), it would likewise be deterred by the prospect that its lower cost in building and operating this new element would be immediately available to its competitors; under TELRIC, the incumbents assert, the lease rate for an incumbent's existing element would instantly drop to match the marginal cost of the entrant's new element once built. According to the incumbents, the result will be, not competition, but a sort of parasitic free-riding, leaving TELRIC incapable of stimulating the facilities-based competition intended by Congress.

We think there are basically three answers to this no-stimulation claim of unreasonableness: (1) the TELRIC methodology does not assume that the relevant markets are perfectly competitive, and the scheme includes several features of inefficiency that undermine the plausibility of the incumbents' no-stimulation argument; (2) comparison of TELRIC with alternatives proposed by the incumbents as more reasonable are plausibly answered by the FCC's stated reasons to reject the alternatives; and (3) actual investment in competing facilities since the effective date of the Act simply belies the no-stimulation argument's conclusion.

[In this part of the opinion, Justice Souter provides a lengthy, technical written discussion of the incumbent's arguments against the FCC's claim that TELRIC will stimulate competition.]

At the end of the day, theory aside, the claim that TELRIC is unreasonable as a matter of law because it simulates but does not produce facilities-based competition founders on fact. The entrants have presented figures showing that they have invested in new facilities to the tune of $55 billion since the passage of the Act (through 2000). The FCC's statistics indicate substantial resort to pure and partial facilities-based competition among the three entry strategies: as of June 30, 2001, 33 percent of entrants were using their own facilities; 23 percent were reselling services; and 44 percent were leasing network elements (26 percent of entrants leasing loops with switching; 18 percent without switching). The incumbents do not contradict these figures, but merely speculate that the investment has not been as much as it could have been under other ratemaking approaches, and they note that investment has more recently shifted to nonfacilities entry options. We, of course, have no idea whether a different forward-looking pricing scheme would have generated even greater competitive investment than the $55 billion that the entrants claim, but it suffices to say that a regulatory scheme that can boast such substantial competitive capital spending over a 4-year period is not easily described as an unreasonable way to promote competitive investment in facilities. . . .

Finally, as to the incumbents' accusation that TELRIC is too complicated to be practical, a criticism at least as telling can be leveled at traditional ratemaking methodologies and the alternatives proffered. . . .

We cannot say whether the passage of time will show competition prompted by TELRIC to be an illusion, but TELRIC appears to be a reasonable policy for now, and that is all that counts. The incumbents have failed to show that TELRIC is unreasonable on its own terms, largely because they fall into the trap of mischaracterizing the FCC's departures from the assumption of a perfectly competitive market (the wire-center limitation, regulatory and development lags, or the refusal to prescribe high depreciation and capital costs) as inconsistencies rather than pragmatic features of the TELRIC plan. Nor have they shown it was unreasonable for the FCC to pick TELRIC over alternative methods, or presented evidence to rebut the entrants' figures as to the level of competitive investment in local-exchange markets. In short, the incumbents have failed to carry their burden of showing unreasonableness to defeat the deference due the Commission. We therefore reverse the Eighth Circuit's judgment insofar as it invalidated TELRIC as a method for setting rates under the Act. . . .

The 1996 Act sought to bring competition to local-exchange markets, in part by requiring incumbent local-exchange carriers to lease elements of their networks at rates that would attract new entrants when it would be more efficient to lease than to build or resell. Whether the FCC picked the best way to set these rates is the stuff of debate for economists and regulators versed in the technology of telecommunications and microeconomic pricing theory. The job of judges is to ask whether the Commission made choices reasonably within the pale of statutory possibility in deciding what and how items must be leased and the way to set rates for leasing them. The FCC's pricing and additional combination rules survive that scrutiny.

The judgment of the Court of Appeals is reversed in part and affirmed in part, and the cases are remanded for further proceedings consistent with this opinion. . .

JUSTICE BREYER, with whom JUSTICE SCALIA joins as to Part VI, concurring in part and dissenting in part.

I agree with the majority that the Telecommunications Act of 1996 (Act or Telecommunications Act) does not require a historical cost pricing system. I also agree that, at the present time, no taking of the incumbent firms' property in violation of the Fifth Amendment has occurred. I disagree, however, with the Court's conclusion that the specific pricing and unbundling rules at issue here are authorized by the Act.

I

The primary goal of the Telecommunications Act is to "promote competition and reduce regulation" in both local and long-distance telecommunications markets. As part of that effort, the Act requires incumbent local telecommunications firms to make certain "elements" of their local systems available to new competitors seeking to enter those local markets. If the incumbents and competitors cannot agree on the price that an incumbent can charge a new entrant, local regulators will determine the price. The regulated price will depend upon the element's "cost." In *AT & T Corp. v. Iowa Utilities Bd.*, this Court held that the Act authorizes the FCC to set rules for determining those prices.

These cases require the Court to review the Commission's rules. Those rules create a "start-from-scratch" version of what the Commission calls a "Total Element Long-Run Incremental Cost" system (TELRIC). In essence, the Commission requires local regulators to determine the cost of supplying a particular incumbent network "element" to a new entrant, not by looking at what it has cost *that incumbent* to supply the element in the past, nor by looking at what it will cost *that incumbent* to supply that element in the future. Rather, the regulator must look to what it would cost *a hypothetical perfectly efficient firm* to supply that element in the future, assuming that the hypothetical firm were to build essentially from scratch a new, perfectly efficient communications network. The only concession to the incumbent's actual network is the presumption that presently existing wire centers—which hold the switching equipment for a local area—will remain in their current locations.

An example will help explain the system as I understand it. Imagine an incumbent local telephone company's major switching center, say, in downtown Chicago, from which cables and wires run through conduits or along poles to subsidiary switching equipment, other electronic equipment, and eventually to end-user equipment, such as telephone handsets, computer modems, or fax machines located in office buildings or private residences. A new competitor, whom the law entitles to use an "element" of the incumbent firm's system, asks for use of such an "element," say, a single five-block portion of this system, thereby obtaining access to 20 downtown office buildings. Under the Commission's TELRIC, the incumbent's "cost" (upon which "rates" must be based) equals not the real resources that the Chicago incumbent must spend to provide the five-block "element" demanded, but the resources that a hypothetical perfectly efficient new supplier would spend were that supplier rebuilding the entire downtown Chicago system, other than the local wire center, from scratch. This latter figure, of course, might be very different from any incumbent's actual costs.

As a reviewing Court, we must determine, among other things, whether the Commission has " 'abuse[d]' " its statutorily delegated " 'discretion' " to create implementing rules. In doing so, we must assume that Congress intended to grant the Commission broad legal leeway in respect to the substantive content of the rules, particularly since the subject matter is a highly technical one, namely ratemaking, where the agency possesses expert knowledge.

Nonetheless, that leeway is not unlimited. It is bounded, for example, by the scope of the statute that grants authority and by the need for the agency to show a "rational connection" between the regulations and the statute's purposes. We must determine whether, despite the leeway given experts on technical subject matter, agency regulations exceed these legal limits. And, reluctantly, I have come to the conclusion that they do. After considering the incumbents' objections and the Commission's responses, I cannot find that "rational connection" between statutory purpose and implementing regulation that the law demands. . . .

. . . The Telecommunications Act is not a ratemaking statute seeking better regulation. It is a deregulatory statute seeking competition. . . .

Nonetheless, the critics argue, the Commission cannot lawfully choose a system that thwarts a basic statutory purpose without offering any significant compensating advantage. They take the relevant purpose as furthering local competition where feasible. They add that rates will further that purpose (1) if they discourage new firms from using the incumbent's facilities or "elements" when it is significantly less expensive, economically speaking, for the entrant to build or to buy elsewhere, and (2) if they encourage new firms to use the incumbent's facilities when it is significantly less expensive, economically speaking, for the entrant to do so. They point out that prices that approximately reflect an *actual* incumbent's *actual* additional costs of supplying the services (or "element") demanded will come close to doing both these things. But prices like the Commission's, based on the costs that a *hypothetical* "most efficient" firm would incur if *hypothetically* building largely from scratch would do neither. Indeed, they would do exactly the opposite, creating incentives that hinder rather than further the statute's basic objective.

First, the critics ask, why, given such a system, would a new entrant ever build or buy a new element? After all, the Commission's rate-setting system sets the incumbent's compulsory leasing rate at a level that would rarely exceed the price of building or buying elsewhere. That is because the Commission's rate-setting system chooses as its basis the hypothetical cost of the most efficient method of providing the relevant service—*i.e.,* the cost of entering a house through the use of electrical conduits or of using wireless (if cheaper in general) and it then applies those costs (based on, say, hypothetical wireless) *as if* they were the cost of the system in place (the twisted pair of wires). Why then would the new entrant use an electrical conduit, or a wireless system, to enter a house when, by definition, the Commission will require the incumbent to lease its pair of twisted wires at an equivalent price or lower— whether or not the incumbent will have to spend more, in fact, to provide the twisted wires? The rules further discourage independent building or buying by assessing a special penalty upon the new entrant that does so, for that entrant will have to worry that soon another newer new entrant will insist upon sharing the incumbent's equivalent of that very element at a still lower regulation-determined price based on subsequent technological developments.

The Commission's system will tend to create instances in which (1) the incumbent's *actual* future cost of maintaining an element (say, a set of wires), will exceed (2) the new entrant's cost of building or buying elsewhere (say, through wireless or wires in electrical conduits) which, in turn, will equal, (or even exceed), (3) the *hypothetical* future "best practice" cost (namely, what the experts decide will, in general, be cheapest). In such a case (or in related cases, where technological improvements, actual or predicted, tend to offset various cost differences), the new entrant will uneconomically share the incumbent's facilities by leasing rather than building or buying elsewhere. And that result, in the assumed circumstances, is wasteful. It undermines the efficiency goal that the majority itself claims the Act seeks to achieve.

Nor is the "sharing" of facilities (*e.g.,* the wire pairs) that this result embodies consistent with the competition that the Act was written to promote. That is because firms that share existing facilities do not compete in respect to the facilities that they share, any more than several grain producers who auction their grain at a single jointly owned market compete in respect to *auction services. . . .*

Second, what incentive would the Commission's rules leave the incumbents either to innovate or to invest in a new "element?" The rules seem to say that the incumbent will share with competitors the cost-reducing benefits of a successful innovation, while leaving the incumbent to bear the costs of most unsuccessful investments on its own. Why would investment not then stagnate? . . .

I recognize that no regulator is likely to enforce the Commission's rules so strictly that investment literally slows to a trickle. Indeed, the majority cites figures showing that in the past several years new firms have invested $30 to $60 billion in local communications markets. We do not know how much of this investment represents facilities, say broadband, for which an incumbent's historical network offers no substitute. Nor do we know whether this number is small or large compared with what might have been. . . .

The criticisms described in Part III are serious, potentially severing any rational relation between the Commission's regulations and the statutory provision's basic purposes. Hence, the Commission's responses are important. Do those responses reduce the force of the criticisms, blunt their edges, or suggest offsetting virtues? I have found six major responses. But none of them is convincing. . . . [Justice Breyer then considers and rejects the FCC's arguments regarding: (1) depreciation; (2) profit regulation; (3) other jurisdictions domestically and internationally; (4) how the "most efficient" firm hypothetical operates; (5) state regulatory discretion; and, (6) how time, through "regulatory lag" will smooth out the regulatory scheme.]

For these reasons, I dissent.

NOTES AND QUESTIONS

1. As noted repeatedly in the readings, the purpose of the Telecommunications Act of 1996 was to stimulate competition in local telephony by granting rights to new entrants. Do you think new entrants should be given, in effect, new property rights? In assessing whether to provide new entrants (also called competitive local exchanges carriers CLECs) with new rights to access, the FCC must also assess whether the failure to provide access might *impair* the provision of services. By regulation the Commission defines "impair" as occurring when "lack of access to [an] element materially diminishes a requesting carrier's ability to provide the services it seeks to offer."[20]

In *U.S. Telecom Ass'n v. FCC*, 20 F.3d 415 (D.C. Cir. 2002) incumbent local exchange carriers (ILECs) challenged FCC orders that adopted uniform national rules that required ILECs to lease a variety of unbundled network elements to CLECs. The FCC did so to accomplish the goals of the Act: " "(1) rapid introduction of competition, (2) promotion of facilities-based competition, investment and innovation, (3) certainty in the marketplace, (4) administrative practicality and (5) reduced regulation." 290 F.3d at 423. On review the D.C. Circuit Court remanded these orders back to the Commission reasoning that while the FCC's goal was to rapidly expand competition through national rules that "Congress did not authorize so open-ended a judgment. It made "impairment" the touchstone. 290 F.3d at 425.

What argument can you make for and against uniform national rules which require an incumbent to make specific property available to new entrants? How does the impairment standard operate here?

2. What ratesetting formula was used in *Verizon*? How does it differ from the traditional rate formula described in Chapter 4? Which would you prefer as a customer? As a shareholder? Why?

---

[20] 15 FCC Recd 3725 (1999).

3. Among the other arguments made by the incumbents in *Verizon* was that TELRIC was constitutionally suspect. They argued that "cost" needed to be based on historical investment or otherwise a taking of property in violation of the Fifth Amendment might occur. The incumbent takings claims was easily dispatched by Justice Souter saying that "this Court has never considered a takings challenge on ratesetting methodology without being presented with specific rate orders alleged to be confiscatory. . . . Undeniably, then, the general rule is that any questions about the constitutionality of rate-setting are raised by rates, not methods. . . ."

Justice Souter is making the traditional distinction between constitutional challenge "on the face" of a statute or rule and an "as applied" challenge. What is the significance of this distinction? Can you never challenge the constitutionality of a statute "on its face"? Or, must you always have a specific application? Does this distinction apply to all Fifth Amendment takings claims? Does it apply to rate cases? Can you think of an example of exceptions to the "general rule" stated by Justice Souter?

C.   REGULATION OF CABLE TELEVISION

Cable television is a product and a service that has similarities both to broadcast television and to telephony. Cable systems escape facile denomination as simply one kind of regulated product or another, thus making regulation complex. As you read the remainder of this chapter, notice the different ways in which regulators view cable television, and how these differing views contribute to alternate theories for its regulation and the choice of multiple regulatory tools. In fact, cable television regulation has been justified by economic arguments of scarcity and natural monopoly as well as by a non-economic public interest argument in the wide dissemination of information.

1.   REGULATORY HISTORY

Primitive cable systems first appeared in the late 1940s and early 1950s. These early systems were confined largely to rural areas, where mountains or unusual topography made television broadcast reception to the region difficult. These early systems, appropriately deemed "community antenna television" (CATV) systems, consisted of little more than an antenna placed at an advantageous location, usually on top of a mountain or big hill, with coaxial cable wires running from the antenna, across telephone or utility poles, or later, buried underground, to individual homes.

Thus, early CATV system operators simply "re-transmitted" television broadcast signals and contained no programming other than that which was available over the airwaves. Therefore, broadcasters had a pecuniary interest in CATV systems, at least in the first decade of its development.[21] The development of cable television led to an increase in the size of the audience for broadcast television. Largely unrestricted by federal or state regulation, CATV systems grew from 70 in 1952 to approximately 550 by 1960. The total number of subscribers to CATV systems increased from 14,000 to over 550,000 during this same period.

---

[21] *See e.g.*, P. PARSONS, CABLE TELEVISION AND THE FIRST AMENDMENT (1987).

By the mid 1960s, improvements in cable technology and the development of microwave relay stations, which allowed CATV systems to import television programming from distant locations, increased the opportunities of, and ultimately began to change the nature of the product offered by CATV operators. Because cable wires were now capable of transmitting twelve channels and long-distance programming could be procured to fill these channels, CATV systems began to function as competitors to broadcast television. This evolution of cable from a technological extension of, and supplement to, broadcast television to one of its competitors, differentiates the term "cable television" from its predecessor CATV system.

Congress' major intervention in the area of telecommunications was in 1934, and had specifically directed the FCC to regulate a number of different kinds of media, including radio, telephone systems, and newspapers. This meant that the FCC had to determine how the 1934 Act applied to television broadcasting and cable television although neither industry existed at the time when Congress passed the legislation. The application to television, however, was more obvious. The 1934 Act authorizes the Commission to regulate entities that broadcast electronic signals. As you read, television signals create the same problem of electrical interference as radio broadcasting. By comparison, cable television is not engaged in broadcasting—cable operators obtain programming by receiving electronic signals and they rebroadcast the programming along a wire grid. Initially, the FCC did not assert jurisdiction over cable television for this reason. After being lobbied by television broadcasters, because they saw the cable industry as a threat, the FCC changed its position. It asserted that it had jurisdiction because the 1934 Act required it to ensure that television broadcasting served the "public interest." The Commission argued that because cable television had the potential to compete unfairly with television broadcasters, it was necessary to regulate cable television to protect broadcast television. Without such protection, the FCC predicted television broadcasters were likely to go out of business, and if this occurred, persons who did not have cable television would be adversely affected. In this manner, the FCC concluded that the "public interest" requirement of the 1934 Act required it to regulate cable television.

You will read more about this rationale later in the chapter. For now you should recognize that the FCC's regulation of cable television was justified under legislation that was signed into law years before cable television was created. For this reason, the FCC continually asked Congress for direction on cable issues as it regulated cable television through various regulations and administrative decisions. Although Congress considered cable legislation several times during this period, the pleas of the FCC were not answered until 1984.

In 1984, Congress passed the Cable Communications Policy Act,[22] which simultaneously codified the established regulatory structure for cable television, dividing regulatory responsibilities between local government and the FCC, and deregulated cable rates for the great majority of all cable companies in the country. Cable companies flourished under the Act, growing at an unprecedented rate and offering more programming services to consumers

---

[22] Pub. L. No. 98-549, 98 Stat. 2780 (1984).

than ever before. Anything that helps cable companies, however, gets the attention of broadcasters, and the major national networks complained loudly to Congress about their perceived loss of market power. Highly vocal consumer groups also played a large role in the period following the 1984 Act, as most homes saw their cable rates increase significantly under the deregulatory environment of the 1984 Act.

In 1992, Congress responded to these concerns by passing the Cable Television Consumer Protection and Competition Act of 1992.[23] This Act re-regulated much of the cable industry, putting into place a regulatory structure more complicated than anything the FCC or cable companies had seen before. The 1992 Act also included a complex form of rate regulation. The FCC had barely begun addressing the enormity of its task before Congress passed the Telecommunications Act of 1996, which overhauled the entire telecommunications field. Nonetheless, many of the provisions from the 1992 Act were unaffected by the 1996 Act, and they remain good law.

At the same time, the 1996 Act also repealed many of the provisions of the 1992 Act, which had reintroduced cable rate regulation after eight years of almost total deregulation under the 1984 Act. The 1996 Act immediately eliminated all rate regulation for small cable system operators and repealed current FCC rules regulating cable rates for other cable system operators on services beyond "basic tier" cable programming by March 1, 1999. The "basic tier" of cable programming consists of the services furnished to all subscribers for the basic cable rate, such as local broadcast network programming, public television channels, and programming provided by local government. All rate regulation, including "basic tier" programming, is also prohibited for any cable system operator facing "effective competition" from comparable video programming services. The 1996 Act broadened the definition of "effective competition" from the 1992 Act to include local telephone companies (LECs) and other multichannel television programming providers.

The 1996 Act also sought to take advantage of the fact telephone and cable companies developed separate wire grids as the result of the historical pattern of regulation. Most residences now have three lines running to their homes: one for electricity, one for telephone service, and one for cable. There have been technological developments that may make it possible for electric utilities and telephone companies to provide cable services and for electrical utilities and cable operators to provide telephone services. FCC regulations have been one reason that this technology has not been exploited. In the early 1970s, the FCC adopted a series of rules prohibiting various kinds of media interests from owning interests in other media outlets. These rules, the "cross-ownership" rules, stemmed from a desire to prevent undue concentration in media ownership within larger markets. One such rule, the "telco-cable" ban, prohibited telephone common carriers from offering cable television services to viewers within the market that they operated. Separate rules also prohibited the control, ownership, or operation of cable television services by national television networks and local broadcasters within the broadcasters' service area. These rules survived both the 1984 Act and the 1992 Act,[24] but Congress

---

[23] Pub. L. No. 102-385, 106 Stat. 1460 (codified in various sections of 47 U.S.C.).

[24] Some of the cross-ownership rules were struck down by courts on First Amendment grounds.

repealed them in 1996 to promote the competition envisioned by the Telecommunications Act, with one very important exception. Local telephone companies are prohibited from acquiring the incumbent cable company in their local service area; otherwise, the "two-wire model" would be owned by a single provider, and the possibility of competition from the other line would be nonexistent.

2. RATE REGULATION

The history of rate regulation of cable television is one of many twists and turns. Rates have been regulated, deregulated, re-regulated, and deregulated again. This section explores the justification for rate regulation, and why rate regulation has this tortured history. More specifically, it considers whether cable television is a natural monopoly or whether it is possible to have competition among cable operators for local customers.

The argument for rate regulation is that cable television is a natural monopoly because cable operators depend on a grid system to deliver programming. As you know from Chapter 4, the existence of a grid is the *sine qua non* of a natural monopoly. Unlike other natural monopolies, however, cable operators do not furnish a service that is a necessity. Moreover, cable operators face competition, at least to some extent, from other forms of entertainment. Furthermore, if Congress' repeal (by the 1996 Act) of the ban prohibiting cable operation by telephone companies creates effective competition in the cable market, rate regulation may be unnecessary. At the end of this section you will be asked to consider whether this reform is likely to have this result.

a. REGULATORY JUSTIFICATION

Cable television regulation has been justified on various grounds. At times, regulation has been based on a scarcity rationale. Different versions of this argument have made their way into the courts. At least one court has analogized the limited space on telephone and utility poles to the spectrum scarcity market failure of radio and broadcasting.[25] Another court has presented the scarcity problem in a slightly different manner: "A city needs control over the number of times its citizens must bear the inconvenience of having its streets dug up and the best times for it to occur. Thus, government and cable operators are tied in a way that government and newspapers are not."[26] Also, cable television is said to suffer from a second market failure: it closely resembles a natural monopoly. The following excerpt describes the characteristics common to most natural monopolies.

See, e.g., Chesapeake and Potomac Tel. Co. v. United States, 830 F. Supp. 909 (E.D. Va. 1993), *aff'd*, 42 F.3d 181 (4th Cir. 1994), *vacated*, 116 S. Ct. 557 (1996); *U.S. West v. United States*, No. C93-1523R (W.D. Wash. June 15, 1994) (slip opinion); *BellSouth Corp. v. United States*, 868 F. Supp. 1335 (N.D. Ala. 1994); *Ameritech Corp. v. United States*, 867 F. Supp. 721 (N.D. Ill. 1994). These decisions have been largely rendered moot by the 1996 Act, which opens up ownership.

[25] *Telesat Cablevision, Inc. v. City of Riviera Beach*, 733 F. Supp. 383 (S.D. Fla. 1991).

[26] *Community Communications v. Boulder*, 660 F.2d 1370, 1377-78 (10th Cir. 1981).

OMEGA SATELLITE PRODS. CO. v. CITY OF INDIANAPOLIS
694 F.2d 119 (7th Cir. 1982)

POSNER, CIRCUIT JUDGE.

The cost of the cable grid appears to be the biggest cost of a cable television system and to be largely invariant to the number of subscribers the system has. We said earlier that once the grid is in place—once every major street has a cable running above it or below it that can be hooked up to the individual residences along the street—the cost of adding another subscriber probably is small. If so, the average cost of cable television would be minimized by having a single company in any given geographical area; for if there is more than one company and therefore more than one grid, the cost of each grid will be spread over a smaller number of subscribers, and the average cost per subscriber, and hence price, will be higher.

If the foregoing accurately describes conditions in Indianapolis . . . it describes what economists call a "natural monopoly," wherein the benefits, and indeed the very possibility, of competition are limited. You can start with a competitive free-for-all—different cable television systems frantically building out their grids and signing up subscribers in an effort to bring down their average costs faster than their rivals—but eventually there will be only a single company, because until a company serves the whole market it will have an incentive to keep expanding in order to lower its average costs. In the interim there may be wasteful duplication of facilities. This duplication may lead not only to higher prices to cable television subscribers, at least in the short run, but also to higher costs to other users of the public ways, who must compete with the cable television companies for access to them. An alternative procedure is to pick the most efficient competitor at the outset, give him a monopoly, and extract from him in exchange a commitment to provide reasonable services at reasonable rates. In essence Omega's antitrust allegations accuse the City of Indianapolis of having taken this alternative route to the monopoly that may be the inevitable destination to which all routes converge.

NOTES AND QUESTIONS

1. Does the existence of a grid justify regulation? Why not let several cable companies compete for subscribers? Should municipalities allow for open entry rather than exclusive franchises? Recall from Chapter 4 that Professor Demsetz argued that government should let the market determine whether the existence of a grid discourages competitors from entering a market. Similarly, Professor Hazlett argues that open entry can increase consumer surplus at no social cost, but at reduced profits for operators.[27] Judge Posner, in the excerpt above, noted that the cable grid was a monopoly. In his treatise, he suggests an alternative to regulation by having the cable company contract with a sufficient number of subscribers (without the necessity of a franchise)

---

[27] Hazlett, *Duopolistic Competition in Cable Television: Implications for Public Policy*, 7 YALE J. REG. 65 (1990).

to enable them to cover production costs, because "[n]o firm would begin building its cable grid until after a period of solicitation, and if in that period a strong consumer preference for one firm was indicated the other firm would sell their subscriber contracts to it."[28]

2. Other analysts argue against open entry because of wasteful duplication.[29] According to this argument, it makes no economic sense to have multiple transmission lines, also known as "over builds." Yet producers of video games, personal computers, and cars enter and are forced out of markets if their investment is imprudent. Why should cable operators be treated differently? What answer is suggested by the concept of the regulatory compact that you studied in Chapter 4?

3. According to one study, there is little empirical evidence of competition among cable operators. Of nine thousand systems in operation, there have been sixty-five examples of over builds and only three instances of competition. Every other case of competition ended by one company being acquired or going out of business.[30] Does this evidence establish that cable television is a natural monopoly?

Is cable television even a monopoly? Cable television is a monopoly only if it has no competition. Does cable television compete with other forms of entertainment, such as movies, home videos, radio, compact disks, and reading? If these other forms of entertainment are competitors, then the cable operator risks losing customers to other forms of entertainment when there is a price increase. Because these other forms of entertainment obviously provide some competition, the key question may be how inelastic is the demand for cable television.

Is "entertainment" the correct market to be used in assessing whether or not cable is a monopoly? Is "information" a better market? Should Congress or the FCC protect cable because it provides the public with information? Does the public have other sources besides cable for information?

As you studied in Chapter 2, the concept of elasticity measures the change in demand caused by a change in price. When prices are inelastic, a seller can raise prices without an exact corresponding decrease in demand. When prices are elastic, as in a perfectly competitive market, the seller will lose all of its customers if it raises its price. How much flexibility does a cable operator have to raise its prices in light of the competition from other forms of entertainment?

4. Does rate regulation contribute to the natural monopoly status of cable systems? The front-end capital intensive nature of cable television usually forces competing companies to charge higher rates, but what happens if regulators require competitors to charge the same (lower) prices as the

---

[28] R. POSNER, ECONOMIC ANALYSIS OF LAW 361 (3rd ed. 1986); *see also* A. KAHN, THE ECONOMICS OF REGULATION: PRINCIPLES AND INSTITUTIONS 359–63 (2d ed. 1988).

[29] *E.g.*, Smiley, *Regulation and Competition in Cable Television*, 7 YALE J. REG. 121 (1990); *see also* Hazlett, *A Reply to Regulation and Competition in Cable Television*, 7 YALE J. REG. 141 (1990) (reply to Smiley).

[30] Bell, *Unbundling: An Alternative to the Current System of Cable Television Franchising*, 21 CUMB. L. REV. 43 (1990).

existing operator? Do regulators face a regulatory catch-22? If they do not regulate, the monopolist will overcharge consumers, but if regulators do control prices, they will prevent additional competition.

b. REGULATORY REFORM

The cable industry has gone through cycles of regulation and deregulation concerning price controls. Local governments were responsible for the first price regulation of cable systems. Rate regulation developed because CATV operators needed permission to place their cable lines over public rights-of-way. In return for this permission, CATV operators would often agree to hold the rates charged for the provision of their services to a level specified in the franchise agreement. As cable television developed through the 1960s, state and local regulators made increasing demands on operators. As cable became more popular, it became an increasingly important matter of the public interest, as well as a potentially lucrative source of revenue for cable operators.

The federal government initially cleared the way for local rate regulation. In 1972, the FCC adopted an order that divided cable television programming into three groups.[31] The FCC delegated to local governments the regulation of rates of the first group of programming, "basic tier" programming, or those "services regularly furnished to all subscribers." Examples of "basic tier" programming today include local broadcast network programming, Public Broadcast Service (PBS) channels, and programming provided by local government. The FCC, however, preempted state and local governments from regulating "auxiliary tier" service, or programming offered on a bundled basis that did not include "basic tier" programming, and the Commission regulated rates for these tiers itself. Current examples of "auxiliary tier" service typically include programming such as ESPN, MTV, and independent superstations like TBS. Finally, the FCC preempted local and state governments from regulating rates charged for programming offered on a "per-program" or "per-channel" basis such as HBO or The Disney Channel. Despite other subsequent changes, this type of programming has been left unregulated.

In the late 1970s and early 1980s, cable operators began to complain to the FCC and Congress that local rate regulation was inhibiting their ability to develop new technology and grow into new markets. The FCC continued to ask Congress for clarification of its authority over and appropriate role in regulating cable television.

Against this regulatory framework, Congress enacted the 1984 Act, which established for the first time a national policy on cable television. This policy had three key features. First, it maintained the FCC's must-carry rules. The next section of this chapter discusses the nature and impact of these rules. Second, Congress sanctioned the FCC's action in adopting the "telco-cable" ban by explicitly adopting it, thus keeping telephone and cable television services separate. The Act also expanded the authority of local governments to pass various kinds of media "cross-ownership" rules, and delegated to the

---

[31] Cable Television Report and Order, 36 F.C.C. 2d 143, 209, 219 (1972), *reconsidered*, 36 F.C.C. 2d 326 (1972).

FCC the authority to promulgate others. Examples of these rules included not only bans on local telephone companies owning or operating cable programming companies and services, but also "media concentration limits," which restricted broadcast and radio companies from owning cable companies in the same market area.

Perhaps the defining policy of the 1984 Act was a decision to "promote competition in cable communications and minimize unnecessary regulation that would impose an undue economic burden on cable systems."[32] Congress adopted an "effective competition" standard, a term not defined in the Act. Instead, it delegated to the FCC the responsibility to establish rules for rate regulation and to decide which cable systems faced "effective competition." All cable systems facing "effective competition" were deregulated following the completion of a two-year transitional period. The few cable systems not satisfying the FCC's definition of "effective competition" were subject to a local rate regulatory structure similar to that which preceded the 1984 Act.[33] The tenor of the Act, combined with the deregulatory spirit of the Reagan administration, created a clear preference for competition within the cable industry. In short, the FCC encouraged competition by opening the market.

The FCC's original definition of "effective competition" echoed this deregulatory spirit. In 1985, it defined "effective competition" as the presence of three unduplicated broadcast signals receivable without a cable hookup by any portion of a market served by a single cable system. This definition operated to deregulate cable on the vast majority of cable systems following the two-year transitional period. Perhaps the FCC's position in narrowly defining "effective competition" of cable systems in terms relating only to broadcasting can best be understood through the comments of Ronald Reagan's first FCC Chairman, Mark Fowler, who stated that television was nothing more than a "toaster with pictures."[34] In other words, Fowler was saying that there was no reason to assume that cable television was different from a product like a toaster in the sense that competition would produce the lowest possible price. Thus, Fowler believed that cable television was simply one of many forms of entertainment and that these other forms of entertainment, such as movies, video rentals, and broadcast television, were sufficient competition to keep cable prices at competitive levels. This standard was modified in 1988 to require that the three signals must be receivable without a cable connection by the entire market served by a cable operator, but this still encompassed most cable systems. In 1991, the FCC beefed up the standard a bit by establishing a two-pronged test. The "broadcast signal" prong requires the availability of six unduplicated signals throughout the market. The "alternate provider" prong requires competition from an alternative multichannel television

---

[32] 47 U.S.C. § 521(6).

[33] Regulation of "regular subscriber service," the 1984 Act's term for "basic tier" service, by local governments was permitted under the Act, but a narrow definition of that term limited the reach of this authority. Furthermore, the 1984 Act granted nonreviewable discretionary five percent increases for those cable systems not facing "effective competition," and limited the ability of local governments to effectively control rates related to "basic tier" service, such as rates for equipment rental and installation fees.

[34] Hickey, *Revolution in Cyberia: As the FCC, the Congress, and Megamedia Redraw the Map, Who Will Tell the People?*, 34 COLUM. JOURNAL. REV. 40 (1995).

provider, such as direct broadcast satellite television (DBS),[35] satellite master antenna television (SMATV),[36] or a home satellite dish (HDS) system.[37] Under either prong of the test, the idea is to measure whether there is sufficient competition for cable operators in the form of alternatives that consumers would regard as substitutes for cable television. If such substitutes exist, then cable operators would operate in a competitive market. For example, if DBS is widely available in a market at reasonable prices, cable operators would be unable to charge more for their services than the DBS system.

Although this standard returned cable rate regulatory authority to local governments, much of the damage of the preceding seven years had already been done. It seemed that everyone, except the cable companies, was unhappy with the results of the 1984 Act, and they all urged Congress to reconsider the issue. Consumer groups complained loudly to Congress that cable rates were spiraling wildly out of control, local regulatory authorities protested their inability to do anything about it, the national networks lamented their declining market share, telephone companies began to seek opportunities within the cable industry and pursue avenues to abolish the "telco-cable" ban, and producers of independent television programming objected to the power of larger vertically-integrated cable companies to discriminate against them. This last complaint is related to the fact that vertically integrated cable operators develop and produce their own programming to show cable subscribers. This gives such operators an economic incentive to discriminate against the programming of independent producers in favor of their own programming.

Congress responded with the 1992 Act, the only act to be passed over a veto by President Bush. Congress noted that prior to the 1991 FCC regulations the rates of 97 percent of cable systems had been deregulated under the guise of "effective competition," but that less than 1 percent of all cable systems actually faced head-to-head competition. Finding that the average monthly rates for basic cable service had increased by 29 percent since deregulation had begun in 1986, an increase of almost three times that of the Consumer Price Index for the same period, Congress reregulated cable rates and reinstituted the cable rate regulatory structure of the pre-1984 Act era, with some variations. At the same time, the 1992 Act maintained the "telco-cable" ban, and contained a host of other complicated provisions specifying the regulatory power of the FCC and local government franchising authorities.

The 1992 Act preserved the 1984 Act's concept of "effective competition," but, in contrast to the 1984 Act, specifically defined the term. Like the 1984 Act, it exempted cable systems from rate regulation facing "effective competition," but reversed the presumption that most cable systems face such

---

[35] DBS systems, used primarily in single-family dwellings, consist of a small receiver used to receive satellite signals that are coordinated and decoded at a separate location owned by the system.

[36] SMATV is a "mini" cable system, used primarily to provide service to private multi-unit dwellings, that combines broadcast signals and satellite signals at a central location into a single line that is run to the individual units.

[37] HDS systems, used primarily in restaurants, bars, and sometimes in single-family dwellings, consist of a large satellite receiver that also decodes direct satellite signals.

competition. Under the 1992 Act, a cable system faces "effective competition" if one of three conditions are met: the cable system is subscribed to by fewer than 30 percent of the households in the franchise area; the cable system faces direct competition from at least two alternative multichannel television providers, each of which is available to at least 50 percent of the households in the franchise area and actually serving at least 15 percent of those households; or, the local government offers some kind of multichannel television programming to at least 50 percent of the households in the franchise area. Under this definition of "effective competition," the rates of "basic tier" service of most cable companies once again are subject to local regulation.

The 1992 Act also contained a provision permitting the FCC to regulate the rates of "cable programming services," the Act's somewhat cryptic way of referring to nonpremium "extended tier" programming beyond the "basic tier." The 1992 Act included within the definition of "cable programming service" any equipment used to receive this service, vesting in the FCC the authority, for the first time, the ability to monitor rates charged for converter boxes and remote controls. In short, the 1992 Act put the FCC back in the cable rate regulation business, which it had been out of for nearly a decade.

Congress, however, soon changed its mind and its approach. The 1996 Act repeals the previous structure of rate regulation and replaces it with one that contains significant deregulation. The Act:

(1) repeals current FCC rules regulating cable rates for most cable system operators beyond "basic tier" cable programming by March 1, 1999;

(2) prohibits all rate regulation, including "basic tier" programming, for any cable system operator facing "effective competition" for comparable video programming services;

(3) permits LECs to offer video programming services either through a traditional cable system, and thus subject themselves to the local and state rate regulation, or by creating an "open video platform" and providing video programming on a "common carrier" basis; and

(4) eliminates immediately all rate regulation for small cable system operators.

Since Congress eliminated rate regulation for cable systems facing "effective competition," it is important to know when such competition exists. The Act broadens the definition of "effective competition" used in the 1992 Act to include all video programming services, offered through a cable system or otherwise by any multichannel television programming provider, including LECs. As you read earlier, LECs are local exchange carriers or local telephone companies.

Congress also chose to permit LECs to be either traditional cable carriers or common carriers. If an LEC chooses the latter option, they are not subject to state or local regulation. Because the Act favors a "two-wire" model for competition in telecommunications services, LECs and cable system operators serving the same market are prohibited from acquiring ownership interests in one another's company.

Finally, consumers are affected by the elimination of rate regulation for small cable system operators. Small cable system operators are those serving fewer than 1 percent of all cable subscribers nationally and with annual revenues of less than $25 million.

As a result of these various provisions, cable systems serving almost 30% of cable subscribers nationally are immediately deregulated.[38] The Senate Committee on Commerce, Science, and Transportation offered the following justification for the Act's deregulatory orientation:

P.L. 104-104, TELECOMMUNICATIONS COMPETITION AND DEREGULATION ACT OF 1995, SENATE REPORT NO. 104-23

Subsection (a) of section 204 of the bill limits the rate regulation currently imposed by the Cable Television Consumer Protection and Competition Act of 1992, Public Law 102-385. Under existing section 623 of the 1934 Act, rates for the basic (broadcast) tier of service, as well as the expanded (cable programming services) tier of service have been regulated by the FCC.

Rate regulation for the basic tier is justified where the cable operator retains its monopoly because, for many consumers, the basic cable tier is their best, and sometimes, only access to over-the-air broadcast stations. The Committee feels strongly that this tier should remain affordable for all those consumers who need to use cable television as an antenna service to receive broadcast signals.

Cable operators argue that rate regulation for the expanded tier, however, does not fall under the same principle. While the expanded tier of service does provide a variety of satellite-delivered programming, some maintain that it is not a consumer necessity. Therefore, rates should only be regulated for those operators that take advantage of their monopoly position to raise rates beyond acceptable levels.

Cable operators argue that cable rate regulation, as implemented by the FCC, has hurt cable's access to capital and the financial markets. Cable is the most logical competitor to telephone companies for residential services. Without access to capital, cable operators believe that they will not be able to spend the necessary funds to rebuild and upgrade their systems to compete with telephone companies for telephone customers, and thus, give consumers greater choices.

On the other hand, consumer groups allege that the cable rate regulations are essential to protecting consumers from unjustified rate increases. Consumer groups note that cable operators borrowed more money in 1994 than they borrowed in 1993, and they note that the major cable companies recently spent millions of dollars in the auctions for new Personal Communications Services (PCS). Consumers also point out that the vast majority of consumers subscribe to expanded tiers of cable service in addition to the basic tier. . . .

Paragraph (2) amends section 623(l)(1). Section 623(l)(1) provides that cable operators subject to effective competition are not subject to rate regulation,

---

[38] Interview with Larry Irving, WASHINGTON TELECOM NEWS, June 5, 1995, at 1, *available at* 1995 WL 6614016.

including regulation of the basic tier. The amendment to the definition of effective competition contained in the bill allows the provision of video services by a local exchange carrier, either through a common carrier video platform, or as a cable operator, in an unaffiliated cable operator's franchise area to satisfy the effective competition test. In other words, under the bill, if a telephone company offers video services in a cable operator's franchise area, the cable operator's basic and expanded tiers of service will not be regulated.

NOTES AND QUESTIONS

1. The FCC's 1972 regulations delegated regulation of the basic tier of cable programming to local governments, implemented federal regulation of the auxiliary tier service, and left charges on the basis of individual programs or channels unregulated. On what grounds can each of these policy choices be defended? Why delegate regulation of the basic tier but have federal regulation of the auxiliary tier? Why regulate the auxiliary tier but not the charges for individual programs or channels?

2. The 1996 Act eliminates rate regulation for anything but "basic tier" programming by March 1, 1999. What is the theory behind this deregulation? Could Congress reasonably decide that cable operators could not charge unreasonable prices for other than "basic tier" programming because there is a high elasticity of demand? Could Congress reasonably decide that there was sufficient competition concerning this type of programming that rate regulation was unnecessary? What is the nature of this competition?

3. What is the policy rationale for the elimination of rate regulation for small cable systems? Are such systems less likely to charge consumers unreasonable prices? Will the elimination of price controls permit small operators to afford to enlarge and modernize their systems?

4. What is the policy rationale for exempting from state and local regulation LECs which provide video programming on a "common carrier" basis? Are such systems less likely to charge consumers unreasonable prices? Is there some other reason for this exemption?

2. ENTRY CONTROLS

The natural monopoly characteristics of cable television render the industry more analogous to local telephone industries than to broadcast television. Does this mean that cable television companies should be regulated as "common carriers" and thus forced to open up their cable lines to everyone, including competitors? This section considers the regulatory justifications for such entry controls.

Initially, the FCC refused jurisdiction over CATV systems in 1958, but it gradually changed its mind and asserted its regulatory authority over cable television.

At first, the FCC reasoned that cable was not a "common carrier," such as a telephone company, and thus subject to regulation pursuant to the authority granted by Congress in Title II of the 1934 Communications Act. Further, the FCC concluded that the operators of CATV systems were not "broadcasters," and thus subject to regulation under Title III of that Act.[39] The Commission reached this conclusion because most cable television does not involve a transmission of radio signals. Instead, most cable operators simply pick up signals with an antenna and transmit them over a grid of wires.

In 1962, however, the FCC reversed its position and asserted authority over some cable systems by virtue of its authority to regulate microwave relay stations, which some cable systems used to import long-distance programming signals. In *Carter Mountain Transmission Corp.*,[40] for example, the Commission denied the application of a company to construct a microwave communication system to transmit television programs from one city to another. The system would have picked up a broadcast using an antenna at the remote location, transmitted the program to the city to be served, and then the program would be distributed through a grid of wires. The appellate court, which upheld the Commission's order, explained its rationale as follows:

> The Commission concluded that it would not serve the public interest, convenience, and necessity to grant appellant's application. Its reasoning was essentially this: that to permit appellant to bring in outside programs for the community antenna systems on the basis proposed would result in the "demise" of the local television station (intervenor KWRB-TV) and the loss of service to a substantial rural population not served by the community antenna systems, and to many other persons who did not choose (or were unable) to pay the cost of subscribing to the community antenna systems; and that the need for the local outlet outweighed the improved service which appellant's proposed new facilities would bring to those who subscribed to the community antenna systems.[41]

In 1966, the FCC extended its jurisdiction to all cable systems, reasoning that regulation of cable was necessary to prevent the gradual deterioration and eventual elimination of broadcast television. The FCC, then, was confronted with two basic issues: Should each communication industry (broadcast television, cable, radio, and telephone) be regulated separately? What obligations did the FCC have to promote and protect each industry? This section examines these issues.

a. CROSS-OWNERSHIP RULES

The FCC maintained separate regulation of communications in part by its so-called telco-cable ban, which prohibited telephone companies from becoming cable operators. The FCC initially based its ban on the argument that the cable industry should have an opportunity to develop.[42] Under this theory, cross-ownership was against the public interest because of the likelihood that cable ownership would be concentrated in the hands of the telephone industry. The FCC feared that this would happen because the telephone companies,

---

[39] *See Frontier Broadcasting Co. v. Collier*, 24 F.C.C. 251 (1959).

[40] 32 F.C.C. 459 (1962).

[41] *Carter Mountain Transmission Corp. v. FCC*, 321 F.2d 359 (D.C. Cir.), *cert. denied*, 375 U.S. 951 (1963).

[42] C. KENNEDY, AN INTRODUCTION TO U.S. TELECOMMUNICATIONS LAW 75-76 (1994).

which had substantially more resources than the fledgling cable operators, would be the first to establish cable grids in most cities and towns. Once this occurred, the FCC believed that the telephone companies would not permit any other cable operators to use their wires, which would establish them as natural monopolists and would concentrate control of cable in the telephone companies.[43]

Under the FCC ban, a telephone company was prohibited from providing cable services within its service area and from licensing pole or conduit space to its own cable affiliates. Independent telephone companies were forced to divest already established cable television services. Telephone companies, however, were allowed to own cable systems outside of their service area and waivers were available for rural areas.

In the 1984 Act, Congress adopted the FCC rules, with one significant change. Congress adopted a less restrictive telco-cable ban. Telephone companies were only forbidden from providing "video programming," such as ESPN or Home Box Office, in their service area.[44] This policy change reflected a shift by the FCC.

During the 1980s, the FCC began to question the wisdom of the cross-ownership ban, in light of its impact on competitiveness in the cable industry.[45] In 1988, the FCC suggested that the primary purpose of the cross-ownership ban of promoting growth of an independent cable industry had been satisfied. It also suggested that telephone company participation in the industry would promote rather than hinder competition. The FCC had another reason to question the telco-cable ban. A number of circuit courts struck down elements of the ban on the ground it violated the First Amendment.[46] Nevertheless, since the 1984 Act had adopted the ban, the FCC did not have authority to change it.

Of course, the 1996 Act authorizes telephone companies to be cable operators. Nevertheless, there are still some ownership restrictions, intended to promote competition. The Act still generally prohibits acquisitions in joint ventures between local telephone companies and cable companies that operate in the same market. It also restricts the local telephone company from owning more than 10 percent in a regional cable operator and vice versa. Nor may the local telephone company in the same market operate a joint venture, provide telecommunication services or video programming directly to subscribers.

b.   MUST-CARRY AND DUPLICATION RULES

With the cross-ownership rules, the FCC attempted to establish the extent to which telephone companies would be competitors of cable operators. The FCC also addressed the extent to which cable operators and broadcast television competed. Specifically, the agency set out to protect broadcasters

---

[43] Application of Telcos, 21 F.C.C. 2d 307 (1970); *See also* KELLOGG, THORNE & HUBER, *supra* note 5, at § 14.4.

[44] 47 U.S.C.A. § 533(b)(1) (1994); *see also* KELLOGG, THORNE & HUBER, *supra* note 5, at § 14.6.

[45] KELLOGG, THORNE & HUBER, *supra* note 5, at § 14.10.

[46] *See supra* note 20.

from cable television by adopting the "must-carry" and "nonduplication" rules. The "must-carry" rules, referred early on by the FCC as simply the "carriage" rules, required cable operators to transmit across its lines the signals of local broadcast companies. The "nonduplication" rules prevented cable operators from transmitting identical programming as that transmitted by local broadcasters. These two rules were relaxed slightly in subsequent FCC orders, but new requirements on cable systems serving the top one hundred television markets substantially limited the ability of these cable systems to import long-distance programming at all.

In the following order, the FCC offers its justification for the must-carry and nonduplication rules. Notice how the FCC justified the implementation of these regulations based upon cable's presumed relationship to broadcasting.

In the Matter of: Amendment of Subpart L, Part 91 to Adopt Rules and Regulations to Govern the Grant of Authorizations in the Business Radio Service for Microwave Stations
SECOND REPORT AND ORDER
2 F.C.C.2d 725 (1966)

[Earlier in this Order the Commission asserted jurisdiction over all community antenna systems whether or not microwave facilities were used.]

24. [The Commission] concluded that CATV serves the public interest when it provides program choices not locally available off the air and acts as a supplement rather than a substitute for off-the-air television service, explaining our principal reasons as follows:

> Because of the prohibitive cost of extending the cables beyond heavily built-up areas, CATV systems cannot serve many persons reached by television broadcast signals. Persons unable to obtain CATV service, and those who cannot afford it or who are unwilling to pay, are entirely dependent upon local or nearby stations for their television service. The Commission's statutory obligation is to make television service available, so far as possible, to all people of the United States on a fair, efficient, and equitable basis. This obligation is not met by primary reliance on a service which, technically, cannot be made available to many people and which, practically, will not be available to many others. Nor would it be compatible with our responsibilities to permit persons willing and able to pay for additional service to obtain it at the expense of those dependent on the growth of television broadcast facilities for an adequate choice of services.

25. Our determination to adopt the carriage and nonduplication requirements rested on two basic grounds: (1) That failure to carry local stations and duplication of their programs are unfair competitive practices, which are inconsistent with the supplementary role of CATV and (2) that these requirements were necessary to ameliorate the risk that the burgeoning CATV industry would have a future adverse impact on television broadcast service, both existing and potential.

26. With respect to the first ground, we found that the CATV system which fails to carry the local station on its system has in practical effect cut off the

station from access to CATV subscribers. We stated: As a competitive practice, the failure or refusal by a CATV system to carry the signal of a local station is plainly inconsistent with our belief that CATV service should supplement, but not replace, off-the-air television service. The cable system that follows such a practice offers the subscriber the benefits of additional television service at the price of blocking or impeding his access to available off-the-air signals. . . .

27. We further pointed out that CATV, though distributing the programs of the television broadcast service, stands outside its normal program distribution process and fails to recognize the reasonable exclusivity for which the local stations have bargained in the program market when it duplicates local programming via the signals of distant stations. We summarized our conclusion that this was unfair and inconsistent with CATV's supplementary role as follows:

> In light of the unequal footing on which broadcasters and CATV systems now stand with respect to the market for program product, we cannot regard a CATV system's duplication of local programming via the signals of distant stations as a fair method of competition. We do not regard the patterns of exclusivity created in the existing system for the distribution of television programs as sacrosanct. We think it apparent, however, that the creation of a reasonable measure of exclusivity is an entirely appropriate and proper way for program suppliers to protect the value of their product and for stations to protect their investment in programs. . . . Nor do we consider the duplication of existing off-the-air service to be consistent with CATV's appropriate role as a supplementary service. Whatever the ultimate impact of CATV competition upon the revenues and operation of competing stations, duplication is highly likely to affect the audience for the specific programs involved. And it does so without generally offering the public a substantially different service. . . .

————

Thus, the FCC regulated cable television as ancillary to the regulation of broadcast television, its apparent nearest media cousin, as within the public interest. Or as clearly stated elsewhere, "The perceived federal interest was primarily the relation of cable to broadcasting rather than an independent purpose of promoting cable as a technology independent of and competitive with broadcasting."[47]

By 1969, the FCC's attitude began to change as it reexamined the assumption that cable would ruin broadcast television in communities by splintering the public interest. The FCC restructured its approach as one of "deliberately structured dualism." This policy recognized that cable television could make important contributions to the public interest. Here is how the Commission explained the change:

---

[47] D. BRENNER ET AL., CABLE TELEVISION AND OTHER NONBROADCAST VIDEO: LAW AND POLICY, § 2.03[4], at 2-14 (CBC looseleaf service).

Over the years, the cable industry has continued to grow and develop. Cable systems are no longer simply auxiliary facilities for retransmitting the signals of broadcast television stations. Rather, they have evolved as providers of a multiplicity of video services from a broad range of program sources, some of which are original to cable. These changes have not gone unnoticed by the Commission. In the Economic Inquiry Report, the Commission recognized that the growth of cable and other program delivery systems such as videocassette recorders (VCRs) was changing the video services market and that cable in particular was no longer an auxiliary or secondary distribution service. The Commission observed that video services were being provided by a more diverse set of media and that this trend was likely to grow and develop to a greater extent in the future. The Commission further stated that it has become clear that the supply of home entertainment and information services could be increased through this greater variety of delivery alternatives. It concluded that with the advent of these new services, the justifications for attempting to control cable had declined accordingly. This change in the nature of cable and the video industry resulted in the Commission's decision to eliminate most of the rules other than must carry that were adopted as part of the comprehensive cable regulatory plan. [48]

In 1986, the Commission issued new regulations concerning the "must-carry" restrictions. The immediate impetus for the new rule was a decision by the District of Columbia Court of Appeals that the Commission's old rule violated the First Amendment. [49] The FCC decided to phase out the must-carry rules and to require cable outlets to provide input selector switches to make it easier for consumers to switch between programming transmitted by cable and by broadcasting. The Commission explained:

The Commission's mandatory signal carriage requirements were ruled constitutionally invalid in *Quincy Cable TV, Inc. v. FCC*. After examination of the record, the Commission determined that the most appropriate course of action in this matter is to adopt a regulatory program that will provide an orderly transition from the current situation where there is need for must carry regulation to its long term objective of developing an environment in which consumers will be able effectively to choose between cable and broadcast television program services. The first part of this two part program requires cable systems to offer their subscribers input selector switches that enable use of an antenna in conjunction with cable service and to implement a consumer education program to inform subscribers that it may be necessary to have off-the-air reception capability to receive all of the available broadcast signals. These requirements are intended to eliminate, over time, the current perceived capability of cable systems to limit their subscribers' access to over-the-air broadcast stations. The second part of this program consists of interim must

---

[48] Amendment of Part 76 of the Commission's Rules Concerning Television Broadcast Signals By Cable Television Systems, Report and Order, 1 FCC Rcd. 864 (1986).

[49] *Quincy Cable TV, Inc. v. FCC*, 768 F.2d 1434 (D.C. Cir. 1985).

carry rules that will expire at the end of five years. These rules will provide for an orderly transition to a market environment where must carry regulations are no longer necessary. During the transition period, the input selector switch requirement and consumer education program will work to gradually supplant must carry rules and assure subscribers' access to local television broadcast stations. . . .[50]

The 1986 Order was immediately challenged before the District of Columbia Circuit Court of Appeals, which struck it down as a violation of the First Amendment. In *Century Communications Corp. v. FCC*, 835 F.2d 292 (D.C. Cir. 1987), the court determined that "the FCC's reimposition of its must-carry rules on a five-year basis clearly furthers neither a substantial governmental interest nor is of brief enough duration to be considered narrowly tailored so as to satisfy the [constitutional] test for incidental restrictions on speech."

The combination of broadcasters' pressure on Congress and the public outcry against exploding cable rates during the 1980s culminated in the Cable Television Consumer Protection and Competition Act of 1992.[51] Although presumed dead, the must-carry rules were nonetheless revived by Congress. Section 4 of the Act requires cable operators to carry "local commercial television stations," which is defined to include all full power television broadcasters that operate within the same television market as the cable system. Large cable systems, or systems with more than 12 active channels and more than 300 subscribers, must set aside up to one-third of their channels for commercial broadcast stations that request carriage. Small cable systems, or systems with more than 300 subscribers but only 12 or fewer active channels, must carry the signals of three commercial broadcast stations. Section 5 of the Act imposes similar requirements regarding the carriage of local public broadcast television stations. Any system with between 13 and 36 channels must carry between one and three public broadcast stations, while a system with 12 or fewer channels must carry one of these stations.

Soon after the Act was passed, the Turner Broadcasting System challenged the constitutionality of the must-carry provisions under the First Amendment. After a three-judge District Court, in a divided opinion, granted summary judgment for the government, a majority of the Supreme Court reviewed the case and returned it to the District Court for further factual findings.[52] A divided panel of the District Court granted summary judgment to Turner Broadcasting. After a direct appeal to the Supreme Court, the Court upheld the must-carry rules by a five-to-four vote in *Turner Broadcasting II*. In the following excerpt from that opinion, the majority summarizes the justifications Congress had for reviving the must-carry rule, and the dissent takes issue with the justifications. The majority and the dissent also disagree concerning whether the Congress had viable, alternative policies that it could have enacted in place of the must-carry rules. In the next section, we will consider the constitutionality of the must-carry rules. At this point, we are interested

---

[50] In the Matter of Amendment of Part 76 of the Commission's Rules Concerning Carriage of Television Broadcast, 1 FCC Rcd. 864 (1986).

[51] Pub. L. No. 102-385, 106 Stat. 1460.

[52] *Turner Broadcasting System, Inc. v. FCC*, 512 U.S. 622 (1994).

in whether such rules can be justified as a policy matter, and whether there are alternative policies that might work better.

TURNER BROADCASTING SYSTEM, INC. v. FCC
(*TURNER BROADCASTING II*)
520 U.S. 180 (1997)

JUSTICE KENNEDY delivered the opinion of the Court

. . . [M]ust-carry was designed to serve "three interrelated interests: (1) preserving the benefits of free, over-the-air local broadcast television, (2) promoting the widespread dissemination of information from a multiplicity of sources, and (3) promoting fair competition in the market for television programming.". . .

The dissent proceeds on the assumption that must-carry is designed solely to be (and can only be justified as) a measure to protect broadcasters from cable operators' anticompetitive behavior. Federal policy, however, has long favored preserving a multiplicity of broadcast outlets regardless of whether the conduct that threatens it is motivated by anticompetitive animus or rises to the level of an antitrust violation. Broadcast television is an important source of information to many Americans. Though it is but one of many means for communication, by tradition and use for decades now it has been an essential part of the national discourse on subjects across the whole broad spectrum of speech, thought, and expression. Congress has an independent interest in preserving a multiplicity of broadcasters to ensure that all households have access to information and entertainment on an equal footing with those who subscribe to cable. . . .

We have no difficulty in finding a substantial basis to support Congress' conclusion that a real threat justified enactment of the must-carry provisions. . . .

. . . [T]here was specific support for [Congress'] conclusion that cable operators had considerable and growing market power over local video programming markets. Cable served at least 60 percent of American households in 1992, and evidence indicated cable market penetration was projected to grow beyond 70 percent. As Congress noted, cable operators possess a local monopoly over cable households. Only one percent of communities are served by more than one cable system. Even in communities with two or more cable systems, in the typical case each system has a local monopoly over its subscribers.

Evidence indicated the structure of the cable industry would give cable operators increasing ability and incentive to drop local broadcast stations from their systems, or reposition them to a less-viewed channel. Horizontal concentration was increasing as a small number of multiple system operators (MSOs) acquired large numbers of cable systems nationwide. The trend was accelerating, giving the MSOs increasing market power. In 1985, the 10 largest MSOs controlled cable systems serving slightly less than 42 percent of all cable subscribers; by 1989, the figure was nearly 54 percent.

Vertical integration in the industry also was increasing. As Congress was aware, many MSOs owned or had affiliation agreements with cable programmers. Evidence indicated that before 1984 cable operators had equity interests in 38 percent of cable programming networks. In the late 1980's, 64 percent of new cable programmers were held in vertical ownership. Congress concluded that "vertical integration gives cable operators the incentive and ability to favor their affiliated programming services". . . .

Cable systems also have more systemic reasons for seeking to disadvantage broadcast stations: Simply stated, cable has little interest in assisting, through carriage, a competing medium of communication. . . . Congress could therefore reasonably conclude that cable systems would drop broadcasters in favor of programmers—even unaffiliated ones—less likely to compete with them for audience and advertisers. . . .

The dissent contends Congress could not reasonably conclude cable systems would engage in such predation because cable operators, whose primary source of revenue is subscriptions, would not risk dropping a widely viewed broadcast station in order to capture advertising revenues. However, if viewers are faced with the choice of sacrificing a handful of broadcast stations to gain access to dozens of cable channels (plus network affiliates), it is likely they would still subscribe to cable even if they would prefer the dropped television stations to the cable programming that replaced them. Substantial evidence introduced on remand bears this out: With the exception of a handful of very popular broadcast stations (typically network affiliates), a cable system's choice between carrying a cable programmer or broadcast station has little or no effect on cable subscriptions, and subscribership thus typically does not bear on carriage decisions. . . .

Appellants posit a number of alternatives in an effort to demonstrate a less-restrictive means to achieve the Government's aims. . . .

. . . [W]e cannot conclude that any of them is an adequate alternative to must-carry for promoting the Government's legitimate interests. First among appellants' suggested alternatives is a proposal to revive a more limited set of must-carry rules, known as the "Century rules" after the 1987 court decision striking them down. Those rules included a minimum viewership standard for eligibility and limited the must-carry obligation to 25 percent of channel capacity. The parties agree only 14 percent of broadcasters added to cable systems under the Cable Act would be eligible for carriage under the Century rules. The Century rules, for the most part, would require carriage of the same stations a system would carry without statutory compulsion. While we acknowledge appellants' criticism of any rationale that more is better, the scheme in question does not place limitless must-carry obligations on cable system operators. In the final analysis this alternative represents nothing more than appellants' " '[dis]agreement with the responsible decisionmaker concerning' . . . the degree to which [the Government's] interests should be promoted." . . .

The second alternative appellants urge is the use of input selector or "A/B" switches, which, in combination with antennas, would permit viewers to switch between cable and broadcast input, allowing cable subscribers to watch broadcast programs not carried on cable. Congress examined the use of A/B switches as an alternative to must-carry and concluded it was "not an enduring or feasible method of distribution and . . . not in the public interest." The data showed that: many households lacked adequate antennas to receive broadcast signals; A/B switches suffered from technical flaws; viewers might be required to reset channel settings repeatedly in order to view both UHF and cable channels; and installation and use of the switch with other common video equipment (such as videocassette recorders) could be "cumbersome or impossible." Even the cable industry trade association (one of appellants here) determined that "the A/B switch is not a workable solution to the carriage problem." The group's engineering committee likewise concluded the switches suffered from technical problems and that no solution "appear[ed] imminent."

. . .

Appellants also suggest a leased-access regime, under which both broadcasters and cable programmers would have equal access to cable channels at regulated rates. Appellants do not specify what kind of regime they would propose, or how it would operate, making this alternative difficult to compare to the must-carry rules. Whatever virtues the proposal might otherwise have, it would reduce the number of cable channels under cable systems' control in the same manner as must-carry. Because this alternative is aimed solely at addressing the bottleneck control of cable operators, it would not be as effective in achieving Congress' further goal of ensuring that significant programming remains available for the 40 percent of American households without cable. Indeed, unless the number of channels set aside for local broadcast stations were to decrease (sacrificing Congress' interest in preserving a multiplicity of broadcasters), additional channels would have to be set aside for cable programmers, further reducing the channels under the systems' control. Furthermore, Congress was specific in noting that requiring payment for cable carriage was inimical to the interests it was pursuing, because of the burden it would impose on small broadcasters. Congress specifically prohibited such payments under the Cable Act.

Appellants next suggest a system of subsidies for financially weak stations. Appellants have not proposed any particular subsidy scheme, so it is difficult to determine whether this option presents a feasible means of achieving the Government's interests, let alone one preferable to must-carry under the First Amendment. To begin with, a system of subsidies would serve a very different purpose than must-carry. Must-carry is intended not to guarantee the financial health of all broadcasters, but to ensure a base number of broadcasters survive to provide service to noncable households. Must-carry is simpler to administer and less likely to involve the Government in making content-based determinations about programming. The must-carry rules distinguish between categories of speakers based solely on the technology used to communicate. The rules acknowledge cable systems' expertise by according them discretion to determine which broadcasters to carry on reserved channels, and (within the Cable Act's strictures) allow them to choose broadcasters with a view to offering program choices appealing to local subscribers. Appellants' proposal would require the Government to develop other criteria for giving subsidies and to establish a potentially elaborate administrative structure to make subsidy determinations.

Appellants also suggest a system of antitrust enforcement or an administrative complaint procedure to protect broadcasters from cable operators' anticompetitive conduct. Congress could conclude, however, that the considerable expense and delay inherent in antitrust litigation, and the great disparities in wealth and sophistication between the average independent broadcast station and average cable system operator, would make these remedies inadequate substitutes for guaranteed carriage. The record suggests independent broadcasters simply are not in a position to engage in complex antitrust litigation, which involves extensive discovery, significant motions practice, appeals, and the payment of high legal fees throughout. An administrative complaint procedure, although less burdensome, would still require stations to incur considerable expense and delay before enforcing their rights. As it is, some public stations have been forced by limited resources to forgo pursuing administrative complaints under the Cable Act to obtain carriage. Those problems would be compounded if instead of proving entitlement under must-carry, the station instead had to prove facts establishing an antitrust violation. . . .

JUSTICE O'CONNOR, with whom JUSTICE SCALIA, JUSTICE THOMAS, and JUSTICE GINSBURG join, dissenting. . . .

Perhaps because of the difficulty of defending the must-carry provisions as a measured response to anticompetitive behavior, the Court asserts an "independent" interest in preserving a "multiplicity" of broadcast programming sources. In doing so, the Court posits existence of "conduct that threatens" the availability of broadcast television outlets, quite apart from anticompetitive conduct. We are left to wonder what precisely that conduct might be. Moreover, when separated from anticompetitive conduct, this interest in preserving a "multiplicity of broadcast programming sources" becomes poorly defined. Neither the principal opinion nor the partial concurrence offers any guidance on what might constitute a "significant reduction" in the availability of broadcast programming. . . .

. . . It is undisputed that the broadcast stations protected by must-carry are the "marginal" stations within a given market; the record on remand reveals that any broader threat to the broadcast system was entirely mythical. Pressed to explain the importance of preserving noncable viewers' access to "vulnerable" broadcast stations, appellees emphasize that the must-carry rules are necessary to ensure that broadcast stations maintain "diverse," "quality" programming that is "responsive" to the needs of the local community. Must-carry is thus justified as a way of preserving viewers' access to a Spanish or Chinese language station or of preventing an independent station from adopting a home-shopping format. Undoubtedly, such goals are reasonable and important, and the stations in question may well be worthwhile targets of Government subsidies. But appellees' characterization of must-carry as a means of protecting these stations, like the Court's explicit concern for promoting " 'community self-expression' " and the " 'local origination of broadcast programming' " reveals a content-based preference for broadcast programming. . .

. . . [T]he availability of less restrictive alternatives—a leased-access regime and subsidies—reinforces my conclusion that the must-carry provisions are overbroad.

Consider first appellants' proposed leased-access scheme, under which a cable system operator would be required to make a specified proportion of the system's channels available to broadcasters and independent cable programmers alike at regulated rates. Leased access would directly address both vertical integration and predatory behavior, by placing broadcasters and cable programmers on a level playing field for access to cable. . . . Accordingly, to the extent that leased access would address problems of anticompetitive behavior, I fail to understand why it would not achieve the goal of "ensuring that significant programming remains available" for noncable households. . . . As noted, a leased access regime would respond directly to problems of vertical integration and problems of predatory behavior. Must-carry quite clearly does not respond to the problem of vertical integration. In addition, the must-carry scheme burdens the rights of cable programmers and cable operators; there is no suggestion here that leased access would burden cable programmers in the same way as must-carry does. In both of these respects, leased access is a more narrowly tailored guard against anticompetitive behavior. Finally, if, as the Court suggests, Congress were concerned that a leased access scheme would impose a burden on "small broadcasters" forced to pay for access, subsidies would eliminate the problem. . . .

NOTES AND QUESTIONS

1. What FCC policies were served by the must-carry rule? Without such a rule, cable companies would be free to negotiate with distant broadcasters to acquire their programming at a lower rate than they paid for local broadcasters. How would such actions impede the FCC's policy of localism? How does a policy of "localism" relate to the FCC's mandate to regulate broadcasting in the "public interest, convenience, and necessity?" Is this an economic or noneconomic justification? If it is a noneconomic justification, which noneconomic goal identified in Chapter 2 does it serve?

2. How does the must-carry rule promote "universal service?" In other words, how does the fact that cable companies rely on subscriptions for their revenue instead of the advertising-financed programming threaten universal service? How does a policy of "universal service" relate to the FCC's mandate to regulate broadcasting in the "public interest, convenience, and necessity?" Is this an economic or noneconomic justification? If it is a noneconomic justification, which noneconomic goal identified in Chapter 2 does it serve?

3. What FCC policies were served by the nonduplication rule? How did such a rule help promote the financial viability of local broadcasters?

4. Justice O'Connor noted that a "leased-access" scheme would be a solution to potential bottlenecks imposed by cable operators which was less intrusive on their First Amendment rights. How would such a system work? What flaws in this approach did the majority identify? Would a system of subsidies for small broadcasters address the problem that some stations could not afford to pay for space on a cable system? Do you prefer this approach or the must-carry rules? Which is better policy, and why?

5. The FCC's 1986 rule, which proposed to phase out the must-carry rules, required that cable operators offer subscribers input selector switches that enable the use of an antenna in conjunction with cable service. Is the FCC's requirement that cable operators install selector switches to permit easier access to broadcast programming reminiscent of our opening discussion of seat belts? Why do you suppose this political compromise failed?

In *Turner Broadcasting II*, the majority discusses this policy proposal as a potential alternative to Congress' choice of must-carry rules. According to Justice Kennedy, what flaws did Congress identify concerning the installation of such "A/B" switches? Do you agree this approach would not work? Why or why not?

6. Justice Kennedy identifies "antitrust enforcement" as a final, alternative policy option. The must-carry rule applies to every cable operator, while the government would use antitrust enforcement only in circumstances where a cable operator was attempting to establish a bottleneck for purposes of eliminating competition in violation of antitrust prohibitions. Yet, Justice Kennedy says that Congress had reasonable grounds to reject this approach. What were its grounds? Do you prefer an antitrust approach? Why or why not?

7. Although the FCC initially attempted to limit the growth of cable television, it made no such efforts to constrain other competitors to broadcasting, such as direct broadcast satellite television, satellite master antenna television, or a home satellite dish system. Is this refusal consistent with the Commission's actions concerning entry regulation of cable television?

8. Generally, the FCC believed that cable television threatened the entire viability of broadcasting. Economically, each viewer that subscribed to a cable television system that did not carry local broadcast programming represented the loss of that viewer for the local broadcast network. The deterioration of this viewer base, in turn, would generate less revenue from advertisers, which would, in turn, lead to a diminishing quality in broadcast programming. By limiting the content of programming provided by, as well as stunting the growth of, cable television, the FCC assured that broadcast television would not be left in cable's dust, at least until Congress acted on the matter.

Can this protectionist paternalistic view of broadcast television as the "favored son" of the FCC be explained by understanding the FCC's confusion over the extent of its authority over the cable industry and its initial reservations whether it had any authority at all? Or was the FCC simply captured by the broadcast industry and doing its bidding? Even if the later is true, did Congress intend for the FCC to protect and preserve the broadcast industry? Remember that Congress' only legal instruction to the Commission was to regulate in the public interest, convenience, and necessity. Why would the government have any more interest in protecting a local broadcaster than, say, a local newspaper (vis-à-vis USA Today, for example)?

9. Another form of "must-carry" rule also aimed at opening access is the Pole Attachments Act,[53] which requires the FCC to set rates and conditions for certain attachments to telephone and electric poles. The US Supreme Court upheld an FCC order requiring pole owners to allow attachments for commingled high-speed Internet and cable services and attachments by wireless services. See *National Cable & Telecommunications Ass'n. v. FCC*, 534 U.S. 327 (2002). Who are the winners and losers under the pole attachment regulations?

---

[53] 42 U.S.C. § 224.

3. FIRST AMENDMENT LIMITATIONS

It did not take long for the cable operators to challenge the must-carry rules established by Congress as a violation of the First Amendment. This litigation generated two trips to the Supreme Court.

In the first case, *Turner Broadcasting I*, which follows, the government made two arguments concerning the Court's scope of review. First, it argued that the Court should review the rules under the same First Amendment standard that it applies to broadcasting. This standard, which was articulated in *Red Lion Broadcasting Co., Inc. v. FCC*, 395 U.S. 367 (1969), adopts a more deferential approach to the regulation of speech in broadcasting than the Court applies in other areas. The Court, however, rejected this argument and gave cable operators the same level of protection as print journalists.

In *Red Lion*, the Court reviewed an FCC regulation, called the "fairness doctrine," which required broadcasters to offer a "reasonable opportunity" for persons to respond when the station had broadcast "an attack on upon their honesty, character, or integrity, or like personal qualities" during the "presentation of views on a controversial subject."[54] The broadcasters had argued that the doctrine violated the First Amendment because broadcasters, like print journalists, had complete freedom to exercise their editorial judgments. The Court refused to equate broadcasters and print journalists because "differences in the characteristics of news media justify differences in the First Amendment standards applied to them." Because of the problem of frequency scarcity, the Court determined that traditional First Amendment standards were inappropriate:

> Where there are substantially more individuals who want to broadcast than there are frequencies to allocate, it is idle to posit an unbridgeable First Amendment right to broadcast comparable to the right of every individual to speak, write, or publish. . . .
>
> . . . A license permits broadcasting, but the licensee has no constitutional right to be the one who holds the license or to monopolize a radio frequency to the exclusion of his fellow citizens.

Because broadcasters operate under government licenses, the Court described them as having a "fiduciary duty" to the public. Thus, when the public interest requires, the FCC can command broadcasters to "present those views and voices which are representative of the community, and which would otherwise be barred from the airwaves."

Second, the government argued that the Court should apply an intermediate level of scrutiny, because the must-carry rules were content neutral. The scope of review that the Court uses to determine the constitutionality of such regulations depends on whether the restrictions are based on the content of the speech. The regulation of the content of speech triggers some form of "strict scrutiny," while content-neutral regulation is analyzed under an "intermediate" level of scrutiny. The Court varies the nature of this intermediate level of scrutiny depending on the First Amendment context in which it is being applied. The Court held that the must-carry rules would not receive strict scrutiny because they were content-neutral.

---

[54] *See* 395 U.S. at 373–74.

TURNER BROADCASTING SYSTEM, INC. v. FCC
(*TURNER BROADCASTING I*)
512 U.S. 622 (1994)

JUSTICE KENNEDY announced the judgment of the Court and delivered the opinion of the Court . . .

We address first the Government's contention that regulation of cable television should be analyzed under the same First Amendment standard that applies to regulation of broadcast television. It is true that our cases have permitted more intrusive regulation of broadcast speakers than of speakers in other media. But the rationale for applying a less rigorous standard of First Amendment scrutiny to broadcast regulation, whatever its validity in the cases elaborating it, does not apply in the context of cable regulation.

The justification for our distinct approach to broadcast regulation rests upon the unique physical limitations of the broadcast medium. As a general matter, there are more would-be broadcasters than frequencies available in the electromagnetic spectrum. And if two broadcasters were to attempt to transmit over the same frequency in the same locale, they would interfere with one another's signals, so that neither could be heard at all. The scarcity of broadcast frequencies thus required the establishment of some regulatory mechanism to divide the electromagnetic spectrum and assign specific frequencies to particular broadcasters. In addition, the inherent physical limitation on the number of speakers who may use the broadcast medium has been thought to require some adjustment in traditional First Amendment analysis to permit the Government to place limited content restraints, and impose certain affirmative obligations, on broadcast licensees. As we said in *Red Lion*, "[w]here there are substantially more individuals who want to broadcast than there are frequencies to allocate, it is idle to posit an unabridgeable First Amendment right to broadcast comparable to the right of every individual to speak, write, or publish."

Although courts and commentators have criticized the scarcity rationale since its inception, we have declined to question its continuing validity as support for our broadcast jurisprudence, and see no reason to do so here. The broadcast cases are inapposite in the present context because cable television does not suffer from the inherent limitations that characterize the broadcast medium. Indeed, given the rapid advances in fiber optics and digital compression technology, soon there may be no practical limitation on the number of speakers who may use the cable medium. Nor is there any danger of physical interference between two cable speakers attempting to share the same channel. In light of these fundamental technological differences between broadcast and cable transmission, application of the more relaxed standard of scrutiny adopted in *Red Lion* and the other broadcast cases is inapt when determining the First Amendment validity of cable regulation. . . .

C

Insofar as they pertain to the carriage of full power broadcasters, the must-carry rules, on their face, impose burdens and confer benefits without reference to the content of speech. Although the provisions interfere with cable operators' editorial discretion by compelling them to offer carriage to a certain minimum number of broadcast stations, the extent of the interference does not depend upon the content of the cable operators' programming. The rules impose obligations upon all operators, save those with fewer than 300 subscribers, regardless of the programs or stations they now offer or have offered in the past. Nothing in the Act imposes a restriction, penalty, or burden by reason of the views, programs, or stations the cable operator has selected or will select. The number of channels a cable operator must set aside depends only on the operator's channel capacity; hence, an operator cannot avoid or mitigate its obligations under the Act by altering the programming it offers to subscribers.

The must-carry provisions also burden cable programmers by reducing the number of channels for which they can compete. But, again, this burden is unrelated to content, for it extends to all cable programmers irrespective of the programming they choose to offer viewers. And finally, the privileges conferred by the must-carry provisions are also unrelated to content. The rules benefit all full power broadcasters who request carriage—be they commercial or noncommercial, independent or network-affiliated, English or Spanish language, religious or secular. The aggregate effect of the rules is thus to make every full power commercial and noncommercial broadcaster eligible for must-carry, provided only that the broadcaster operates within the same television market as a cable system.

It is true that the must-carry provisions distinguish between speakers in the television programming market. But they do so based only upon the manner in which speakers transmit their messages to viewers, and not upon the messages they carry: Broadcasters, which transmit over the airwaves, are favored, while cable programmers, which do not, are disfavored. Cable operators, too, are burdened by the carriage obligations, but only because they control access to the cable conduit. So long as they are not a subtle means of exercising a content preference, speaker distinctions of this nature are not presumed invalid under the First Amendment.

That the must-carry provisions, on their face, do not burden or benefit speech of a particular content does not end the inquiry. Our cases have recognized that even a regulation neutral on its face may be content-based if its manifest purpose is to regulate speech because of the message it conveys.

Appellants contend, in this regard, that the must-carry regulations are content-based because Congress' purpose in enacting them was to promote speech of a favored content. We do not agree. Our review of the Act and its various findings persuades us that Congress' overriding objective in enacting must-carry was not to favor programming of a particular subject matter, viewpoint, or format, but rather to preserve access to free television programming for the 40 percent of Americans without cable. . . .

In unusually detailed statutory findings, Congress explained that because cable systems and broadcast stations compete for local advertising revenue, and because cable operators have a vested financial interest in favoring their affiliated programmers over broadcast stations, cable operators have a built-in "economic incentive . . . to delete, reposition, or not carry local broadcast signals." Congress concluded that absent a requirement that cable systems carry the signals of local broadcast stations, the continued availability of free local broadcast television would be threatened. . . .

This overriding congressional purpose is unrelated to the content of expression disseminated by cable and broadcast speakers. Indeed, our precedents have held that "protecting noncable households from loss of regular television broadcasting service due to competition from cable systems," is not only a permissible governmental justification, but an "important and substantial federal interest."

The design and operation of the challenged provisions confirm that the purposes underlying the enactment of the must-carry scheme are unrelated to the content of speech. The rules, as mentioned, confer must-carry rights on all full power broadcasters, irrespective of the content of their programming. They do not require or prohibit the carriage of particular ideas or points of view. They do not penalize cable operators or programmers because of the content of their programming. They do not compel cable operators to affirm points of view with which they disagree. They do not produce any net decrease in the amount of available speech. And they leave cable operators free to carry whatever programming they wish on all channels not subject to must-carry requirements. . . .

In short, Congress' acknowledgment that broadcast television stations make a valuable contribution to the Nation's communications system does not render the must-carry scheme content-based. The scope and operation of the challenged provisions make clear, in our view, that Congress designed the must-carry provisions not to promote speech of a particular content, but to prevent cable operators from exploiting their economic power to the detriment of broadcasters, and thereby to ensure that all Americans, especially those unable to subscribe to cable, have access to free television programming—whatever its content.

———

Having concluded that the intermediate standard of scrutiny was appropriate in *Turner Broadcasting I*, the Court vacated the lower court's decision and remanded the case to the district court to do the fact finding necessary to apply the scope of review announced in *United States v. O'Brien*, 391 U.S. 367 (1968). According to *O'Brien*

a government regulation is sufficiently justified if it is within the constitutional power of the Government; it furthers an important or substantial interest; if the government interest is unrelated to the suppression of free speech; and if the incidental restriction on alleged First Amendment freedoms is no greater than is essential to the furtherance of that interest.

The Supreme Court required the district court to conduct a more detailed inquiry into whether the economic health of local broadcasting would be in jeopardy with the "must-carry" rules, and if so, whether the specific rules "burden more speech than is necessary to further the government's legitimate interests."

On remand, the United States District Court for the District of Columbia concluded that the must-carry provisions of the 1992 Act satisfied the intermediate scrutiny standard. In doing so, the court relied heavily on the Supreme Court's admonition that "courts are compelled to accord substantial deference to Congress' predictive judgments." In *Turner II*, the Supreme Court affirmed the decision by a five-to-four vote. As you will read, the majority and dissent disagreed concerning how much deference was due Congress under the heightened scrutiny the Court employed.

TURNER BROADCASTING SYSTEM, INC. v. FCC
(*TURNER BROADCASTING II*)
117 S. Ct. 1174 (1997)

JUSTICE KENNEDY delivered the opinion of the Court.

. . . We begin where the plurality ended in *Turner [Broadcasting I]*, applying the standards for intermediate scrutiny enunciated in *O'Brien*. A content-neutral regulation will be sustained under the First Amendment if it advances important governmental interests unrelated to the suppression of free speech and does not burden substantially more speech than necessary to further those interests. As noted in *Turner [Broadcasting I]*, must-carry was designed to serve "three interrelated interests: (1) preserving the benefits of free, over-the-air local broadcast television, (2) promoting the widespread dissemination of information from a multiplicity of sources, and (3) promoting fair competition in the market for television programming." We decided then, and now reaffirm, that each of those is an important governmental interest. We have been most explicit in holding that " 'protecting noncable households from loss of regular television broadcasting service due to competition from cable systems' is an important federal interest." Forty percent of American households continue to rely on over-the-air signals for television programming. Despite the growing importance of cable television and alternative technologies, " 'broadcasting is demonstrably a principal source of information and entertainment for a great part of the Nation's population.' " We have identified a corresponding "governmental purpose of the highest order" in ensuring public access to "a multiplicity of information sources." And it is undisputed the Government has an interest in "eliminating restraints on fair competition . . ., even when the individuals or entities subject to particular regulations are engaged in expressive activity protected by the First Amendment." . . .

A

On our earlier review, we were constrained by the state of the record to assessing the importance of the Government's asserted interests when "viewed in the abstract." The expanded record now permits us to consider whether the must-carry provisions were designed to address a real harm, and whether those provisions will alleviate it in a material way.

[The Court reviewed the evidence before Congress and the District Court which indicated that "the economic health of local broadcasting is in genuine jeopardy and in need of the protections afforded by must-carry." The earlier excerpt from *Turner Broadcasting I* described some of this evidence. Based on the evidence, the majority had "no difficulty in finding a substantial basis to support Congress' conclusion that a real threat justified enactment of the must-carry provisions." The majority also dismissed the dissent's prediction that cable systems would not engage in predation against broadcasters.]

This is not a case in which we are called upon to give our best judgment as to the likely economic consequences of certain financial arrangements or business structures, or to assess competing economic theories and predictive judgments, as we would in a case arising, say, under the antitrust laws. . . . The issue before us is whether, given conflicting views of the probable development of the television industry, Congress had substantial evidence for making the judgment that it did. We need not put our imprimatur on Congress' economic theory in order to validate the reasonableness of its judgment.

2

The harm Congress feared was that stations dropped or denied carriage would be at a "serious risk of financial difficulty," and would "deteriorate to a substantial degree or fail altogether." Congress had before it substantial evidence to support its conclusion. Congress was advised the viability of a broadcast station depends to a material extent on its ability to secure cable carriage. One broadcast industry executive explained it this way:

> "Simply put, a television station's audience size directly translates into revenue—large audiences attract larger revenues, through the sale of advertising time. If a station is not carried on cable, and thereby loses a substantial portion of its audience, it will lose revenue. With less revenue, the station cannot serve its community as well. The station will have less money to invest in equipment and programming. The attractiveness of its programming will lessen, as will its audience. Revenues will continue to decline, and the cycle will repeat."

Empirical research in the record before Congress confirmed the " 'direct correlation [between] size in audience and station [advertising] revenues,' " and that viewership was in turn heavily dependent on cable carriage. . .

To be sure, the record also contains evidence to support a contrary conclusion. Appellants (and the dissent in the District Court) make much of the fact that the number of broadcast stations and their advertising revenue continued to grow during the period without must-carry, albeit at a diminished rate. Evidence introduced on remand indicated that only 31 broadcast stations actually went dark during the period without must-carry (one of which failed after a tornado destroyed its transmitter), and during the same period some 263 new stations signed on the air. New evidence appellants produced on remand indicates the average cable system voluntarily carried local broadcast stations accounting for about 97 percent of television ratings in noncable households. Appellants, as well as the dissent in the District Court, contend that in light of such evidence, it is clear "the must-carry law is not necessary to assure the economic viability of the broadcast system as a whole."

This assertion misapprehends the relevant inquiry. The question is not whether Congress, as an objective matter, was correct to determine must-carry is necessary to prevent a substantial number of broadcast stations from losing cable carriage and suffering significant financial hardship. Rather, the question is whether the legislative conclusion was reasonable and supported by substantial evidence in the record before Congress. In making that determination, we are not to "re-weigh the evidence de novo, or to replace Congress' factual predictions with our own." Rather, we are simply to determine if the standard is satisfied. If it is, summary judgment for defendants-appellees is appropriate regardless of whether the evidence is in conflict. We have noted in another context, involving less deferential review than is at issue here, that " 'the possibility of drawing two inconsistent conclusions from the evidence does not prevent . . . [a] finding from being supported by substantial evidence.'

Although evidence of continuing growth in broadcast could have supported the opposite conclusion, a reasonable interpretation is that expansion in the cable industry was causing harm to broadcasting. . . .

Despite the considerable evidence before Congress and adduced on remand indicating that the significant numbers of broadcast stations are at risk, the dissent believes yet more is required before Congress could act. It demands more information about which of the dropped broadcast stations still qualify for mandatory carriage, about the broadcast markets in which adverse decisions take place, *post*, and about the features of the markets in which bankrupt broadcast stations were located prior to their demise. The level of detail in factfinding required by the dissent would be an improper burden for courts to impose on the Legislative Branch. That amount of detail is as unreasonable in the legislative context as it is constitutionally unwarranted. "Congress is not obligated, when enacting its statutes, to make a record of the type that an administrative agency or court does to accommodate judicial review." . . .

B

The second portion of the *O'Brien* inquiry concerns the fit between the asserted interests and the means chosen to advance them. Content-neutral regulations do not pose the same "inherent dangers to free expression" that content-based regulations do, and thus are subject to a less rigorous analysis, which affords the Government latitude in designing a regulatory solution. Under intermediate scrutiny, the Government may employ the means of its choosing " 'so long as the . . . regulation promotes a substantial governmental interest that would be achieved less effectively absent the regulation,' " and does not " 'burden substantially more speech than is necessary to further' "

The must-carry provisions have the potential to interfere with protected speech in two ways. First, the provisions restrain cable operators' editorial discretion in creating programming packages by "reduc[ing] the number of channels over which [they] exercise unfettered control." Second, the rules "render it more difficult for cable programmers to compete for carriage on the limited channels remaining."

Appellants say the burden of must-carry is great, but the evidence adduced on remand indicates the actual effects are modest. Significant evidence indicates the vast majority of cable operators have not been affected in a significant manner by must-carry. Cable operators have been able to satisfy their must-carry obligations 87 percent of the time using previously unused channel capacity; 94.5 percent of the 11,628 cable systems nationwide have not had to drop any programming in order to fulfill their must-carry obligations; the remaining 5.5 percent have had to drop an average of only 1.22 services from their programming; and cable operators nationwide carry 99.8 percent of the programming they carried before enactment of must-carry. Appellees note that only 1.18 percent of the approximately 500,000 cable channels nationwide is devoted to channels added because of must-carry; weighted for subscribership, the figure is 2.4 percent. Appellees contend the burdens of must-carry will soon diminish as cable channel capacity increases, as is occurring nationwide.

Appellants posit a number of alternatives in an effort to demonstrate a less-restrictive means to achieve the Government's aims. . . . This " 'less-restrictive-alternative analysis . . . has never been a part of the inquiry into the validity' " of content-neutral regulations on speech . . .

[Although the majority denied that a less-restrictive-alternative analysis was part of the inquiry, it examined several alternatives suggested by the appellants. The earlier excerpt of *Turner Broadcasting II* indicated the grounds on which the Court determined these options were not viable.]

III

Judgments about how competing economic interests are to be reconciled in the complex and fast-changing field of television are for Congress to make. Those judgments "cannot be ignored or undervalued simply because [appellants] cas[t] [their] claims under the umbrella of the First Amendment." Appellants' challenges to must-carry reflect little more than disagreement over the level of protection broadcast stations are to be afforded and how protection is to be attained. We cannot displace Congress' judgment respecting content-neutral regulations with our own, so long as its policy is grounded on reasonable factual findings supported by evidence that is substantial for a legislative determination. Those requirements were met in this case, and in these circumstances the First Amendment requires nothing more. . . .

JUSTICE O'CONNOR, with whom JUSTICE SCALIA, JUSTICE THOMAS, and JUSTICE GINSBURG join, dissenting. . . .

[The dissent disputed the need for the must-carry rules.] Neither the principal opinion nor the partial concurrence offers any guidance on what might constitute a "significant reduction" in the availability of broadcast programming. The proper analysis, in my view, necessarily turns on the present distribution of broadcast stations among the local broadcast markets that make up the national broadcast "system." Whether cable poses a "significant" threat to a local broadcast market depends first on how many broadcast stations in that market will, in the absence of must-carry, remain available to viewers in noncable households. It also depends on whether viewers actually watch the stations that are dropped or denied carriage. The Court provides some raw data on adverse carriage decisions, but it never connects that data to markets and viewership. Instead, the Court proceeds from the assumptions that adverse carriage decisions nationwide will affect broadcast markets in proportion to their size; and that all broadcast programming is watched by viewers. Neither assumption is logical or has any factual basis in the record. . . .

In my view, the statute is not narrowly tailored to serve a substantial interest in preventing anticompetitive conduct. . . . Congress has commandeered up to one third of each cable system's channel capacity for the benefit of local broadcasters, without any regard for whether doing so advances the statute's alleged goals. To the extent that Congress was concerned that anticompetitive impulses would lead vertically integrated operators to prefer those programmers in which the operators have an ownership stake, the Cable Act is overbroad, since it does not impose its requirements solely on such operators. An integrated cable operator cannot satisfy its must-carry obligations by allocating a channel to an unaffiliated cable programmer. And must-carry blocks an operator's access to up to one third of the channels on the system, even if its affiliated programmer provides programming for only a single channel. . . .

Finally, I note my disagreement with the Court's suggestion that the availability of less-speech-restrictive alternatives is never relevant to *O'Brien*'s narrow tailoring inquiry. . . .

. . . [T]he availability of less restrictive alternatives—a leased-access regime and subsidies—reinforces my conclusion that the must-carry provisions are overbroad. . . .

———

Turner I and *Turner II* review the FCC's regulations of cable television particularly in relationship to broadcast television. If cable is going to be a major player in the television market, the FCC has decided through the must-carry rules to promote competition by assisting broadcast television to stay in the market.

Beyond the must-carry rules, the FCC also attempted to maintain competition in this industry by restricting market share by television stations. The FCC adopted two rules to do this. The National Television Station Ownership (NTSO) Rule prohibited any entity from controlling television stations with a combined potential audience exceeding 35% of the households in the United States. The Cable/Broadcast Cross-Ownership (CBCO) Rule prohibited a cable system from carrying the signal of any broadcast station if the cable system owned a broadcast station in the same local market. Together with the must-carry rule, the CBCO rule effectively prohibited common ownership of a broadcast station and a cable system in the same local market.

Both rules were challenged. Network broadcasters–Fox, CBS, NBC, and Viacom challenged the NTSO rules; Time Warner challenged the CBCO rules, and, all petitioners said both rules violated the First Amendment. The D.C.

Circuit Court, per Chief Judge David Ginsburg held that: (1) The Commission's decision to retain both parties was arbitrary, capricious and contrary to law; (2) the NTSO rule was remanded for further consideration, and (3) the CBCO rule was vacated.

FOX TELEVISION STATIONS, INC. V. FCC
280 F.3d 1027 (D.C. Cir. 2002)

. . .The Commission gave three primary reasons for retaining the NTSO Rule: (1) to observe the effects of recent changes to the rules governing local ownership of television stations; (2) to observe the effects of the increase in the national ownership cap to 35%; and (3) to preserve the power of affiliates in bargaining with their networks and thereby allow the affiliates to serve their local communities better. The Commission also stated that it believed repealing the rule would "increase concentration in the national advertising market"—presumably to the detriment of competition—and "enlarge the potential for monopsony power in the program production market"— presumably to the detriment of both competition and diversity.

The effect upon petitioners Fox and Viacom of the Commission's decision to retain the NTSO Rule was direct and immediate. Viacom's acquisition of CBS brought its audience reach to 41%; only a stay issued by this court has enabled Viacom to avoid divesting itself of enough stations to come within the 35% cap. Similarly, the Rule is preventing Fox from going forward with its purchase of Chris-Craft Industries, which purchase would enable Fox to reach more than 40% of the national audience. . . .

In the *1998 Report* the Commission decided that retaining the CBCO Rule was necessary to prevent cable operators from favoring their own stations and from discriminating against stations owned by others. The Commission also determined that the CBCO Rule was "necessary to further [the] goal of diversity at the local level." The Rule, according to the Commission, contributes to the diversity of viewpoints in local markets by preserving the voices of independent broadcast stations, which provide local news and public affairs programming.

The effect upon Time Warner of the Commission's decision to retain the CBCO Rule was significant. Although Time Warner has not identified any specific transaction it would have consummated but for the CBCO Rule, the Rule is preventing it from acquiring television stations in markets, such as New York City, where it owns a cable system. Time Warner asserts that "obvious procompetitive efficiencies" would result from "combining" a television station in that area with its all-local-news cable programming service, NY1. Time Warner also argues that the CBCO Rule hinders its "WB" network from competing with networks that own stations in major television markets. . . .

III. The NTSO Rule

The networks assert that the Commission's decision to retain the NTSO Rule was contrary to § 202(h) and arbitrary and capricious in violation of the APA; alternatively they contend the Rule violates the First Amendment.

A. Section 202(h) and the APA

The networks argue that the Commission's decision not to repeal the NTSO Rule was arbitrary and capricious and contrary to § 202(h) for three reasons: (1) the Rule is fundamentally irrational, and the Commission's justifications for retaining it are correlatively flawed; (2) the Commission failed meaningfully to consider whether the Rule was "necessary" in the public interest; and (3) the Commission failed to explain why it departed from its previous position that the Rule should be repealed.

1. Is the Rule irrational?

The networks advance three reasons for thinking that retention of the NTSO Rule was irrational: The 35% cap is if anything less justified than the aggregate limitation upon cable system ownership we held a violation of the First Amendment in *Time Warner Entertainment Co., L.P. v. FCC,* 240 F.3d 1126 (2001) (*Time Warner II*); the Commission has provided no persuasive reason to believe retention of the Rule is necessary in the public interest; and retention of the Rule is inconsistent with some of the Commission's other recent decisions.

Time Warner II. According to the networks, "[t]he logic of *Time Warner II* applies with even greater force here." They contend that the television station ownership cap of 35% is more severe than the cable system ownership cap of 30% struck down in *Time Warner II,* because unlike cable systems "broadcasters face intense competition from numerous stations in each local market" and the 35% cap is measured in terms of homes potentially rather than actually served. In response, the Commission, supported by intervenors NAB and NASA, notes two distinctions between *Time Warner II* and this case: The 30% cap in *Time Warner II* was set by the Commission whereas the 35% cap at issue here was set by the Congress; and the provision of the Cable Act at issue in the prior case limited the extent to which the Commission could regulate in furtherance of diversity, whereas § 202(h) mandates that a rule necessary "in the public interest"—including the public interest in diversity—be retained.

The networks are right, of course, that a broadcaster faces more local competition than does a cable system. We must also acknowledge that under the cap expressed in terms of a "potential audience reach" of 35%, an owner of television stations cannot in practice achieve an audience share that approaches 35% of the national audience. Nonetheless, we find the networks' reliance upon *Time Warner II* less than convincing for two reasons, one advanced by the Commission and one not. As the Commission points out, we concluded in *Time Warner II* that the 1992 Cable Act limited the agency's authority to impose regulations solely in order to further diversity in programming, whereas no such limitation is at work in this case. Additionally, in *Time Warner II* we reviewed the challenged regulations under first amendment "intermediate scrutiny," which is more demanding than the arbitrary and capricious standard of the APA.

The networks next argue that neither safeguarding competition nor promoting diversity generally can support the Commission's decision to retain the NTSO Rule. . . .

As to competition, the networks note that there is no evidence "that broadcasters have undue market power," such as to dampen competition, in any relevant market. The Commission attempts to rebut the point, but to no avail. In its brief the agency cites a single, barely relevant study. . . . The study plainly does not, however, suggest that broadcasters have undue market power. . . .

As to diversity, the networks contend there is no evidence that "the national ownership cap is needed to protect diversity" and that in any event § 202(h) does not allow the Commission to regulate broadcast ownership "in the name of diversity alone." The Commission, again supported by intervenors NAB and NASA, persuasively counters the statutory point: In the context of the regulation of broadcasting, "the public interest" has historically embraced diversity (as well as localism). . . . First, the Commission failed to explain why it was no longer adhering to the view it expressed in the *1984 Report* that national diversity is irrelevant. Second, the Commission's passing reference to national diversity does nothing to explain why the Rule is necessary to further that end.

As to the Commission's three more specific reasons for retaining the NTSO Rule, the networks contend that each is inadequate. The Commission stated that retaining the cap was necessary so it could: (1) observe the effects of recent changes in the rules governing local ownership of television stations; (2) observe the effects of the national ownership cap having been raised to 35%; and (3) preserve the power of local affiliates to bargain with their networks in order to promote diversity of programming. We agree with the networks that these reasons cannot justify the Commission's decision.

The first reason is insufficient because there is no obvious relationship between relaxation of the local ownership rule—which now permits a single entity to own two broadcast stations in the same market in some situations,— and retention of the national ownership cap, and the Commission does nothing to suggest there is any non-obvious relationship.

The Commission, with the support of intervenors NAB and NASA, argues that it was required to defer to the decision of the Congress to set the initial ownership cap in the 1996 Act at 35%. . . . This legislative history is no basis whatever for the Commission's decision. . . .

Nor does the Commission's third reason—that the Rule is necessary to strengthen the bargaining power of network affiliates and thereby to promote diversity of programming—have sufficient support in the present record.

In sum, we agree with the networks that the Commission has adduced not a single valid reason to believe the NTSO Rule is necessary in the public interest, either to safeguard competition or to enhance diversity. Although we agree with the Commission that protecting diversity is a permissible policy, the Commission did not provide an adequate basis for believing the Rule would in fact further that cause. We conclude, therefore, that the 1998 decision to retain the NTSO Rule was arbitrary and capricious in violation of the APA. . . .

In sum, we hold that the decision to retain the NTSO Rule was both arbitrary and capricious and contrary to § 202(h) of the 1996 Act. The networks argue that this requires us to vacate the Rule rather than merely to remand the case to the agency for further consideration. As will be discussed below, we disagree, and for this reason we must go on to consider the networks' first amendment challenge to the NTSO Rule which, if successful, without question would require that the Rule be vacated.

[The Court finds that the NTSO rule does not violate the First Amendment.]

IV. The CBCO Rule

Time Warner's principal contention is that the CBCO Rule is an unconstitutional abridgment of its first amendment right to speak. Time Warner also argues that the Commission's decision to retain the Rule was arbitrary and capricious and contrary to § 202(h). Because we agree that the retention decision was arbitrary and capricious as well as contrary to § 202(h), and that this requires us to vacate the Rule, we do not reach Time Warner's first amendment claim.

A. Section 202(h) and the APA

Time Warner raises a host of objections to the Commission's decision to retain the CBCO Rule. The Commission is largely unresponsive to these arguments; to the extent it is responsive, it is unpersuasive.

First, Time Warner argues that the Commission impermissibly justified retaining the Rule on a ground, namely that cable/broadcast combines might "discriminate against unaffiliated broadcasters in making cable-carriage decisions," different from the one it gave when it promulgated the Rule, namely, that "cable should be protected" from acquisition by networks bent upon pre-empting new competition. The Commission does not respond but even so we think the argument is clearly without merit. Nothing in § 202(h) suggests the grounds upon which the Commission may conclude that a rule is necessary in the public interest are limited to the grounds upon which it adopted the rule in the first place.

Next, Time Warner argues that the Commission applied too lenient a standard when it concluded only that the CBCO Rule "continues to serve the public interest," and not that it was "necessary" in the public interest. Again the Commission is silent, but this time we agree with Time Warner; the Commission appears to have applied too low a standard. The statute is clear that a regulation should be retained only insofar as it is necessary in, not merely consonant with, the public interest.

Finally, Time Warner attacks the specific reasons the Commission gave for retaining the Rule. All three reasons relate either to competition or to diversity, and we have grouped them below accordingly.

1. Competition

The Commission expressed concern that a cable operator that owns a broadcast station: (1) can "discriminate" against other broadcasters by offering cable/broadcast joint advertising sales and promotions; and (2) has an incentive not to carry, or to carry on undesirable channels, the broadcast signals—including the forthcoming digital signals—of competing stations. Addressing the first concern, Time Warner argues that the Commission failed both to explain why joint advertising rates constitute "discrimination—which is simply a pejorative way of referring to economies of scale and scope"—and to "point to substantial evidence that such 'discrimination' is a nonconjectural problem." Addressing the second concern (in part), Time Warner contends that refusals by cable operators to carry digital signals must not be a significant problem because the Commission has declined to impose must-carry rules for duplicate digital signals. Both of Time Warner's points are plausible—indeed the first is quite persuasive—and we have no basis upon which to reject either inasmuch as the Commission does not respond to them.

Next, Time Warner gives four reasons for which the Commission's concern about discriminatory carriage of broadcast signals is unwarranted. First, must-carry provisions, already ensure that broadcast stations have access to cable systems; indeed, the Commission pointed to only one instance in which a cable operator denied carriage to a broadcast station (Univision). Second, competition from direct broadcast satellite (DBS) providers makes discrimination against competing stations unprofitable. Third, the Commission failed to explain why it departed from the position it took in the *1992 Report,* where it said that the CBCO Rule was not necessary to prevent carriage discrimination. Fourth, because a cable operator may lawfully be co-owned with a cable programmer or a network, the Rule does little to cure the alleged problem of cable operators having an incentive to discriminate against stations that air competing programming.

In response the Commission concedes it did not address Time Warner's second and third points—competition from DBS services and the contradiction of the *1992 Report*: "Since the Commission did not address any of these issues in the *1998 Report,* counsel for the Commission are not in a position to respond to Time Warner's claims concerning these issues." The same might have been said of Time Warner's fourth point. These failings alone require that we reverse as arbitrary and capricious the Commission's decision to retain the CBCO Rule.

The only argument to which the Commission does respond is that the Univision incident alone cannot justify retention of the Rule: The Commission first points to its predictive judgment that there would be more discrimination without the CBCO Rule and then points out that the availability of behavioral remedies does not necessarily preclude it from imposing a structural remedy. We acknowledge that the court should ordinarily defer to the Commission's predictive judgments, and we take the Commission's point about remedies. In this case, however, the Commission has not shown a substantial enough probability of discrimination to deem reasonable a prophylactic rule as broad as the cross-ownership ban, especially in light of the already extant conduct rules. A single incident since the must-carry rules were promulgated—and one that seems to have been dealt with adequately under those rules—is just not enough to suggest an otherwise significant problem held in check only by the CBCO Rule.

We conclude that the Commission has failed to justify its retention of the CBCO Rule as necessary to safeguard competition. The Commission failed to consider competition from DBS, to justify its change in position from the *1992*

Report, and to put forward any adequate reason for believing the Rule remains "necessary in the public interest."

2. Diversity

As for retaining the Rule in the interest of diversity, the Commission had this to say: "Cable/TV combinations . . . would represent the consolidation of the only participants in the video market for local news and public affairs programming, and would therefore compromise diversity." Time Warner argues that this rationale is contrary to § 202(h), as well as arbitrary and capricious, for essentially three reasons.

First, Time Warner contends that § 202(h), by virtue of its exclusive concern with competition, plainly precludes consideration of diversity and that, in any event, it should be so interpreted in order to avoid the constitutional question raised by the burden the CBCO Rule places upon the company's right to speak. Second, Time Warner argues that the increase in the number of broadcast stations in each local market since the promulgation of the CBCO Rule in 1970 renders any marginal increase in diversity owing to the operation of the Rule too slight to justify retaining it. Finally, Time Warner asserts that the decision to retain the Rule cannot be reconciled with the *TV Ownership Order,* in which the Commission concluded that a single entity may own two local television stations as long as there are eight other stations in the market and one of the two stations coming under common ownership is not among the four most watched stations.

The Commission responds feebly. First, it does not address Time Warner's argument that diversity may not be considered under § 202(h), but that is of little moment because it adequately addressed essentially the same argument when it was presented by the networks in connection with the NTSO Rule: A rule may be retained if it is necessary "in the public interest"; it need not be necessary specifically to safeguard competition. Second, the Commission concedes that it decided to retain the Rule without considering the increase in the number of competing television stations since it had promulgated the Rule in 1970. The Commission gives no explanation for this omission, yet it is hard to imagine anything more relevant to the question whether the Rule is still necessary to further diversity.

Finally, the Commission makes no response to Time Warner's argument that the concern with diversity cannot support an across-the-board prohibition of cross-ownership in light of the Commission's conclusion in the *TV Ownership Order* that common ownership of two broadcast stations in the same local market need not unduly compromise diversity. The Commission does object that Time Warner failed to raise this argument before the agency, but it appears that Time Warner did what it could to bring the argument to the Commission's attention. The *TV Ownership Order* was issued in August, 1999, after the close of the comment period, but almost a year before the *1998 Report* was issued (in June, 2000). A few months thereafter Time Warner proffered supplemental comments raising this point but the Commission declined to consider them. For this reason, we find the Commission's forfeiture argument unpersuasive. Even if it was proper for the agency to refuse to accept the comments, however, it does not follow that the agency was free to ignore its own recently issued *TV Ownership Order*. Yet the Commission made no attempt in the *1998 Report* and makes no attempt in its brief to harmonize its seemingly inconsistent decisions.

In sum, the Commission concedes it failed to consider the increased number of television stations now in operation, and it is clear that the Commission failed to reconcile the decision under review with the *TV Ownership Order* it had issued only shortly before. We conclude, therefore, that the Commission's diversity rationale for retaining the CBCO Rule is woefully inadequate.

B. Remedy

. . . Because the probability that the Commission would be able to justify retaining the CBCO Rule is low and the disruption that vacatur will create is relatively insubstantial, we shall vacate the CBCO Rule.

NOTES AND QUESTIONS

1. The last section reviewed four cable regulations—the "must-carry," non-duplication, NTSO, and CBCO rules. How does each operate? Who are the industry winners and losers under the operation of each rule? How do consumers fair under the rules? Is the public interest served? How?

2. Whose free speech rights do the must-carry rules limit? How are cable operators adversely affected? How are cable programmers (*i.e.*, those persons who produce programming to be shown on cable) adversely affected? Is the First Amendment being used to protect the commercial interests of private actors? Should it be so used? Can alcohol and tobacco companies make similar First Amendment arguments?

3. As discussed briefly in Chapter 4, the Court ordinarily applies strict scrutiny to the regulation of speech, but as you read, it has made an exception for broadcasting. On what grounds did the Court refuse in *Turner Broadcasting I* to apply *Red Lion* to cable operators? What is the difference between broadcasting and cable that justifies the difference in the scope of review?

4. Professor Smolla has noted the important First Amendment implications of the Court's refusal to apply *Red Lion* to cable operators: "[*Turner Broadcasting I*], of course, treated the must-carry regulations before the Court as content-neutral regulations, and thus applied the intermediate *O'Brien* standard to those provisions. By clear implication, therefore, the Court would have applied the strict scrutiny test to any content-based regulation of cable programming."[55]

5. The must-carry rules favor one class of media, broadcasters, over another, cable operators. In light of this favoritism, on what grounds did the Court hold that the rules had a neutral impact? Did Congress regulate cable operators because it favored the content of broadcasters' speech, or because cable networks give operators a "bottleneck" or "gatekeeper" form of control over most programming delivered into viewers' homes? Why does the intent of Congress matter?[56]

---

[55] R. SMOLLA, SMOLLA AND NIMMER ON FREEDOM OF SPEECH § 27:11 at 27-18 (3rd ed. 1996).
[56] *See id.*, § 27:10 at 27-11.

6. The majority and the dissent in *Turner II* strongly disagreed whether the law furthers a "substantial governmental interest" as required by *O'Brien*. Do the majority and dissenting justices apply the same level of deference? Do you think that the majority was too lenient in accepting the justifications that the government offered in support of the must-carry rules?

7. The majority and dissent in *Turner II* also disagreed whether "the incidental restriction on alleged First Amendment freedoms is no greater than is essential to furtherance of that interest." The dissent claimed that the must-carry rules failed this requirement for two reasons. First, the rules were overbroad because they applied to cable operators who did not seek to take advantage of their gatekeeping control to gain a competitive disadvantage over local broadcasters. Second, there were less restrictive alternatives that Congress had failed to adopt. What response did the majority give to each argument? Do you find the majority's response persuasive?

———

D. THE FUTURE OF TELECOMMUNICATIONS

With the passage of the 1996 Act, Congress has recognized the technological convergence of telecommunications industries. The technological boundaries between long-distance telephone service, regional telephone service, cable service, computer technology, and other communications services is becoming increasingly blurred. One observer predicts:

> Innovation in the telecommunications industry is occurring so rapidly that the same services today can be carried by different technologies and industries. Within 10 to 20 years, to refer to these technologies as separate sectors will be meaningless. These many voice, video, and data services are rapidly combining to create a new communications medium commonly known as the "information highway." Once in place, this highway will allow Americans to use these combined services right from the living room through their television sets, telephones or computers.[57]

The original assumption behind regulation of many of the individual technologies was that the firms which provided the services were natural monopolies. Now, however, technological innovation is rapidly introducing competition where none existed before. The government's reassessment of its role in light of these changes is appropriate and timely. Indeed, critics argue that the government has been slow to recognize recent developments and this failure has retarded the development of the information highway.

Although technological advances have eroded the original justification for rate regulation, the government's role is not necessarily at an end. First, we do not yet know the extent to which competition will reach every corner of telecommunications. For example, the assumption is that local telephone companies will become cable operators, but it remains to be seen to what

---

[57] Thierer, *Time To Free Up Both Phone and Cable*, CONSUMERS' RESEARCH MAGAZINE, Oct. 1, 1994, at 14.

extent this occurs. Second, the elimination of one regulatory problem—natural monopoly—does not mean the end to all regulatory problems. For one thing, the problem of "bottlenecks" can slow the spread of competition. When one competitor must depend on the cooperation of another competitor to deliver its services or product, the potential for anticompetitive behavior is strong. As you now know, the government can address this problem using entry controls. Further, the government might be able to assist the creation and spread of competition by requiring companies in a position to be a bottleneck to be common carriers. Finally, even in the short and midterms, technological innovation continues apace. Is fiber optic technology more like quadrophonic sound or CD technology? Will fiber optic transmission soon be surpassed by microwave transmission? What are the regulatory consequences of these changes?

Even without the problem of bottlenecks, the government has a role in terms of antitrust enforcement. Indeed, since the 1996 Act was passed, there has been a significant number of mergers and acquisitions in the telecommunications industry. In April 1996, for example, the parent companies of two RBOCs, Pacific Telesis Group and SBC Communications, agreed to a $16 billion merger. Later that month, Bell Atlantic Corporation and Nynex also agreed to merge, forming the second-largest telecommunications company in the country behind AT&T.[58] Within three months of the signing of the Act, the seven BOCs became five, with future mergers looming. Mergers within the local telephone industries were not the only ones occurring. In February 1996, US West, Inc., one of the former BOCs that has not merged with another former BOC, agreed to purchase Continental Cablevision, Inc. for approximately $11 billion, making US West the third largest cable operator in the country.[59] In April 1996, video-service provider MFS Communications Inc. agreed to buy the world's largest Internet service provider, UUNet Technologies Inc., for approximately $2 billion. UUNet serves as the primary pathway for The Microsoft Network, America Online, and Compuserve.[60] Then, in August, MFS merged with WorldCom, Inc., a company that operates a nationwide grid of fiber-optic telephone lines, in a $14 billion deal. The new company, MFS WorldCom, will be able to provide local telephone service, long-distance telephone service, and Internet access service on a single bill.

Although the antitrust implications of these mergers are beyond the scope of this book, it is easy enough to see the important issues that they create. With the continued consolidation of telecommunications companies, will we see a return to the monopolistic practices of AT&T before 1983? Is it possible that *fewer* companies will result in *increased* competition? Recall the fierce competition in the long-distance telephone service arena, which is dominated largely by only three companies: AT&T, MCI, and Sprint. Moreover, will antitrust enforcement be sufficient to ensure a competitive telecommunications

---

[58] *See* Birritteri, *Crossing the Competition Threshold: The Telecommunications Act of 1996*, N.J. BUS., June 1, 1996; Lee & Camia, *Telecom's Fast Start: Mergers Raise Questions About New Law's Effect on Competition*, THE DALLAS MORNING NEWS, May 19, 1996; Abrahms, *Bell Atlantic, Nynex Agree to Giant Merger*, THE WASHINGTON TIMES, Apr. 22, 1996.

[59] *US West: Slip in Stock Won't Kill Cable Deal*, THE OMAHA WORLD-HERALD, July 19, 1996.

[60] Norris, *Time Spurs MFS Deal, Boss Says $2 Billion Lands Internet Hookup*, THE OMAHA WORLD-HERALD, May 1, 1996.

marketplace, or will Congress have to step into the fray again, regulating telecommunications?

Since that flurry of activity the telecommunications market, indeed all the technology markets, and the market as a whole have collapsed. We might even be more precise and suggest that between Enron and WorldCom the energy and telecommunications industries are chiefly to blame for our market woes at the time of writing this book. In addition to both being network industries and formerly regulated by command-and-control regulations, both industries were (and are) being aggressively deregulated. What continuing lessons lie in this tale? Did firms like Enron and WorldCom, and all like associated firms, exploit the deregulatory environment too aggressively? Too unscrupulously? What are the lessons for regulators' law and policy?

Chapter 7

ECONOMIC RENTS: WEALTH DISTRIBUTION AND HOUSING RENTALS

Chapter 4 considered the justification for regulation that controls the prices that monopolies can charge. Price-setting regulation has also been used, along with related types of regulation, to address the problem of "rents" or the excess profits earned by those who sell a good or service that is in short supply. This chapter discusses the justification and methods of regulating markets where there may be economic rents. As you will determine, the justification for this type of economic regulation is not based on market failure, but on equitable and redistributional values.

A. REGULATORY JUSTIFICATIONS

Although most of us have at one time or another paid "rent" to a landlord, economists use the term "rent" in a different manner. The concept of "rent" is related to a firm's incentives to remain in a particular business. A seller is willing to continue selling a good or service as long as it earns enough money to pay all of its costs of production, including an acceptable return on its investment, which can be considered its "profit." This return or profit can also be described as an "opportunity cost." Opportunity costs represent the amount of money a seller could earn in some alternative business with the same degree of risk. In common terminology, unless a firm is earning at least as much "profit" as it would earn in another business of the same risk, it will switch to that other business.

In economics, the term "rent" refers to the amount of money that a firm earns over and above its costs, including its opportunity costs. Therefore, it is the amount of money a seller earns above what is necessary for that seller to remain in a market. In a sense, it is the amount of "excess" profit or profit unnecessary to keep the seller in its current business. As we saw in Chapter 4, a monopolist in an unregulated market earns "rents," because the prices it charges will produce income in excess of the monopolist's actual costs and its opportunity costs. The possibility of earning rents, however, is not limited to a monopolist; a seller can also earn *pure* rents or *economic* rents.

A seller can earn *pure* rents if it is selling a good or service that has a fixed supply, such as land, or if it is selling a good or service the supply of which cannot increase quickly, such as apartment housing. Normally, when the demand for a product increases, we can expect supply to increase as well. The supply increases because the increased demand for the product will bid up its price, and the higher prices will encourage production of an additional supply of the product. As the supply increases, the price will eventually fall. But if the supply of the product or service is fixed, the price will remain high, because no new supply will be forthcoming. The difference between the price charged before demand increased and the price charged after the increase in demand constitutes rent. We can infer from the seller's willingness to sell at the lower price that it was previously earning enough money to recover its actual costs and to recoup its "opportunity" costs. Thus, the additional income produced by the new, higher price is unnecessary to keep the seller in the market.

To illustrate the concept of pure rents, consider why the very best professional athletes earn so much money. These persons would remain athletes as long as they earned slightly more playing sports than their next best business opportunity. However, the best professionals earn millions of dollars more than the next best job they would be qualified to hold could pay. This is because the athlete possesses something in very short supply— extraordinary athletic ability. Since the supply of athletes with such superior skills is relatively small, and grows only slowly, demand for such skills has bid up the salaries of such athletes into millions of dollars. The difference between what they are paid as athletes and what they would earn in some other occupation constitutes "pure" rents.

A firm can earn *economic* rents if it controls a source of supply that costs less than the amount paid by other sellers for their sources of supply. For example, an oil firm that takes its oil from Alaska, the North Sea, or other relatively inaccessible spots will have spent more money to develop its source of supply than a firm that has discovered oil in Texas. Those firms with expensive oil development costs will have to charge more money for that oil in order to recover their actual and opportunity costs. As long as the demand for oil exceeds the supply of low cost oil, the market price for oil will be higher than if every seller had the same low costs as the Texas producers. Since the firm with Texas oil will charge the market price for its oil, the amount of money it will earn will exceed its costs (because the firm's cost of discovering the oil is less). In this manner, the firm with the less expensive source of supply can earn rents.

Chapter 4 indicated that monopolized markets are inherently inefficient because the monopolist charges higher prices than would exist in a competitive market. Regulating the monopolist's price makes the market more efficient, because it reproduces (at least in theory) the price conditions that would have prevailed in a competitive market. Unlike the situation in a monopolized market, where high prices are the product of *abnormal* competitive conditions, the high prices in markets with scarce goods or services are the product of *normal* market conditions. When something is scarce, its high price will allocate it to the persons who desire it the most, as evidenced by their willingness to pay its high price. This is efficient in the sense that the market allocates scarce goods to their highest valued use.

If high prices for scarce goods are produced by normal competition, what are the justifications for the regulation of rents? In essence, rent control is aimed at wealth transfers and is based on three related justifications.[1]

First, regulation reflects a judgment that rents are the result of "plain luck" rather than wise investment decisions or other desirable behavior. For

---

[1] These justifications are discussed in S. Breyer, Regulation and Its Reform 22 (1982).

example, you will shortly read about the imposition of windfall profits taxes on domestic oil producers during the OPEC oil embargo in 1973. During the embargo, the members of the Organization of Petroleum Exporting Countries (OPEC) limited their international oil sales as a response to the war between Israel and its Arab neighbors. This action, which precipitated a market price that was five to six times higher than the pre-embargo price, generated substantial rents for domestic oil producers. When this happened, it is likely that domestic producers earned rents. We can make this assumption because the producers had been willing to sell their oil for much less money prior to the embargo. Since oil producers did not engage in exploration in anticipation of a future Arab oil embargo, they were the lucky recipients of an unanticipated political event.

Compare the situation of some professional athletes who, as noted earlier, earn substantial rents. Yet, no one (except the owners of sports teams) appears to support regulation of how much these men and women can earn. Unlike the oil producers, however, the athletes' success is the product of more than good luck. It represents thousands of hours of practice and hard work.

Second, regulation reflects a judgment that the income transfer from consumers to sellers is regressive because income is transferred from persons who have less wealth to persons who have more. During the OPEC embargo, for example, there was a wealth transfer from millions of consumers who could not avoid buying gasoline despite the increase in price to the smaller number of persons who owned stock in the oil producers. Such investors are likely wealthier than many of these consumers.

Third, the wealth transfer associated with rents is not only regressive, but it can amount to millions of dollars. The wealth transfer from consumers to oil producers during the oil embargo is a good example. When the amounts are this large, regulation is justified on the ground that the government should capture "windfall" rents for the benefit of the consumers or the country as a whole.

In addition to these three justifications, regulation may also seek to address problems of economic hardship created by a sudden and unexpected increase in prices for consumers who were unable to plan for the changes. The suddenness of a price increase may cause consumers to cut back drastically on other expenditures or to invade their savings. This hardship can be particularly severe if the price rise involves a product for which demand is relatively inelastic, such as gasoline or housing.

B. REGULATORY METHODS

In the United States, three types of regulatory methods have been used to control rents. In Chapter 4, we examined cost-of-service ratemaking and price caps, which are related to a regulated entity's current costs. Historically-based price controls, which forbid sellers from charging more than the price they charged as of a certain date specified by regulators, are another form of regulation. This regulatory tool was employed nationwide during World War II, the Korean War, and during the Nixon administration. It is also used in some cities to control the cost of rental housing. The third control is a windfall profits tax that captures economic rents. This approach was used by the Carter administration in response to the OPEC oil embargo of 1973. This section describes the regulation of rents by historical price controls and by a windfall profits tax.

As an introduction to this discussion, one must realize that each tool has certain advantages and disadvantages as summarized in Table 7-1. In the table, the third column (Price Level) refers to the price that consumers will pay for goods or services that are in short supply. The term "cost" means that consumers will pay a price that reflects the producers' costs (including opportunity cost). The term "rent" means that consumers will pay a price that reflects both the producers' cost and their rent (excess profit).

Table 7-1

RENTS IN MARKETS AND UNDER REGULATION				
Situation	*Example*	*Price Level*	*Advantages*	*Disadvantages*
Unregulated Market	Athletic Compensation	Rent	Efficient rationing	Product or service to highest bidder
Cost-of-Service Ratemaking	Electricity	Cost	Eliminates rents	High administrative costs
Windfall Profits Tax	Oil	Rent	Efficient rationing Rents used for public purpose	High cost to consumers Reduces supply
Historical-Based Price Controls	Rental Housing	Cost	Eliminates rents Avoids high consumer costs	Pressure for exemptions Protects incumbents Inhibits new entry

Note in the table that the different regulations have different effects. Regulations which have the effect of keeping costs down, such as cost-of-service ratemaking or price controls, can create shortages because demand for that product will be greater than the amount producers are willing to supply. Producers have a disincentive to supply the market because rewards are less. Another way of explaining market changes in reaction to regulation is through supply shifts. A tax which increases the cost of a good will drive marginal producers from the market, thus shrinking the supply available. A subsidy, of course, will have the opposite effect. Marginal producers will be drawn to the market in order to increase their profitability.

Any rents that do exist are distributed to different groups. Market pricing, for example, distributes rents to producers. Cost-of-service ratemaking and price controls effectively protect consumers and taxes are returned to the public treasury. The effect of prices and distribution of rents through government allocation depends upon how the allocation program is designed.

1.   HISTORICALLY-BASED PRICE CONTROLS

This section starts with a brief history of the use of historically-based price controls. It then describes two significant problems that arise in conjunction with this regulatory method. First, regulators must devise some way to grant exemptions. Second, they must also have a method to ration goods and services.

a.   PRICE CONTROLS DURING WORLD WAR II AND THE KOREAN WAR

In 1942, Congress passed the Emergency Price Control Act,[2] which established the Office of Price Administration (OPA), under the direction of the Price Administrator appointed by the President. The Act's goals were:

> to stabilize prices and to prevent speculative, unwarranted, and abnormal increases in prices and rents; to eliminate and prevent profiteering, hoarding, manipulation, speculation, and other disruptive practices resulting from abnormal market conditions or scarcities caused by or contributing to the national emergency; to assure that defense appropriations are not dissipated by excessive prices; to protect persons with relatively fixed and limited incomes, consumers, wage earners, investors, and persons dependent of life insurance, annuities, and pensions, from undue impairment of their standard of living; to prevent hardships to persons engaged in business, . . . and to the Federal, State, and local governments, which would result from abnormal increases in prices; to assist in securing adequate production of commodities and facilities; to prevent a post emergency collapse of values; . . .

The Administrator was authorized, after consultation with representative members of an industry, to promulgate regulations fixing prices of commodities which "in his judgment will be generally fair and equitable and will effectuate the purposes of [the] Act" when, in his judgment, their prices "have risen or threaten to rise to an extent or in a manner inconsistent with the purposes of [the] Act." Congress also instructed the Administrator that prices, wages, and salaries were to be stabilized so far as practicable on the basis of levels which existed on September 15, 1942. The Administrator issued maximum price regulations for particular industries until the General Price Regulation, issued April 30, 1942, forbade the sale of most commodities at prices in excess of the highest price charged by the seller during March 1942.[3]

In September 1950, a few months after the Korean War started, Congress enacted the Defense Production Act,[4] providing for the imposition of

---

[2] 56 Stat. 23 (1942).

[3] 7 Fed. Reg. 3153 (1942).

[4] 64 Stat. 798 (1950).

production, allocation, price, and wage controls. As in the case of the World War II controls, Congress intended that the regulations address the problem of inflation caused by the demands placed on the economy to produce goods to be used in the war effort. The OPA was restaffed in order to carry out the necessary regulation and, after a slow start, caused in part because Congress had required a test of "voluntary" methods before wage and price regulations could be used, it promulgated a General Ceiling Price Regulation in January 1951.[5] The regulation froze prices at the highest level charged by individual sellers during a one-month period between December 1950 and January 1951.

The country's latest experience with nationwide wage and price controls occurred during the Nixon administration. The Economic Stabilization Act of 1970 authorized the President "to issue such orders and regulations as he may deem appropriate to stabilize prices, rents, wages, and salaries at levels not less than those prevailing on May 25, 1970," with any adjustments necessary to "prevent gross inequities."[6] According to a congressional report, the purpose of the act was to address the fact that, at a 6 percent rate, inflation was "still on a rampage in our economy."[7] The report criticized the "economic game plan" of the Nixon administration for dealing inadequately with the intertwined problems of high inflation and high unemployment and offered the president the alternative of wage-price controls as a solution. The Republicans accused the Democrats of passing the legislation in order to embarrass the President. To the Democrats' likely surprise, President Nixon went on nationwide television in August 1971 to announce a ninety-day freeze on wages and prices while his administration created a wage-price control program. The Cost of Living Council was established as the agency responsible for the regulatory program.[8]

b. EXEMPTIONS

The political and market pressure to provide relief from historically-based price controls is strong. Regulators in all three cases found it necessary to permit price increases, because some sellers became squeezed between rising costs and frozen prices.

Producers' costs (and prices) increased for several reasons.[9] First, certain products and services were exempt from the price freeze. Thus, the price of these products was permitted to increase. Agricultural commodities, for example, were exempted, because their price fluctuated widely depending on factors such as the weather and perishability. Further, if a product not subject to the price freeze was an input for another producer, the secondary producer's costs rose. Second, regulators also encouraged the production of some products by exempting them from the freeze. Third, wages (which were subject to a different set of controls) slowly rose as some categories of workers were exempt. Employers who had to pay higher wages pressured the government to expand the categories exempt from price controls. If administrators had

---

[5] 16 Fed. Reg. 808 (1951).

[6] 84 Stat. 799 (1970).

[7] H.R. REP. No. 91-1330 (1970).

[8] Exec. Order No. 11,615, 36 Fed. Reg. 15,727 (1971).

[9] BREYER, *supra* note 1, at 62.

not allowed price increases, these sellers would have stopped selling some goods and services as they became increasingly unprofitable.

Once regulators began to permit some price increases, the price rule became "historical price plus (certain allowable) costs."[10] In a country the size of the United States, the problem for regulators was how to gear up to determine which price and wage increases would be allowed. Administering the program that granted the exceptions to the frozen prices and wages became a logistical and legal nightmare.

Once regulators started to grant exemptions to frozen prices on the grounds a seller's production costs had increased, historically-based price regulation moved closer to being "cost-of-service" ratemaking. The new price was set at "current" cost. At this point in the administration of all three programs, many of the problems which plague cost-of-service ratemaking began to appear. For example, if a seller can recoup increases in its production costs, its incentive to reduce those costs is eliminated. In World War II, regulators sought to avoid this problem by not allowing price increases in manufacturing industries when costs went up, unless a price increase was necessary to maintain "reasonable" industry profits.[11] This solution, however, produced its own set of problems, associated with the issues of how to determine what constituted a cost and what was a "reasonable" profit. Of course, this is also a problem in "cost-of-service" ratemaking.

c. RATIONING

Price controls present another difficult problem. Before long, shortages of some products are likely to develop, for several reasons.[12] Some shortages are caused by the failure to permit sellers to pass on increases in their production costs. Even if the regulator permits price increases, delays in the approval process can create shortages. Once regulators approve price increases, another type of shortage is created. Goods already in stock or made from inventoried materials will be cheaper than goods or manufactured items to which new prices apply. Since consumers will prefer the lower-priced goods or products to the higher-priced ones, there will be a shortage of the less expensive items. Regulators can solve this problem by the sale of all goods (old and new) at the higher price, but this will permit sellers to earn rents on the old goods.

Unless the government is to leave allocation decisions concerning shortages to the seller, it must create some type of rationing system. The system might be as simple as first come, first served or as elaborate as determining which allotments would be most in the public interest. (The subject of government rationing is taken up in Chapter 10.) Even with government rationing, however, black markets and other forms of seller cheating, such as that described in the following case, *M. Kraus & Brothers v. United States,* are inevitable. For example, dairy industry officials testified after World War II that between 50% and 80% of all butter was sold on the black market.[13]

---

[10] *Id.*

[11] *Id.* at 63.

[12] *Id.* at 66–67.

[13] *Id.* at 68.

M. Kraus & Brothers, offers some insight into the practical difficulties of implementing widespread wage and price controls. The legal issue was whether the defendant corporation was denied due process because the regulations promulgated by the government did not put it on notice that the type of commercial practices in which it engaged was a violation. Note that the majority and dissent disagree concerning how much foresight can be expected of an administrative agency charged with the extraordinary task of implementing a wage and price control program for the entire economy.

M. KRAUS & BROTHERS v. UNITED STATES
327 U.S. 614 (1946)

MR. JUSTICE MURPHY announced the conclusion and judgment of the Court.

The problem here is whether the petitioner corporation was properly convicted of a crime under the Emergency Price Control Act of 1942.

The petitioner is engaged in the wholesale meat and poultry business in New York City. Poultry is a commodity subject to the provisions of Revised Maximum Price Regulation No. 269, promulgated by the Price Administrator pursuant to Section 2(a) of the Emergency Price Control Act of 1942. . . .

The theory of the Government is that [during Thanksgiving in November 1943] the petitioner was guilty of an evasion of the price limitations set forth in this particular regulation if it required the purchase of chicken feet and skin as a necessary condition to obtaining the primary commodity, the poultry. This practice is commonly known as a "combination sale" or a "tying agreement." It is argued that the petitioner thereby received for the poultry the ceiling price plus the price of the secondary commodities, the chicken parts. . . .

The jury acquitted petitioner's president but convicted the petitioner on nine counts. Petitioner was fined $2,500 on each count, a total of $22,500. The conviction was affirmed by the court below. . . . In our opinion, however, the conviction must be set aside.

Section 205(b) of the Emergency Price Control Act of 1942 imposes criminal sanctions on "Any person who willfully violates any provision of section 4 of this Act." Section 4(a) of the Act in turn provides that "It shall be unlawful . . . for any person to sell or deliver any commodity, . . . in violation of any regulation or order under section 2. . . ." Section 2(a) authorizes the Price Administrator under prescribed conditions to establish by regulation or order such maximum prices "as in his judgment will be generally fair and equitable and will effectuate the purposes of this Act." Section 2(g) further states that "Regulations, orders, and requirements under this Act may contain such provisions as the Administrator deems necessary to prevent the circumvention or evasion thereof."

The Price Administrator, pursuant to Section 2(a), issued Revised Maximum Price Regulation No. 269 on December 18, 1942, which regulation was in effect at the time the poultry sales in question were made. Section 1429.5 of this regulation, referred to in the information, stems from Section 2(g) of the Act. It is entitled "Evasion" and reads as follows: "Price limitations set forth in this Revised Maximum Price Regulation No. 269 shall not be evaded whether by direct or indirect methods, in connection with any offer, solicitation, agreement, sale, delivery, purchase or receipt of, or relating to, the commodities prices of which are herein regulated, alone or in conjunction with any other commodity, or by way of commission, service, transportation, or other charge, or discount, premium, or other privilege or other trade understanding or otherwise.". . .

This delegation to the Price Administrator of the power to provide in detail against circumvention and evasion, as to which Congress has imposed criminal sanctions, creates a grave responsibility. . . . [T]he Administrator's provisions must be explicit and unambiguous in order to sustain a criminal prosecution; they must adequately inform those who are subject to their terms what conduct will be considered evasive so as to bring the criminal penalties of the Act into operation. . . .

. . . The only issue bearing upon the regulation which is open in this criminal proceeding is whether the Administrator did in fact clearly and unmistakably prohibit tying agreements of this nature by virtue of the language he used in Section 1429.5. That issue we answer in the negative.

Section 1429.5, so far as here pertinent, provides that price limitations shall not be evaded by any method, direct or indirect, whether in connection with any offer or sale of a price-regulated commodity alone "or in conjunction with any other commodity," or by way of any trade understanding "or otherwise." No specific mention is made of tying agreements or combination sales. . . .

Mr. Justice Black, dissenting.

We were at war in 1943. Scarcity of food had become an acute problem throughout the nation. To keep the public from being gouged the government had set ceiling prices on food items. Congress had made it a crime to sell food above these ceiling prices. When Thanksgiving Day approached there were not enough turkeys to supply the demand of the many American families who wanted to celebrate in the customary style.

. . . This meat shortage was felt acutely during the Thanksgiving season, when petitioner instead of his usual 100 to 150 cars of turkeys received only one car. When the retail butchers and poultry market proprietors came clamoring for their share of the small supply (which the defendant rationed among them) they found that along with the turkeys which they wanted so badly petitioner gave and charged them for large amounts of chicken feet, skins and gizzards which they had not asked for at all and which for the most part they had never before sold as separate items. While the butchers paid in addition to the ceiling price charged for the turkeys the price charged for the chicken skins and feet, they did so only because they understood that unless they bought these unwanted items they could get no turkeys. . . .

. . . In promulgating this regulation the Administrator could not possibly foresee every ingenious scheme or artifice the business mind might contrive to shroud violations of the Price Control Act. The regulation does not specifically describe all manner of evasive device. The term "tying agreement" nowhere appears in it and a discussion of such agreements is irrelevant. We need not decide whether what petitioner did would have violated every possible hypothetical regulation the Administrator might have promulgated. The regulation here involved prohibits every evasion of the Price Control Act. . . .

NOTES AND QUESTIONS

1. Was the majority expecting too much of the government, or was it appropriate to insist that the government give clearer guidance concerning the boundaries of what types of behavior violated the law? Can sellers be expected to look for ways to evade price regulations? If so, are regulators hampered if they must write regulations which specifically prohibit whatever evasions sellers might think up?

2. Regarding Justice Black's dissent, he says that scarcity of food had become an acute national problem. Was that problem aggravated by price ceilings? If so, what was the justification for such ceilings?

3. Concerning the difficulties of implementing wage and price controls, Justice Stephen Breyer concludes:

> The problems that accompany historically price-based pricing methods are serious and increase in severity the longer regulation stays in effect. Misallocation, shortage, and enforcement problems become increasingly serious. . . . [T]he virtue of the historically price-based system rests in its ability to control the prices of hundreds or thousands of producers and products, while avoiding the firm-by-firm approach of cost-of-service ratemaking. It is difficult to see, in the case of economic-wide controls, any practical alternative.[14]

Breyer also notes that the system works best in wartime, when citizens are more prepared to cooperate voluntarily and will more readily tolerate the administrative problems that accompany the program. Do you agree? Are Breyer's conclusions supported by the situation being litigated in *Kraus*? Does the fact that *Kraus* was a criminal proceeding affect your answer to the previous question?

4. As Chapter 5 discussed, interstate natural gas pipelines are regulated by the Federal Energy Regulatory Commission (FERC), and local distribution companies are regulated by state utility commissions or local communities. In both instances, the regulators employ cost-of-service ratemaking, because these companies are considered natural monopolies. At one time, gas producers were also regulated by FERC (and its predecessor the Federal Power Commission (FPC)) using cost-of-service ratemaking. But unlike interstate or intrastate distribution companies, these producers are not a natural monopoly. In fact, there are hundreds of such producers. The justification for regulation was that producers were in a position to earn rents.[15] Given the large number of producers, how is it likely that they were in a position to earn rents? Does the fact that the producers have different costs of production, depending, for example, on the age of their wells, offer an explanation? Based on what you learned about the methodology of cost-of-service ratemaking, can you explain how it eliminates (at least in theory) the possibility that gas producers would earn rents?

5. Cost-of-service ratemaking was responsible for, or at least contributed to, a serious natural gas shortage in the middle of the 1970s. For a number

---

[14] *Id.* at 70.

[15] *Id.* at 243.

of reasons, including the fact that the FPC underestimated future drilling costs, the highest price the Commission established for new gas was not high enough to encourage enough new exploration to meet a rising demand for natural gas. This problem was exacerbated by FPC regulatory policy, which permitted interstate pipelines to average all gas costs and resell at that price. Thus, if a pipeline purchased old gas at a less expensive price and new gas at a more expensive price, it would charge its customers based on its average price for the two types of gas. In other words, the rent the interstate pipeline earned by selling old gas at a higher price than the pipeline paid for it was used to sell new gas at a lower price than the pipeline paid for it. Thus, an interstate pipeline could afford to sell new gas at below its cost, if it had enough old gas to offset the loss. As Stephen Breyer explains, "This system, by holding the price of new gas below its cost, encouraged customers to demand new natural gas, despite the possibility that they might have used other fuels that in terms of real resources were less costly to produce."[16] In this manner, the FPC increased demand for natural gas and caused what supplies existed to be used up faster than if new gas had been sold at a price that reflected how much the new gas cost the pipeline.

2. WINDFALL PROFITS TAXES

An alternative to controlling rents by historically-based price controls or cost-of-service ratemaking is to use a tax-based regulatory system. This approach was used to regulate oil prices in the wake of the OPEC oil embargo in 1973. At that time, the members of OPEC withheld oil from the market in retaliation for support by the United States of Israel in its seven-day war with the Arab countries. To address the windfall profits that the embargo created for domestic oil producers, the Carter administration established a wellhead tax on oil.[17] It categorized oil according to cost (including opportunity cost), set a tax equal to the difference between such cost and the world market price for oil, and allowed the resale price to rise to the world market level.

When oil prices increased after Iraq's invasion of Kuwait in 1990, a similar problem arose. The supply of oil was reduced because the United States organized an embargo of oil from Iraq and supplies from Kuwait were disrupted by the war. Since producers in the United States had been willing to sell their oil at lower prices before the war (implying that previously prices were sufficient to cover their costs), these producers earned pure rents at the higher prices. The existence of these rents produced calls for a windfall profits tax similar to the one imposed by the Carter administration. Consider the following arguments for a tax:

---

[16] *Id.* at 252.

[17] Crude Oil Windfall Profits Tax Act of 1980, Pub. L. No. 96-22, 94 Stat. 229.

SILVIO CONTE, . . . OR TAX EXCESS PROFITS, NEW YORK TIMES, SEPTEMBER 10, 1990, AT A15[*]

Has the recent rise in oil prices ruled out a hike in energy taxes? Not necessarily. While higher prices make it harder to tax consumers — a regressive way to go anyway — there is an alternative that is pro-consumer and appropriate under today's circumstances: the windfall-profits tax.

For weeks now, we have been reaching into our wallets to pay much higher prices for gasoline — and, soon, for heating oil — even though it would have been months before those higher prices reached consumers. We have seen it time and time again: retail energy prices respond immediately to price increases but very slowly to price decreases. There are only two words to describe the process: price gouging.

As the price of imported oil escalates, the windfall to domestic producers of oil grows and grows. The artificially inflated world price of oil increases the price that domestic producers can charge, even though the cost of production remains the same.

This windfall is direct profit to oil companies, and the amount can be substantial. According to one recent estimate, a rise in oil prices of $7 a barrel would increase the value of U.S. oil production by $21 billion a year. That's gravy on the plates of Big Oil at the expense of American consumers.

We should skim a bit off the top to help reduce the Federal deficit and protect consumers from having to bear the brunt of deficit reduction. That is one of the benefits of the windfall-profits tax. It is an excise tax that does not get passed through to the consumer. Because the price of oil is determined on the world market, it would not be economical for companies to raise the price of domestic oil to recover the tax. They would have no market for their oil.

Based on recent history, the windfall-profits tax is a proven revenue raiser. Between 1980 and 1988, the original windfall-profits tax generated approximately $80 billion in gross Federal revenues.

Preliminary estimates indicate that several billion dollars in new Federal revenues could be raised from a windfall-profits tax. True, when and if the price of crude oil falls back below a certain level, revenues would decline. However, even a short-term leveling off of the current upsurge could generate substantial revenues. Some could even be directed to programs aimed at protecting low-income consumers; heating assistance and weatherization, for instance.

In our free enterprise system, profits in the regular course of business are expected and encouraged. Windfall profits generated by an international crisis and price gouging at the expense of consumers are intolerable and should be taxed.

NOTES AND QUESTIONS

1. Oil companies defended the rapid increase in domestic gasoline prices after Iraq's invasion on the ground that it cost the companies more to purchase new supplies of oil. Does this answer justify the higher prices, or is there a flaw in the argument?

2. How does a windfall tax plan compare to cost-of-service ratemaking or historically-based price controls? On the one hand, it is more efficient, because it permits the price of a commodity to rise to the market level. As a result, the market will allocate the scarce supply of the commodity to those persons who pay the most for it. No government rationing plan is necessary. On the other hand, because the price is permitted to rise to the market level, the commodity may be priced higher than many consumers can afford. This result can be mitigated, however, if the government uses the proceeds of the windfall profits tax to subsidize the purchase of gasoline and heating oil by low income consumers. Would you prefer a windfall profits tax to historically-based price controls, if there is such a rebate to consumers? How likely is it that the rebate will significantly lessen the economic dislocation to low income consumers?

3. Although economists favor the use of a tax to regulate rents because it leads to more "efficient" markets, it should not be assumed that it is necessarily easier to administer.

The operation of a tax can be illustrated by assuming that a producer has Q_1 of oil to sell, and it cost him P_c per unit to produce. His total cost would be: $(Q_1 \times P_c)$. When the producer sells the oil, it would obtain P_w, or the world price per unit. Thus, total revenue would be: $(Q_1 \times P_w)$. To calculate the producer's rents, you would subtract his costs from his revenue:

(1) $(Q_1 \times P_w) - (Q_1 \times P_c) = $ rents   where:

(2) $(P_w - P_c) \times Q_1 = $ rents $Q_1 = $ quantity of oil for sale by the producer

$P_w = $ world price per unit

$P_c = $ producer's cost per unit

To calculate producer's tax, what two pieces of information would you need? You would need P_w and P_c. But obtaining this information is not nearly as simple as it might seem. Take the P_w, or the world price per unit. Since the world price for oil fluctuates, the regulator must determine how often to make adjustments. What happens if the regulator fails to make adjustments often enough? What is the difficulty of making adjustments too often? In addition, the regulator must also determine which world price to use, since there are different types of oil, and they sell at different prices. What would be the consequences if the regulator used only one type or took an average of the various types?

Although calculation of P_w presents some problems, they are not nearly as serious as the problems associated with how you calculate P_c, or the costs of producing the oil. How can the regulator determine a company's costs, including its opportunity costs? Would this require cost-of-service ratemaking? Would it be sufficient to assume that some price charged in the past (before the inflation) was an accurate measure of P_c? If the latter method is used, the regulator must determine which oil was produced (*i.e.*, discovered) before the inflation of prices and which oil was produced after the inflation. Needless to say, the oil companies will argue that oil characterized by the administrator as "old" is really "new," and therefore not associated with any rents. The administrator must therefore have some type of process to reconcile these claims.

C.   CASE STUDY: RENTAL HOUSING

The previous materials indicated that in the past the government has regulated rents in several different industries. The following section is a case study of a current regulatory program: the use by local governments of price controls on rental housing. The wisdom of rent controls for rental housing is a hotly debated topic. The following excerpts indicate the arguments used by each side in this debate.

RICHARD A. EPSTEIN, RENT CONTROL AND THE THEORY OF EFFICIENT REGULATION, 54 BROOKLYN LAW REVIEW 741, 761–70 (1988) *

Let us begin with the static analysis, which assumes that the supply of housing within a given community is fixed, so that the only question is its allocation. For sake of argument I shall assume that the market is competitive in form, a good approximation of all rental markets. Competitive markets have the virtue of always forcing each resource user to measure his demand for the resource against the strongest best rival claim, so that at renewal the tenant in possession has to decide whether the rental demanded is worth it to him in terms of benefits foregone. . . . The nonrenewal of leases should not be regarded as a bad social event because someone else with a greater willingness to pay now enjoys the unit. . . .

The introduction of the rent control statute of necessity changes the decision function for the tenant in ways that frustrate the social welfare. No longer will the tenant compare the subjective use of the property to its market value, which represents a minimum estimate of the subjective use of some rival tenant. Instead the tenant will compare the subjective value of leasehold renewal with the lower regulated rent. Whenever the subjective valuation is greater than the regulated price, but lower than the market one, there is an allocative blunder, as the private decision to remain ignores the greater cost inflicted upon some potential rival. The larger the gap between the market and the regulated price, the greater the divergence between private and social cost.

Nonetheless, turnover will occur whenever the subjective value to the tenant falls below the regulated rental. The question is who gets the vacant unit given that demand under regulation is far in excess of supply. Since rents cannot move freely upward, nonprice systems of allocation will be used. Where the landlord controls the process, there will be a tendency to select those tenants

---

* Reprinted by permission.

with very low risk. Hence the system favors friends and connections, the way in which I got my Columbia College apartment in 1963. If this approach is blocked, then a queue will form for the now available units, and prospective tenants will vie for a place at the front, which can be obtained by making side payments to the right person. Hence the common practice of paying key money to vacating tenants, or of greasing the palm of the superintendent, again as happened with me in New York in 1963. Rent control thus introduces distortions on the ending of old leases and forming of new ones. Applied in countless cases in large cities, it leads to stagnation and social dislocation.

B. For Cause Provisions . . .

In the ordinary unregulated market, the landlord has little incentive to manipulate for cause requirements in order to remove a well-behaved tenant. . . .

However, the rent control laws radically increase the landlord's returns from for cause dismissal. . . . Small deviations from the leasehold provisions therefore are no longer small items for the parties to resolve by informal adjustments. The landlord has strong incentives to exploit minor breaches in order to escape rent control laws. . . .

C. Long-Term Investment

. . . Even if new construction is exempt from the statute, existing rent control laws give a loud and clear signal that old policies may be reversed so that future units may be subject to similar restrictions. That prospect is, moreover, far from negligible because once those units are occupied, their residents add a new class of voters to the rolls whose interests can no longer be ignored in the political calculus. All rent control statutes thus depress the future total return of any investment. Reduced returns mean reduced investments, so that rent control statutes only exacerbate the housing shortages they are said to alleviate.

D. The Political Dimension

. . . Instead of having competitive markets make the decision, the law must necessarily introduce political formulas whereby the majority of voters within the jurisdiction, subject only to loose constitutional rate of return constraints, determine the formula for allowable increases. The political battles are often ugly, acrimonious, and uncivilized. The costs are extensive, given the very wide bargaining range between the market and the minimum allowable regulated rents. Factional struggle can dissipate the gains that are otherwise generated by voluntary exchange.

W. DENNIS KEATING, COMMENTARY ON "RENT CONTROL AND THE THEORY OF EFFICIENT REGULATION," 54 BROOKLYN LAW REVIEW 1223, 1224–27 (1988) *

. . . Epstein chooses to ignore the housing problems that have given rise to rent control. For example, in its 1988 report to Congress, the National Housing Task Force cited such serious problems as the declining stock of affordable housing and the increasing number of tenants, millions, mostly poor, living in substandard housing and paying very high proportions of their income for rent. These conditions preceded rent control in New York City and they remain very serious problems. Of course, rent control protects not only poor but also moderate and middle-income tenants, most of whom would otherwise be subject to extreme rent fluctuations in tight housing markets. . . .

. . . Epstein does not discuss the reality of the housing situation in which the market does not provide affordable housing and the government does not provide adequate housing subsidies. The reality is that many citizens, especially lower income tenants, must pay dearly for what is all too often substandard housing. . . .

Epstein does not recognize a right to security of tenure unless it results from private negotiations between landlord and tenant in the form of a lease. However, for many tenants the right to negotiate such protection is illusory since they lack the individual or organized power to obtain much protection against displacement. Most residential leases are short-term. In those housing markets with low vacancy rates, high demand for apartments and condominiums, and wide income differences, the housing market frequently leads to gentrification which displaces those lower-income tenants unable to compete economically.

MICHAEL J. MANDEL, DOES RENT CONTROL HURT TENANTS?: A REPLY TO EPSTEIN, 54 BROOKLYN LAW REVIEW 1267, 1268–74 (1988) *

Imagine two types of rent control laws. The first law, which I will call strict rent control, will set nominal rents for all apartments, both old and new. There will be no adjustment for inflation or for rising operating costs. Strict rent control laws are very common in textbooks and figure prominently in attacks on rent control, but are almost nonexistent in reality. The only important United States example of strict rent control was New York City between the end of World War II and 1969.

The second law, which I will call moderate rent control, will allow regulated rents to rise with inflation and increased operating costs and will exempt new construction from regulation. Moderate rent control laws are very common in reality, and almost never discussed in textbooks. There are at least one hundred communities which have some form of a moderate rent control law. . . .

---

* Reprinted by permission

* Reprinted by permission.

Moreover, a moderate rent control law may even increase the supply of rental housing. This apparently counterintuitive implication is actually very sensible. A moderate rent control law, by limiting the rent increases on old apartments, protects tenants in old apartments. Some of these tenants would have either moved out of the rental market or taken smaller apartments if the rents had been allowed to rise to the market level.

The result is that moderate rent control increases the demand for rental apartments, or put another way, new tenants are chasing a smaller pool of available apartments. In either case, the rent control law will drive the rents on unregulated apartments above where they would be without the law.

. . . Faced with the fact that all existing laws exempt new construction from regulation, Epstein is forced to shift to a much weaker form of attack — the claim that "existing rent control laws give a loud and clear signal that old policies may be reversed so that future units may be subject to similar restrictions." . . .

It seems clear that rent control is not a perverse public policy which hurts everyone. There are winners and there are losers, and it is important to identify who is who. On the landlord side the losers are people who owned rental housing at the time the original rent control law was passed, and the winners are builders of new apartments (who reap the benefit of higher rents). People who bought rent controlled buildings after the law was passed deserve no sympathy, since their purchase price reflected the status of the building.

On the tenant side, the elderly and long-term stable households benefit from the low levels of their original rent. People just entering the rental market and renters who move frequently tend to pay higher rents (especially in cities with vacancy decontrol) or face long housing searches. Often this means that low-income households do not receive as much protection from rent regulation.

Rent control has a special role to play in neighborhoods undergoing gentrification. In a rapidly appreciating housing market, rent control can afford some protection to middle-and lower-income tenants, keeping a mix of people in gentrifying areas. Moreover, limiting residential rent increases may also provide some protection for small business and light industry. Regulation of apartment rents may prevent the switching of land and buildings to residential uses — a tactic which becomes highly profitable when gentrification occurs.

MARGARET JANE RADIN, RESIDENTIAL RENT CONTROL, 15 PHILOSOPHY AND PUBLIC AFFAIRS 350, 351–52, 359–70 (1986) *

In short, classic price theory suggests that imposition of rent control will exacerbate the housing shortage that gave rise to the high rents that gave rise to the imposition of rent control, and at the same time will encourage landlords to supply lower-quality housing. No wonder rent control is anathema to economists who espouse this picture. The cure is not only worse than the disease, it is a worse case of the same disease.

From the predictions of this empirical model the normative conclusion that there ought not to be rent control seems, for some, to follow as a matter of course. There is a misallocation of resources when landlords take their units off the market to enter some other business which is less preferred, while people who are willing to rent at the market price cannot find apartments to rent and must go elsewhere. Social welfare is not maximized, and therefore the arrangement is bad.

This is clearly a simple kind of utilitarian analysis. It assumes utility maximization is measured by wealth maximization, and it assumes that housing may be treated normatively like any other market commodity. But even for an economist who accepts both assumptions, the conclusion condemning rent control is too sweeping. If the landlords can collude to extract high prices, then rent control may merely bring prices down to the competitive level. Even if the landlords cannot collude, if they are reaping high "rents" in the economic sense, making them lower prices to the competitive level should result in no restriction of supply or other misallocation of resources.

A more complex ethical analysis might question the two assumptions and find the normative conclusion barring rent control not so obvious. Might the level of efficiency losses be outweighed by other gains? Might some right of tenants "trump" the utility analysis? . . .

[T]he main normative issue seems to be this: where rent control lowers rents at the landlord's expense (that is, thereby decreasing the landlord's profit), is that just?[5] . . .

III. The Argument From the Tenant as Individual

Most of us, I think, feel that a tenant's interest in continuing to live in an apartment that she has made home for some time seems somehow a stronger or more exigent claim than a commercial landlord's interest in maintaining the same scope of freedom of choice regarding lease terms and in maintaining a high profit margin. Where rising rents are forcing out tenants and where landlords have significant economic rents, that is, one feels the tenant's claim is stronger than the landlord's.[12] Even where significant economic rents are not present, so that some landlords are forced to leave the business, one may still feel that the tenant's expectation or desire to continue in her home is more important than the commercial landlord's expectation or desire to continue in the landlord business over some other business that will yield a

---

[5] The same normative issue arises in the context of legal habitability rights, insofar as they attempt to raise quality (hence the landlord's costs) while not raising the price to the tenant. . . .

[12] . . .There could be tenants who don't much care whether or not they stay very long in one residence. Why grant them a price break against landlords who care very much about their profit levels? If such a subclass of tenants can be singled out, it can be exempted from rent control (for example, an exemption for transient accommodations). . . .

There could also be tenants who would value the money they might get by "selling" back to the landlord their rent-control rights more than they value a right to keep their apartments. This could come about if we made rent control waivable by the tenant, and if circumstances were such that the landlord would charge a lower price "up front" for a non-rent-controlled apartment, knowing she could raise the rent at will, than she would charge for a rent-controlled apartment, knowing she would be stuck with the original price for as long as the tenant stayed. Then some tenants might choose to waive rent control in exchange for lower initial rent. . . .

better return. We do not recognize any general right to remain in a specific business such that regulation of the industry would be prohibited if regulation would operate to force some of the less efficient suppliers out of that market and into others. . . .

Let me refer to the situation where the tenant stands to lose an established home and the landlord is purely commercial as "standard circumstances." To the extent there does exist the intuitive appeal for preserving the tenant's home in standard circumstances that I postulate here, it can be understood in terms of the distinction between personal and fungible property that I elaborated in an earlier article.[14] Property that is "personal" in this philosophical sense is bound up with one's personhood, and is distinguishable from property that is held merely instrumentally or for investment and exchange and is therefore purely commercial or "fungible." One way to look at this distinction is to say that fungible property is fully commodified, or represents the ideal of the commodity form, whereas personal property is at lest partially noncommodified.

Personal property describes specific categories in the external world in which holders can become justifiably self-invested, so that their individuality and selfhood become intertwined with a particular object. The object then cannot be replaced without pain by money or another similar object of equivalent market value; the particular object takes on unique value for the individual. Only a few special objects or categories of objects are personal property. Other property items, which can be replaced by their equivalents or money at no pain to the holder, are merely fungible, that is not bound up with personhood. When a holding is fungible, the value for the holder is the exchange or market value, not the object *per se*; one dollar bill is as good as another, or the equivalent in stocks or bonds, or any other item with market value. When a holding is personal, the specific object matters, and the fact that it matters is justifiable. . . .

IV. The Argument from Tenant Community . . .

Consider the idea that a predominantly tenant community is justified in enacting rent control to avoid dispersion of the community to other and cheaper markets. Under what circumstances would this justification hold? To justify control on this ground would seem to require the general condition (1) that real community (in the spiritual sense) may be preserved even at some expense to fungible property interests of others, at least where the group affirms through local political action like rent control that it seeks continuity; and the specific condition (2) that a particular rent-controlled jurisdiction is indeed such a tenant community. In addition, the argument is strengthened if (3) the community will certainly be dispersed unless rent control is imposed. . . .

Assuming that the community may be preserved when it exists, at least where the group affirms through local political action like rent control that it seeks continuity, there arises the specific question (2) of when a rent-controlled

---

[14] *See* Margaret Jane Radin, "Property and Personhood," *Stanford Law Review* 34, no. 5 (May 1982): 957.

jurisdiction is in fact such a community. Without a more well-developed theory of community, it is not possible to outline the indicia of community. But it seems there are particular intuitions we can feel fairly confident about, even without a fully developed theory. Sometimes, for example, tenants are primarily members of one ethnic group who interact in ways that form a cohesive and defined group. On the other hand, perhaps a very high turnover rate might convince us we are not dealing with a real community. Sometimes, the case of elderly people on fixed incomes being squeezed out of their long-term homes by younger, wealthier people is especially sympathetic. Of course, the elderly people may have remained strangers to each other during their years of residence, in which case their claims would have to rest on individualism. But it is perhaps more likely that over the years they have developed ties of friendship and support that unite them into a group or community. . . .

EDGAR O. OLSEN, IS RENT CONTROL GOOD SOCIAL POLICY?, 67 CHICAGO-KENT LAW REVIEW 931, 931–33, 944–45 (1991)*

Rent control has been a major type of governmental housing regulation throughout the world for many years. In the United States, it has been the exception rather than the rule. It existed throughout the country during and immediately after the Second World War, but by the early 1950s it had been abandoned almost everywhere. During the remainder of the 1950s and 1960s, it existed only in a few cities in the State of New York, most notably New York City. There was a resurgence of rent control during the 1970s and early 1980s when rates of inflation were high. Over 200 localities in the United States currently have some form of rent regulation, and more than ten percent of all rental units are subject to rent control. Controls now exist in six states (California, Connecticut, Maryland, Massachusetts, New Jersey, and New York) and the District of Columbia. New York City accounts for thirty-nine percent of all rent controlled units; Los Angeles, seventeen percent; San Francisco, seven percent; and Washington, D.C., four percent. . . .

It is important to recognize at the outset that different rent control ordinances have different provisions and these differences can lead to different results. For example, almost all jurisdictions automatically increase the ceiling rent each year, some by a fixed percentage and others by a fraction of the increase in the Consumer Price Index. However, these percentages and fractions differ greatly across localities. Los Angeles allows one hundred percent of the increase in the CPI; Berkeley only sixty-two percent. Some jurisdictions with rent control allow rents to be increased for new tenants without limit, others limit the increase, and still others allow no increase. If landlords are allowed to set rents freely when units turn over, it is to be expected that rent control will not lead to any substantial transfer of wealth from owners of rental housing to their tenants. Instead it will lead to higher initial rents and a slower rate of increase in rents for sitting tenants. Thus the transfers will be from tenants who move frequently to those who seldom

---

* This article first appeared in 67 CHI.-KENT L. REV. 754–931, 931–933 (1991) [Copyright © 1992]. Reprinted by special permission of Chicago-Kent College of Law, Illinois Institute of Technology and by permission of the author.

move. The Los Angeles ordinance has this feature, and the major studies of it support this conjecture. The best estimate of the more recent study is that rent control has lowered the mean rent in Los Angeles by seven dollars per month but that it has increased the mean rent of those who have been living in their apartment one or two years by twenty-eight dollars per month.

The available evidence suggests that the majority of ordinances in the United States today have little effect on rents and hence do not, to any great extent, have the ill effects often attributed to rent control. There is little to be said for such ordinances. An administrative cost is incurred to produce a small amount of haphazard redistribution. Since proponents of rent control usually argue that these ordinances should be made more stringent in order to have the effects that they desire, this paper will focus on the desirability of more restrictive laws.

Attempts to justify rent control in the legal literature leave much to be desired. Keating asserts that housing is a fundamental right, but he does not tell us to what type of housing people have a right and why. He also offers the usual popular arguments for housing subsidies to low-income households, namely "the declining stock of affordable housing and the increasing number of tenants, millions, mostly poor, living in substandard housing and paying very high proportions of their income for rent." Since existing studies suggest that housing subsidies to low-income households and rent control have the exact opposite effect on consumption patterns, it is difficult to understand how they can have the same justifications. Furthermore, it is not clear why all of the phenomena mentioned are considered problems. If low-income households decided to place a higher value on housing (that is, to spend a higher proportion of their income on it), the housing stock would be upgraded and the stock of affordable housing as usually measured would decline. Keating does not explain why this would be bad. Dobkin says that "[r]ent controls are necessary to protect people who through no fault of their own would otherwise be priced out of decent housing." There are several problems with this argument. First, rent control is not limited to people who are priced out of decent housing. The majority of renters are not poor, and the majority of low-income renters live in adequate housing. Second, rent control is not necessary to attain this end since it could also be achieved by providing households that are priced out of decent housing with housing subsidies financed by broad-based taxes. Finally, we might ask why people should be protected from this outcome. . . .

Despite the gaps in our knowledge of the effects of rent control, the case against this type of government action is fairly strong. No compelling justification has been offered for financing benefits to tenants by an implicit tax on landlords. There is no satisfactory explanation of why the magnitude of this tax on equally wealthy people should depend on the proportion of their assets held in the form of rental housing. The pattern of benefits is equally indefensible. Among households living in controlled units when rent control is enacted, the richest households receive the largest benefits. Among households who move into controlled housing later, there is no discernible relationship between benefit and household characteristics and the variance in benefit among similar households is large. In short, rent control is a poorly focused redistributive device.

It is also highly inefficient. The benefits of a mature rent control ordinance to tenants is far less than its cost to landlords because it leads to distortions in the consumption patterns of tenants and the production decisions of landlords. The majority of tenants occupy a unit whose overall desirability is less than that of the unit that they would occupy if given a cash grant by their landlord, while a significant minority occupy a better unit. Furthermore, many tenants live in units whose particular characteristics are not well suited to their current circumstances. That is, rent control leads to haphazard changes in consumption patterns. Finally, theoretical reasoning suggests that rent control leads to higher costs of producing housing services in both the controlled and uncontrolled sectors. It induces some units to be undermaintained and (perhaps) others to be overmaintained. It induces too many people to be homeowners, imposes greater search costs on tenants, increases the risks facing providers of housing services, and affects the location of new construction in an urban area.

NOTES AND QUESTIONS

1. Why do housing shortages of the type identified by Keating create economic rents for landlords? Why does the supply of housing only expand slowly? Besides the time lag necessary to build new apartments, are there other reasons why the supply of housing might lag behind demand? Even if the supply of housing (eventually) expands, why will some landlords still earn rents?

2. According to Keating and Mandel, how do rent controls redistribute wealth? Why are these redistributions socially desirable? Mandel mentions rent control has a "special role" to play in neighborhoods undergoing gentrification? Is he suggesting that there is another justification for rent control in such neighborhoods besides wealth redistribution? According to Radin, what is this other justification? More generally, do you find Professor Radin's noneconomic justifications for rent control persuasive? How do these justifications relate to the justifications offered at the beginning of this chapter?

3. Olsen acknowledges that landlords might be wealthier than tenants, but he objects to the idea that this justifies a redistribution of wealth from one group to the other. He argues it is not justifiable to finance government programs by a tax based on characteristics such as occupation. He argues that the burden of helping poor persons should be financed by broad-based taxes. How would a supporter of rent controls respond to this argument? Are there good reasons for singling out landlords for this wealth redistribution?

4. Mandel posits that there are "strict" rent controls and "moderate" rent controls. Do you see an analogy between "strict" and "moderate" rent controls and, respectively, historically-based pricing and cost-plus pricing?

5. If as Epstein claims, rent control actually reduces the amount of housing, it would appear to be a counterproductive policy. On what basis does Mandel deny that rent control causes a shortage of housing? On what basis does Mandel claim that rent control might stimulate the construction of new rental housing? What is Epstein's argument? Whose arguments do you find more convincing and why?

6. Although Professor Epstein is a libertarian, rent control is also opposed by liberal voices, such as the *New York Times*. Consider the following editorial:

> Many upper-and middle-income families pay rents much lower than they would without regulations. In a freer market, many of them would have moved as children grew up, opening their former homes to others with lower incomes. Some families in the highest income groups became even richer by buying apartments they rented, reselling them later at 10 and 15 times what they paid.
>
> Behold the losers. They include owners of small apartment houses who expected to retire on the rental income. Often, their costs exceeded regulated rent; many have lost their properties in mortgage or tax foreclosures. The losers also include their former tenants, who often clung desperately to their fading apartments after rent collection stopped. Homeowners also are losers to rent regulations. It diminishes the taxable value of apartment houses, requiring higher taxes on owner-occupied homes.
>
> Perversely, many poor families are the harshest losers. Rent regulation does not protect those who live in undesirable apartments that have frequently changed hands. Trying to make landlords alone subsidize housing for the poor is an inadequate, evasive substitute for targeted rent assistance grants subsidized by society. A municipal program of rent subsidies is needed for families not aided by Federal and state programs. . . .[18]

Does the New York Times oppose all rent control or rent control for upper-and middle-income persons? Would it be desirable to maintain rent control for poor persons? How could you justify this change? Why should landlords who earn economic rents from poor persons be regulated while landlords who earn rents from upper-and middle-income persons are not regulated?

7. Epstein claims that the "larger the gap between the market and regulated price, the greater the divergence between private and social cost." Recall that one of the advantages of markets is that goods and services move to persons who value them more, as indicated by their willingness to pay higher prices for the goods or services. Epstein is indicating that, while rent controls increase the wealth of the person living in an apartment, they decrease the net wealth of society. Why does this occur?

How is this argument related to an editorial observation of the *New York Times* that rent controls have a tax impact? The *Times* pointed out that, because rent controls artificially depress the taxable value of rental buildings, the owners of such buildings pay lower taxes than they would in a free market. The newspaper argued that this was unfair to persons who lived in buildings without such controls, because they were forced to pay $100 million more in higher taxes than they would if rental controls were lifted.

Epstein claims that rent controls also reduce social wealth by encouraging tenants and landlords to engage in economically unproductive activity. What are these activities? Why are they economically counterproductive?

---

[18] *How Rent Control Hurts The Poor*, NEW YORK TIMES, May 30, 1989, at A1 (national edition). Copyright © 1989 by The New York Times Co. Reprinted by permission.

8. Keating complains that Epstein does not recognize a tenant's lack of bargaining power in many markets, which prevents renters from negotiating lease provisions against displacement. In the late 1960s and early 1970s, the law witnessed the expansion of "tenant rights" in both the common law and in legislation. In some jurisdictions, exculpatory clauses were prohibited, landlords were required to have cause for eviction, and tenants could withhold rent if the premises were not properly maintained.[19] What is the regulatory justification for these actions? Is there a market flaw or is the protection of tenants justified on some noneconomic basis? How does the economic and political analysis in the previous excerpts apply to these developments?

9. If rent control is difficult to justify on a policy basis, what are the political factors that have led to its imposition or maintenance? Likewise, does politics explain the preference of cities for price controls instead of windfall profits taxes? Consider the recent experience of the city of New York. In 1997, New York State legislators believed that the time was ripe to let the sun set on rent controls. New York politics is such that the legislators met significant resistance from Mayor Guiliani and Governor Pataki who favored gradual elimination. As a result, lawmakers passed new legislation to keep the state's rent control system in place for at least six more years, while granting more expansive vacancy and luxury decontrols.[20]

Under the Rent Regulation Reform Act of 1997, most of the people currently living in rent-regulated apartments will be able to keep those protections for as long as they live there. However, landlords can now have rent controls removed on apartments where the rent is at least $2,000 a month and the tenant's annual income in the past two years was at least $175,000, down from the previous threshold of $250,000. Also under the new law, an apartment that previously rented for $2,000 or more per month and is subsequently vacated is no longer subject to rent stabilization and the landlord may charge the next tenant market value. Where the rent is not $2,000 per month, after a vacancy a landlord can now increase rents at least 20%.[21] Finally, under the new law, current occupiers of rent regulated apartments may pass on the apartment with its protections to their successors, but only as far as one generation past the current occupant, or in the future, one generation past the original leaseholder. Previously, many critics of rent control pointed out that rent controlled apartments never became available because they were continuously passed on to any living relative who would then occupy the apartment for another lifetime, adding to the unavailability of affordable housing.

---

[19] See *Javins v. First Nat'l Realty Corp.*, 428 F.2d 1071 (D.C. Cir. 1970) (warranty of habitability as set by housing code implied in residential lease); *see also* Komesar, *Return To Slumville: A Critique of the Ackerman Analysis of Housing Code Enforcement and the Poor*, 82 YALE L.J. 1175 (1973); Ackerman, *More On Slum Housing and Redistribution Policy: A Reply To Professor Komesar*, 82 YALE L.J. 1194 (1973); Ackerman, *Regulating Slum Housing Markets On Behalf of the Poor: Of Housing Codes, Housing Subsidies and Income Redistribution*, 80 YALE L.J. 1093 (1971).

[20] Rent Regulation Reform Act of 1997, N.Y. Laws 116 § 1 et seq.

[21] Richard Perez-Pena, *Lawmakers Take Up Bill to Continue Rent Rules*, N.Y. TIMES, at A1 (June 20, 1997).

D.   CONSTITUTIONALITY

Conservative commentators such as Professor Epstein have urged the Supreme Court to declare rent control to be unconstitutional, as a taking of property without adequate compensation.[22] Such laws have also been attacked as a violation of substantive due process on the ground that they are not rationally (reasonably) related to the goals to be achieved by the regulations. This section considers the extent to which the Due Process Clause and the Takings Clause limit the government's authority to regulate economic rents.

BLOCK v. HIRSH
256 U.S. 135 (1921)

MR. JUSTICE HOLMES delivered the opinion of the Court. . . .

[The landlord Hirsh sought to recover possession of part of a building from the tenant Block, but Block claimed lawful possession because of a District of Columbia statute giving him the right to remain after the expiration of the lease. The Court upheld the regulation against arguments that it violated substantive due process and constituted a taking.]

. . . The main point against the law is that tenants are allowed to remain in possession at the same rent that they have been paying, unless modified by the Commission established by the act, and that thus the use of the land and the right of the owner to do what he will with his own and to make what contracts he pleases are cut down. But if the public interest be established, the regulation of rates is one of the first forms in which it is asserted, and the validity of such regulation has been settled since *Munn v. Illinois,* 94 U.S. 113. . . .

Machinery is provided to secure to the landlord a reasonable rent. It may be assumed that the interpretation of "reasonable" will deprive him in part at least of the power of profiting by the sudden influx of people of Washington caused by the needs of Government and the war, and thus of a right usually incident to fortunately situated property. . . . If the tenant remained subject to the landlord's power to evict, the attempt to limit the landlord's demands would fail.

Assuming that the end in view otherwise justified the means adopted by Congress, we have no concern of course with the question whether those means were the wisest, whether they may not cost more than they come to, or will effect the result desired. It is enough that we are not warranted in saying that legislation that has been resorted to for the same purpose all over the world, is futile or has no reasonable relation to the relief sought.

NOTES AND QUESTIONS

1. In *Block,* the Court refers to *Munn v. Illinois,* which you studied in Chapter 4. Why does the guarantee of a "reasonable rate of return" satisfy the regulatory takings issue in *Block?*

---

[22] See R. EPSTEIN, TAKINGS: PRIVATE PROPERTY AND THE POWER OF EMINENT DOMAIN (1985).

2. The ordinance in *Block* limited the landlord's ability to evict tenants who were willing to pay the amount of rent that the ordinance allowed. Why did not this interference with the landlord's property rights constitute a "taking"? In *Penn Central*, decided years later, the Court indicated that "a use restriction on real property may constitute a 'taking' if [it is] not reasonably related to the effectuation of a substantial public purpose. . . ." What substantial public purpose did this restriction serve?

PENNELL v. CITY OF SAN JOSE
485 U.S. 1 (1988)

CHIEF JUSTICE REHNQUIST delivered the opinion of the Court. . . .

The City of San Jose enacted its rent control ordinance (Ordinance) in 1979 with the stated purpose of "alleviat[ing] some of the more immediate needs created by San Jose's housing situation. These needs include but are not limited to the prevention of excessive and unreasonable rent increases, the alleviation of undue hardships upon individual tenants, and the assurance to landlords of a fair and reasonable return on the value of their property."

At the heart of the Ordinance is a mechanism for determining the amount by which landlords subject to its provisions may increase the annual rent which they charge their tenants. A landlord is automatically entitled to raise the rent of a tenant in possession by as much as eight percent; if a tenant objects to an increase greater than eight percent, a hearing is required before a "Mediation Hearing Officer" to determine whether the landlord's proposed increase is "reasonable under the circumstances." The Ordinance sets forth a number of factors to be considered by the hearing officer in making this determination, including "the hardship to a tenant."

. . . In essence, appellants' claim is as follows: § 5703.28 of the Ordinance establishes the seven factors that a Hearing Officer is to take into account in determining the reasonable rent increase. The first six of these factors are all objective, and are related either to the landlord's costs of providing an adequate rental unit, or to the condition of the rental market. Application of these six standards results in a rent that is "reasonable" by reference to what appellants contend is the only legitimate purpose of rent control: the elimination of "excessive" rents caused by San Jose's housing shortage. When the Hearing Officer then takes into account "hardship to a tenant" pursuant to § 5703.28(c)(7) and reduces the rent below the objectively "reasonable" amount established by the first six factors, this additional reduction in the rent increase constitutes a "taking." This taking is impermissible because it does not serve the purpose of eliminating excessive rents — that objective has already been accomplished by considering the first six factors — instead, it serves only the purpose of providing assistance to "hardship tenants." In short, appellants contend, the additional reduction of rent on grounds of hardship accomplishes a transfer of the landlord's property to individual hardship tenants; the Ordinance forces private individuals to shoulder the "public" burden of subsidizing their poor tenants' housing. . . .

We think it would be premature to consider this contention on the present record. As things stand, there simply is no evidence that the "tenant hardship clause" has in fact ever been relied upon by a Hearing Officer to reduce a rent below the figure it would have been set at on the basis of the other factors set forth in the Ordinance. . . .

Appellants also urge that the mere provision in the Ordinance that a Hearing Officer may consider the hardship of the tenant in finally fixing a reasonable rent renders the Ordinance "facially invalid" under the Due Process and Equal Protection Clauses, even though no landlord ever has its rent diminished by as much as one dollar because of the application of this provision. The standard for determining whether a state price-control regulation is constitutional under the Due Process Clause is well established: "Price control is 'unconstitutional . . . if arbitrary, discriminatory, or demonstrably irrelevant to the policy the legislature is free to adopt. . . .'" In other contexts we have recognized that the Government may intervene in the marketplace to regulate rates or prices that are artificially inflated as a result of the existence of a monopoly or near monopoly, or a discrepancy between supply and demand in the market for a certain product. Accordingly, appellants do not dispute that the Ordinance's asserted purpose of "prevent[ing] excessive and unreasonable rent increases" caused by the "growing shortage of and increasing demand for housing in the City of San Jose," is a legitimate exercise of appellees' police powers. *Cf. Block v. Hirsh,* 256 U.S. 135, 156 (1921) (approving rent control in Washington, D.C., on the basis of Congress' finding that housing in the city was "monopolized"). They do argue, however, that it is "arbitrary, discriminatory, or demonstrably irrelevant" for appellees to attempt to accomplish the additional goal of reducing the burden of housing costs on low-income tenants by requiring that "hardship to a tenant" be considered in determining the amount of excess rent increase that is "reasonable under the circumstances" pursuant to § 5703.28. As appellants put it, "The objective of alleviating individual tenant hardship is . . . not a 'policy the legislature is free to adopt' in a rent control ordinance."

We reject this contention, however, because we have long recognized that a legitimate and rational goal of price or rate regulation is the protection of consumer welfare. Indeed, a primary purpose of rent control is the protection of tenants. *See, e.g., Bowles v. Willingham,* 321 U.S. 503, 513, n. 9 (1944) (one purpose of rent control is "to protect persons with relatively fixed and limited incomes, consumers, wage earners . . . from undue impairment of their standard of living"). Here, the Ordinance establishes a scheme in which a Hearing Officer considers a number of factors in determining the reasonableness of a proposed rent increase which exceeds eight percent and which exceeds the amount deemed reasonable. . . . The first six factors of § 5703.28(c) focus on the individual landlord — the Hearing Officer examines the history of the premises, the landlord's costs, and the market for comparable housing. Section 5703.28(c)(5) also allows the landlord to bring forth any other financial evidence — including presumably evidence regarding his own financial status — to be taken into account by the Hearing Officer. It is in only this context that the Ordinance allows tenant hardship to be considered and, under § 5703.29, "balance[d]" with the other factors set out in § 5703.28(c). Within this scheme, § 5703.28(c) represents a rational attempt to accommodate the conflicting interests of protecting tenants from burdensome rent increases while at the same time ensuring that landlords are guaranteed a fair return on their investment. We accordingly find that the Ordinance, which so carefully considers both the individual circumstances of the landlord and the tenant before determining whether to allow an additional increase in rent over and above certain amounts that are deemed reasonable, does not on its face violate the Fourteenth Amendment's Due Process Clause. . . .

JUSTICE SCALIA, with whom JUSTICE O'CONNOR joins, concurring in part and dissenting in part.

I agree that the tenant hardship provision of the Ordinance does not, on its face, violate . . . the Due Process Clause. . . . I disagree, however, with the Court's conclusion that appellants' takings claim is premature. I would decide that claim on the merits, and would hold that the tenant hardship provision of the Ordinance affects a taking of private property without just compensation in violation of the Fifth and Fourteenth Amendments. . . .

The Fifth Amendment of the United States Constitution, made applicable to the States through the Fourteenth Amendment provides that "private property [shall not] be taken for public use, without just compensation." We have repeatedly observed that the purpose of this provision is "to bar Government from forcing some people alone to bear public burdens which, in all fairness and justice, should be borne by the public as a whole."

Traditional land-use regulation (short of that which totally destroys the economic value of property) does not violate this principle because there is a cause-and-effect relationship between the property use restricted by the regulation and the social evil that the regulation seeks to remedy. Since the owner's use of the property is (or, but for the regulation, would be) the source of the social problem, it cannot be said that he has been singled out unfairly. Thus, the common zoning regulations requiring subdividers to observe lot-size and set-back restrictions, and to dedicate certain areas to public streets, are in accord with our constitutional traditions because the proposed property use would otherwise be the cause of excessive congestion. The same cause-and-effect relationship is popularly thought to justify emergency price regulation: When commodities have been priced at a level that produces exorbitant returns, the owners of those commodities can be viewed as responsible for the economic hardship that occurs. Whether or not that is an accurate perception of the way a free-market economy operates, it is at least true that the owners reap unique benefits from the situation that produces the economic hardship, and in that respect singling them out to relieve it may not be regarded as "unfair." That justification might apply to the rent regulation in the present case, apart from the single feature under attack here.

. . . Appellants' only claim is that a reduction of a rent increase below what would otherwise be a "reasonable rent" under this scheme may not, consistently with the Constitution, be based on consideration of the seventh factor — the hardship to the tenant as defined in § 5703.29. I think they are right.

Once the other six factors of the ordinance have been applied to a landlord's property, so that he is receiving only a reasonable return, he can no longer be regarded as a "cause" of exorbitantly priced housing; nor is he any longer reaping distinctively high profits from the housing shortage. The seventh factor, the "hardship" provision, is invoked to meet a quite different social problem: the existence of some renters who are too poor to afford even reasonably priced housing. But that problem is no more caused or exploited by landlords than it is by the grocers who sell needy renters their food, or the department stores that sell them their clothes, or the employers who pay them their wages, or the citizens of San Jose holding the higher-paying jobs from which they are excluded. And even if the neediness of renters could be regarded as a problem distinctively attributable to landlords in general, it is not remotely attributable to the particular landlords that the ordinance singles out — namely, those who happen to have a "hardship" tenant at the present time, or who may happen to rent to a "hardship" tenant in the future, or whose current or future affluent tenants may happen to decline into the "hardship" category. . . .

The politically attractive feature of regulation is not that it permits wealth transfers to be achieved that could not be achieved otherwise; but rather that it permits them to be achieved "off budget," with relative invisibility and thus relative immunity from normal democratic processes. San Jose might, for example, have accomplished something like the result here by simply raising the real estate tax upon rental properties and using the additional revenues thus acquired to pay part of the rents of "hardship" tenants. It seems to me doubtful, however, whether the citizens of San Jose would allow funds in the municipal treasury, from wherever derived, to be distributed to a family of four with income as high as $32,400 a year — the generous maximum necessary to qualify automatically as a "hardship" tenant under the rental ordinance. The voters might well see other, more pressing, social priorities. And of course what $32,400-a-year renters can acquire through spurious "regulation," other groups can acquire as well. Once the door is opened, it is not unreasonable to expect price regulations requiring private businesses to give special discounts to senior citizens (no matter how affluent), or to students, the handicapped, or war veterans. Subsidies for these groups may well be a good idea, but because of the operation of the Takings Clause our governmental system has required them to be applied, in general, through the process of taxing and spending, where both economic effects and competing priorities are more evident.

NOTES AND QUESTIONS

1. In *Pennell*, the majority refused to hear the takings issue because the plaintiff had filed a facial challenge to the statute. This refers to the fact that the provision that the plaintiff attacked had not yet been applied to anyone. The majority indicated its preference to consider the takings issue if, and when, the city applied the seventh factor to a specific landlord. The Court was applying the "ripeness" doctrine, which is a matter of judge-made or common law. It permits the courts to refuse to hear an issue that can arise at a later date in order to avoid premature consideration of the issue. When a court applies the "ripeness" doctrine, it anticipates the same issue will arise at another time in a posture that will make it more concrete and less abstract. On what ground did the majority decide the takings claim was not ripe? Is the implication of the majority's refusal to hear the claim that the statute was not invalid on its face?

2. In *Pennell* and the following cases, the Court refers to Takings Clause cases that are outside of the line of cases, such as *Munn v. Illinois*, that address the constitutionality of ratemaking. In these other cases, the Court draws a distinction between a physical invasion of property by the government and regulations that adversely affect the value of property. When the government physically takes possession of an interest in property for some public, purpose, it must compensate the owner whether or not the interest taken constitutes an entire parcel of land or merely a part of the land, and whether or not the government's occupation of the property is temporary or not. *See, e.g., Loretto v. Teleprompter v. Manhattan CATV Corp.*, 458 U.S. 419 (1982) (appropriation of part of a rooftop to provide cable TV access for apartment tenants constitutes a taking for which compensation is owed). When the government enacts a restriction on land use, by comparison, the Court does not employ a per se rule as it does in cases of physical invasion. Instead, it applies a multifactor test as the following notes explain.

3. The Court's regulatory takings jurisprudence dates back to *Pennsylvania Coal Co. v. Mahon*, 260 U.S. 393 (1922), in which a coal company challenged a Pennsylvania statute which banned mining under the surface of a home or apartment when the mining could cause the ground to subside and threaten the dwelling. The Court recognized that the government might owe compensation because of the impact of a regulation, which adversely affected the coal company's property rights to mine the coal under the surface of the land. Justice Holmes declared, "The general rule at least is that while property may be regulated to a certain extent, if regulation goes too far it will be recognized as a taking." He continued:

> Government hardly could go on if to some extent values incident to property could not be diminished without paying for every such change in the general law. As long recognized, some values are enjoyed under an implied limitation and must yield to the police power. But obviously the implied limitation must have its limits or the contract and due process clauses are gone. One fact for consideration in determining such limits is the extent of the diminution. When it reaches a certain magnitude, in most if not in all cases there must be an exercise of eminent domain and compensation to sustain the act. So the question depends upon the particular facts. The greatest weight is given to the judgment of the legislature but it always is open to interested parties to contend that the legislature has gone beyond its constitutional power.

Holmes' pronouncements in *Pennsylvania Coal* went against the grain of takings jurisprudence at the time. At that time, government could exercise two strong powers that affected property. Government could exercise its police power regulation for which no compensation was due, or it could exercise its power of eminent domain which required compensation for the taking of private property. Holmes recognized a third category of government power called "regulatory takings" which would receive compensation.

What reason did Justice Holmes give for not applying a per se test to regulatory takings? What reason did he give for holding that a regulation can go "too far" and constitute a taking of property without compensation?

4. Ever since *Pennsylvania Coal*, the Court has struggled to determine when a regulation goes "too far" and constitutes a taking of property. The current test is set out in *Penn Central Transportation Co. v. New York City*, 438 U.S. 104 (1978), which upheld the refusal of New York City Landmarks Preservation Commission to approve plans for construction of 50-story office building over Grand Central Terminal, which had been designated a "landmark." The Court explained that the test was essential ad hoc:

> While this Court has recognized that the "Fifth Amendment's guarantee . . . [is] designed to bar Government from forcing some people alone to bear public burdens which, in all fairness and justice, should be borne by the public as a whole," this Court, quite simply, has been unable to develop any "set formula" for determining when "justice and fairness" require that economic injuries caused by public action be compensated by the government, rather than remain disproportionately concentrated on a few persons. Indeed, we have frequently observed that whether a particular restriction will be rendered invalid by the government's failure to pay for any losses proximately caused by it depends largely "upon the particular circumstances [in that] case.

Based on its prior opinions, the Court identified three factors as relevant to whether the government owed compensation: "The economic impact of the regulation on the claimant and, particularly, the extent to which the regulation has interfered with distinct investment-backed expectations are, of course, relevant considerations. So, too, is the character of the governmental action." Regarding the last criteria, the Court added, "[A] use restriction on real property may constitute a 'taking' if [it is] not reasonably necessary to the effectuation of a substantial public purpose. . . ."

It upheld the ordinance on the ground it stopped well short of destroying the economic value of the land to its owner. The law did not interfere with the company's use of the railroad terminal, it only partially limited its ability to build an addition, and it gave the company valuable "transferable developmental rights" which would be used on other parcels of nearby land.

5. In *Pennell*, Justice Scalia was prepared to hold the ordinance invalid on its face? On what basis did he hold that the landlords did not "cause" the problem that the seventh factor was attempting to solve? How did Justice Scalia distinguish the first six factors which he determined were constitutional?

6. The nexus requirement that Justice Scalia applies in his dissent is drawn from *Nollan v. California Costal Commission*, 483 U.S. 825 (1987), which involved the refusal of the California Costal Commission to grant a building permit to a landowner unless the landowner granted the state an easement to permit the public to access the beach across a portion of the person's property. Had the landowner agreed to the condition, there would have been a physical occupation of a portion of the person's property by the state. Nevertheless, since the state did not occupy the land directly, the Court treated the case as involving a regulatory takings issue. But it also applied a heightened nexus requirement, holding that the conditional granting of a permit does not effect a taking if it " 'substantially advance[s] legitimate state interests' and does not 'den[y] an owner economically viable use of his land.' " By comparison, in *Penn Central*, the Court only required that a use restriction be "reasonably necessary to the effectuation of a substantial public purpose.

7. In *Pennell*, Justice Scalia seeks to extend the heightened "nexus" require-ment of *Nollan* because he applies it in a different factual context — the constitutionality of a rent control ordinance. He then limits the state's authority to regulate under the takings clause to cases in which the state is addressing some problem that the owner's use of the property creates for other persons. *See Dolan v. City of Tigard*, 512 U.S. 374 (1994) (requiring that the impact of conditions extracted for granting a permit be "roughly proportional" to the problems that use of the property poses for the public.) How does Justice Scalia defend this interpretation of the takings doctrine? What does he mean when he says that the "politically attractive" feature of the seventh factor is that "it permits wealth transfers to be achieve that could not be achieved otherwise; but rather that it permits them to be achieved 'off budget'." Under Justice Scalia's approach, is wealth redistribution in the housing market a legitimate public interest or a legitimate justification for government interven-tion into a market? *See Hawaii Hous. Auth. v. Midkiff,* 467 U.S. 229 (1984) (state statute transferring title in real property from lessors to lessees for compensation does not violate Takings Clause and is constitutional). Would you favor such an interpretation of the Takings Clause?

8. In *Block* and *Pennell*, the Court held that price controls for rental housing did not violate substantive due process. What did the Court identify as the rational basis for the regulation in *Block* ? In light of *Block*, the plaintiff in *Pennell* tried a novel argument. On what basis did the landlord claim that the San Jose ordinance violated due process; that is, why was the seventh factor "arbitrary, capricious, and demonstrably irrelevant" to the elimination of economic rents? What was the Court's response? Why did the "seventh" factor in the statute have a rational connection to a legitimate purpose of government?

SEAWALL ASSOCIATES v. CITY OF NEW YORK
542 N.E.2d 1059 (N.Y. Ct. Appeals),
cert. denied, 110 S. Ct. 500 (1989)

HANCOCK, JUDGE. . . .

After years of encouraging the demolition and redevelopment of SRO properties [which are single room occupancy hotels where poor persons live, eat, and sleep in one room]—which the City of New York considered substan-dard housing—the City abandoned its policy when it found that the stock of low-cost rental housing was shrinking at an alarming rate. . . .

[To address this condition the city passed a series of laws which were similar in content. One was Local Law No. 9.] The main provisions of Local Law No. 9 are as follows:

> *Moratorium.* The conversion, alteration and demolition of SRO multiple dwellings are prohibited; the moratorium extends for five years and is renewable for additional five-year periods as the City Council deems necessary. SRO property owners must rehabilitate and make habitable every SRO unit in their buildings, and lease every unit

to a "bona fide" tenant ("rent-up" obligation) at controlled rents; an owner is presumed to have violated these requirements if any unit remains vacant for a period of 30 days. . . .

Buy-Out and Replacement Exemptions. An owner may purchase an exemption from the moratorium by payment of $45,000 per unit (or such other amount as the Commissioner of the Department of Housing Preservation and Development determines would equal the cost of a replacement unit) or by providing an equal number of replacement units approved by the Commissioner.

Hardship Exemption. The amount of payment or the number of replacement units required for an exemption may be reduced at the discretion of the Commissioner, in whole or in part, if "there is no reasonable possibility that such owner can make a reasonable rate of return," defined as a net annual return of 8½% of the assessed value of the property as an SRO multiple dwelling. . . .

In our opinion, the provisions of Local Law No. 9, which not only prevent the SRO property owners from developing their properties by replacing the existing structures, but also compel them to refurbish the structures and keep them fully rented, impose on the property owners more than their just share of such societal obligations. Whether viewed as effecting a physical or regulatory taking, Local Law No. 9, we believe, violates the "Takings" Clauses of the Fifth Amendment of the Federal Constitution and article I, § 7 of the New York State Constitution.

A

Plaintiffs contend that Local Law No. 9 has resulted in a physical occupation of their properties and is, therefore, a per se compensable taking. . . .

Whether the mandatory "rent-up" obligations of the antiwarehousing provision effect a physical taking depends upon the nature and extent of their interference with certain essential property rights. Here, the claimed physical taking is the City's forced control over the owners' possessory interests in their properties, including the denial of the owners' rights to exclude others. Local Law No. 9 requires the owners to rent their rooms or be subject to severe penalties; it compels them to admit persons as tenants with all of the possessory and other rights that status entails; it compels them to surrender the most basic attributes of private property, the rights of possession and exclusion. This, plaintiffs contend, constitutes a physical occupation of private property for public use, similar to encroachments on structures or land such as the mandated installation of CATV cables and fixtures (*see, Loretto v. Teleprompter Manhattan CATV Corp.,* [458 U.S. 419]), the permanent flooding from the construction of a dam, or the invasion of air space and resulting interference with the land use below by continuous low altitude airplane flights. Defendants argue that a physical taking must entail the kind of palpable invasion involved in those cases and, therefore, that the deprivation of intangible property rights alone, such as that resulting from coerced tenancies, is not enough. We disagree. Where, as here, owners are forced to accept the occupation of their properties by persons not already in residence, the resulting deprivation of rights in those properties is sufficient to constitute a physical taking for which compensation is required. . . .

Although the Supreme Court has not passed on the specific issue of whether the loss of possessory interests, including the right to exclude, resulting from tenancies coerced by the government would constitute a per se physical taking, we believe that it would. Indeed, it is difficult to see how such forced occupancy of one's property could not do so. By any ordinary standard, such interference with an owner's rights to possession and exclusion is far more offensive and invasive than the . . . installation of the CATV equipment in *Loretto*.

Contrary to defendants' contentions, the decisions of the Supreme Court and this court upholding rent control and similar regulations of housing conditions and other aspects of the landlord-tenant relationship do not undermine plaintiffs' claims of per se physical takings. Indeed, those decisions have no bearing on the question here—whether forcing plaintiffs to rent their properties to strangers constitutes a physical taking. It is the nature of the intrusion which is determinative—i.e., that it deprives the owners of their rights to possession and exclusion—not the beneficial purpose of the regulation or the extent of the police power which authorizes it. . . .

We conclude that Local Law No. 9 has effected a *per se* physical taking because it "interfere[s] so drastically" with the SRO property owners' fundamental rights to possess and to exclude. The law requires nothing less of the owners than "to suffer the physical occupation of [their] building[s] by third part[ies]."

B

Even if Local Law No. 9 were not held to effect a physical taking, it would still be facially invalid as a regulatory taking. . . .

. . . Unquestionably, the effect of the law is to strip owners of SRO buildings—who may have purchased their properties solely to turn them into profitable investments by tearing down and replacing the existing structures with new ones (as plaintiffs claim they have)—of the very right to use their properties for any such purpose. Owners are forced to devote their properties to another use which, albeit one which might serve the City's interests, bears no relation to any economic purpose which could be reasonably contemplated by a private investor.

Finally, Local Law No. 9, particularly in those provisions prohibiting redevelopment and mandating rental, inevitably impairs the ability of owners to sell their properties for any sums approaching their investments. Thus, the local law must also negatively affect the owners' right to dispose of their properties. By any test, we think these restrictions deny the owners "economically viable use" of their properties. . . .

We agree with plaintiffs, moreover, that Local Law No. 9 does not pass the other threshold test for constitutional validity of regulatory takings: that the burdens imposed substantially advance legitimate State interests. Of course, the end sought to be furthered by Local Law No. 9 is of the greatest societal importance—alleviating the critical problems of homelessness. The question here, however, concerns the means established by the local law purportedly to achieve this end. In other words, can it be said that imposing the burdens of the forced refurbishing and rent-up provisions on the owners of SRO properties substantially advances the aim of alleviating the homelessness problem? Is there a sufficiently close nexus between these burdens and "the end advanced as the justification for [them]"?

Defendants contend that by increasing the availability of SRO units the antiwarehousing and moratorium measures will provide more available low-cost housing and, thereby, further the aim of alleviating homelessness; this relationship between means and ends, they argue, supplies the required "close nexus". . . . [But] the SRO units are not earmarked for the homeless or for potentially homeless low-income families, and there is simply no assurance that the units will be rented to members of either group. . . .

The heavy exactions imposed by Local Law No. 9 must "substantially advance" its putative purpose of relieving homelessness. No such showing of this required "close nexus" has been made. Rather, the nexus between the obligations placed on SRO property owners and the alleviation of the highly complex social problem of homelessness is indirect at best and conjectural. Such a tenuous connection between means and ends cannot justify singling out this group of property owners to bear the costs required by the law toward the cure of the homeless problem. . . .

BELLACOSA, JUDGE (dissenting). . . .

It would seem fundamental that a law that has no real impact upon a person does not deprive that person of a constitutional right. The majority, however, ignores that the SRO law will have varied [e]ffects on different landowners. Perhaps there are properties subject to this law for which SRO operation is the highest and best use. For other SRO operations, 8½% may be a generous rate of return. It is likely that there are SRO owners who have never intended to further develop or differently develop their property. Of course, these persons are not before the court and, if they were, their interests might well be served by upholding the SRO law. Yet, without a record or the means to assess the differing impacts and with no attempt to make this assessment, the majority holds that Local Law No. 9 facially results in a regulatory taking with respect to every SRO dwelling in the City of New York. Resisting the blanket approach and using the concrete facts of an individual case is not a novel approach, especially in this area of constitutional law. . . .

. . . The Supreme Court routinely rejects preenforcement taking challenges—conceptually and functionally equivalent to facial attacks—to the constitutionality of legislative enactments. Relevantly and bluntly, that court recently [in *Pennell v. San Jose*] rejected a facial challenge to a rent-control law, stating: "We have found it particularly important in takings cases to adhere to our admonition that 'the constitutionality of statutes ought not be decided except in an actual factual setting that makes such a decision necessary.' "

The Supreme Court's "admonition" is particularly pertinent in this case where the declaration of facial unconstitutionality is overinclusive and rooted in a record devoid of specific and relevant facts. The conclusion that the antiwarehousing and rental provisions are a forced occupation, effecting a per se physical taking, contradicts the way high courts have treated their functionally and conceptually equivalent rent-control and regulatory statutes—by repeatedly finding them constitutional, at least facially. This contrary holding negates an as-applied analysis which could support findings in appropriate cases that some SRO's are currently being operated at their highest and best use, thus suffering no economic disadvantage under the law; or that, by reason of the hardship provision, may never be subject to the moratorium. There is no way of knowing on this record the extent to which landlords are economically affected or how profitable the dwelling units might be. . . .

. . . Physical invasion cases are special because of the nature and quality of the governmental intrusion on a private party's property rights. A simple bright line rule applies: "any permanent physical occupation is a taking." "[W]hen the 'character of the governmental action' is a permanent physical occupation of property, [the Supreme Court's] cases uniformly have found a taking to the extent of the occupation, without regard to whether the action achieves an important public benefit or has only minimal economic impact on the owner." The moratorium law at issue does not effect a physical taking because on its face it is not permanent in its individual application or in its limited five-year duration. . . .

Equally inapplicable is the regulatory taking approach. . . .

No litmus test is available to determine what constitutes a legitimate State interest or what type of nexus "between the regulation and the state interest satisfies the requirement that the former 'substantially advance' the latter," but it is clear that "a broad range of governmental purposes and regulations satisfies these requirements.". . .

There is no disagreement that Local Law No. 9 is of the "greatest societal purpose" because it cannot be seriously disputed that preserving SRO housing stock and stanching the growing ranks of the City's shelter-less population is a legitimate governmental interest of the highest, most critical order. . . .

When it is clear—as in this case—that a law substantially advances a self-evidently legitimate governmental interest, the test to be applied in considering a facial challenge is simplified: "[a] statute regulating the uses that can be made of property effects a taking if it 'denies an owner economically viable use of his land.'" The SRO moratorium law effects no such deprivation. Indeed, it guarantees a fair minimum return, among a whole host of other economic balancing features. Government regulation almost always limits the maximization of the economic aggrandizement from private property ownership. Local Law No. 9 concededly places substantial restraints on the destruction or redevelopment of SRO buildings. But I would find dispositive of this takings challenge that the law leaves the owners in possession and guarantees them a whole web of economic concessions or "give-backs," including the minimum profit of 8½% of the assessed value of the property per year.

Appellant owners and some amici argue nevertheless that properties could be put to more profitable uses if their destruction or redevelopment options were unimpeded. The simple answer to that proposition is that a property owner is not constitutionally guaranteed the most profitable use. . . .

YEE v. CITY OF ESCONDIDO, CALIFORNIA
503 U.S. 519 (1992)

JUSTICE O'CONNOR delivered the opinion of the Court.

Petitioners own mobile home parks in Escondido, California. They contend that a local rent control ordinance, when viewed against the backdrop of California's Mobile home Residency Law, amounts to a physical occupation of their property, entitling them to compensation under the first category of cases discussed above.

I

The term "mobile home" is somewhat misleading. Mobile homes are largely immobile as a practical matter, because the cost of moving one is often a significant fraction of the value of the mobile home itself. They are generally placed permanently in parks; once in place, only about 1 in every 100 mobile homes is ever moved. A mobile home owner typically rents a plot of land, called a "pad," from the owner of a mobile home park. The park owner provides private roads within the park, common facilities such as washing machines or a swimming pool, and often utilities. The mobile home owner often invests in site-specific improvements such as a driveway, steps, walkways, porches, or landscaping. When the mobile home owner wishes to move, the mobile home is usually sold in place, and the purchaser continues to rent the pad on which the mobile home is located.

In 1978, California enacted its Mobilehome Residency Law. The legislature found "that, because of the high cost of moving mobilehomes, the potential for damage resulting therefrom, the requirements relating to the installation of mobilehomes, and the cost of landscaping or lot preparation, it is necessary that the owners of mobilehomes occupied within mobilehome parks be provided with the unique protection from actual or constructive eviction afforded by the provisions of this chapter."

The Mobilehome Residency Law limits the bases upon which a park owner may terminate a mobile home owner's tenancy. These include the nonpayment of rent, the mobile home owner's violation of law or park rules, and the park owner's desire to change the use of his land. While a rental agreement is in effect, however, the park owner generally may not require the removal of a mobile home when it is sold. The park owner may neither charge a transfer fee for the sale, [or] disapprove of the purchaser, provided that the purchaser has the ability to pay the rent. . . .

In the wake of the Mobilehome Residency Law, various communities in California adopted mobile home rent control ordinances. The voters of Escondido did the same in 1988 by approving Proposition K, the rent control ordinance challenged here.

II

Petitioners do not claim that the ordinary rent control statutes regulating housing throughout the country violate the Takings Clause. Instead, their argument is predicated on the unusual economic relationship between park owners and mobile home owners. Park owners may no longer set rents or decide who their tenants will be. As a result, according to petitioners, any reduction in the rent for a mobile home pad causes a corresponding increase in the value of a mobile home, because the mobile home owner now owns, in addition to a mobile home, the right to occupy a pad at a rent below the value that would be set by the free market. Because under the California Mobile-home Residency Law the park owner cannot evict a mobile home owner or easily convert the property to other uses, the argument goes, the mobile home owner is effectively a perpetual tenant of the park, and the increase in the mobile home's value thus represents the right to occupy a pad at below-market rent indefinitely. And because the Mobilehome Residency Law permits the mobile home owner to sell the mobile home in place, the mobile home owner can receive a premium from the purchaser corresponding to this increase in value. The amount of this premium is not limited by the Mobilehome Residency Law or the Escondido ordinance. As a result, petitioners conclude, the rent control ordinance has transferred a discrete interest in land—the right to occupy the land indefinitely at a submarket rent—from the park owner to the mobile home owner. Petitioners contend that what has been transferred from park owner to mobile home owner is no less than a right of physical occupation of the park owner's land.

This argument, while perhaps within the scope of our regulatory taking cases, cannot be squared easily with our cases on physical takings. The government effects a physical taking only where it requires the landowner to submit to the physical occupation of his land. . . .

But the Escondido rent control ordinance, even when considered in conjunction with the California Mobilehome Residency Law, authorizes no such thing. Petitioners voluntarily rented their land to mobile home owners. At least on the face of the regulatory scheme, neither the city nor the State compels petitioners, once they have rented their property to tenants, to continue doing so. To the contrary, the Mobilehome Residency Law provides that a park owner who wishes to change the use of his land may evict his tenants, albeit with 6 or 12 months notice. Put bluntly, no government has required any physical invasion of petitioners' property. Petitioners' tenants were invited by petitioners, not forced upon them by the government. While the "right to exclude" is doubtless, as petitioners assert, "one of the most essential sticks in the bundle of rights that are commonly characterized as property," we do not find that right to have been taken from petitioners on the mere face of the Escondido ordinance. . . .

On their face, the state and local laws at issue here merely regulate petitioners' use of their land by regulating the relationship between landlord and tenant. "This Court has consistently affirmed that States have broad power to regulate housing conditions in general and the landlord-tenant relationship in particular without paying compensation for all economic injuries that such regulation entails." . . . Such forms of regulation are analyzed by engaging in the "essentially ad hoc, factual inquiries" necessary to determine whether a regulatory taking has occurred. In the words of Justice Holmes, "while property may be regulated to a certain extent, if regulation goes too far it will be recognized as a taking." *Pennsylvania Coal Co. v. Mahon.*

Petitioners emphasize that the ordinance transfers wealth from park owners to incumbent mobile home owners. Other forms of land use regulation, however, can also be said to transfer wealth from the one who is regulated to another. Ordinary rent control often transfers wealth from landlords to tenants by reducing the landlords' income and the tenants' monthly payments, although it does not cause a one-time transfer of value as occurs with mobile homes. Traditional zoning regulations can transfer wealth from those whose activities are prohibited to their neighbors; when a property owner is barred from mining coal on his land, for example, the value of his property may decline but the value of his neighbor's property may rise. The mobile home owner's ability to sell the mobile home at a premium may make this wealth transfer more visible than in the ordinary case, but the existence of the transfer in itself does not convert regulation into physical invasion.

The same may be said of petitioners' contention that the ordinance amounts to compelled physical occupation because it deprives petitioners of the ability to choose their incoming tenants.[*] Again, this effect may be relevant to a regulatory taking argument, as it may be one factor a reviewing court would wish to consider in determining whether the ordinance unjustly imposes a burden on petitioners that should "be compensated by the government, rather than remain[ing] disproportionately concentrated on a few persons." But it does not convert regulation into the unwanted physical occupation of land. Because they voluntarily open their property to occupation by others, petitioners cannot assert a per se right to compensation based on their inability to exclude particular individuals. . . . [The Court refused to consider whether the ordinance constituted a regulatory taking because it had not granted review on that issue.]

TAHOE-SIERRA PRESERVATION COUNCIL, INC. V. TAHOE REGIONAL PLANNING AGENCY
122 S.Ct. 1465 (2002)

JUSTICE STEVENS delivered the opinion of the Court.

The question presented is whether a moratorium on development imposed during the process of devising a comprehensive land-use plan constitutes a *per se* taking of property requiring compensation under the Takings Clause of the United States Constitution. This case actually involves two moratoria ordered by respondent Tahoe Regional Planning Agency (TRPA) to maintain the status quo while studying the impact of development on Lake Tahoe and designing a strategy for environmentally sound growth. . . . As a result of these two directives, virtually all development on a substantial portion of the property subject to TRPA's jurisdiction was prohibited for a period of 32 months. . . .

---

[*] Strictly speaking, the Escondido rent control ordinance only limits rents. Petitioners' inability to select their incoming tenants is a product of the State's Mobilehome Residency Law, the constitutionality of which has never been at issue in this case. (The State, moreover, has never been a party.) But we understand petitioners to be making a more subtle argument—that before the adoption of the ordinance they were able to influence a mobile home owner's selection of a purchaser by threatening to increase the rent for prospective purchasers they disfavored. To the extent the rent control ordinance deprives petitioners of this type of influence, petitioners' argument is one we must consider.

. . . Land-use regulations are ubiquitous and most of them impact property values in some tangential way—often in completely unanticipated ways. Treating them all as *per se* takings would transform government regulation into a luxury few governments could afford. By contrast, physical appropriations are relatively rare, easily identified, and usually represent a greater affront to individual property rights.[19] . . .

. . . In the decades following [*Pennsylvania Coal Co.*], we have "generally eschewed" any set formula for determining how far is too far, choosing instead to engage in " 'essentially ad hoc, factual inquiries.' . . . Justice Brennan's opinion for the Court in *Penn Central* did, however, make it clear that even though multiple factors are relevant in the analysis of regulatory takings claims, in such cases we must focus on "the parcel as a whole":

> " 'Taking' jurisprudence does not divide a single parcel into discrete segments and attempt to determine whether rights in a particular segment have been entirely abrogated. In deciding whether a particular governmental action has effected a taking, this Court focuses rather both on the character of the action and on the nature and extent of the interference with rights in the parcel as a whole—here, the city tax block designated as the 'landmark site.' "
>
> This requirement that "the aggregate must be viewed in its entirety" . . . clarifies why restrictions on the use of only limited portions of the parcel, such as set-back ordinances or a requirement that coal pillars be left in place to prevent mine subsidencewere not considered regulatory takings. In each of these cases, we affirmed that "where an owner possesses a full 'bundle' of property rights, the destruction of one 'strand' of the bundle is not a taking." . . .

Certainly, our holding that the permanent "obliteration of the value" of a fee simple estate constitutes a categorical taking does not answer the question whether a regulation prohibiting any economic use of land for a 32-month period has the same legal effect. . . . Petitioners . . . [argue] we can effectively sever a 32-month segment from the remainder of each landowner's fee simple estate, and then ask whether that segment has been taken in its

---

[19] According to THE CHIEF JUSTICE's dissent, even a temporary, use-prohibiting regulation should be governed by our physical takings cases because . . . "from the landowner's point of view," the moratorium is the functional equivalent of a forced leasehold. Of course, from both the landowner's and the government's standpoint there are critical differences between a leasehold and a moratorium. Condemnation of a leasehold gives the government possession of the property, the right to admit and exclude others, and the right to use it for a public purpose. A regulatory taking, by contrast, does not give the government any right to use the property, nor does it dispossess the owner or affect her right to exclude others.

. . . THE CHIEF JUSTICE stretches *Lucas'* "equivalence" language too far. For even a regulation that constitutes only a minor infringement on property may, from the landowner's perspective, be the functional equivalent of an appropriation. *Lucas* carved out a narrow exception to the rules governing regulatory takings for the "extraordinary circumstance" of a permanent deprivation of all beneficial use. The exception was only partially justified based on the "equivalence" theory cited by his dissent. It was also justified on the theory that, in the "relatively rare situations where the government has deprived a landowner of all economically beneficial uses," it is less realistic to assume that the regulation will secure an "average reciprocity of advantage," or that government could not go on if required to pay for every such restriction. But as we explain, these assumptions hold true in the context of a moratorium.

entirety by the moratoria. . . . Petitioners' "conceptual severance" argument is unavailing because it ignores *Penn Central's* admonition that in regulatory takings cases we must focus on "the parcel as a whole." We have consistently rejected such an approach to the "denominator" question. . . .

. . . Nevertheless, we will consider whether the interest in protecting private property owners from bearing public burdens "which, in all fairness and justice, should be borne by the public as a whole," justifies creating a new rule under these circumstances.

. . . [T]he ultimate constitutional question is whether the concepts of "fairness and justice" that underlie the Takings Clause will be better served by one of these categorical rules or by a *Penn Central* inquiry into all of the relevant circumstances in particular cases. From that perspective, the extreme categorical rule that any deprivation of all economic use, no matter how brief, constitutes a compensable taking surely cannot be sustained. Petitioners' broad submission would apply to numerous "normal delays in obtaining building permits, changes in zoning ordinances, variances, and the like," as well as to orders temporarily prohibiting access to crime scenes, businesses that violate health codes, fire-damaged buildings, or other areas that we cannot now foresee. Such a rule would undoubtedly require changes in numerous practices that have long been considered permissible exercises of the police power. . . .

. . . In rejecting petitioners' *per se* rule, we do not hold that the temporary nature of a land-use restriction precludes finding that it effects a taking; we simply recognize that it should not be given exclusive significance one way or the other.

A narrower rule that excluded the normal delays associated with processing permits, or that covered only delays of more than a year, would certainly have a less severe impact on prevailing practices, but it would still impose serious financial constraints on the planning process. . . .

It may well be true that any moratorium that lasts for more than one year should be viewed with special skepticism. But given the fact that the District Court found that the 32 months required by TRPA to formulate the 1984 Regional Plan was not unreasonable, we could not possibly conclude that every delay of over one year is constitutionally unacceptable. Formulating a general rule of this kind is a suitable task for state legislatures. In our view, the duration of the restriction is one of the important factors that a court must consider in the appraisal of a regulatory takings claim, but with respect to that factor as with respect to other factors, the "temptation to adopt what amount to *per se* rules in either direction must be resisted." There may be moratoria that last longer than one year which interfere with reasonable investment-backed expectations, but as the District Court's opinion illustrates, petitioners' proposed rule is simply "too blunt an instrument," for identifying those cases. We conclude, therefore, that the interest in "fairness and justice" will be best served by relying on the familiar *Penn Central* approach when deciding cases like this, rather than by attempting to craft a new categorical rule.

. . .[The majority upheld the constitutionality of the moratorium because the plaintiffs had made a facial attack on it and had argued that the mere enactment of a temporary moratorium constituted a per se takings. Having found that the moratorium was not invalid on its face, the Court upheld the law.]

CHIEF JUSTICE REHNQUIST, with whom JUSTICE SCALIA and JUSTICE THOMAS join, dissenting.

For over half a decade petitioners were prohibited from building homes, or any other structures, on their land. Because the Takings Clause requires the government to pay compensation when it deprives owners of all economically viable use of their land, and because a ban on all development lasting almost six years does not resemble any traditional land-use planning device, I dissent. . . .

JUSTICE THOMAS, with whom JUSTICE SCALIA joins, dissenting.

. . . A taking is exactly what occurred in this case. No one seriously doubts that the land use regulations at issue rendered petitioners' land unsusceptible of *any* economically beneficial use. This was true at the inception of the moratorium, and it remains true today. These individuals and families were deprived of the opportunity to build single-family homes as permanent, retirement, or vacation residences on land upon which such construction was authorized when purchased. The Court assures them that "a temporary prohibition on economic use" cannot be a taking because "logically . . . the property will recover value as soon as the prohibition is lifted." But the "logical" assurance that a "temporary restriction . . . merely causes a diminution in value," is cold comfort to the property owners in this case or any other. After all, "*[i]n the long run* we are all dead." John Maynard Keynes, Monetary Reform 88 (1924). . . .

NOTES AND QUESTIONS

1. In *Seawall* the city had not entered any SRO hotel and occupied it. Nevertheless, *Seawall* held that the ordinance constituted a physical taking because, under the traditional conception of property, the most important of the various rights of an owner is the right to exclude others from occupying or using the property. In other words, the majority in *Seawall* sees this case as one involving the property ownership bundle of rights (such as the right to sell, etc.), and, specifically, the elimination of one of these rights—the right to exclude others—which is enough to constitute a physical taking. In *Yee*, the land owner also argued that it had lost the right to exclude. According to the plaintiff, how did the local rent control ordinance and the state Mobilehome Residency Law combine to have this impact? The Court in *Yee* holds that it does not have to reach the issue of whether the loss of a possessory interest constitutes a physical taking because the landowner had not lost that right. Why not? Can *Yee* and *Seawall* be distinguished?

2. The *Seawall* majority opinion recognizes that the United States Supreme Court has not passed on the specific issue of whether loss of a possessory interest, such as the right to exclude, constitutes a *per se* physical taking. In *Yee*, as the last question observed, the Court avoided this issue. In *Tahoe-Sierra Preserve*, however, the majority observed that "where an owner possesses a full 'bundle' of property rights, the destruction of one 'strand' of the bundle is not a taking." Does this sentence indicate that the Court would not have decided this aspect of *Seawell* in the same way as the *Seawall* majority?

3. Should the Court hold that the government must pay compensation when a regulation results in the loss of a possessory interest? Should the government be required to pay for the loss of any possessory interest, or only certain possessory interests, such as the right to exclude? If you agree with Professor Epstein, who takes the position that the government should pay compensation for the loss of any interest,[23] what is the likely impact of this position on the government's capacity to regulate? If you think the Court should require the government to pay only for the loss of some interests, how should the Court distinguish between the loss of interests for which compensation is and is not paid?

4. In *Seawell*, the majority struck down a "temporary" moratorium on the conversion of SRO hotels to other types of uses as a per se takings. In *Tahoe-Sierra Preserve*, the majority holds that a moratorium on the development of land is not a "per se" takings, although it may constitute a takings in a particular case. If *Seawell* had been decided after *Tahoe-Sierra Preserve*, would it have come out the same way? Could the court have decided that the moratorium was a per se takings? Can *Seawell* be distinguished from *Tahoe-Sierra Preserve*?

5. In *Seawall*, the majority also holds that the ordinance is facially invalid as a regulatory taking. One ground for this holding is that the landowners are deprived of any economically viable use of their property. The dissent objects that they are entitled to a minimum of an 8½ percent rate of return, and may be entitled to additional compensation. According to the majority, this guarantee is not sufficient to save the statute. Why not? Do you agree with the majority's reason?

6. In *Seawall*, the second ground that the statute is facially invalid is because the burdens imposed do not advance legitimate state interests. In his dissent in *Pennell*, Justice Scalia uses a similar analysis to strike down the rent control statute. In both cases, the opinions take the position because the landowners are not the "cause" of the problem that the government is trying to solve, they are being forced to bear public burdens which should be borne by the public as a whole. How did the majority and dissent in *Seawall* differ concerning whether the landowners caused the problem of "homeless people" in New York City? Which opinion do you find most persuasive and why?

7. The notes following *Pennell* discussed Justice Scalia's attempt to create a heightened "nexus" test under the Takings Clause and to restrict regulation of the use of land to problems that the use of the land created for other persons. By comparison, although *Penn Central* requires that the government have a legitimate purpose of its regulation, it is only necessary that the regulation is "reasonably necessary" to effectuate a "substantial public purpose." Under the heightened requirement, the regulation must "substantially advance" a legitimate state interest. How does this type of test applied affect your answer to the previous question? Is the type of regulation in *Seawell* unconstitutional under the heightened "nexus" test and constitutional under the less demanding *Penn Central* test? Does the nature of the test affect how much deference

---

[23] Epstein, *supra* note 22.

the Supreme Court (or state supreme courts) give to legislative decisions to regulate land usage? Do you think the founders intended the Court to be extra vigilant in its protection of landowners under the Takings Clause?

8. Property rights advocates have lobbied state legislatures around the country to pass takings legislation. Eighteen states have passed such legislation and at least twenty-four other states have considered such proposals.[24] The majority of laws require state and/or local agencies to evaluate their regulations to determine if such regulations could generate constitutional takings.[25] Five states have laws which provide for different thresholds of compensation for regulatory takings: Florida (whenever regulation imposes an "inordinate burden" on the use of any property); Louisiana (20 percent reduction in the value of agricultural property and forest land); North Dakota (50 percent loss in the value of any property); Mississippi (40 percent reduction in the value of agricultural property and forest land); and Texas (25 percent reduction in the value of any property).[26] None of these laws, however, require compensation when the state is regulating a land use that would constitute a nuisance.

Do you favor a requirement that a state must compensate a landowner when the impact of regulation exceeds some threshold? Why or why not? Do you favor a requirement that agencies analyze whether proposed regulations would constitute a taking? Is it anything more than a symbolic gesture? Why do the states that require compensation make an exception for land use that would constitute a nuisance? Do you agree with this distinction?

9. The Taking Clause has been the subject of considerable debate in the academic literature.[27] What is the Court's appropriate role in protecting private property under the Takings Clause? Are those Justices, such as Justice Scalia, who support a more protecting Takings Clause seeking to reestablish substantive due process in a new guise? Or is there a difference between the Due Process and Takings Clauses that justifies a more aggressive enforcement of the latter?

---

[24] The information in this note is based on Jost, *Property Rights,* 5 CQ RESEARCHER 515 (1995); *Land-Use Regulation—Compensation Statutes—Florida Creates Cause of Action for Compensation of Property Owners When Regulation Imposes "Inordinate Burden,"* 109 HARV. L. REV. 542 (1995).

[25] Delaware, Idaho, Indiana, Kansas, Missouri, Tennessee, Utah, Virginia, West Virginia, and Wyoming have takings impact assessment laws. Arizona passed legislation requiring state agencies to conduct similar analyses, but this statute was rejected by referendum in 1994.

[26] Texas's law permits invalidation of the regulatory restrictions as an alternative to compensation when property loss reaches a requisite level of severity. A sixth state, Washington, passed a law requiring compensation for any diminution in property value, but it was later rejected by referendum.

[27] Besides Professor Epstein's contribution, *supra* note 22. see W. FISCHEL, REGULATORY TAKINGS: LAW, ECONOMICS AND POLITICS (1995); B. ACKERMAN, PRIVATE PROPERTY AND THE CONSTITUTION (1977); Sax, *Takings, Private Property and Public Rights,* 81 YALE L.J. 149 (1971); Michelman, *Property, Utility, and Fairness: Comments on the Ethical Foundations of "Just Compensation" Law,* 80 HARV. L. REV. 1165 (1967); Sax, *Takings and the Police Power,* 74 YALE L.J. 36 (1964); Dunham, *A Legal and Economic Basis for City Planning,* 58 COLUM. L. REV. 650 (1958).

Chapter 8

EXCESSIVE COMPETITION: AIRLINE REGULATION AND FARM PROGRAMS

Transportation services were regulated for years in this country in the belief that it was necessary to prevent "excessive competition." Without regulation, the fear was that market conditions would force sellers to cut their prices to the point that many of them would go out of business. The few sellers remaining in business would then be able to charge prices higher than they could have charged in a more competitive market. In the late 1970s and early 1980s, transportation was almost entirely deregulated in recognition that regulation harmed consumers by keeping prices artificially high. Nevertheless, the government continues to intervene in other markets, such as agriculture, based on the idea that government should address the impact of too much competition.

This chapter will discuss whether regulation is an appropriate response to excessive competition. If price regulation is inappropriate, as many analysts believe, why did Congress adopt airline regulation in the first place, or, in the case of agricultural prices, why does Congress refuse to return to a market without government intervention? One answer is that Congress and federal regulators are responding to the political power of agricultural interests. Agricultural interests, like the airlines before them, are able to obtain "rents" from government regulation—they earn rates of return that exceed the profit they could earn in a competitive market.

A. AIRLINE REGULATION

The federal government and the states no longer subject the airline, train, bus, or trucking industries to price controls or to licensing in order to control of entry and exit. We illustrate and discuss the remarkable change from regulation to deregulation of these industries by examining what happened in the airline industry.[1] We first examine the justifications for regulation and deregulation and the results of deregulation. We will then consider whether additional government regulation may be necessary to address problems that have arisen in the deregulated market.

1. REGULATION

The initial justification for airline regulation was based on the need for government subsidies to support the industry. As the subsidies became less

---

[1] Readers interested in a fuller account of this story should see S. MORRISON & C. WINSTON, THE EVOLUTION OF THE AIRLINE INDUSTRY (1995); T. PETZINGER, HARD LANDING: THE EPIC CONQUEST FOR POWER AND PROFITS THAT PLUNGED THE AIRLINES INTO CHAOS (1995); B. PETERSON & J. GLAB, RAPID DESCENT: DEREGULATION AND THE SHAKE-OUT IN THE AIRLINES (1994).

important (and eventually were phased out), "excessive competition" became the new rationale for regulation.

a. REGULATION AND SUBSIDIES

The airline business started in the United States as a "dangerous, seat-of-the-pants, heavily subsidized mail delivery service."[2] Under the Kelly Airmail Act of 1925, the Post Office was authorized to award contracts for airmail service by competitive bidding and to provide a subsidy that was not to exceed four-fifths of airmail revenues. The subsidy, which totaled $7 million by 1930, stimulated public demand for airmail was a great boon to the fledgling industry. Soon, however, the subsidies gave way to scandal. In May 1930, Walter Brown, President Hoover's Postmaster General, invited key airline executives to a meeting to divide up the principal air routes throughout the country. This collusion was in violation of a law that required competitive bidding. As a result of what became known as the "spoils conference," the Big Four—United, American, TWA, and Eastern—were earning about $20 million of federal subsidies by 1933. When the scandal was made public, then Senator Hugo Black chaired hearings in the Senate that ultimately resulted in regulation of the industry.

In response to the spoils conference, Congress established the Civil Aeronautics Board in 1938.[3] Modeled after the Interstate Commerce Commission (ICC), the CAB had five members (with no more than three from the same political party) appointed by the President with the concurrence of the Senate for six-year terms. Congress delegated to the Board power to control exit and entry (by granting and revoking certificates of public convenience and necessity), establish prices (by approving or amending tariffs filed by carriers), set mail rates and award contracts, and control mergers and acquisitions.

b. REGULATION AND EXCESSIVE COMPETITION

The original impetus for regulation was the chaotic competitive atmosphere of the early industry. These conditions also provided the rationale for regulation as the industry matured and subsidies were reduced and eventually ended. Advocates of regulation argued that airline services were prone to excessive competition. This defense of regulation was based on the fact that airlines have significant economies of scale for each flight. Once the decision is made to fly an airplane between two cities, whether the airplane flies with three passengers or ninety-three, the costs to the airline are about the same, except perhaps for marginal differences in fuel costs. In order to attract additional customers and fill up their airlines, proponents of regulation predicted that airlines would keep lowering their fares. In this manner, unrestrained competition would drive down the price and erode airline profitability.

---

[2] R. Vietor, Contrived Competition: Regulation and Deregulation in America 24 (1994). The following history of airline regulation is drawn from this source and from A. Brown, the Politics of Airline Deregulation 102–03, 106–10 (1987); Carstensen, *Evaluating "Deregulation" of Commercial Air Travel: False Dichotomization, Untenable Theories, and Unimplemented Premises,* 46 Wash. & Lee L. Rev. 109, 110–15 (1989).

[3] Civil Aeronautics Act of 1938, P.L. 75-706, 52 Stat. 973 (1938). The Board was originally named the Civil Aeronautics Authority.

More specifically, the proponents of regulation warned that unrestrained competition would have two deleterious effects. Financially weak competitors would go out of business because their profits would not be sufficient to sustain them or they would be purchased by financially stronger companies. Other competitors would seek mergers to decrease the level of competition and permit them to earn higher profits. Once these events transpired, airlines would raise prices in markets with little or no competition. As Professor Dempsey explains, those who favored regulation thought they were protecting consumers from the related evils of destructive competition and monopoly:

> The consumer . . . sees things go from bad to worse, as an unstable pack of anemic, bankrupt carriers becomes a sleek, powerful, price-discriminating monopoly or oligopoly. In the view of early advocates of regulation these two phenomena, destructive competition and powerful monopolies, were simply two sides of the same coin. The purpose of regulation, under these circumstances, was to eliminate this Hobson's choice for consumers: preventing the potential threats to safety, service and investment posed by destructive competition on the one hand, and the price-gouging and price discrimination associated with market power in a consolidated industry, on the other.[4]

Price regulation created the rationale for controlling entry and exit. Once prices were fixed, the only method that airlines had to compete was to offer new services. One such service was more frequent flights because it offered customers more convenience and less crowded planes. If one firm added additional flights, competitors also would respond by adding new flights. This type of competition—adding new flights—increased an airline's costs more than if it filled up existing flights. As noted earlier, the cost to the airline of adding new passengers to an existing flight is small. Since the CAB was charged with the responsibility of promoting industry growth and welfare, it used licensing in order to control exit and entry controls to ensure that airlines filled up existing planes before they started adding new flights.

Airlines, however, resorted to service competition only because they could not adjust their fares without CAB approval.[5] If an airline had been able to control its own prices (as it can do now), it would not have added new flights in order to attract additional customers. Instead, it would have attempted to fill existing flights by cutting its prices. If lowering prices did not fill up an existing flight, the airline would have attempted to move underutilized planes to another route where there was greater demand. Thus, in a competitive market, the government does not have to use licensing in order to ensure that planes are filled up. The CAB, however, did not employ price competition to eliminate excess capacity because of the idea that unrestrained competition would produce the evils mentioned previously.

---

[4] P. DEMPSEY, FLYING BLIND: THE FAILURE OF AIRLINE DEREGULATION 4 (Economic Policy Institute 1990).

[5] S. BREYER, REGULATION AND ITS REFORM 220 (1982).

2. DEREGULATION

In the 1960s and 1970s, the concept of destructive competition came under attack. The attack occurred first in the scholarly literature, where economists and others argued that competition would produce lower prices and better quality service for consumers.[6] First, analysts disputed that excessive competition would cause airlines to merge to earn higher profits. This prediction was based on studies that found that, although airlines had significant economies of scale for individual planes, there were no similar economies of scale for an airline company as a whole. Unless big firms have significant cost advantages over small firms, there is no motive for small firms to merge in order to become larger.[7] Second, analysts predicted that, even if mergers led to domination of markets by one or two sellers, these airlines would keep their prices at or near levels that would prevail in more competitive markets, or markets with a larger number of sellers. This second prediction was based on the theory of "contestability."[8]

According to the concept of "contestability," even if airline companies dominated a market, they would not raise their prices above competitive levels because of the threat of *potential* entry. In other words, if existing firms attempted to charge prices higher than would prevail in a competitive market, new entry would be attracted by the prospect of competing away some of the high profits earned by the existing firms. These new entrants would take business away from the existing firms by offering flights at lower prices. They would remain in the market until the one or two original airlines matched their prices, and then they would leave the market for some other, more profitable opportunity.[9]

The second attack on the concept of destructive competition came on the political front. Senator Edward Kennedy chaired subcommittee hearings organized by Stephen Breyer, who was then on leave from the Harvard Law School, that called public attention to the academic criticisms of regulation. A report based on the hearings concluded that deregulation would enlarge the range of price and service options for consumers, enhance carrier productivity and efficiency, and increase the economic health of the industry.[10] The report was influential because of its source: although it is conservatives who are naturally distrustful of government regulation, Senator Kennedy's actions signaled to

---

[6] *See, e.g.*, D. WYCKOFF & D. MAISTER, THE DOMESTIC AIRLINE INDUSTRY (1977); REGULATION OF AIR FARES AND COMPETITION AMONG THE AIRLINES (P. MacAvoy & J. Snow eds., 1977); R. BURKHARD, CAB — THE CIVIL AERONAUTICS BOARD (1974); G. DOUGLAS & J. MILLER, ECONOMIC REGULATION OF DOMESTIC AIR TRANSPORT: THEORY AND PRACTICE (1974); W. JORDAN, AIRLINE DEREGULATION IN AMERICA: EFFECTS AND IMPERFECTIONS (1970); R. CAVES, AIR TRANSPORTATION AND ITS STUDY: AN INDUSTRY STUDY (1967); S. RICHMOND, REGULATION AND COMPETITION IN THE AIR TRANSPORTATION INDUSTRY (1961); Levine, *Is Regulation Necessary: California Air Transportation National Regulatory Policy*, 74 YALE L.J. 1416 (1965).

[7] *See, e.g.*, CAVES, *supra* note 6, at 56–61.

[8] See generally W. BAUMOL, J. PANZAR, & R. WILLIG, CONTESTABLE MARKETS AND THE THEORY OF INDUSTRY STRUCTURE (1980).

[9] DEMPSEY, *supra* note 4, at 8; *see* Brenner, *Airline Deregulation — A Case Study in Public Policy Failure,* 16 TRANSP. L.J. 179, 186–88 (1988).

[10] Senate Subcomm. on Administrative Practice & Procedure, Civil Aeronautics Board Practices and Procedures, 96th Cong., 1st Sess. (1976), *reprinted in* 41 J. AIR L. & COMM. 697 (1975).

liberals that they, too, should support deregulation. At about the same time, President Carter appointed a proponent of deregulation, Professor Alfred Kahn of Cornell University, to be chair of the CAB. As CAB chair, Kahn worked tirelessly to convince Congress of the benefits of deregulation. Since the agency charged with regulation was in favor of its own abolition, Kahn's efforts also had an important impact.

Congress responded by passing the Airline Deregulation Act of 1978[11] with overwhelming bipartisan support. After the CAB supervised the transition to a competitive market, it was abolished.[12] Price regulation and entry and exit controls were eliminated, but the government's authority to approve airline mergers was retained and transferred to the Department of Transportation.[13]

NOTES AND QUESTIONS

1. How does the theory of excessive competition relate to the marginal costs of flying an airplane? Did the initial chaotic experience of the airline industry make the theory of "excessive competition" more credible? Consider Professor Levine's argument:

> In 1938, it appeared to the general public and the Congress that uncontrolled markets did not work very well for the public over the long run. Although markets produced low prices during the Depression years, many producers went out of business. The airline business was relatively new, Congress had little experience with it, and there was no reason not to apply general skepticism about markets to airlines. Doubts about airline markets were reinforced by the fact that firms were continuing to attempt entry. Notwithstanding this dismal picture, a modern analyst would say that these firms were looking past the Depression at a bright future for a new technology. But it seemed to Congress that mistakenly optimistic entrepreneurs were seeking profitable operations where none were possible, draining away resources needed for further extension of the airline system in fruitless and profitless competitive struggles for existing business. Firms which had invested substantial resources in pioneering air transportation would become the innocent victims of still another example of market competition run riot.
>
> It was therefore not difficult for the airline industry to persuade Congress and the public that the fledgling airline industry would go the way of many other Depression-era firms and that the full potential of aviation could not be developed in a free-market environment. This would be both inefficient and unfair. Whether the industry sincerely believed this, merely hoped for the benefits of cartelization, or both, is immaterial. It made its case. . . .[14]

---

[11] Pub. L. 95-504, 92 Stat. 1705 (1978). Congress also deregulated air cargo transportation. Air Cargo Deregulation Act of 1977, Pub. L. 95-163, 91 Stat. 1278.

[12] Civil Aeronautics Board Sunset Act of 1984, Pub. L. No. 99-443, 98 Stat. 1703.

[13] 49 U.S.C. § 1551(b)(1)(C) (1988).

[14] Levine, *Revisionism Revised: Airline Deregulation and the Public Interest*, 44 L. CONTEMP. PROBS. 179, 191–94 (Winter, 1981). Copyright © 1981 by Duke University School of Law. Reprinted by permission.

2. The theory of excessive competition predicted that without regulation consumers would be at the mercy of only a few carriers, which would charge very high prices. On what grounds did the proponents of deregulation argue that the industry would remain competitive and consumers would enjoy lower prices?

3. Airline deregulation was only one form of transportation deregulation. During this same period of time, Congress also passed legislation that deregulated interstate railroad, truck, and bus services.[15] Most states followed with deregulation of intrastate railroad, truck, and bus services.[16]

3. AFTER DEREGULATION

Deregulation had several major impacts on the airline industry. Deregulation generated lower prices overall, but many passengers ended up paying higher fares than other passengers due to lack of competition and the airlines' use of fare discrimination. After deregulation, there was a flood of new entrants, but most of these new airlines eventually went broke. New entry continues but new airlines continue to fail and go out of business. The major airlines have been subject to similar instability. Most of the major airlines in existence at the time of deregulation have gone out of business and only six major airlines remain (American, Continental, Delta, Northwest, United and U.S. Air). These airlines have developed hub and spoke systems, which increased their efficiency, but which also created an opportunity to avoid competition. Finally, many smaller cities no longer have airline service or they only have small commuter airlines, which offer infrequent flights at high prices.

a. LOWER PRICES

By the middle of the 1980s, economists found deregulation had produced substantial consumer benefits. For example, a 1986 report by the Brookings Institution concluded that deregulation caused at least a $6 billion improvement in the welfare of travelers. The study found that "the benefits from deregulation largely accrue to business travelers because of improved service convenience . . . and to frequency improvements in low-density markets." It estimated that the reduced time between departures has saved business travelers approximately $4 billion annually. The other $2 billion in benefits was attributed to savings in fares, primarily for the non-business traveler. The analysts derived this estimate using 1983 fares as a base and retroactively calculating what fares would have been in 1977 if deregulation had been in

---

[15] Surface Freight Forwarder Deregulation Act of 1986, Pub. L. 99-521, 100 Stat. 2993; Shipping Act of 1984, Pub. L. 98-237, 98 Stat. 67; Bus Regulatory Reform Act of 1982, Pub. L. 97-261, 96 Stat. 1102; Household Goods Transportation Act of 1980, Pub. L. 96-454, 94 Stat. 2011; Motor Carrier Act of 1980, Pub. L. 96-292, 94 Stat. 793; Staggers Rail Act of 1980, Pub. L. 96-448, 94 Stat. 1895; Railroad Revitalization and Regulatory Reform Act Amendments of 1976, Pub. L. 94-210, 90 Stat. 31.

[16] *See* Dempsey, *Transportation Deregulation — On a Collision Course*, 13 TRANSP. L.J. 329, 361–63 (1984); Freeman & Bullock, *State Regulatory Responses to Federal Motor Carrier Regulation*, 35 U. FLA. L. REV. 69 (1983).

place. The study compared these hypothetical 1977 fares with actual fares that year to calculate the claimed savings.[17]

The availability of more flights on more routes at lower fares fundamentally changed the nature of air travel in the United States. In the prior regulated environment, airline travel had been the preserve of the well-to-do and the government-protected air carriers generally focused on providing quality service to those persons who could afford to pay the high fares. As a result of more flights from more locations at lower prices, airlines obtained an ever-broadening base of air travelers. "In the aggregate, culturally and sociologically, airline travel became familiar and passengers' awe with airplane travel was replaced with a no-nonsense expectation of getting to a destination cheaply, quickly, and safely."[18]

The lower fares resulted primarily from an increase in competition.[19] New airlines, such as Midway Airlines, America West and People Express, quickly emerged after deregulation. Unlike older competitors, which were saddled with expensive labor agreements dating back to the regulatory era, the new entrants had lower base salaries, an entry-level work force, and greater flexibility in the utilization of personnel, which enabled them to "cream-skim" busy routes by attracting customers away from established airlines on the basis of low-cost, no frills service.

b. INSTABILITY AND CONSOLIDATION

Deregulation produced lower prices, but it also produced bankruptcies and mergers since airlines no longer had the CAB to ensure their survival.[20] By the mid-1990s, most of the upstart airlines had gone out of existence and most of the pre-deregulation major carriers had a similar fate. There were fifty-one mergers and acquisitions in the airline industry between 1979 and 1988. During this period, fifteen independent airlines had been merged into six carriers. Moreover, five of the largest airlines at the time of deregulation, including Pan Am and Eastern, went out of business. A second wave of new airlines emerged in the 1990s including Kiwi International, ValuJet, Reno, Morris Air, Vanguard and MarkAir, and carriers that took the names of airlines that had gone out of business, such as Braniff, Midway and Frontier, but many of these airlines had gone out of business at the end of the decade. And there was further instability and consolidation among the major carriers. American purchased TWA in January 2000, and United Airlines attempted to merge with US Airways in May 2000. After the Department of Justice thwarted the merger, both airlines eventually went into bankruptcy.

As this record indicates, the airline industry has been particularly susceptible to changes in economic conditions. A recession and higher oil prices

---

[17] S. MORRISON & C. WINSTON, THE ECONOMIC EFFECTS OF AIRLINE DEREGULATION (1986); *see also* T. MOORE, U.S. AIRLINE DEREGULATION: ITS EFFECTS ON PASSENGERS, CAPITAL AND LABOR (1985); E. BAILEY, D. GRAHAM, & D. KAPLAN, DEREGULATING THE AIRLINES (1985); Moore, *U.S. Airline Deregulation: Its Effects on Passengers, Capital and Labor,* 24 J. L. & ECON. 1 (1986).

[18] Ravitch, *Re-Regulation and Airline Passenger Rights,* 67 J. AIR L. & COM. 935, 960–61 (2002).

[19] *See* Dempsey, *Predation, Competition and Antitrust Law: Turbulence in the Airline Industry,* 67 J. AIR L. & COM. 685, 703–07 (2002); Ravitch, *supra* note 18, at 990.

[20] *On A Wing and a Fare: Deregulation Decoded,* NEW YORK TIMES, Nov. 5, 1995, at E5 (national edition); Murray, In a Tailspin, NATIONAL JOURNAL, Oct. 12, 2002.

contributed to a $10 billion dollar loss between 1990 and 1992. The industry's profitability increased by 1995 when the economic had improved. By 2002, however, airlines lost $7.7 billion, attributable in part to another economic downturn and the residual effects of September 11.

c. HUB AND SPOKE SYSTEM

The merger and bankruptcy trend in the airline industry is one significant post-deregulation development. Another is the development of the "hub and spoke" system. Soon after deregulation, carriers adopted particular cities as hubs in order to coordinate flights and maximize the number of persons flying on any one airplane.[21] Airlines use smaller planes to bring passengers to their hub and then transfer all persons bound for the same destination to the same airplane. This also permits an airline to use larger planes, which are more efficient than flying the same number of passengers on two or more smaller planes.

The hub and spoke system has turned out to be both a benefit and a detriment for consumers. Consumers benefit from more efficient aircraft usage (because fuller planes reduce costs and permit airlines to charge lower fares), additional service (the majority of cities with air service now have more frequent flights), additional competition for many pairs of cities (because consumers can make connections from different hubs), and from being able to use the same airline for their entire flight (passengers frequently switched airlines under regulation).[22] The merger trend in the airline industry is related to the development of the hub and spoke system. Proponents of deregulation now concede that they overlooked scale economies that airlines can obtain by becoming larger when they predicted before deregulation that the airlines lacked economic incentives to merge into larger units.[23] This promise of increased economic efficiency was one reason why the Department of Transportation failed to turn down any merger proposal that the airlines presented to it.

Nevertheless, the hub and spoke system also has a downside for consumers. With the development of the hub and spoke system, airline markets have turned out to be less contestable than the proponents of deregulation had predicted. As explained earlier, the theory of "contestability" predicts that the potential of new competition will restrain airlines that dominate a market (a hub) from raising their prices above competitive levels. According to the theory, if a dominate airline were to raise its prices above competitive levels, new competition would come into the market and drive prices back down to prior levels or below. The hub system, however, became a way for airlines to avoid competition. Because the major airlines largely adopted different hubs, they avoided head-to-head competition and established market domination at their hub airports. As a result, all but four hub airports are now dominated by a single airline, which accounts for 60 percent to 80 percent of landings,

---

[21] Hahn & Kroszner, *The Mismanagement of Air Transport: A Supply Side Analysis*, 95 PUB. INTEREST 102 (1989).

[22] See Cushman, *Support for Airline Deregulation*, N.Y. TIMES, Feb. 14, 1990, at C1 (national edition).

[23] Levine, *Surprises of Airline Deregulation,* 78 AEA PAPERS & PROC. 316, 432 (1988).

takeoffs, and passengers at a particular hub.[24] In Atlanta, for example, Delta has 72 percent of the market, while Northwest's market share in Minneapolis is 80 percent.[25] Studies have shown that prices are considerably higher in hub cities in which one or two airlines originate most of the flights out of that city.

The General Accounting Office (GAO) compared fares at airports dominated by one or two carriers and airports with more competition. On average, the fares adjusted for flight distances, were 31 percent higher at the airports having less competition.[26] More recently, the Department of Transportation reported, "In the absence of competition, the major carrier is able to charge fares that exceed its fares in non-hub markets of comparable distance and density by upwards of 40 percent."[27]

d. FARE DISCRIMINATION

The airline's use of fare discrimination was another post-deregulation development that had both a good and bad impact for consumers. Although deregulation produced lower fares, they are usually subject to numerous restrictions, including the infamous requirement of "staying over on a Saturday" night. Consumers unable to qualify under these restrictions pay much higher fares. As a result, about 60 percent of passengers pay less or equal to the average fare, while about 13 percent pay more than 1.5 times the average fare. Since large companies can usually negotiate with the airlines to avoid the restrictions on lower fares, smaller businesses and non-business travelers primarily pay the higher unrestricted fares.

Airline prices vary because the carriers practice "yield management." Through yield management, tickets are divided into groups of different prices. Depending on the ultimate destination of the passenger, the number of tickets already sold, and the number of days remaining before the flight, the airline will sell higher-or lower-priced tickets to fill the flight. In this manner, the airline attempts to get each passenger to pay the highest possible fare.[28] For example, business travelers will pay higher fares to avoid the requirement of a Saturday stay-over because they wish to be home on weekends.

The extent to which airlines can depend on fare restrictions is influenced by the degree of competition. The major airlines have relied on their dominance of hubs to raise prices to business travelers, but this tactic became less viable as the economy declined and fewer people flew after the events of September 11. Moreover, as booking airline tickers over the Internet became more widespread, customers were less willing to pay high fares or abide by restrictions to the extent that they could buy tickets from discount airlines

---

[24] DEMPSEY, *supra* note 4, at 16.

[25] McCarthy, *Major Airlines Find Their 'Fortress Hubs' Aren't Impenetrable*, WALL STREET JOURNAL, Feb. 6, 1996, A1 (Midwest Edition).

[26] General Accounting office, Airline Deregulation: Barriers To Entry Continue to Limit Competition in Several Key Markets 20 (1996).

[27] Department of Transportation, Requests for Comments in Docket OST-98-3717 (Apr. 6, 1998), *cited in* Dempsey, *supra* note 19, at 697.

[28] See Uchitelle, *Off Course*, NEW YORK TIMES MAGAZINE, Sept. 1, 1991, at 25; Kahan, *Confessions of an Airline Deregulator*, THE AMERICAN PROSPECT, Winter 1992, at 38.

at lower prices with fewer restrictions. To meet such competition, the major airlines lowered their prices to non-business travelers and attempted to make up the difference by raising fares for business travelers, but business travelers generally resisted paying the higher fares and the major airlines lost considerable business as a result.[29]

e. SHORT TRIPS AND REMOTE AREAS

Another function of deregulation is higher fares for short trips. Under regulation, the CAB subsidized the cost of short flights, and flights to remote areas, by permitting airlines to charge higher prices for other flights. The cross-subsidy ensured that the cost of these types of flights was not exorbitant. After deregulation, fares increased once airlines set prices based on their high costs. When demand fell as a result, the major carriers abandoned many of these routes. Commuter carriers replaced them in some cases, and there is no longer air service in other cases.

NOTES AND QUESTIONS

1. Richard Kuttner argues that the events after deregulation prove the validity of the excessive competition rationale?

> Either there is genuine competition—in which case passengers get good deals and carriers go broke—or the airlines find ways to accumulate monopoly power and consumers get snookered. Sometimes, as in the case of U.S. Airways, there is simultaneously the worst of both worlds: monopoly power over and exorbitant prices on some routes without enough income to make up for the ruinous competition on others.[30]

Do the events after deregulation support Kuttner's conclusion? Robert Crandall of American Airlines contends that airline markets will remain competitive. According to Crandall, "15 domestic airlines would create less competition than three domestic airlines."[31] Does the validity of Crandall's argument depend on the extent to which the three carriers compete against each other? How does the existence of hubs dominated by one or two carriers affect your answer?

2. Can the nation afford to have an instable airline industry? Judge Richard Cudahy notes:

> The airlines are part of the transportation infrastructure. Does this mean that, if a financial crisis impends, they properly can be subsidized? . . . If the airlines are threatened with economic ruin, there are a number of possible remedies, ranging from subsidies at one end of the spectrum to nationalization at the other.[32]

---

[29] Levine, *No Clear Way Forward For Airlines*, NEW YORK TIMES, Dec. 6, 2002, at A33.

[30] Kuttner, *Useless Airways*, THE AMERICAN PROSPECT, Sept. 9, 2002, at 2.

[31] Uchitelle, *supra* note 28, at 26.

[32] Cudahy, *Full Circle in the Formerly Regulated Industries?*, 33 LOY. U. CHI. L.J. 767, 780–81 (2002).

The reader will recall that the original impetus for regulation was to ensure that government subsidies to the fledgling airline industry were not misused. Have we come full circle?

3. The loss of airline service or low-cost airline service is a significant impediment to economic development in rural areas. Gary Collins notes:

> "The free market is the best system by which to solve the air service situation," said Senator Charles Grassley, who then demanded to know what the industry intended to do for Iowa, a state with a small, spread-out population that's not showing any signs of getting larger. When you rely on the magic of the marketplace, this is exactly the kind of place that turns out to be a toad. . . .
>
> The sparse service and high cost of tickets to relatively low-demand destinations is an obsession with many of our nation's elected officials. It ruins their hopes for economic development, and its hurtful, like discovering that your beloved daughter can't get a date for the prom. [33]

Should the government provide a subsidy to continue airline service to some destinations? After deregulation, the federal government did subsidize air service to some remote locations, but these subsidies are being phased out. [34] What, if any, public interest is there in providing subsidies for airline transportation to remote areas?

4. Economic regulation has often been used to establish cross-subsidies. The CAB, as noted, established a rate structure that subsidized flights to remote areas and short-distance flights. As Chapter 6 discussed, some telephone consumers in metropolitan areas pay higher rates in order to ensure those persons living in remote areas have affordable telephone service. Economists criticize such subsidies on the ground they are inefficient because the prices do not reflect the cost of providing the good or service. Once a cross-subsidy is eliminated, consumers can expect prices to rise for goods or services that are more expensive to provide. In some cases, consumers will not be able to afford the higher price and sellers will exit the market because of the lack of demand.

If the government must offer a subsidy, economic analysts generally prefer that it should be paid directly to the recipient. Although the direct subsidy distorts the price of the subsidized service, it does not also distort the price of other services in the way that a cross-subsidy would do.

5. Should airline tickets be based on the "value" to the consumer (e.g., willingness to pay) or on the "cost" to the airline on transporting the passenger? Alfred Kahn, who (as noted earlier) ushered in deregulation as Chairman of the CAB, defends the price discrimination created by yield management. [35] He acknowledges that "[r]egulators and would-be reregulators . . . hate price discrimination," but argues that "different prices are not discriminatory if they merely reflect different costs." Kahn contends, "There's a rough justice when business travelers who make last-minute reservations and who value frequent, conveniently scheduled flights pay above-average fares. That kind of

---

[33] Collins, *Fly the Lonely Skies*, New York Times, Feb. 13, 2001, at A31.

[34] Brooke, *Budget Cuts Threaten Air Links to Remote Areas*, New York Times, Sept. 6, 1995, at A1 (national edition).

[35] Kahn, *The New Deal On Fares Deserves Applause*, N.Y. Times, May 17, 1992, at F13.

service is more costly to provide than, say, a single daily wide-bodied flight with every seat filled." Donald Pevsner contends that yield management permits the airlines to gouge some consumers.[36] He recommends that Congress restore rate regulation so that the Department of Transportation can determine if airline fares are "just and reasonable."

Is it "fair" that consumers pay different prices for the same flight? Or is Professor Kahn correct, that the differences in price reflect differences in service? Is discriminatory pricing an adequate policy reason to re-regulate the airlines?

6. The competitive turmoil caused by deregulation may have caused some airlines to skimp on safety precautions in order to save money. The investigation of Valujet, a low-cost airline, after one of its planes crashed into the Florida Everglades, revealed that the airline's cost cutting concerning the handling of dangerous cargo may have played a role in the crash.[37] More recently, the lack of effective security by the airlines apparently contributed to the events of September 11. In order to save money, airlines apparently tried to economize on the level of security that was provided.[38]

7. Congress initially assigned the responsibility for airline safety to the CAB, but this function was transferred to the Federal Aviation Administration (FAA) in 1958,[39] out of concern that giving the CAB the responsibility for both promoting the success of the air transportation industry and regulating its safety created an institutional conflict of interest. Nevertheless, the FAA has been criticized as being too cozy with the airlines because it is likewise required to "provide for the regulation and promotion of civil aviation in a manner as to best foster its development and safety. . . ."[40] Whatever the validity of this criticism, it cannot be denied that deregulation has caused a growth in air traffic that has sorely tested the FAA's capacity to regulate the safety of the industry.

4. REGULATORY REFORM

The deregulation of the airline industry was based on the assumption that a competitive market would emerge that would produce lower prices and better service for consumers. There are clear consumer benefits associated with deregulation, but this does not necessarily mean that airline markets are free of problems that might benefit from regulatory attention. Thus, airline markets after deregulation present the same two fundamental issues that have been asked throughout this book: First, are there problems that justify government intervention; second, if so, what regulatory tool or tools would work best?

---

[36] Pevsner, *And Mislead the Flying Public*, N.Y. TIMES, Apr. 19, 1992, at F11.

[37] Bryant, *Airline, Frequently Praised, Will Not Get New Scrutiny*, NEW YORK TIMES, May 13, 1996, at A10 (national edition).

[38] *See* Just, *Cut-Rate Security: How the Airlines Privatized the Nation's Safety*, THE AMERICAN PROSPECT, Oct. 22, 2001, at 15.

[39] Federal Aviation Act of 1958, 72 Stat. 731 (1958).

[40] See Feaver, *A New Route to Safety*, WASHINGTON POST WEEKLY EDITION, Aug. 12-18, 1996, at 22.

As mentioned earlier, the major carriers employ a hub and spoke system to channel passengers to various cities. Carriers have been able to dominate hubs for several reasons. One, as discussed earlier, is judicious use of price cuts to match the prices of competitors that attempt to enter a market. (There are also allegations that such price-cutting may be in violation of the antitrust laws, as discussed below.) Other reasons relate to the structure of the airline market. Airlines seeking to compete in markets dominated by one or two carriers have been stymied by the lack of landing slots and gates. In order to fly into an airport, a potential competitor requires a "landing slot," or an easement from the airport's owner to land an airplane during a specific period of the day. Airports can support only a limited number of landings (and take-offs) in any given period of time, and current market occupants usually control existing "landing slots." After the landing, the new entrant must have a gate at which the plane can be parked and the passengers unloaded (or "deplaned," as the airlines insist on describing it). Like landing slots, existing gates are often leased by current market occupants. The government can respond to the bottleneck problem presented by gates and landing slots by several means. Consider following responses.

a. EXPANSION

In 1990, Congress passed legislation that might constitute one solution to the previous problem. It authorized airports to charge passenger taxes to pay for airport expansion,[41] which could lead to additional competition at some airports if the proceeds are used to build additional runways and gates. This approach, however, is subject to several constraints. First, the airport must have sufficient room to build an additional runway. Second, the decision to expand an airport can be politically controversial. Although the local business community generally favors new construction, nearby neighbors will likely oppose such plans because of increased noise, air pollution and automobile congestion.[42] Finally, as the next excerpt indicates, existing tenants may be in a position to stymie expansion plans.

KIRK VICTOR, HUB CAP, NATIONAL JOURNAL, MAY 12, 1990, AT 1145–46 *

Further impeding airports' expansion efforts are 20-year and 30-year leases with airlines that contain so-called majority-in-interest clauses. These clauses give the airlines significant influence over airport-expansion projects; the airports, in return, receive through these agreements a guaranteed source of revenue.

Congress's General Accounting Office (GAO) last year surveyed leases at 185 airports. Kenneth M. Mead, the GAO's director of transportation issues, testified in September that these provisions usually give an airline that performs most operations at an airport "a veto power over airport expansion, thus possibly preventing the construction of new gate space."

---

[41] Aviation Safety and Capacity Expansion Act of 1990, 49 U.S.C.A. App. § 1513(e).

[42] Victor, *Hub Cap*, NAT'L J., May 12, 1990, at 1145–46.

"The more restrictive an agreement the airport signs, the greater the commitment the airlines will make to continue revenue-generating operations at the airport," Mead told the Senate Commerce, Science and Transportation Subcommittee on Aviation.

Majority-in-interest clauses are in effect at 55 U.S. airports, including 15 of the 27 largest airports, Mead said. In 14 cases, he said, the agreements give a single airline a veto over airport expansion. . . .

"The dominant airlines [at hubs] have the ability to stop projects from going forward where they may believe it not to be in their best interest to add new capacity, because maybe they have all the capacity they need but don't want a new competitor to come in," charged Robert Wigington, senior vice president for government and economic affairs of the Airport Operators Council International. The Washington group represents local, regional and state governmental bodies that own and operate U.S. airports.

Airline representatives have a different view. Asked whether a major airline should have such influence over development at an airport at which it carries a large share of the traffic, William J. Burhop, vice president for federal affairs at American Airlines Inc., said: "You betcha, and why the hell not? It is that user of that airport that is paying for the growth of that airport. . . . We're the ones that are paying for it. We're bringing in the passengers who pay the ticket tax and who pay the fares, a portion of which goes to landing fees." . . .

Paul Schoelhamer, vice president of government affairs at Northwest Airlines Inc., dismissed . . . charges [that airlines oppose expansion] and pointed out that Northwest is working with county officials in Detroit to begin a $1 billion expansion that will create "a whole lot more gates not only for us but for a lot of other people. . . . I don't see any basis for the idea that carriers use facility constraints to keep competitors out intentionally."

Notwithstanding such reassurances, Denver officials seem less than charitable in assessing the motives behind the past opposition to the new airport from United and Continental. Doughty said that the carriers had "argued that market share and market control was not the issue, [but] we feel that [they opposed the airport because] having a bigger facility where more airlines could compete with them probably wasn't in their interest." . . .

———

b. AUCTIONS AND LOTTERIES

To the extent that the government can create new runways, regulators will confront the issue of how these new spots should be allocated. Under an auction scheme, an airport decides on the ideal capacity and then it allocates landing slots to the highest bidder for slots that are not already grandfathered. At the current time, aircraft pay landing fees based on their weight, which means that small private planes and regional jets pay less to land than the largest commercial planes. The result is inefficient because it encourages smaller planes to occupy landing slots that could otherwise be used by larger airlines carrying more persons.[43]

---

[43] See *Ending Gridlock at La Guardia*, New York Times, Apr. 9, 2001, at A20.

Robert Frank discusses the advantages of this approach:

> In 1979, the Civil Aeronautics Board called for carriers to offer cash payments, free tickets or other rewards to induce volunteers to relinquish their seats on oversold flights. Passengers could decide for themselves how important it was to avoid waiting. . . .
>
> Scare landing slots. . .can be allocated in essentially the same way. Rather than give them away by lottery, the FAA could sell them to the highest-bidding airlines. If the market value of a slot were, say, $5,000, carriers would have to charge travelers on a 20 passenger flight $250 more for a one-way ticket, while those on a 200-passenger flight would have to pay only $25 extra. Passengers on smaller flights thus have a strong incentive to divert to less crowded times or less crowded airports.

Frank concedes, "Granted, this doesn't do much for passengers from Ames, Iowa, who want to visit New York City. But they can still fly to nearby airports, especially in West Chester or Long Island." He concludes, "And if aviation authorities really wanted to help the citizens of small communities, they could sell scare slots to the highest bidders, then give cash compensation to those communities that suffered as a result."[44]

c.   CONGESTION PRICING

Some economists have criticized the recent legislation authorizing airport authorities to charge departure taxes that could be used for airport expansion as wasteful. At most airports, the vast majority of takeoffs and landings occur early in the morning and during early evening, in order to accommodate business travelers. At most other times, airport facilities are almost unused. Instead of building new capacity, economists propose that airports adopt "congestion pricing," which would base takeoff and landing fees paid by air carriers on the time of day. DOT has proposed to permit airports to charge higher landing fees during rush hours, to relieve airport congestion and reduce delays in cities where many routes intersect.[45] This concept is explained further in the next excerpt:

STEVEN MORRISON & CLIFFORD WINSTON, ENHANCING THE PERFORMANCE OF THE DEREGULATED AIR TRANSPORTATION SYSTEM, BROOKINGS PAPERS: MICROECONOMICS 84–85, 99 (1989)[*]

Congestion and delays impose significant costs on passengers and carriers. . . . Besides reregulation, proposed remedies include limiting operations at major airports and constructing new airports.

It is certainly true that deregulation and the current macroeconomic expansion have caused a tremendous surge in air travel in the past ten years.

---

[44] Frank, *Scare Slots? Hold an Auction*, NEW YORK TIMES, Dec. 13, 2000, at A27.

[45] Cushman, *U.S. Plan Raises Airport Fee To Reduce Rush-Hour Delay*, N.Y. TIMES, Nov. 22, 1991, at A9.

[*] Reprinted by permission.

This surge and the accelerated development of hub-and-spoke operations have placed a great strain on the major airport's capacity. But airport congestion exists largely because of a failure to price the use of, and make appropriate investments in, scarce runway capacity and air traffic control. . . . [W]e find that replacing current landing fees, which are based primarily on weight, with marginal-cost landing fees, which account for an aircraft's contribution to congestion, would generate at least $3.8 billion in annual net benefits largely accrued in time savings. . . . Efficient pricing alone or in combination with efficient investment would significantly reduce the strain on airport capacity, eliminate the perceived need to limit flight operations, and postpone the expensive construction of new airports. . . .

Optimal Runway Pricing and Investment

. . . Basically, each take off and landing imposes costs on other users in the form of delay. For runway use to be optimal, users must be charged fees that reflect the (external) costs that they impose on other users and on the airport authority. These are called marginal-cost fees. In the long run, capacity should be added until the extra cost of the added capacity equals the attendant reduction in delay costs. This is the basis for optimal runway investment. . . .

Economists have advocated airport congestion pricing for at least twenty years. The recent explosion in air traffic makes its adoption imperative. The long-standing political concerns that have mitigated against congestion pricing may now be outweighed by new political realities. The public's plea for an end to flight delays and the need for more efficient expenditure of limited federal funds may be the basis for a political consensus that could make congestion pricing, and thus an improvement in the deregulated air system's performance, a real possibility.

———

d. REGULATION OF SLOTS AND GATES

Although the FAA does not appear likely to restructure the current system of ownership of slots and gates, there have been legislative proposals that would makes these changes. One proposal would delegate regulation over gate allocation to the Department of Transportation:[46]

(c) *Gate Usage at Certain Airports.* — . . .

(2). *DOT Allocation.* — Not later than 180 days after the date of enactment of this section, the Secretary [of Transportation] shall establish, by regulation, a procedure under which the Secretary may direct the operator of a concentrated airport to take such actions as may be necessary (including modification of existing contracts for the use of gates at the airport) to provide an eligible air carrier which petitions the Secretary for the right to use a gate at the airport during hours at which the gate is not being used. . . .

---

[46] H.R. 2074, 102nd Cong., 1st Sess. (1991); *see also* S. 2312, 102nd Cong., 2d Sess. (1992).

(e) *Definitions* . . .

(1). *Concentrated Airport.* — The term "concentrated airport" means an airport at which 1 or 2 air carriers have the right to use 60 percent of more of the gates.

A more radical proposal would have Congress pass a law prohibiting an airline from dominating more than 60% of the gates, landings, takeoffs, and passengers at more than a single airport. Further, an airline with a hub monopoly would be prohibited from having more than 25% of the gates, landings, takeoffs, and passengers at any other airport.[47]

e. REGULATION OF SERVICE

Members of Congress have proposed a number of bills that would regulate various aspects of airline service.[48] The assumption behind these proposals is that there is insufficient competition in the airline industry to guarantee acceptable levels of services and that regulation is therefore necessary. For example, the bills address what rights a flyer should have and how the airlines will have to compensate flyers for delays, cancellations, and other service-related items. Some bills, for example, would require prohibit airlines from selling non-refundable tickets. The airline lobby was able to head off the passage of any legislation by agreeing to adopt a joint commitment for improved service. The industry then incorporated new service terms in their contracts with passengers, although it is unlikely that a consumer would afford to sue over a contract violation since any remedy would be less than the cost of bringing the lawsuit.

NOTES AND QUESTIONS

1. A Brookings Institution study of airline deregulation estimated that an additional $2.5 billion in benefits were still available under deregulation if the industry became more competitive.[49] If consumers would benefit from more competition, what is the best way to accomplish this result? Which of the four solutions to a lack of landing slots and gates—expansion, auctions, congestion pricing, or restructuring slots and gates—is most likely to increase competition? Will there ever be enough competition to guarantee customers adequate service or is government regulation necessary?

2. Airlines, as you read, may have been able to stymie airport construction because they have exclusivity clauses that give them a veto over expansion plans. Are these clauses "efficient?" Consider the following argument:

> To run a hub properly—the efficient form of competition—an airline needs to ensure that it receives a great deal (and often the vast majority) of an airport's resources. It needs many gates near each other, access to rapid baggage handing, availability of repair facilities,

---

[47] DEMPSEY, *supra* note 4, at 51.

[48] *See* Ravitch, *supra* note 18, at 939–977; Field, *Bills Would Make Skies Friendlier*, U.SA TODAY, March 29, 1999, at 3B.

[49] Morrison & Winston, *Enhancing the Performance of the Deregulated Air Transportation System,* BROOKINGS PAPERS: MICROECONOMICS 1989, at 58.

and a good deal of other inputs. Exclusionary clauses are an effective way of ensuring that these services are received. Majority-in-interest clauses also often require the largest carrier to cover a large degree of the financial risk inherent in an airport's operation. . . . Given such responsibility, it is only natural that the carrier possesses the ability to limit its risk exposure by preventing overexpansion on the past of the airport authority. Thus, exclusionary clauses, while generating barriers to entry, also generate important efficiencies. . . . [50]

3. Morrison and Winston note the "long-standing political concerns that have mitigated against congestion pricing." What are these concerns? Do you favor congestion pricing? Is there any reason not to charge someone who wishes to fly when large numbers of other persons also wish to fly (thereby contributing to congestion problems) more money to fly (by charging the person's airline a higher takeoff or landing fee) than someone who is willing to fly in the middle of the day (and who thereby not only does not contribute to congestion problems, but helps eliminate them)?

4. Would you favor the use of congestion pricing in other situations where the lack of capacity causes congestion and delays? Consider the following analysis of traffic congestion:

The classic economist's prescription for dealing with traffic is for the government to impose "congestion fees," tolls for using roads during period of overcrowding. With modern technology, such tolls could even be collected without tollbooths: an electronic sensor could pick up the signal from a tiny gizmo on your dashboard, or a low powered laser could read a bar code on your windshield. The fees could be rebated to the public. . . . Most of those deterred from rush-hour driving would be more than compensated for their inconvenience through the rebate scheme. Those who continued to drive would be compensated for the extra tolls with a much faster trip to work. [51]

This is not entirely hypothetical. The Mayor of London, England has proposed a £7.50 charge for driving a car into the most congested areas of central London. [52] Would you favor this proposal? Are there "long-standing political concerns" that have deterred adoption of congestion pricing for highways?

5. Air carriers have engaged in various actions that have the potential to reduce competition. At least some of these actions may be subject to the antitrust laws, and the government has pursued some antitrust remedies. [53] Critics claim, however, that the government has not been vigilant enough in using the antitrust laws to protect and promote competition. The antitrust laws are implicated in two ways.

First, after deregulation, Congress assigned that responsibility to the Department of Transportation to approve mergers between airline companies.

---

[50] Kleit, *Competition Without Apology: Market Power and Entry in the Deregulated Airline Industry*, REGULATION, Summer, 1991, at 72–73.

[51] Krugman, *The Reform Obsession*, NEW YORK TIMES MAGAZINE, Apr. 7, 1996, at 36

[52] Harper, *Livingston Plans £7.50 Traffic Charge*, GUARDIAN, July 24, 2000, at 9.

[53] *E.g.,* Tolchin, *Suit by U.S. Says 8 Airlines Used Computer Fare Lists to Fix Prices*, NEW YORK TIMES, Dec. 22, 1992, at A1 (national edition).

Critics maintain that the DOT has been insufficiently vigilant in stopping mergers with anticompetitive potential.

Second, there are allegations that the airlines have managed to maintain their dominance in hubs by engaging in predatory pricing, which involves "the sacrifice of short-term profits in the expectation that these losses will be recouped in the future through the realization of monopoly profits."[54] Once competitors are driven out of business, the survivor firm will gain not only market share, but market power, which permits it to raise prices above competitive levels. Economists, however, are generally dubious about the willingness of firms to engage in predatory pricing. They note that once the survivor firm raises prices, it will attract new competition, which will prevent it from maintaining its market power for very long. In light of this analysis, the courts have had difficulty devising an appropriate test for when predatory conduct occurs, and antitrust scholars differ concerning the extent to which such conduct should be regulated.[55]

B. FARM PROGRAMS

The idea that "excessive competition" justifies government control of prices and entry in transportation is now discredited. But this concept remains the justification for the expensive farm programs supported by the federal government. The nature of the regulatory process in agricultural markets is quite complex. Our limited objective here is to permit you to consider the concept of excessive competition in another context. In particular, we ask you to consider the following issue: Is there a market flaw (excessive competition) that justifies the billions of dollars that consumers and taxpayers spend as the result of farm programs, or is it more likely that these programs are continued because of the political power of agribusiness?

1. THE HISTORY OF REGULATION

Prior to the depression in the 1930s the federal government had limited involvement in agricultural markets. The government's primary aim was to improve productivity through research and education.[56] Congress established support for land grant colleges in 1862 (Morrill Act), a system of state agricultural experiment stations in 1887 (Hatch Act), a cooperative federal-state Agricultural Extension Service in 1914 (Smith-Lever Act), and the teaching of vocational agriculture in highs schools in 1917 (Smith-Hughes Vocational Education Act).

a. NEW DEAL PROGRAMS

The roots of today's farm programs date back to the Great Depression.[57] Farm incomes in the early 1900s were unusually high as the result of food

---

[54] S. ROSS, PRINCIPLES OF ANTITRUST LAW 55-56 (1993).

[55] *Id.* at 56–57.

[56] E. PASOUR, AGRICULTURE AND THE STATE: MARKET PROCESSES AND BUREAUCRACY 49 (1990).

[57] P. NAVARRO, THE POLICY GAME: HOW SPECIAL INTERESTS ARE STEALING AMERICA 108–13 (1984).

and commodity demands generated by World War I. But when European farmers resumed production after the Armistice, domestic farm prices fell by more than 40% between 1919 and 1922. Because American farmers continued to produce large quantities of food, prices remained low for the remainder of the 1920s. In the 1930s, the Great Depression wreaked havoc among farmers already weakened by the events of the preceding decade. Books like *The Grapes of Wrath* dramatically illustrated this misery.

When President Roosevelt signed the Agricultural Adjustment Acts of 1933 and 1938, he established the foundation of today's programs. For the first time, the government began direct cash payments to producers. The objective was to raise farm incomes in a period of falling farm prices. The budget for the Department of Agriculture (USDA) increased to $1.2 billion in fiscal year 1935 from only $172 million in 1929.[58]

Once the government set a price higher than the market price, farmers were encouraged to overproduce a food or commodity. Can you explain why? Because the surpluses that resulted would further lower the market price of the commodity (and increase the amount of money the government would have to pay in price supports), the Roosevelt administration also established supply controls. Again, why? Peter Navarro explains:

> The controls included in the acts ranged from "plowing every third row under" to destroying part of the surpluses. The idea was to raise prices artificially through price supports to boost farm income and then eventually reduce supply through controls to ensure that the market price rose above support levels. Hence controls would eventually obviate the need for the support system's drain on the treasury—or so it was thought.[59]

b. POST-WAR PROGRAMS

Farm income rose during World War II when the United States furnished food and clothing to its military forces and its allies. Nevertheless, the government continued and expanded its support of the farm economy based on the justifications discussed later in the chapter.

Between 1933 and 1996, Congress enacted at least twenty-five major pieces of legislation designed to affect price and production. Some of these programs continued the government's efforts to increase productivity through education and research, while others continued and expanded income support programs and production limitations. Numerous commodities have been affected, including cotton, wool, sugar, tobacco, milk, rice, wheat, corn, soybeans, honey, and mohair (though not livestock, poultry, and vegetables).

Income support: The government has used various methods to support the income of farmers. Under "target price supports," USDA sets annual target prices for crops such as wheat, feed grains, and rice based on projections of supply and demand as well as the income needs of farmers. If the market price

[58] PASOUR, *supra* note 56, at 75.

[59] NAVARRO, *supra* note 57, at 109.

was less than the target price, the government provided a deficiency payment, equal to the difference between the market price and target price.

The government also provides income support by use of "nonrecourse loans." Under this system, a farmer takes out a government loan equivalent to the amount of money the farmer would receive under the support price for a food or commodity. If that food or commodity can be sold for more than the amount of the loan, the farmer is required to repay the loan. If, however, the farmer earns less than the loan, the farmer is entitled to default on the loan, and the government becomes owner of the crop. Because the loan is "nonrecourse" in this circumstance, the government will not force the farmer to repay the loan.

The government has also permitted groups of farmers to join agricultural cooperatives to jointly market their products without violating antitrust laws. Pursuant to the Agricultural Marketing Agreement Act of 1937,[60] Congress empowered the Department of Agriculture to issue "marketing orders" in order to maintain marketing conditions and fair prices for commodities. These orders are a form of economic regulation, which displaces competition. The orders promote collective action rather than independent competition. These orders can require uniform prices, set quality and quantity standards, determine the grade and size of a commodity, and allocate any surplus that might depress market prices. For example, about 80 percent of Grade A milk in the United States is sold to purchasers (daily producers) under federal marketing orders. Most of the rest is marketed under similar state orders. Under each order, a regulator establishes a minimum price for fluid milk. Farmers sell as much milk as is demanded at the minimum price and the rest is channeled into manufacturing uses. The orders also involve joint research and development projects, inspection procedures, and standardized packaging requirements. In addition, the marketing orders have been imposed to collect funds from affected producers to be used for research and development as well as to be used for advertising promotion.

Production limits: The government has also resorted to protection controls in the form of acreage allotments or marketing quotas. When American agriculture took a nose dive in the 1980s, for example, the Reagan administration responded with the Payment-in-Kind (PIK) Program, which paid farmers to reduce the number of acres they cultivated. Some farmers received cash payments to reduce production, and others received surplus crops, which they were permitted to sell.

c. THE 1996 AGRICULTURAL IMPROVEMENT AND REFORM ACT (FAIR ACT)

In 1996, Congress passed a major revision of federal support for agriculture.[61] Initially, the new legislation was intended to phase out farm subsidies over a period of time in order to allow the agricultural market to function in a traditional free market system. However, the 1996 FAIR Act was only temporary by design, legislated to last only 7 years. The FAIR Act established

---

[60] 7 U.S.C. § 601 *et seq.* (1994).

[61] Pub. L. No. 104-127, 110 Stat. 888 (1996).

a fixed, slightly declining system of payments to farmers through the year 2002. Total payments were to start at $5.6 billion and decline to $4 billion in the last year of the program.

Farmers obtained two significant advantages from the new program. First, they are eligible for these government subsidies regardless of the level of farm prices. In fact, farmers were able to sell their commodities at record level prices in 1996.[62] Second, the legislation abolished government-mandated production controls, permitting farmers to plant as much as they desired, and thus dubbing the legislation the "Freedom to Farm Act." The new legislation continued existing programs for sugar, peanuts, and dairy products, although farmers of these products received additional income support.[63]

Despite the apparent desire to end the agricultural welfare program being run by the federal government, a decline in the market price of commodities in 1997 caused a rise in the amount of direct payments government would make to farmers. Critics of FAIR reported that once prices fell sharply in 1997, farmers received much less support than under previous legislation. Congress responded with emergency ad hoc legislation that included new disaster relief and crop insurance subsidies, and most importantly, supplemental annual appropriations. These new appropriations would cause direct government payments to farmers to increase to over $20 billion each year during the final three years of the legislation. Direct governmental payments to farmers provided more than 40% of net farm income during that same period.[64]

d. THE FARM SECURITY AND RURAL INVESTMENT ACT OF 2002

On May 13, 2002, President Bush signed the Farm Security and Rural Investment Act of 2002 ("The 2002 Farm Bill").[65] A Congressional election year law, the 2002 Farm Bill diverges from the free market ideas of the 1996 Federal Agricultural Improvement Act (FAIR) by creating guaranteed levels of aid to farmer that vastly exceed previous aid packages. In total, the 2002 Farm Bill authorized $73.5 billion in new spending over its ten-year lifespan, putting the government on course to spend approximately $20 billion annually to aid American agriculture. According to preliminary cost estimates from the Congressional Budget Office, the 2002 Farm Bill authorizes somewhere between $111 billion to $117 billion to be spent on Agriculture Department programs through the year 2007.[66]

2. THE JUSTIFICATION FOR REGULATION

Now that we have described the history of farm regulation down to the present time, what policies are furthered through these programs? Can the enormous amount of money that is spent on farm price supports be justified

---

[62] Epstein, *Farm Bill A Bumper Crop of Handouts*, ARIZONA REPUBLIC, Mar. 26, 1996, at B5.

[63] Price Supports Continue to Milk Producers, USA TODAY, Feb. 28, 1996, at 10A.

[64] Orden, *Reform's Stunted Crop*, REGULATION, April 1, 2002, Vol. 25, Issue 1.

[65] Pub. Law No. 107-171, 116 Stat. 134 (2002).

[66] Rogers, *House Passes Massive Farm Bill -With Billions in Subsidies, Measure is Partial Retreat From Free Market Policies*, THE WALL STREET JOURNAL, May 3, 2002, at A12.

or is it simply the product of the political power of agricultural interests and the politicians who represent them?

The original justification for farm programs was the deep depression of the farm economy during the 1920s and 1930s.[67] The Roosevelt administration wanted to prop up farm incomes to keep farmers in business and ensure adequate food to feed the nation. At the same time, income support was a general economic stimulus because such a large percentage of the population lived on farms. In 1935, there were 6.8 million farmers in the United States, which meant that one-quarter of the population lived on farms.[68]

Although World War II ended the farm depression, supporters argued that farm programs should continue because free markets were subject to excessive competition, which creates a boom and bust cycle.[69] At the start of the cycle, farmers will expand production in an attempt to maximize their income. Overproduction forces down commodity prices and farm income, which forces farmers out of business. Shortages develop because there are fewer farmers, which will drive up prices. Farm production will eventually expand to meet demand and then the cycle will start over. As a result of the cycle, farm program supporters argue that a free market will not produce food and fiber at stable, affordable prices.

Farm markets are subject to overproduction because farmers have the capacity to produce more food and fiber than is demanded. Farm productivity has expanded dramatically because of technological innovations, such as mechanization, improved quality of seeds, and the development of new pesticides and herbicides. By comparison, the demand for food and fiber, which is a product of the size of the population and its wealth, has grown more slowly. This imbalance is said to produce a chronic oversupply, which puts downward pressure on farm incomes.[70] At the same time, farmers are threatened by the risks inherent in farming. They are subject to wide swings in economic outcomes due to national and global forces of nature (weather, insects, etc.), money exchange markets and government policies, which make it difficult to survive financially.

If farm programs make it less likely that farmers will go out of business during periods of low farm prices, market cycles should be mitigated. Although low prices will reduce supply, farm income will remain stable because of the price supports. Because lower prices will not drive as many farmers out of business, more farmers will be in a position to respond to shortages by additional planting.

Advocates for farm programs also assert that "family farming" is a "way of life" worthy of protection in and of itself.[71] This claim has strong historical origins. As we quoted Arthur Schlesinger, Jr. in Chapter 1, Thomas Jefferson

---

[67] Meyer, The E.C. Common Agricultural Policy (unpublished manuscript).

[68] Learn, Martin, & McCalla, *American Farm Subsidies: A Bumper Crop*, 84 PUB. INTEREST 66, 70 (1986).

[69] NAVARRO, *supra* note 57, at 121–22; PASOUR, *supra* note 56 at 18.

[70] PASOUR, *supra* note 56, at 61.

[71] *See generally* J. Antle & D. Sumner (eds.), THE ECONOMICS OF AGRICULTURE: SELECTED PAPERS OF D. GALE JOHNSON (2 vols. 1996).

"saw America as a paradise of small farms, a rural Arcadia with every freeholder secure under his own vine and fig tree.'" Jefferson himself wrote, "'Those who labor in the earth are the chosen people of God. . . . Corruption of morals in the mass of cultivators is a phenomenon of which no nation has furnished an example."[72] Legislators endorse this Jeffersonian concept of the virtue and importance of family farming. The preamble to one food program, for example, states that "'the maintenance of the family farm system of agriculture is essential to the social well being of the nation."[73]

NOTES AND QUESTIONS

1. Given the complexity of agricultural markets, and the regulation of them, assessing whether regulation is necessary to stabilize farm markets is difficult based on the limited materials used here, or perhaps even with wider exposure to such information. What is clear is that federal and state governments are not likely to end agricultural price-setting or subsidy programs any time soon. These programs will therefore remain the most prominent example of price-setting justified on the basis of excess competition.

2. Why are agricultural markets cyclical? Does the impact of these cycles on consumers warrant government intervention? The government does not augment the income of other types of producers or manufacturers in order to mitigate businesses cycles. Is there something special about agricultural markets that require such intervention?

3. Are farm price support programs justified on an economic basis, a non-economic basis, or both? Why should the country be concerned that farmers will go out of business because of conditions beyond their control? Is it a matter of fairness to help farmers because they are subject to changes in economic conditions, climate, and other factors? Or is there some market flaw that farm price supports address? Is it realistic that the country would face food shortages if we did not have economic price support programs?

4. Why is preserving the family farm a legitimate policy objective? Other types of family businesses have been unable to compete successfully with the national chains that dominate retailing and food sales. For example, after Walmart comes to town, small retailers are quickly driven out of business. Yet, the country has not chosen to save these businesses. A recent commentator cites three arguments generally given for preserving family farms. First, family farming is simply a "way of life" that should be protected because it is valuable in and of itself. Second, family farming most efficiently contributes to the critical agricultural sector of our economy. Finally, family farms should be preserved because this is a way of preserving rural areas and that this is the most appropriate use of rural land.[74] Do you agree?

---

[72] THOMAS JEFFERSON, NOTES ON VIRGINIA, IN BASIC WRITINGS OF THOMAS JEFFERSON 161 (P. Foner ed. 1944), *quoted in* Bahls, *Preservation of Family Farms — The Way Ahead*, 45 DRAKE L.J. 311, 232 (1997).

[73] Agricultural and Food Act of 1981, Pub. L. No. 97-98, 95 Stat. 1213 (codified as amended at 7 U.S.C. § 2266 (1994)), *quoted in* Hamilton, *Reaping What We Have Sown: Public Policy Consequences of Agricultural Industrialization and Legal Implications of a Changing System*, 45 DRAKE L. REV. 289, 323 (1997).

[74] Bahls, *supra* note 72, at 322–23.

3. REGULATORY REFORM

Although agricultural markets are subject to cyclical conditions which threaten farmers, critics claim that the extraordinary cost of farm programs subsidized at the federal or state level very likely exceeds their benefits. They also doubt the value of maintaining the "family farm" and contend existing programs fail to achieve this objective in any case. Consider the following evaluation of farm programs offered by the Department of Agriculture at the start of the Bush administration:

UNITED STATES DEPARTMENT OF AGRICULTURE, FOOD AND AGRICULTURAL POLICY: TAKING STOCK FOR THE NEW CENTURY 6–7, 47–51 (2001)

More than seven decades of farm policy have provided a rich, full experience upon which to draw as we contemplate appropriate 21st century policies for our industry. . . .

Many of the program approaches since the 1930s proved not to work well or not at all, produced unexpected and unwanted consequences, became far costlier than expected, and have been continually modified in our long succession of farm laws. The Federal Agricultural Improvement and Reform (FAIR) Act of 1996 removed much of the decades-old program structure, provided unparalleled farmer decision-making flexibility through "decoupled" benefits, and set a new example throughout the world for providing domestic farm sector support. While that approach still is arguably the least market- and resource-use-distorting approach available, its direct payments do share some unintended effects with price support programs, namely, the artificial inflation of farm land prices. The effect clearly has been exacerbated by the size of payments in recent years, some $28 billion in the last 4 years above the amount provided in the 1996 law.

Because of their historical evolution, current program benefits still are largely directed to specific commodity producers reaching only about 40 percent of our farms. And, there still is no direct relationship between benefits received and financial status of the farm.

Our current broad-scale, commodity-oriented approach to farm support does not recognize existing wide differences in production costs, marketing approaches, or overall management capabilities that delineate competitive and noncompetitive operations. For example, highly efficient commercial farms benefit enormously from price supports, enabling them to expand their operations and lower costs even more. Other farms have not received enough benefits to remain viable and have been absorbed along the way.

Another unintended consequence of current programs stems from the increasing disconnect between land ownership and farm operation. While program benefits were intended to help farm operators, most support eventually accrues to landowners, in the short run through rising rental rates and in the longer term through capitalization into land values. For many farm operators, renting land is a key strategy to expand the size of the business and capture the size economies, as evidenced by 42 percent of farms renting land in 1999. Clearly, operators farming mostly rented acreage may receive little benefit from the programs. . . .

Principles for Farm Policy

Pay heed to lessons learned. Above all, effective farm policies for the new century must build upon the lessons learned form over seven decades of rich experience with the farm programs. Even the most carefully designed government intervention distorts markets and resource allocation, produces unintended consequences, and spreads benefits unevenly. We cannot afford to keep relearning the lessons of the past.

Recognize our new operating environment. Our farm sector and food system operate today in a new and evolving business and social environment. It is a competitive, consumer-driven environment, global and rapidly changing with enormous implications for the place and role of the farm sector in the overall food system. It is highly interdependent, blending the efforts of many industries to add value to farm sector products.

Continually expand our commitment to open markets. The United States is thoroughly committed to market-oriented policies, well understood to serve the best long-term interests of all stakeholders in the food system and society at large. Markets have continually demonstrated their superiority to other alternatives in guiding allocation of resources, investment, and production in patterns that are most beneficial to society at large. Still, this commitment needs to be renewed and expanded. . . .

Accommodate and build on the farm sector's wide diversity. Effective agricultural policies must recognize the wide diversity in the farm sector itself, in terms of size, location, financial status, crop and livestock products produced, managerial abilities, income sources, and goals and aspirations. The problems faced by these groups are widely different and require solutions tailored effectively to address particular needs. Failure to do so only exacerbates the problems and postpones the day of reckoning.

Provide a market-oriented economic safety net for farmers. The national recognition that the farm sector is both unique and essential is long standing and widely held. The result is a parallel commitment to policies that support open markets and those that prevent precipitate downturns in the farm sector. Thus, these programs must conform to basic public policy principles including effectiveness, transparency, equity, consistency, and comprehensiveness. Current policies now take several forms, including countercyclical loans, crop and revenue insurance, and direct payments, but they could be constructed with other programs (such as tax-deferred income accounts) that fully comply with such principles. . . .

The Economic "Safety Net"

While strong arguments can be made for solutions for specific problems, common principles apply to all programs that support the diversity of American farms. Foremost, our strongly held view is that agricultural policy must recognize that the marketplace is the best guide for allocating resources and provides the most objective reward for efficiency and good management. But, that does not rule out helping farmers and ranchers when unexpected events beyond their control occur and cause output or income to plummet. The challenge, of course, is to provide an adequate safety net without encouraging sustained dependence on government. Safety net interventions should not obscure needed adjustments in outputs and markets that inevitably must occur, nor should they fail to reflect that the functioning of competitive markets must cover the entire food system in today's dynamic, consumer-driven agriculture.

The idea of a "safety net" is becoming much more encompassing than the traditional price and income support. This modern view has been dramatically emphasized in recent years, when we have seen the entire agriculture infrastructure placed under great stress from food safety concerns and the potentially devastating losses to producers (food-and-mouth disease and BSE in Europe, for example). These and other events have underscored the need for protection from plant and animal diseases and pests, new research on testing, more widespread monitoring, research to maintain and improve competitiveness in world markets, buttressing the foundation for sanitary and phytosanitary measures in trade agreements, and generating more attention to food safety and the integrity of the entire food system. Arguably, the policy focus on the past 4 years has distracted us from focusing on these fundamental aspects of a safety net for the entire food system for the benefit of not only the farmer but the consuming public as well.

———

To what extent does the 2002 Farm Bill meet the goals and criticisms of the previous report? What are its advantages and disadvantages?

Budget Stability: Proponents of the 2002 Farm Bill espouse the budgetary stability created by the new agricultural legislation in that it prevents the need for the annual ad hoc appropriations legislation that Congress has felt necessary under the FAIR Act in order to provide American farmers some measure of income stability.[75] In fact, Title I of the 2002 Farm Bill seeks to stabilize farming income through the continued use of fixed annual payments to farmers, loan price supports, and a revised target-price program similar to those in existence prior to the 1996 FAIR Act.[76]

Although it is impossible to predict whether or not specific legislation will actually accomplish the goals its sets forth, it seems likely that the 2002 Farm Bill will at least accomplish its goal of providing more concrete budgetary figures regarding agricultural spending to allow for more accurate economic projections. In providing levels of aid that are substantially similar to those provided by ad hoc legislation over the last few years, it appears this goal of budgetary stability is reachable.

---

[75] Secretary of Agriculture Ann M. Veneman, *Letters to the Editor: In Defense of the Farm Bill,* THE WALL STREET JOURNAL, May 28, 2002, at A19.

[76] Rogers, *Congress's Agriculture Measure to Aid More Than Just Farmers,* THE WALL STREET JOURNAL, April 29, 2002, at A4.

Nonetheless, it is impossible to foresee certain economic changes that may cause a change in the level of aid required by farmers, such as the severe drop of commodities prices in 1997. The 2002 Farm Bill will only provide budgetary stability if Congress can prevent itself from passing ad hoc appropriations legislation for agricultural spending similar to those bills Congress has promulgated since 1997. Considering the lack of budgetary restraint Congress has shown in the past, only time will tell if the 2002 Farm Bill has accomplished its goals of budgetary stability.

Rural Development: Another of the goals of the Farm Security and Rural Investment Act of 2002 is rural development. Title VI of the 2002 Farm Bill provides $1.03 billion in federal funds ensure Americans may maintain their rural existence without being handicapped by a lack of technology or business funding.[77] Congress has earmarked $100 million to make available funds to businesses to provide rural consumers with high-speed, high-quality broadband service. In addition, the 2002 Farm Bill budget allows $100 million to provide $280 million in guarantees for rural business investment companies to provide equity investment for businesses. Finally, in light of recent events and the increased concern over safety and terrorist activities, Congress has provided $50 million in funding to train rural firefighters and emergency personnel.

Cost: The most often heard complaint regarding the Farm Security and Rural Investment Act of 2002 is its largesse. Many critics claim the bill creates upward of a 70 percent increase in agricultural spending. While this figure is technically accurate when viewing spending authorized by the 1996 FAIR Act in comparison with the 2002 Farm Bill, that statement is somewhat misleading. When one considers the annual emergency appropriates bills passed by Congress to give aid to farmers, the 2002 Farm Bill is basically maintaining present aid levels. If Congress can prevent itself from appropriating even more funds each year, the 2002 Farm Bill should account for no considerably larger agricultural spending than previous years. However, critics are wary of the 2002 Farm Bill because it approves a high level of agricultural spending and provides no guarantee that more funds will not be appropriated.

Distribution of Benefits: The other major concern about the increased agricultural spending in the 2002 Farm Bill is one that is very familiar. Who is really getting the money? History has shown us that a considerable portion of the subsidies go to huge agribusinesses, not the small, family-farmer whom politicians claim Americans need to save by subsidizing the income of these small farms. The federal government has distributed approximately $71 billion in agricultural subsidies over the last five (5) years. Approximately two-thirds (2/3) of that $71 billion went to only ten (10) percent of United States farms.[78]

By basing payment on acreage, not need, government has no choice by to give larger sums of money to large farms. History has shown that increased

---

[77] Farm Bill Conference Summary, April 30, 2002, *available at* agriculture.senate.gov/Briefs/2001FarmBill.conframe.htm.

[78] *The Farm State Pig-Out, Review and Outlook* (Editorial), THE WALL STREET JOURNAL, May 2, 2002, at A14.

guaranteed subsidies lead to increased production. The increased production leads to even lower prices, causing a need for even greater subsidies. These businesses realize that they can make the most money by utilizing the target-price payments and loan deficiency payments. They can harvest huge surpluses of crops that have no market and be paid a set amount for those surpluses by the government through the use of the aforementioned programs.

These large-scale farmers also defeated a measure that would have limited the amount of loan deficiency payments to $275,000 per farm per year. The 2002 Farm Bill sets a limit of $360,000 per farm per year for loan deficiency payments and provides a loophole to write off much more if necessary.[79] The free spending does not end there. The 2002 Farm Bill increases crop payments to North Dakota by 68 percent this year alone and by over 60 percent over the life of the bill.[80] In a Congressional election year where control of the Senate is thought to hinge upon elections in such farm states as South Dakota, Iowa, Missouri, and Arkansas, keeping farming constituents happy is a top priority for politicians seeking to maintain or gain control of the senior house of Congress.

Environmental Protection: Another major provision of the 2002 Farm Bill is the greatly increased commitment to environmental protection found in the Title II – Conservation section of the bill. According to the Congressional Budget Office, the 2002 Farm Bill allocates approximately 20% of the $73.5 billion in new spending to Conservation programs.[81] Title II reauthorizes most existing conservation program while enacting several new ones. For example, the current Environmental Quality Incentives Program (EQIP), which seeks to encourage farmers and ranchers to adopt environmentally friendly practices by providing education, technical assistance and financial assistance, will see a budgetary increase from $200 million in FY2002 to $1.3 billion in FY2007. The new programs include the Conservation Security Program, which will provide payments to farmers for maintaining or adopting structural and land management practices that address a wide range of national and local environmental resource concerns.

While the 2002 Farm Bill goes far beyond any previous conservation legislation, it is difficult to determine if the new bill will provide better environmental protection. The new bill does provide considerably more funding to existing programs than they have received, but there appears to be very little innovation in the 2002 Farm Bill regarding conservation. The 2002 Farm Bill focuses more on increasing funding and amending existing programs than on creating new programs.

It appears that by passing the 2002 Farm Bill, Congress has resigned itself to continued use of subsidies, likely in increased amounts, to make American farmers economically secure. Should history repeat itself, and there is substantial evidence that history does repeat itself, the 2002 Farm Bill may create

---

[79] Rogers, *House Passes Massive Farm Bill -With Billions in Subsidies, Measure is Partial Retreat From Free-Market Policies*, THE WALL STREET JOURNAL, May 3, 2002, at A12.

[80] Congressman Earl Pomeroy, *Congressman Earl Pomoroy Newsroom*, May 7, 2002, www.house.gov/pomoroy/prfbnorthdakota.html.

[81] Zinn, *Soil and Water Conservation Issues*, Issue Brief for Congress, May 17, 2002, Congressional Research Service.

budgetary stability over the life of the bill, but it appears the 2002 Farm Bill will also create an even greater need for agricultural subsidization. It appears that Congress has chosen to focus on short-term goals such as budgetary stability as opposed to developing an agricultural policy that will reduce American farmers' dependency upon subsidies. According to Rep. John Boehner (R) – Ohio, "We're going back to what we know didn't work."[82] Does history repeat itself?

NOTES AND QUESTIONS

1. We have learned some interesting things about the regulation of agriculture chiefly that it is historically persistent, economically questionable, and seemingly politically stable. If policymakers were writing on a clean slate, what type of policy would they write? Would a pristine policy eliminate or continue support programs and why? If farmers are subject to boom-and-bust cycles and to the vagaries of nature and world markets, does a more fully developed insurance program hedging against financial risk make more sense? If so what role, if any, should the federal government play? What would the insurance cover? Should target support payments continue to protect "family farmers?" Should support payments be used to encourage and reward farm efficiencies? Invention? Environmental protection?

2. How does Secretary Veneman's farm policy differ from the FAIR Act and from the New Deal farm program?

3. Compare the 2002 Farm Bill with the FAIR Act. Which is more market-oriented? Arguably Republicans and conservatives are more market-oriented than Democrats and liberals (although we hasten to add this difference is simply a matter of degree). How, then, do you explain the more market-oriented Clinton approach compared with the less market-oriented Bush program?

4. Who are the winners and losers under the 2000 Farm Bill? What does Secretary Veneman mean by "safety net?" In providing a safety net, should large-scale farmers be subsidized more, less, or the same as small-scale farmers?

How does this "safety-net" differ from what we ordinarily consider to be a welfare program?

5. Although price supports have stayed relatively intact, there have been significant effects of agricultural deregulation under the 1996 Agricultural Act. Under federal price guarantees, farmers were left with relatively narrow decisions about what to plant. With their deregulation farmers can engage in crop switching and in planting fields that were once left fallow under price supports. As a consequence, farmers familiar with planting one crop need advice on new crops as well as new investment in different seed, machinery, chemicals, and other supplies. As a result, more money is at risk and, as always, farmers are dependent on the weather. Excessively bad weather, of course, ruins a crop. Excessively good weather brings too much to market, thus lowering prices. Not surprisingly, futures markets are particularly

---

[82] Rogers, *supra* note 79.

vigorous given the great degree of uncertainty. The mediating force in this new dynamic agricultural market is the transition payments under the Act. The 2002 Farm Bill seems to have returned to more traditional policies.

6. In a recent book, Bruce L. Gardner arrives at some conclusions about agricultural policy.[83] Gardner writes that there are certain facts about agriculture, including that farm population has declined, that we have roughly one-third the number of farms today that we had in 1930; at the same time, agricultural output has doubled which means that farm size has increased. He also notes that acreage has remained relatively constant and productivity has increased at a sustained rate since 1940. Finally, farm household income, which historically had been less than non-farm income in the first half of the 20th century has now reached parity. He also notes that farms have changed their economic structure. They have become more specialized, larger, have concentrated on particular forms of production, and have diversified sources of farm household income. This is especially true with smaller farm households:

> Farms selling less than $100,000 annually in farm products, which amounted to 80 percent of all farms in the late 1990s, earn more than 90 percent of their household income from off-farm sources. This in itself means that the returns from agricultural production will be heavily concentrated in the larger farms; indeed, in 1996, farms with more than $250,000 in sales (less than 10 percent of all farms) accounted for more than 85 percent of net cash income.

In short, we have seen an increase in productivity and an increase in farm income. Gardner goes on to explain that there are four possible factors for the situation including: (1) new agricultural technology; (2) sophisticated agricultural commodity markets; (3) integration of farm people into non-farm economy; and, (4) government policies including commodity programs. He further notes that an important feature of the growth in farm income is integration of farm and non-farm economies.

4. POLITICS AND REGULATION

If the current farm programs are difficult to defend on policy grounds, why have they been continued and even expanded? Do farm programs serve private, rather than public, interests? Are benefits of a program concentrated among a relatively small group of persons, and are the costs spread out over thousands of persons? Do the interest groups whose members receive the benefits dominate the political process? By comparison, is there little opposition, because the individual cost to any person is so small? The cost to the taxpayers as a whole, however, can be quite large.

Professor Pasour explains the dynamics of client politics concerning agricultural legislation:

> Suppose one hundred people go out to eat. Compare the likely behavior of each individual under two different situations. In the first procedure, each person pays his own bill; in the second the bill is divided

---

[83] B. GARDNER, AMERICAN AGRICULTURE IN THE TWENTIETH CENTURY: HOW IT FLOURISHED AND WHAT IT COST (2002).

evenly. Each individual has an incentive to spend more in the latter case since eating a one-dollar desert under the check-splitting arrangement, for example, would cost the individual only one cent (rather than one dollar). This check splitting arrangement in the collective-choice process leads to "pork barrel" legislation in agriculture and other areas. Since the amount a legislative district will pay toward a diary price-support program (or other federally funded project) is very small relative to its total cost, every representative in Congress has an incentive to obtain income transfers for farmers (and other special-interest groups) in his or her legislative district.[84]

Moreover, as Pasour explains, the committee structure in Congress creates an additional incentive to support farm interests:

> The analogy of the federal budget to a dinner check can be carried on step further. Suppose the check is divided evenly among the large group but the ordering will be done by committee so there will be separate committees for drinks, appetizers, entrees, salads, and desserts. Since each person is able to serve on the committee of his (or her) choice, lushes end up on the drinks committee, vegetarians on the salad committee, sweet-tooths on the dessert committee, and so. This arrangement further exacerbates the tendency toward overordering and overspending. The arrangement just described closely resembles the committee structure of the U.S. Congress.[85]

As Pasour indicates, farm-state legislators dominate the agricultural committees in both houses. This has two effects. First, it guarantees support for farm programs in those committees. Second, members of the agricultural committees are able to engage in log-rolling with other committees which seek to extend other federal benefits.[86]

NOTES AND QUESTIONS

1. In a newspaper account of the signing of the 2002 Farm Bill, it was reported:

> President Bush this morning reversed six years of Republican efforts to wean farmers from huge government subsidies signing into law a bill that increased those federal payments by at least $83 billion over the next 10 years. Mr. Bush signed the bill at the Eisenhower Executive Office Building next door to the White House before traveling here. "It's not a perfect bill, I know that," he told farm state lawmakers. "But, you know, no bill ever is." Mr. Bush also said the bill would provide a safety net for farmers "without encouraging overproduction and depressing prices' while giving farmers an opportunity 'to plan and operate based on market realities, not government dictates."[87]

---

[84] PASOUR, *supra* note 56, at 55.

[85] *Id.* at 55–56.

[86] W. BROWNE, ET. AL., SACRED COWS AND HOT POTATOES: AGRARIAN MYTHS IN AGRICULTURAL POLICY 128 (1992).

[87] Sanger, *Reversing Course, Bush Signs Bill Raising Farm Subsidies*, N.Y. TIMES, May 14, 2002, at A16.

2. The continuation of farm subsidies has persisted through Democratic and Republican presidential administrations and Congresses. Why? Perhaps the answer to the question about the persistence of farm subsidies was given in the article just quoted in which Sanger writes:

> Many of his aides, speaking on condition of anonymity, said signing the bill was painful for a president who came to office promoting a government commitment to free markets. But one senior official traveling with Mr. Bush here today said it would have been 'political suicide in the November election' to stand in the way of farm-state politicians who demanded huge increases in federal support after years of declining farm prices.

3. Professor Kelley[88] opposes means-testing for farm programs because they will then have the functions and attributes of welfare. He worries that the country will be unwilling to support generous payments to farmers if the payments are perceived as "welfare." Kelley's insight is confirmed by the fact that critics of farm programs (and other similar government subsidies) characterize them as "corporate welfare" in the hope that this term will generate public opposition.

5. REGULATORY TOOLS

As noted, a fundamental tool of United States farm policy involves financial support for specific products through various means such as counter-cyclical payments, direct payments, and non-recourse loans.[89] The following provisions of the 1996 FAIR Act and the 2002 Farm Bill set out those commodity provisions.

---

[88] Kelly, *Rethinking The Equities of Federal Farm Programs*, 14 N. ILL. L. REV. 659 (1994).

[89] These terms are defined by the Department of Agriculture for the 2002 Farm Bill as follows:

Counter-cyclical payments: Counter-cyclical payments are available to eligible commodities under the 2002 Farm Act whenever the effective commodity price is less than the target price. The effective price is equal to the sum of (1) the higher of the national average farm price for the marketing year, or the commodity national loan rate and (2) the direct payment rate for the commodity. The payment amount for a farmer equals the product of the payment rate, the payment acres, and the payment yield. Payments are considered counter-cyclical since they vary inversely with market prices.

Direct payment: Fixed payments provided under the 2002 Farm Act for eligible producers of wheat, corn, barley, grain sorghum, oats, upland cotton, rice, soybeans, other oilseeds, and peanuts. Producers enroll annually int he program to receive payments based on payment rates specified in the 2002 Farm Act and their historic program payment acres and yields.

Nonrecourse loan program: Provides commodity-secured loans to producers for a specified period of time (typically 9 months), after which the producer may either repay the loan and accrued interest or transfer ownership of the commodity pledged as collateral to the Commodity Credit Corporation (CCC) as full settlement of the loan, without penalty. These loans are available on a crop year basis for wheat, feed grains, cotton, peanuts, tobacco, rice, and oilseeds. Sugar processors are also eligible for nonrecourse loans. Participants in commodity loan programs agree to store and maintain a certain quantity of a commodity as loan collateral, for which they receive loan funds from the CCC based on the announced commodity-specific, per-unit loan rate. The loans are called nonrecourse because, at the producer's option, the CCC has no recourse but to accept the commodity as full settlement of the loan. For those commodities eligible for marketing loan benefits, producers may repay the loan at the world price (rice and upland cotton) or posted county price.

Commodity programs were established in the early decades of the 20th Century for the purpose of supporting and stabilizing markets. More precisely for the purpose of supporting and stabilizing farmers' income. These programs began in the early 1920s and became entrenched during the New Deal and continue to this day for such products as dairy, sugar and grains.

The regulatory tool of choice for commodity programs is quantity or supply control. If a regulator wishes to prop up a farmer's income, how does a supply control achieve that end? Quite simply, prices rise as supply decreases. The next question is: How can supply be decreased? One method is through acreage allotments, which restrict the areas in which a farmer can plant. Do acreage restrictions control supply? Not necessarily, especially if a farmer can coax more product from an acre. Another method is to simply restrict the amount that a farmer can sell on the market. But what about excess supply? Should farmers be allowed to place such excess on foreign markets at world prices? Below are excerpts for peanut commodity programs in the Fair Act of 1996 and the Farm Bill of 2002. Which regulatory tools are contained in these excerpts? Which are supply controls? What other controls are used?

FEDERAL AGRICULTURAL IMPROVEMENT AND REFORM ACT OF 1996

P.L. 104-127, 110 Stat. 922

(a) QUOTA PEANUTS.—

(1) AVAILABILITY OF LOANS.–The Secretary shall make nonrecourse loans available to producers of quota peanuts.

(2) LOAN RATE.–The national average quota loan rate for quota peanuts shall be $610 per ton.

(3) INSPECTION, HANDLING, OR STORAGE.–The loan amount may not be reduced by the Secretary by any deductions for inspection, handling, or storage.

(4) LOCATION AND OTHER FACTORS.–The Secretary may make adjustments in the loan rate for quota peanuts for location of peanuts and such other factors as are authorized by section 162.

(5) OFFERS FROM HANDLERS.–If a producer markets a quota peanut crop, meeting quality requirements for domestic edible use, through the marketing association loan for two consecutive marketing years and the Secretary determines that a handler provided the producer with a written offer, upon delivery, for the purchase of the quota peanut crops at a price equal to or in excess of the quota support price, the producer shall be ineligible for quota price support for the next marketing year. The Secretary shall establish the method by which a producer may appeal a determination under this paragraph regarding ineligibility for quota price support.

(b) ADDITIONAL PEANUTS.—

(1) IN GENERAL.–Subject to paragraph (2), the Secretary shall make nonrecourse loans available to producers of additional peanuts at such rates as the Secretary finds appropriate, taking into consideration the demand for peanut oil and peanut meal, expected prices of other vegetable oils and protein meals, and the demand for peanuts in foreign markets.

(2) LIMITATION.–The Secretary shall establish the support rate on additional peanuts at a level estimated by the Secretary to ensure that there are no losses to the Commodity Credit Corporation on the sale or disposal of the peanuts.

(3) ANNOUNCEMENT.— The Secretary shall announce the loan rate for additional peanuts of each crop not later than February 15 preceding the marketing year for the crop for which the loan rate is being determined.

(c) AREA MARKETING ASSOCIATIONS.—

   (1) WAREHOUSE STORAGE LOANS.—

      (A) IN GENERAL.–In carrying out subsections (a) and (b), the Secretary shall make warehouse storage loans available in each of the producing areas (described in section 1446.95 of title 7 of the code of Federal Regulations (January 1, 1989)) to a designated area marketing association of peanut producers that is selected and approved by the Secretary and that is operated primarily for the purpose of conducting the loan activities. The Secretary may not make warehouse storage loans available to any cooperative that is engaged in operations or activities specified in this section and section 358e of the Agricultural Adjustment Act of 1938 (7 U.S.C. 1359a).

      (B) ADMINISTRATIVE AND SUPERVISORY ACTIVITIES.— An area marketing association shall be used in administrative and supervisory activities relating to loans and marketing activities under this section and section 358e of the Agricultural Adjustment Act of 1938 (7 U.S.C. 1359a).

      (C) ASSOCIATION COSTS.— Loans made to the association under this paragraph shall include such costs as the area marketing association reasonably may incur in carrying the association under this section and section 358e of the Agricultural Adjustment Act of 1938 (7 U.S.C. 1359a).

   (2) POOLS FOR QUOTA AND ADDITIONAL PEANUTS.—

      (A) IN GENERAL.–The Secretary shall require that each area marketing association records are area and segregation for quota peanuts handled under loan and for additional peanuts placed under loan, except the separate pools shall be established for Valencia peanuts produced in New Mexico. . . .

FARM SECURITY AND RURAL INVESTMENT ACT OF 2002

P.L. No. 107-171, 116 Stat. 134   –Peanuts

In this subtitle:

(1) BASE ACRES FOR PEANUTS.–The term "base acres for peanuts" means the number of acres assigned to a farm by historic peanut producers pursuant to section 1302(b).

(2) COUNTER-CYCLICAL PAYMENT.–The term "counter-cyclical payment" means a payment made under section 1304.

(3) EFFECTIVE PRICE–The term "effective price" means the price calculated by the Secretary under section 1304 for peanuts to determine whether counter-cyclical payments are required to be made under that section for a crop year.

(4) DIRECT PAYMENT–The term "direct payment" means a payment made under section 1303.

(5) HISTORIC PEANUT PRODUCER.–The term "historic peanut producer" means a producer on a farm in the United States that produced or was prevented from planting peanuts during any or all of the 1998 through 2001 crop years.

(6) PAYMENT ACRES.–The term "payment acres means–

    (A)   for the 2002 crop of peanuts, 85 percent of the average acreage determined under section 1302(a)(2) for an historic peanut producer; and

    (B)   for the 2003 through 2007 crops of peanuts, 85 percent of the base acres for peanuts assigned to a farm pursuant to section 2302(b)

(7) PAYMENT YIELD.–The term "payment yield" means the yield assigned to a farm by historic peanut producers pursuant to section 1302(b).

(8) PRODUCER.–The term "producer" means an owner, operator, landlord, tenant, or sharecropper that shares in the risk of producing a crop on a farm and is entitled to share in the crop available for marketing from the farm, or would have shared had the crop been produced. In determining whether a grower of hybrid seed is a producer, the Secretary shall not take into consideration the existence of a hybrid seed contract and shall ensure that program requirements do not adversely affect the ability of the grower to receive a payment under this subtitle.

(9) SECRETARY.–The term "Secretary" means the Secretary of Agriculture.

(10) STATE.–The term "State" means each of the several States of the United States, the District of Columbia, the Commonwealth of Puerto Rico, or any other territory or possession of the United States.

(11) TARGET PRICE.–The term "target price" means the price per ton of peanuts used to determine the payment rate for counter-cyclical payments.

(12) UNITED STATES.–The term "United States," when used in a geographical sense, means all of the States.

(a) AVERAGE YIELD AND ACREAGE AVERAGE FOR HISTORIC PEANUT PRODUCERS.–

(1) DETERMINATION OF AVERAGE YIELD.–

(A) IN GENERAL.–The Secretary shall determine, for each historic peanut producer, the average yield for peanuts on each farm on which the historic peanut producer planted peanuts for harvest for the 1998 through 2001 crop years, excluding any crop year in which the producer did not plant or was prevented from planting peanuts.

(B) ASSIGNED YIELDS.–For the purposes of determining the 4-year average yield for an historic peanut producer under this paragraph, the historic peanut producer may elect to substitute for a farm, for not more than 3 of the 1998 through 2001 crop years in which the producer planted peanuts on the farm, the average yield for peanuts produced in the county in which the farm is located for the 1990 through 1997 crop years.

(2) DETERMINATION OF ACREAGE AVERAGE.–

(A) IN GENERAL.–The Secretary shall determine, for each historic producer, the 4-year average of the following:

(i) Acreage planted to peanuts on each farm on which the historic peanut producers planted peanuts for harvest for the 1998 through 2001 crop years.

(ii) Any acreage on each farm that the historic peanut producer was prevented from planting to peanuts during the 1998 through 2001 crop years because of drought, flood, or other natural disaster, or other condition beyond the control of the historic peanut producer, as determined by the Secretary. . . .

(b) ASSIGNMENT OF AVERAGE YIELDS AND AVERAGE ACREAGE TO FARMS–

(1) ASSIGNMENT BY HISTORIC PEANUT PRODUCERS–The Secretary shall give each historic peanut producer an opportunity to assign the average peanut yield and average acreage determined under subsection (a) for each farm of the historic peanut producer to cropland on that farm or another farm in the same State or a contiguous State. . . .

(c) PAYMENT YIELD.–The average of all of the yields assigned by historic peanut producers under subsection (b) to a farm shall be considered to be the payment yield for that farm for the purpose of making direct payments and counter-cyclical payments under this subtitle.

(d) BASE ACRES FOR PEANUTS.–Subject to subsection (e), the total number of acres assigned by historic peanut producers under subsection (b) to a farm shall be considered to be the farm's base acres for peanuts for the purpose of making direct payments and counter-cyclical payments under this subtitle.

(a) PAYMENT REQUIRED–

(1) 2002 CROP YEAR.–For the 2002 crop year, the Secretary shall make direct payments under this section to the historic peanut producers.

(2) SUBSEQUENT CROP YEARS.–For each of the 2003 through 2007 crop years for peanuts, the Secretary shall make direct payments to the producers on a farm to which a payment yield and base acres for peanuts are assigned under section 1302.

(b) PAYMENT RATE.–The payment rate used to make direct payments with respect to peanuts for a crop shall be equal to $36 per ton. . .

(a) PAYMENT REQUIRED–

(1) IN GENERAL.–During the 2002 through 2007 crop years for peanuts, the Secretary shall make counter-cyclical payments under this section with respect to peanuts if the Secretary determines that the effective price for peanuts is less than the target price for peanuts.

(2) 2002 CROP YEAR.–If counter-cyclical payments are required for the 2002 crop year, the Secretary shall make the payments to historic peanut producers.

(3) SUBSEQUENT CROP YEARS.–If counter-cyclical payments are required for any of the 2003 through 2007 crop years for peanuts, the Secretary shall make the payments to the producers on a farm to which a payment yield and base acres for peanuts are assigned under section 1302

(b) EFFECTIVE PRICE.–For purposes of subsection (a), the effective price for peanuts is equal to the sum of the following:

(1) The higher of the following:

(A) The national average market price for peanuts received by producers during the 12-month marketing year for peanuts, as determined by the Secretary.

(B) The national average loan rate for a marketing assistance loan for peanuts in effect for the applicable period under this subtitle.

(C) The payment rate in effect under section 1303 for the purpose of making direct payments.

(c) TARGET PRICE.–For purposes of subsection (a), the target price for peanuts shall be equal to $495 per ton. . . .

(a) NONRECOURSE LOANS AVAILABLE.–

    (1) AVAILABILITY.–For each of the 2002 through 2007 crops of peanuts, the Secretary shall make available to producers on a farm nonrecourse marketing assistance loans for peanuts produced on the farm. The loans shall be made under terms and conditions that are prescribed by the Secretary and at the loan rate established under subsection (b).

    (2) ELIGIBLE PRODUCTION.–The producers on a farm shall be eligible for a marketing assistance loan under this subsection for any quantity of peanuts produced on the farm.

NOTES AND QUESTIONS

1. What is the purpose of the peanut commodity program? How does it work under each act? Which regulatory tools are employed in each act? What are the economic consequences? How does the peanut commodity program further U.S. farm policy as set out in Secretary Veneman's report?

2. The basic question then is: What is the objective of a commodity program? The basic objective is to provide farmers with some income stability. There are two ways that this can be done. The first is through supply management to reduce supply by taking acreage out of production. The second way of maintaining a farmer's income is through subsidy or a direct payment of some sort. What are the consequences on supply, production, and income of supply management programs? What are the effects of a subsidy on supply, price, and income? As a farmer, would you choose supply management or subsidy?

Part III
Social Regulation

In Part II, we concentrated on economic regulation and the specific regulatory tools that the government uses for that function. In Part III, we turn our attention to social regulation. This designation is based on two distinctions. First, most economic regulation generally dates back to the New Deal and has as its goal the correction of market conditions that threaten the economic welfare of citizens. Most social regulation, by comparison, dates back to the late 1960s and early 1970s and has as its goal the correction of market conditions that are discriminatory, unjust, or unsafe. Also, some significant areas of social regulation, such as food and drug safety laws, date back to the New Deal or the Progressive Era, but these laws were changed in significant ways during the 1960s and early 1970s.

Professor Christopher Jencks notes the rise of social regulation:

When I arrived in Washington as a very junior editor at the New Republic in 1961, the term "social policy" was not part of America's political vocabulary.

. . . Except for the Social Security Act, the federal government had almost no policies or programs for solving social problems. It was not trying to reduce poverty or end discrimination against minorities. It did not play a significant role in educating the young, caring for the sick, or preventing violent crime. Nor was it doing anything to discourage teenage parenthood, to encourage couples to marry before they had children, or to keep couples with children together.[1]

Second, most economic regulation is guided primarily by an efficiency criterion, although, as Chapter 7 detailed, the regulation of rents has a primarily noneconomic justification. Social regulation, by comparison, consists of a greater mix of social goals. Indeed, for many types of social regulation, there is often a lively debate concerning the extent to which efficiency or noneconomic goals should guide decisionmaking.

Economic regulation emphasizes efficiency and addresses issues of supply, demand, and price. Further, economic regulation can be analyzed largely in terms of classical or neoclassical micro and macroeconomics. Social regulation, by way of contrast, in addition concerns itself with the social cost issues and with the distributional consequences of regulatory policies. Social regulation, then, can be analyzed largely in terms of welfare economics.

Although social regulation often involves both economic and noneconomic goals, we again rely on market failure as the organizing principle in Part III. As the following table indicates, market failures are spillover costs, inadequate information, scarcity, and public goods. Government responds to these

---

[1] C. JENCKS, RETHINKING SOCIAL POLICY: RACE, POVERTY, AND THE UNDERCLASS 1 (1992).

market failures with three basic regulatory tools: standard setting, licensing, and public funding.

SOCIAL REGULATION			
MARKET FAILURES	*REGULATORY TOOLS*		
	Standard Setting	*Licensing*	*Public Financing*
Spillover Costs	Environmental Protection (Chapter 9)		
Inadequate Information		Prescription Drugs (Chapter 10) Occupational Licensing (Chapter 10)	
Scarcity		Radio and Television Broadcasting (Chapter 11) Adoption (Chapter 11)	
Public Goods			Welfare and Subsidies (Chapter 12) Public Education (Chapter 13)

Thus, this part examines how government uses standard setting to regulate health hazards in the workplace and environmental pollution (Chapter 9); licensing to control inadequate information in the drug industry and in professional occupations (Chapter 10); licensing to address the problem of scarcity in the context of radio and television broadcasting and adoption (Chapter 11); public funding to create public goods concerning welfare and other subsidies (Chapter 12) and concerning public education (Chapter 13).

Chapter 9

SPILLOVER COSTS: ENVIRONMENTAL PROTECTION

Environmental regulation constitutes a significant change in how private markets are regulated. Prior to the mid-1960s, citizens relied on state tort law to protect themselves (and their property) from environmental hazards. Beginning in the 1960s, it became clear that this form of environmental regulation was insufficient to address broader problems. Environmentalists pointed to polluted air, water, and workplaces as proof that additional regulation was necessary. Authors such as Rachel Carson,[1] Barry Commoner,[2] and Aldo Leopold[3] popularized these claims. Congress responded with significant legislation, including the National Environmental Policy Act of 1969,[4] the Clean Air Act,[5] and the Clean Water Act,[6] among several other environmental protection laws.[7]

This chapter addresses four basic elements of environmental protection. First, we explain the economic justification for environmental regulation. Second, we discuss the roll of tort law as a response to this type of market failure. Third, we raise the issue of why Congress rejected reliance on a cost-benefit test to set the level of environmental regulation. Fourth, we study standard setting, which is the regulatory tool used most often to implement environmental protection, and discuss possible alternatives to standard setting, such as pollution taxes, as potentially more appropriate regulatory tools.

We begin our discussion with a description of the economics of "spillover costs." Though market failure is not the only justification for environmental protection, it is still an extremely important justification. Before you can consider other defenses of environmental regulation, you should understand the nature and limits of this approach.

---

[1] RACHEL CARSON, SILENT SPRING (1962).

[2] BARRY COMMONER, THE CLOSING CIRCLE — MAN, NATURE, AND TECHNOLOGY (1971).

[3] ALDO LEOPOLD, A SAND COUNTY ALMANAC (1968).

[4] 42 U.S.C. §§ 4321–4370a.

[5] 42 U.S.C. §§ 7401–7626.

[6] 33 U.S.C. §§ 1251–1387.

[7] See C. CAMPBELL-MOHN, B. BREEN, & J. FUTRELL, ENVIRONMENTAL LAW: FROM RESOURCES TO RECOVERY, § 1.2 (1993); S. HAYES, BEAUTY, HEALTH, AND PERMANENCE: ENVIRONMENTAL POLITICS IN THE UNITED STATES 1955-1985 (1987); Caulfield, *The Conservation and Environmental Movements: An Historical Analysis*, in ENVIRONMENTAL POLITICS AND POLICY (J. Lester ed., 1989).

A. THE ECONOMICS OF SPILLOVER COSTS

The following hypothetical illustrates the definition of spillover costs and explains why it constitutes a market flaw. Assume that there is a factory that manufactures a chemical called "benzene." During the manufacturing process, some benzene escapes and poses a health risk to factory workers. The pollution adversely affects the health of the workers by increasing their risk of becoming ill with cancer.

The discussion of spillover costs starts with the economic incentives of the factory. Table 9-1 reviews the concepts of marginal cost, marginal revenue, and total revenue. To illustrate our example, it assumes that the factory can manufacture between one and five barrels of benzene.

Table 9-1

FACTORY COST AND REVENUE			
Barrels of Benzene	*Marginal Cost*	*Marginal Revenue*	*Total Revenue*
1	1	6	6
2	1	4	10
3	1	2	12
4	1	1	13
5	1	.5	13.5

The concepts of marginal cost (MC) and marginal revenue (MR) were discussed in Chapter 2. Marginal cost is the cost of making one more barrel, and marginal revenue is the amount for which the additional barrel can be sold. Marginal revenue declines as the supply of benzene goes up, because as supply expands, the price falls. (It is assumed, however, that the factory will sell the first barrel at a higher price than the second barrel.) How many barrels will the factory make? A producer will increase the quantity of a commodity for sale until the MC of producing another unit exceeds the marginal revenue. In this case, the factory will produce four barrels, which is where its MC (1) equals its MR (1).

Now we can bring workers into the picture. In our example, we assume that workers eventually become ill because of their exposure to benzene, and as a result, their earnings are reduced, because they are unable to work as long as if they had remained well. It is further assumed that the amount of pollution increases as the number of barrels is increased, and, as a result, the workers lose more revenue as production increases. From the point of view of the workers, benzene production is a "spillover cost" because it reduces their earnings. In other words, one of the costs of making the benzene—reduced earnings—spills over, in the sense that the cost is borne by the workers and not the factory. (Of course workers have additional costs, such as the expense of paying for medical treatment. But, for now, we will assume that lost earnings is the only "cost" to workers.)

Another name for spillover costs is "externalities." This term reflects the fact that the cost of the reduced earnings is "external" to the factory, since it does not pay for injury to workers. By comparison, the costs of producing the benzene that the factory does pay are called "internal" costs. Table 9-2 illustrates the relationship between the external and internal costs of manufacturing benzene.

Table 9-2

INTERNAL AND EXTERNAL PRODUCTION COSTS					
Internal Cost (Borne by Factory)			External Cost (Borne by Workers)		
Barrels of Benzene	Marginal Cost	Total Internal Cost	Marginal Lost Revenue	Total External Cost	Total Costs
1	1	1	1	1	2
2	1	2	2	3	5
3	1	3	3	6	9
4	1	4	4	10	14
5	1	5	5	15	20

The reason that an externality constitutes a market failure is that if the factory had to pay the total cost of manufacturing four barrels (14), it would produce fewer barrels. For example, assume that a tort system has been introduced, and that now the workers can hold the factory liable for the reduced earnings attributable to the factory's pollution. In this case, the factory's costs and revenues would be as shown in Table 9-3. Now that the factory is responsible for paying for the workers' reduced earnings, the factory will produce only two barrels, because it would cost more to produce a third barrel (4) than the revenue it would bring in (2).

Unless the price charged for a commodity reflects the actual cost of producing it, it will be overproduced, which constitutes a market failure. It will be overproduced in the following sense. If the cost of manufacturing benzene does not include external costs (the revenue lost by ill workers), the manufacturer will produce more benzene than if it had to pay such costs. As Table 9-1 reveals, the manufacturer will produce four barrels in this circumstance. By comparison, Table 9-3 demonstrates that the manufacturer will produce only two barrels if the tort system forces it to pay for workers' lost revenue. This "overproduction" harms society for the following reason. If manufacturers proceed as described in Table 9-1 (and each produces four barrels), the price of benzene will be lower than if they proceed as in Table

9-3 (and each produces two barrels). The price will be lower because manufacturers will supply more benzene in the first circumstance than in the second. The lower price will lead to greater consumption than would occur if the manufacturers had to pay for *both* the internal and external costs. The greater consumption is inefficient because it is a waste of resources. Society is using resources, such as raw materials and labor, that would be put to other purposes if benzene were properly priced. That is, the benzene market is producing a larger quantity of the chemical than would be produced if the price of benzene reflected the total cost of producing it. Thus, it is undesirable for society to sell a product at a price that does not reflect the external costs associated with its production.

Table 9-3

FACTORY COSTS AND REVENUES WITH TORT DAMAGES

Barrels of Benzene	Marginal Direct Cost	Marginal Tort Cost	Total Marginal Cost	Marginal Revenue
1	1	1	2	6
2	1	2	3	4
3	1	3	4	2
4	1	4	5	1
5	1	5	6	.5

1. COASE'S THEOREM

Until Ronald Coase published *The Problem of Social Cost,*[8] economic analysts assumed that the problem of externalities required a tort system that would force producers like the benzene factory to pay for the damage that their activities caused others. Professor Coase, however, argued that the parties in the position of the factory and the workers would negotiate a solution that would have the same result as the imposition of a tort remedy. For example, we noted earlier that if the workers have no legal right to stop the factory from polluting, the factory will manufacture four barrels. If the workers have a legal right to stop the pollution, however, the factory will not be able to produce any barrels without the agreement of the workers. In these circumstances, the factory would pay the workers not to assert their right to stop the pollution. The factory is willing to reimburse the workers for reduced earnings as long as the cost of reimbursement is less than the revenue that an additional barrel of benzene will generate. Thus, using the previous numbers, we can predict the outcome of the bargain between the factory and the workers, as Table 9-4 demonstrates.

[8] Coase, *The Problem of Social Cost*, 3 J.L. & ECON. 1 (1960).

Table 9-4

FACTORY COSTS AND REVENUES AFTER CONTRACT WITH WORKERS				
Barrels of Benzene	Marginal Direct Cost	Indirect Marginal Cost	Total Marginal Cost	Marginal Revenue
1	1	1	2	6
2	1	2	3	4
3	1	3	4	2
4	1	4	5	1
5	1	5	6	.5

In Table 9-4, the factory's indirect marginal cost is how much the workers will charge the factory to produce one or more barrels. The workers will charge the factory the amount of earnings that they lose because of an increase in pollution. Thus, the factory's indirect marginal cost is the same as the workers' marginal loss in revenue as the number of barrels increases.

The factory will make two barrels, because the marginal revenue from making a third barrel (2) is less than the cost of paying the workers (3) for lost earnings if a third barrel is produced. Because the factory has to pay for the workers' lost earnings, the workers' legal right to stop the pollution eliminates the overproduction of barrels that would occur in a market without such a right.

Coase's article generates three insights concerning externalities. First, the market, aided by a property rule which specifies whether the factory has the legal right to pollute, or the workers have the legal right to stop the pollution, can address spillover costs, and no government regulation may be required. (We will discuss shortly the circumstances under which this insight is not accurate.) Second, the arrangement between persons like the workers and factory will be "efficient" in the sense that it eliminates overproduction. Third, overproduction will be eliminated regardless of what property rule is adopted. Society can choose to have a property rule that the factory is not allowed to pollute. But it can also adopt a property rule that permits the factory to pollute. In this second case, the factory would still end up producing only two barrels. Can you see why? Refer back to the last chart. The workers could afford to give up income to reduce its production of barrels to two. At that point the revenue the workers would gain by a further reduction in the number of barrels manufactured (3) is less than the revenue (4) that the factory would forgo if it made one less barrel.

2. TORT RULES — CALABRESI AND MELAMED

Shortly after the Coase article was published, Professors Calabresi and Melamed challenged Coase's indifference concerning which property rule is adopted.[9] They also contended that there are reasons for favoring a regulatory solution to externalities, despite Coase's argument that reliance on markets may be sufficient.

a. COMMON LAW OPTIONS

Calabresi and Melamed started their analysis by recognizing that there are two property law and two tort options to address the problem of externalities, as indicated by Table 9-5. Under option (1), there is a property rule that workers have a right to stop pollution of the factory, and under option (2), the property rule permits the factory to pollute. As noted, Coase hypothesizes that under either arrangement the factory will produce two barrels. Under option (3), there is a tort rule which permits the workers to recover compensation for their reduced earnings attributable to the factory's pollution. We noted earlier that this rule will also result in the production of two barrels. The tort rule under option (4) entitles the factory to compensation for its lost earnings attributable to a reduction in pollution. Option (4) may seem like a strange idea to you, but eminent domain is a common example of this option. A community can condemn a land use it finds objectionable, as long as the landowner is compensated for the community's decision to take the land. This option, however, is not limited to eminent domain. A community could reimburse a firm for lost revenue attributable to a reduction in pollution. For example, the government could permit the firm to deduct the lost revenue from the taxes it owes. Option (4) will also lead to the production of two barrels. Do you see why?

Table 9-5

PROPERTY VERSUS TORT OPTIONS		
Parties	*Legal Options*	
	Property Rules	*Tort Rules*
Workers	(1) Right to stop pollution	(3) Right to receive compensation
Factory	(2) Right to pollute	(4) Right to receive compensation

b. TRANSACTION COSTS

Thus, in theory, the choice of whether to address an externality by property or tort rules seems to make no difference. Moreover, the choice of which property

---

[9] Calabresi & Melamed, *Property Rules, Liability Rules and Inalienability: One View of the Cathedral*, 85 HARV. L. REV. 1089 (1972). *See also* Symposium, *Property Rules, Liability Rules, and Inalienability: A Twenty-Five Year Retrospective*, 106 YALE L.J. 2083 (1997); Kaplow & Shavell, *Property Rules Versus Liability Rules: An Economic Analysis*, 109 HARV. L. REV. 713 (1996); Ayres & Talley, *Solomonic Bargaining: Dividing a Legal Entitlement to Facilitate Coasean Trade*, 104 YALE L.J. 1027 (1995).

or tort rule also seems to make no difference. All four options lead to the production of two barrels. However, one insight of Calabresi and Melamed is that these options can lead to different results if there are transaction costs.

Coase's analysis assumes that there will be no significant economic impediments that would prevent persons in the position of the workers and factory from entering into contract negotiations. If, however, there are reasons why contract negotiations would be costly, these "transaction costs" could prevent a bargain from taking place or alter the outcome of the bargaining. This point can be illustrated by assuming that the factory's pollution impacts hundreds of workers who are engaged in working at the factory, which raises the cost of bargaining.

To illustrate the effect of transaction costs, we start with identifying the relationship between the factory's marginal revenue and the degree to which the factory is polluted. This relationship is illustrated by Figure 9-1 on the following page.

In Figure 9-1, the vertical axis measures the factory's marginal revenue gained by the factory as output increases, and the horizontal axis measures the degree of pollution in the workplace as output increases. Thus, the workplace becomes more polluted as the factory expands output. At the same time, the factory earns additional revenue from the additional output, but its marginal revenue falls, because as the supply of benzene increases, the price the factory can charge decreases.

Figure 9-1: Factory's Marginal Revenue

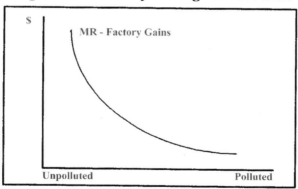

Figure 9-2 illustrates the marginal revenue lost by workers as pollution increases. The vertical axis in Figure 9-2 measures the marginal revenue lost by workers and the horizontal axis measures the degree of pollution in the workplace.

Figure 9-2: Workers' Marginal Revenue

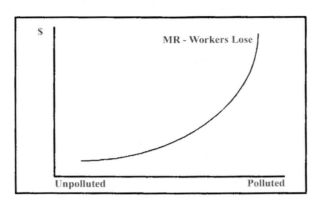

As the factory becomes more polluted, the workers lose additional earnings because there is more pollution.

When the two charts are combined in Figure 9-3, you can find the point where the two lines intersect, which indicates how much pollution will result after the parties bargain. Under either property rule, the amount of pollution will end up at Q. If the workers have the legal right to stop the factory from polluting, we can expect the factory to agree to compensate the workers for reduced earnings up to the point where the two lines intersect. At that point, the factory's revenue from an increase in production is less than the money lost by the workers because of the increased pollution. If the workers have no legal right to stop the factory from polluting, we can expect the workers to agree to compensate the factory for a reduction in output up to the point where the two lines intersect. At that point, the workers increase in earnings (from a further decrease in pollution) is less than the money lost by the factory because of decreased production.

Figure 9-3: Optimal Amount of Pollustion

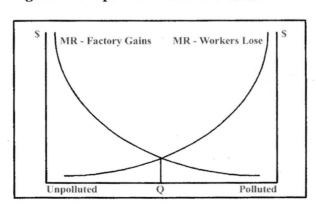

The economist considers the intersection to be the "optimal" amount of pollution. Why? To the right of the intersection, society has lost earnings that are more valuable than the value of the benzene being produced. To the left, we have the opposite situation. Where the lines intersect, society has exactly the amount of health and benzene that it wishes, and neither is under produced or over produced.

If transaction costs are taken into account, however, bargaining will not lead to an optimal amount of pollution. Figure 9-4 illustrates how transaction costs can prevent the parties from reaching a bargain that achieves the optimal level of pollution.

Figure 9-4: Effect of Transaction Cost

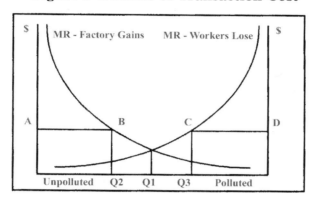

The area under the lines marked A-B-Q_2 represents the transaction costs (legal fees, etc.) that the factory must pay to negotiate with the workers. Because of these transaction costs, the amount of pollution will be at Q_2. At this point, the revenue that the factory could earn from additional output is worth more than the revenue that the workers would lose. But this difference is exceeded by the transaction costs the factory owner would have to pay in order to obtain an agreement to expand production further. If the workers have to pay the transaction costs, represented by the area under the lines Q_3-C-D, the amount of pollution will be Q_3.

Note that transaction costs not only prevent society from reaching an optimal amount of pollution, but that the property rule determines whether the amount of pollution will be Q_2 or Q_3. There will be less pollution if the workers can prevent the factory from polluting than under the opposite arrangement.

c. DISTRIBUTIONAL CONSEQUENCES

Calabresi and Melamed also argued that government regulation (tort law) may be a preferable process than private markets (property law) on grounds of equity. For example, assume there is a factory that uses cheap coal in its manufacturing process and is polluting a wealthy section of a community. It employs low income workers to produce a product that is purchased primarily by poor persons. If the homeowners have a right to stop the pollution, what is the likely outcome? The factory will not be able to afford to purchase a right to pollute if the value of the pollution to the factory is less than the value of the harm the pollution causes to the wealthy landowners. This result is efficient, but it also has significant consequences in terms of the distribution of wealth in the community. Under a property right that the homeowners can stop the pollution, the factory could go out of business, and the workers would lose their jobs. If the homeowners have a tort right to be compensated for damage to their property, the results are the same.

If the factory had a property right to pollute, the homeowners would pay the factory to reduce the amount of pollution (which it could do by purchasing more expensive coal). This result is also efficient, and it has the second advantage of avoiding the possible shutdown of the factory. But this assumes that transaction costs will not prevent the parties from negotiating. If this is the case, there is only one common law option that serves the goals of both efficiency and equity: a tort rule that the factory has the right to receive compensation for reducing its pollution.

NOTES AND QUESTIONS

1. The Coase Theorem is a staple of law and economics and should be familiar to all property students. In fact, according to an empirical study, Coase's *The Problem of Social Cost* is the most cited article in law reviews by almost twice that of the next most popular article.[10] Curiously, nowhere in his famous article did Professor Coase actually formulate a theorem. Rather, that was done by his followers.[11]

2. Coase recognized that an efficient outcome may not occur if there are transaction costs which impede bargaining between the parties. Thus, the Coase Theorem is at least, if not more valuable for what it does not address as for what it does. A concise formulation of the theorem is: If there are zero transaction costs, the efficient outcome will occur regardless of the choice of legal rule.[12] To reformulate slightly, the Coase Theorem holds that who holds the legal right is irrelevant for efficiency purposes in a world of zero transaction costs. For Coase, people will bargain until they reach the most efficient solutions. What Coase does not say or claim is that such a world (without transaction costs) does in fact exist.[13] As important, Coase does not deny that the existence of transaction costs has both distributional and efficiency consequences. Moreover, because transaction costs exist, the placement of the legal right is significant. Recall the discussion of the bargaining between the workers and the factory. The placement of the legal right determines who pays whom. In other words, the distribution of wealth is directly affected. Further, the placement of the legal right determines who bears the bulk of transaction costs. In the benzene hypothetical, if the factory has the legal right to pollute,

---

[10] Krier & Schwab, *The Cathedral at Twenty-Five: Citations and Impressions*, 106 YALE L.J. 2121 (1997).

[11] *See* R. COASE, THE FIRM, THE MARKET AND THE LAW chs. 5–6 (1990).

[12] A. MITCHELL POLINSKY, AN INTRODUCTION TO LAW AND ECONOMICS 12 (1983).

[13] Hovenkamp, *Marginal Utility and the Coase Theorem*, 75 CORNELL L. REV. 783, 786–87 (1990).

then the workers must bear the cost of getting together and bargaining with the factory.

3. Another problem is that individuals may not behave as Coase theorized because they engage in strategic behavior, or attempt to obtain an outcome which favors them and which may not be efficient. Moreover, such behavior may prevent a bargain from being struck.[14] For example, a polluter may not engage in good faith bargaining with those injured by the pollution when there is a financial advantage to this behavior. Nevertheless, it is precisely the relevance of the Coase Theorem that it permits analysts to demonstrate the impact of such factors as transaction costs, failure to seek "efficient" solutions, and strategic behavior.

4. Robert Ellickson investigated a variety of disputes arising from the damage caused by escaped cattle in Shasta County, California. He concludes that informal social understandings may replace the type of bargaining the Coase predicted:

> Shasta County neighbors, it turns out, do not behave as Coase portrays them as behaving. . . . Neighbors in fact are strongly inclined to cooperate, but they achieve cooperative outcomes not by bargaining from legally established entitlements, as [Coase] supposes, but rather by developing and enforcing adaptive norms of neighborliness that trump formal legal entitlements. Although the route chosen is not the one that [Coase] anticipates, the end reached is exactly the one that Coase predicted: coordination to mutual advantage without supervision by the state.[15]

Can you think of other examples of other informal social norms that produce cooperation that addresses spillover costs? Are such norms powerful enough that we do not need to rely on government to address the problem of externalities in most cases?

5. Calabresi and Melamed warn that different approaches to an environmental problem can have different distributional consequences.[16] Should society favor environmental programs that have a distributional impact that favor the poor? Or, should the impact on wealth of environmental policies be ignored, and the problems of poverty addressed through other means?

3. TORT VERSUS STANDARD SETTING

The Calabresi and Melamed analysis suggests two justifications for a tort approach to externalities: this approach can be more efficient and equitable. Regulation can be more efficient because the government is not subject to the transaction costs that inhibit an appropriate bargain from taking place

---

[14] *See* J. TOMAIN & J. HICKEY, ENERGY LAW AND POLICY 45–46 (1989); Hovenkamp, *supra* note 13, at 788–93.

[15] R. ELLICKSON, ORDER WITHOUT LAW: HOW NEIGHBORS SETTLE DISPUTES 3–4 (1991).

[16] For a discussion of the distributional impacts of environmental policy, see Tomain, *Distributional Consequences of Environmental Regulation: Economics, Politics, and Environmental Policy,* 1 KAN. J.L. & PUB. POL'Y 101 (1991); Michelman, *Property, Utility and Fairness: Comments on the Ethical Foundations of "Just Compensation Law,"* 80 HARV. L. REV. 1165 (1968).

between affected parties. Moreover, regulation can be designed in a way to promote equitable goals, as we will discuss in more detail later in this chapter.

When government regulates, however, it has the choice between tort law—a form of government regulation—and standard setting—another method of regulation. As the introduction mentioned, since the 1970s the government has relied primarily on standard setting, instead of tort remedies, to reduce pollution and other health-and safety-related externalities. There are several reasons for this choice.[17] First, the chemical, biological, physiological, and other scientific evidence required to establish a causal connection between exposure to pollution and harm from such exposure is often highly technical and difficult, if not impossible, for the most conscientious judge or layman to understand. Moreover, judges would try so few pollution cases that most would not develop expertise in assessing the complex data that is commonly involved. Second, tort litigation is too fortuitous an event to constitute the basis of a reliable pollution abatement program. For example, some plaintiffs who are injured may not sue or they may be hampered in litigating liability by a lack of resources. Third, courts are not equipped for the type of surveillance necessary to ensure that polluters are in compliance with pollution reduction orders.

Perhaps the most important limitation of tort law is that court proceedings are limited to the parties involved, which inhibits the judge from considering the interest of the public, who are not parties in the case. Professor Hines explains this limitation in terms of water pollution:

> The effect of an alleged pollution situation on the interests of the public frequently may not be a part of either side's case. To be sure, any judge worthy of his bench constantly considers the implications of his decisions to the welfare of the general community, but a judge is not omniscient and is generally limited in his knowledge of a problem to the evidence that has been produced in the cases tried before him. Considering the pollution problem in its totality, interests of the public in conserving and restoring the quality of the community's water may considerably overshadow the interests of the parties to any particular dispute. When such a situation occurs, a sound pollution control program requires that the facts relating to the public point of view be ferreted out and that these facts be judged in the light of the community's water quality policy. Even the most enlightened court, using all of the information gathering techniques at its disposal, is not well suited to this undertaking.[18]

Finally, standard setting has the advantage that it is preventative because it addresses the risks posed by environmental and other hazards. Congress has authorized environmental and other regulators to act on the basis of anticipated harm, which permits regulators to reduce personal and environmental risks on the basis of incomplete knowledge about the extent of those harms. In other harms, Congress permits regulators to act when the courts

---

[17] See Hines, *Nor Any Drop To Drink: Public Regulation of Water Quality,* 52 Iowa L. Rev. 186, 196–201 (1966).

[18] *Id.* at 201.

might be stymied by a lack of conclusive information about the causal relationship between a hazard and the illnesses it causes. As John Applegate has pointed out, regulation therefore changed government regulation in a fundamental way: "Regulation based on risk permits regulatory action based on *ex ante* collective danger rather than *ex post* injury, and also operates preventatively to avert injury to the public as a whole."[19]

In light of these limitations, what role can and should tort law play in the regulation of spillover costs or externalities? Consider the following analysis.

CHRISTOPHER P. SCHROEDER, LOST IN TRANSLATION: WHAT ENVIRONMENTAL REGULATION DOES THAT TORT LAW CANNOT DUPLICATE, 41 WASHBURN LAW JOURNAL 583, 598–602 (2002) *

There are certain types of environmental harms that are objects of public concern and yet largely evade the tort system because of the doctrinal restrictions of the tort regime. Tort will not be able to address these situations well. On the other hand, there is a paradigm case of harm that tort is relatively well equipped to address. The more the features of an environmental risk resemble the features of the paradigm case of harm or injury tort was originally developed to handle, the better tort is in addressing the environmental risk. Contrariwise, as the features of an environmental risk deviate from the paradigm, the harder it is for tort to address those risks absent wholesale restructuring of tort doctrine.

The paradigm tort case involves a single plaintiff suing a single defendant for a well-documented and significant harm. This is frequently called a bipolar structure, and Ernest Weinrib is correct in asserting that it is the implicit model that the core of tort doctrine assumes. Among those core doctrines of tort is the principle that the plaintiff bears the burden of demonstrating by a preponderance of the evidence that the defendant was the cause-in-fact of her harm. Of course, civil litigation forms in general, and tort in particular, are themselves flexible instruments, and it is totally familiar that tort suits can involve numerous plaintiffs and defendants. Tort acquires this flexibility by augmenting basic doctrine with supplemental provisions to deal with the complications involved, including doctrines distinguishing several from joint and several liability, doctrines of contribution and apportionment, rules regulating joinder of plaintiffs, procedures and standards for creating and maintaining class actions and the like.

In developing the supplemental doctrines necessary to move beyond the bipolar case, so as to deal with harms as they actually arise in the world around us, one fundamental feature of tort has remained constant. Tort innovations have scarcely changed the cause-in-fact requirement. When the harm context implicates a number of defendants, the plaintiff is always faced with the burden of showing that the cause-in-fact of her harm came from within the totality of the defendants' actions, and almost always cannot

---

[19] Applegate, *The Perils of Unreasonable Risk: Information, Regulatory Policy, and Toxic Substances Control*, 91 COLUM. L. REV. 261, 273 (1991).

* Reprinted with permission.

recover any amount from a defendant unless she can demonstrate that an action of that specific defendant at least contributed to her harm. In part to relieve some of the pressure modern cases put on the cause-in-fact requirement, tort has innovated within damages doctrine, recognizing a right of recovery for costs such as medical monitoring or cancerphobia. These techniques provide some measure of relief for plaintiffs who have been exposed to potential harm by the otherwise actionable conduct of the defendant by finding a way to characterize a harmful effect that the defendant has caused.

One classification scheme with which to characterize environmental risks can be generated by distinguishing between those that involve single versus numerous parties. On the defendant's side, the source of the plaintiff's harm can emanate from numerous sources—increased lead levels from auto pollution is an example. On the plaintiff's side, the harm that defendants cause can be spread over a wider and wider geographical area, potentially implicating more and more people. Acid rain or global warming are good examples. We can visualize the possible plaintiff-defendant arrangements with the help of Table 1.

EFFECTS

		Concentrated	Diffuse
ORIGINS	Concentrated	Trespass; "old" nuisances; "signature" toxic harm	Tall stack air pollution; non-signature toxic emissions
	Diffuse	Contaminated groundwater; Superfund site	Criteria air pollutants; non-signature toxic emissions

Table 1

The origins (defendants) and the effects (plaintiffs) of environmental harm actually vary along a continuum, but the Table marks out the ideal types, and this serves a useful illustrative purpose.

First, note that the bipolar paradigm, in the upper left hand box, fits some modern environmental risks as well as older types of tort situations. A particular toxic emission can come from a concentrated set of sources and the toxic substance can be the predominant source of a particular type of harm, as for instance asbestos is with respect to mesothelioma. Here we have a "signature" tort. In such a case, there will often be a straight causal link from a downstream case of mesothelioma back to one or a few sources. Long latency periods confound problems of proof, to be sure, but the case fits the idealized bipolar model fairly well.

Cases in the upper right, those with diffuse effects from concentrated origins, face some doctrinal difficulties in tort. The fundamental one arises in situations where harm falls broadly on a large group and any individual harm does not rise above a threshold necessary to constitute an actionable injury. In that case, the sources of the harm may be causing harm that in the aggregate justifies intervention, but no one will be able to litigate. Even if this doctrinal threshold is passed, plaintiffs with small injuries face daunting and unattractive transaction costs of litigation. While class action devices can ameliorate some of the transaction costs problem, cases of only moderate individual injury remain difficult to bring.

Lower left cases, concentrated effects from diffuse origins, present different doctrinal problems, especially ones having to do with the cause-in-fact requirement. Joint and several liability can provide plaintiffs with one way around an individualized cause-in-fact showing; this has the practical effect of shifting the burden onto the defendants to figure out a way to apportion the plaintiff's loss among themselves, or for individual defendants to disprove a causal connection between their acts and the plaintiff's harm. The range of cases to which joint and several liability applies is under continual pressure from defendants claiming it to be unfair.

Cases in the lower right, diffuse effects from diffuse origins, pose the greatest challenges for tort. Ozone, for example, is produced from precursors that themselves originate from numerous sources, including stationary and mobile sources, both local and remote. Plaintiffs having asthma attacks face insurmountable difficulties in identifying and bringing into court enough defendants sufficient even to capture a bare majority of the human origins of causes of asthma attacks, let alone the entire group of responsible sources. Sustaining the burden of showing that plaintiff's harm resulted from the actions of the defendants will thus prove quite difficult. Compounding the problem of absent defendants is the fact that asthma attacks can be caused by factors other than manmade elevated ozone. The manmade causes of asthma attacks may actually be a small enough fraction of total expected asthma attacks that the plaintiff could not prevail on cause-in-fact even if she had 100 percent of the human origins of ozone present as defendants.

Background rates of injury can make toxic cases instances of diffuse effects as well. Seeing how requires a little elaboration, because from the ex post perspective of tort, a suit for injury of the type expected from toxic exposure would wait until harm had occurred. At that point, the case would look like a case of concentrated effects, and hence one that tort might at least in some halting way handle. The difficulty is that in a case in which the effects caused by the manmade risks remain hidden within a slightly elevated background rate, we cannot tell whether a given case of harm originates in something done by the defendant(s) or in some other causes, including natural ones. Because the tort is non-signature, we cannot trace any harm back to any specific human origin, so the effects of defendants' risky behavior will remain spread out among the entire exposed population as risk exposure, rather than as identifiable concentrated harm. When the contribution of the defendant to the total expected incidence of harm is significant but small, it will be possible to say that the defendant more likely than not caused some harm, but impossible to say which harm. This concatenation of elements has led some commentators to urge a cause of action for having exposed people to risk. So far, however, the common law tort system has remained quite resistant to such an innovations.

Cases in this final category of environmental risks, then, are likely to remain impervious to the doctrines of tort. Yet such risks—diffuse effects from diffuse origins—are among some of the most important objects of regulatory attention today. In cases such as these, shifting from regulation to tort would be tantamount to abandoning efforts to reduce the prevalence or magnitude of such risks.

NOTES AND QUESTIONS

1. In which of the categories identified by Professor Schroeder would you locate lawsuits concerning automobile accidents? Is there any problem with causality in such lawsuits? Although the automobile accident would appear to be a paradigm case for tort law, according to Schroeder's typology, Congress nevertheless created the National Highway Safety Administration (NHTSA) in 1966, as Chapter 1 related. If it was not problems of proof, what was the justification for Congress' decision to create a regulatory regime to augment tort law?

2. Professor Keith Hylton argues that tort law has "some important properties to make it superior to statute-based regulatory systems as a system of environmental protection."[20] One advantage of tort law relates to "agency costs." Hylton observes that, unlike plaintiffs' lawyers, whose interests are correlated with tort victims, "[p]ublic enforcement agents do not always have the right incentives" because they "are motivated by paychecks and promises of promotion within the public enforcement agency." A second advantage relates to information. As you learned in Section A, the goal of regulation according to economic theory is to replicate a Coasian bargain. The government can do this by using a cost-benefit test to set the level of regulation. Hylton argues that tort law is preferable to agency regulation because "a public regulatory scheme could not hope to match the negligence system in terms of its scope, detail, and encapsulation of private information." That is, the government is not as good at obtaining information about costs and benefits of regulation before there is a spillover as the tort system is in collecting the information after the spillover occurs. Thus, tort law, with its superior access to information, will do a better job of matching costs and benefits.

Do you agree with Hylton that these are disadvantages of agency regulation? Assuming that he is correct, would you agree that tort law is superior to agency regulation as a response to spillover costs or externalities?

B. WORKPLACE HEALTH: A CASE STUDY

In this section, we examine in more detail each of the concepts discussed above by analyzing the problem of protecting workers from the dangers of workplace pollution. In 1970, Congress passed the Occupational Safety and Health Act,[21] creating the Occupational Safety and Heath Administration (OSHA). Prior to the establishment of OSHA, workers were protected by market transactions of the type Professor Coase described, and by workers'

---

[20] Hylton, *When Should We Prefer Tort Law to Environmental Regulation?*, 41 WASHBURN L.J. 515 (2002).

[21] 29 U.S.C. §§ 651–78 (1988).

compensation, a form of a state tort remedy. Before describing OSHA and its regulatory powers, these other approaches to protecting workers are considered.

1. PROPERTY RULES — WAGE PREMIUMS

Coase hypothesized that, under a regime of property rules, market transactions will adjust an externality to an optimal or efficient amount. According to economic theory, such a market process exists concerning employment markets.[22]

Economic theory predicts that workers will seek safer jobs unless employers compensate them for the workplace risks that accompanying a more dangerous job. In other words, workers will seek a wage premium sufficient to reimburse them for the costs of any future accidents, including the loss of any compensation. Since a worker gives up the "wage premium" to work in a safer place, the worker who leaves a risky job is "willing to pay" (in terms of foregone compensation) the amount of the premium to work in safer conditions.

Economists claim to have verified the existence of such wage premiums by empirical studies, which have found a positive association between the level of safety risks in an industry and its wage rates. For example, one analyst concludes that these studies

> indicate labor markets operating as they should. Although they do not exist in a paradigm labor market, workers are being rewarded for risk bearing and there are wage benefit tradeoffs. There are workers, who are risk adverse, have information about job risk, and collect for bearing risk.[23]

Another analyst concludes, "Economists since the time of Adam Smith have noted that individuals require higher wages to accept jobs they view as hazardous. . . . Analysis of actual employment patterns yields consistent evidence with this traditional view."[24]

The size of wage premiums is typically small. Professor Viscusi, for example, has found that annual compensation for all job safety risks equals about $400 per worker.[25] Although the compensation is low, analysts extrapolate from such data that workers are willing to pay between $3.0 and 7.0 million dollars to prevent one premature death. A small wage premium is the equivalent of this much larger amount because the premium is paid for a relatively small risk. For example, if one worker out of ten thousand workers will die annually from a particular safety risk, a $400 wage premium is the equivalent of a $4.0 million value of life. The value of a life is calculated by dividing the $400 wage

---

[22] *See* P. Dorman, Markets and Morality: Economics, Dangerous Work, and the Value of Human Life 35–36 (1996); R. Smith, The Occupational Safety and Health Act: Its Goals and Achievements 26–28 (1976).

[23] Worrall, *Compensation Costs, Injury Rates, and the Labor Market, in* Safety and the Workforce: Incentives and Disincentives in Workers Compensation 13 (J. Worrall ed., 1979).

[24] W. Viscusi, Employment Hazards: An Investigation of Market Performance 271 (1979).

[25] W. Viscusi, Fatal Tradeoffs: Public & Private Responsibilities for Risk 40 (1992).

premium by the fatality risk (.0001), which results in a $4.0 million valuation for a life saved.

Others, however, are skeptical that workers receive wage premiums that adequately compensate them for the risks that they face. Some of the reasons for this skepticism are suggested in the following excerpt.

THOMAS O. MCGARITY & SIDNEY A. SHAPIRO, OSHA'S CRITICS AND REGULATORY REFORM, 31 WAKE FOREST LAW REVIEW 587, 605–07 (1996) *

. . . A wage premium is the extra compensation that an employer must pay for hazardous work to keep an employee from taking less risky alternative employment. Some economists believe that wage premiums have a greater impact on workplace safety than OSHA because total wage premiums (estimated to be about $69 billion) greatly exceed the amount of fines that OSHA assesses. . . .

Researchers who have tested the correlation between employee compensation and injury data have concluded that workers in risky jobs receive higher wages after controlling for education, experience, and other market characteristics of safety hazards. There are no reliable similar studies for occupational illnesses because of the lack of accurate data about the extent of such risks, but other evidence, discussed below, suggests that fewer workers receive wage premiums for occupational health risks.

Workers typically receive relatively small wage premiums. James Robinson found that workers exposed to significant risks of occupational injuries received annual wage premiums of about $300 to $500, which amounted to a 5% to 8% increase of the earnings of unexposed blue collar workers. Viscusi found that annual compensation for all job risks totaled about $400. Although Robinson describes such premiums as "modest," Viscusi finds them "impressive" because he is convinced that the average workplace risk is not very large. Factoring in what he believes to be the limited nature of the risk, he estimates that workers receive a premium of $1 to $1.5 million per fatality and $10,000 per injury in 1969 dollars. Viscusi's calculations, however, probably overstate hazard pay. If the risks are greater than the injury data that Viscusi relies upon, workers are less compensated than he calculates. As noted earlier, existing data understate the extent of workplace fatalities and injuries.

Wage premiums do not fully compensate most workers for two reasons. First, the amount of additional compensation that a worker will seek for hazardous work is a function of the worker's knowledge and understanding of existing risks. The existence of wage premiums indicates that workers have some knowledge of workplace risks, but the extent of that knowledge is limited. Using national survey data, Robinson found that 33% to 50% of workers in occupations with high rates of disabling injuries and illnesses reported that they faced no significant safety or health hazards. Although workers were more likely to recognize cancer risks in industries where such risks were high, only 12% to 33% considered themselves exposed to a significant risk. Even workers with some knowledge of workplace risks must be able to discern marginal differences in risks to bargain effectively for appropriate hazard pay. Such distinctions are especially difficult to make in the context of occupational illness, where huge uncertainties befuddle attempts to predict the precise effects of health risks on longevity and the quality of life once a disease has manifested itself. Finally, a worker's evaluation of risk may be distorted by psychological defects in the way individuals process risk information.

Second, the additional compensation that a worker can obtain for hazardous work is a function of the worker's bargaining power. An employee who can be fired at the whim of an employer cannot be very demanding in seeking hazard pay. This is especially true in jobs in which employees can be easily replaced and for which alternative jobs are not readily available. Many hazardous jobs have these characteristics. Robinson found that if education and skill levels are ignored, hazardous jobs pay 20% to 30% less than safe employment. This discrepancy indicates that persons with training and education avoid such jobs because safer employment pays more. The pool of labor for hazardous jobs therefore consists of "disadvantaged workers who are willing to accept health and safety risks in return for very modest amounts of compensation." Poorly educated and low skilled workers may also hesitate to leave dangerous jobs because the risk pay is inadequate. Even skilled workers may be hesitant to change jobs when that may entail loss of health benefits, pension rights, seniority, the necessity of becoming familiar with a new employer, and the expense and disruption of relocation.

2. TORT RULES — WORKERS' COMPENSATION

Wage premiums constitute "ex ante" compensation for health and safety risks because wages are paid before any injury is incurred. Under state workers' compensation systems, "ex post" compensation is available on a no-fault basis, once it is determined that an injury or disease is work-related. In the 1920s and 1930s, the states adopted workers' compensation when it became apparent that state court judges had erected numerous difficult barriers to recovery under tort law. Employer support for a no-fault approach was obtained by prohibiting workers covered by workers' compensation from suing the employer for any remedy other than the benefits under that system.

Workers' compensation funds are supported by charges levied on employers. Theoretically, the size of the premium is based on the relative safety of workplaces, as measured by reported employee injuries and illnesses. In this manner, employers end up paying the costs of the injuries and illnesses associated with their workplaces. They will therefore engage in preventative safety efforts as long as such efforts are less costly than the payments that they are required to make to the workers' compensation fund. As the following analysis indicates, however, the actual performance of workers' compensation is different than this theoretical model.

THOMAS O. MCGARITY & SIDNEY A. SHAPIRO, OSHA'S CRITICS AND REGULATORY REFORM, 31 WAKE FOREST LAW REVIEW 587, 599–602 (1996) *

In the minds of many economists, workers' compensation must be more influential in promoting workplace safety than OSHA, because compensation payments total $50 to $60 billion as compared to about $10 million in OSHA fines. But these numbers do not tell the entire story. Despite the large cost of workers' compensation, employers pay for only a portion of the costs of occupational accidents and for almost none of the costs of occupational illness. Moreover, the evidence on the extent to which workers' compensation induces employers to take safety precautions is at best equivocal.

a. *Uncompensated injuries and illnesses.* Workers' compensation has never been structured to compensate workers completely for the cost of their injuries and illnesses. Indeed, the level of compensation in most states varies inversely with the seriousness of the injury. Compensation for temporary disabilities is controlled by statutorily prescribed formulas that limit compensation to less than the direct wage losses of disabled employees.[78] Additionally, compensation for permanent partial disability "rarely" equals the total wage loss of any employee, and compensation for fatalities is often less than for temporary and permanent disabilities. Furthermore, neither the loss of fringe benefits nor nonpecuniary losses to workers and their families are factored into the compensation awards.

Under workers' compensation, employers are not likely to be held responsible for the social costs of workplace-induced illness. Studies indicate that only 2% to 3% of all workers' compensation payments are for occupational disease, and only about 5% of all occupational disease victims receive compensation. Two factors account for this exceedingly low compensation rate. First, workers and their physicians often fail to recognize that many illnesses are work-related. Second, when claims are filed, they are usually successfully contested by employers because of the difficulty of proving causation and because many states have restrictive standards for recovery. The few disease victims that do prevail face the same statutory limitations on compensation amounts that injury victims must endure.

Even if more workers were compensated at higher rates, employers would still lack a strong economic incentive to take protective action. A manager's decision to invest in disease prevention is not based on current compensation expenses, which are a result of past actions, but on the likelihood that the investment will prevent future illness. Since occupational diseases are frequently characterized by long latency periods between exposure and disease onset, the manager can discount heavily the consequences and spend little or nothing on prevention. . . .

---

[78] Workers typically receive two-thirds of their pre-injury gross earnings up to a maximum of 100% of the state average weekly wage. Workers who earn more than 150% of the state's weekly wage will therefore collect less than two-thirds of their own wage. Thus, the level of wage replacement is the least adequate for the highest wage earners, such as persons who work in the construction industry, which is also one of the nation's most dangerous industries.

b. *Empirical evidence.* The empirical evidence suggests that workers' compensation arrangements do not stimulate employers to take effective safety and health precautions. The extraordinary increase in workers' compensation costs over the last twenty years has failed to stimulate an improvement in workplace safety of a similar magnitude. Although compensation costs rose 600% (from $6 billion to $62 billion) between 1971 and 1992, injury and fatality rates declined far less (by 57% and 75%), and the lost workday injury rate increased (by 75%). These trends suggest that workers' compensation creates limited safety incentives.

Econometric testing appears to support this conclusion. Of sixteen empirical tests, only one could establish that workers' compensation had a positive safety impact. Studies generally found the converse to be true: injury rates rise when benefit levels increase.

Two theories explain why workers' compensation has failed to produce safer workplaces. One explanation attributes this failure to employer behavior and the other to employee behavior.

i. *Employer behavior.* Employers may fail to take safety precautions for two reasons. First, insurance for workers' compensation accurately reflects the employer's safety experience only for the largest firms. Second, a rational employer will use other options to reduce compensation payouts when they are less expensive than taking safety precautions.

Insurance attenuates the relationship between risk and cost because the price of insurance for many firms does not reflect, or only partially reflects, their claims experience. The relationship of premiums to claims experience varies inversely with the size of the firm, with the smallest firms paying premiums that have no relationship to their actual claims experience.[99] Thus, although small businesses have the highest injury rates, they also have the least economic incentive to take safety precautions. Some researchers have established that a firm's response to increases in compensation rates differs between large and small firms, but other researchers have been unable to verify such an "experience-rating" effect.

Employers can take two different steps to reduce compensation payments, both of which can be less expensive than taking safety precautions. First, employers can try to discourage claims by pressuring employees not to file claims, delaying the completion of necessary paperwork, aggressively contesting claims, and persuading employees who file claims to return to work prematurely. Second, employers can engage in political activity to obtain workers' compensation reform. At the behest of business lobbies, most states

---

[99] Smaller employers, who constitute the majority of purchasers of all insurers, have class-based premiums. The cost of insurance for these employers is based on the claims experience of a class of similar employers. Because small firms have so few employees, insurance companies view individual claims experience as too random to have any predictive value. These firms have only a weak economic incentive to take safety precautions because their actual claims experience will have little effect on their future premiums. Larger firms, which pay premiums based in part on claim losses, have a greater incentive to engage in injury prevention. The extent to which these firms are rated according to their claims experience depends on the credibility or predictive value of that experience. It is only the largest employers that pay rates that are based entirely on their claims experience. These firms, and firms that self-insure, have the greatest economic incentive to reduce workplace risks.

have passed amendments that eliminate or reduce the obligation of employers to make compensation payments. A smaller number of states have also adopted various types of injury prevention and safety requirements. . . .

ii. *Employee behavior.* Economists are inclined to attribute the absence of a clear correlation between increased workers' compensation costs and injury reduction to employee behavior. According to the "moral hazard" explanation, workers are less vigilant and therefore suffer more (and more serious) injuries because higher benefits diminish the personal economic risks associated with such injuries. This theory would be more persuasive if workers did not have strong economic and other incentives to avoid injuries. As indicated earlier, workers receive less, sometimes far less, than the actual costs of their injuries and illnesses. More importantly, the moral hazard theory reflects a bizarre view of human nature under which the prospect of money in the future will persuade people to risk severe pain, hospitalization, dismemberment, and even death in the present.

According to a more plausible "reporting" theory, higher compensations only increase the number of accident reports, not the absolute number of injuries. Since workers lose less income if they miss work, they may report more injuries and stay home longer. Increased benefits might also induce more cases of outright fraud. Yet even the reporting theory may lack explanatory power, because an employee's decision on whether to file a claim will probably not be based exclusively on an assessment of the economic worth of benefits. Some studies have found that higher workers' compensation levels reduce injuries after controlling for reporting effects, but other studies have found no safety improvement. Finally, there is no empirical evidence at all to suggest that a significant portion of the increase in workers' compensation costs can be attributed to fraud.

NOTES AND QUESTIONS

1. Earlier you read Professor Schroeder's analysis of when tort law is more and less suitable to regulate spillover costs. Does his analysis explain any of the constraints that limit the efficacy of workers compensation in reducing workplace illnesses and injuries?

2. What are the key differences between tort law and workers compensation in terms of the level of deterrence and compensation that each generates? How do these differences impact the efficacy of workers compensation in reducing workplace illnesses and injuries?

3. Professor Kip Viscusi notes that "[w]hereas government regulation imposed negligible fines—on the order of less than $10 million per year—the safety incentives created by the market and by social insurance were considerably greater."[26] By market incentives, Viscusi means the "wage premiums" that you read about in the last section. By social insurance, Viscusi is referring to workers compensation, which he says imposes insurance premiums on firms in excess of $30 billion per year. Viscusi observes: "Especially for large firms, these premiums are linked to the firms' safety performance, providing incentives for safety improvements. Indeed, estimates of the effect of workers'

---

[26] K. VISCUSI, FATAL TRADEOFFS: PUBLIC & PRIVATE RESPONSIBILITIES FOR RISK 11–12 (1992).

compensation on death risks indicates that workplace fatality risks would be 20 to 30 percent higher in the absence of the workers' compensation incentives."

Is there a way to reconcile Viscusi's argument about the significance of workers compensation in reducing workplace injuries and the criticism of it by Professors McGarity and Shapiro in the excerpt you read? Does Professor Viscusi establish the insignificance of government regulation by citing the small amount of fines that employers pay for violating workplace regulations?

4. Professor Martha McCluskey points out that from the late 1980s through the 1990s, many states enacted legislation imposing substantial restrictions on workers compensation benefits available to injured workers.[27] The restrictions were justified as necessary to "restore a sound economic balance to the system." She observes, "By using economic efficiency as a rationale for workers compensation reforms, policymakers have tried to disguise decisions to *shift* costs to workers as decisions to *save* overall costs." Does economic theory support restricting the damages that employers pay workers under workers compensation costs to less than the full amount of their injuries or illnesses? In what sense does reducing damages "shift" the cost of illnesses and injuries from employers to workers?

3. GOVERNMENT REGULATION — OSHA STANDARDS

In the late 1960s, the level of workplace injuries and illnesses strongly suggested that the previous methods of addressing this problem were not sufficient. In 1968, the Johnson administration, pushed by the labor unions, drafted a bill that would have empowered the Department of Labor to establish and enforce workplace occupational safety and health standards. The bill, however, met stiff resistance from industry, which argued that most industrial accidents were attributable to human error, and that federal involvement would be an unwarranted interference with "states' rights." The legislative initiative was given new life by support from the Nixon administration, which was seeking to lure blue collar support away from the Democrats, and by a mine disaster, which had killed eighty-eight miners. In light of these events, industry moved from opposing federal legislation to a strategy of obtaining a regulatory system with which it could live.[28]

As regulatory regimes go, the Occupational Safety and Health Act is reasonably uncomplicated. Its purpose is "to assure as far as possible every working man and woman in the Nation safe and healthful working conditions."[29] A "general duty clause" requires every employer "to furnish to each of his employees employment and a place of employment which are free from recognized hazards that are causing or are likely to cause death or serious physical harm to his employees."[30] Employers must also comply with health

---

[27] McCluskey, *The Illusion of Efficiency in Workers' Compensation "Reform,"* 50 RUTGERS L. REV. 657 (1998).

[28] Kelman, *Occupational Safety and Health Administration, in* THE POLITICS OF REGULATION (J. Wilson ed., 1980); J. PAGE & M. O'BRIEN, BITTER WAGES: RALPH NADER'S STUDY GROUP REPORT ON DISEASE AND INJURY ON THE JOB (1973).

[29] 29 U.S.C. § 651.

[30] *Id.* § 654(a)(1).

and safety standards promulgated by OSHA. Any standard must establish conditions and practices that are "reasonably necessary or appropriate" to provide "safe or healthful employment."[31] In addition, any health standard—a standard that concerns toxic materials or harmful physical agents—must be established in a way that "most adequately assures, to the extent feasible, on the basis of the best available evidence, that no employee will suffer material impairment of health or functional capacity even if such employee has regular exposure to the hazard dealt with in such standard for the period of his working life."[32] Congress required that both safety and health standards prescribe the use of labels, emergency treatments, and "proper conditions and precautions of safe use and exposure." In addition, where appropriate, OSHA is required to prescribe suitable protective equipment, control or technological procedures, monitoring requirements, and time and frequency of medical examinations.[33]

C.   THE COST-BENEFIT DEBATE

The OSHA statute, as described above, requires the agency to establish the level of protection against health hazards that "most adequately assures, to the extent feasible" that no employee will suffer a "material impairment of health or functional capacity even if such employee has regular exposure to the hazard" addressed by the regulation. This approach to setting the level of permissible exposure to a hazard is known as "technology-based" regulation. It determines the level of exposure by reference to the level of protection that is achievable by an existing protective technology. In the case of OSHA, feasibility refers to both technological and economic feasibility.[34] A level of protection is infeasible if it requires "protective devices unavailable under existing technology" or if it made "financial viability generally impossible." A regulation, however, is still feasible even if it is "financially burdensome and affect[s] profit margins adversely." *Industrial Union Department v. Hodgson*, 499 F.2d 467, 447–48 (D.C. Cir. 1974).

Besides OSHA's mandate, Congress has relied on technology-based standards to establish the level of protection in most environmental laws. For example, the Clean Air Act (CAA) specifies that each state containing a nonattainment area must require existing stationary sources of air pollution to implement all "reasonable available control technology" as expeditiously as practicable.[35] A nonattainment area is one that does not meet national ambient air quality standards (NAAQS) established by EPA. In addition, Congress often directs the agency to make adjustments in the level of regulation

---

[31] *Id.* § 652(8).

[32] *Id.* § 655(b)(5).

[33] *Id.* § 655(b)(7).

[34] For a discussion feasibility, see M. ROTHSTEIN, OCCUPATIONAL SAFETY AND HEALTH LAW §§ 77–78 (3rd ed. 1990); OCCUPATIONAL SAFETY AND HEALTH LAW 594–602 (S. Bokat & H. Thompson III eds. 1988).

[35] 42 U.S.C. § 7502(c)(1). Sources subject to this requirement may actually become subject to even more stringent controls under other provisions of the statute if controls on other kinds of sources do not bring an area into compliance with the CAA's national ambient air quality standards.

indicated by a model technology. The 1996 amendments to the Safe Drinking Water Amendments of 1996, for example, require EPA to set a maximum contaminant level (MCL) which comes as close as "feasible" to achieving the level at which no known or anticipated adverse health effects will occur, allowing an adequate margin of safety.[36]

This method of setting the level of regulation differs from the level of regulation that economic theory prefers. When wage premiums and workers compensation fail to induce employers to invest in safety and health improvements, government can rely on regulation to accomplish the same result. The economic goal of such regulation is to obtain the same result as would have occurred if workers were fully compensated for occupational illnesses. As discussed earlier, economic theory predicts that workers will demand wage premiums to compensate them for health risks, or seek workers compensation for unabated risks. In response, an employer will reduce such risks until it is less expensive to pay wages and compensation than to undertake additional health precautions. When wage premiums and workers compensation do not function in this efficient manner, employers will invest too little money in safety and health improvements. Regulators can address this shortfall by ordering employers to undertake safety and health precautions up to the point where the costs of such improvements exceed their benefits. If benefits are measured as the value of the improvements to workers, administrative regulation will produce the same investment in health precautions as efficient labor markets.

Since the goal of regulation according to economic theory is to replicate the results that would have occurred if workers and employers had struck an appropriate bargain, the goal of a cost-benefit test is to achieve the outcome of the type of bargain that Professor Coase described in his famous article. Why did Congress reject this approach? Why did it prefer a technology-based approach? As the following materials indicate, these questions have been the subject of an ongoing controversy between the critics and supporters of the technology-based approach to environmental protection.

1. THE "COTTON DUST" CASE

It took a Supreme Court decision to verify that Congress had chosen a technology-based approach for OSHA regulation. In *American Textile Manufacturers Institute v. Donovan*, 452 U.S. 490 (1981), known as the *Cotton Dust* case, the Court reviewed an OSHA standard that required manufacturers of cotton thread to reduce the amount of cotton dust to which workers were exposed. Long-term exposure to cotton dust causes lung diseases which make it difficult to breathe. The employers had argued that OSHA's standard was illegal because OSHA had failed to establish that its benefits exceed its costs. OSHA responded that such an interpretation of its mandate would be inconsistent with the requirement that it protect workers to the extent that is feasible. The following excerpt indicates the basis for these arguments and the reasons why the Court sided with OSHA.

---

[36] 42 U.S.C. § 300g-1(b)(4)(A)–(B). Feasible means "feasible with the use of the best technology, treatment techniques, and other means" that EPA finds are available. Ibid., § 300g-1(b)(4)(D).

AMERICAN TEXTILE MANUFACTURERS INSTITUTE v. DONOVAN
452 U.S. 490 (1981)

JUSTICE BRENNAN delivered the opinion of the Court.

Congress enacted the Occupational Safety and Health Act of 1970 (Act) "to assure so far as possible every working man and woman in the Nation safe and healthful working conditions. . . ." The Act authorizes the Secretary of Labor to establish, after notice and opportunity to comment, mandatory nationwide standards governing health and safety in the workplace. In 1978, the Secretary, acting through the Occupational Safety and Health Administration (OSHA), promulgated a standard limiting occupational exposure to cotton dust, an airborne particle byproduct of the preparation and manufacture of cotton products, exposure to which induces a "constellation of respiratory effects" known as "byssinosis." This disease was one of the expressly recognized health hazards that led to passage of the Act. . . .

Petitioners in these consolidated cases, representing the interests of the cotton industry, . . . contend in this Court, as they did below, that the Act requires OSHA to demonstrate that its Standard reflects a reasonable relationship between the costs and benefits associated with the Standard. Respondents, the Secretary of Labor and two labor organizations, counter that Congress balanced the costs and benefits in the Act itself, and that the Act should therefore be construed not to require OSHA to do so. They interpret the Act as mandating that OSHA enact the most protective standard possible to eliminate a significant risk of material health impairment, subject to the constraints of economic and technological feasibility. . . .

II

The principal question presented in these cases is whether the Occupational Safety and Health Act requires the Secretary, in promulgating a standard pursuant to § 6(b)(5) of the Act to determine that the costs of the standard bear a reasonable relationship to its benefits. Relying on §§ 6(b)(5) and 3(8) of the Act, petitioners urge not only that OSHA must show that a standard addresses a significant risk of material health impairment, but also that OSHA must demonstrate that the reduction in risk of material health impairment is significant in light of the costs of attaining that reduction. Respondents on the other hand contend that the Act requires OSHA to promulgate standards that eliminate or reduce such risks "to the extent such protection is technologically and economically feasible." To resolve this debate, we must turn to the language, structure, and legislative history of the Act. . . .

A.

The starting point of our analysis is the language of the statute itself. Section 6(b)(5) of the Act, (emphasis added), provides:

"The Secretary, in promulgating standards dealing with toxic materials or harmful physical agents under this subsection, shall set the standard which most adequately assures, *to the extent feasible*, on the basis of the best available evidence, that no employee will suffer material impairment of health or functional capacity even if such employee has regular exposure to the hazard dealt with by such standard for the period of his working life."

Although their interpretations differ, all parties agree that the phrase "to the extent feasible" contains the critical language in § 6(b)(5) for purposes of these cases.

The plain meaning of the word "feasible" supports respondents' interpretation of the statute. According to Webster's Third New International Dictionary of the English Language 831 (1976), "feasible" means "capable of being done, executed, or effected." Thus, § 6(b)(5) directs the Secretary to issue the standard that "most adequately assures . . . that no employee will suffer material impairment of health," limited only by the extent to which this is "capable of being done." In effect then, as the Court of Appeals held, Congress itself defined the basic relationship between costs and benefits, by placing the "benefit" of worker health above all other considerations save those making attainment of this "benefit" unachievable. Any standard based on a balancing of costs and benefits by the Secretary that strikes a different balance than that struck by Congress would be inconsistent with the command set forth in § 6(b)(5). Thus, cost-benefit analysis by OSHA is not required by the statute because feasibility analysis is. . . .

When Congress has intended that an agency engage in cost-benefit analysis, it has clearly indicated such intent on the face of the statute. . . . These and other statutes demonstrate that Congress uses specific language when intending that an agency engage in cost-benefit analysis. Certainly in light of its ordinary meaning, the word "feasible" cannot be construed to articulate such congressional intent. We therefore reject the argument that Congress required cost-benefit analysis in § 6(b)(5).

B.

Even though the plain language of § 6(b)(5) supports this construction, we must still decide whether § 3(8), the general definition of an occupational safety and health standard, either alone or in tandem with § 6(b)(5), incorporates a cost-benefit requirement for standards dealing with toxic materials or harmful physical agents. § 3(8) of the Act (emphasis added), provides:

"The term 'occupational safety and health standard' means a standard which requires conditions, or the adoption or use of one or more practices, means, methods, operations, or processes, *reasonably necessary or appropriate* to provide safe or healthful employment and places of employment."

Taken alone, the phrase "reasonably necessary or appropriate" might be construed to contemplate some balancing of the costs and benefits of a standard. Petitioners urge that, so construed, § 3(8) engrafts a cost-benefit analysis requirement on the issuance of § 6(b)(5) standards, even if § 6(b)(5) itself does not authorize such analysis. We need not decide whether § 3(8), standing alone, would contemplate some form of cost-benefit analysis. For even if it does, Congress specifically chose in § 6(b)(5) to impose separate and additional requirements for issuance of a subcategory of occupational safety and health standards dealing with toxic materials and harmful physical agents: it required that those standards be issued to prevent material impairment of health *to the extent feasible*. Congress could reasonably have concluded that *health* standards should be subject to different criteria than *safety* standards because of the special problems presented in regulating them.

Agreement with petitioners' argument that § 3(8) imposes an additional and overriding requirement of cost-benefit analysis on the issuance of § 6(b)(5) standards would eviscerate the "to the extent feasible" requirement. Standards would inevitably be set at the level indicated by cost-benefit analysis, and not at the level specified by § 6(b)(5). For example, if cost-benefit analysis indicated a protective standard of 1,000 ug/m 3 PEL, while feasibility analysis indicated a 500 ug/m 3 PEL, the agency would be forced by the cost-benefit requirement to choose the less stringent point. We cannot believe that Congress intended the general terms of § 3(8) to countermand the specific feasibility requirement of § 6(b)(5). Adoption of petitioners' interpretation would effectively write § 6(b)(5) out of the Act. We decline to render Congress' decision to include a feasibility requirement nugatory, thereby offending the well-settled rule that all parts of a statute, if possible, are to be given effect. . . .

C.

The legislative history of the Act, while concededly not crystal clear, provides general support for respondents' interpretation of the Act. The congressional Reports and debates certainly confirm that Congress meant "feasible" and nothing else in using that term. Congress was concerned that the Act might be thought to require achievement of absolute safety, an impossible standard, and therefore insisted that health and safety goals be capable of economic and technological accomplishment. Perhaps most telling is the absence of any indication whatsoever that Congress intended OSHA to conduct its own cost-benefit analysis before promulgating a toxic material or harmful physical agent standard. The legislative history demonstrates conclusively that Congress was fully aware that the Act would impose real and substantial costs of compliance on industry, and believed that such costs were part of the cost of doing business. . . .

2. ECONOMIC ARGUMENTS

OSHA regulation under its "feasibility" standard is controversial.[37] Although economists have generally supported occupational health regulation, because employers underinvest in prevention, they favor health regulation only insofar as it passes a cost-benefit test. They recommend that Congress amend the OSHA act to mandate this requirement.

---

[37] *Compare* T. McGarity & S. Shapiro, Workers at Risk: The Failed Promise of the Occupational Safety Administration (1993) (supporting the standard) *with* J. Mendeloff, The Dilemma of Toxic Substance Regulation: How Overregulation Causes Underregulation at OSHA (1988) [cited hereinafter as Overregulation] (criticizing the standard); J. Mendeloff, An Economic and Political Analysis of Occupational Safety and Health (1980) (same).

Economists have leveled the same criticism at other environmental regulation because Congress has not subjected EPA's authority to a cost-benefit test. For example, the Clean Air Act (CAA) and the Federal Water Pollution Control Act (FWPCA) also rely to a significant extent on a technology-based standard. These statutes have been implemented by requiring polluters to install the "best available technology" (BAT) to reduce pollution. Like OSHA's feasibility standard, the BAT mandate requires EPA to seek the highest level of protection that existing technologies can provide.

Congress' insistence on using technology-based regulation for environmental risks has its critics, but others stoutly defended its choice. The supporters contend that technology-based regulation is rational, and that it stands up well when compared to reliance on a cost-benefit test. This dispute has produced an extensive literature on cost-benefit analysis.[38] The next two sections describe the basic arguments in this debate.

The critics of the current approach contend it wastes society's resources to order employers to undertake more regulatory protection than a cost-benefit test would indicate. They also argue that OSHA habitually over regulates or orders more regulation than a cost-benefit test would permit.[39] In order to measure the economic "benefits" of an OSHA regulation, or any other government regulation, economic analysts multiply the number of lives that a regulation is estimated to save times the value of those lives to society. To the extent that data are available, analysts will also estimate the monetary benefit of the number of non-fatal illnesses that the regulation is estimated to prevent. The total value of these "benefits" is then compared to the estimated cost of regulation—i.e., an estimate of how much money employers will spend on its implementation.

Economists employ a variety of techniques for specifying the value of a human life. The two most prominent are the "human capital" method and the "willingness-to-pay" approach. Under the human capital approach, the economist estimates the total future earnings of the person whose life is being valued and discounts that number to its present value.[40] This discounting process recognizes that money earned in the future is worth less today. This is because if you invest an amount of money today in a bank or similar investment, it will be worth more in the future, since it will earn interest each year it is invested. The human capital approach yields values ranging from $100,000 to $500,000 for the life of a worker. This approach, however, likely

---

[38] In addition to the citations in the remainder of this section, the literature includes *Symposium*, 150 U. PA. L. REV. 1343–1553 (2002); Sunstein, *Cost-Benefit Default Principles*, 99 MICH. L. REV. 1651 (2001); McGarity, *A Cost-Benefit State*, 50 ADMIN. L. REV. 7 (1998); Heinzerling, *Regulatory Costs of Mythic Proporations*, 107 YALE L.J. 1981 (1998); Sunstein, *Legislative Forward: Congress, Constitutional Moments, and the Cost-Benefit State*, 48 STAN. L. REV. 247 (1996); McGarity, *Media Quality, Technology, and Cost-Benefit Strategies for Health and Environmental Regulation,* 46 LAW & CONTEMP. PROBS. 159 (1983); *see generally* T. McGARITY, REINVENTING RATIONALITY: THE ROLE OF REGULATORY ANALYSIS IN THE FEDERAL BUREAUCRACY (1991).

[39] *See, e.g.,* OVERREGULATION, *supra* note 37.

[40] *See* M. CONNERTON & M. MACCARTHY, COST-BENEFIT ANALYSIS & REGULATION: EXPRESSWAY TO REFORM OR BLIND ALLEY (1982); Vaupel, *On the Benefits of Health and Safety Regulation, in* THE BENEFITS OF HEALTH AND SAFETY REGULATION (G. Ferguson & E. LeVeen eds., 1981); Sagoff, *The Principles of Federal Pollution Control Law,* 71 MINN. L. REV. 19 (1986).

undervalues human life, because a person's value to society is clearly worth more than his salary.[41]

The other method of valuing human life, the willingness-to-pay method, attempts to measure what the person at risk would be willing to pay for reducing his or her mortality risk. One measure of willingness-to-pay is the wage premiums that workers receive for working in dangerous conditions. Since any worker would have to sacrifice that premium to work in safer conditions, workers who leave the job are willing to pay (in terms of foregone compensation) the amount of the premium to work in safer conditions. Relying on his own and other economic studies of wage premiums, Professor John Mendeloff calculates the value of a human life at $2.5 million.[42] Other analysts have established a value of as low as $1 million, and as high as between $5.4 and $6.8 million.[43]

Professor Mendeloff has compared the cost of saving one life under each of nine OSHA standards to the $2.5 million dollar value of a life. The results, reported on the following page in Table 9-6,[44] indicate that only OSHA's asbestos standard meets a cost-benefit test. Mendeloff's methodology was to divide the estimated cost of each standard (column 2) by the number of cancer deaths that the standard was likely to prevent (column 1). The result was the cost per cancer death avoided (column 3). For example, because the asbestos standard costs $173 million and saves 396 lives, the standard costs $0.4 million for each cancer death it prevents. Since the standard costs less to save a life ($.4 million) than the value of a human life ($2.5 million), the asbestos standard meets a cost-benefit test. By comparison, all of the other standards in Table 9-6 cost more than $2.5 million per live saved and therefore do not pass a cost-benefit test. The accuracy of Mendeloff's calculations has been challenged. Consider the objections raised in the next excerpt.

---

[41] *See* Graham & Vaupel, *The Value of A Human Life: What Difference Does It Make, in* WHAT ROLE FOR GOVERNMENT?: LESSONS FROM PUBLIC POLICY RESEARCH (R. Zeckhauser & D. Leebart eds., 1983).

[42] OVERREGULATION, *supra* note 37, at 51.

[43] Moore & Viscusi, COMPENSATION MECHANISMS FOR JOB RISKS: WAGES, WORKER'S COMPENSATION, AND PRODUCT LIABILITY 80 (1990); *see* Early, *What's A Life Worth?,* WASH. POST MAG., June 9, 1985.

[44] OVERREGULATION, *supra* note 37, at 22.

Table 9-6

Standard	Annual		
	Cancer Deaths Prevented	Total Cost (in millions)	Cost Per Cancer Death Avoided (in millions)
Asbestos	396	$173	$0.4
Vinyl Chloride	1	$40	$40
Coke Over Emissions	8-36	$200 - $400	$6 - $50
Benzene	6-21	$94 - $188	$4.5 - $32
DBCP	Not available	$6	Not available
Arsenic	5-20	$95 - $190	$4.8 - $38
Acrylonitrile	7	$18 - $37	$2.6 - $5.2
Lead	Not available	$460 - $690	Not available
Ethylene Oxide	4-16	$18 - $36	$1.1 - $9

MENDELOFF'S EVIDENCE OF OVERREGULATION

SIDNEY A. SHAPIRO & THOMAS O. MCGARITY, NOT SO PARADOXICAL: THE RATIONALE FOR TECHNOLOGY-BASED REGULATION, 1991 DUKE LAW JOURNAL 729, 731–36 *

On the cost side, Mendeloff's principal problem is his reliance on cost estimates that are based, for the most part, on notoriously inaccurate before-the-fact predictions. . . . Attempts to validate cost projections in light of subsequent experience have been sparse, but the evidence that does exist suggests that pre-implementation cost estimates are often far too high.

The inadequacies of Mendeloff's cost estimates pale in comparison with his failure to grapple with the exceedingly complex and value-laden issues inherent in estimating or measuring health and environmental regulations' benefits. To begin with, current techniques for risk assessment simply do not have the power to permit anything approximating precise calculations of the number of lives saved by a health or safety standard.[17]

---

* Reprinted by permission.

[17] Epidemiological studies of groups of humans who have historically received greater than normal exposures to chemicals can provide some direct evidence of risk, but these studies are notoriously inconclusive. Moreover, the validity of virtually any animal study can be significantly challenged by such questions as the appropriateness of extrapolating from high-dose animal exposures to low-dose human exposures, the choice of the particular species, the validity of test designs, and the applicability of exposure routes. In addition, few studies can satisfactorily surmount the problems inherent in calculating the number of persons exposed to any chemical. This information is expensive to obtain, and OSHA must heavily rely upon employers for this critical piece of the puzzle.

For example, the predictions of cancer risk assessment models can vary over ten orders of magnitude. Translated into economic terms, the difference between some low and high estimates of cancer risk approximates the difference between the price of a cup of coffee and the national debt.

The vinyl chloride standard . . . exemplifies the imprecision in risk measurement particularly well. In calculating that the vinyl chloride standard saves only one life per year, Mendeloff makes several assumptions that belittle the impact of the standard.[21] In fact, given the uncertainties in the information and the primitive state of current knowledge about environmental carcinogenesis, an estimate of twenty or even forty lives per year saved by the vinyl chloride standard would be equally plausible. Under this alternative calculation, the vinyl chloride standard costs under $1 to $2 million per life saved, which is well within the cost range that most persons, including Mendeloff, would consider reasonable.

In addition, Mendeloff fails to factor many benefits of health and safety regulation, other than the saving of lives, into his cost-benefit calculus. For example, Mendeloff does not attempt to measure the value of reducing the number of non-fatal illnesses, the lost productivity attributable to occupational disease, or the welfare and social security payments made to workers who become ill. Mendeloff also fails to consider adequately other "soft variables" benefits, such as the emotional loss to the injured workers' loved ones. Mendeloff argues that the "willingness to pay" measurement of benefits includes these benefits because workers factor the potential cost of the consequences of occupational illness into the payment they demand. No empirical evidence yet supports this claim. Moreover, the suggestion that people accurately consider the possible future loss of productivity when they engage in risky conduct, let alone the loss of grieving relatives, seems on its face highly implausible.

The vagaries inherent in calculating the benefits of a health or safety standard extend beyond the uncertainties in estimating the number of lives saved, the number of illnesses prevented, and the amount of pain avoided. The dollar-for-dollar comparisons that . . . Mendeloff . . . advocate[s] require that the numerical estimates of risk be multiplied by the dollar value of avoiding each of those unattractive outcomes. Thus, Mendeloff calculates the value of a human life as $2.5 million, relying on a "willingness-to-pay" measurement defined by the wage premium that workers receive for working in dangerous conditions. However, most wage premium studies (and all of those used by Mendeloff) are based on safety hazards, not health risks.

---

[21] To support his estimate, Mendeloff cites a study that relied on an early epidemiological study of workers exposed to vinyl chloride. This study estimated that only two deaths would be prevented each year by the current vinyl chloride standards. However, the study depends on the astounding assumption that the twenty-one angiosarcoma deaths definitively attributed to vinyl chloride exposure through 1976 constituted all of the deaths caused by vinyl chloride during the preceding forty years. Mendeloff also interprets an Environmental Protection Agency (EPA) risk assessment based upon animal bioassays to conclude that only two cancers per year would be prevented by the standard. But to reach this result, he reduced EPA's predictions by a factor of eight to take into account the fact that workers are only exposed for eight hours per day for forty-five years. Yet given that the EPA risk assessment could easily be off by a factor of ten, that estimate might just as easily be twenty or even forty cancers per year.

The little empirical evidence available on wage premiums for occupational illness is suspect for three reasons. First, most studies pre-date the implementation of OSHA's hazard communication standard.* Even with the hazard communication standard, many workers are still not apprised of all of the health risks to which they are exposed. Second, even assuming the availability of full information, most workers would be unable to wade through the extraordinarily complex risk data to form rational conclusions about the extent of risks in the workplace. Even if workers could understand the data, they would likely undervalue low-probability/high consequence risks based on the familiar "it-can't-happen-to-me" theory. In this case, "risk premium" measures of small risks to life would generally be too low. Finally, wage premium studies assume that workers make free and unconstrained choices. Unfortunately, low-paid workers in hazardous industries where there are no (or weak) unions may act more out of desperation than choice.

In addition, basing calculations of benefits on supposed wage premiums entails two controversial value judgments. First, most economists (although not Mendeloff) believe in discounting future health benefits to present value. Yet in cases of toxic substance exposure, where the onset of disease can be delayed by as much as thirty years, this practice effectively ignores the risk altogether.

Second, most of those who advocate application of health, safety, and environmental regulation to a quantitative cost-benefit litmus test apparently prefer a "willingness-to-pay" measure of the benefits of a health or environmental regulation to a "willingness-to-sell" approach. [But] . . . "willingness-to-sell" approach [is] the better measure . . . because it is not limited by the wealth of the beneficiaries of regulation. . . .

Given the vast technical uncertainties and anchorless moral judgments reflected in the cost-benefit calculations for health and safety standards, basing important public policy decisions on these quantitative cost-benefit comparisons is patently unreasonable.

––––

While Mendeloff concedes at least some of these objections, he argues that the cost of OSHA's standards exceeds their benefits by such a large magnitude that it is likely that OSHA engages in overregulation. Moreover, Mendeloff defends the use of cost-benefit analysis on the ground that it is better than doing nothing. He observes that absolute safety is beyond the financial capability of any society, that tradeoffs are therefore inevitable, and that it borders on dishonesty to suggest otherwise. Economists also argue that regulations that cost too much deprive society of resources with which to support different safety or health improvements or other desirable activities. Peter Asch amplifies:

> Those who are "done dirty" by the system are not likely to be helped
> by rendering the system more wasteful. The venerable analogy is to

––––

* Editor's note: OSHA's hazard communication standard requires employers to furnish employees with information about the chemicals to which they are exposed. *See* 54 Fed. Reg. 6886 (1989).

the economic "pie." Efficiency maximizes the size of the pie. An unfair economy might give Ms. Jones too small a slice, but she is unlikely to be helped by inefficient policies that reduce the pie size.[45]

Asch and other economists recognize that society may wish to help those who are "done dirty"—those who are injured by accidents and illnesses that are not prevented—but they object to using the regulatory system to do so. As Asch's reference to the economic pie suggests, economists argue that regulation beyond what is indicated by a cost-benefit test is inefficient and reduces economic welfare. If society is to help such injured or ill persons, economists prefer that any redistribution of wealth be done outside of the context of regulatory protection. They oppose using regulation for this purpose because it is "inefficient" which has the disadvantage of decreasing society's wealth. That is, it reduces the "size of the pie." Referring to Ms. Jones in the previous quote, Ash concludes, "She would, of course, be helped by a policy that taxes Mr. Rich in order to provide her with benefits; but such a redistribution of welfare, however, desirable it may be, does not argue for inefficiency."

3. NONECONOMIC ARGUMENTS

As Asch's comment indicates, economists are unwilling as a normative matter to accept the legitimacy of regulation that does not meet a cost-benefit test despite the problems in calculating costs and benefits. Regulation that does *not* meet a cost-benefit test, however, can be defended on distributional grounds, as the following excerpt explains.

SIDNEY A. SHAPIRO & THOMAS O. MCGARITY, NOT SO PARADOXICAL: THE RATIONALE FOR TECHNOLOGY-BASED REGULATION, 1991 DUKE LAW JOURNAL 729, 739–42 *

Economists defend the use of cost-benefit standards in formulating social policy on risk reduction by arguing that, in some cases, it is less expensive for society when employers pay compensation for illnesses rather than spending money to prevent them. This argument, however, ignores the ethical distinction between preventing death and compensating the victim's family after death occurs. As the Supreme Court's *Cotton Dust* reading of the OSHA Act's legislative history indicates, Congress apparently had this in mind when it rejected cost-benefit analysis for OSHA health standards. In addition, placing the entire burden of less stringent cost-benefit-based standards on workers is inequitable. Even if milder standards would ultimately make more resources available to society, there is no reason why workers should not be fully compensated for the losses they sustain that could have been prevented under more stringent standards. In other words, the resources saved by a switch to less stringent standards should go to the injured workers, rather than to the employers or their customers. Yet few economists advocate redistributing the efficiency gains of cost-benefit approaches to workers.

---

[45] P. Asch, Consumer Safety Regulation: Putting a Price on Life and Limb 59 (1988).

* Reprinted by permission.

Indeed, economic analysts respond that the distributional consequences of their prescriptions are beyond their bailiwick. For example, Mendeloff recognizes that the winners of a policy prescription do not necessarily have to pay the losers for their losses under his cost-benefit approach:

> Those who die because society rejects inefficient lifesaving programs will not be around to benefit from the bigger pie. Does this fact require condemnation of any policy that stops short of a maximum effort to prevent deaths? No. It is inevitable that public policy will create losers who are beyond the reach of compensation. But this fact should spur thinking about who the losers are and how we feel about their plight.

Surviving family members of workers whose deaths could have been prevented at a cost somewhat greater than the economist's optimal expenditure will take no comfort in the assurance that the loss of their loved one will stimulate scholars to think more about how society should feel about their plight.

When the distributional consequences of a cost-benefit regulatory world are considered, it becomes obvious that cost-benefit approaches undercompensate workers in two ways. First, cost-benefit analysts underestimate the value of a life. Second, compensation systems pay workers less than the full value of their lives, as defined by economists. Indeed, some workers are not compensated at all. Although public policy may inevitably create some losers beyond the reach of compensation, the cost-benefit approach creates too many uncompensated losers when compared with technology-based approaches.

In a world where workers are seldom fully compensated for occupational illness, the merit of a technology-based approach is that it reduces the need for victims to resort to the compensation system to a much larger degree than does the cost-benefit approach. Under the cost-benefit approach, significant financial burdens fall on those who are least able to sustain them, i.e., workers and their families. In comparison, the additional costs imposed by technology-based standards are passed on to consumers or absorbed by stockholders. The individual impact of these costs on any one consumer or stockholder is insignificant compared to the burden imposed on uncompensated or under-compensated workers and their families, who are forced to absorb the entire cost of their illnesses. Protecting workers with technology-based standards may be more costly to society than compensating them after-the-fact. But in the absence of a realistic mechanism to ensure adequate compensation, fairness demands that workers be protected from incurring the costs of illness where possible.

Mendeloff and other economic critics have difficulty believing that Congress really rejected the use of cost-benefit analysis. Because no rational consumer would pay twenty-five dollars in a private market for something that is worth only twenty dollars, the economist assumes that voters also intend for their representatives to reject policies whose costs exceed their "economic" benefits.

However, the economist fails to understand that public, social decisions provide citizens with an opportunity to give certain things a higher valuation than they would otherwise choose to give them in their private activities or in their capacity as individuals. In public forums, individuals are often willing to vote for outcomes that economic analysis would characterize as inefficient because these outcomes can confirm and serve important noneconomic values. As consumers, we may dislike paying more for manufactured products because of the costs of protecting workers, but as citizens we can rationally vote for these types of costly and (by the economist's "willingness-to-pay" measure) irrational goals. We vote in favor of such costly goals because they permit us to reaffirm our ideal that preventable occupational diseases are not merely inefficient—they are *wrong*.

NOTES AND QUESTIONS

1. What factors make it difficult to measure the costs and benefits of an OSHA health regulation? How do the difficulties of measuring the benefits relate to the reliability of scientific testing concerning risk and to the difficulty of calculating what a human life is worth?

2. In the *Cotton Dust* case, for what reason did the Supreme Court reject the argument that OSHA standards had to comply with a cost-benefits test? On what grounds might Congress have decided not to use a cost-benefit test to constrain OSHA rulemaking? Arguments that cost-benefit analysis "should" be used to guide regulatory decisionmaking are "normative," because they are based on value judgments about the proper extent of regulation in our society. What are the normative arguments for cost-benefit analysis? Why is "over-regulation" bad for society? How does cost-benefit analysis prevent overregulation? What are the normative criticisms of cost-benefit analysis? Do you find these persuasive? Why, or why not?

3. The normative debate is about the extent to which we should choose to make public policy decisions based exclusively on economic values. Do you base decisions in your life exclusively on economic values? What factors do you consider concerning whether to: (1) purchase a new car; (2) take a new job; and (3) get married? What role do economic factors such as costs and benefits play in each of these questions? Where is economics determinative, where does it have less weight, and where does it have no weight? To the extent that you consider costs and benefits, how easy are they to quantify? What do your answers suggest concerning the extent to which we should use cost-benefit analysis to guide regulatory decisionmaking concerning pollution?

4. One of the normative criticisms mentioned earlier is that a "willingness-to-sell" measurement should be used to value a life, rather than a "willingness-to-buy" measurement, because "willingness-to-sell" does not depend on a person's wealth.[46] Thus, it could be expected that individuals will sell their right to a safe workplace for more money than they would (or can) pay for a safe workplace. One reason analysts use "willingness-to-buy" is the availability of data; no similar data exists for "willingness-to-sell." Should we use a "willingness-to-buy" measure, because no data exists for another method of measurement, or should we avoid the use of cost-benefit analysis, because we lack data for a "willingness-to-pay" measurement?

---

[46] For more on this criticism of cost-benefit analysis (and others), *see* Kennedy, *Cost-Benefit Analysis of Entitlement Problems: A Critique,* 33 STAN. L. REV. 387 (1981); Lovins, *Cost-Risk-Benefit Assessment in Energy Policy,* 45 GEO. WASH. L. REV. 911 (1980). For a response to Kennedy, see Markovits, *Duncan's Do Nots: Cost-Benefit Analysis and the Determination of Legal Entitlements,* 36 STAN. L. REV. 116 (1984).

5. How is technology-based regulation responsive to the normative criticisms of cost-benefit analysis? Two supporters of technology-based regulation offer this answer:

> [T]echnology-based approaches . . . reflect a considered *normative* choice about the proper balance between lives and monetary costs. Acknowledging that society cannot vest workers with an unqualified right to an absolutely safe workplace, one may rationally assert that workers do have a right to insist that employers "do the best they can" to protect human health. In other words, society can decide that risky behavior is to be reduced beyond the point indicated by a cost-benefit test. Indeed, society may choose to limit its protection of workers only at the point where it would cause industry substantial economic dislocation.[47]

6. The *Cotton Dust* case was not the only Supreme Court challenge involving OSHA's mandate to protect workers. The *Cotton Dust* case addressed the issue of what level of regulation did Congress require the agency to adopt once it had identified some substance as potentially dangerous to workers. In *Industrial Union Department v. American Petroleum Institute*, 448 U.S. 607 (1980), the Court considered what type of evidence OSHA must produce that a substance is dangerous in order to have the authority to regulate. The case addressed OSHA's attempt to reduce the exposure of workers to benzene. OSHA's regulation set an exposure limit of 1 ppm (parts per million), but the scientific evidence only established an empirical relationship between cancer and benzene exposure at levels of 10 ppm or higher. OSHA, however, cited the testimony of cancer experts that, although there was no reliable scientific data that benzene caused cancer at levels below 10 ppm, this possibility could not be dismissed.

A deeply divided Supreme Court rejected OSHA's approach. Writing for a plurality of three judges, Justice Stevens concluded that implicit in OSHA's mandate was the requirement that OSHA had to make a threshold finding that benzene posed a "significant" risk to workers at 1 ppm. Justice Stevens found that because OSHA had not quantified the risk to workers at 1 ppm, it had not established that benzene posed a significant risk. Justice Powell, who concurred in the result, said that he was willing to accept expert scientific opinion as proof of "significant risk," but only if OSHA first proved that quantifiable evidence is not available, which it had not done.

7. Professor Cass Sunstein offers the following defense of the plurality's actions:

> . . . The language of the statute provides that the Secretary must assure, "to the extent feasible," that "no employee will suffer material impairment of health as a result of exposure to toxic substances." If the words are taken outside of their context, they are most naturally read to require the Secretary to regulate even minor risks to the point where the industry would be endangered by the regulation. . . . The

---

[47] Shapiro & McGarity, *Not So Paradoxical: The Rationale For Regulation*, 1991 DUKE L. REV. 729; *see* Schroeder, *In the Regulation of Manmade Carcinogens: If Feasibility Analysis is the Answer, What is the Question?*, 88 MICH. L. REV. 1483, 1504 (1990).

"significant risk" requirement—an aggressive construction of the statute—provides a salutary check on extremely costly regulation that does little good.[48]

8. By comparison, Justice Marshall, who dissented in *Industrial Union Department*, contended that the plurality's interpretation would unduly hamper OSHA's capacity to protect workers:

> . . . The plurality ignores the plain meaning of the Occupational Safety and Health Act of 1970 in order to bring the authority of the Secretary of Labor in line with the plurality's own views of proper regulatory policy. The unfortunate consequence is that the Federal Government's efforts to protect American workers from cancer and other crippling diseases may be substantially impaired. . . . In this case the Secretary of Labor found, on the basis of substantial evidence, that (1) exposure to benzene creates a risk of cancer, chromosomal damage, and a variety of nonmalignant but potentially fatal blood disorders, even at the level of 1 ppm; (2) no safe level of exposure has been shown; (3) benefits in the form of saved lives would be derived from the permanent standard; (4) the number of lives that would be saved could turn out to be either substantial or relatively small; (5) under the present state of scientific knowledge, it is impossible to calculate even in a rough way the number of lives that would be saved, at least without making assumptions that would appear absurd to much of the medical community; and (6) the standard would not materially harm the financial condition of the covered industries. . . .
>
> The critical problem in cases like the ones at bar is scientific uncertainty. While science has determined that exposure to benzene at levels above 1 ppm creates a definite risk of health impairment, the magnitude of the risk cannot be quantified at the present time. The risk at issue has hardly been shown to be insignificant; indeed, future research may reveal that the risk is in fact considerable. But the existing evidence may frequently be inadequate to enable the Secretary to make the threshold finding of "significance" that the Court requires today. If so, the consequence of the plurality's approach would be to subject American workers to a continuing risk of cancer and other fatal diseases, and to render the Federal Government powerless to take protective action on their behalf. Such an approach would place the burden of medical uncertainty squarely on the shoulders of the American worker, the intended beneficiary of the Occupational Safety and Health Act. . . .

9. Other environmental statutes are constructed like OSHA's mandate in that, Congress indicates a "statutory trigger" and a "statutory standard." The trigger establishes the evidentiary burden that an agency has to meet in order to regulate a toxic substance or other hazard. In OSHA's case, it most prove that a significant risk exists. Congress defines these triggers in different ways and thereby assigns a burden of proof that is easier or more difficult for the

---

[48] C. Sunstein, After the Rights Revolution: Reconceiving the Regulatory State 181 (1990).

agency to meet. The easier the burden is to meet the easier it is for the agency to protect the public or the environment. Second, Congress specifies a statutory standard or an indication of the level or stringency of regulation. As noted earlier, Congress has generally relied on a technology-based approach to set the level of regulation. In OSHA's case, it must establish the maximum level of protection that is "feasible." In additional to technology-based standards, Congress also relies on "open-ended balancing." These standards requires an agency to consider a number of factors, including regulatory costs and benefits, in setting the level of regulation, but Congress does not indicate the weight to be assigned to each factor. Thus, the agency is not required to balance costs and benefits.[49]

D. REGULATORY REFORM

Proponents of regulatory reform would replace technology-based standards with a requirement that health and safety standards must meet a cost-benefit test. They would also place greater reliance on market-based approaches to regulation.[50] These techniques are of two types. One change would be to rely on taxes and fees and the other is to utilize "emissions trading" and related programs.

1. TAXES AND FEES

So far you have studied three methods by which the government can address the problem of spillover costs. The government can rely on market transactions, tort remedies, or government regulation in the form of safety and health standards. Reformers would like the government to use a fourth method: taxes or fees. Under this approach, an entity would be required to pay an amount equal to the amount of spillover costs it creates.[51] To avoid this charge, the firm would engage in preventative efforts until the costs of such actions exceeded the amount of the charge. For example, recall the benzene factory and the workers. Assume the government assessed a tax on the factory equal to the spillover costs, or the revenue lost by the workers. The factory would reduce the number of barrels of benzene it produced until it became less expensive for it to pay the taxes than to take preventative efforts. In other words, the tax works in a similar fashion to giving the workers a tort remedy, except that it is assessed by the government and does not require those affected by the externality to sue. And, like the tort remedy, the tax in theory forces the producer to assume as internal costs all of the costs attributable to the production of a commodity. Unlike the tort remedy, however, the tax creates revenue that can be used by the government for social purposes.

Thus, Congress could require employers to pay a tax based on workplace illnesses that they fail to prevent. Employers would reduce the exposure of

---

[49] For a more detailed description of the two aspects of environmental regulation, see S. SHAPIRO & R. GLICKSMAN, RISK REGULATION AT RISK: RESTORING A PRAGMATIC APPROACH (2003).

[50] See Richards, *Framing Environmental Policy Instrument Choice*, 10 DUKE ENVTL' L. & POL. FORUM 221 (2000); Keohane, Revesz & Stavins, *The Choice of Regulatory Instruments in Environmental Policy*, 22 HARV. ENVT'L L. REV. 313 (1998)

[51] See Brennan & Johnson, *Pollution Control by Effluent Charges: It Works in the Federal Republic of Germany, Why Not in the U.S.?*, 40 NAT'L RESOURCES J. 645 (2000).

workers to toxic substances covered by the tax up to the point where it is less expensive to pay the tax than take additional precautions. If the amount of tax is equal to the value of the improvement to workers, the tax would produce the same investment in health precautions as efficient labor markets. As you will read in more detail shortly, reformers prefer this approach because, as compared to OSHA regulation, a tax is a more efficient method by which to reduce workplace risks. Under OSHA standards, all employers must comply with the level of safety that OSHA specifies regardless of the cost of compliance. Under a tax approach, an employer would have the option of paying the tax if it was less expensive than the cost of abatement of a hazard.

2. EMISSIONS TRADING

Emissions trading affects the extent to which individual firms reduce pollution, but it does not affect the overall reduction of pollution that is achieved. The aim is to reduce the overall cost of pollution abatement by permitting firms to adjust the level of abatement based on the cost of the abatement.

a. EXTERNAL TRADING

One form of emissions trading allows firms which are willing to undertake more abatement than regulations require to sell pollution rights to firms that wish to undertake less abatement than the regulations require. For reasons that will be made clear, this technique will not work in the context of workplace pollution, but it has considerable potential concerning environmental pollution. In the 1990 amendments to the Clean Air Act (CAA), for example, Congress adopted emissions trading for some types of pollution.[52]

For external emissions trading, a firm is assigned permits to dispose of a certain amount of pollution. It can sell all or some of these permits, or it can purchase additional permits. Despite this trading, the total amount of pollution should not change. If a firm sells some of its permits, it will have to reduce the amount of pollution it emits because it has fewer permits to pollute. Conversely, the firm that bought the permits can emit more pollution. The advantage of this approach is efficiency. A firm will sell permits if the cost of reducing pollution is less than the money it can earn from selling permits. Conversely, a firm will buy permits if the cost of the permits is less than its pollution abatement costs. In this manner, firms that have lower pollution reduction costs will undertake more abatement than firms that have higher costs. This should reduce the total cost of pollution abatement. Thus, the public obtains the same level of abatement, but at a lower cost. By comparison, emissions trading would not be useful in the workplace context because those affected by workplace pollution would not be indifferent to how much each employer abates.[53]

---

[52] Pub. L. No. 101-549, 104 Stat. 2399 (1990); *see* Stevenson, *Trying A Market Approach to Smog*, N.Y. TIMES, May 25, 1992, at C1.

[53] *See* Remy and Revesz, *Markets and Geography: Designing Marketable Permits Schemes to Control Local and Regional Pollutants*, 28 ECOLOGY L.Q. 569 (2000).

b. INTERNAL TRADING

Emissions trading can also occur within the context of just one firm. These programs permit a polluter to increase the pollution emitted from one source if there is a corresponding reduction from another source. This flexibility permits firms to undertake more pollution abatement where it can be done in the least expensive manner.

The "bubble concept" is one such method. In rules adopted to prevent the serious deterioration of air quality in areas which already meet the requirements of the CAA (known as "PSD" areas), EPA permits a firm to choose which sources of pollution within a facility it would reduce. Prior to the bubble program, EPA required uniform reductions for every smokestack, vent, and loading and transfer operation within an industrial facility, regardless of the relative cost of reducing emissions from each source. Under the bubble approach, a firm is told the total reduction in pollution that it must achieve, and it is then free to achieve that reduction by concentrating its efforts on the sources that can be reduced at the least cost. In *Chevron U.S.A., Inc. v. Natural Resources Defense Council, Inc.,* 467 U.S. 837 (1984), which is discussed in Chapter 3, the Supreme Court approved the bubble concept as consistent with EPA's mandate under the CAA. In 1987, two economists estimated that the forty-two bubbles that EPA had approved resulted in savings of about $300 million.[54]

3. ADVANTAGES

In the following excerpt, Professor Sunstein summarizes the case for market-based incentives, which he argues are superior to technology-based regulation, such as that used by OSHA.

CASS R. SUNSTEIN, ADMINISTRATIVE SUBSTANCE, 1991 DUKE LAW JOURNAL 607, 627–29, 637–42 *

A large source of regulatory failure in the United States is the use of rigid, highly bureaucratized "command-and-control" regulation. The resulting programs dictate national control strategies for hundreds, thousands, or even millions of companies and individuals in an exceptionally diverse nation. Command-and-control regulation is a dominant part of American government in such areas as environmental protection and occupational safety and health.

In the environmental context, command-and-control approaches usually take the form of regulatory requirements of the "best available technology" (so-called BAT requirements). BAT strategies pervade federal law. Indeed, they are a defining characteristic of the regulation of the air, water, and workplace conditions.

One of the many problems with BAT strategies is that they systematically ignore the enormous differences among plants, industries, and geographical areas in the United States. In view of these differences, nationally uniform

---

[54] Hahn & Hester, *The Market for Bads: EPA's Experience with Emissions Trading,* 3/4 REGULATION 48, 50 (1987)

* Reprinted by permission.

technological requirements are wildly inefficient. It does not seem sensible to impose identical technological requirements on diverse industries—regardless of whether they are polluted or clean, populated or empty, or expensive or cheap to clean up.

The problems go deeper still. BAT requirements usually apply only to new entrants in the market. By requiring all new industries to adopt costly technology while allowing existing plants and industries to conform to more lenient standards, BAT strategies penalize new products. In this way, they discourage investment and perpetuate old, dirty technology. In the environmental arena, for example, BAT strategies discourage new pollution control technologies by requiring that industries adopt new technology for no financial gain. Under the BAT approach, a company that innovates in this area will simply have to invest more in pollution control. BAT requirements punish such companies for their development of new control technology, rather than rewarding them. In addition, BAT strategies are extremely expensive to enforce, imposing extraordinary monitoring burdens on agencies that employ them.

Perhaps worse, by focusing on the technology at the end of the pipe, BAT strategies are aimed at superficial symptoms rather than underlying causes of pollution. For example, the EPA has forced coal-fired power plants to adopt costly "scrubbing" strategies to deal with sulfur dioxide emissions that cause acid rain. A far better approach would use financial incentives to encourage American consumers and industries to increase energy conservation and efficiency, and to shift to cleaner, renewable fuels.

Most fundamentally, the BAT approach is severely deficient from the standpoint of a well-functioning political process. BAT strategies ensure that citizens and representatives will focus their attention on largely incidental and nearly impenetrable questions about currently available technologies, rather than on the appropriate levels of reduction. Technological debates are singularly ill-suited for democratic resolution. They also distract attention from the central issue of determining the appropriate degree and nature of regulatory protection. Moreover, the focus on "means" increases the power of well-organized private groups, by allowing them to use regulation to serve their own parochial ends. The promotion of ethanol (helpful to corn farmers although not necessarily to environmental protection) and scrubbers (helpful to the eastern coal industry although not necessarily to air quality) are prominent examples of interest group influence on BAT-focused systems.

In these respects, BAT strategies are emblematic of a large problem in current regulation. Centralization at the national level diminishes opportunities for citizen participation; it also promotes struggles among well-organized factions. The focus on technological details and sensational incidents ensures that public education about risk levels and risk comparisons will be incomplete and episodic. These characteristics of contemporary administrative law fall far short of guaranteeing democratic control over decisions about how best to characterize and to achieve social goals. [Professor Sunstein suggests some of the ways in which market-incentive approaches could replace command-and-control approaches:]

a. *Emissions trading programs.* An important and increasingly used incentive-based system is "emissions trading." Under emissions trading programs, polluters who exceed air pollution standards can purchase permits from other polluters who are below the maximum levels. Polluters may legally exceed the regulatory standards if they obtain a permit to do so. If the emissions trading program is correctly administered, a region will meet the same pollution standards overall; those who pollute too much will be balanced by those who reduce more than they must. The price of the permits is determined by the market. . . .

In one bold stroke, a system of tradeable permits would create market-based disincentives to pollute and market-based incentives for pollution control. By enlisting the aid of private markets, this system would reward rather than punish technological innovation in pollution control. . . .

Some argue that emissions trading should be rejected on the theory that it creates a "license to pollute," or that it wrongly treats clean air or water like any other commodity traded on markets. . . .

. . . As a first approximation, a flat ban on an activity may well be preferable to a cash payment for resulting harm, assuming that there are no transaction costs (such as enforcement expenditures), when and only when the right level of the underlying activity is zero. The right level of assaults and poisonings seems to be zero. It would therefore be absurd to allow people to assault and poison others as long as they are willing to compensate people for the harm. Such a strategy would be inconsistent with the underlying goal of eliminating the conduct altogether.

By contrast, the appropriate emissions level for many pollutants is well above zero. For example, complete elimination of sulfur dioxide emissions would cause a severe energy shortage—one that would dramatically increase poverty, health risks, unemployment, and inflation. In this respect, a ban on sulfur dioxide emissions would be difficult to justify. For those pollutants whose continued emission is necessary to achieve desirable social goals, a fee, designed to bring about the optimal emissions level, makes far more sense than a ban. . . .

b. *Taxation.* The simplest reform strategy to control pesticides and other toxic substances would be to impose a tax on their use. Through this single step, people would decrease their use of pesticides. This strategy would encourage the use of alternative methods of pest control, including those that do not rely on chemicals. Perhaps funds collected from a pesticide tax could be allocated to help farmers use biological techniques efficiently.

Taxation can also be used to decrease automobile emissions. Instead of existing regulations that impose technological requirements on new cars (which are often ineffective and difficult to monitor, and which create incentives to keep old cars on the road longer), Congress should adopt broad plans to reduce dependence on the automobile. Strategies might include "old car" taxes or increased gasoline taxes. . . .

It is not sufficient to respond that gasoline taxes (or any other efforts that require actors to internalize the social costs of their harmful activity) would be "regressive," in the sense that the poor would feel their effects more sharply than the well-to-do. To be sure, any effort to use incentives is likely to be harder on those with few resources than on those with many. Indeed, any strategy to control many social problems will increase prices, and thus hit the poor especially hard. For at least three reasons, however, a system requiring an activity to reflect its true social costs should not be deemed illegitimate merely because it has more severe consequences for the poor.

First, well-functioning markets ensure that the prices of products reflect their social costs. Any pricing system, in any market, works against the poor in the sense that poor people are less able to pay for commodities than are those with greater resources. . . .

When government refuses to ensure that products (like energy) reflect their environmental costs, the result is analytically the same as a government decision to fix prices. Such a refusal will lower the price of the resulting products, and some poor people will always benefit from lower prices. But such a result is hardly a desirable approach to the problem of poverty, any more than an across-the-board, governmentally mandated ten percent reduction in the price of (say) automobiles and soap, which it rather resembles.

Second, the pollution tax is no more regressive than command-and-control strategies. Suppose, for example, that government continues to require expensive, statutorily specified antipollution devices for new cars. This system also imposes costs that will ultimately be reflected in prices—but in a more arbitrary, less predictable, and less visible way than a direct tax. . . .

Third, and finally, a failure to require enterprises to bear the full environmental and social costs of their activities is not a sensible redistribution strategy. The class of beneficiaries simply does not correspond to the category of needy people. A government subsidy that lowers the cost of sources of carbon-dioxide and other greenhouse gases benefits people who use those harmful substances. These beneficiaries are not the people who can legitimately claim government support. For all these reasons, the apparently regressive character of any "pollution tax" does not count as a reason against its use.

c. *Deposits*. Deposits might be especially useful in the regulation of solid and hazardous waste. The current waste control regulations ensure that neither producers nor consumers of waste materials pay disposal costs; neither has an incentive to reduce waste. A deposit system, however, would make it more expensive to dispose of substances in landfills or in the oceans, by requiring that those who handle waste pay a deposit, refundable in whole or in part upon a showing of safe disposal and recycling. The government would thus encourage recycling and discourage the accumulation of solid and hazardous waste.

4. DISADVANTAGES

Other analysts have cautioned that a market-incentives approach is not necessarily the nirvana that its proponents allege. Consider the following criticisms of Professor Sunstein's endorsement of a tax-based approach as superior to technology-based regulation in occupational safety and health.

SIDNEY A. SHAPIRO & THOMAS O. MCGARITY, NOT SO PARADOXICAL: THE RATIONALE FOR TECHNOLOGY-BASED REGULATION, 1991 DUKE LAW JOURNAL 729, 745–51 [*]

Specifically, in discussing market-based incentives, Sunstein asserts that "[i]f the ultimate goal is to reduce pollution sharply, then we should simply issue few permits." He also assumes that risks from toxic substances could easily be reduced by simply assessing high taxes on, for examples, toxic waste disposal and automobile emissions. These optimistic assessments may underestimate the difficulties inherent in estimating risks and benefits. In addition, the incentive-based approach adds new uncertainties to the prediction of the number of permits and level of taxes necessary to achieve a given level of risk reduction, on top of the already existing uncertainties about how various levels of exposure to toxic substances affect humans and the environment. Unless agencies are prepared to tolerate potentially high exposures and/or devastating short-term economic consequences during the time it takes for the system to reach "steady state," proceedings examining the level of tax or the issuable number of permits are likely to be highly contentious. Moreover, because industry will likely resist any change to the status quo, especially if it requires immediate outlays, implementation of any market-based program is likely to be slow. . . .

In addition to providing a speedier approach to regulation, BAT strategies, when compared to market-based approaches, stack up well on other instrumental grounds. A comparison of Sunstein's four indictments of BAT with the probable implementation difficulties of a market-based approach indicates that BAT is not nearly as oafish as Sunstein suggests, and that market-based approaches are not nearly as neat.

First, Sunstein argues that because BAT strategies ignore the enormous differences among plants in industries and among geographical areas, these strategies are "wildly inefficient." According to Sunstein, emissions trading programs perform more efficiently because they allow firms with high abatement costs to buy additional permits to pollute from firms with low abatement costs. However, BAT systems do not operate in the blind manner that Sunstein indicates. No agency ignores the types of geographical and intra-industry differences Sunstein cites. Rather, agencies utilize a system of variances to account for these differences. Emissions trading may be less expensive to administer than the relatively cumbersome system of variances, and the variance process can be abused to allow unjustified departures from the national standards. However, characterizing the BAT approach as "wildly" inefficient is an inaccurate overstatement of BAT's performance in practice.

Moreover, Sunstein fails to discuss the administrative costs associated with the reforms that he proposes. For example, because we do not know exactly how much abatement a pollution or injury tax would cause, the tax would likely have to be adjusted several times to meet the abatement goals. Aside from the problem of whether Congress (or any legislature) would be willing to alter the tax after it has been initially set, the costs associated with these

---

[*] Reprinted by permission.

changes must be factored into any comparison of BAT and market-related incentives.

Second, Sunstein argues that BAT strategies are "extremely expensive to enforce, imposing extraordinary monitoring burdens" on EPA and OSHA. But this is not reality. BAT strategies are less expensive to enforce because inspectors are only required to determine whether a firm has installed the required technology and continues to operate it properly. By comparison, emissions trading and pollution taxes require inspectors to monitor constantly the amount of pollution that a plant emits. In many cases, monitoring all the possible discharge points for air and water pollution will be far more expensive and difficult than identifying whether a firm is using a required technology. In the air pollution context, the incentive-based approach would create an incentive to abuse the system by hiding emissions in all but the very simplest plants.

Third, Sunstein contends that because BAT strategies impose stricter regulatory requirements on new plants and industries than old ones, they penalize new products and thereby perpetuate old, dirty technology. In contrast, pollution taxes and marketable permits would, according to Sunstein, induce firms to invest in new technologies. To the extent the system is adequately policed to ensure that firms do not avoid paying the taxes in the first place, or cheat by emitting in excess of their permits, we agree with this assessment. However, the current income tax system, with its monument to the ingenuity of tax avoidance, does not inspire optimism on this point.

Finally, Sunstein objects to using regulation to pursue redistributive objectives, because it is less efficient in obtaining these objectives than more direct redistribution techniques. Thus, if society prefers to shift the costs of occupational disease from workers to their employers, Sunstein would advocate revamping workers' compensation rather than using BAT strategies to accomplish this goal. Although we have already expressed normative objections to choosing compensation over prevention, we also believe that compensation is unlikely to be increased to the point where it fully compensates workers for their injuries and illnesses.

First, fifty states must act to reform workers' compensation; this fact alone makes significant reform unlikely. In addition, experience indicates that states are unlikely to increase benefits any time soon. In the face of employer threats to relocate to states less inclined to redistribute wealth from employers to employees, most states will be unwilling to become the first to reform their workers' compensation laws. Congress could possibly overcome these difficulties by federalizing workers' compensation, but it is unlikely to take such a drastic step in the near future because of political considerations. Congress might more feasibly enact an injury tax and make the proceeds available to the states to augment workers' compensation funding for both injuries and diseases. Although this could be a positive step drawing on the incentive-based approach and accomplishing redistributive goals, it would not address the more pressing problem of uncompensated workplace diseases.

Yet even this step is unlikely to provide full compensation for workers for injuries and illnesses. Workers' compensation systems have been designed to keep an employee from starving, rather than to compensate the worker for medical expenses and lost wages. Thus, if Sunstein intends to ensure that workers' compensation, an injury tax, or some combination of the two forces employers to bear the full costs of the injuries and illnesses they cause, he should forthrightly press for the revolutionary recasting of current workers' compensation regimes that this would require.

Even with its problems, technology-based regulation compares favorably with market-related incentives from a strictly instrumental perspective. We therefore consider a more incremental path to occupational safety and health reform more likely. Congress might be persuaded to authorize OSHA to use BAT, while at the same time allow OSHA to regulate more stringently if necessary to reduce or eliminate significant workplace risks. Unlike drastic workers' compensation reform, this step would protect workers before they are injured, and reduce the number of illnesses for which employees would never be fully compensated because of difficulties in establishing cause-effect relationships between workplace exposures and individual diseases.

NOTES AND QUESTIONS

1. Assume that your city council determines that it will soon run out of space to bury garbage. The council is considering the following options: (1) mandating that bottles, cans, etc., be recycled in separate containers at curbside for pickup by city workers; (2) raising monthly fees for picking up garbage by $20 per household to pay for the costs of a new landfill; (3) charging households for garbage pickup based on the number of containers of garbage that city workers collect. Which solution or solutions would you favor and why?

2. There is a considerable debate in the literature over the merits of technology-based regulation versus market incentives.[55] Professor Sunstein argues that BAT regulation is "wildly inefficient" because every firm is required to engage in the same level of abatement regardless of its costs. On what grounds do Professors McGarity and Shapiro deny this charge? Assuming that Professor Sunstein's charge is accurate, how would taxes or fees remedy the problem? What problems do Professors McGarity and Shapiro foresee with a tax approach?

3. On what ground does Professor Sunstein contend that BAT regulation discourages innovation? What response is given by Professors McGarity and Shapiro? Assuming that Professor Sunstein's contention is accurate, how would taxes encourage more innovation?

4. Professor Sunstein also maintains that reliance on economic incentives is preferable to BAT regulation because such programs require as their starting point an explicit decision concerning what levels of pollution are acceptable. By comparison, BAT focuses on what technology exists to reduce a pollutant. Why is a focus on the acceptable level of pollution an advantage?

---

[55] *See, e.g.,* Steinzor, *Toward Better Bubbles and Future Lives: A Progressive Response to the Conservative Agenda for Reforming Environmental Law,* 32 ENVT'L L. REP. 11421 (2002); Thompson, *Political Obstacles to Implementation of Emissions Markets,* 40 NAT'L RESOURCES J. 645 (2000); Cole & Grossman, *When is Command-and-Control Effective? Institutions, Technology, and the Comparative Efficiency of Alternative Regulatory Regimes for Environmental Protection,* 1999 WIS. L. REV. 887; Driesen, *Is Emissions Trading An Economic Incentive Program?: Replacing the Command and Control/Economic Inventive Dichotomy,* 55 WASH. & LEE. L. REV. 289 (1998).

According to Professor Sunstein, how would this focus make environmental decisionmaking more democratic?[56] What response do Professors McGarity and Shapiro make? Why do they regard the need to determine an acceptable level of pollution as a disadvantage of market incentives?[57]

5. If emissions trading works in the manner indicated by its proponents, is there any policy reason why it should not be adopted? Can anyone object to a program that achieves the same level of abatement at less cost? Consider Steven Kelman's warning that we should be "hesitant about the use of economic incentives in environmental policy out of concerns about the *kind of society we help create* when we choose to change over to doing so." For example, Kelman notes, "If a society uses economic incentives in environmental policy, it fails to make a statement stigmatizing polluting behavior. If one believes that people may justifiably wish the societies they live in on occasion to make approbatory or stigmatory statements about certain behaviors, and if one further believes that polluting behavior should be stigmatized, then one has reason to be concerned with using economic incentives in environmental policy." Kelman cites three grounds for having a social process that stigmatizes polluting behavior by declaring it illegal:

> First, such stigmatization provides an occasion for a social statement expressing a judgment condemning such behavior, a judgment that pleases environmentalists. Second, such stigmatization encourages development of preferences that attach a strong weight to high environmental quality. Third, such stigmatization encourages compliance by polluters with environmental demands.[58]

6. Charles Schultze, one of the earliest supporters of market incentives, disputes Kelman's assertion concerning the importance of stigmatizing behavior that produces pollution. He argues that "If I want to cut down on pollution, indignant tirades about social responsibility can't hold a candle to schemes that reduce the profits of firms that pollute." According to Schultze, the reason is simple: "Harnessing the 'base' motive of material self-interest to promote the common good" is "perhaps *the* most important social invention that mankind has yet achieved."[59]

7. With whom do you agree? Should we rely on economic incentives to reduce spillover costs or are there good reasons to rely on standard-setting such as BAT regulations?

---

[56] For support of Sunstein's conclusion that market incentives promote more democratic decisionmaking, see Ackerman & Stewart, *Reforming Environmental Law: The Democratic Case for Market Incentives*, 13 COLUM. J. ENVTL. L. 171 (1988); Ackerman & Stewart, *Reforming Environmental Law*, 37 STAN. L. REV. 1333 (1985).

[57] For an argument that economic incentives may not promote more democratic decisionmaking, see Heinzerling, *Selling Pollution, Forcing Democracy*, 14 STAN. ENVT'L L.J. 300 (1995).

[58] S. KELMAN, WHAT PRICE INCENTIVES: ECONOMISTS AND THE ENVIRONMENT 27, 46–47 (1981).

[59] C. SCHULTZE, THE PUBLIC USE OF THE PRIVATE INTEREST 18 (1977).

Chapter 10

INADEQUATE INFORMATION: DRUG AND OCCUPATIONAL LICENSING

A market will operate in an efficient manner only when buyers have adequate information about the products and services they purchase. If a consumer lacks product or service information, the person may end up purchasing a good or service that is not of the quality the consumer assumed. When this happens, the consumer will at least be disappointed, and worse, the person may be injured, if the product or service turns out to be dangerous to that person. If the consumer had accurate information at the time of the purchase, the person would not have purchased the product or service, or at least would not have paid the same price for it. When consumers lack information, the market will be inefficient, because products or services will be overproduced. With accurate information, less of the product or service would have been sold.

This chapter focuses on two prominent examples of regulation used to address the problem of inadequate information: the regulation of prescription drugs by the Food and Drug Administration (FDA) and occupational licensing by state boards or agencies. FDA controls the market entry of prescription drugs because drug manufacturers are required to have a license to sell their products in interstate commerce. FDA also has the authority to seize a drug and remove it from the market under certain conditions. Similarly, state boards engaged in occupational licensing control entry by prohibiting the marketing of services without a license, and they have the authority to revoke a license under certain conditions. In both cases, the primary justification for regulation is that certain types of defects in markets limit the extent and type of information available to consumers concerning the products and services they purchase.

There is, however, another way to respond to the problem of inadequate information. The government can simply order sellers or professionals to disclose certain types of information to consumers as a condition of selling the product or service.

This chapter will consider why there is inadequate consumer information in some markets, and what response the government should make. The second issue involves the question of whether the government should require sellers to provide additional information, which leaves the decision whether to buy a product entirely with the consumer, or whether the government should prohibit the sale of a product unless the seller obtains a license from the government, which prevents consumers from buying products that are not licensed.

A. JUSTIFICATIONS FOR REGULATION

An unregulated market will operate efficiently only if certain conditions exist. As Chapter 2 explained, an efficient market is one that produces exactly the types and quantities of goods or services demanded by consumers. But a market will operate in this fashion only if consumers have adequate information about the qualities of the products they wish to purchase. When information is limited, consumers buy products that, if they had better information, they would not purchase, or they would purchase in smaller quantities. This permits sellers to charge a higher price for the product than they could obtain in a more efficient market.[1]

The problem posed by inadequate information can be demonstrated by considering a market for a hazardous product.[2] In Figure 10-1, consumers who are uninformed concerning the hazard will generate demand curve D1 given supply curve S. As a result, the market will produce quantity Q1. If consumers become "moderately" informed about the hazard, demand will fall to D2, which will produce quantity Q2. If consumers become "highly" informed, demand will fall to D3, which will produce quantity Q3. When consumers are "highly" informed—in the sense that they understand the risk that a product poses—more consumers will prefer to purchase a safer substitute (or do without the product) than in a market with less product information.

Figure 10-1: Relationship of Information and Quanitity Demanded

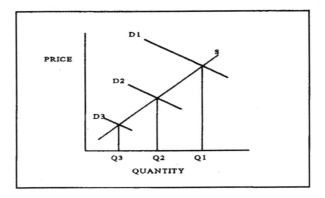

Three types of defects operate to limit the information available to consumers in unregulated markets. Consumers may not demand information about a product because the cost of the information is more than consumers are willing to pay. But even if consumers are willing to pay for information about a product, two other defects can prevent them from obtaining it. Sellers may find it to their advantage to limit or distort information about some products, and third parties may find it unprofitable to sell accurate information to consumers about the quality of those products.

---

[1] D. Weimer & A. Vining, Policy Analysis: Concepts And Practice 69–77 (2d ed. 1992); Stigler, *The Economics of Information,* 69 J. Pol. Econ. 213, 220 (1961).

[2] *See* P. Asch, Consumer Safety Regulation: Putting A Price On Life And Limb 4 (1988).

1. CONSUMER DEMAND

The amount of information available concerning a product is a function of consumer incentives to demand product or service information. Consumers will demand information when the value of the information is greater than their "search costs," or the cost of obtaining the information. For example, consumers will do little or no research concerning which ball-point pen will last the longest, because the cost of obtaining the information is likely to exceed any savings that obtaining the information would make possible. Because of high search costs, consumers also are unable to demand information that could protect them from serious injuries. For example, consumers cannot, unaided, evaluate the potential effectiveness or dangers of a drug, nor would it make any sense for the consumer to obtain a pharmacy or medical degree in order to be able to do so. A consumer can consult a physician, which involves less expensive search costs, but the person cannot readily evaluate the competence of the doctor either.

Economists refer to the services provided by physicians, lawyers, and other similar service providers as "credence goods" because it is the service provider who determines the how much of the good or service the buyer needs.[3] Buyers of credence goods not only cannot assess how much of the good that they need, they are not in a position to determine how well the service was performed, which can encourage opportunistic behavior on the part of the seller. The risk that automobile shops will recommend unnecessary repairs is a good example of such behavior.

Consumer search costs are also affected by information asymmetries exploited by sellers. For example, consumers are not in a position to demand third-party information about chemicals, because they lack accessible chemical identity data:

> A fundamental information asymmetry in the chemicals market is created by the fact that the chemical producer knows what the chemical is, while the buyer does not. Without the chemical identity, the buyer cannot seek assistance in developing information independently. Chemical manufacturers [are] . . . "riding" on consumer ignorance; they benefit by not providing toxicity data, at the expense of consumer uncertainty and injury. Absent regulation, the information is likely to remain undisclosed and unexamined, since the interests of its holders are adverse to those of the beneficiaries of disclosure.[4]

2. SELLER INCENTIVES

Even if consumers demand information, sellers will have an economic incentive to limit or skew information in four types of cases. It will not be in a firm's interest to disclose information when disclosure will help a firm's competitors, reveal defects in the firm's product or service, or decrease demand for the product or service, regardless of who makes or furnishes it, or when

---

[3] *See* Hadfield, *Bias in the Evolution of Legal Rules,* 80 Geo. L.J. 583 (1992).

[4] Lyndon, *Information Economics and Chemical Toxicity: Designing Laws To Produce and Use Data,* 87 Mich. L. Rev. 1795, 1815 (1989).

the cost of producing and releasing the information is less than the additional revenue that its release will generate.[5]

In some cases, sellers will recognize that supplying the information will help competitors more than themselves. Sellers therefore restrict or alter such information in order to protect sales of their own product. A food manufacturer, for example, may be reluctant to label the fat content of a food that is high in cholesterol as a means of blocking comparisons with other labeled products. Another example involves pharmaceutical drugs. Before FDA required drug manufacturers to do so, they did not print the generic (general scientific) name of their product, as well as the brand name, in advertising or on the label. FDA's labeling requirement makes it possible for consumers to recognize more easily when competitors sell the same drug for a lower price under a different brand name or under the generic name.[6] Sellers may also skew the information provided. Selling a product in a different sized box or a different weight than competitors makes it difficult for consumers to make price comparisons unless the store utilizes unit pricing.

In other cases, sellers of defective or dangerous products deliberately mislead consumers by conveying false information or by omitting a key fact. Market forces can police this behavior to some extent in two ways. First, sellers who mislead consumers may develop a reputation for shoddy workmanship, which will alert consumers not to purchase their products. Reputation, however, is less important for sellers that do not depend on repeat business, such as transient home repair companies. Other sellers are protected from developing a poor reputation because consumers are often unable to tell they have received poor service. Medical providers and lawyers are in this category.[7]

Second, competitors would appear to have an incentive to expose false or misleading claims in order to protect their own sales.[8] Nevertheless, Professor Pitofsky points out that "in the scores of proceedings in which the FTC successfully challenged the truth of major advertising themes, there was not a single instance in which rivals used their own access to channels of consumer information to expose deceptions."[9] Pitofsky cites several reasons why companies fail to expose shoddy practices by their competitors—including the risk that the competitors will retaliate.

Sellers may also decline to provide information about their products because any increase in their own sales will be offset by a general decline in consumer demand. For example, cigarette manufacturers did not voluntarily advertise low tar and nicotine brands, which may be safer to smoke, because calling the consumers' attention to the risks of smoking would have decreased the

---

[5] *See* Beales, Craswell, & Salop, *The Efficient Regulation of Consumer Regulation,* 24 J.L. & Econ. 491, 492 (1981); Rothschild, *Models of Market Organization with Imperfect Information: A Survey,* 81 J. Pol. Econ. 1283, 1284–86 (1973); Nelson, *Information and Consumer Behavior,* 78 J. Pol. Econ. 311, 312 (1970).

[6] S. Breyer, Regulation And Its Reform 27 (1982).

[7] R. Posner, Regulation Of Advertising By The FTC 5 (1973).

[8] *Id.* at 5–6.

[9] Pitofsky, *Beyond Nader: Consumer Protection and the Regulation of Advertising,* 90 Harv. L. Rev. 661, 667 (1977).

overall demand for cigarettes. Similarly, airlines do not advertise that they have had fewer crashes than their competitors out of a concern of decreasing consumer demand for their service.

3. INFORMATION IS A PUBLIC GOOD

Sellers are not the only source of information concerning their products. Consumers can consult *Consumer Reports,* published by Consumers Union, or other independent sources of information. The availability of third-party sources of information is limited, however, by the "public goods" characteristic of information. When the purchaser of a private good, such as a candy bar, consumes it, it is of no value to subsequent consumers. By comparison, public goods are products or services that can be used by more than one person. Information is a public good, because those who purchase information can give or resell it to other consumers. When one consumer reads *Consumer Reports,* he or she does not destroy its value to other consumers. Firms who sell information, therefore, face the problem that their customers can easily become their competitors. Sellers will be reluctant to invest in the production of information for resale, unless the confidentiality of information can be protected through contract arrangements.[10] For example, firms that produce market survey information about consumer attitudes and preferences require those who purchase the information to sign a confidentiality agreement. Because Consumers Union is a not-for-profit organization, it does not have this disincentive.

NOTES AND QUESTIONS

1. Are consumers in the market for legal services poorly informed, moderately well informed, or well informed about the quality of legal services? Do corporate purchasers of legal services have more information about service quality than individual consumers? Which of the previous factors limit the amount of information that is available? How does consumer information about legal services compare to information available concerning automobile repair, plumbing, and health care?

2. Consumers can sustain a welfare loss when they purchase a product without adequate information. Professor Ogus offers the following illustration:

> Suppose I have to choose between two brands of suntan lotion. Brand A costs £1.00 but its use carries a small risk (1/1000) of a skin disorder. Brand B is identical except that there is no such risk and it costs me £1.20. Assuming that I evaluate the average adverse consequences of a skin disorder at £300 and am risk-neutral, which brand will I choose? If I remain uninformed of the risk, I will certainly prefer to buy Brand A since £1.00 is less than £1.20. However, once the hidden cost (the risk of the skin disorder = 0.001 × £300 = £0.30) is added, the real cost of Brand A to me is £1.30. If legislation forced the manufacturers of Brand A to disclose the risk and I make a rational decision on the basis of that information, I will gain £0.10 by buying Brand B.[11]

---

[10] Lyndon, *supra* note 4, at 1810.

[11] A. Ogus, Regulation: Legal Form and Economic Theory 122 (1994).

3. Although the tort system provides incentives for sellers to disclose accurate and complete information, why is it that additional regulation is thought to be necessary? What are the limitations of the tort system in promoting accurate and complete information? One problem is the ability of firms to earn "fraud rents," which are obtained when a firm defrauds consumers knowing that, because of the small amount of money involved, individual consumers are highly unlikely to sue. Another problem is that tort law assumes that consumers act in a rational manner when presented with information that may not be true.[12]

4. REGULATION WHEN CONSUMERS HAVE ADEQUATE INFORMATION

Is the government justified in regulating a product because consumers fail to act on the information available to them? Most, if not all, of those persons who ride motorcycles are aware that riding without a helmet is extremely dangerous, and yet many continue to do so. Should they be required by law to wear helmets? Car passengers know that they are safer when they wear seat belts, and yet many do not do so. Should they be required by law to wear seat belts? Does it matter whether such activities impact anyone but the person who engages in the activity?

There are two possible justifications for regulation in the situation where consumers have adequate information, but do not act on it. One is that the activity harms not only the person doing it, but others as well. The Department of Transportation has banned smoking on all domestic air flights on the ground that secondary smoke harms others in the plane.[13] States which require the use of motorcycle helmets and seat belts defend such laws on the ground that the failure to take these precautions drives up the insurance costs of all those who drive.[14] This type of justification was discussed in Chapter 9 as an "externality" or "spillover cost."

The other justification for regulation when consumers have adequate information about product quality is referred to as "paternalism." This justification argues that, even if consumers have adequate information, they fail to act rationally based on the information, because of such factors as addiction, habits, or myopia.[15] For example, many smokers probably do not act on information about the dangers of smoking, because they are addicted. In addition, young cigarette smokers erroneously discount the consequences of their behavior, because young people generally do not realistically assess their chances of dying.

---

[12] See Hasen, *Efficiency Under Information Asymmetry: The Effect of Framing on Legal Rules,* 38 UCLA L. REV. 391 (1990).

[13] 55 Fed. Reg. 8364 (1990).

[14] ASCH, *supra* note 2, at 82–83.

[15] Sunstein, *Legal Interferences With Private Preferences,* 53 U. CHI. L. REV. 1129, 1158–66 (1986).

5. WHAT IS THE ROLE OF ADVERTISING?

In 1996, the liquor industry ended a 60-year voluntary ban on hard-liquor advertisements on television. In response, regulators at the Federal Communications Commission (FCC) considered banning hard-liquor ads, requiring broadcasters to allot time for counter advertisements or channeling the ads into time shows with few young watchers.[16] Assuming the FCC has the legal authority to ban such advertisements, what is the public interest in taking this action? If an efficient market requires adequate information, how do you justify advertising bans which restrict the dissemination of truthful information to consumers? Does liquor advertising provide useful information to consumers, or does it have some other purpose?

Economists generally assume that consumers have clear, stable preferences, but inadequate knowledge of what will best satisfy them. Under this viewpoint, there is consumer sovereignty, since advertising cannot convince consumers to purchase something they do not already desire.[17] Professor Galbraith, however, challenges consumer sovereignty by distinguishing between "physical needs" and "psychic satisfactions" or "contrived wants." He argues that a person's psychic or contrived wants are often created by advertising and salesmanship. This makes the producer, not the consumer, sovereign.[18]

NOTES AND QUESTIONS

1. Does the fact that consumers continue smoking with full knowledge of its dangers justify banning cigarette smoking? Is there any limit to regulating human behavior based on a paternalism justification? Should Congress ban all dangerous activities, such as hang gliding, for example?[19] If not, where do you draw the line between activities that the government is justified in regulating on the basis of paternalism and those that it is not?

2. What are the limits of the spillover rationale? Is the government entitled to regulate any activity that has an impact on other people. For example, should Congress ban cigarette smoking on the ground that it drives up the costs of health insurance for everyone?

3. Is the government more justified in regulating on the basis of paternalism if it is addressing the behavior of children? Consider smoking again. What is the justification of laws that ban the sale of cigarettes to persons under the age of 18?

4. What is your understanding of the effect of advertising on you? Do you believe that mainstream economic theory or Galbraith's theory best describes

---

[16] MacLachlan, *Law Murky On Stopping Liquor Ads*, NATL L.J., Nov. 25, 1996, at 1.

[17] J. RHODES, THE ECONOMIST'S VIEW OF THE WORLD: GOVERNMENT, MARKETS & PUBLIC POLICY 148 (1985).

[18] J. GALBRAITH, ECONOMICS, PEACE, AND LAUGHTER 68–71 (1971).

[19] *See* Kennedy, *Cost-Benefit Analysis of Entitlement Programs: A Critique*, 33 STAN. L. REV. 387, 398–400 (1981) (discussing whether regulation can be justified any time one person's activities adversely affect another person); *see also* O'Reilly, *A Consistent Ethic of Safety Regulation: The Case For Improving Regulation of Tobacco Products*, 3 AD. L.J. 215 (1989) (discussing the possible methods of regulating tobacco products).

consumer demand for products such as liquor? Consider the same question in the context of advertising for soft drinks or beer. Do such advertisements provide information about the quality of the product that consumers can use to evaluate whether to purchase it? Indeed, why do consumers need to rely on advertising at all concerning such products?

5. What is the cost to you of determining whether you like the taste of a specific brand of soft drink? How high are your search costs? If you like the taste, you will buy the same brand again, and if you do not, you will not. Yet, soft drink and beer advertisers spend hundreds of millions of dollars a year on advertising. Presumably, such advertisements are associated with an increase in sales, or sellers would not purchase the advertising. Are they attempting to create demand, as Professor Galbraith suggests?

B. REGULATORY RESPONSES TO INADEQUATE INFORMATION

The government generally relies on two regulatory tools it can use to address the problem of inadequate information: licensing and standard setting. As Table 10-1 indicates, each method can be used either to require the seller to disclose additional information or to set minimum standards that a product or service must meet before it can be sold.

Table 10-1

RESPONSES TO INADEQUATE INFORMATION		
Regulatory Method	Require Information Disclosure	Require Minimum Quality
Licensing	SEC: securities prospectus	FDA: new drug regulation States: occupational licensing
Standard Setting	FDA: food labels OSHA: chemical labels	EPA: pesticide regulation FDA: food contaminant tolerances FDA: pesticide contaminant tolerances

The government can use licensing in two ways. First, as a condition of selling a specific product, regulators can require sellers to provide additional or accurate information. The Securities and Exchange Commission (SEC), for example, establishes what information must be disclosed to securities consumers as a condition of marketing a security.[20] The SEC will individually screen the information provided to potential securities customers in a prospectus and a company cannot sell securities until the SEC approves its prospectus. Persons selling securities without appropriate disclosures are subject to

---

[20] 15 U.S.C. § 77(j) (1988).

financial penalties.[21] Second, the government can use standard setting, or promulgate a regulation, to require sellers to provide additional or accurate information in conjunction with the sale of a group of products or a type of service. This type of regulation is "generic" in the sense that it establishes standards for a group of products rather than approving information on a case-by-case basis as the SEC does. FDA relies on standard setting to regulate the content of food labeling.[22] Mislabeled foods can be seized.[23] The Occupational Safety and Health Administration (OSHA) has established a standard which requires employers to disclose to employees the names of the chemicals to which they are exposed, as part of its mandate to protect employees from toxic chemicals.[24] Firms violating regulations mandating disclosure are subject to fines.[25]

The preceding types of regulation leave it to consumers to determine whether to purchase a product based on the information the government requires to be disclosed. For example, the SEC will approve any prospectus as long as it is true and leave it up to the consumer to judge the soundness of the security offered for sale. For other products, the government prohibits the marketing of products or services that do not meet qualifications concerning minimum quality. This regulation can also be carried out by licensing or by standard setting. Licensing involves entry and exit controls: the individual approval of each product or service. The two types of regulation that are the focus of this chapter—FDA regulation of prescription drugs and occupational licensing—are examples of entry controls that set minimum qualifications. By comparison, standard setting involves setting generic standards for a group of products or a type of service. For example, Congress has required FDA to set a standard or tolerance level for unavoidable food contaminants, such as aflatoxin (a naturally occurring food contaminant which is toxic when eaten above minimum doses) in peanuts, that considers "the extent to which the use" of the substance "is required or cannot be avoided" and the ways in which it may harm the consumer.[26] Similarly, FDA promulgates standards which limit the amount of pesticide residues in food.[27] In both cases, FDA is authorized to seize food products that contain food contaminants in levels in excess of those permitted in a regulation.[28]

Since the problem of inadequate information can be addressed either by mandating disclosure or by entry and exit controls, the choice of which approach is preferable is a common policy issue. If the government requires additional information to be provided to consumers, it enhances the capacity of consumers to make their own product choices. If the government uses entry and exit controls, it restricts the capacity of consumers to make their own choices. For this reason, economists typically favor regulatory programs based

---

[21] *Id.* § 77(i).

[22] 21 U.S.C. § 341 (1988).

[23] *Id.* § 334.

[24] Hazard Communications Standard, 29 C.F.R. 1910.1200 (1990).

[25] 29 U.S.C. § 10 (1988).

[26] 21 U.S.C. § 346 (1988).

[27] 7 U.S.C. § 136(b) (1988).

[28] *Id.* § 136(k).

on information disclosure, unless such programs will not work for some reason. This choice is highlighted in the materials that follow on FDA and occupational licensing.

C. CASE STUDY: NEW DRUG REGULATION

One good example of product licensing is the regulation of new drugs by the FDA, an agency located within the Department of Health and Human Services. As noted, when licensing is used to protect consumers from inadequate information, the regulator interposes between the consumer and the manufacturer. Unless and until FDA approves a drug for sale that has not been previously marketed, consumers will not have access to it. As you will read below, patients with incurable illnesses such as AIDS object to the FDA denying access to drugs and argue that they should be able to use any therapy.

This section considers the justification for FDA regulation, or what market flaw justifies the use of licensing. It also considers whether patients should have access to drug therapies not approved by FDA and how the FDA process might be reformed to speed up drug approval.

1. REGULATORY SCHEME

Federal regulation of pharmaceutical drugs is based on three landmark statutes: the Pure Food and Drugs Act of 1906, the Food, Drug and Cosmetic Act of 1938, and, amending the 1938 Act, the Kefauver-Harris Amendments of 1962. Each statute was passed in reaction to a public outcry concerning the safety of food and drugs.[29]

The 1906 Act[30] resulted from the longtime efforts of Dr. Harvey Wiley, then director of the Division of Chemistry of the U.S. Department of Agriculture (USDA), and of "muckraking journalists," to call public attention to patent medicines that contained harmful or addictive substances and to adulterated food products commonly sold to consumers.[31] Legislative reform was blocked by industry, however, until President Roosevelt joined the fight after reading *The Jungle,* Upton Sinclair's exposé of shocking conditions in the meat packing industry.

The inadequacy of the 1906 Act became apparent after FDA, which was then located in USDA, had difficulty controlling dangerous patent medicines. In order to prove that a drug was misbranded, FDA had to prove that the seller's therapeutic claims were both false and fraudulent. Despite journalistic exposés revealing this problem,[32] legislative reform was stymied until 107 persons died after taking a popular drug, Elixir Sulfanilamide, which was mixed with diethylene glycol, a toxic substance. Congress responded to the

---

[29] *See generally* P. TEMIN, TAKING YOUR MEDICINE: DRUG REGULATION IN THE UNITED STATES 18–57, 120–26 (1980); Weimer, *Organizational Incentives: Safe–and Available–Drugs, in* REFORMING SOCIAL REGULATION: ALTERNATIVE STRATEGIES 22–29 (L. Graymer & F. Thompson eds., 1982).

[30] Pub. L. No. 59-384, 34 Stat. 768.

[31] O. ANDERSON, THE HEALTH OF A NATION: HARVEY WILEY AND THE FIGHT FOR PURE FOOD (1958).

[32] *E.g.,* A. KALLET & F. SCHLINK, 100,000,000 GUINEA PIGS: DANGERS IN EVERYDAY FOOD, DRUGS, AND COSMETICS (1932).

disaster by passing the Food, Drug, and Cosmetic Act of 1938 which gave USDA the authority to seize drugs that were not safe and prevent their future sale. [33]

In the 1950s, Senator Estes Kefauver held a series of widely publicized hearings that revealed that many drugs still were of questionable safety and efficacy and that drug advertising was frequently misleading. [34] Public concern increased in reaction to press reports that a disproportionate number of birth defects were associated with women who had taken Thalidomide, a sedative, during their pregnancy. Although the drug had been widely distributed in Europe and Great Britain, Dr. Frances Kelsey of FDA had managed to delay its approval in the United States. Nevertheless, the fact that the drug was distributed in this country for testing purposes created sufficient public concern that Congress unanimously passed the 1962 Kefauver-Harris Amendments to the 1938 Act. [35]

Under the 1962 Amendments, manufacturers are prohibited from selling a drug in interstate commerce until FDA has approved it for sale. A "new" drug is one whose composition is not generally recognized as safe and effective for use under the conditions prescribed, recommended, or suggested in the labeling of the drug. The FDA may only approve the drug if its sponsor establishes, for the therapeutic use or uses for which it will be advertised and promoted, that the drug is safe and that there is "substantial evidence" that it is effective. [36] Meeting the previous requirements involves a rigorous process consisting of both animal and human testing. [37] Once a drug is licensed, the law gives FDA the authority to seize the drug and prevent its future sale if the agency has information (not available to it at the time of approval) that it is not safe or effective for the conditions for which it is prescribed. FDA, however, has the burden of proving the lack of safety or efficacy. By comparison, the sponsor of the drug has the burden of establishing the safety and efficacy of a drug during the initial licensing process.

The decision whether to approve a drug can involve a complex risk/benefit decision. The reason is that every drug has the potential to cause a set of physiological effects in the body, some of which are beneficial and some of which are adverse. [38] The dysfunctional aspects result from the fact that a drug may react with some other body process than the one for which it has been designed. The adverse effects, often termed adverse reactions or side effects, can range in seriousness from a relatively mild result, such as drowsiness, to a serious reaction including death.

Because of these potentially serious consequences, no drug can be considered absolutely safe. This means that, when the FDA judges a drug to be safe

---

[33] 52 Stat. 1040 (1938).

[34] Quirk, *The Food and Drug Administration, in* THE POLITICS OF REGULATION 197–98 (J. Wilson ed., 1980); M. MINTZ, THE THERAPEUTIC NIGHTMARE (1965).

[35] Pub. L. No. 87-781, 76 Stat. 780 (1962). *See* M. NADEL, THE POLITICS OF CONSUMER PROTECTION 128 (1971); Quirk, *supra* note 34, at 199.

[36] 21 U.S.C. §§ 321(p), 355(d) (1988).

[37] 21 C.F.R. §§ 310–14 (1990); *see* J. GIBSON, MEDICATION, LAW AND BEHAVIOR 125–45 (1976).

[38] GIBSON, *supra* note 37, § 8.1.1, at 86; M. DIXON, DRUG PRODUCT LIABILITY § 6.10[5], at 46 (1977).

during its licensing process, the agency makes a decision that the benefit of the drug, in terms of its expected therapeutic effect, outweighs the risk that one of the nonbeneficial side effects may occur. If the test on a drug leads the FDA to the conclusion that the drug is, on the whole, beneficial, the drug is considered "safe" for its intended use.

The risk/benefit decision for a drug is particularly complex because the question of the drug's benefit always depends on the particular use or uses to which the drug will be put. For example, medical evidence now has established that an antibiotic called "Chloromycetin" will cause a fatal blood disease in one out of every 24,000 persons who take it. [39] Thus, given the wide variety of alternative methods of treating mild infections, the use of Chloromycetin for such infections cannot be considered safe. By comparison, it is generally medically accepted that the drug's use to treat typhoid is safe, since the mortality rate of the disease, without use of the drug, is about 20%.

Given that the risk/benefit ratio of Chloromycetin varies so widely, the FDA is faced with a dilemma. On the one hand, the drug is needed to treat typhoid. On the other hand, the risk/benefit ratio may be unfavorable when the drug is used against other diseases. To resolve this kind of problem, the FDA requires that the drug label, the package insert, and drug advertisements all contain sufficient information about the hazards of a drug like Chloromycetin to alert the physician to the shifting risk/benefit ratios posed by the drug. [40]

This information about potential health hazards is conveyed to the physician by the use of several descriptive categories in the drug's label. One such category, "contraindications," tells the physician that the drug should not be given to certain types of patients if an alternative method of treatment exists. There will also be information pertaining to "precautions" which can be taken to avoid the occurrence of a side effect. The physician will also be informed of other facts relevant to his prescribing decision under a heading of "warnings." Finally, there will be a list of side effects apparently caused by the drug that were observed in the testing process. [41] Once FDA approves a drug, the decision whether to prescribe it, and for what conditions, is up to a patient's physician. FDA's regulatory authority extends only to the shipment of drugs in interstate commerce, and it does not have the legal authority to restrict the use of a drug to the conditions indicated in its label.

Once FDA approves Chloromycetin for sale, for example, a physician would be free to prescribe the drug for some condition other than typhoid even through the FDA recommends against such a practice. If a patient is injured by taking a drug for a nonapproved purpose, the person can sue the physician for malpractice and argue that the drug therapy was inappropriate.

2. REGULATORY JUSTIFICATION

Although a patient purchases a drug, it is the physician who makes the product selection. Section A described the reasons why consumers may lack

[39] Merrill, *Compensation for Prescription Drug Injuries,* 59 VA. L. REV. 1, 17–20 (1973).

[40] GIBSON, *supra* note 37, § 9.1, at 160; DIXON, *supra* note 38, § 6.10[4], at 39.

[41] GIBSON, *supra* note 37, § 9.2.1, at 169–71; DIXON, *supra* note 38, § 6.10[4], at 44.

sufficient information to judge accurately the quality of a product like a new drug. Which of those market flaws are present in drug markets?

One market flaw is that physicians, despite years of training, may not be in a position to judge accurately the risk/benefit ratio of a drug without FDA regulation. In the absence of scientific testing, which is statistically validated, physicians are unable to judge accurately whether a drug's use is efficacious. Although a physician may perceive that a drug benefits patients, such "anecdotal" evidence is scientifically unreliable.

Another potential market flaw is that drug companies occasionally will falsify their research results.[42] For example, a news report in 1992 revealed that tainted data played a role in FDA's 1982 approval of Halcyon, which is one of the world's leading sleep remedies. FDA relied on a key clinical study that was conducted in part by a physician who had fabricated patient records and related data in other clinical studies. The physician's role was obscured at the time by the pharmaceutical company that sponsored the study, and FDA did not discover the false data until ten years later.[43] In another incident, three FDA officials, three industry employees, and two companies were convicted in 1989 under bribery and other laws for the falsification of data submitted to FDA.[44]

3. DRUG LAG AND THE AIDS CRISIS

The rigorous evidentiary requirements put in place by the 1962 amendments have significantly slowed the development of new drugs. Physicians have argued that this delay, which is called "drug lag," has harmed patients by denying ill persons access to new therapies.[45] Economists have asserted that the costs of FDA regulation, in terms of delayed access to new therapies, outweigh the benefits of new drug regulation, in terms of protection of consumers against ineffective and unsafe drugs.[46] Although it is clear that the drug approval process proceeds slowly, others have disputed that consumers are harmed as a result of drug lag.[47]

Until recently, one cause of drug lag has been FDA's political situation. As noted, drugs have side effects, and some of these are severe. When FDA had approved a drug in the past, and unanticipated side effects were found after the drug was marketed, the agency was the subject of vigorous criticism by Congress. This potential made FDA cautious about approving a drug until questions about potential side effects were resolved. Dr. Alexander Schmidt, who served as a Commissioner of FDA, explained this effect:

---

[42] *See* Shapiro, *Divorcing Profit Motivation from New Drug Research: A Consideration of Proposals to Provide FDA with More Reliable Test Data,* 1978 DUKE L.J. 154.

[43] *Halcyon Takes Another Hit: Tainted Data Played a Key Role in FDA Approval,* NEWSWEEK, Feb. 17, 1992, at 58.

[44] Hilts, *A Guardian of U.S. Health Is Failing Under Pressures,* N.Y. TIMES, Dec. 4, 1989, at A1.

[45] *E.g.,* W. WARDELL & L. LASAGNA, REGULATION AND NEW DRUG DEVELOPMENT (1975).

[46] *E.g.,* S. PELTZMAN, REGULATION OF PHARMACEUTICAL INNOVATION (1974).

[47] *E.g.,* Schifrin, *Lessons from the Drug Law: A Retrospective Analysis of the 1962 Drug Regulations,* 5 HARV. J.L. & PUB. POL'Y 91 (1982); Department of Health, Education, and Welfare, Review Panel on New Drug Regulation, Final Report 28–30 (May 1977).

[W]hen it comes to pure unadulterated and directly applied "pressure" on FDA, the industry can't hold a candle to Congress, and that pressure is very one-sided and biased.

For example, in all of FDA's history, I am unable to find a single instance where a Congressional committee investigated the *failure* of FDA to approve a new drug. However, the times when hearings have been held to criticize our approval of new drugs have been so frequent that we have been unable to count them.

The message to FDA could not be clearer. Whenever a controversy over a new drug is resolved by its approval, the Agency and the individuals involved likely will be investigated. Whenever such a drug is disapproved, no inquiry will be made. The Congressional pressure for our *negative* action is, therefore, intense.[48]

Dr. Schmidt concluded, "What I see as a seriously unbalanced and deleterious pressure can be remedied only by a Congressional and public recognition that the *failure* to approve an important new drug can be as detrimental to the public health as the approval of a potentially bad drug."[49]

The political pressure on FDA was unbalanced in part, because persons denied access to new drug therapies were not organized in a manner that permitted them to lobby for faster approval. Such persons were widely dispersed across the country, which made it difficult for them to organize. Moreover, they did not already belong to groups which demanded quicker access to new drug therapies on their behalf. This situation, however, changed dramatically with the onset of the AIDS epidemic, as David Vogel relates:

As a result of the AIDS crisis, for the first time [FDA] is being challenged politically by a group of articulate and well-organized people who want to facilitate the approval of new drugs. Organizations defending homosexual rights now criticize the FDA on grounds remarkably similar to those of conservatives in the *Wall Street Journal* and of businessmen in publications of the Pharmaceutical Manufacturers Association (PMA). Because of the political mobilization of potential customers of currently unavailable drugs, the advocates of strict drug-approval now find themselves on the defensive for the first time in three decades.

. . . Three things made the politics surrounding the medical treatment of AIDS unique. First, unlike virtually all of the diseases whose sufferers had been previously harmed by FDA drug-approval policies, AIDS was fatal. Second, because the disease was new, no existing drugs were available to treat it. Third, and most important, those who suffered from delays in the FDA's approval of drugs to treat AIDS were vocal and politically powerful. . . .[50]

---

[48] Schmidt, *The FDA Today: Critics, Congress, and Consumerism*, 29 FOOD DRUG COSM. L.J. 575, 581 (1974) (emphasis in original).

[49] *Id.* (emphasis in original).

[50] Vogel, *AIDS and the Politics of Drug Lag*, 96 PUB. INTEREST 73, 73–74, 76 (1989).

4. FDA REFORM

FDA has adopted several reforms in response to the advocates for an AIDS remedy and other critics of slow drug approval. After reading about these efforts, you are asked to assess whether people who are terminally ill, such as AIDS patients, or who have debilitating diseases with no known treatment, such as Alzheimer's disease, should have unlimited access to unproven drug therapies.

In May 1987, the FDA promulgated a regulation establishing a "Treatment Investigational New Drug Exemption (treatment IND)."[51] This regulation allows a drug manufacturer to make promising new therapies available to desperately ill persons while the manufacturer is still testing the drugs to obtain FDA approval. Despite FDA's intention to make drugs available sooner, critics argued that the treatment IND was not an adequate response to the AIDS crisis for two reasons.[52] First, they claimed that FDA was unwilling to approve treatment INDs until the very end of drug testing, or just before commercial approval. Second, they objected to the fact that FDA had restricted access to "immediately life-threatening" situations, which made the policy useless to persons who wanted access to drugs that prevented the onset of AIDS—for those infected with the virus, but who did not yet have AIDS-related symptoms.

In reaction to this criticism, FDA adopted a new regulation in 1992 that expanded the availability of new drugs through a "parallel track" for persons with AIDS.[53] This regulation makes promising new drugs available to AIDS patients and those persons with other HIV-related diseases at the same time a manufacturer begins testing such drugs on humans. A manufacturer must test the drug in humans to establish that it is safe and effective. In 1992, FDA also issued "accelerated approval" regulations for new drugs and biologics to be used for life-threatening or serious illnesses.[54] These rules established a fast-track approval process for such drugs. FDA also agreed to approve certain drugs on the basis of laboratory data or physical measurements rather than evidence of a reduced incidence of disease. For example, FDA might approve a drug intended to reduced cholesterol, if it actually had this effect, instead of waiting for evidence that those who took such drugs had a reduced incidence of heart attacks.

In 1997, Congress passed the FDA Modernization Act, which codified the previous FDA regulations and practices intended to increase patient access to experimental drugs and medical devices and to accelerate agency review of important new medications.[55] The law also renewed FDA's authority to charge prescription drug user fees, which are fees charged by FDA to to review new drug applications. The idea is that FDA can more quickly review such

---

[51] 99 Fed. Reg. 19,466 (1987).

[52] Note, *The Need for Improved Access to Experimental Drug Therapy: AIDS Activists and Their Call for a Parallel Track Policy*, 4 AD. L.J. 589, 609–10 (1991).

[53] 57 Fed. Reg. 13,250 (1992).

[54] 57 Fed. Reg. 58,942 (1992).

[55] Food and Drug Administration Modernization Act of 1997, Pub. L. 105-115, Nov. 21, 1997, 111 Stat. 2296.

applications with the additional staff paid for by such fees, which in turn reduces drug lag.

Are these reforms sufficient or should ill persons have access to new therapies whether or not FDA has approved them? Consider the arguments raised in the next two excerpts.

JOHN J. SMITH, SCIENCE, POLITICS, AND POLICY: THE TACRINE DEBATE, 47 FOOD & DRUG LAW JOURNAL 511, 529–530 (1992)*

There are two extremes for any new drug approval system: a purely scientific approach and an approach based entirely on public choice. Between these two extremes lie hybrid systems that incorporate features of both science and public choice.

A drug approval system based exclusively on scientific factors presumably would rely heavily on the results of clinical studies, allowing the treatment use of new drugs only after safety and efficacy are established. The standards and review priority for various drugs would be based on objective criteria ostensibly removed from subjective considerations. Discussion of these objective criteria would take place, but would involve only informed members of the scientific community and not the general public.

A drug regulation system based entirely on public choice would permit a patient to obtain any drug he or she desired, free from government interference. Manufacturers could label their products and make product claims as they saw fit. Consumers would have little recourse against drugs which were not safe and/or effective, other than to discontinue use of the drug or pursue a tort or products liability claim against the drug's manufacturer.

The public choice model is largely supported by HIV/AIDS advocates, who believe that the individual patient should have the right to decide whether the benefits of an unproven but potentially effective treatment outweigh the risks. This point of view is reflected in the explicit statements of HIV/AIDS advocates and in their strong emphasis on interest group advocacy. As part of their advocacy, the HIV/AIDS lobby attempts to gain access to drug products that patients feel they have a right to have. A drug regulatory scheme which stresses interest group advocacy therefore will approach a pure public choice model.

Between science and public choice theories lie hybrid new drug approval systems that incorporate aspects of both models and address two fundamental concerns. One of these concerns is that the public is not in a position to judge the safety or effectiveness of a medication. The other is that patients, caretakers, and other interested parties have a genuine stake in the treatment of disease, and should have some input on government's drug regulatory decisions which greatly affect their lives.

The FDA's traditional new drug regulatory scheme is a hybrid system because it stresses science while incorporating some public choice input. However, that scheme is not the only possible mixture of science public choice.

---

* Reprinted with permission of the Food and Drug Law Institute (1997).

For example, a hybrid regulatory system where the government guaranteed only the truth of drug labeling and placed no additional limits on drug distribution would emphasize public choice over science. While the FDA is not explicitly moving toward such a "truth in labeling" regulatory scheme, the agency is allowing public choice (in form of interest group advocacy) to play a greater role in the new drug approval process.

GEORGE J. ANNAS, FAITH (HEALING), HOPE, AND CHARITY AT THE FDA: THE POLITICS OF AIDS DRUG TRIALS, 34 VILLANOVA LAW REVIEW 771, 789–97 (1989) *

Randomized clinical trials (RCT) are the "gold standard" upon which experimental treatments are judged useful, worthless or dangerous. [In a randomized clinical trial, a new drug is compared with a placebo or other drug, each being assigned at random to comparable patients. In a double blind study, neither the physician nor the patient knows who is getting the new drug and who is getting the placebo.] . . . This view is widely endorsed in the scientific community. The trend has been to try to develop methods to evaluate surgery and other therapies by RCT as well, in an effort to improve the quality of care by eliminating costly therapies that provide no benefit. . . .

. . . FDA . . . should continue to insist on a scientifically valid randomized clinical trial before certifying drugs safe and effective. All consumer protection legislation is to some degree paternalistic, but in this case it is also realistic. FDA certification of the safety and efficacy of drugs recognizes that the public is in no position to judge the value or usefulness of many medications and that many are dangerous and have serious side effects (which is one reason we also license physicians and require some drugs be available only upon a physician's prescription). Furthermore, drug manufacturers have another social role: to create and sell new products. Their role is not consumer protection.

Libertarians and those with extreme views of individual autonomy, and even some free marketers, object to FDA regulation, equating "pursuit of quackery" with "life, liberty, and the pursuit of happiness." True autonomy requires adequate and accurate information upon which to base decisions. This is simply impossible in the absence of responsible scientific study and properly designed clinical trials. It is appropriate to concentrate energies and resources in the time of an epidemic. It is also appropriate to assign AIDS drug testing a very high priority and to assure adequate governmental funding for the development and testing of drugs that might be effective. . . . But it is not appropriate or ultimately helpful to AIDS sufferers to rush inadequately tested drugs to market. . . .

. . . The excuse that patients are dying without treatment and have "nothing to lose" will not do. Terminally ill patients can be harmed, misused and exploited. Realistic discussion of death and accurate education about the status of unproven AIDS drugs and the reason randomized clinical trials are needed is in order. It is not compassionate to make quack remedies easily available to those who can pay for them. True compassion demands that we

---

* Reprinted with permission of author and copyright holder.

allocate the money and staff necessary to do meaningful scientific research, and that when valid clinical trials demonstrate that a therapy is "safe and effective," we make it available to all who need it regardless of their ability to pay, not that we help supply dying patients with false promises and useless drugs.

NOTES AND QUESTIONS

1. What are the arguments for and against the FDA reforms? Recall the reasons why Congress created FDA regulation. Have FDA's actions been consistent with those goals? How should we weigh the risk of delay versus the risk of too-early approval? Consider the following comment:

> Henry Miller, a former FDA official recently blasted the agency in a *National Review* article as slow and politically-motivated. But when I asked him about the study showing France and Britain with triple the number of drug recalls as the U.S., Miller replied that he wouldn't mind more recalls if it meant getting drugs through [FDA] more quickly. Considering the devastation that a bad drug can cause—Clometacin was withdrawn in France after 130 reports of hepatitis, including nine deaths; Indomethacin-R was withdrawn in Britain after 717 adverse reactions and 36 deaths—this is hardly a trade-off most of us would make.[56]

What about the "devastation" caused by a person's inability to get access to a therapy while it is being tested? Should the patient (and the person's physician) decide the degree of risk the person is willing to undertake in order to get better? Are patients (and their physicians) in a position to assess such risks accurately? Is protection of such patients based on lack information or on paternalism (such patients are desperate and cannot accurately weigh the risks)?

2. A report by the Government Accounting Office (GAO) found that more than one-half of the new drugs approved for marketing in this country had some severe or fatal side effects not found in testing, or not reported until years after the medications have been widely used.[57] What do these facts suggest about the tradeoff between faster and slower FDA approval of new drugs?

3. Economists have attempted to measure the costs and benefits of FDA regulation. Specially, they have attempted to measure whether the current regulatory system adds expense to the drug approval process without producing any corresponding gain in drug safety. These studies have been almost uniformly critical of FDA regulation. For example, Robert Hahn and John Hird estimate that FDA regulations give rise to a deadweight loss of between

---

[56] Shenk, *Warning: Cutting the FDA could Be Hazardous to Your Health*, THE WASHINGTON MONTHLY, Jan./Feb., 1996, at 23; *but see* Greg Critser, *What's the Rush to Approve Drugs*, USA TODAY, Jan. 18, 2000, at 15A; Schwartz, *Are New Drugs Landing on the Shelves Too Fast?*, WASHINGTON POST, Mar. 29, 1999, at 29 (weekly edition).

[57] General Accounting Office, FDA Drug Review: Postapproval Risks 1965–85 (1990); *see* Hilts, *Dangers of New Drugs Go Undetected, Study Says*, N.Y. TIMES, May 5, 1990, at A10.

$1.5 and 3.0 billion a year.[58] In other words, consumers would be better off by that amount of money if they had earlier access to new drug therapies; consumers are worse off by that amount of money after taking into account the benefits of a drug lag (i.e., more deliberate approval) including less fraud and fewer unanticipated side-effects.

4. A study for the Congressional Research Service found that it was difficult to measure the success of the FDA reforms:

> Evaluating the benefits derived from these reform measures can be problematic when FDA and the pharmaceutical industry emphasize different statistical outcomes in assessing improvement or decline. For example, in 1995 the agency announced that it had approved 85 new drugs and licensed biological products during the previous year. The median review time for the 62 new drug approvals and the 23 approved vaccines and biological products was 19 and 12.2 months respectively. Of the approved drugs and biologics, 22 were new molecular entities (NMEs) or products containing an active substance that had never been marketed in the United States.

> FDA reported median drug approval times as follows: a 21 percent shorter review time for 62 new drug approvals; 12.2 months in 1994 versus 23.4 months in 1993 for vaccines and other biological products; and 17.5 months in 1994 versus 23 months the year before for 22 NMEs. FDA also claimed it had made "significant reductions" in the 1994 approval times for drugs and biologics.

> In contrast, the Pharmaceutical Research and Manufacturers of America (PhRMA) disregarded FDA's approval time reductions, and instead emphasized that the agency had approved fewer pharmaceutical products during that same time period. Such contrasting portrayals are not unusual, but it is important to note that these data represent changes measured over a single year, and a fuller evaluation of regulatory improvements necessarily requires longer term results.[59]

5. In order to expedite FDA's approval process, Congress passed the Prescription Drug User Fee Act (PDUFA) in 1992,[59] which authorizes the agency to assess drug companies "user fees." FDA uses the fees to offset some of the costs of the drug application review process. The fees permitted FDA, among other improvements, to hire more drug reviewers.

6. In *United States v. Rutherford*, 442 U.S. 544 (1979), the Supreme Court upheld FDA's authority to deny a drug therapy to a terminally ill patient because its manufacturer had not established its safety and efficacy. The drug,

---

[58] Hahn & Hird, *The Cost and Benefits of Regulation: Review and Synthesis*, 8 YALE J. ON REG. 233, 276–77 (1991). Hahn and Hird updated an earlier study by Professor Peltzman. *See* S. PELTZMAN, REGULATION OF PHARMACEUTICAL INNOVATION (1974).

[59] B. RANDELL, CRS REPORT FOR CONGRESS: DRUG REGULATION: HISTORICAL OVERVIEW AND CURRENT REFORM PROPOSALS (Jan. 17, 1996).

[59] P.L. No. 102-571, 106 Stat. 4491 (1992); *see* Kuhlik, *Industry Funding of Improvements in the FDA's New Drug Approval Process: The Prescription Drug Use Fee Act of 1992*, 47 FOOD & DRUG L.J. 483 (1992).

Laetrile, was a popular, but unproven, therapy for cancer. The Court of Appeals concluded that an implied exemption from the Food, Drug and Cosmetic Act was justified because the Act's safety and efficacy requirements had no reasonable application to terminally ill patients. The Court disagreed because the efficacy requirement is not limited to the capacity to cure. It also applies to whether a drug is effective in prolonging life, improving physical condition, or reducing pain. The Court also noted, "An otherwise harmless drug can be dangerous to any patient if it does not produce its purported therapeutic effect. If any individual suffering from a potentially fatal disease rejects conventional therapy in favor of a drug with no demonstrable curative properties, the consequences can be irreversible." Finally, the Court noted that the intent of the Food, Drug and Cosmetic Act was to protect consumers against fraudulent claims by drug sponsors, and that this activity was even more important in the case of terminally ill patients, who might be more susceptible to such claims.

7. Some terminally ill patients claim that the failure of FDA to license unproven therapies violates their constitutional rights. This argument is usually grounded on a privacy right to the medical therapy of one's choice. The federal government is authorized under the Commerce Clause to regulate new drugs, unless such actions would violate other constitutional provisions. As Chapter 4 related, the Supreme Court requires, as a matter of substantive due process, that legislation bear a rational relationship to the goals and purposes for which it was enacted. There is no doubt that the FDCA passes this minimal test. However, as Chapter 4 explained, the Court will apply stricter scrutiny if legislation impacts on a fundamental constitutional right, such as the right of privacy, or a property or liberty interest within the scope of the Fifth Amendment. Such legislation is constitutional only if it is narrowly drawn to support a "compelling state interest." For liberty interests, the Court appears to balance the state's interest against the burden on the liberty interest.

The question of whether the right to a medical treatment is part of the fundamental right of privacy, or a liberty interest, has not been addressed by the Supreme Court. In *Rutherford v. United States*, 438 F. Supp. 1287, 1299–1300 (W.D. Okla. 1977). the district court held that, by denying cancer patients the right to use Laetrile, FDA had infringed constitutionally protected privacy interests. That court reasoned:

> [I]t appears uncontrovertible that a patient has a right to refuse cancer treatment and should he decide to forgo conventional treatment, does he not possess a further right to enlist such nontoxic treatment, however unconventional, as he finds to be of comfort, particularly where recommended by a physician? . . .
>
> When certain "fundamental rights" are invoked herein, regulation may be justified only by a "compelling state interest" and legislative enactments "must be narrowly drawn to express only the legitimate state interests at stake." By denying the right to use a nontoxic substance in connection with one's own personal health-care, FDA has offended the constitutional right to privacy.

The Tenth Circuit in *Rutherford*, 616 F.2d 455, 457 (10th Cir. 1980). however, overruled the district court's decision that FDA's action was unconstitutional. After the Supreme Court remanded the case to consider the constitutional challenge, it held:

> [T]he trial court held that the petitioners had a right "to be left alone" or a constitutional right to permit them, as terminally ill cancer patients, to take whatever treatment they wish to take regardless of whether FDA regarded the medication as "effective" or "safe."
>
> . . . [T]he decision by the patient whether to have a treatment or not is a protected right, but his selection of a particular treatment, or least a medication, is within the area of governmental interest in protecting public health.

The circuit court thus rejected the district court's conclusion that the right to medical treatment was a "fundamental" right. The court apparently then decided that the government's interest in regulating new drugs outweighed any liberty interest a patient might have in choosing a therapy.

8. As noted, the Supreme Court has not addressed the right to refuse treatment. But in *Cruzan v. Director of Mo. Pub. Health Servs.*, 492 U.S. 917 (1989), the Court held that, while a patient in a persistent vegetative state has a "liberty" interest in refusing medical treatment, the state's interest in preserving life justified a requirement that an incompetent patient's intent to refuse treatment be proven by clear and convincing evidence. This suggests that the Court is unlikely to regard the right to medical treatment as a privacy right. In *Cruzan,* the Court was willing to consider the right to refuse treatment only as a liberty interest. A similar conclusion would seem to follow with respect to the right to receive treatment. *Cruzan* also suggests that any right to medical treatment will be balanced against the state's interest in regulating public health.

9. The United States Supreme Court also has held that patients do not have a right to physician-assisted suicide. In *Washington v. Glucksberg*, 117 S. Ct. 2258 (1997), the Court ruled that the Due Process Clause is not violated by a state ban on physician-assisted suicide. Similarly, in *Vacco v. Quill*, 117 S. Ct. 2293 (1997), the Court upheld that the Equal Protection Clause was not violated by a New York statute outlawing physician-assisted suicide. Both of these decisions recognize the right to refuse treatment. Nevertheless, they kept the state legislative bans against suicide in place.

D.　CASE STUDY: OCCUPATIONAL LICENSING

Many professions are regulated by occupational licensing. The regulatory agency, which is typically called a licensing board or commission, engages in two functions. First, it controls entry into the occupation by reviewing the credentials of applicants, investigating and accrediting their training (usually by reliance on private accrediting bodies), and examining the academic and practical qualifications of applicants, often by testing. Second, it promulgates standards of practice for the profession, investigates charges of violations of the standards, and conducts hearings as to whether a violator's license should be revoked.[60]

The first forms of occupational licensing appeared in colonial times, when auctioneers and peddlers were licensed by local communities, while modern occupational licensing started in the late nineteenth century, as Illinois' experience indicates.[61] In 1881, Illinois set up a Board of Pharmacy and prohibited anyone except a registered pharmacist from retailing, compounding, or dispensing drugs, medicines, or poisons. The practice of dentistry was subjected to regulation in the same year, and a board, consisting of five practicing dentists, was charged with its enforcement. An 1877 Illinois law required a license for the practice of medicine. In 1897, Illinois created a State Board of Examiners of Architects. In 1899, the state added midwives, coal miners, and veterinarians, plus chiropractors and osteopaths.

Many states in the 1880s licensed plumbers, barbers, and blacksmiths. Laws regulating undertakers, embalmers, and funeral directors soon followed. In 1894, Virginia established a state board of embalming, consisting of five members to be appointed by the governor. Only registered embalmers could practice embalming thereafter. By 1900, some twenty-four states had passed similar legislation. The current extent of occupational licensing is suggested by the list in Table 10-2.[62]

---

[60] G. ROBINSON, E. GELLHORN, & H. BRUFF, THE ADMINISTRATIVE PROCESS 689–90 (3rd ed. 1986).

[61] L. FRIEDMAN, A HISTORY OF AMERICAN LAW 397–98 (1973).

[62] The source of the chart is Gellhorn, *The Abuse of Occupational Licensing,* 44 U. CHI. L. REV. 6 (1976).

Table 10-2

NUMBER OF STATES THAT REGULATE CERTAIN OCCUPATIONS		
Abstractor 12	Hearing aid dealer 41	Physical therapy assistant 6
Acupuncturist 12	Landscape architect 35	Physician's assistant 25
Aerial duster 8	Librarian 23	Plumber 30
Ambulance attendant 32	Marriage counselor 6	Polygraph examiners 21
Auctioneer 24	Masseur 15	Private detective 35
Audiologist 30	Medical lab technician 8	Private patrol agent 17
Boiler inspector 26	Medical lab director 15	Psychologist 48
Chauffeur 34	Midwife 28	TV technician 4
Collection agent 22	Milk sampler 30	Radiologic technician 10
General contractor 20	Mine foreman 19	Sanitarian 33
Specialty contractor 5	Projectionist 6	School bus driver 12
Well driller 31	Naturopath 11	Securities agent 49
Driving instructor 40	Nursing home	Shorthand reporter 13
Electrician 15	administrator 49	Social worker 20
Elevator inspector 12	Occupational therapist 10	Soil tester 7
Funeral director 29	Occupational therapy	Surveyor 49
Employment agency 49	assistant 6	Tree surgeon 11
Engineer 49	Optician 19	Veterinarian 16
Forester 12	Outfitter 4	Watchmaker 10
Geologist 9	Pest control applicator 23	Watchman/guard 9
Guide 24	Pesticide applicator 18	Weather modifier 21
Harbor pilot 25	Pharmacist's assistant 17	Weighmaster 21

1. JUSTIFICATION FOR REGULATION

Occupational licensing is justified on the grounds discussed earlier: asymmetrical consumer information and spillover costs.

In an unregulated market, consumers will often have less information about the quality of the service than the producer. This asymmetry can create excessive demand for service that is of low quality:

> In the case of medicine, for example, . . . the consumer cannot evaluate beforehand whether or not Dr. X is a competent physician; in fact, the consumer may not be able to evaluate the abilities of Dr. X after treatment because numerous factors other than the treatment may contribute to the consumer's health. In addition, the consumer is in a poor position to evaluate how much of Dr. X's services that he or she needs. . . . Is surgery required, or are there other less radical alternatives?
>
>   Faced with these alternatives, a consumer would normally engage in an agency relationship with a third party. Faced with the purchase of stocks, for example, the consumer hires a broker for advice. In the present example, the only agent is Dr. X. The consumer trusts Dr. X to tell him or her how much medical treatment is needed.
>
>   . . . [But] Dr. X, as agent, has an incentive to recommend more services than the consumer needs because these services will be

purchased from Dr. X, the seller. Regulation . . . is therefore needed, to prevent an excessive demand for the product.[63]

Excessive demand for poor quality service is related to the fact that the consumer does not have the skills to prejudge the quality of a service. Lacking such skills, there is a greater risk that the consumer will purchase a service that is of poor quality, or even that is dangerous to the person. For example, "a dentist might do actual long-run damage to a patient's teeth, or an abstractor may miss a lien on property sold to a consumer."[64]

The second potential market flaw is a spillover cost, or externality. An externality can arise when a consumer purchases a poor quality service and, as a result, a third person is harmed. For example, a person who hires an incompetent architect may endanger the lives of persons who use a building, or a person who employs an incompetent plumber risks the health of others in the community through the spread of disease.[65]

Despite these justifications, economists have generally been critical of occupational licensing. They charge that it produces a variety of evils.[66] First, occupational licensing restricts the free flow of labor from one occupation to another by creating barriers to entry such as examinations, education, apprentice programs, and so on. These roadblocks make markets less efficient by preventing labor from flowing freely to those occupations with the greatest returns. Second, occupational licensing raises the cost of services. As long as supply is restricted and demand remains constant or increases, the price of a regulated service will rise. Third, as a result of restricted entry and high prices, members of the regulated occupation will receive economic rents. This occurs because consumers will pay higher prices than they would in a competitive market.

The extent to which the barriers to entry are harmful to consumers depends on the answer to two questions. First, does the occupational licensing effectively weed out incompetent providers? Second, are there less restrictive alternatives that will protect consumers?

Effective regulations: Critics are skeptical that occupational licensing protects consumers because regulation is associated in many cases with barriers that lack any redeeming benefits for consumers, such as nonsense requirements, useless examinations, or a lack of reciprocity. As Professor Gellhorn found:

> In California, a license to cut hair can be won only after the completion of a long apprenticeship, graduation from a barber college, and success in an examination that in past years has demanded knowledge of such esoteric things as the chemical composition of bones and the name of the muscle that is inserted in the hyoid bone. Illinois purportedly tests a would-be barber's knowledge of, among other things, physiology, electricity, anatomy, and barber history. . . .

---

[63] K. Meier, Regulation: Politics, Bureaucracy, and Economics 175–76 (1985).

[64] *Id.* at 176.

[65] *Id.* at 177.

[66] *Id.* at 181.

. . . Some states insist that only an American citizen can qualify to become, for instance, a pharmacist, chiropodist, tree surgeon, embalmer, bill collector, or osteopath—evidencing a type of xenophobia which reached a severe pitch in state legislatures in the late 1930s when European refugees began arriving in large numbers during a time of job scarcity. Other laws provide that, regardless of national citizenship, a licensee must have been a resident of the license-issuing state for a substantial period of time—although the relationship between prior residence and occupational qualification may be undiscoverable, as in the case of optometrists, accountants, masseurs, and dentists. . . . Occupational licenses have also been conditioned upon residency in political subdivisions smaller than a state. Twenty-eight states provide for the licensing of plumbers, but in most of these states the plumbers have managed to prevent licensing on a state-wide basis. Instead, the licenses are issued by cities, which impose municipal residence requirements aimed at excluding "outsiders" from the local job market.[67]

The origin of indefensible barriers to entry is not hard to find—those who benefit from such regulation are more likely to be politically active than those who pay for it. Milton Friedman explains:

[P]eople in the same trade, like barbers or physicians, all have an intense interest in the specific problems of this trade and are willing to devote considerable energy to doing something about them. On the other hand, those of us who use barbers at all, get barbered infrequently and spend only a minor fraction of our income in barber shops. . . . Hardly any of us are willing to devote much time going to the legislature in order to testify against the iniquity of restricting the practice of barbering. . . . The public interest is widely dispersed. In consequence, in the absence of any general arrangements to offset the pressure of special interests, producer groups will invariably have a much stronger influence on legislative action and the powers that be than will the diverse, widely spread consumer interest.[68]

Less restrictive alternatives: Besides the issue of whether occupational licensing is effective, there is also the question of whether less restrictive alternatives can protect consumers adequately. States have two alternative options: registration and certification.[69]

Under registration, everyone who sells a specified service must register with an agency. Since anyone who wishes can register, there is no barrier to entry. Registration permits the agency to receive complaints about the providers of a service and suspend registration if warranted. Without registration, the provider can no longer operate.

Under certification, a regulatory agency offers an examination for those who wish to be certified. Any individual who passes the examination and meets

---

[67] Gellhorn, *supra* note 61, at 14–15.

[68] M. FRIEDMAN, CAPITALISM AND FREEDOM 143 (1962), *quoted in* Gellhorn, *supra* note 61, at 16 n.35.

[69] MEIER, *supra* note 62, at 179–80.

other criteria set by the agency can hold himself or herself out as a "certified" member of the profession. Since persons who wish to sell a service without certification can do so, it is not a barrier to entry. For example, anyone who wishes can sell the service of preparing tax returns, but those with accounting degrees who have passed an examination can advertise that they are "certified public accountants" (CPAs). The previous options are not mutually exclusive.[70] For example, lawyers are licensed in all states; they may also be certified in some states as specialists in some area like tax law. Likewise, physicians are both licensed to the general practice of medicine and certified as specialists. Critics argue that, if some form of consumer protection is justified at all concerning some occupations, registration or certification is preferable. For example, a consumer has the option under certification of purchasing services from an individual who is certified as competent by an agency, but if the consumer feels that the price charged by certified providers is too high, the person still has the option of purchasing the service from a noncertified provider. Thus, consumers are free to purchase services from the lower-cost tax preparer, or from the higher-cost CPA.

NOTES AND QUESTIONS

1. Additional proof cited by critics that occupational licensing serves only to protect those being regulated from competition is the fact that so many disparate professions are licensed. Professor Gellhorn observes, "[T]he founding fathers . . . would, however, have been aghast to learn that in many parts of the country today aspiring bee keepers, embalmers, lightning rod salesmen, septic tank cleaners, taxidermists, and tree surgeons must obtain official approval before seeking the public's patronage. After examining the roster of those who must receive official permission to function, a cynic might conclude that virtually the only people who remain unlicensed in at least one of the United States are clergymen and university professors, presumably because they are nowhere taken seriously."[71]

2. Another problem with irrelevant licensing requirements is that they exclude ethnic minorities from entering a profession, as Professor Gellhorn points out:

> Licensing tests are often administered solely in English, so that Spanish-speaking citizens and foreign-born residents encounter special difficulty. In some instances, indeed, written tests may be altogether inapposite means of determining whether an applicant possesses a requisite degree of skill. Many economically deprived young people cannot easily meet the qualifications demanded of applicants, such as paying tuition to pseudo-professional schools or undergoing needlessly prolonged periods of apprenticeship.[72]

3. Milton Friedman maintains that all occupational regulation should be deregulated. He argues that consumers have other methods to obtain information concerning the quality of a product, such as experience, when numerous

---

[70] *Id.* at 180.

[71] Gellhorn, *supra* note 61, at 6.

[72] *Id.* at 18.

purchases are made, or talking with relatives and friends, when there is a one-time purchase. Friedman also contends that there are few or no externalities for most occupations. In those instances where externalities do exist, such as health care or engineering, Friedman says that spillover costs are limited by the fact that consumers can obtain information by other means and by the existence of tort remedies.[73] Do you agree with Friedman's argument? Should states end all occupational licensing? Consider Professor Gellhorn's response:

> Painful economic experiences might ultimately lead consumers of services to locate the most efficient, most trustworthy suppliers. Meanwhile, however, many persons would suffer avoidable wounds to person or purse. The anonymity of large urbanized American society prevents the kind of informed choice which may have been possible when clients, patients, and customers could rely with reasonable confidence upon neighbors' opinions of professionals and tradesmen. For that reason I accept the view that in some occupations some kind of quality control may be needed to protect the uninformed against blatant incompetents, wily charlatans, and persons whose past delinquencies suggest the probability of future corrupt conduct.[74]

Although Professor Gellhorn does not favor the end of regulation, he suggests that in many cases alternatives to licensing be used. Do you agree? Look at the list of occupations listed in Table 10-2. Which of these would you deregulate completely? Which would you subject to registration or certification as an alternative?

4. If occupational licensing is retained as the method of regulation, critics propose that the membership of licensing boards be changed to guard against rent-seeking by the occupation being regulated. Most licensing boards are composed of members of the profession. A few states, however, appoint consumer representatives to such boards. Do you favor this reform? How likely is it to work? Consider the following analysis:

> If a major problem with occupational regulation is that consumer interests are rarely considered, then one possible solution is to require consumer or public representatives on the regulatory boards. California, for example, requires public members on many of its regulatory boards, including a voting majority on 15 boards. Where public representation is used in states other than California, however, it is generally only used halfheartedly. Rarely are consumers given a majority on the board — usually one or at most two seats. This voting disadvantage means that, on serious disagreements, the regulated occupation usually has access to a voting majority. Second, public members on a regulatory board may be no different from general consumers; they can probably be snowed by professional expertise. As one regulator said, after we spend some time educating a public member, he or she votes correctly. . . .[75]

---

[73] FRIEDMAN, *supra* note 60, at 157.

[74] Gellhorn, *supra* note 61, at 25.

[75] MEIER, *supra* note 62, at 197.

5. Charles Peters, editor of the *Washington Monthly,* proposes a plan to solve the problem of weak consumer representation on medical licensing boards:

> Certainly it doesn't seem likely that the medical licensing boards will do much to control the sins of their peers. . . .
>
> But I have a solution to this, . . . [T]he average trial lawyer does become an expert on the sins of doctors. In malpractice cases, he has to learn enough about medicine to understand why things go wrong in the operating room and elsewhere in the practice of medicine. If medical licensing boards were dominated by laymen with enough trial lawyers among them to cross-examine the doctors accused of malpractice, there would be none of the self-protective guild mentality that now lets the guilty escape. . . .[76]

Do you support Peters' proposal? Would a similar plan work for other professions? For example, should lawyers who do tort work in the construction area be placed on boards that regulate architects?

2. REGULATION OF LAWYERS

Earlier, you were asked whether consumers in the market for legal services are poorly informed, moderately well informed, or well informed about the quality of legal assistance which they purchase. This section examines the regulation of lawyers as a case study in occupational licensing. Since every state licenses lawyers, legislators have reached the decision that licensing is necessary to ensure that consumers receive services of at least minimum quality. But do the existing methods of licensing serve the public or the regulated industry? Does the occupational licensing of lawyers weed out incompetent practitioners? Are there less restrictive alternatives that would protect consumers? The following excerpt will assist you in considering these issues.

REED OLSEN, DEAN LUECK, & MICHAEL RANSOM, WHY DO STATES REGULATE ADMISSION TO THE BAR? ECONOMIC THEORIES AND EMPIRICAL EVIDENCE, 14 GEORGE MASON LAW REVIEW 253, 255–272 (1991)*

I. Admission to the Bar

Professional associations of lawyers—the precursor of modern bar associations—arose in England during the Middle Ages. Prior to and during the colonial American period, English lawyers studied at Inns of Court. The Inns controlled the admission and educational requirements for the legal profession. In the early history of the United States (including much of the colonial period), the legal profession retained much of the English legal structure. In fact, many American lawyers were trained in England. Local groups of lawyers formed bar associations in New York State as early as 1747. During this time, however, these groups did not have effective control over the educational or

---

[76] Peters, *Tilting At Windmills,* WASH. MONTHLY, May 1990, at 10.

* Copyright © 1991 George Mason Law Review. Reprinted by permission.

other requirements for admission to practice law and were largely social organizations.

Although states have always regulated the practice of law, there was a rather dramatic decline in professional licensing rules during the period between the Revolutionary War and the Civil War. Many states had initially required some formal education or formal apprenticeship, but by the time of the Civil War, these requirements were severely weakened, if not altogether abolished. . . .

After the Civil War, formal professional organizations reemerged. These organizations sought to persuade states to impose restrictions on those who could practice law. Formal bar associations arose during the end of the 19th Century as "professional organization[s] for promoting the practice of a learned art in the spirit of public service." The American Bar Association (ABA) was organized in 1878, largely by members of the Bar Association of the City of New York. State bar associations emerged after the ABA; by 1900, 43 states had such associations. By 1936, the state bars and the ABA began to coordinate their activities.

Despite the increasing authority of the ABA and state bar associations, admission to practice law was relatively unregulated during the early 1900s. Most lawyers did not attend law school, and no state required a law degree to practice law. Early law training programs typically were not affiliated with universities. However, in 1899, Harvard Law School initiated the first three-year requirements for a law degree, heralding a trend toward university law training. Soon thereafter, the ABA began to accredit law schools and states began requiring bar examinations. Simultaneously, the use of other methods to gain admission to practice law began to decline. . . .

By 1985, regulations governing admission to the bar were quite formal and varied considerably between jurisdictions. These regulations can be divided into six general categories: educational requirements, rules governing reciprocity of bar admission between jurisdictions, residency requirements, the use of multistate exams, the level of exam fees charged bar applicants, and the difficulty of the state bar exam.

The stringency of educational requirements varies dramatically between jurisdictions. A few states (California, Maine, New York, Virginia, Washington, and Wyoming) have no specific degree requirements. Thirty-five states impose the most stringent educational regulation; they require bar applicants to hold a law degree from a law school approved by the ABA. Two states, West Virginia and Wisconsin, still have a diploma privilege, whereby bar admission is granted to graduates of certain preferred law schools within the state without a bar examination requirement. . . .

Reciprocity rules determine how a lawyer can become a member of a particular jurisdiction's bar when that lawyer is already a member of another bar. Of the 51 jurisdictions in the United States, 36 practice some form of reciprocity. Of these 36, 6 offer a special, shortened version of the bar exam for practicing attorneys who are members of another state's bar. Other states allow some practicing attorneys to join the bar on "motion" without taking the bar exam. Since 1920, however, less than 10 percent of annual bar admissions were granted on motion.

In the past, states imposed residency requirements on bar applicants. The three types of proof of residency that a jurisdiction could require were: (1) the applicant must establish legal residency, (2) the applicant must reside in the state but not be a legal resident, or (3) the applicant must declare an intent to reside in the state before taking the bar exam. . . .

Two multistate exams may be required for admission to the bar for any particular jurisdiction. The Multistate Professional Responsibility Exam (MPRE) is a 50 question multiple-choice legal ethics exam designed by the National Conference of Bar Examiners, and is administered nationally, rather than by each individual state. Thirty jurisdictions require that their applicants take and pass the MPRE; however, the percentage of correct answers required to pass the MPRE varies from a low of 65 percent for Illinois to a high of 85 percent for Nevada, Minnesota, and Arizona. The Multistate Bar Exam (MBE) is a six hour, 200 question multiple-choice exam that covers a variety of topics. Only 4 states do not require that their bar applicants take this exam.

All jurisdictions require examinees to pay fees before taking the bar exam. These fees vary significantly between jurisdictions. Moreover, the fees may be different for residents and nonresidents as well as for recent law school graduates and practicing attorneys. In 1985, fees ranged from a low of $20 for residents and nonresidents taking the West Virginia bar exam to a high of $490 for practicing lawyers taking the bar exam in Utah.

Finally, the difficulty of the bar exam varies across jurisdictions. Exam difficulty is commonly measured by the relative passage rates for each jurisdiction's exam. For example, consider the average passage rates for the July bar exam from 1981 to 1984. Georgia and California had rates below 50 percent, while 5 states had rates in excess of 90 percent. . . .

II. Competing Theories of Professional Licensure . . .

Both the capture theory and the public interest theory offer simple, yet plausible, explanations for the existence of professional licensure. The simple capture theory suggests that professionals control the rules that govern professional licensure in an attempt to increase their income; the public interest theory suggests that professional licensure arises in response to public demand to correct market failures. In the face of competing theories that explain professional licensure, the decision as to which is correct is problematic and ultimately an empirical issue. . . .

Mounting evidence suggests that both professionals and the public have an impact on professional licensure. . . .

III. Empirical Evidence

. . . The capture theory suggests that the main intent of professional licensure is to enhance professionals' income by limiting the entry of new professionals who, if allowed to practice, would compete with existing professionals and reduce the price of legal advice. Thus, under the capture theory, professional licensure is expected to: (1) limit the entry (supply) of practicing professionals; (2) increase the price charged for professional services; and, (3) increase the income of existing professionals.

In contrast, the public interest theory suggests that professional licensure serves to increase the quality of the services provided by the licensed profession. Thus, under the public interest theory, the empirical evidence would be expected to reflect a positive correlation between professional licensure and the quality of professional services. Unfortunately, quality is quite difficult to measure, especially for professional services, making empirical tests difficult. As a result, most empirical studies that test the relevance of the capture and public interest theories have focused on the impact that professional licensure has on the price of professional services, the level of professional income, and the supply of professionals. . . .

Previous empirical studies yield no consistent picture of the impact of professional licensure on prices, income or supply. This inconclusive result weakens support for the capture theory. . . . [Our results], as with the earlier research discussed above, provide little support for the simple capture theory. Contrary to capture theory predictions, bar admission regulations do not consistently increase fees or incomes, or limit the entry of new lawyers in the data set presented here. Like other researchers, however, we cannot accurately measure the quality of legal services with our data. Therefore, the public interest theory is not directly tested.

———

Educational requirements are one of the six categories of regulations identified in the previous excerpt. Most states require that an applicant for admission to the bar be a graduate of an accredited law school. In the following case, *In re Hansen*, which concerns the requirement that a person graduate from an ABA-accredited law school, the Minnesota Supreme Court performs two functions. First, it determines as a constitutional matter whether the decision of the Bar Examiners denies equal protection to Mr. Hansen. Regarding this function, even the dissenting justices conceded that Mr. Hansen did not raise a "serious" constitutional challenge to Minnesota's regulation.

Second, the court also functions as a regulator, because the legislature has delegated to it the responsibility for determining the eligibility rules. In Minnesota (as in other states), the court is assisted in this function by committees composed of lawyers, such as the State Board of Bar Examiners, to which the opinion refers. In this capacity, the court splits concerning whether it should waive the requirement that Mr. Hansen be a graduate of an ABA-accredited law school in order to be eligible to take the bar examination. As you read the case, consider what policies are served by such a restriction.

IN RE HANSEN

275 N.W.2d 790 (Minn. 1978)

KELLY, JUSTICE.

This case comes before the court pursuant to petitioner's request for review of a decision by the State Board of Law Examiners (Board) that petitioner would not be allowed to sit for the Minnesota State Bar examination because he had not graduated from an approved law school as required by Rule II(4) of the Supreme Court Rules for Admission to the Bar. We affirm.

Petitioner, originally a Minnesota resident, is a 1977 graduate of Western State University College of Law (Western State), San Diego, California. . . .

In the fall of 1976, when petitioner was a senior student at Western State, he applied to the Board for permission to sit for the July, 1977 bar examination. The Board denied his application because he was not a graduate of an approved law school. According to the Rules for Admission to the Bar, an approved law school is one "that is provisionally or fully approved by the Section of Legal Education for Admissions to the Bar of the American Bar Association." . . .

This case presents the following issues for decision: (1) Whether Rule II(4) of the Supreme Court Rules for Admission to the Bar is constitutional; and, (2) Whether, granting its constitutionality, the requirement of graduating from an ABA-accredited law school should be waived in this case.

Petitioner and Western State, as *amicus curiae,* suggest that Minnesota's rule requiring proof of graduation from an ABA-approved law school as a prerequisite to sitting for the bar examination is unconstitutional under both the due process and the equal protection clauses of the Fourteenth Amendment to the United States Constitution. We disagree. . . .

All United States Supreme Court decisions concerning state regulation of the practice of law recognize that a state has a substantial interest in the qualifications of those it admits to the legal profession. . . .

The test that emerges from these cases is that, despite the strong interest of the applicant in being able to practice law, the state can regulate admission as long as such regulation is reasonably related to its interest in a competent bar. A procedure is reasonable as long as it is not arbitrary and capricious. Only if the complainant is a member of a suspect class or if the procedure at issue violates a fundamental right must the state demonstrate a compelling state interest for its system of regulation to pass constitutional muster.

The procedure being challenged in this case is Minnesota's requirement that an applicant wishing to take the bar examination demonstrate, among other things, that he graduated from a law school which is provisionally or fully accredited by the American Bar Association. Although there have been numerous challenges over the years to educational requirements similar to those of Rule II, both state and federal courts have consistently found such requirements to be constitutional. . . .

Clearly, it is reasonable for Minnesota to require proof that an applicant's legal education was of a high quality as a general prerequisite to admission to the bar. Similarly, it is neither arbitrary nor capricious for us to measure the quality of legal education with the same standards as those utilized by the ABA. . . . Thus, petitioner's argument that Rule II(4) is an unconstitutional violation of the due process clause of the Fourteenth Amendment has no merit.

Likewise, we find no violation of the equal protection clause. Under traditional equal protection analysis classifications will be upheld as long as they are reasonably related to some legitimate governmental purpose. We have already established that the distinction between graduates of accredited and nonaccredited law schools is reasonably related to ensuring a competent bar. . . .

Petitioner and Western State both argue that whether or not the court decides that Rule II(4) is unconstitutional, petitioner still deserves to have the requirement waived. . . .

The . . . basis for petitioner's claim to a waiver is the fact that he has passed the California bar examination and been admitted to practice law in the State of California. The mere passage of a bar examination in another state, however, does not necessitate a waiver of the educational rule of the state in which petitioner now seeks to practice. We do not believe that passage of a bar examination is necessarily an equivalent measure of the characteristics of legal education which are important in the accrediting decision.

YETKA, JUSTICE (dissenting).

While I agree that this case, in my opinion, does not pose a serious constitutional challenge to Rule II(4) of the Supreme Court Rules for Admission to the Bar, I believe the facts of this situation justify our waiving the requirement that the applicant graduate from an ABA-accredited law school. . . .

I regret to see Minnesota refuse applicant's petition because there is much to be said for a rule that would allow Any applicant who has passed the bar examination of Any other state and has been admitted to practice in that state to take the bar examination of any other state in the union. Why these barriers? What state or states do we fear are so lenient in their admission standards that we will not permit their lawyers to even take our examination? If our examination is tough enough to screen out the unqualified applicants, we need not have concern for anyone who wishes to take it. And if it is not tough enough to do so, there is little reason for the existence of the bar examination at all. . . .

I would waive the rule and allow petitioner to take our bar examination.

OTIS, JUSTICE (dissenting).

I join in the dissent of MR. JUSTICE YETKA. Western had no opportunity to become accredited prior to 1977, by which time Bryan Hansen was ready to graduate. This is not a case where the ABA has declined to approve a law school, and we are not justified in assuming Western fails to meet ABA standards. All of the evidence strongly suggests Hansen is a highly qualified candidate for admission to our bar. We establish no precedent by permitting him to sit for the examination since the ABA ban on accrediting proprietary schools has now been lifted. This is not a proper case for us to adopt a rigid and inflexible attitude to vindicate our rules.

NOTES AND QUESTIONS

1. As you read, only two states waive the requirement of a bar examination for graduates of the state's law schools. What is the purpose of the bar examination? Are regulators concerned that law schools might graduate incompetent lawyers? Did the legislatures in West Virginia and Wisconsin conclude that their law schools could be trusted to weed out incompetent practitioners, but the schools in other states could not? Or did they determine that students graduating from the local law schools would be sufficiently familiar with state law, but other lawyers had to be tested to ensure such knowledge?

2. Is it likely a state supreme court, or a federal court, would ever strike down an occupational licensing statute as a violation of equal protection, unless strict scrutiny was applied? Does this mean that lawyers effectively regulate themselves? Is this good for society?

3. Physicians take a national licensing examination. Is there some reason why states continue to rely on their own local examinations at least to some extent? Do local laws differ sufficiently to justify a separate examination?

4. A litigant's ability to appeal constitutional decisions like *Hansen* has been limited by the Supreme Court. The Court has held that appeals of state court decisions arising out of judicial proceedings must be taken to the United States Supreme Court under 28 U.S.C. § 1257 (1988), even if those challenges allege that the state court's action was unconstitutional. *District of Columbia Ct. of Appeals v. Feldman,* 460 U.S. 462, 486 (1983). The Court, however, will hear such appeals only if it grants certiorari, which would seem unlikely in most cases.

5. The antitrust laws constitute a potential limitation on occupational licensing of lawyers, but licensing decisions are generally immunized from the antitrust laws under the "state action" doctrine announced in *Parker v. Brown,* 317 U.S. 341 (1943). *See, e.g., Hoover v. Rowin,* 466 U.S. 558, 567–74 (1984). *Parker* held that Congress had not intended to use the antitrust laws "to restrain a state or its officers or agents from activities directed by its legislature." *Id.* at 350–51. Thus, "a state may be free to determine for itself how much competition is desirable, provided that it substitutes adequate public control whenever it has weakened competition."[77] When a state authorizes its supreme court to promulgate rules governing occupational licensing, it meets the previous test, and the rules are exempt from antitrust review. *Bates v. State Bar of Ariz.,* 433 U.S. 350, 360 (1977). When state action is carried out by state boards or agencies, the courts will engage in a case by case review to determine if a specific decision is made pursuant to state action. *Hoover,* 466 U.S. at 568. In those cases where the Court has applied the antitrust laws, such as the decision that the Virginia Bar Association violated the antitrust laws by promulgating minimum price schedules, it found that the

---

[77] P. Areeda & D. Turner, Antitrust Law § 213a, at 72 (1978).

decisionmaker was not closely supervised by any state entity. *Goldfarb v. Virginia State Bar,* 421 U.S. 773, 791 (1975).

6. In 1987, the California Bar created the Public Protection Committee (Committee) to identify areas for deregulation of the legal profession. The Committee recommended abolishing the prohibition of the lay practice of law and permitting persons to practice law without meeting educational requirements or following ethical restraints. Instead, lay practitioners would be required only to register with a state agency. The Bar authorized the release of the Committee's report, but did not approve its contents.[78] Consider the following issues raised by the report:

(1) What market flaw or flaws does the occupational licensing of lawyers address, and are these economically significant for consumers?

(2) What are the arguments for and against the practice of law by laypersons as recommended by the California Committee? In particular, assess whether poorer consumers have adequate access to legal assistance, and whether the previous proposal would increase such access.

(3) Should the practice of law be allowed by laypersons in some areas where practice is standardized?

(4) As an alternative reform, should laypersons be appointed to the majority of positions on the state's licensing board?

In answering question (3), consider the conclusion of one researcher that "there is reason to believe that standardized or standardizable legal services form a large portion of the practice of many lawyers."[79] According to the researcher, the most standardized areas of law include uncontested divorces, preparation of wills and trusts, preparation of income tax returns, probate services, and certain real estate matters. The next level of standardization includes uncontested adoptions, simple personal bankruptcies, collections, changes of name, and incorporations of small businesses. He concludes that, because many types of law practice require less legal expertise, lay practitioners can competently perform them. Another commentator suggests this analogy: "[D]octors and dentists, like lawyers, cost too much; and while no one suggests letting an untrained person operate, lay people, under the supervision of registered nurses, instead of licensed ophthalmologists and otolaryngolists, screen school children for vision and hearing defects."[80]

E. FIRST AMENDMENT RESTRICTIONS

The authority of the government to address informal market defects is constrained by First Amendment restrictions. The First Amendment is implicated because when the government limits the advertising message of a seller, it is restricting that person's right to engage in speech. In effect, it

---

[78] Note, *Deregulation of the Practice of Law: Panacea or Placebo?,* 42 HASTINGS L.J. 203, 205–06, 224 (1990)

[79] Engel, *The Standardization of Lawyers' Services,* 1977 AM. B. FOUND. RES. J. 817, 842–43.

[80] *Deregulation of the Practice of Law, supra* note 77, at 243. For a skeptical look at the regulation of lawyers, *see* R. POSNER, OVERCOMING LAW 39–70 (1995) (discussing the legal profession as a medieval guild and then as a modern cartel).

is banning that person from making certain claims in order to protect consumers. For example, a state might attempt to prohibit advertising concerning liquor prices, or it might prohibit lawyers from advertising about prices. Both of these restrictions were the subject of the Supreme Court cases, as you will read shortly. In both cases, the states attempted to justify the restrictions on the basis of consumer protection.

Commercial speech to promote products was not accorded First Amendment protection until 1976, when the Supreme Court decided *Virginia State Board of Pharmacy v. Virginia Citizens Consumer Council, Inc.*, 425 U.S. 748 (1976), which struck down a state prohibition on price advertising of drugs by pharmacies. In 1977, the Court struck down a similar ban on price advertising by lawyers in *Bates v. State Bar of Arizona*, 433 U.S. 350 (1977).

Although the application of the First Amendment to commercial speech is no longer in doubt, the Court is unsettled concerning what level of scrutiny to apply. The next two cases indicate the nature of this disagreement. How this disagreement is ultimately resolved will determine the scope of state regulation of advertising.

CENTRAL HUDSON GAS & ELECTRIC CORPORATION
v.
PUBLIC SERVICE COMMISSION OF NEW YORK
447 U.S. 557 (1980)

Mr. Justice Powell delivered the opinion of the Court.

This case presents the question whether a regulation of the Public Service Commission of the State of New York violates the First and Fourteenth Amendments because it completely bans promotional advertising by an electrical utility.

I

In December 1973, the Commission, appellee here, ordered electric utilities in New York State to cease all advertising that "promot[es] the use of electricity." The order was based on the Commission's finding that "the interconnected utility system in New York State does not have sufficient fuel stocks or sources of supply to continue furnishing all customer demands for the 1973-1974 winter."

Three years later, when the fuel shortage had eased, the Commission requested comments from the public on its proposal to continue the ban on promotional advertising. Central Hudson Gas & Electric Corp., the appellant in this case, opposed the ban on First Amendment grounds. After reviewing the public comments, the Commission extended the prohibition in a Policy Statement issued on February 25, 1977. . . .

II

The Commission's order restricts only commercial speech, that is, expression related solely to the economic interests of the speaker and its audience. The First Amendment, as applied to the States through the Fourteenth

Amendment, protects commercial speech from unwarranted governmental regulation. Commercial expression not only serves the economic interest of the speaker, but also assists consumers and furthers the societal interest in the fullest possible dissemination of information. In applying the First Amendment to this area, we have rejected the "highly paternalistic" view that government has complete power to suppress or regulate commercial speech. "[P]eople will perceive their own best interests if only they are well enough informed, and . . . the best means to that end is to open the channels of communication rather than to close them. . . ." Even when advertising communicates only an incomplete version of the relevant facts, the First Amendment presumes that some accurate information is better than no information at all.

Nevertheless, our decisions have recognized "the 'commonsense' distinction between speech proposing a commercial transaction, which occurs in an area traditionally subject to government regulation, and other varieties of speech." The Constitution therefore accords a lesser protection to commercial speech than to other constitutionally guaranteed expression. The protection available for particular commercial expression turns on the nature both of the expression and of the governmental interests served by its regulation.

The First Amendment's concern for commercial speech is based on the informational function of advertising. Consequently, there can be no constitutional objection to the suppression of commercial messages that do not accurately inform the public about lawful activity. The government may ban forms of communication more likely to deceive the public than to inform it, or commercial speech related to illegal activity.

If the communication is neither misleading nor related to unlawful activity, the government's power is more circumscribed. The State must assert a substantial interest to be achieved by restrictions on commercial speech. Moreover, the regulatory technique must be in proportion to that interest. The limitation on expression must be designed carefully to achieve the State's goal. Compliance with this requirement may be measured by two criteria. First, the restriction must directly advance the state interest involved; the regulation may not be sustained if it provides only ineffective or remote support for the government's purpose. Second, if the governmental interest could be served as well by a more limited restriction on commercial speech, the excessive restrictions cannot survive.

Under the first criterion, the Court has declined to uphold regulations that only indirectly advance the state interest involved. In both *Bates* and *Virginia Pharmacy Board*, the Court concluded that an advertising ban could not be imposed to protect the ethical or performance standards of a profession. The Court noted in *Virginia Pharmacy Board* that "[t]he advertising ban does not directly affect professional standards one way or the other." In *Bates*, the Court overturned an advertising prohibition that was designed to protect the "quality" of a lawyer's work. "Restraints on advertising . . . are an ineffective way of deterring shoddy work."

The second criterion recognizes that the First Amendment mandates that speech restrictions be "narrowly drawn." The regulatory technique may extend only as far as the interest it serves. The State cannot regulate speech that poses no danger to the asserted state interest, nor can it completely suppress information when narrower restrictions on expression would serve its interest as well. For example, in *Bates* the Court explicitly did not "foreclose the possibility that some limited supplementation, by way of warning or disclaimer or the like, might be required" in promotional materials. . . .

In commercial speech cases, then, a four-part analysis has developed. At the outset, we must determine whether the expression is protected by the First Amendment. For commercial speech to come within that provision, it at least must concern lawful activity and not be misleading. Next, we ask whether the asserted governmental interest is substantial. If both inquiries yield positive answers, we must determine whether the regulation directly advances the governmental interest asserted, and whether it is not more extensive than is necessary to serve that interest.

III

We now apply this four-step analysis for commercial speech to the Commission's arguments in support of its ban on promotional advertising. . . . We accept without reservation the argument that conservation, as well as the development of alternative energy sources, is an imperative national goal. Administrative bodies empowered to regulate electric utilities have the authority—and indeed the duty—to take appropriate action to further this goal. When, however, such action involves the suppression of speech, the First and Fourteenth Amendments require that the restriction be no more extensive than is necessary to serve the state interest. In this case, the record before us fails to show that the total ban on promotional advertising meets this requirement.

44 LIQUORMART, INC. v. RHODE ISLAND
116 S. Ct. 1495 (1996)

JUSTICE STEVENS announced the judgment of the Court and delivered the opinion of the Court with respect to Parts I, II, and VIII . . .

Last Term we held that a federal law abridging a brewer's right to provide the public with accurate information about the alcoholic content of malt beverages is unconstitutional. Rubin v. Coors Brewing Co., 514 U.S. 476, 491 (1995). We now hold that Rhode Island's statutory prohibition against advertisements that provide the public with accurate information about retail prices of alcoholic beverages is also invalid. Our holding rests on the conclusion that such an advertising ban is an abridgment of speech protected by the First Amendment and that it is not shielded from constitutional scrutiny by the Twenty-first Amendment.

I

In 1956, the Rhode Island Legislature enacted two separate prohibitions against advertising the retail price of alcoholic beverages. The first applies to vendors licensed in Rhode Island as well as to out-of-state manufacturers, wholesalers, and shippers. It prohibits them from "advertising in any manner whatsoever" the price of any alcoholic beverage offered for sale in the State; the only exception is for price tags or signs displayed with the merchandise within licensed premises and not visible from the street. The second statute applies to the Rhode Island news media. It contains a categorical prohibition against the publication or broadcast of any advertisements—even those referring to sales in other States—that "make reference to the price of any alcoholic beverages.". . .

IV

As our review of the case law reveals, Rhode Island errs in concluding that *all* commercial speech regulations are subject to a similar form of constitutional review simply because they target a similar category of expression. The mere fact that messages propose commercial transactions does not in and of itself dictate the constitutional analysis that should apply to decisions to suppress them.

When a State regulates commercial messages to protect consumers from misleading, deceptive, or aggressive sales practices, or requires the disclosure of beneficial consumer information, the purpose of its regulation is consistent with the reasons for according constitutional protection to commercial speech and therefore justifies less than strict review. However, when a State entirely prohibits the dissemination of truthful, nonmisleading commercial messages for reasons unrelated to the preservation of a fair bargaining process, there is far less reason to depart from the rigorous review that the First Amendment generally demands.

Sound reasons justify reviewing the latter type of commercial speech regulation more carefully. Most obviously, complete speech bans, unlike content-neutral restrictions on the time, place, or manner of expression, are particularly dangerous because they all but foreclose alternative means of disseminating certain information. . . .

The special dangers that attend complete bans on truthful, nonmisleading commercial speech cannot be explained away by appeals to the "commonsense distinctions" that exist between commercial and noncommercial speech. Regulations that suppress the truth are no less troubling because they target objectively verifiable information, nor are they less effective because they aim at durable messages. As a result, neither the "greater objectivity" nor the "greater hardiness" of truthful, nonmisleading commercial speech justifies reviewing its complete suppression with added deference.

It is the State's interest in protecting consumers from "commercial harms" that provides "the typical reason why commercial speech can be subject to greater governmental regulation than noncommercial speech." Yet bans that target truthful, nonmisleading commercial messages rarely protect consumers from such harms. Instead, such bans often serve only to obscure an "underlying governmental policy" that could be implemented without regulating speech. In this way, these commercial speech bans not only hinder consumer choice, but also impede debate over central issues of public policy. Precisely because bans against truthful, nonmisleading commercial speech rarely seek to protect consumers from either deception or overreaching, they usually rest solely on the offensive assumption that the public will respond "irrationally" to the truth. The First Amendment directs us to be especially skeptical of regulations that seek to keep people in the dark for what the government perceives to be their own good.

V

In this case, there is no question that Rhode Island's price advertising ban constitutes a blanket prohibition against truthful, nonmisleading speech about a lawful product. There is also no question that the ban serves an end unrelated to consumer protection. Accordingly, we must review the price advertising ban with "special care," mindful that speech prohibitions of this type rarely survive constitutional review.

The State argues that the price advertising prohibition should nevertheless be upheld because it directly advances the State's substantial interest in promoting temperance, and because it is no more extensive than necessary. Although there is some confusion as to what Rhode Island means by temperance, we assume that the State asserts an interest in reducing alcohol consumption.

In evaluating the ban's effectiveness in advancing the State's interest, we note that a commercial speech regulation "may not be sustained if it provides only ineffective or remote support for the government's purpose." For that reason, the State bears the burden of showing not merely that its regulation will advance its interest, but also that it will do so "to a material degree." The need for the State to make such a showing is particularly great given the drastic nature of its chosen means—the wholesale suppression of truthful, nonmisleading information. Accordingly, we must determine whether the State has shown that the price advertising ban will *significantly* reduce alcohol consumption.

We can agree that common sense supports the conclusion that a prohibition against price advertising, like a collusive agreement among competitors to refrain from such advertising, will tend to mitigate competition and maintain prices at a higher level than would prevail in a completely free market. Despite the absence of proof on the point, we can even agree with the State's contention that it is reasonable to assume that demand, and hence consumption throughout the market, is somewhat lower whenever a higher, noncompetitive price level prevails. However, without any findings of fact, or indeed any evidentiary support whatsoever, we cannot agree with the assertion that the price advertising ban will significantly advance the State's interest in promoting temperance. . . .

JUSTICE SCALIA, concurring in part and concurring in the judgment.

I share Justice THOMAS's discomfort with the *Central Hudson* test, which seems to me to have nothing more than policy intuition to support it. I also share Justice STEVENS's aversion towards paternalistic governmental policies that prevent men and women from hearing facts that might not be good for them. On the other hand, it would also be paternalism for us to prevent the people of the States from enacting laws that we consider paternalistic, unless we have good reason to believe that the Constitution itself forbids them.

I will take my guidance as to what the Constitution forbids, with regard to a text as indeterminate as the First Amendment's preservation of "the freedom of speech," and where the core offense of suppressing particular political ideas is not at issue, from the long accepted practices of the American people.

The briefs and arguments of the parties in the present case provide no illumination on that point; understandably so, since both sides accepted *Central Hudson*. . . .

Since I do not believe we have before us the wherewithal to declare *Central Hudson* wrong—or at least the wherewithal to say what ought to replace it—I must resolve this case in accord with our existing jurisprudence, which all except Justice THOMAS agree would prohibit the challenged regulation. I am not disposed to develop new law, or reinforce old, on this issue, and accordingly I merely concur in the judgment of the Court. . . .

JUSTICE THOMAS, concurring in Parts I, II, VI, and VII, and concurring in the judgment.

In cases such as this, in which the government's asserted interest is to keep legal users of a product or service ignorant in order to manipulate their choices in the marketplace, the balancing test adopted in *Central Hudson Gas & Elect. Corp. v. Public Service Comm'n. of N.Y.* should not be applied, in my view. Rather, such an "interest" is *per se* illegitimate and can no more justify regulation of "commercial" speech than it can justify regulation of "noncommercial" speech. . . .

I do not join the principal opinion's application of the *Central Hudson* balancing test because I do not believe that such a test should be applied to a restriction of "commercial" speech, at least when, as here, the asserted interest is one that is to be achieved through keeping would-be recipients of the speech in the dark. Application of the advancement-of-state-interest prong of *Central Hudson* makes little sense to me in such circumstances. Faulting the State for failing to show that its price advertising ban decreases alcohol consumption "significantly," as Justice STEVENS does, *ante,* at 1510 (emphasis deleted), seems to imply that if the State had been *more successful* at keeping consumers ignorant and thereby decreasing their consumption, then the restriction might have been upheld. This contradicts *Virginia Bd. of Pharmacy's* rationale for protecting "commercial" speech in the first instance.

Both Justice STEVENS and Justice O'CONNOR appear to adopt a stricter, more categorical interpretation of the fourth prong of *Central Hudson* than that suggested in some of our other opinions, one that could, as a practical matter, go a long way toward the position I take. The State argues that keeping information about lower priced alcohol from consumers will tend to raise the total price of alcohol to consumers (defined as money price plus the costs of searching out lower priced alcohol), thus discouraging alcohol consumption. In their application of the fourth prong, both Justice STEVENS and Justice O'CONNOR hold that because the State can ban the sale of lower priced alcohol altogether by instituting minimum prices or levying taxes, it cannot ban advertising regarding lower priced liquor. Although the tenor of Justice O'CONNOR's opinion (and, to a lesser extent, that of Justice STEVENS' opinion) might suggest that this is just another routine case-by-case application of *Central Hudson*'s fourth prong, the Court's holding will in fact be quite sweeping if applied consistently in future cases. The opinions would appear to commit the courts to striking down restrictions on speech whenever a direct regulation (*i.e.,* a regulation involving no restriction on speech regarding lawful activity at all) would be an equally effective method of dampening demand by legal users. But it would seem that directly banning a product (or rationing it, taxing it, controlling its price, or otherwise restricting its sale in specific ways) would virtually always be at least as effective in discouraging consumption as merely restricting advertising regarding the product would be, and thus virtually all restrictions with such a purpose would fail the fourth prong of the *Central Hudson* test. This would be so even if the direct regulation is, in one sense, more restrictive of *conduct* generally. In this case, for example, adoption of minimum prices or taxes will mean that those who, under the current legal system, would have happened across cheap liquor or would have sought it out, will be forced to pay more. Similarly, a State seeking to discourage liquor sales would have to ban sales by convenience stores rather than banning convenience store liquor advertising; it would have to ban liquor sales after midnight, rather than banning advertising by late-night liquor sellers; and so on.

JUSTICE O'CONNOR, with whom THE CHIEF JUSTICE, JUSTICE SOUTER, and JUSTICE BREYER join, concurring in the judgment.

Rhode Island prohibits advertisement of the retail price of alcoholic beverages, except at the place of sale. The State's only asserted justification for this ban is that it promotes temperance by increasing the cost of alcoholic beverages. I agree with the Court that Rhode Island's price-advertising ban is invalid. I would resolve this case more narrowly, however, by applying our established *Central Hudson* test to determine whether this commercial speech regulation survives First Amendment scrutiny.

Under that test, we first determine whether the speech at issue concerns lawful activity and is not misleading, and whether the asserted governmental interest is substantial. If both these conditions are met, we must decide whether the regulation "directly advances the governmental interest asserted, and whether it is not more extensive than is necessary to serve that interest."

Given the means by which this regulation purportedly serves the State's interest, our conclusion is plain: Rhode Island's regulation fails First Amendment scrutiny.

Both parties agree that the first two prongs of the *Central Hudson* test are met. Even if we assume, *arguendo,* that Rhode Island's regulation also satisfies the requirement that it directly advance the governmental interest, Rhode Island's regulation fails the final prong; that is, its ban is more extensive than necessary to serve the State's interest.

As we have explained, in order for a speech restriction to pass muster under the final prong, there must be a fit between the legislature's goal and method, "a fit that is not necessarily perfect, but reasonable; that represents not necessarily the single best disposition but one whose scope is in proportion to the interest served." While the State need not employ the least restrictive means to accomplish its goal, the fit between means and ends must be "narrowly tailored." The scope of the restriction on speech must be reasonably, though it need not be perfectly, targeted to address the harm intended to be regulated. The State's regulation must indicate a "carefu[l] calculat[ion of] the costs and benefits associated with the burden on speech imposed by its prohibition." The availability of less burdensome alternatives to reach the stated goal signals that the fit between the legislature's ends and the means chosen to accomplish those ends may be too imprecise to withstand First Amendment scrutiny. If alternative channels permit communication of the restricted speech, the regulation is more likely to be considered reasonable. . . .

The fit between Rhode Island's method and this particular goal is not reasonable. If the target is simply higher prices generally to discourage consumption, the regulation imposes too great, and unnecessary, a prohibition on speech in order to achieve it. The State has other methods at its disposal—methods that would more directly accomplish this stated goal without intruding on sellers' ability to provide truthful, nonmisleading information to customers. Indeed, Rhode Island's own expert conceded that " 'the objective of lowering consumption of alcohol by banning price advertising could be accomplished by establishing minimum prices and/or by increasing sales taxes on alcoholic beverages.' ". . .

NOTES AND QUESTIONS

1. All of the Justices agree that there is no First Amendment protection for commercial speech that does not accurate inform the public about lawful activities. Why is such speech not entitled to First Amendment protection? On what basis does Justice Powell distinguish such speech in *Central Hudson*.

2. In *Central Hudson*, the Court adopted a four-part test that imposed an intermediate level of scrutiny that was less strict that the strict scrutiny it applies in cases involving noncommercial speech. In *44 Liquormart*, Justice Stevens, joined by Justices Kennedy and Ginsburg, said a strict scrutiny test should apply when a state prohibits the dissemination of truthful, nonmisleading commercial messages. Justice Thomas would make such restrictions "per se" illegitimate. Justice O'Conner, joined by Chief Justice Rehnquist and Justices Souter and Breyer, applied the *Central Hudson* intermediate level of scrutiny. What is the impact of the various tests on the state's authority to restrict truthful, nonmisleading commercial speech? Under Justice Thomas' approach the government could never engage in such a restriction. Under Justice Steven's approach, such restrictions will almost always be unconstitutional since the government must have a compelling reason for such restrictions. Under *Central Hudson*, by comparison, the government must assert only a "substantial" interest, although it must also adopt the least restrictive means necessary to accomplish its purpose.

3. To what extent should the Supreme Court defer to a state or Congress concerning the need to restrict commercial speech that is truthful and nonmisleading? Is Justice Thomas' correct that the government would never have a legitimate rationale for keeping people in the dark? What grounds did Justice Thomas suggest for his position in *44 Liquormart*? If not, should the

Court apply strict scrutiny or is the intermediate level of scrutiny adopted in *Central Hudson* appropriate because commercial speech is somehow different than other types of speech? How well did the Court justify choosing an intermediate level of scrutiny in *Central Hudson*? On what grounds does Justice Stevens adopt strict scrutiny in *44 Liquormart*?

4. In *Thompson v. Western States Medical Center*, 122 S.Ct. 1497 (2002), the Supreme Court invalidated a federal statute that prohibited pharmacists from advertising the fact that they compounded certain types of drugs in their pharmacies. Compounding is a process by which a pharmacist combines or mixes ingredients to make a medication tailored for an individual's special needs. Since neither party in the law suit challenged the application of the *Central Hudson* framework, all of the Justices applied it, but they split 5-4 over the constitutionality of the restriction. Justice O'Connor, writing for herself and three other members of the court, carefully reviewed the government's justifications for the ban and found that they were not sufficiently persuasive. Justice Thomas concurred but wrote separately to stress his belief that the Court should overrule *Central Hudson*. Justice Breyer reviewed the government's evidence for the advertising ban and found it to be sufficiently persuasive to uphold the restriction.

5. FDA generally prohibits a pharmaceutical manufacturer from advertising a prescription drug to physicians (or consumers) for therapeutic uses other than those approved by FDA. For example, can a representative of a pharmaceutical manufacturer give a physician a copy of an article from a medical journal that suggests a drug is efficacious for a therapy that is not approved by FDA?[81] What interest does the government have in restricting such information? If the government's purpose was to discourage to discourage the use of drugs approved for some types of therapy from being prescribed for other therapies not approved by the agency, would that be sufficient to meet the *Central Hudson* tests? Recall from earlier in the chapter that Congress established FDA regulation because it believed that physicians were not in a good position to assess the efficacy of a drug without prior approval by FDA. Are FDA restrictions on the advertising of drugs for purposes not approved by FDA unconstitutional? Professor Gilhooley suggests that unless FDA can regulate the advertising of therapies not approved by the agency a manufacturer has no incentive to test new therapies and gain FDA approval.[82] Is this sufficient to sustain such restrictions under the *Central Hudson* tests?

6. Some countries ban cigarette advertising in magazines and cigarette advertising on television is banned in the United States and other countries. Are such restrictions constitutional in this country? If the state of Rhode

---

[81] *See Washington Legal Foundation v. Friedman*, 13 F. Supp. 2d 51 (D.D.C. 1998), *amended sub. nom. Washington Legal Found. v. Henley*, 56 F. Supp. 2d 81 (D.D.C. 1999), *vacated in part and appeal dismissed*, 202 F.3d 331 (D.C.Cir. Feb 11, 2000) (holding FDA could not preclude manufacturers from distributing reprints of "bona fide" peer-review journal articles although it could require conspicuous disclosure that the therapy discussed in the article was not approved by FDA); *see also Pearson v. Shalala*, 164 F.3d 650 (D.C. Cir. 1999) (holding FDA must consider the use of disclaimers about the lack of supporting studies and FDA approval concerning health claims made by dietary supplement manufacturers, rather than preclude claims that had not been approved by FDA).

[82] *See* Gilhooley, *Constitutionalizing Food and Drug Law*, 74 TULANE L. REV. 815, 337 (2000).

Island cannot ban the advertising of low liquor prices on the ground that such advertising encourages excess consumption of alcohol, can the federal government ban such advertisements on television or in magazines on the ground that the ads encourage smoking? Can you distinguish smoking from the sale of liquor on the ground that cigarette advertisements are misleading rather than truthful advertising? Is it misleading to advertise cigarettes by attempting to associate them with good times, thin people, and rebellion against authority, as the cigarettes companies are apparently trying to do? Can you justify a ban on cigarette advertising on the ground that it will encourage children to smoke? Is such a ban the narrowest means available to stop teenage smoking?[83]

---

[83] *See Anneuser-Bush, Inc. v. Schmoke*, 101 F.3d 325 (4th Cir. 1996) (upholding a city ordinance prohibiting the advertisement of alcoholic beverages in areas where children are expected to walk to school or play in their neighborhood as reasonable time, place and manner restrictions).

Chapter 11

GOVERNMENT ALLOCATION: RADIO AND TELEVISION LICENSING AND ADOPTION

In a competitive market system, the forces of supply and demand allocate goods and services to those who will pay the most money for them. In some instances, however, a public choice has been made to replace market allocation with allocation by the government. This chapter considers when the government should replace market allocation, who should be eligible to obtain the product or service the government is allocating, and what nonmarket method of allocation should be used.

According to economic theory, we assume that resources are put to their best use if they go to the person who is willing to pay the most for them. If you are willing to pay more than anyone else for a baseball card, economic theory assumes that you must get more satisfaction or utility out of owning the card than anyone else. For this reason, reliance on market allocation raises several issues. Is it important to make sure that goods and services go to those who would gain the most satisfaction out of them? Does this guarantee that society has made the *best* use of scarce resources? Or, is the best use to ensure that people who cannot afford to pay as much are also able to obtain the good or service?

When the government replaces market transactions with some form of government allocation, the purpose is to serve some noneconomic goal. In Chapter 2, we discussed four such goals: prohibit objectionable exchanges, eliminate price as the basis of exchange, remedy the distribution of wealth, and subject exchanges to collective values. In this chapter, you can determine which, if any, of these goals justify the current regulatory systems for radio and television licensing and for adoption.

If government allocation is justified, regulators must resolve two issues. First, what method of allocation is to be used to determine which persons will receive a good or service? If the government is to allocate a service or commodity, it has several means of doing so. It can allocate under a public interest standard, under a queue (first-come, first-serve), by a lottery, or by auctioning off the good or service. Unlike the other options, the last choice shares with private market allocation the feature of allocating the good or service to persons who can pay the most for it. The difference is that the government can establish conditions for the purchase of the good or service which must be met before a person is allowed to purchase, retain, or transfer it.

Second, as just discussed, the government can establish terms or conditions concerning who is eligible to receive a good or service that it allocates. The government can create such conditions for an auction, but it can also create them for the other methods of allocation. For example, as you will read in more detail, states investigate the suitability of parents to engage in adoption, and only those parents who are judged to be acceptable are eligible to adopt a child. But once the parents qualify, then adoption is usually based on a queue and the prospective parents who have been waiting the longest are eligible for the next adoption.

A. RADIO AND TELEVISION LICENSING

As you read in Chapter 6, the first law regulating radio communications dates back to 1912,[1] but the modern era in communications regulation began with the Radio Act of 1927,[2] which addressed the problem that the signals of many radio stations vying for too few broadcasting bands canceled each other out and listeners heard nothing. "With everybody on the air, nobody could be heard."[3] The Act created the Federal Radio Commission and gave it the authority to classify radio stations, assign frequencies to each class of broadcasters, such as radio, ship-to-shore communication, or police radio, and to each individual station within a class, and determine their power, hours of operation, and geographical service area. The Communications Act of 1934 reconstituted the FRC as the Federal Communications Commission (FCC) and gave the new agency control of radio stations, as well as all other forms of radio communication, including telephone, telegraph, and cable.[4] The structure of the FCC has remained essentially unchanged since 1934. It is comprised of five commissioners (formerly seven), no more than three of whom can be from the same political party. Commissioners are appointed by the President, with the approval of the Senate, for terms of five years.[5]

Congress acted because, without government allocation of the radio frequency, no one could be heard. This reality justifies government regulation, but it does not answer two additional issues associated with government allocation. What method of allocation should the FCC use and what qualifications should it establish concerning eligibility to obtain and retain broadcast licenses?

1. METHOD OF ALLOCATION

Although the FRC (and later the FCC) were created to address the problem of electronic interference among stations, Congress gave the agency broad authority to determine "whether the public interest, convenience, and necessity will be served" by the award of a broadcast license to a particular applicant.[6] The FCC has used this authority to attempt to pick the "best"

---

[1] 37 Stat. 302 (1912).

[2] 44 Stat. 1162 (1927).

[3] *National Broadcasting Co. v. United States*, 319 U.S. 190, 212 (1943).

[4] 48 Stat. 1064 (1934) (codified at 47 U.S.C. §§ 301–32).

[5] 47 U.S.C. § 154.

[6] *Id.* § 309(a).

applicant for a radio or television license. For this purpose, the FCC holds a hearing (known as a "comparative hearing") which compares the attributes of the applicants for a license. But, as the following excerpt explains, there are five different assignment mechanisms that the agency can use, and each has particular advantages and disadvantages.

WILLIAM KUMMEL, SPECTRUM BIDS, BETS, AND BUDGETS: SEEKING AN OPTIMAL ALLOCATION AND ASSIGNMENT PROCESS FOR DOMESTIC COMMERCIAL ELECTROMAGNETIC SPECTRUM PRODUCTS, SERVICES AND TECHNOLOGY, 48 FEDERAL COMMUNICATIONS LAW JOURNAL 511, 524–528 (1996) *

At one time or another, the FCC has used five different assignment methods: first-come/first-served, comparative hearings, user fees, random selection, and competitive bidding. Each method offers unique benefits and distinct constraints upon public interest, convenience, and necessity. . . .

1. First-Come/First-Served

First-come/first-served is the default assignment method. If the FCC does not receive "mutually exclusive applications" then it awards a license to the first qualified applicant. Processing costs are low. Legal challenges are limited to contesting whether the applicant is qualified. Limited legal challenges and limited administrative work make processing very quick. However, service competition, speed, universality, and diversity are likely to be low. Successful licensees are effective applicants, quick to locate and apply for available frequencies, rather than well-capitalized, capable service providers. Low levels of invested capital promote service delay by creating relatively more attractive speculative rather than service opportunities. Subsequently, fewer services will be developed; spectrum use is likely to be less efficient and intensively used; and public financial benefit will be minimal with no revenue but very low administrative costs. However, with low capital requirements, licensee diversity should improve. Control functions, including licensee criteria, antitrafficking restrictions, minimum capital requirements, and service deadlines, should mitigate or at least minimize some of these undesired conditions. In sum, first-come/first-served neither provides an efficient or effective use of spectrum nor insures public interest, convenience, and necessity.

2. Comparative Hearings

Comparative hearings provide a marginal advantage over first-come/first-served. Authorized under Section 309(b) of the Communications Act, administrative hearings are conducted before administrative law judges. Administrative cost and time increase significantly as qualifications must be checked and critically compared. While direct revenue increases slightly with administrative application fees, net revenue does not improve and may decline due to administrative costs. Licensing time increases with additional administrative steps and legal challenges. Comparative hearings that examine qualifications, prior operations, and ownership character likely result in awarding licenses to parties with service ability and experience as well as diversity in ownership and management. Licensees' up-front invested capital requirements increase due to additional costs of preparing, presenting, and defending qualifications for comparative hearings as well as incurring opportunity costs for lost competitions. This provides additional, but limited, incentive to develop the frequency. Additional economic activity increases the taxable income base, producing a gain in indirect revenue to the public from additional tax revenue. In sum, comparative hearings are an inefficient distribution method as they do not achieve optimal use or public interest.

3. User Fees

User fees offer significant advantages over comparative hearings. . . .

User fees are difficult to price. Without a developed private market to establish the free market price of electromagnetic spectrum, the FCC would have to calculate "shadow prices"—the prices users would be willing to pay for a service not privately sold—for all frequencies to be assigned. The federal government is very good at pricing core commodity products with consistent physical properties and large, established markets. Electromagnetic spectrum, however, is an inconsistent and speculative product with different frequency bands having significantly different physical properties and value varying by use. Therefore, even if a private market exists, spectrum does not lend itself to consistent, predictable pricing. . . . The inefficiencies of establishing a market price would produce higher costs and risks. Users would seek higher rates of return on capital.

Compared to comparative hearings, public revenues would increase. Significantly greater capital requirements and stable fees would reduce speculation by licensees thereby inducing faster building of systems. Universality of service, particularly in rural areas with lower density and lower incomes, would improve as licenses in these areas would cost comparatively less than those in major metropolitan areas with higher density and higher income, thereby reducing development costs. Spectrum use and efficiency would be higher due to increased investment in technology which would serve to offset the additional licensing costs. In sum, user fees prove more desirable than first-come/first-served and comparative hearings.

4. Random Selection

In 1981, Congress authorized the FCC to use random selection to assign electromagnetic spectrum. Spectrum lotteries, as conducted by the FCC, proved a significant step backward in developing spectrum use, efficiency, and equity. The FCC failed to implement substantive screening requirements. Unchecked speculation produced "license mills" charging small investors 10 to 100 times filing costs. Returns on investment were "virtually nonexistent" given the odds, often facially defective applications, and the limited practical use of the winnings. In 1991, the North American Securities Administrators

Association issued a bulletin citing wireless lotteries as the largest investor fraud in the nation.

Random selection, even with additional controls such as must-build, holding, and antitrafficking requirements, and increased application fees, remains unattractive. The assignment method reduces public income, defers development, limits diversity and universality, and promotes inefficient use. Random selection produces no direct public revenue while incurring high aggregate government and applicant administrative expenses. It defers development as unqualified, undercapitalized, and inexperienced parties, spurred by low investment requirements, win frequencies that require repackaging to become useful assets. Without a market, diversity declines. Universality suffers as qualified licensees avoid unattractive rural properties. Spectrum use and efficiency decline because many licenses will be in the hands of speculators rather than operators, or additional licenses are needed to construct a useful band of frequencies. In sum, random selection is less attractive than first-come/first-served, comparative hearings, or user fees.

5. Competitive Bidding

Under Section 309(j) of the Communications Act, the FCC initiated in 1994 competitive bidding for . . . [personal communications services (PCS), direct broadcast satellite (DBS), multipoint distributional service (MDS), and specialized mobile radio (SMR)]. Competitive bidding proves the market mechanism of choice. First, public revenue, in the short-and long-term, is maximized as the fair market value of the electromagnetic spectrum less auction administrative expenses goes to the U.S. Treasury, and taxes rise due to increased economic activity. Second, speed of development increases because high licensing costs induce successful bidders to launch services as soon as possible to recover large initial investment. Third, universality of service increases as low prices of rural licenses reduce development costs and attract investors unable or unwilling to make capital requirements necessary to develop major metro licenses. Fourth, high levels of spectrum efficiency and use are achieved as high spectrum costs foster large investments in technology to expand capacity. . . .

————

Of the five methods of assigning radio frequencies, the FCC for years used "comparative hearings" to select the "best" applicant for a radio or television license when more than one application has been filed for the same frequency. In 1996, however, Congress eliminated comparative hearings for license renewals of existing broadcast stations, providing instead that the FCC was to renew a license, without considering competing applications, as long as the incumbent broadcaster had "served the public interest," committed no "serious violations" of the FCC rules, and did not commit any other violations "which, if taken together, would constitute a pattern of abuse."[7] This change in effect

---

[7] 47 U.S.C. § 309(k).

grants existing broadcasters virtually perpetual licenses because few broadcasters flout the FCC rules and the FCC is highly unlikely to find that an incumbent broadcaster was not operating in the public interest. Nevertheless, it may not constitute a significant policy change because the FCC almost always renewed the licenses of broadcasters under the prior law.[8]

When Congress authorized the FCC in 1981 to employ a "system of random selection" to choose among qualified applicants for a new broadcast license, the Commission debated whether to replace comparative hearings with a lottery as the allocation method for new television licenses. When the FCC asked for public comments on replacing comparative proceedings with a lottery, among the reasons it offered for choosing a lottery were the following.

NOTICE OF PROPOSED RULEMAKING, AMENDMENT OF THE COMMISSION'S RULES TO ALLOW THE SELECTION FROM AMONG COMPETING APPLICANTS FOR NEW AM, FM, AND TELEVISION STATIONS BY RANDOM SELECTION (LOTTERY), 54 FEDERAL REGISTER 11,416 (1989)

1. The Commission initiates this proceeding to consider revising the system used to award licenses for new broadcast facilities. Specifically, it is proposing the use of a random selection or lottery procedure for new AM, FM, and television broadcast stations instead of the present comparative hearing process.

2. After more than 20 years of experience in using the existing comparative hearing procedures to select among mutually exclusive applicants for new broadcast stations, several difficulties, discussed in more detail below, have become apparent. First, this selection process frequently operates to delay service to the public significantly without providing substantial offsetting benefits in terms of selecting a "better" applicant. In addition, the process unduly drains the Commission's limited administrative resources as well as the resources of potential licensees. Moreover, the public may never benefit from our ultimate selection because the permittee decides, or is forced by unforeseen circumstances, to modify its proposed operation, the nature of its ownership, or proposed involvement in management, or is compelled to assign the permit, without profit, to a third party. Finally, even when there is no change in the proposed operation of the station or subsequent assignment of the permit, it is highly questionable whether this elaborate and costly process actually results in a material benefit to the public. This is especially true in those cases where the comparative distinction between a winning and losing applicant, both of whom are basically qualified, is marginal.

3. In view of these difficulties with the current system, we are inviting comment on whether use of the random selection procedures ("lotteries") prescribed by section 309(I) of the Communications Act would, on balance, better serve the public interest without any diminution (or, at most, without any significant diminution) in the quality of service provided to the public. We have already exercised our statutory authority to use random selection procedures in many of those radio services hampered by application backlogs,

---

[8] *See* Krattenmaker, *The Telecommunications Act of 1996*, 29 CONN. L. REV. 123, 156–157 (1996).

and from a legal standpoint, it is our tentative conclusion based on the statutory language of section 309(I) itself, that we have the authority to use these procedures to award licenses in other broadcast services.

4. In order to appreciate fully our reasons for considering revision of the existing process in choosing between competing applicants, it is necessary to understand the complexity and expense involved in that adjudicatory process. As detailed in paras. 5–13 of the Notice, that process involves the time, money, and energy spent on filing motions to enlarge issues, oppositions, and replies; on discovery procedures; on hearing preparation and the hearing itself; on preparation and filing of proposed findings of fact and conclusions of law; on the Administrative Law Judge's (ALJ) Initial Decision selecting a comparative winner; on filing exceptions and reply exceptions to the Initial Decision and awaiting decision by the Review Board; on filing Applications for Review and other responsive pleadings to the full Commission; on the Commission's decision; and, in some instances, appealing the Commission's decision to the U.S. Court of Appeals and, less often, on filing for review of the Court of Appeals' decision with the U.S. Supreme Court.

5. The adjudicatory procedures can be so intricate and time-consuming that cases which employ all of the possible steps available as part of the comparative hearings process can take three to five years or more to complete after the case has first been designated for hearing. Even cases which are concluded by settlement agreement prior to the issuance of an Initial Decision can be time-consuming and costly. . . .

6. While the Commission recognizes that the comparative hearing procedures are designed to ensure that all parties are afforded maximum due process consistent with the requirements of the Administrative Procedure Act, the overriding questions are whether this process is superior or inferior to a lottery selection method, after analyzing the respective costs and benefits of both procedures, and, therefore, which process operates better to serve the public interest.

7. Moreover, it is essential to ascertain whether the existing process results in discernibly better service to the public than an alternative procedure. The object of the existing elaborate process is to use the comparative qualification criteria to select the applicant that will best serve the public interest. These criteria and qualitative enhancements include, inter alia, (1) the extent to which an applicant would diversify ownership of the mass media; (2) whether owners would be integrated into management positions at the proposed station; (3) whether the integrated personnel are present or proposed local residents of the community of license or service area of the proposed station; (4) whether such integrated owners are minorities or females; (5) whether they have past broadcast experience or past participation in civic activities; (6) the broadcast record of the applicant; (7) proposed program service; (8) the daytimer preference; and (9) comparative coverage proposals. On the basis of the evidence adduced, the ALJ awards preferences, based on these criteria that range from "very slight" to "slight" to "moderate" to "substantial" to "overwhelming" and then determines, on an overall basis, the best applicant.

8. [W]e have tentatively concluded . . . that, generally, the criteria do not lend themselves to consistent and easily predictable results, and that the

process often functions to produce only marginal benefits to the public. . . . Therefore, the process is viewed as inconsistent, unpredictable, and as producing results which appear arbitrary in nature.

9. Another reason for concern with the effectiveness of the comparative hearing process lies with the extent to which changed circumstances may undermine the basis for a final comparative selection. . . . Equally significant, even though a comparative hearing had resulted in the selection of what appeared to be the best qualified applicant, legitimate changed circumstances may occur which could prevent that entity from ever providing service to the public, and instead, could result in transfer of the permit to a third party that had no connection with the prior hearing.

10. [W]e believe that a lottery procedure would be substantially superior to comparative hearings. First, the statutory lottery would significantly simplify the process of selecting among mutually exclusive applications. Procedurally, there would be no need for lengthy and complex comparative hearings. Rather, applications would be screened for completeness prior to the lottery, and, only after a tentative selectee had been chosen, would parties be able to file petitions to deny against the winner. Such petitions would be limited to the basic qualifications of the tentative selectee. . . .

11. A second advantage of the random selection process is that it would be more objective and, therefore, easier to administer than comparative hearings. This is because a lottery system would substantially reduce, if not eliminate, the need to resolve cases on exceedingly narrow or insignificant factors and would rely, instead, on the preferences mandated by the statute.

12. Third, a lottery approach would speed up the licensing process. For example, based upon our review of 39 cases designated for hearing in 1982, we found that there was a 32.5 month average period of time from the filing of the successful application to grant of a construction permit. By way of contrast, by examining 58 lottery winners that filed applications in the June, 1987, low power television window, the average time from filing to grant for 44 of these construction permits granted so far was 14 months. . . .

13. Fourth, a lottery system would be less expensive to applicants and to the Commission. This is because applicants would avoid many of the often substantial fees for legal services, transportation costs, and assorted administrative expenses. Likewise, the Commission can use fewer personnel and other administrative resources to implement the lottery than comparative hearings.

14. Fifth, because we have no reason to believe that our comparative criteria (and, indeed any alternative comparative criteria) necessarily leads to "better" licensees and "better" service to the public, we do not believe that the quality of licensees and the service they provide to the public would deteriorate under a lottery process. Our experience in selecting licensees through lottery in other services (such as low power television) does not suggest any such degradation in licensees or public service. . . .

In 1990, the FCC dropped the idea of awarding broadcast licenses on the basis of a lottery. It explained its decision in the following order.

AMENDMENT OF THE COMMISSION'S RULES TO ALLOW THE SELECTION FROM AMONG COMPETING APPLICANTS FOR NEW AM, FM, AND TELEVISION STATIONS BY RANDOM SELECTION (LOTTERY), 5 FEDERAL COMMUNICATION COMMISSIONS RECORD 4002 (1990)

1. On January 30, 1989, the Commission adopted a Notice of Proposed Rule Making in this proceeding, inviting comment on the possible use of random selection or lottery procedures in lieu of comparative hearings to select among competing applicants for new AM, FM, and television stations. The Notice questioned whether lotteries would, on balance, better serve the public interest as a licensing mechanism than the current comparative hearing process. A critical issue was whether lotteries could achieve efficiencies in the licensing process without resulting in any diminution in the quality of service provided to the public.

2. The vast majority of the commentators in this proceeding oppose the use of lottery procedures for licensing new broadcast stations, arguing that this would disserve the public interest. They variously contend that awarding licenses by chance would (1) conflict with the statutory obligation to grant licenses in the public interest to the best applicant; (2) promote the filing of speculative and sham applications; (3) increase the number of applications and thereby burden the Commission's resources; (4) reverse the small growth rate in minority ownership; and (5) contravene recent appropriations legislation prohibiting modification or elimination of comparative preferences for minority or female ownership. While the commentators recognize shortcomings in the comparative hearing process, they believe that it has been a rational means for selecting licensees and should be retained and reformed before a lottery approach is tried.

3. After reviewing this record, we agree with the commentators that it would at this time best serve the public interest to focus on reforming the traditional comparative hearing process. We are concerned that any potential gains in efficiency that may be achieved by use of a lottery would be outweighed by the possible reduction in quality of broadcasting licensees and service to the public. Therefore, we will terminate the lottery proceeding and seek instead to improve the efficiency and integrity of our current comparative hearing process for the grant of new broadcasting facilities. . . .

SEPARATE STATEMENT OF COMMISSIONER ERVIN S. DUGGAN

Re: Amendment of the Commission's Rules to Allow the Selection from Among Competing Applicants for New AM, FM, and TV Stations by Random Selection

I'm delighted that the Commission has decided to conduct a decent burial for its earlier Rule Making on the possible use of random selection or a lottery for new AM, FM and television stations—delighted, because lotteries are a terrible idea. The Commission has a statutory obligation to grant licenses to the best applicants, and I cannot imagine how this mandate can be obeyed by something so willy-nilly as lotteries. . . . I cannot support proposals whose unspoken assumption is that a broadcast license is simply an income-producing asset like any other—like a widget factory or a peanut farm. A broadcast license, to my mind, is a sacred trust and should be granted with exquisite care. So to the idea of lotteries, I say good riddance.

———

Although the FCC has not considered the use of an auction for allocating radio and television licenses, Glen Robinson, an administrative law professor and former FCC Commissioner, endorsed an auction in the following opinion, which he issued while he was at the Commission.

CENTRAL FLORIDA
60 F.C.C.2d 372, 443–47 (1976)

. . . In the circumstances here a simple lottery is a sensible method of choosing among qualified applicants (those meeting minimal, threshold standards), but an even better mechanism would be an auction among such applicants. An auction combines the simplicity of the lottery with two additional virtues: one, it would allow the public to recoup the economic value of the benefits conferred upon private licensees; two, unlike a lottery an auction measures the intensity of individual preferences, in accordance with the prevalent standard for allocating resources in our economic system.

Auctioning frequencies is not, of course, a new idea though it could not be said to have a wide following. I concede that for the Commission to implement an auction scheme would push its present legislative powers to the limits; nevertheless, administrative action to implement some such scheme cannot be dismissed out of hand. Legal considerations aside, however, proposals to auction licenses to the highest bidder have been criticized on grounds of social policy. It is said, for example, than an auction (1) would be an abandonment of "public interest considerations," (2) could lead to the view that the winning bidder has a property right in the license, and (3) "would favor the wealthy." None of these objections seems to me compelling.

The first objection is a little vague but it seems to harbor both a misunderstanding of how the auction system would work as well as a misunderstanding of how the present system does work. An auction system need not, and in my proposal would not, eliminate all inquiry into licensee qualifications. I do not propose (nor do I know of any auction proponent who proposes) to waive minimum standards of fitness or eligibility for anyone who comes in with enough cash. On the contrary, only those applicants who meet the basic legal and character qualifications for licensees would be eligible to bid. Thus, under any circumstances, successful bidders at auction would be at least as well qualified as licensees whose applications are uncontested. When all is said and done, that is all we can realistically expect from the comparative hearing process also. The idea that comparative hearings really select out the "best" candidate is naive. Seldom is there any single "best" candidate; more often than not, the candidates are, for all practicable purposes, fungible. In any case, history shows that the comparative process, despite adjustments made in it over the years, is not designed to discover "the best," and even where the best may be selected there is no mechanism (other than the general rule against trafficking) which prevents the winner from ultimately selling out to a less qualified candidate.

As to the second objection, that an auction would lend credence to the view that licenses are a property right, it is sufficient to respond that such a property right does in fact exist as a consequence of the historic practice of renewing licenses except for misbehavior. To pretend otherwise is to blink reality. What needs to be considered is, what follows once we recognize this reality? I believe what follows is a reconsideration of the basis on which such property rights are acquired, and it is this that leads me to the proposed auction.

Finally, the objection that an auction would favor rich over poor hardly seems a decisive objection since the same can be said of any pricing system. Why is it, for example, any more pertinent to broadcast licenses than land or mineral leases or the use of dialysis machines? In any case, it is indulging fantasy to pretend that an open pricing system would lead to greater control of licenses by the rich than does the present system, given the current expense of obtaining a license, particularly in the context of a comparative hearing. Anyone who believes that the comparative hearing process is available to everyone regardless of wealth must also be willing to believe in Santa Claus. Indeed, it is not a great exaggeration to describe the comparative hearing process as, in effect, a bidding system, except that money goes not to the owner of the resource, the public, but to lawyers representing the contestants. As a practical matter the poor are excluded from the present system far more effectively than they would be from an auction system, because of the difficulties of raising the capital necessary to engage in such an uncertain venture as applying, and competing, for a license. Given the profitability of broadcast stations, lending institutions are ordinarily well disposed to advance the requisite capital to buy a station, or even to build it once a clear license grant has been made. One need not be wealthy to obtain such financial support, because the security for it lies in the relatively low-risk, and high-profit character of the enterprise. The real problem lies in raising the capital necessary *to compete* for a contested license, a high-risk, low profit enterprise. It is in this latter respect that the present system most effectively screens out the poor. This is quite senseless as well as discriminatory: the risk capital is required not because of the risks inherent in the enterprise itself but because of risks in an artificial licensing process which shows no demonstrable relationship to superior performance or public service in the operation of the station.

NOTES AND QUESTIONS

1. Commentators have long criticized the FCC for failing to produce coherent standards for determining who is entitled to a radio or television license. In 1962, Henry Friendly, a prominent jurist, wrote that the FCC uses "an arbitrary set of criteria whose application . . . is shaped to suit the cases of the moment."[9] Another observer described the FCC proceedings as "unpredictable, excessively discretionary, complex and baffling, deficiently consonant with the rule of law, and producing results that seem inconsistent from case to case."[10] Why should the lack of such standards be regarded as a problem? How does the lack of standards contribute to difficulty in planning in the broadcast industry and the potential for unfairness?

Why has the FCC been unable to define standards for the allocation of radio and television licenses? When he was an academic, Justice Breyer suggests that the problem is the agency's mandate. The responsibility to regulate in the "public interest, convenience, and necessity" is such a broad mandate that there is no agreement concerning what the agency should be doing.[11] Do you agree?

2. What reasons, besides the difficulty of defining standards for awarding licenses, did the FCC identify as in favor of a lottery? Do you find these convincing? Why did the FCC decide to reject the lottery proposal? Do you accept their reasons? Why or why not?

3. What is the impact of Congress' decision not to subject existing broadcasters to comparative renewal hearings? Can the FCC really pick the "best" candidate from among competitive applicants for an existing license? Would the FCC be in any better position to make this determination in a renewal proceeding than an initial licensing proceeding?

4. Should Congress amend the Federal Communications Act to allocate broadcast licenses by auction? What are the advantages of using an auction? What are the disadvantages? As Robinson points out, one advantage is that an auction "allow[s] the public to recoup the economic value of the benefits conferred upon private licensees. . . ." In other words, an auction permits the public to capture the "rents" now earned by successful broadcast applicants. Why do those who currently have broadcast licenses earn "rents?" What are the other advantages and disadvantages of an auction?

Both Robinson and Kummel endorse an auction as the best method for the FCC to make allocations, yet Congress has resisted this advice concerning broadcasting. Many observers attribute Congress' reluctance to the political power of the broadcast industry. Are there reasons why broadcasters might have more influence with Congress than other interest groups?

5. In the Telecommunications Act of 1996, Congress required the FCC to allocate digital television licenses to existing television broadcasters, and it

[9] H. FRIENDLY, THE FEDERAL ADMINISTRATIVE AGENCIES: THE NEED FOR BETTER DEFINITION OF STANDARDS 54 (1962).

[10] Anthony, *Towards Simplicity and Rationality in Comparative Broadcast Licensing Proceedings,* 24 STAN. L. REV. 1, 39 (1971).

[11] S. BREYER, REGULATION AND ITS REFORM 70 (1982).

prohibited the FCC from allocating such licenses by the use of auctions.[12] Digital television, or high definition television (HDTV), provides viewers with much higher resolution (*i.e.*, lifelike picture) and CD-quality sound. At the end of a transition period, however, Congress required that a television broadcaster surrender either its digital television license or its analog license to the FCC to be reallocated to another owner. Thus, Congress not only refused to rely on an auction system to allocate the new digital licenses, but it gave them away free to existing broadcasters.

Congress' decision was highly controversial. Broadcasters defend the decision on the ground that the new broadcast rights were not new licenses, but rather upgrades of old licenses. They and the FCC envisioned that stations would use their new broadcast rights to convert over time from analog to digital broadcasting and, while the new spectrum was being developed, stations could still broadcast over their old analog licenses. Broadcasters also argued that auctions would put them in deep financial straits and that many broadcasters could not afford the transition costs and would be eliminated from the market. Critics characterized Congress' decision as the largest corporate giveaway in history since the value of the spectrum given away to broadcasters was estimated at the time to have a value of $37 to $70 billion dollars. How do you assess the arguments for and against auctions, particularly the broadcasters' argument that this would be too costly and some of them would go out of business?[13]

6. Assuming that an auction is adopted, what property rights does a winning bidder obtain? Spectrum winners, like other FCC licensees, are subject to the 1934 Communications Act, which authorizes the FCC to revoke a license if it serves the public interest. Thus, as the following comment indicates, there may be problems down the road:

> Auction winners seem all too happy to get whatever rights are on offer, however ill-defined. Perhaps they are counting on the agency's past restraint in interfering with spectrum licenses—the FCC has seldom refused to renew a broadcast license even through broadcasters enjoy nothing more than a vague "renewal expectancy." . . .
>
> The undiminished resolve of bidders, however, does not diminish the problem. The fuzziness of the rights given auction winners may not matter until they need to exercise them to the fullest extent or the FCC tries to abridge them. When it comes to a head, however, this uncertainty will compromise the desired efficiency benefits from auctions, and the goals of revenues for federal coffers.[14]

The commentator recommends that Congress establish "full-fledged" property rights to the spectrum for auctions winners, but he acknowledges that this

---

[12] 47 U.S.C. § 336.

[13] See Koerner, Onward Christian Moguls: The Lord and the FCC Provide For A Televangelical Bonanza, AMERICAN PROSPECT, Jan. 1–14, 2002, at 32; Goodman, Digital Television and the Allure of Auctions: The Birth and Stillbirth of DTV Legislation, 49 FED. COMM. L.J. 517 (1997); Symposium, Telecommunications Law: Unscrambling the Signals, Unbundling the Law, 97 COLUM. L. REV. 819 (1997).

[14] Michalopoulos, *Money for Nothing? Spectrum Auction Winners Paid A Lot, But What They Got Is Far From Clear*, LEGAL TIMES, Sept. 23, 1996, at 20.

"may unduly inhibit the FCC's flexibility" in regulating a scarce resource. He proposes that, as a substitute, Congress should require

> a contract between the FCC and the auction winner that would fully and clearly delineate its rights and obligations. The government follows this practice in auctioning mineral leasing rights to federal lands. The lease agreements seem to have worked well in protecting [leasing rights]. Recently, for example, the Court of Claims found that the government had breached its contract obligations by imposing a moratorium on oil exploration in areas covered by such agreements.[15]

How does the lack of clear property rights impede an auction system? What impact will such confusion have on the amount of money that the government can raise and on the efficiency of the system?[16]

7. How far should the government go in relying on an auction approach? Should winning bidders be permitted to resell their license to firms who would use the spectrum for a different use. This step would have important ramifications concerning how the radio spectrum is used and how much competition exists in various communications markets. Consider:

> [F]ive years ago the FCC staff estimated that a transfer of spectrum used by a single television station in Los Angeles to cellular phone service would raise the spectrum's value by $1 billion. [Although some FCC officials want] to give winning bidders the right to use it as they please[,] . . . the new "personal communications service" companies— some of whom paid a fortune for licenses—are lobbying hard to block added competition. . . .
>
> At the heart of the matter . . . lies a fundamental tension between consumer and producer interests. Writ large, the job of the FCC is to reduce economic scarcity, allocating communication spectrum in ways that generate the most value for consumers. On the other hand, . . . "anyone who already has spectrum doesn't want to make it less scarce because scarcity drives up the market price."[17]

For example, if a Los Angeles television station made such a transfer, there would be one less location on the spectrum for television stations, which would affect the auction price for L.A. television licenses. The diminished supply of licenses would lead to a higher auction price for the remaining licenses. Thus, any license holder with a license dislikes scarcity because it drives up the market price for the license that the license holder must repurchase.

Thus, the FCC controls not only who should possess individual licenses, but it also determines how to divide up the radio spectrum among competing uses, such as television broadcasting versus cellular phone service. Should the government divide up the spectrum into various uses, or should it permit the market to make such choices?

---

[15] *Id.*

[16] *See* Ayres & Balkin, *Legal Entitlements as Auctions: Property Rules, Liability Rules, and Beyond*, 106 YALE L.J. 703 (1996).

[17] Passell, *Big Brother Wants To Manage the Broadcast Spectrum Again*, NEW YORK TIMES, Feb. 6, 1997, at C2 (national edition).

2. ELIGIBILITY CRITERIA

Congress authorized the FCC to prescribe the "nature of the service to be rendered by each class of licensed applicant" as the "public interest, convenience, and necessity requires."[18] The "willful" failure to comply with any such requirements can be grounds for revocation of a license, and the FCC considers a station's compliance in determining whether renewal of a license is in the public interest.

Applicants for a radio or television broadcast license must satisfy a number of technical requirements concerning, for example, location of the broadcast facility within the community to be served, the extent to which the broadcast signal can be heard throughout that community, and the quality of the applicant's equipment. Applicants must also meet certain nontechnical requirements. For example, corporate owners must be of good character, the majority of corporate owners must be United States citizens, applicants must have sufficient resources to build and run the station, and applicants must have demonstrated a propensity to deal honestly with the Commission and to comply with the FCC Act.[19] Concerning the last requirement, the FCC determines whether applicants have any felony convictions, or adjudicated antitrust violations concerning anticompetitive behavior involving mass communications.[20]

Beyond these technical and nontechnical requirements, what conditions of eligibility criteria should the FCC enforce? What does the "public interest" demand?[21] The FCC currently relies on market forces to shape the type of programming that broadcasters present to adults.[22] This is a policy shift. At one time, the FCC had several types of regulations that were intended to influence what programming was presented. In the materials which follow, you can determine the grounds for the FCC deregulation and whether you agree with the Commission's hands-off policy. By comparison, Congress and the FCC have increased the regulation of children's programming. Congress has required the FCC to protect children from indecent and violent programming and to promote more hours devoted to educational television for children. What is the justification for this increased regulatory activity? If the market can be trusted to influence what adults see on television, why are regulatory controls necessary concerning what children view? Moreover, assuming children require protection, what regulatory methods are best employed to achieve these goals? The following materials also address these issues.

a. ADULT PROGRAMMING

The FCC in recent years has backed away from its oversight of programming content for adults. Professor Hamilton explains:

---

[18] 47 U.S.C. § 303(b).

[19] *Character Qualifications In Broadcasting*, 102 F.C.C.2d 1179, *reconsideration denied*, 1 F.C.C.R. 421 (1986).

[20] *Character Qualifications In Broadcast Licensing*, 67 Rad. Reg. 2d (P & F) 107 (1990).

[21] *See Symposium: Television Self-Regulation and Ownership Regulation: The American Experience*, 13 CARDOZO ARTS & ENT. L.J. 645 (1995).

[22] T. KRATTENMAKER & L. POWE, REGULATING BROADCASTING PROGRAMMING (1994).

Throughout the 1980s the metaphor of the market guided the decisions of the Federal Communications Commission. Then-Chairman Mark Fowler declared that television was simply a "toaster with pictures" and adopted the position that the same market mechanisms which work in the market for private goods (such as toasters) would also work in the broader information marketplace of television broadcasting. To those who bemoaned the lack of public affairs or educational programming, he pointed out that viewer preferences determined programming outcomes and that any lack of programming stemmed from a lack of demand. As he put it: "The public's interest, then, defines the public interest."[23]

In one of its first "deregulatory" actions, the FCC ruled that a radio station could change its entertainment format without the agency's approval. In the following opinion, the Supreme Court affirmed the agency's decision. As you read the decision, consider what are the policy arguments for and against requirements concerning the entertainment format.

FCC v. WNCN LISTENERS GUILD
450 U.S. 582 (1981)

JUSTICE WHITE delivered the opinion of the Court.

Sections 309(a) and 310(d) of the Communications Act of 1934 (Act) empower the Federal Communications Commission to grant an application for license transfer or renewal only if it determines that "the public interest, convenience, and necessity" will be served thereby. The issue before us is whether there are circumstances in which the Commission must review past or anticipated changes in a station's entertainment programming when it rules on an application for renewal or transfer of a radio broadcast license. The Commission's present position is that it may rely on market forces to promote diversity in entertainment programming and thus serve the public interest. . . .

I

. . . Following public notice and comment, the Commission issued a Policy Statement pursuant to its rulemaking authority under the Act. The Commission concluded in the Policy Statement that review of format changes was not compelled by the language or history of the Act, would not advance the welfare of the radio-listening public, would pose substantial administrative problems, and would deter innovation in radio programming. . . . The Commission also emphasized that a broadcaster is not a common carrier and therefore should not be subjected to a burden similar to the common carrier's obligation to continue to provide service if abandonment of that service would conflict with public convenience or necessity.

The Commission also concluded that practical considerations as well as statutory interpretation supported its reluctance to regulate changes in

---

[23] Hamilton, Private Interests in *"Public Interest" Programming: An Economic Assessment of Broadcast Incentives*, 45 DUKE L.J. 1177, 1177 (1996).

formats. Such regulation would require the Commission to categorize the formats of a station's prior and subsequent programming to determine whether a change in format had occurred; to determine whether the prior format was "unique"; and to weigh the public detriment resulting from the abandonment of a unique format against the public benefit resulting from that change. The Commission emphasized the difficulty of objectively evaluating the strength of listener preferences, of comparing the desire for diversity within a particular type of programming to the desire for a broader range of program formats and of assessing the financial feasibility of a unique format. . . .

II

. . . It is common ground that the Act does not define the term "public interest, convenience, and necessity." The Court has characterized the public-interest standard of the Act as "a supple instrument for the exercise of discretion by the expert body which Congress has charged to carry out its legislative policy." Although it was declared in *National Broadcasting Co. v. United States* that the goal of the Act is "to secure the maximum benefits of radio to all the people of the United States," it was also emphasized that Congress had granted the Commission broad discretion in determining how that goal could best be achieved. The Court accordingly declined to substitute its own views on the best method of encouraging effective use of the radio for the views of the Commission. . . . Furthermore, we recognized that the Commission's decisions must sometimes rest on judgment and prediction rather than pure factual determinations. In such cases complete factual support for the Commission's ultimate conclusions is not required, since " 'a forecast of the direction in which future public interest lies necessarily involves deductions based on the expert knowledge of the agency.'

The Commission has provided a rational explanation for its conclusion that reliance on the market is the best method of promoting diversity in entertainment formats. The Court of Appeals and the Commission agree that in the vast majority of cases market forces provide sufficient diversity. The Court of Appeals favors Government intervention when there is evidence that market forces have deprived the public of a "unique" format, while the Commission is content to rely on the market, pointing out that in many cases when a station changes its format, other stations will change their formats to attract listeners who preferred the discontinued format. The Court of Appeals places great value on preserving diversity among formats, while the Commission emphasizes the value of intraformat as well as interformat diversity. Finally, the Court of Appeals is convinced that review of format changes would result in a broader range of formats, while the Commission believes that Government intervention is likely to deter innovative programming.

In making these judgments, the Commission has not forsaken its obligation to pursue the public interest. On the contrary, it has assessed the benefits and the harm likely to flow from Government review of entertainment programming, and on balance has concluded that its statutory duties are best fulfilled by not attempting to oversee format changes. This decision was in major part based on predictions as to the probable conduct of licensees and the functioning of the broadcasting market and on the Commission's assessment of its capacity to make the determinations required by the format doctrine. The Commission concluded that " '[e]ven after all relevant facts ha[d] been fully explored in an evidentiary hearing, [the Commission] would have no assurance that a decision finally reached by [the Commission] would contribute more to listener satisfaction than the result favored by station management.' " It did not assert that reliance on the marketplace would achieve a perfect correlation between listener preferences and available entertainment programming. Rather, it recognized that a perfect correlation would never be achieved, and it concluded that the marketplace alone could best accommodate the varied and changing tastes of the listening public. These predictions are within the institutional competence of the Commi

. . . The Commission's position on review of format changes reflects a reasonable accommodation of the policy of promoting diversity in programming and the policy of avoiding unnecessary restrictions on licensee discretion. . . .

III

. . . A major underpinning of its Policy Statement is the Commission's conviction, rooted in its experience, that renewal and transfer cases should not turn on the Commission's presuming to grasp, measure, and weigh the elusive and difficult factors involved in determining the acceptability of changes in entertainment format. To assess whether the elimination of a particular "unique" entertainment format would serve the public interest, the Commission would have to consider the benefit as well as the detriment that would result from the change. Necessarily, the Commission would take into consideration not only the number of listeners who favor the old and the new programming but also the intensity of their preferences. It would also consider the effect of the format change on diversity within formats as well as on diversity among formats. The Commission is convinced that its judgments in these respects would be subjective in large measure and would only approximately serve the public interest. It is also convinced that the market, although imperfect, would serve the public interest as well or better by responding quickly to changing preferences and by inviting experimentation with new types of programming. Those who would overturn the Commission's Policy Statement do not take adequate account of these considerations. . . .

We decline to overturn the Commission's Policy Statement, which prefers reliance on market forces to its own attempt to oversee format changes at the behest of disaffected listeners. . . .

JUSTICE MARSHALL, with whom JUSTICE BRENNAN joins, dissenting.

. . . The Policy Statement completely forecloses any possibility that the Commission will re-examine the validity of its general policy on format changes as it applies to particular situations. Thus, even when it can be conclusively demonstrated that a particular radio market does not function in the manner predicted by the Commission, the Policy Statement indicates that the Commission will blindly assume that a proposed format change is in the "public interest." This result would occur even where reliance on the market to ensure format diversity is shown to be misplaced, and where it thus appears that action by the Commission is necessary to promote the public interest in diversity. This outcome is not consistent with the Commission's statutory responsibilities. . . .

This "safety valve" feature is particularly essential where, as here, the agency's decision that a general policy promotes the public interest is based on predictions and forecasts that by definition lack complete factual support. . . .

. . . [I]n examining renewal applications, the Commission has considered claims that a licensee does not provide adequate children's programming, or programming for women and children, or for a substantial Spanish-American community, or that the licensee has ignored issues of significance to the Negro community, or has not provided programming of specific interest to residents of a particular area. In each case, the Commission reviewed submissions ranging from general summaries to transcripts of programs, to determine whether the licensee's programming met the public-interest standard. . . .

NOTES AND QUESTIONS

1. Is there any justification for FCC regulations that establish the type of programming which broadcasters present? As one group of commentators point out, "Timber produced in the national forests is a public resource (*i.e.*, owned by the public); does this mean that the Forest Service should regulate the use to which it is put?"[24] Can the case of broadcasting be distinguished from the sale of timber on public lands? That is, does the public have some interest in how broadcasters perform that would not apply to other public resources, such as timber?

2. The FCC believes that the market is adequate to promote diversity in programming.[25] But how responsive are radio and television stations to viewers' interests? How much variety is there in the radio stations to which you listen? Is there some reason to believe that radio and television markets do not fit the perfectly competitive model? Moreover, is the outcome of a perfectly competitive market the one that society wants? Consider Professor Sunstein's analysis:

> . . . The first problem is that because of the crucial importance of advertising for programming decisions, the link between listener or viewer desires and broadcasting performance is less tight than in ordinary markets. The purchaser of the product is in significant part the advertiser rather than the listening public; the public is often the product to be sold rather than the purchaser. There is a connection between the public's tastes and advertising decisions, but that connection is not always close, especially when advertisers have their own distinctive agendas.
>
> The second problem is that even in places with a fair number of broadcasters, people with unusual tastes might be completely unaccommodated, even though it would be possible to provide services for

---

[24] G. ROBINSON, E. GELLHORN, & H. BRUFF, THE ADMINISTRATIVE PROCESS 291 (2nd ed. 1986).
[25] *See* Fowler & Brenner, *A Marketplace Approach to Deregulation,* 60 TEX. L. REV. 207 (1982).

them without high cost to others. Suppose that 85% of listeners in a certain community like popular music, but that 15% want classical music or news; suppose too that there are only five stations. It may well be that the market will provide five popular music stations, dividing the 85% majority. This is so even though a system of four such stations and one for the minority of 15% would be a significantly better way of satisfying public desires in view of the fact that the decrease from five to four would not really harm the 85% majority.[26]

Do Professor Sunstein's arguments establish that there are market flaws that require FCC regulation concerning adult programming?

3. Are there noneconomic reasons why the FCC should regulate programming? Professor Sunstein defends the right of society to establish broadcast policies that would not necessarily be promoted by market forces. He notes that the "voting public appears to want (a) to ensure more diversity in broadcasting than the market provides, (b) to promote high-quality or public affairs programming notwithstanding consumption decisions, and (c) to counteract the sometimes harmful preference-shaping effects of broadcasting decisions through regulatory controls."[27] Do you agree?

4. The majority opinion indicates the grounds on which the FCC eliminated its format inquiry in licensing. What were the FCC's justifications? The dissent indicates one objection to the FCC's new policy. Is this a legitimate complaint? Should the FCC be concerned whether small audiences obtain programming? Why or why not? Is programming diversity in television of less of concern now that most cable providers have dozens of channels? Should the FCC take into account that many people cannot afford cable?

5. In a subsequent action, the FCC eliminated "ascertainment" procedures that had required radio stations to conduct interviews with leaders of significant community groups and members of the public to ascertain community needs and interests. The Commission also eliminated guidelines that had limited the number of commercials that a radio station could run, restricted the amount of time devoted to commercials, and required stations to keep detailed program logs. The FCC, however, continued the requirement that radio stations provide programs concerning issues of public importance.[28] A panel of the D.C. Circuit affirmed the FCC's decision, except concerning a record-keeping requirement.[29]

6. The FCC also took analogous steps to deregulate television broadcasting. It eliminated ascertainment procedures, nonentertainment programming guidelines, and limits on the amount of time devoted to commercials, including a prohibition against infomercials.[30] As in the *WNCN Listeners Guild* case,

---

[26] C. SUNSTEIN, AFTER THE RIGHTS REVOLUTION: RECONCEIVING THE REGULATORY STATE 185 (1990); *see also* Baker, *Giving the Audience What It Wants,* 58 OHIO ST. L.J. 316 (1997) (critiquing claims that the market gives people the media that they want).

[27] *Id*. at 185.

[28] *Deregulation of Radio,* 84 F.C.C.2d 968, *reconsidered,* 87 F.C.C.2d (1981).

[29] *Office of Commun. of United Ch. of Christ v. FCC,* 707 F.2d 1413 (D.C. Cir. 1983); *see also Office of Commun. of United Ch. of Christ v. FCC,* 779 F.2d 702 (D.C. Cir. 1985) (remanding FCC's revised record-keeping requirement).

[30] *Deregulation of Commercial Television,* 98 F.C.C.2d 1076 (1984).

these deregulation decisions were premised on the FCC's belief that market-place forces would adequately force radio and television stations to reflect community needs and preferences. Once again, a panel of the D.C. Circuit affirmed the FCC's deregulation, except the panel held that the Commission did not have an adequate rationale for its elimination of rules concerning the commercialization of children's programming. These rules restricted advertising on children's programming because young children do not always understand the difference between programming and commercials. For example, the rules prohibited the same cartoon characters being used in both a program and commercials.[31]

7. In another deregulatory move, the Commission jettisoned the 38-year-old "fairness" doctrine. The doctrine had assigned television stations two responsibilities. They were obligated to present programming that addressed controversial subjects, and they were obligated to afford a reasonable opportunity for the presentation of contrasting views on such issues. The FCC concluded that the doctrine was unconstitutional as a violation of free speech, and that it was against the public interest, because, among other defects, it discouraged stations from presenting controversial programming. The FCC found that the doctrine produced a chilling effect by placing significant burdens on stations that would air numerous programs on controversial issues. The Commission also thought that the doctrine was no longer necessary because the number of broadcast outlets had increased significantly.[32]

8. The question of reliance on market forces versus regulation has been involved in another policy issue—whether the FCC should take affirmative steps to diversify ownership of broadcast facilities. In *Metro Broadcasting, Inc. v. FCC*, 497 U.S. 547 (1990), the Supreme Court upheld preferences designed to benefit minority applicants for broadcasting licenses. The Court, which applied an intermediate level of scrutiny, accepted diversity of broadcast ownership as an "important" governmental interest. The government had argued that increasing the number of minority owners would benefit all viewers by increasing available viewpoints. Recent cases, however, have cast doubt on the constitutionality of such a policy.[33] Nevertheless, Congress' most recent enactment concerning the distribution of the spectrum gives favored status to racial minorities and women as well as small businesses and rural telephone companies.[34]

---

[31] *Action for Children's T.V. v. FCC*, 821 F.2d 741 (1987).

[32] *See Syracuse Peace Council v. FCC*, 867 F.2d 654 (D.C. Cir. 1989) (upholding FCC decision to abrogate fairness doctrine); *see generally* Rainey, *The Public's Interest in Public Affairs Discourse: A Critical Review of the Public Interest Duties of the Electronic Media*, 62 Geo. L.J. 269 (1993).

[33] *See Adarand Constructors, Inc. v. Penna*, 515 U.S. 200 (1995) (establishing strict scrutiny fo reviewing racial classifications); *Lutheran Church-Mo. Synod v. FCC*, 141 F.3d 344 (D.C. Cir. 1998) (invaliding an FCC equal employment opportunity program designed to benefit minorities and women under strict scrutiny); *Lamprecht v FCC*, 958 F, 2d 382 (D.C. Cir. 1992) (finding an equal protection violation where the FCC awarded extra credit, based on gender, to a woman seeking a license to build a radio station, using the intermediate scrutiny standard of *Metro Broadcasting*).

[34] 47 U.S.C. § 309(j)(4)(D) (establishing that the FCC shall "ensure that small businesses, rural telephone companies, and businesses owned by members of minority groups and women are given the opportunity to participate in the provision of spectrum-based services, and, for such purposes, consider the use of tax certificates, bidding preferences, and other procedures.")

9. Broadcasters are less likely to respond to the programming preferences of small groups of persons because advertisers generally prefer large audiences. The FCC could require broadcasters to serve such groups, as part of their public interest obligation, but the Commission has given up on this approach, as you have seen. Public television is also a way to serve such audiences. Since it is not-for-profit, public television has more flexibility to put on programming that would not attract advertisers. But it must raise the money to support such programming. Obtaining contributions is subject to the problem that public television cannot exclude viewers who do not contribute.

Public broadcasting also receives public funding, but many in Congress would like to end this subsidy. What arguments can be made for and against the subsidy? Why is it fair to require taxpayers, who may not watch public television, to contribute to its cost? One proposal is to replace public funding with a tax on broadcasters. Would you favor this proposal? Why or why not? How does the fact that broadcasters do not have to pay for their licenses affect your answer?

b. CHILDREN'S TELEVISION

Although Congress acquiesced in the FCC's efforts to end regulation concerning adult programming, it has taken an active role in television programming watched by children. In 1990, Congress directed the FCC to consider the extent to which a licensee "has served the educational needs of children" in applications to renew commercial and noncommercial television broadcast licenses.[35] In 1992, Congress prohibited indecent radio or television broadcasts outside of "safe harbor" hours, which now extend from 10 p.m. to 6 a.m, and, in 1996, it required that all television sets larger than thirteen inches contain computer chips that permit parents to deny access to programming that contains "sexual, violent, or other indecent material about which parents should be informed before it is displayed to children."[36] These devices are commonly called "V-chips," because they are intended to permit parents to prevent children from watching excessively violent television shows, but the chips can read any type of electronic labeling which broadcasters attach to programming. Thus, for example, parents could block access to programming based on its sexual content if broadcasters were required to engage in the appropriate electronic labeling of such programs.

This section explores this new activism through the lens of efforts to limit children's access to excessively violent programming. The usual issues will be raised. First, why is regulation necessary? In adult programming, the FCC relies on market forces to direct programming. What is different about programming watched by children that requires governmental intervention? Second, if the government should act, what regulatory method will work the best? Finally, what are the constitutional boundaries of government action?

---

[35] Children's Television Act of 1990, Pub. L. No. 101-437, 104 Stat. 996; *see* Hayes, *The Children's Hour Revisited: The Children's Television Act of 1990*, 46 FED. COMM. L.J. 293 (1994).

[36] Telecommunications Act of 1992, Pub. L. No. 102-356, § 16, 106 Stat. 949, 954 (1992); *see Action for Children's Television v. FCC*, 58 F.3d 654 (D.C. Cir. 1995) (en banc); Telecommunications Act of 1996 § 551, Pub. L. No. 104-104, 110 Stat. 56, 139–142.

To what extent does the First Amendment constrain the censorship of violence on television?

(1) MARKET FAILURE

Experts believe that some children are adversely affected by exposure to violence in television programs:

> In 1969 the National Commission on the Causes and Prevention of Violence concluded that a "constant diet of violent behavior on television has an adverse effect on human character and attitudes." In 1972, a Surgeon General's Advisory Committee also found a causal connection between TV violence and aggressive behavior; a 1982 Surgeon General's update reinforced that conclusion. Later studies — 188 of them involving 244,000 children — supported the American Medical Association's conclusion that "TV's massive daily diet of symbolic violence is an environmental hazard," a risk factor threatening the health and welfare of American children and youth. . . ."[37]

You should recognize this problem as a "spillover" or "externality," as Professor Hamilton explains:

> Both indecent and violent television programs may involve negative externalities if they are viewed by children. . . . The social science literature suggests that viewing violent television programs may lead some children in the short run to behave more aggressively and in the long run to behave more violently. However, the social costs from crime and aggression engendered by television are not reflected in the programming calculus of broadcasters or advertisers. Instead, a broadcaster considering whether to air a violent program will calculate the number of likely viewers and multiply this figure by the advertising revenues realized by marketing these viewers to advertisers. In simplified terms, profits from the program are: (Advertising rate per thousand viewers $\times$ Number of thousands of viewers) -(Production costs of the program), and broadcasters will choose to air programs that maximize these profits. On the other hand, if broadcasters factored in the expected costs of violence to society in their programming decisions, returns on these shows would be lowered and their production made less likely. [38]

Thus, broadcasters lack an economic incentive to take into account the societal impact of violent programming. This is not, however, the only market flaw. Those who argue for regulation contend that broadcasters are also subject to a "race to the bottom" with respect to violence.[39] That is, any broadcaster which attempts to limit the amount of violence on television will lose its audience to other broadcasters who are willing to broadcast such programming. As Judge Patricia Wald observes, "The fact is 'violence sells.'

---

[37] Wald, *Doing Right By Our Kids: A Case Study in the Perils of Making Policy On Television Violence,* 23 U. BALT. L. REV 397, 399 (1995).

[38] Hamilton, *supra* note 23, at 1183.

[39] Hundt, *The Public's Airwaves: What Does The Public Interest Require of Television Broadcasters,* 45 DUKE L.J. 1089, 1091 (1996).

. . . The business of television and its cable competitors is to sell audiences to advertisers, and historically violence increases audiences."[40]

But is regulation justified even if violence on television has these undesirable effects? After all, as Judge Patricia Wald asks, "Why can't parents handle this crisis by controlling what their children watch? To paraphrase the old television public service announcement: Where are your parents tonight?"[41] Judge Wald offers the following reaction concerning the role of parents.

PATRICIA M. WALD, DOING RIGHT BY OUR KIDS: A CASE STUDY IN THE PERILS OF MAKING POLICY ON TELEVISION VIOLENCE, 23 UNIVERSITY OF BALTIMORE LAW REVIEW 397, 403–404 (1995)*

. . . [This is] not an altogether foolish question; columnist Anna Quindlen asks: "Kids and violent TV, violent TV and violence, violence and kids. The only people missing from this discussion are the parents. Where are we? Gone. Abdicated." Why, she comments, as in the case of poisonous cleaners stored under the sink, don't parents themselves take responsibility for their kids' television watching? A representative of the Annenberg School of Communications, on the other hand, calls the notion of parental control "an upper middle class conceit. Passing the buck to parents is the greatest cop-out of this industry."

These two views are not necessarily inconsistent. No matter what corrective action industry and/or government takes—short of an impossible blanket ban on violence—the parental role should still be critical. The autonomy of the family to set its own child-rearing standards, barring neglect or abuse, is a constitutional freedom recognized by the Supreme Court. Parents are as varied as our society, and differ radically in what they want their kids to watch, including how much violence and what kind, by whom and against whom. Some parents are actually quite sanguine. A cover story a few months ago in the Washington Post entitled "Group Portrait with Television, One Family's Love Affair with the Tube" told of an upper middle class family in Gaithersburg, Maryland with two young kids and six television sets that were on up to seventeen hours a day. The obviously devoted parents didn't worry about television sex or violence; there were no forbidden shows; the children were well-adjusted and doing fine in school. "If the kids have a question, [the stay-at-home mother stated], they'll ask it, and if they don't they'll probably get bored and change the channel." Unfortunately, all kids don't have a resident mother to run to with questions; a large percent of inner-city children are indiscriminate latch-key consumers of television fare.

And even otherwise attentive and caring parents complain that they don't have the time to act as full-time "gatekeepers" on television. While some, like the family in Gaithersburg, do not worry at all, most parents—and certainly children without parental supervision—need some outside help to control the amount and type of violence available at the flick of a switch. . . .

---

[40] Wald, *supra* note 37, at 410–11.

[41] *Id.* at 403.

(2) REGULATORY OPTIONS

If government should react to the problem of children's exposure to violence on television, what solution(s) should the government adopt? The FCC can evaluate a broadcaster's programming when the firm applies for a renewal, it can limit the hours during which violent programming is shown ("safe harbors"), or it can promulgate regulations that permit parents to use the V-chips in televisions to block access to violent (or other undesirable) programming.

License renewal: The next excerpt discusses the possibility that the FCC could address this problem in the licensing renewal process. As you will see, this approach is problematic, but technology may aid the FCC.

JAMES T. HAMILTON, PRIVATE INTERESTS IN "PUBLIC INTEREST" PROGRAMMING: AN ECONOMIC ASSESSMENT OF BROADCASTER INCENTIVES, 45 DUKE LAW JOURNAL 1177, 1186–89 (1996) *

Chairman Hundt has noted that the license renewal process has devolved into a process of nearly automatic approval. The definitions of "public interest" standards are vague, leaving broadcasters free to pursue a low-cost strategy of compliance that does not significantly increase the probability that they will provide programs with positive externalities. The Chairman has argued that broadcasters should be required to satisfy certain clear public interest standards as a condition for license renewal. For example, in the area of children's educational programming, the Chairman has proposed a require- ment of three hours per week for licensed broadcast stations. If requirements for broadcast licenses are in fact made more explicit, an additional way to ensure compliance is to provide the public with a larger role in monitoring contract performance.

Currently, viewers can participate in the license renewal process by review- ing a broadcast station's public inspection file. Maintained at the station, the file contains a listing of public affairs issues the station is covering that are of concern to the community, a listing of educational children's programs that the station believes demonstrate compliance with the Children's Television Act, data on political advertising sales, equal employment opportunity infor- mation on workforce composition, and viewer complaints. Additional informa- tion on station ownership and performance, including a history of fines for regulatory violations, is maintained at the FCC's Washington office.

The dispersion of information and the lack of a consistent reporting format currently make it costly for viewers to determine how a broadcast station is complying with the statutory public interest standards. The FCC could remedy this by requiring stations to report information electronically to the agency, which could in turn maintain an Internet-accessible database of station information (including viewer complaints). Admittedly, the logic of collective action suggests that the majority of viewers will never use this data. However, local PTAs, national media organizations, local journalists, and some viewers

---

will use the information to monitor station performance more closely. Consider the transformation of the debate over the provision of children's television programming that would likely occur if such a database were available. Viewers or interest groups could determine how the provision of such programming varied within markets and across ownership types. They could study the degree to which stations shirked their public interest requirements by preempting educational programs and scheduling them for early morning hours. They could also examine which programs were claimed to be educational, so such programs could be studied for their content. Individuals could also use data on children's programming to determine whether stations which schedule low levels of educational programming for children are also more likely to schedule their community service programs at the earliest hours and to offer violent programming in hours with large numbers of children in the viewing audience.

By lowering the transaction costs to viewers of monitoring station performance, the FCC could increase the incentives for broadcasters to comply with public interest requirements. Stations will be less likely to claim that "Geraldo" or "Beverly Hills 90210" are educational for children if such claims are likely to be seen by viewers. During the era of the New Deal, Justice Louis Brandeis supported the provision of information to the public on the grounds that "sunlight . . . is the best of disinfectants." The Internet offers the FCC the opportunity to extend this principle to electronic reporting of station data. The future of digital broadcasting may also provide the Commission with an opportunity to alter incentives to comply with public interest standards. If part of the spectrum continues to be allocated rather than auctioned, the future ability of local stations to offer multiple programs at once may give the FCC the chance to provide a credible sanction for those who do not comply with public interest standards. At present, although it can issue fines for violation of specific regulations, the FCC's single major enforcement tool is license denial. License denial is not a credible threat to broadcasters who fail to broadcast in the "public interest" because it is such a blunt instrument. If the agency could deny a station part of its allotment of multiple programming signals, however, the FCC would have additional flexibility to penalize stations which failed to follow the public interest terms of their licenses.

———

Safe harbors: As you read earlier, Congress and the FCC have addressed the issue of indecent programming by limiting the hours during which it can be shown to times where children are less likely to be in the audience. A similar approach could be adopted concerning violent programs. Since children are less likely to be up late at night to watch television, the FCC could require broadcasters to limit violence on television until after some point in time, such as 9:00 or 10:00 p.m. Of course, some children will be up to watch such programs. Moreover, the FCC would have to define somehow what programming is too violent to be shown at earlier hours. Social scientists may be able to help:

Research . . . indicates that the impact of violent programming varies according to the nature and context of the programming. Children are more likely to emulate violence if it is seen as realistic or perpetrated by a hero. They are also more likely to be affected if the violence is rewarded or left unpunished or if the negative outcomes of violence are not shown.

Researchers have recently developed a coding scheme for violent programming based on these media effects. Under this scheme, violent programming is defined according to the different contexts in which violence is presented. The scheme incorporates information on the perpetrator, action, and target of the violence and codes for such elements as whether the violence is portrayed in a realistic context or whether the violence is rewarded or punished. Social science research on violent programming, which is conducted largely in the laboratory, where aggressive behaviors rather than criminal acts are observed, admittedly cannot pinpoint the exact damage likely to be caused by a particular program. However, the research does indicate generally which programs and which types of acts within programs are more likely to be damaging to children.[42]

V-chip: The last option is the V-chip. Although Congress required television manufacturers to include such chips, it did not mandate that broadcasters send the signals necessary to activate such systems. Thus, there is still an open issue concerning how this approach might be used to stem the tide of television violence available to children's viewing. The idea of the V-chip is to lower the "search costs" of adults who wish to supervise their children. In the next excerpt, Professor Balkin characterizes this solution in terms of how consumers "filter" what information they want to see and not see. The V-chip, as Balkin further explains, is problematic, because of the issue of who will rate programming and how.

J. M. BALKIN, MEDIA FILTERS, THE V-CHIP, AND THE FOUNDATIONS OF BROADCAST REGULATION, 45 DUKE LAW JOURNAL 1131, 1148–50, 1165–75 (1996) *

IV. FILTERING AND THE MASS MEDIA

Broadcast communication is a linear stream of information in a predetermined and unchangeable order sent out at a predetermined and unchangeable time. This form of communication limits the ways one can filter information. There are basically only three: turning the receiver off completely, turning it on only at designated times, or changing the channel. Parental blocking is similarly limited. Parents can control children's viewing habits by turning the television off at specified times or forbidding children to watch certain channels. If children insist on watching television when their parents are not at home or cannot supervise them, parents have no choice other than to remove the television entirely. Because the number of filtering solutions is

---

[42] Hamilton, *supra* note 23, at 1183.

limited, there is a poor fit between desirable filtering mechanisms and practical excludability. Only very coarse filters can be made to work. This coarseness is the distinctive characteristic of broadcast media.

Consider the problem from the perspective of a single broadcast station attempting to organize information for the benefit of its viewers. Other than simply not broadcasting a program, the only means of organizing information is to segment it by time. And that is precisely what broadcasters do. They put different types of programming on sequentially, so that viewers can choose what programs to watch by time period. Broadcasters then try to turn these limitations to their advantage, through strategic scheduling of programs as regular series at preordained times, through the use of special blocks of programming, or through repeated showings. . . .

Not surprisingly, temporal filtering is also a major method of FCC regulation. Examples are the Prime Time Access Rule and the safe harbor provisions. These regulations organize programming in sequences of time and require that some programs not appear at certain times. They act like blocking or organizing filters. . . .

The V-chip and similar technologies promise to change the nature of broadcast media because they offer the possibility of new types of filtering mechanisms. They help the broadcast media become more like the library or the video store, although the former will never be the same as the latter two. The approximation would work best if broadcast and cable could offer literally hundreds of channels, so that there would always be something to watch as an alternative to blocked-out material, and so that the same or similar programs would be available at different times. Perhaps the best approximation would be a pay-per-view system, in which each home could order any available programming at any time of day. (This system could also be priced as a flat fee if that were economically feasible.) We are not yet at that point in video delivery. But we may well be in a few years' time. . . .

VIII. THE V-CHIP AND THE DELEGATION OF INFORMATIONAL FILTERING

. . . [T]he deeper problems that the V-chip raises . . . concern the power over individual thought and national culture that arises with increasingly powerful forms of delegation of informational access. . . .

The regulatory apparatus surrounding the V-chip will work an enormous new delegation of informational filtering to a centralized bureaucracy, whether one operated by the federal government or one operated by private industry. This new bureaucracy will be entrusted with the task of devising and implementing filters for virtually all of the television programs available in the United States. It will have to determine both the salient characteristics of all programming and evaluate which programs fit within the boundaries defined by these characteristics. These characteristics and these evaluations will in turn be employed by viewers and, more importantly, by advertisers, cable providers, video rental stores, public libraries, television production companies, writers, composers, and directors. As these evaluations become commonly employed, further choices and social arrangements will then be organized around them. In this way, the divisions of the cultural and informational world created by the custodians of the V-chip, however innocent, will be amplified throughout our culture, shaping and skewing the social world in unforeseen ways. . . .

I want to focus on three basic kinds of effects. The first has to do with what characteristics are salient in forming categories—for example, bad language or nudity. The second has to do with coarseness—how fine-grained the filtering categories are. The third concerns equivalency—what kinds of things are seen as parts of equivalent categories.

The first problem of any ratings system is what characteristics count in making programming unsuitable for children. . . .

. . . Many people would probably be content with a ratings system that, even if not guaranteed to be nonideological, would at least be doggedly centrist. That is probably the best reason to have an industry-sponsored ratings system, which will cater to the tastes (or, more appropriately, the fears) of advertisers. But if ratings guidelines are entrusted to a federally appointed television advisory committee, there is no guarantee of even this. Rather, the protection of family values through a ratings system is likely to take on decidedly different political spins under successive administrations. Nothing prevents a future committee from changing its mind about ratings guidelines if they should prove unsatisfactory or outmoded. And if the FCC has control over who sits on such an advisory committee, the guidelines produced by that committee will probably change over time depending on the regnant political forces (including subsequent Presidential appointments to the Commission). . . .

Coarseness of the ratings system is a second major concern. The current motion picture ratings system is perhaps the best example of how coarseness operates in practice. The MPAA currently offers a rating system featuring six categories—Unrated, G, PG, PG-13, R, and NC-17. . . .

If, as seems likely, the V-chip system uses ratings as coarse as the MPAA, the broadcast world will display similar effects. The MPAA ratings resemble the anthropologist's two basic categories of the sacred and the profane. There is a category of that which is suitable for children (taking the role of the sacred) and a category in which everything else—violence, bad language, nudity, homosexuality—gets thrown in indiscriminately (the profane). What is profane is then subdivided not by kind of expression but by degree of profaneness, resulting in a world consisting of what is sacred, a bit profane, a lot profane, and seriously profane.

On the other hand, if substantive categories are increasingly differentiated, the system produces a different set of incentives. It may pay for the director to produce a film with increased violence but not sexual content, and vice versa, because a change at the margins is better reflected in the ratings system. Of course, the more categories are added, the more difficult it becomes for parents to operate the system. As noted earlier, one of the most important constraints on the V-chip system will be ensuring ease of use to technologically-challenged adults. So the result is likely to be a compromise between coarseness and adequacy of ratings.

A third and final set of problems with any ratings system concerns equivalency. Even after the basic categories are determined, any ratings system will have to decide what gets coded within each category. More important for present purposes, it will have to decide what gets coded as possessing equal levels of inappropriateness. Like decisions about the categories themselves, these decisions cannot avoid political controversy; they are likely to have wide-ranging effects.

Take, for example, discussions of homosexuality or of safe sex as a means of preventing AIDS. How should these be coded in a ratings system? And what should they be coded as equivalent to? Some parents would see a big difference between such discussions and a sexually titillating love scene, while other parents would find both categories equally unsuitable for people under the age of eighteen. Now imagine a made-for-television movie that depicts a fictional cover-up by the church hierarchy of child abuse allegations made against Catholic priests, and a movie in which Freddy Krueger murders a hapless teenage couple having sex in the woods at midnight. It is not difficult to imagine different groups of parents disagreeing heatedly about the relative inappropriateness for children of these two examples. . . .

Nevertheless, it is possible that events will play out quite differently. If cable bandwidth is expanded—for example, through digital delivery systems—there may be room for several different ratings systems. Groups like the Christian Coalition may offer their own ratings system using V-chip technology, employing their own conception of what is family-friendly and what is not. Consumers can then subscribe to the ratings system of their choice, much as they now subscribe to magazines like TV Guide. More over, an explosion of space on cable systems promises the possibility of filtering systems based on any number of programming criteria. The only limitation upon would-be filterers is their ability to catalogue and categorize the millions of hours of materials that will eventually exist for television, and their ability to gain sufficient market share to underwrite the costs of rating this material. . . .

NOTES AND QUESTIONS

1. Assuming that violence on television adversely affects children, as the evidence apparently establishes, why is it not sufficient for the government to educate parents of this fact? If parents were so informed, would there be fewer children watching violence on television? Why or why not?

2. Judge Wald suggests that, although the problems created by television violence are widely recognized, there is no easy solution on the horizon:

> It has always been—and probably always will be—conceptually and practically difficult to disentangle children's problems from the broader social problems affecting society as a whole. The problem of television violence inevitably incites ideological, legal, and economic disputes. . . . [T]he best we seem able to do is to lurch towards partial solutions likely to inspire as much dissatisfaction as satisfaction.[43]

---

[43] Wald, *supra* note 37, at 404.

What are the regulatory options and what problems do they present? Is Judge Wald correct that the best we can do is adopt partial solutions that many persons will dislike?

3. A newspaper editorial complains that the "V-chip is still little-known and little-promoted despite all of the political chatter." One problem, according to the editorial, is that "[l]ess than 10% of parents with children age 2 to 17 own a set equipped with the chip; 39% have never heard of it . . ." The editorial admits that "it will take time for the V-chip to filter into homes, but "there's fresh evidence that broadcasters haven't been willing to wait before ratcheting up the raunchiness of their programs" and that "evening television programming has become far racier in the past decade." The editorial concludes, "The industry brought into the rating and V-chip system, even promising the FCC that it would help 'educate the public.' Instead, broadcasters have turned up the dial on set and foul language."[44]

What is your impression of how racy evening television has become? Do you see the V-chip as a suitable method for parents to control what their children may watch or do you even see any problem with children watching the current programming?

4. The FCC debated how to implement Congress' requirement that the Commission assess how well a television broadcaster served the educational needs of children before renewal of its license. Commission members favored mandating a minimum number of hours per week of educational programming, but split concerning the method by which the regulations would be implemented. The dispute was resolved when President Clinton intervened and negotiated a compromise to which the broadcasters agreed. The policy requires three hours of educational children's television per week, but it permits some exceptions.[45]

(3)   FIRST AMENDMENT CONSTRAINTS

Government efforts to limit violence on television must be consistent with the First Amendment. As indicated in our previous coverage of this area, the Supreme Court will permit the government to regulate certain types of speech if the government can meet a heightened standard of scrutiny. The level of scrutiny depends on the nature of the speech and the type of restrictions which the government employs. Moreover, in balancing the government's interest and the impact on speech, the Court considers whether the government has chosen the least restrictive means to accomplish its objectives.

Although it is not possible in the space available to discuss these First Amendment implications in detail, the next two cases, *FCC v. Pacifica Foundation* and *Action for Children's Television v. FCC*, will permit you to address the general issues that regulation of violence on television present. In the first, the Court considers the government's authority to control the broadcast of "indecent" programming. The Court holds that the indecent

---

[44] USA TODAY, Apr. 12, 2000, at 28A.

[45] Landler, *FCC Plan for Children's Television Loses Support of Key Member*, N.Y. TIMES, July 11, 1996, at C1 (national edition); Mifflin, *TV Broadcasters Agree to 3 Hours of Children's Educational Programs a Week*, N.Y. TIMES, July 30, 1996, at A6 (national edition).

nature of the speech does not itself justify regulation, but that safe harbor regulation is justified by the government's interest in protecting children in the special context of broadcasting.

FCC v. PACIFICA FOUNDATION
438 U.S. 726 (1978)

JUSTICE STEVENS delivered the opinion of the Court.

[This case concerns a satiric humorist named George Carlin, who recorded a twelve-minute monologue entitled "Filthy Words" before a live audience in a California theater. He began by referring to his thoughts about "the words you couldn't say on the public, ah, airwaves, um, the ones you definitely wouldn't say, ever." He proceeded to list those words and repeat them over and over again in a variety of colloquialisms. At about two o'clock in the afternoon on Tuesday, October 30, 1973, a New York radio station, owned by the Pacifica Foundation, broadcast the "Filthy Words" monologue. A few weeks later a man, who stated that he had heard the broadcast while driving with his young son, wrote a letter complaining to the Commission. He stated that, although he could perhaps understand the "record being sold for private use, I certainly cannot understand the broadcast of same over the air that, supposedly, you control."

The FCC issued an order that Pacifica had violated the FCC Act's ban on the use of "any obscene, indecent, or profane language by means of radio communications." Although the Commission did not issue any sanctions against the broadcaster, it did say that it might take the broadcaster's violation of the Act into account when it sought renewal of its license. After the order was issued, the Commission was asked to clarify its ruling prohibiting the broadcast of the seven dirty words used by Carlin. It responded that it had not intended an absolute prohibition, but rather sought to limit the broadcast of such words to times during the day when children were unlikely to be listening.]

The words of the Carlin monologue are unquestionably "speech" within the meaning of the First Amendment. It is equally clear that the Commission's objections to the broadcast were based in part on its content. The order must therefore fall if, as Pacifica argues, the First Amendment prohibits all governmental regulation that depends on the content of speech. Our past cases demonstrate, however, that no such absolute rule is mandated by the Constitution.

The classic exposition of the proposition that both the content and the context of speech are critical elements of First Amendment analysis is Mr. Justice Holmes' statement for the Court in *Schenck v. United States:* "We admit that in many places and in ordinary times the defendants in saying all that was said in the circular would have been within their constitutional rights. But the character of every act depends upon the circumstances in which it is done. . . . The most stringent protection of free speech would not protect a man in falsely shouting fire in a theater and causing a panic. It does not even protect a man from an injunction against uttering words that may have all the effect of force. . . . The question in every case is whether the words used are used in such circumstances and are of such a nature as to create a clear and present danger that they will bring about the substantive evils that Congress has a right to prevent." . . .

. . . [T]he fact that society may find speech offensive is not a sufficient reason for suppressing it. Indeed, if it is the speaker's opinion that gives offense, that consequence is a reason for according it constitutional protection. For it is a central tenet of the First Amendment that the government must remain neutral in the marketplace of ideas. If there were any reason to believe that the Commission's characterization of the Carlin monologue as offensive could be traced to its political content—or even to the fact that it satirized contemporary attitudes about four-letter words—First Amendment protection might be required. But that is simply not this case. These words offend for the same reasons that obscenity offends. Their place in the hierarchy of First Amendment values was aptly sketched by Mr. Justice Murphy when he said: "Such utterances are no essential part of any exposition of ideas, and are of such slight social value as a step to truth that any benefit that may be derived from them is clearly outweighed by the social interest in order and morality."

Although these words ordinarily lack literary, political, or scientific value, they are not entirely outside the protection of the First Amendment. Some uses of even the most offensive words are unquestionably protected. Indeed, we may assume, arguendo, that this monologue would be protected in other contexts. Nonetheless, the constitutional protection accorded to a communication containing such patently offensive sexual and excretory language need not be the same in every context. . . .

We have long recognized that each medium of expression presents special First Amendment problems. And of all forms of communication, it is broadcasting that has received the most limited First Amendment protection. Thus, although other speakers cannot be licensed except under laws that carefully define and narrow official discretion, a broadcaster may be deprived of his license and his forum if the Commission decides that such an action would serve "the public interest, convenience, and necessity.". . .

The reasons for these distinctions are complex, but two have relevance to the present case. First, the broadcast media have established a uniquely pervasive presence in the lives of all Americans. Patently offensive, indecent material presented over the airwaves confronts the citizen, not only in public, but also in the privacy of the home, where the individual's right to be left alone plainly outweighs the First Amendment rights of an intruder. Because the broadcast audience is constantly tuning in and out, prior warnings cannot completely protect the listener or viewer from unexpected program content. To say that one may avoid further offense by turning off the radio when he hears indecent language is like saying that the remedy for an assault is to run away after the first blow. One may hang up on an indecent phone call, but that option does not give the caller a constitutional immunity or avoid a harm that has already taken place.

Second, broadcasting is uniquely accessible to children, even those too young to read. Although Carlin's written message might have been incomprehensible to a first grader, Pacifica's broadcast could have enlarged a child's vocabulary in an instant. Other forms of offensive expression may be withheld from the young without restricting the expression at its source. Bookstores and motion picture theaters, for example, may be prohibited from making indecent material available to children. . . .

———

The safe harbor regulation litigated in *Pacifica* limited the broadcast of "seven dirty words" to safe harbor hours. After the Congress and the FCC banned the broadcast of any "indecent" speech outside of the safe harbor hours of midnight to 6:00 a.m., the D.C. Circuit ruled on the constitutionality of the regulation. The majority justified the regulation based on the protection of children, although Judge Edwards in his dissent objected to the government's lack of proof that exposure to indecent programming was harmful to children. Note that he emphasized that, as compared to studies on the impact of violence on children, there is little evidence linking indecency and antisocial behavior. The majority and the others dissenters differed concerning whether the government had chosen the least restrictive means available to serve this interest.

ACTION FOR CHILDREN'S TELEVISION v. FCC
58 F.3d 654 (D.C. Cir. 1995) (en banc)

BUCKLEY, CIRCUIT JUDGE:

We are asked to determine the constitutionality of section 16(a) of the Public Telecommunications Act of 1992, which seeks to shield minors from indecent radio and television programs by restricting the hours within which they may be broadcast. Section 16(a) provides that, with one exception, indecent materials may only be broadcast between the hours of midnight and 6:00 a.m. The exception permits public radio and television stations that go off the air at or before midnight to broadcast such materials after 10:00 p.m. . . .

Unlike cable subscribers, who are offered such options as "pay-per-view" channels, broadcast audiences have no choice but to "subscribe" to the entire output of traditional broadcasters. Thus, they are confronted without warning with offensive material. This is "manifestly different from a situation" where a recipient "seeks and is willing to pay for the communication. . . ."

In light of these differences, radio and television broadcasts may properly be subject to different—and often more restrictive—regulation than is permissible for other media under the First Amendment. While we apply strict scrutiny to regulations of this kind regardless of the medium affected by them, our assessment of whether section 16(a) survives that scrutiny must necessarily take into account the unique context of the broadcast medium.

1. The compelling Government interests . . .

The Commission identifies three compelling Government interests as justifying the regulation of broadcast indecency: support for parental supervision of children, a concern for children's well-being, and the protection of the home against intrusion by offensive broadcasts. Because we find the first two sufficient to support such regulation, we will not address the third.

Petitioners do not contest that the Government has a compelling interest in supporting parental supervision of what children see and hear on the public airwaves. Indeed, the Court has repeatedly emphasized the Government's fundamental interest in helping parents exercise their "primary responsibility for [their] children's well-being" with "laws designed to aid [in the] discharge of that responsibility." This interest includes "supporting parents' claim to authority in their own household" through "regulation of otherwise protected expression."

Although petitioners disagree, we believe the Government's own interest in the well-being of minors provides an independent justification for the regulation of broadcast indecency. The Supreme Court has described that interest as follows:

> It is evident beyond the need for elaboration that a State's interest in safeguarding the physical and psychological well-being of a minor is compelling. A democratic society rests, for its continuance, upon the healthy, well-rounded growth of young people into full maturity as citizens. Accordingly, we have sustained legislation aimed at protecting the physical and emotional well-being of youth even when the laws have operated in the sensitive area of constitutionally protected rights.

While conceding that the Government has an interest in the well-being of children, petitioners argue that because "no causal nexus has been established between broadcast indecency and any physical or psychological harm to minors," that interest is "too insubstantial to justify suppressing indecent material at times when parents are available to supervise their children." That statement begs two questions: The first is how effective parental supervision can actually be expected to be even when parent and child are under the same roof; the second, whether the Government's interest in the well-being of our youth is limited to protecting them from clinically measurable injury.

As Action for Children's Television argued in an earlier FCC proceeding, "parents, no matter how attentive, sincere or knowledgeable, are not in a position to really exercise effective control" over what their children see on television. . . .

With respect to the second question begged by petitioners, the Supreme Court has never suggested that a scientific demonstration of psychological harm is required in order to establish the constitutionality of measures protecting minors from exposure to indecent speech. In *Ginsberg* [*v. New York*, 390 U.S. 629 (1968)], the Court considered a New York State statute forbidding the sale to minors under the age of 17 of literature displaying nudity even where such literature was "not obscene for adults. . . ." The Court observed that while it was "very doubtful" that the legislative finding that such literature impaired "the ethical and moral development of our youth" was based on "accepted scientific fact," a causal link between them "had not been disproved either." The Court then stated that it "d[id] not demand of legislatures scientifically certain criteria of legislation. We therefore cannot say that [the statute] . . . has no rational relation to the objective of safeguarding such minors from harm."

In *Bethel School District No. 403 v. Fraser*, 478 U.S. 675 (1986), the Court did not insist on a scientific demonstration of psychic injury when it found that there was a compelling governmental interest in protecting high school students from an indecent speech at a high school assembly. It noted that its prior cases "recognize the obvious concern on the part of parents, and school authorities acting in loco parentis, to protect children—especially in a captive audience—from exposure to sexually explicit, indecent, or lewd speech." . . .

Finally, we think it significant that the Supreme Court has recognized that the Government's interest in protecting children extends beyond shielding them from physical and psychological harm. The statute that the Court found constitutional in *Ginsberg* sought to protect children from exposure to materials that would "impair[] [their] ethical and moral development." Furthermore, although the Court doubted that this legislative finding "expresse[d] an accepted scientific fact," it concluded that the legislature could properly support the judgment of

> parents and others, teachers for example, who have [the] primary responsibility for children's well-being . . . [by] . . . assessing sex-related material harmful to minors according to prevailing standards in the adult community as a whole with respect to what is suitable material for minors.

2. Least restrictive means . . .

Recognizing the Government's compelling interest in protecting children from indecent broadcasts, Congress channeled indecent broadcasts to the hours between midnight and 6:00 a.m. in the hope of minimizing children's exposure to such material. Given the substantially smaller number of children in the audience after midnight, we find that section 16(a) reduces children's exposure to broadcast indecency to a significant degree. We also find that this restriction does not unnecessarily interfere with the ability of adults to watch or listen to such materials both because substantial numbers of them are active after midnight and because adults have so many alternative ways of satisfying their tastes at other times. Although the restrictions burden the rights of many adults, it seems entirely appropriate that the marginal convenience of some adults be made to yield to the imperative needs of the young. We thus conclude that, standing alone, the midnight to 6:00 a.m. safe harbor is narrowly tailored to serve the Government's compelling interest in the well-being of our youth.

B. The Public Broadcaster Exception

Section 16(a) permits public stations that sign off the air at or before midnight to broadcast indecent material after 10:00 p.m. Petitioners argue that section 16(a) is unconstitutional because it allows the stations to present indecent material two hours earlier than all others. . . .

Whatever Congress's reasons for creating it, the preferential safe harbor has the effect of undermining both the argument for prohibiting the broadcasting of indecent speech before that hour and the constitutional viability of the more restrictive safe harbor that appears to have been Congress's principal objective in enacting section 16(a). . . .

Congress has failed to explain what, if any, relationship the disparate treatment accorded certain public stations bears to the compelling

Government interest—or to any other legislative value—that Congress sought to advance when it enacted section 16(a). . . . Here, Congress and the Commission have backed away from the consequences of their own reasoning, leaving us with no choice but to hold that the section is unconstitutional insofar as it bars the broadcasting of indecent speech between the hours of 10:00 p.m. and midnight. . . .

HARRY T. EDWARDS, CHIEF JUDGE, dissenting: . . .

. . . With respect to the alleged interest in protecting children, although the majority strains mightily to rest its finding of harm on intuitive notions of morality and decency (notions with which I have great sympathy), the simple truth is that "[t]here is not one iota of evidence in the record . . . to support the claim that exposure to indecency is harmful—indeed, the nature of the alleged 'harm' is never explained." There is significant evidence suggesting a causal connection between viewing violence on television and antisocial violent behavior; but, as was conceded by Government counsel at oral argument in this case, the FCC has pointed to no such evidence addressing the effects of indecent programming. With respect to the interest in facilitating parental supervision, the statute is not tailored to aid parents' control over what their children watch and hear; it does not, for example, "segregate" indecent programming on special channels, . . . nor does it promote a blocking device which individuals control. Rather, section 16(a) involves a total ban of disfavored programming during hours when adult viewers are most likely to be in the audience. . . .

. . . I find it incomprehensible that the majority can so easily reject the "public broadcaster exception" to section 16(a), and yet be blind to the utterly irrational distinction that Congress has created between broadcast and cable operators. No one disputes that cable exhibits more and worse indecency than does broadcast. And cable television is certainly pervasive in our country. Today, a majority of television households have cable, and over the last two decades, the percentage of television households with cable has increased every year. However, the Government does not even attempt to regulate cable with the same heavy regulatory hand it applies to the broadcast media. There is no ban between 6 a.m. and midnight imposed on cable.

WALD, CIRCUIT JUDGE, with whom ROGERS and TATEL, CIRCUIT JUDGES, join, dissenting: . . .

. . . I agree with Chief Judge Edwards that the primary government interest here must be in facilitating parental supervision of children. Although the Supreme Court has recognized the government's own interest in protecting children from exposure to indecency, it has never identified this interest as one that could supersede the parental interest. The government's protective responsibility in a matter of morals is, as the majority recognizes, "complementary" to that of parents. Thus, although the majority speaks broadly of the government's independent interest in shielding children from indecency, it recognizes—as it must—that this interest is circumscribed; absent neglect or abuse, it cannot rise above the parental interest in child rearing. In the end, the majority admits the government's own interest in children is limited to "shielding minors from being exposed to indecent speech by persons other than a parent."

The majority is right: the government's primary if not exclusive interest is in "shielding minors from being exposed to indecent speech by persons other than a parent." Given the significant First Amendment rights of adults at stake, moreover, the government has a constitutional responsibility to key its response to the presumed harm from indecency to facilitating parental control, rather than to government censorship per se. When most parents are presumably able to supervise their children, adult viewers should have access to the speech to which they are entitled.

Because the government can pursue whatever legitimate interests it has in protecting children by facilitating parental control, I do not believe that it can impose a valid ban during any hours it pleases solely because some children are in the audience. Nor do I believe that we can throw up our hands at the assumed impossibility of parental supervision simply because large numbers of children have television sets in their own room. Either or both of these excuses would justify a 24-hour ban as easily as the current 18-hour ban. Reasoning along these lines totally ignores the adult First Amendment interest that the majority purportedly recognizes and, effectively, gives the government unharnessed power to censor.

Instead, the scope of any safe harbor can only be responsibly justified in the terms that the government emphasized at oral argument. Counsel for the government maintained that its primary interest is in assisting parents to control their children's viewing and that the function of a safe harbor is to support this interest by identifying for parents a reasonable time period during which they must exert their supervisory function. A safe harbor, so tailored, may well be a constitutionally acceptable means of furthering society's interest in protecting children. Advancement of this justification, however, requires careful tailoring of a sort completely neglected by the government. Though it may be entirely logical for the government to assist parents by purging the airwaves of indecency during certain hours when parental supervision typically is at a low ebb, the government should be put to the task of demonstrating that the banned hours are based on a showing that these are the times of preponderant children viewing and the times when parents are otherwise absorbed in work in or out of the home. . . .

NOTES AND QUESTIONS

1. What reasons does the Court give in *Pacifica* to justify FCC regulation of indecent programming? Do these additional reasons apply equally to cable broadcasting?[46] In *Action for Children's Television*, Judge Edwards concluded that Congress' failure to establish safe harbor hours for indecent programming

---

[46] *See United States v. Playboy Entertainment Group Inc.*, 529 U.S. 803 (2000) (striking down § 505 of the Telecommunications Act of 1996, which required cable companies to fully scramble sexually-oriented programming, because the government failed to show the provision to be the least restrictive means of achieving its objectives and the provision was subject to strict scrutiny as content-based regulation); *Denver Educ. Telecommunications Consortium, Inc. v. FCC*, 518 U.S. 727 (1996) (upholding one provision of the Cable Television Consumer Protection and Competition Act of 1992 (Act), which permitted cable operators to decide whether to broadcast certain material, because the material might be viewed by children, but striking down other provisions because they were not appropriately tailored to achieve the government's purpose.)

on cable indicated that the government lacked valid reasons for such regulations for broadcast television. Do you agree? Can cable be distinguished? What basis did Judge Buckley offer for distinguishing the two mediums?

2. How did Judge Buckley characterize the government's interest in protecting children from observing indecent programming? On what basis did Judge Wald disagree with this characterization? Judge Edwards asserted that there was no empirical evidence in the record to support the claim that children are harmed by exposure to indecent programming. He noted that, unlike violence, for which such evidence exists, scientists have not established a link between indecency and antisocial behavior. Why were the majority unconcerned with the lack of empirical evidence?

3. Based on the D.C. Circuit's approval of safe harbor regulations for indecent programming, would the courts approve safe harbor regulations for violence on television? Consider the arguments of Reed Hundt, a former FCC Chairman:

> [*Action for Children's Television*] upheld the channeling of indecency, and the main difference between violence and indecency, as Judge Edwards has stated, is that the harmful effects of violence are better established, so that the governmental interest is even clearer. A second difference is that indecency often involves language, whereas violence usually does not. Accordingly, the depiction of violence is farther from the core of the First Amendment. Indeed, although I see why burning a draft card is a form of symbolic speech, it is hard to see, for example, how the visual depiction in "Friday the 13th" of someone wearing a mask beheading someone else in an extraordinarily gruesome fashion has much of anything to do with free speech. . . . Because the Supreme Court made clear in *Pacifica* that indecent material may be regulated, as the en banc D.C. Circuit has just confirmed in [*Action for Children's Television*], it is therefore permissible to regulate television violence.[47]

Do you agree with this analysis? Is your answer affected by the fact that the V-chip offers a less restrictive method to regulate violence than safe harbor hours?

4. Is use of the V-chip consistent with the First Amendment? Consider the following censorship issues:

> From one perspective, there is no problem with the government designing a content-based information organization system and leaving it up to private parties to decide whether to accept or reject it. For example, there is nothing unconstitutional about the development of the Library of Congress cataloguing system or its near universal acceptance in public and private libraries as a means of organizing information. The problem comes when the government insists that information must be organized according to content in a certain way or it cannot be published at all. And when the government uses

---

[47] Hundt, *supra* note 39, at 1125–26.

threats, whether overt or concealed, to achieve this result, constitutional values are surely implicated.[48]

Thus, for example, can the government forbid the broadcasting of unrated programs? If not, can the government require that such programs be relegated to safe harbor periods? Moreover, who is to do the rating of programs? If the government undertakes the rating, or even if it delegates it to a private party, is the government engaged in prior restraint of speech? The government might be able to avoid this difficulty if producers rate their own programs, but will such a system be credible? Finally, does the government's interest in protecting children outweigh any censorship that might occur?

5. In *44 Liquormart, Inc. v. Rhode Island*, 116 S. Ct. 1495 (1996), found in Chapter 10, the Court struck down an advertising ban on liquor prices. In a subsequent case, *Anheuser-Busch, Inc. v. Schmoke*, 101 F.3d 325 (3rd Cir. 1996), also discussed in Chapter 10, the court upheld a Baltimore city ordinance which banned the placement of outdoor liquor advertising in areas where children play or walk to school. To what extent do these cases offer a useful analogy concerning the validity of safe harbor hours for violence on television?

6. The Supreme Court has wrested with a similar issue in the context of children's access to the Internet. In *Reno v. American Civil Liberties Union*, 521 U.S. 844 (1997), the Court declared the Communications Decency Act of 1996 to be unconstitutional because it effectively "suppress[ed] a large amount of speech that adults ha[d] a constitutional right to receive and to address one another" in seeking to "deny minors access to potentially harmful speech." In response, Congress passed the Child Online Protection Act, which the Court reviewed in *Ashcroft v. American Civil Liberties Union*, 122 S.Ct. 1700 (2002), but it did not definitively resolve the constitutionality of the act.

B. ADOPTION

Government allocation is not limited to broadcast facilities. Other types of market transactions are also banned. For example, we do not permit the sale of babies. Some policy analysts, however, argue that this is a mistake and urge greater reliance on market principles for adoption. After the following material, you can decide whether there should be market allocation concerning these services.

ELIZABETH M. LANDES & RICHARD A. POSNER, THE ECONOMICS OF THE BABY SHORTAGE, 7 JOURNAL OF LEGAL STUDIES 323, 324–45 (1978) *

Students of adoption agree on two things. The first is that there is a shortage of white babies for adoption; the second is that there is a glut of black babies, and of children who are no longer babies (particularly if they are physically or mentally handicapped), for adoption. . . .

---

[48] Balkin, *Media Filters, the V-Chip, and the Foundation of Broadcast Regulation,* 45 DUKE L.J. 1131, 1159 (1996).

* Copyright © 1978 by the University of Chicago. Reprinted by permission.

Students of adoption cite factors such as the declining proportion of illegitimate children being put up for adoption as the "causes" of the baby shortage. But such factors do not create a shortage, any more than the scarcity of truffles creates a shortage; they merely affect the number of children available for adoption at any price. At a higher price for babies, the incidence of abortion, the reluctance to part with an illegitimate child, and even the incentive to use contraceptives would diminish because the costs of unwanted pregnancy would be lower while the (opportunity) costs to the natural mother of retaining her illegitimate child would rise.

The principal suppliers of babies for adoption are adoption agencies. Restrictive regulations governing nonagency adoption have given agencies a monopoly (though not a complete one) of the supply of children for adoption. However, while agencies charge fees for adoption, usually based on the income of the adoptive parents, they do not charge a market-clearing (let alone a monopoly-profit-maximizing) price. This is shown by the fact that prospective adoptive parents applying to an agency face waiting periods of three to seven years. And the (visible) queue understates the shortage, since by tightening their criteria of eligibility to adopt a child the agencies can shorten the apparent queue without increasing the supply of babies. Thus some demanders in this market must wait for years to obtain a baby, others never obtain one, and still others are discouraged by knowledge of the queue from even trying. Obtaining a second or third baby is increasingly difficult.

The picture is complicated, however, by the availability of independent adoptions. An independent adoption is one that does not go through an agency. Most independent adoptions are by a relative, for example a stepfather, but some involve placement with strangers and here, it would seem, is an opportunity for a true baby market to develop. However, the operation of this market is severely curtailed by a network of restrictions, varying from state to state (a few states forbid independent adoption by a nonrelative) but never so loose as to permit outright sale of a baby for adoption. . . .

The foregoing analysis suggests that the baby shortage and black market are the result of legal restrictions that prevent the market from operating freely in the sale of babies as of other goods. This suggests as a possible reform simply eliminating these restrictions. However, many people believe that a free market in babies would be undesirable. . . . The objections to baby selling must be considered carefully before any conclusion with regard to the desirability of changing the law can be reached.

A. Criticisms Properly Limited to the Black Market

We begin with a set of criticisms that in reality are applicable not to the market as such, but only, we believe, to the *black* market. The first such criticism is of the high price of babies and the bad effects that are alleged to flow from a high price, such as favoring the wealthy. This criticism of the use of the price system is based on the current prices in the black market. There is no reason to believe that prices would be so high were the sales of babies legalized. On the contrary, prices for children of *equivalent quality* would be much lower. . . .

Also, because the adoption agencies give substantial emphasis to the employment and financial situation of adoptive parents, a baby market might actually provide more opportunities for the poor to adopt than nonprice rationing does. If we were correct that the (acquisition) costs of babies in a lawful and competitive market would often be small, perhaps no more than the cost of an automobile, low-income families who would normally be considered financially ineligible by adoption agencies would be able in a free market to obtain a child.

Another prevalent criticism of the market, and again one that pertains primarily to the operations of the black market, is that fraud and related forms of dishonesty and overreaching pervade the market method of providing children for adoption. It is contended, for example, that the health of the child or of the child's mother is regularly misrepresented and that frequently after the sale is completed the seller will attempt to blackmail the adoptive parents. Such abuses are probably largely the result of the fact that the market is an illegal one. Sellers cannot give legally enforceable guarantees of genealogy, health, or anything else to the prospective parents, and even the seller's adherence to the negotiated price is uncertain given the buyer's inability to enforce the contract of sale by the usual legal procedures. . . .

To be sure, there are probably inherent limitations on the use of legal remedies to protect purchasers even in a legal baby market. For example, consideration of the welfare of the child might lead courts to refuse to grant rescission to a buyer as a remedy for breach of warranty (i.e., allow him to return the child). And courts might be reluctant to order specific performance of a contract to put up a child for adoption. However, similar limitations are a traditional feature of remedies for personal-service contracts, yet do not appear to prevent effective enforcement of those contracts. Why should they do so in the case of baby sale contracts?

The foregoing analysis also enables us to place in perspective allegations that the sellers in the baby black market include a number of ex-convicts and other unsavory types and that the market reveals commercial "trafficking" at its ugliest. An illegal market will naturally attract people who are less sensitive to the threat of criminal punishment than is normal and this group may include a large proportion of ex-convicts. But these characteristics of the market are an artifact of its illegality.

This analysis suggests a qualification to our earlier conclusions that legalizing the baby market would result in a reduction in the price of babies below the current black market level: the conclusion refers to a *quality-adjusted* price. The current illegality of baby selling reduces the benefits of transacting to the buyer by depriving him of the contractual protections that buyers in legal markets normally receive. Prospective adoptive parents would presumably be willing to pay more for a child whose health and genealogy were warranted in a legally enforceable instrument than they are willing to pay under the present system where the entire risk of any deviation from expected quality falls on them. Thus the effect of legalizing the baby market would be not only to shift the marginal cost of baby production and sale downward but to move the demand curve for adoptive children upward. Conceivably these movements could cancel each other out, resulting in no change from the current black-market prices, but even if they did consumer satisfaction would be increased. The same price would buy a higher-quality package of rights.

B. Criticisms of a Legal Market

We now consider criticisms of baby selling that are applicable to a legal market rather than just to the present illegal market. The first is that the rationing of the supply of babies to would-be adoptive parents by price is not calculated to promote the best interests of the children, the objective of the adoption process. This criticism cannot be dismissed as foolish. The ordinary presumption of free-enterprise economics is no stronger than that free exchange will maximize the satisfaction of the people trading, who in this case are the natural and adoptive parents. There is no presumption that the satisfactions of the thing traded, in most instances a meaningless concept, are also maximized. If we treat the child as a member of the community whose aggregate welfare we are interested in maximizing, there is no justification for ignoring how the child's satisfactions may be affected by alternative methods of adoption.

Very simply, the question is whether the price system would do as good a job as, or a better job than, adoption agencies in finding homes for children that would maximize their satisfactions in life. While there is no direct evidence on this point, some weak indirect evidence is provided in a follow-up study of independent adoptions which suggest that children adopted privately do as well as natural children. . . .

This conclusion is reinforced by the way in which adoption agencies screen. Agencies attempt to allocate children only to "fit" or caring parents. But after determining the pool of fit, or eligible-to-adopt, couples, they allocate available children among them on a first-come, first-served basis. The "fittest" parents are not placed at the head of the queue.

Further, and perhaps most important, agencies have no real information on the needs of a particular child they place for adoption beyond its need for love, warmth, food, and shelter. One cannot read from the face of a newborn whether he or she will be of above or below normal intelligence, or be naturally athletic, musical, or artistic. Hence agencies cannot be presumed to match these very real, if inaccessible, qualities of infants with the qualities of the adoptive parents any more effectively than a market would.

One valuable function agencies may perform is screening out people whose interest in having children is improper in an uncontroversial sense — people who wish to have children in order to abuse or make slaves of them. The criminal statues punishing child abuse and neglect would remain applicable to babies adopted in a free market, but the extreme difficulty of detecting such crimes makes it unlikely, at least given current levels of punishment, that the criminal statutes alone are adequate. This may make some prescreening a more effective method of prevention than after-the-fact punishment. But the logical approach, then, is to require every prospective baby buyer to undergo some minimal background investigation. This approach would be analogous to licensing automobile drivers and seems as superior to the agency monopoly as licensing is to allocating automobiles on a nonprice basis.

Moreover, concern with child abuse should not be allowed to obscure the fact that abuse is not the normal motive for adopting a child. And once we put abuse aside, willingness to pay money for a baby would seem on the whole a reassuring factor from the standpoint of child welfare. Few people buy a car or a television set in order to smash it. In general, the more costly a purchase, the more care the purchaser will lavish on it. Recent studies suggest that the more costly it is for parents to obtain a child, the greater will be their investment in the child's quality attributes, such as health and education. . . .

Another objection to the market for babies is the alleged vulnerability of both natural and adoptive parents to overreaching by middlemen. Parenthood is thought to be so emotional a phenomenon that people cannot reason about it in the same way they reason about the goods and services normally traded in the market. But many of those goods and services, such as medical care, also involve a strong emotional component, yet it has rarely been thought appropriate to exclude such goods from market exchange. And studies of marriage and procreation have shown that people in fact calculate in family matters, whether implicitly or explicitly, in the same way they do when purchasing ordinary goods and services.

Other objections to legalizing the market in babies are more symbolic than pragmatic. For example, to accord a property right in the newborn child to the natural parents seems to some observers to smack of slavery. But allowing a market in adoptions does not entail giving property rights to natural parents for all purposes. Laws forbidding child abuse and neglect would continue to be fully applicable to adoptive parents even if baby sales were permitted. Further, we are speaking only of sales of newborn infants, and do not suggest that parents should have a right to sell older children. The creation of such a right would require identification of the point at which the child is sufficiently mature to be entitled to a voice in his placement. However, the question is largely academic given the lack of any significant market for adopting older children.

Moreover, it is incorrect to equate the possession of property rights with the abuse of the property, even if the property is a human being. For example, a serious problem with foster care is the foster parents' lack of any property rights in the foster child. The better the job the foster parents do in raising the child, the more likely are the natural parents to reclaim the child and thereby prevent the foster parents from reaping the full fruits of their (emotional as well as financial) investment. This possibility in turn reduces the incentive of foster parents to invest in foster children, to the detriment of those children's welfare. . . .

The emphasis placed by critics on the social costs of a free market in babies blurs what would probably be the greatest long-run effect of legalizing the baby market: inducing women who have unintentionally become pregnant to put up the child for adoption rather than raise it themselves or have an abortion. Some of the moral outrage directed against the idea of "trafficking" in babies bespeaks a failure to consider the implications of contemporary moral standards. At a time when illegitimacy was heavily stigmatized and abortion was illegal, to permit the sale of babies would have opened a breach in an otherwise solid wall of social disapproval of procreative activity outside of marriage. At the same time, the stigma of illegitimacy, coupled with the illegality of abortion, assured a reasonable flow of babies to the adoption market. Now that the stigma has diminished and abortion has become a constitutional right, not only has the flow of babies to the (lawful) market contracted but the practical alternatives to selling an unwanted baby have increasingly become either to retain it and raise it as an illegitimate child, ordinarily with no father present, or to have an abortion. What social purposes are served by encouraging these alternatives to baby sale?

The symbolic objections to baby sale must also be compared with the substantial costs that the present system imposes on childless couples, aborted fetuses (if they can be said to incur costs), and children who end up in foster care. In particular, many childless couples undergo extensive, costly, and often futile methods of fertility treatment in order to increase their chances of bearing a child. Some people produce unhealthy offspring (due to various genetic disorders) because of their strong desire to have children. And no doubt many people settle for childlessness because of the difficulties of obtaining an adopted child. . . .

IV. Interim Steps Toward a Full-Fledged Baby Market

We close by speculating briefly on the possibility of taking some tentative and reversible steps toward a free baby market in order to determine experimentally the social costs and benefits of using the market in this area. Important characteristics of a market could be simulated if one or more adoption agencies, which typically already vary their fees for adoption according to the income of the prospective parents, would simply use the surplus income generated by the higher fees to make side payments to pregnant women contemplating abortion to induce them instead to have the child and put it up for adoption.

This experiment would yield evidence with respect to both the demand and supply conditions in the adoption market and would provide information both on the value that prospective adoptive parents attach to being able to obtain a baby and on the price necessary to induce pregnant women to substitute birth for abortion. Follow-up studies of the adopted children, comparing them with children that had been adopted by parents paying lower fees, would help answer the question whether the payment of a stiff fee has adverse consequences on the welfare of the child.

Some states appear not to limit the fees that adoption agencies pay to natural parents. The experiment we propose could be implemented in such states without new legislation.

J. ROBERT S. PRICHARD, A MARKET FOR BABIES?, 34 UNIVERSITY OF TORONTO LAW JOURNAL 341, 348–57 (1984) *

Market Failure Objections

The first line of reaction of the proposal for a baby market is to meet it on its own terms. That is, a critic might ask whether or not this is a situation in which the market would in fact produce optimal results even if the other categories of objections canvassed below are found unpersuasive. A number of doubts might be raised.

First, there is a problem that "good" babies may drive out the "bad." At present, given the shortage of babies, childless couples are prepared to adopt children who are available although, in the eyes of the adopting parents, less than perfect. If the market proposal were adopted, the supply of children with highly desired characteristics would increase and the demand for other children would diminish. This would presumably increase the number of unadopted children suffering from retardation, birth defects, and other undesired characteristics who would subsequently become foster-children. This would presumably reduce the level of welfare of both these children and society in general and must be counted as a substantial negative effect of the market proposal.

Second, there may be some significant information imperfections in the proposed market. While the market mechanism would encourage the disclosure of information concerning the newborns, there would, of course, be an incentive for mothers to disclose the good information and withhold the bad. . . .

Distributive Concerns . . .

An alternative formulation of the distributive concern is that the rich would get all the "good" babies. In response it should first be noticed that the objection seems to assume that this does not happen already, thus ignoring the reality that one's income and wealth are generally thought by adoption agencies to be important variables in determining one's suitability for parenthood. The objection also seems to ignore the prospect of an increased supply of "good" babies which one would anticipate under the market system. That is, if supply were held fixed, the concern might be persuasive in that the rich would presumably be better able to pay in order to satisfy their desires for children with characteristics found most desirable by adopting parents. However, under the market system the supply of such children would presumably be dramatically increased, leaving the rich with what they want but also leaving many others fully satisfied. Again, the objection seems unpersuasive.

Any arguments as to distributive effects of the proposal must also be counterbalanced by the distributive effect identified earlier of a shift in rents to the suppliers of children, that is, mothers, who would be drawn from a generally poorer class and away from the crooks, shady lawyers, shady

---

* Reprinted by permission of the author and the publisher.

physicians, and others who at present trade on the tragedy of the existing regulatory failure and the fears of pregnant women.

One way of testing whether the issue of the distributive impact of the market proposal goes to the core of one's objection to it is to ask whether one would feel better about the proposal if the market were made wealth neutral as opposed to wealth sensitive. If not, then distributive arguments are probably not the central source of one's intuitive opposition to the proposal.

Cost of Costing

Another principled objection to the market focuses on one of its inevitable aspects: the creation of prices. The concern is that a market for babies would generate negative secondary consequences as a result of the fact that a market mechanism by definition generates explicit prices. In particular, the pricing of babies might violate two principles, each of which we hold dear. The first is that life is infinitely valuable — "a pearl beyond price." With prices of $3,000 per baby, the reality of the limited price of life (at least at the point of creation) and the ideal of the infinitely valuable would contrast starkly. The second principle is that all lives are equally valuable. With higher prices for white than non-white children, and higher prices for healthy than sick children, and other similar forms of price differentials, the reality and the ideal would again clash.

The concern here is real but difficult to evaluate. It is but one example of a much more general problem of public policy. Whenever life is at stake the difficulties of pricing and of costing must be faced. Thus, whether it is the standard of care in tort law, the design of a Pinto, highway design, or medical research one cannot avoid implicitly or explicitly dealing with the price of life. Perhaps it is the degree of explicitness that would be inherent in this scheme that gives rise to the vigor of the opposition. It may also be that the differences in prices would correspond with differences which we strive particularly hard to overcome by means of other social policies. That is, to the extent that differences in price fell along racial grounds, to adopt a policy of a market for babies would be directly contradictory to the wide range of social policies designed to minimize discrimination on racial grounds. . . .

The Absence of a Relationship Between Willingness to Pay and Quality of Parent

Another line of attack on the proposal would be to point out that while willingness to pay for a commodity may be the best measure of desire, people may desire children for the wrong reasons. That is, someone may wish to acquire a child for the purpose of beating or otherwise abusing it, rather than loving it or caring for it. This is no doubt true, but again does it go the heart of the problem? Presumably the same perverted desires motivate people to give birth naturally. We do not in Canadian society require an ex ante check on the reasons for having natural children, and thus one must question why ex ante review of suitability for parenting should be required under the market scheme. However, even if some ex ante scheme is desired (as it is under the existing regulatory mechanism), it is, of course, not inconsistent with having a market scheme of allocation. That is, it would be quite simple to require anyone wishing to make a bid in the baby market first to obtain a parenting certificate from some regulatory agency. This license would be granted or denied on the basis of whether or not one met the minimum necessary qualifications for parenting. There would be no limit on the number of certificates granted. If this step were adopted, it is difficult to see how the divergences of willingness to pay and quality of parent would be any more extreme under the market for babies proposal than under the existing regulatory mechanism. . . .

The Improper Objective

The market for babies proposal would meet what is at present the unmet demand of childless couples who wish to adopt a child and are unable to do so as a result of the insufficient supply of children. A critic might suggest that the proposal is directed towards a social end which is misconceived from the start. That is, it can be argued that the purpose of the existing process is not to meet the desires of childless couples for children, but rather to take care of a limited number of unwanted newborns, with the merely incidental side effect of bringing great joy and happiness to childless couples. Under the latter formulation the number of couples satisfied or left dissatisfied is largely irrelevant to our judgment about the allocative mechanism, since it is assumed that the function of the system is to distribute those babies which are produced as a by-product of the existing sexual and marital activities and rules. The success of the mechanism should therefore be judged in terms of the welfare of the unwanted newborns, not that of childless couples. Furthermore, any system which would increase the supply of such children requiring adoption would be directly counter-productive in terms of the objective of designing a system whose sole function is the distribution of unwanted babies.

This line of argument is compelling if it is accepted that no weight should be give to the preferences of childless couples. How such a judgment could be taken, though, is somewhat more problematic, since it is not at all clear what value is being preserved or promoted by means of denying this fundamental happiness to the large number of couples left childless under the existing scheme. If it were possible to identify that value, perhaps all the other concerns about the market solution might be derived from it.

MARGARET JANE RADIN, MARKET-INALIENABILITY, 100 HARVARD LAW REVIEW 1849, 1879–81, 1925–26 (1987) *

In some cases market discourse itself might be antagonistic to the interests of personhood. . . .

What is wrong with this rhetoric? . . . [F]or all but the deepest enthusiast, market rhetoric seems intuitively out of place here, so inappropriate that it is either silly or somehow insulting to the value being discussed.

One basis for this intuition is that market rhetoric conceives of bodily integrity as a fungible object. A fungible object is replaceable with money or other objects. A fungible object can pass in and out of the person's possessions without effect on the person as long as its market equivalent is given in exchange. To speak of personal attributes as fungible objects—alienable "goods"—is intuitively wrong. . . . Bodily integrity is an attribute and not an object. We feel discomfort or even insult, and we fear degradation or even loss of the value involved, when bodily integrity is conceived of as a fungible object.

Systematically conceiving of personal attributes as fungible objects is threatening to personhood because it detaches from the person that which is integral to the person. Such a conception makes actual loss of the attribute easier to countenance. . . . If my bodily integrity is an integral personal attribute, not a detachable object, then hypothetically valuing my bodily integrity in money is not far removed from valuing *me* in money. For all but the [market enthusiast], that is inappropriate treatment of a person. . . .

. . . If we permit babies to be sold, we commodify not only the mother's (and father's) babymaking capacities . . . but we also conceive of the baby itself in market rhetoric. When the baby becomes a commodity, all of its personal attributes—sex, eye color, predicted I.Q., predicted height, and the like— become commodities as well. . . . [T]o conceive of infants in market rhetoric is . . . to conceive of the people they will become in market rhetoric, and to create in those people a commodified self-conception.

NOTES AND QUESTIONS

1. Professor Prichard raises the issue of whether a market for babies would be subject to market failures. What type of market failures does he identify? Are there others he does not mention? Are these amenable to regulation? For example, Posner and Landes concede that some adoptive parents may mistreat babies, but they contend that the answer is to screen parents who are allowed to enter the adoption market.

2. Would you object to the interim steps proposed by Posner and Landes to test out their theory that a market system would increase the number of babies available for adoption without placing the babies in harm's way? If the answer is yes, do you have some noneconomic reason for opposing a market system? One such concern, identified by Prichard (and admitted by Posner and Landes), is that the wealthy could outbid the poor for available babies. Posner and Landes doubt that this would happen. They predict that, if the cost of adopting babies were increased, there would be more babies for adoption, provided that mothers received a fee for offering a baby for adoption. Thus, the price of adoption would be reasonable, such as the price of a new car. In Chapter 2, we noted that as price increases, so does supply. Is there any reason to think that this "economic rule" would not apply in this context? Do you agree that paying mothers to put their babies up for adoption would make it possible for more persons to adopt children? Assuming that the price would not be within the means of many Americans, is wealth a grounds for objecting to a market system?

3. Professor Radin's objection is fundamental: the use of price demeans children and harms our social fabric. What are Professor Prichard's responses to this argument? Do you find them satisfactory?

4. Professor Prichard notes that the market system would have the advantage that the money spent on adoption would shift to "suppliers of children, that is, mothers, who would be drawn from a generally poorer class and away from the crooks, shady lawyers, shady physicians, and others who at present trade on the tragedy of the existing regulatory failure and the fears of pregnant women." Do you agree this is an advantage? Professor Radin, who opposes an adoption market, finds that the fact that poor women might benefit from such a market creates a dilemma:

> [I]s women's personhood injured by allowing or by disallowing commodification of sex and reproduction? The argument that commodification empowers women is that recognition of these alienable entitlements will enable a needy group—poor women—to improve their relatively powerless, oppressed condition, an improvement that would be beneficial to personhood. . . .
>
> The rejoinder is that, on the contrary, commodification will harm personhood by powerfully symbolizing, legitimating, and enforcing class division and gender oppression. . . .
>
> But the surrejoinder is that noncommodification of women's capabilities under current circumstances, represents not a brave new world of human flourishing, but rather a perpetuation of the old order that submerges women in oppressive status relationships. . . .
>
> These conflicting arguments illuminate the problem with the prophylactic argument for market-inalienability. If we now permit commodification, we may exacerbate oppression of women—the suppliers. If we now disallow commodification—without . . . large scale redistribution of social wealth and power—we force women to remain in circumstances that they themselves believe are worse than becoming sexual market-suppliers. Thus, the alternatives seem subsumed by a need for social progress. . . .
>
> Whether one analogizes paid surrogacy to the sale of sexual services, or to baby selling, the underlying concerns are the same. First, there is the possibility of further oppression of poor or ignorant women, which must be weighed against a possible step toward their liberation through economic gain through a new alienable entitlement. . . . Second, there is the possibility that human surrogacy should be completely prohibited because it expresses an inferior conception of human flourishing. Third, there is the possibility a domino effect of commodification in rhetoric that leaves us all inferior human beings.[49]

5. Medical science has made tremendous strides in the transplantation of human organs. In many medical areas, the medical technology for such transplants is sufficiently well developed that the principal problem is now a lack of organs. Consider the following hypothetical, which addresses how scarce organs ought to be distributed:

---

[49] Radin, *Market-Inalienability*, 100 HARV. L. REV. 1849, 1916–17, 1930. Copyright © 1978 University of Chicago. Reprinted by permission. *See, also* M. RADIN, CONTESTED COMMODITIES (1996).

The year is 2015. The good news is that medical scientists have perfected the mechanical heart. The bad news is that, for the foreseeable future, only 150 hearts can be produced each year. You are chairperson of a congressional committee that is attempting to determine how the machines ought to be distributed. Your choices are: (1) first-come, first-serve; (2) a lottery; (3) an auction; or (4) assignment by an administrative agency created for that purpose according to a "public interest" standard. Which method should the country adopt?

Which method of distribution do you favor and why?

6. The first-come, first-serve method is a general description of the method now used to allocate donated human organs. Hospitals responsible for the allocation process typically allocate an organ to the person who has been waiting the longest for it among the group of persons whom the physicians believe can benefit from the transplant. What are the advantages of this approach? What are the disadvantages? Why might a lottery be a fairer method of allocation than first-come, first-serve? What are the disadvantages to a lottery?

What are the advantages of a market system?[50] What are the disadvantages? One advocate of a market system has offered the following analysis of government allocation:

> Much of what we observe about the structure and organization of the human-tissue industry can be traced to two features of current regulation: the insistence on altruistic donation and the failure to specify the "owner" of the donated tissue, to whom its economic value would accrue.
>
> The failure to specify clear property rights to tissue means that in principle there is nothing to prevent middlemen from reaping the value of donated tissue. Nonprofit organ-procurement agencies, for-profit transplant surgeons, and others therefore compete very intensely—and inefficiently—to acquire a property right to the tissue. . . .
>
> To understand this, it is helpful to consider other activities that involve common resources. Analyses of commercial fishing, to take one example, conclude that the economic value of the free resource—the fish—rarely reaches the consumer. Instead it is dissipated: if the fishermen can collude, they limit their fishing and charge higher

[50] For further reading, see Blair & Kaserman, *The Economics and Ethics of Alternative Cadaveric Organ Procurement,* 8 YALE J. REG. 403 (1991); Guttmann, *The Meaning of "The Economics and Ethics of Cadaveric Organ Procurement Policies,"* 8 YALE J. REG. 453 (1991); Calabresi, *Do We Own Our Bodies?,* 1 HEALTH MATRIX 5 (1991); Murray, *Are We Morally Obligated To Make Gifts Of Our Bodies?,* 1 HEALTH MATRIX 19 (1991).

A new system of organizing the network for organ sharing was adopted in 1999. *See* Stolberg, *Agreement Allows New System for Organ Sharing,* NEW YORK TIMES, Nov. 12, 1999, at A1. The new system requires the United Network for Organ Sharing, which is the nonprofit agency responsible for coordinating distribution of organs under contract to the federal government, to share organs across the regional areas into which the country is divided for purposes of distributing organs. When an organ becomes available, it is offered first within the region in which it became available and then regionally or in some cases nationally. Under prior arrangements, someone in a region, who was not as ill as someone in a nearby region, might have received the organ instead.

monopoly prices; if they cannot collude, they engage in inefficient activities such as overfishing. In either case, the retail price of a can of tuna fish may not reflect the fact that the fish itself was free. . . .

7. When Congress banned organ sales, it made organs a free resource to users. Yet organs are not free from society's point of view. The following scenario illustrates the wastefulness of treating human tissue as if it were a free resource in the commons. Suppose that a transplant surgeon is willing to pay up to $50,000 for a particular type of human tissue, because a patient is willing to pay him that sum on top of the fee for the surgery. If perfect markets exist, the $50,000 will go to the donor of the tissue. If they do not, the surgeon must convince someone to donate the tissue. He would prefer to do this at no cost, but if he cannot, he will still be willing to spend up to $50,000 to procure the tissue somehow. He might for example, pay for television solicitations to attract donors, charter a private plane to visit them, or hire lawyers to represent him in conflicts with other surgeons seeking the tissue. Although these expenditures would all be legal (and would be rational for the surgeon, who can collect his surgical fee only if he has tissue to transplant), they are wasteful from society's point of view. Why is a noncommercial system preferable if the money generated by tissue production goes not to the donor but to a surgeon, a television studio, an aviator, or a lawyer?[51]

[51] Thorne, *Tissue Transplants: The Dilemma of the Body's Growing Value,* 98 THE PUBLIC INTEREST 37, 37–48 (Winter, 1990). Copyright © 1990 by National Affairs, Inc. Reprinted by permission.

Chapter 12

PUBLIC GOODS: SOCIAL WELFARE PROGRAMS AND SUBSIDIES

A. SOCIAL WELFARE PROGRAMS

The United States is a welfare state. An expansive web of social welfare programs totaling over $850 billion guards millions of Americans. Table 12-1 indicates the components of this support according to the latest available data.

Table 12-1

FEDERAL SOCIAL WELFARE PROGRAMS (in billions of dollars)	
Social Insurance (1995)	*Means-Tested* (1998)
Social Security • OASDI (331.6) • Medicare (164.7) Public Employee Retirement (67.0) Railroad Retirement (8.1) Unemployment Compensation (5.2) Workers Compensation (3.0) Other Programs (0.2)	Medical Benefits (113.8) • Medicaid (100.2) Cash Aid (73.8) • TANF (29.7) • SSI (27.3) • Income Tax Credit Refunds (25.3) Food Benefits (33.4) • Food Stamps (20.4) • School Lunches (5.2) Housing Benefits (26.9) Education Aid (17.0) Services (7.3) Job Training (3.8) Energy Assistance (1.3)
TOTAL: $579.8	TOTAL: $277.3

Source: Statistical Abstract of the United States (2002), tables 601, 605

Table 12-1 indicates several significant aspects of the social welfare programs. The first is that eligibility is determined in one of two ways. A person is entitled to benefits in the column marked "Social Insurance" because the person and the person's employer have contributed to the cost of the program. There are no income tests to qualify for one of these programs. Social security is the largest of this category of social welfare programs. Its two principle components are payments to the disabled and elderly (OASDI) and medical assistance to the same persons (Medicare). In the other category of programs, a person must be below a certain income level in order to qualify for benefits. Thus, the government determines eligibility by some form of "means" testing.

A second significant aspect of social benefits is that some are in the form of cash payments and others provide in-kind benefits. Social insurance programs, with the exception of Medicare, provide cash benefits to recipients. Medicare reimburses physicians for services provided to the elderly. All of the means-tested programs, except those marked "cash aid" provide in-kind services. For example, food benefits are in the form of food stamps, which can be exchanged for food at grocery stores or school lunches. Similarly, housing benefits are in the form of vouchers that can be exchanged for housing or in government-owned housing that is directly provided to recipients. Cash aid is largely composed of three programs: Temporary Aid to Needy Families (TANF), Social Security assistance (SSI) to low-income persons who are aged, blind or disabled, and income tax refunds for persons who earn below a certain amount of money (Income Tax Credit Refunds). You can also note that means-tested programs provide a variety of types of assistance, including medical care, food, housing, education, job training, and others, while social insurance programs, with the exception of Medicare, provide money directly to the recipients.

There is a third important aspect to how social welfare is structured in the United States. The federal government administers some programs, delegates the management of others to the states, and still others are jointly administered. As discussed in more detail later, welfare reforms that occurred in 1996 are notable, in part, because they ceded to the states more autonomy in the design of programs to support poor families.

The structure of social welfare is the result of policy choices the country has made concerning who is eligible for various programs and how these programs should be administered. Thus, for example, all social insurance programs, except Medicare, provide cash aid to the recipients, while many of the means-tested programs provide in-kind aid only. Social welfare policies have changed over the country's history, and continue to change. In this section, you will study the general justifications for social welfare programs, the history of such programs, the two dominant models of welfare policy ("social insurance" and "means-tested" assistance) and three specific reform issues (dependency, devolution, and aid to immigrants.

1. JUSTIFICATIONS FOR SOCIAL WELFARE

Two general arguments have been advanced to support the use of government as an instrument for transferring wealth among citizens. One justification is that social welfare programs constitute a "public good," which is a market failure rationale. The other arguments justify social welfare on the basis of equity and fairness.

a. PUBLIC GOOD JUSTIFICATIONS

A public good is one that can be consumed by many people at the same time. For example, while only one person can eat a candy bar, the United States Army protects the security of everyone in the United States simultaneously. One person's consumption of the protection the army offers does not prevent anyone else from also enjoying that benefit. By comparison, a candy bar is a private good, because one person's consumption prevents anyone else from consuming the candy bar.

There are two types of public goods: excludable and nonexcludable. If a public good is excludable, persons who do not pay for the goods can be excluded from obtaining any benefit from them. For example, although one person's attendance at a movie does not prevent others from also watching it (assuming the move theater is not full), it is easy to prevent persons who do not pay for the movie from seeing it. By comparison, the existence of an army creates nonexcludable benefits for everyone in a country, and there is no practical way to exclude from protection those who do not pay.

Any effort to create an army in a private market would fail because there is no way to exclude nonpayers from obtaining the benefits provided by the army's protection. In the economic literature, such persons are known as "free riders." A free-rider will not pay for a public good, such as the army, because it is economically rational not to do so. As long as others pay for the public good, they have no means to exclude the free riders from also obtaining the benefits of the good. As a result, no one will pay, because everyone will wait for someone else to act. That is, everyone will attempt to gain a "free ride" on someone else's payment. The government, however, can avoid this result by purchasing public goods and paying for them with compulsory taxation.

The public goods rationale can justify governmental efforts at redistribution in three ways. First, governmental transfer programs solve the free rider problem that otherwise would frustrate private attempts at charity. Thus, income redistribution is "collective charity." Second, income transfer programs can be understood as a means to ensure social stability. Finally, income redistribution can also be understood as a form of social insurance.

Free rider problem: Although donors to a charity might like to see income inequity reduced, no one person acting alone can make a significant contribution toward the reduction of inequality. If inequality is to be reduced, it must be a collective effort. But without a guarantee that others will participate, few or no donors may participate in a private charity, because of the free rider effect. Donors can overcome this problem by choosing to have the government collect their donations in the form of taxes.

The free rider problem can be described as a "Prisoner's Dilemma." This analytical construct, or "game" as policy analysts call it, establishes that people acting in their own self-interest can be worse off if they do not cooperate.[1]

The following situation illustrates this model. Suppose that you and Molly, your confederate, are about to stand trial for a crime. You must decide whether to turn state's evidence and testify against Molly. You receive the following offer from the district attorney: If Molly remains silent, you will go free if you testify, and receive a one-year sentence if you keep silent. If Molly testifies, you will receive a nine-year sentence if you testify, and a ten-year sentence if you keep silent. You know that Molly has been offered the same deal, but you are not allowed to talk with her.

---

[1] *See* R. HARDIN, COLLECTIVE ACTION 22–30 (1982); R. LUCE & H. RAIFFA, GAMES AND DECISIONS 94–102 (1957).

The following matrix describes the previous information:

		Molly	
You	**Testify**		**Keep Silent**
Testify		9 yrs	10 yrs
	9 yrs	0 yrs	
Keep Silent		0 yrs	1 yr
	10 yrs	1 yr	

The upper left-hand quadrant, for example, shows that if you and Molly both testify, you both will receive nine years. According to the lower right quadrant, if you both keep silent, each of you will receive a year.

Note that your dominant strategy is to testify. A strategy is dominant when it is at least as good as, and sometimes better than, any alternative strategy, no matter what anyone else does. Molly's dominant strategy is also to testify. Thus, without some means of cooperating, you will both end up with a nine-year penalty. If you could cooperate, however, each of you would end up with only a one year penalty, because you would both agree to remain silent.

The following example considers the public goods problem as a Prisoner's Dilemma.[2] Suppose that you have been asked to contribute $100 towards the construction of a local school. The same request is made of your 999 neighbors. Your return on your investment is your portion of the external benefits that the school will generate for your community. Assume this return is only $1. It is therefore economically rational for you to refuse to contribute the $100. But if you do contribute, you will not only gain a $1 return, but all of your neighbors will also gain a $1 return on your investment of $100. Thus, your $100 donation generates $1,000 for the entire community. Nevertheless, there is no economic incentive for you to contribute. Your neighbors are in the same position. They also lack an incentive to contribute, because they will get back only $1 for their investment.

The return on investment in this hypothetical can be diagrammed as in the following matrix (the top figure in each quadrant represents the return for each neighbor; the bottom figure represents your return). If neither you nor your neighbors contribute, there are no benefits (top left quadrant). If you contribute, but your neighbors do not, you will lose $99 (bottom left quadrant). Your contribution generates $1 of benefit for everyone, but you lose $99 because you contributed $100 and obtained a return of $1. If your neighbors contribute and you do not (top right quadrant), you gain $999 because you get a return of $1 from each $100 investment by each of the 999 neighbors. Each of your neighbors gains $899. In this circumstance, each neighbor

---

2 This example is based on D. SCHMIDTZ, THE LIMITS OF GOVERNMENT: AN ESSAY ON THE PUBLIC GOODS ARGUMENT 62–65 (1991).

obtains a $999 return from the others' investment, but each also contributed $100, which produces a net gain of $899. Finally, if both you and your neighbors donate (bottom right quadrant), everyone gains $900. You and each of your neighbors obtains a $1000 return from each others' investment, but you and each of your neighbors contributed $100, which produces a net gain of $900.

You	Each of your 999 neighbors	
	Do Not Contribute	Contribute
Do Not Contribute	$0	$899
	$0	$999
Contribute	$1	$900
	($99)	$900

What is your dominant strategy? If you do not contribute, you will either gain nothing (right top quadrant) or $999 (left top quadrant). If you do contribute, you will lose $99 (left bottom quadrant), or gain $900 (right bottom quadrant). Thus, you are better off not making the donation. Since all of your neighbors would also have the same strategy, no one will donate the money, and the community will not gain any of the external benefits generated by having a school.

You might realize that you and your neighbors will be worse off if none of you makes a donation. But note that if you act unilaterally to give $100, you will be worse off. What you need is some assurance that if you give $100, each of your neighbors will do likewise. If you and your neighbors agree that your local government can levy a $100 tax on each of you, the Prisoner's Dilemma is solved.

Social stability and investment: Income transfers can also be viewed as producing two other types of public goods. One is a benefit in the form of increased social stability. The other is protection of citizens against future economic uncertainty. This explanation considers such programs to be a form of insurance, by which citizens seek to protect themselves against the uncertainty inherent in a market economy. Programs such as unemployment, and workers' and disability compensation, could be explained in this manner. But the explanation could also be used to defend non-work-related transfer programs. For example:

> Many of the things that people might desire protection against are commonly referred to as "accidents of birth." A person who contracts multiple sclerosis will face a more constrained set of options than someone who does not. A transfer program from those who do not have multiple sclerosis to those who do might be conceptualized as not truly a transfer program, but as the outcome of a type of insurance contract

that everyone would agree to, if they had to participate in some genetic lottery. This would represent social insurance applied to individual rather than industrial situations.[3]

b. EQUITY AND FAIRNESS

An argument for redistribution can also be made as a matter of social preference for some degree of income equality. The economist Herbert Simon spoke up for this justification when he said that he found inequality beyond a certain degree to be "distinctly evil or unlovely."[4] Understood in this manner, the welfare system can be viewed as the result of citizens having preferences for different degrees of inequality, with the median preference winning out in a collective choice process.[5]

Social justice theorists such as John Rawls have offered a principled basis for social welfare programs.[6] Rawls asks what choices persons would make about the basic institutional arrangements in their society if these choices were made before they had a good idea of their comparative income prospects. Relying on this hypothetical construct, which he calls the *veil of ignorance,* Rawls argues that it is plausible that individuals might make a different choice concerning social arrangements relating to income if they knew only the structure of that income, and not their particular location within that structure, than if they knew their actual or probable location. Under such circumstances, he reasons that people would prefer what he calls the *difference principle,* which holds that increases in the degree of inequality are to be supported only if they result in higher incomes for the least well-off members of society. Professor Wagner explains:

> The difference principle is sometimes referred to as the *maximin principle,* to indicate that in choosing among alternative social arrangements relating to income, the one to be chosen is the one which maximizes the minimum income. For instances, consider a model in which there are two people, or two sets of people, and compare two regimes governing the production and distribution of income. Under one regime—call it egalitarian regime—total income is $100, with the richer and poorer members of society receiving $60 and $40 respectively. Under the other regime—call it a liberal regime—total income is $120, with the richer and the poorer members of society receiving $90 and $30 respectively. The maximin principle would select the egalitarian over the liberal regime, because the poorer member of society has a larger income under the egalitarian regime.[7]

---

[3] R. WAGNER, TO PROMOTE THE GENERAL WELFARE: MARKET PROCESSES VS. POLITICAL TRANSFERS 38 (1989).

[4] H. SIMON, PERSONAL INCOME TAXATION 19 (1938).

[5] Breit, *Income Redistribution and Efficiency Norms, in* REDISTRIBUTION THROUGH PUBLIC POLICY (Hochman & Peterson eds., 1974).

[6] J. RAWLS, A THEORY OF JUSTICE (1975).

[7] WAGNER, *supra* note 3, at 34-35.

NOTES AND QUESTIONS

1. Do you find one policy justification for welfare more convincing than the others? Can there be more than one justification for the welfare state? Or, do the different justifications lead to a different amount of wealth redistribution?

2. Although social welfare programs can be justified on both economic and noneconomic grounds, the method of justification can lead to different policy decisions. Under the economic rationale, spending on welfare would be subject to a cost-benefit test. In economic terms, it is useful to spend money on welfare as long as the benefits from this investment (in terms of greater economic productivity, reduced crime, etc.) are greater than the cost of the welfare programs. By comparison, analyzing welfare in terms of noncommodity values may justify spending more money on welfare than would be indicated under a cost-benefit test. This would be true even if the level of spending did not eliminate all of the effects of poverty.

Is it appropriate to apply a cost-benefit test to determine the amount that the government should spend on that program? How should we determine how much to spend if our goal is equity or fairness?

3. The Prisoner's Dilemma explanation assumes that a person has only an economic motivation for making a charitable contribution and that it is economically irrational for people to make any contribution to a charity. Are people solely motivated by economic motives when they make such contributions? If so, how does a charity ever raise any money? Is it fair to say that the free rider effect makes it more difficult for charities to raise money?

4. Critics of the public goods justification argue that some public goods can be produced without government intervention. For example, David Schmidtz proposes the use of "assurance contracts" to overcome free rider problems:

> The purpose of the contract is to give each party an assurance that his contribution will not be wasted on a public goods project that is financially undersupported. . . . To provide such an assurance, the contract incorporates a feature similar to a "money-back guarantee." The contract is enforceable against a contractor if and only if the rest of the group agrees to contribute enough to ensure that the project's total funding is sufficient [to make the project viable]. . . . The contract assures the individual that if the rest of the group does not agree to contribute enough, the individual contributes nothing.[8]

For example, charities for muscular dystrophy or lung disease usually announce a fund-raising target and then rely on telethons or door-to-door solicitation to raise the money. Schmidtz recommends that instead a charity should announce its fund-raising goal and guarantee that pledges will not be collected until and unless the total amount reaches the announced target. How does the "assurance contract" solve the free rider problem? Is this solution one which can be applied to support for the poor? Why or why not?

---

[8] SCHMIDTZ, *supra* note 2, at 66.

2. HISTORY OF SOCIAL WELFARE

This social consensus that some social welfare programs are justified does not mean that social welfare is noncontroversial. Indeed, the opposite is true. While generally no one would accept the idea of permitting people to starve or to go without essential medical care, there is considerably less of a consensus concerning the size of social welfare programs and how they should be structured. This lack of agreement is reflected in the history of social welfare in this country.

The treatment of the poor in England influenced social welfare in this country until the Great Depression, when the New Deal fundamentally changed the approach to welfare. Further modifications occurred in the Kennedy and Johnson administrations. Most recently, the Congress enacted welfare reforms in 1996 which made fundamental changes in federal welfare policy.

a. THE ENGLISH LEGACY

The Elizabethan Poor Laws, adopted in the 1600s, distinguished the able-bodied poor, who were to be put to work (even if they were children), and the impotent poor, who were the only persons eligible for direct assistance. This policy was firmly rooted in the belief that "[t]o be poor was not merely the result of social circumstances or the fate of nature; lurking in the background must be some element of slothfulness."[9]

These arrangements lasted in England for nearly two hundred years, "but eventually [these] institutions, locally financed and adapted to a pre-industrial economy, came under pressure from population growth, increased social mobility, industrialization and economic fluctuations. By 1795 food shortages and inflation resulting from war and bad harvests had spread poverty from the unemployed to those in work, giving rise to various local initiatives . . . that . . . extended aid to people in work."[10] Assistance to the poor came under attack from critics, such as Bentham, who believed it caused moral degeneracy among recipients, and Malthus, who argued that poor relief would cause excessive population growth. Although a 1832 Royal Commission endorsed the continuation of poor relief, it insisted that the amount of assistance, and the manner in which it was administered, should place recipients in a worse position than the employed. The Poor Law Amendment Act of 1834 endorsed these principles, which led the government to discourage claims for relief by making the acceptance of assistance highly unpleasant and stigmatizing.[11]

The responsibility for caring for the poor in this country reflected English approaches and attitudes. Early local arrangements included the giving of food, incarceration in almshouses, or indentured service. As the number of poor persons increased, particularly in the cities, because of industrialization and urbanization, reliance on almshouses or workhouses replaced other forms of relief. Most states eventually passed laws designating workhouses as the

---

[9] A. BERNEY, J. GOLDBERG, J. DOOLEY, & D. CARROLL, LEGAL PROBLEMS OF THE POOR 591 (1975).

[10] N. BARR, THE ECONOMICS OF THE WELFARE STATE 14 (2d ed. 1993).

[11] *Id.* at 15.

primary method of caring for the poor, but the responsibility for financing and operating them was left to local communities. The impotent poor did not receive special attention until early in the 1900s when states began to establish pensions for the blind, aged, and widows. These provisions were not mandatory, however, and implementation was a local (usually a county) option. Only a few states shared the cost for such pensions with local government.[12]

b. SOCIAL SECURITY ACT OF 1935

The philosophy and structure of public assistance inherited from the English lasted until the Great Depression, when the New Deal reacted to the substantial poverty in the country. By 1933, as much as 25% of the workforce was unemployed; millions of families lost their homes, and thousands of people stood in bread lines each day.[13] The government's initial efforts were to provide jobs on public work projects. This step reflected the reluctance inherited from the English to support those who did not work. This approach, however, was not enough, as Professor Rodgers explains:

> By 1935 the crisis had deepened. The Works Project Administration (WPA) had provided jobs for millions of U.S. citizens, but some 8 million males were still unemployed. It has been estimated that the WPA provided jobs to only one out of every four applicants. Those millions who could not find work, along with the aged, handicapped, and orphans, turned to state and local governments for assistance. Many of the states could not handle the burden. Some cut the size of the grants so that more of the needy could receive some assistance. Others abolished all assistance. The state of New Jersey offered the indigent licenses to beg.[14]

The Roosevelt administration acted to stem the widespread poverty with two initiatives labeled the "Second New Deal." One was deficit spending to stimulate economic growth, and the other was the Social Security Act of 1935. The Act had two components. First, there was a scheme of "social insurance" to assist workers who were temporarily out of work or who were retired. Second, there were "categorical" programs to assist children and persons who could not work because of physical disabilities.

Social insurance: The social insurance programs were conceived as providing compensation to those persons whose incomes were interrupted by unemployment,[15] disability,[16] and retirement.[17] The Act also provided benefits for the survivors of persons eligible for retirement and disability benefits.[18] The goal of these programs was to establish a floor of income to cushion

---

[12] BERNEY, ET AL., *supra* note 9, at 593; F. PIVEN & R. CLOWARD, REGULATING THE POOR: THE FUNCTIONS OF PUBLIC WELFARE 45–49 (1971); *see* POVERTY AND PUBLIC POLICY IN MODERN AMERICA 1–40 (D. Critchlow & E. Hawley eds., 1989).

[13] Rodgers, *The American Welfare System in Transition, in* FUTURES FOR THE WELFARE STATE 298 (N. Furniss ed., 1986).

[14] *Id.* at 298.

[15] 42 U.S.C. §§ 1101-09.

[16] *Id.* § 416(I)(1).

[17] *Id.* §§ 401-33.

[18] *Id.*

the effects on a wage earner and that person's family when the person was unable to work. These programs supplemented workers' compensation, adopted by the states in the 1920s and 1930s, to compensate employees unable to work because of workplace accidents. Workers not covered by Social Security, such as some public workers and railroad employees, were given their own retirement systems, as Table 13-1 indicates.

These programs were described by the Roosevelt administration as "social insurance" in order to maximize public support for them. This description was based on the fact that employees (or their employers) were required to contribute to the insurance fund, and only those who had contributed (or whose employer had contributed) were eligible for benefits.

In 1965, Congress created another important "social insurance" program. The Social Security Act Amendments of 1965 established Medicare, which is a mandatory federal program to finance hospital and related services for retired and other Social Security beneficiaries, funded through payroll deductions.[19] Congress also created a voluntary federal program covering physician and outpatient services, financed by a monthly premium paid by persons receiving Social Security benefits and supplemented by general federal revenues.

Categorical assistance: The Social Security categorical programs established during the New Deal replaced state and local general assistance for four categories of poor persons: the elderly (Old Age Assistance); the blind (Aid to the Blind); the disabled (Aid to the Permanently and Totally Disabled), and dependent children (Aid to Families of Dependent Children (AFDC)). Congress reorganized the first three programs in 1973, and they became Supplemental Security Income (SSI).[20] Though these programs were originally created by the 1935 Act, they were not perceived as "social" programs but

> were perceived to be nothing more nor less than "welfare relief"— largess from the state. The persons who received assistance from the "categorical" programs were not perceived as having contributed directly to a fund from which the assistance was withdrawn. They were provided assistance not because of a preemptive right flowing from previous contributions, but rather because of their debilitating indigency. The monies appropriated for such relief came from general revenue funds and not from a special fund created by compulsory insurance taxation.[21]

Consistent with this orientation, the categorical insurance programs have always relied on a means-test to determine eligibility.

The New Deal revolutionized the country's approach to social welfare benefits because Social Security and other retirement programs were available on a basis other than means-testing. The New Deal was less revolutionary, however, in two other respects. First, it relied on state administration of the means-tested programs created by the 1935 Act. Second, it did not address

---

[19] Pub. L. 89-97, 79 Stat. 286 (codified at 42 U.S.C. §§ 1395-96).

[20] Pub. L. 92-603, 86 Stat. 1465 (1973) (codified at 42 U.S.C. §§ 601-76, 1381–85).

[21] BERNEY, ET AL., *supra* note 9, at 593.

the problems of the poor, other than those persons who came within the categorical programs.

Although the New Deal relied on state administration of means-tested programs, the federal government regulated state administration. Federal supervision reflected the fact that taxpayers at the national level largely financed the categorical programs. This arrangement turned out to be less than satisfactory, since it created multiple layers of legislation and regulations and therefore generated state-federal conflicts. The 1973 legislation creating SSI, mentioned earlier, was a response to this conflict. It moved administration of all of the categorical programs except AFDC to the Department of Health and Human Services (HHS) in the federal government.

Congress has created joint administration of the newer federal programs, notably Medicaid, which provides medical care services for the indigent. In these programs, the states are given some discretion to determine eligibility, but the federal government has established minimum criteria that the states must meet.

States are also involved in social benefits administration in another way. The Social Security Administration (SSA) will hire state agencies as contractors to perform some of the screening services necessary to determine whether a person is eligible for a program. When states perform this latter role, they do not have any discretion to determine eligibility—their role is to apply the federal standards.

c. NEW FRONTIER AND GREAT SOCIETY PROGRAMS

The drafters of the 1935 Act acknowledged the existence of additional persons living in poverty, but they expected economic expansion would take care of the problem of underlying poverty.[22] Although this expectation turned out to be wrong, the plight of the other poor was not recognized as a serious, national problem until the 1960s.

In the 1960s, civil rights advocates were among the first to sound the alarm that "many U.S. citizens of all races were ill-housed, ill-clothed, medically neglected, malnourished, and even suffering from hunger."[23] While politicians and bureaucrats were initially skeptical, the work of policy analysts such as Michael Harrington, author of *The Other America,* and Dwight McDonald, author of "The Invisible Poor" in the *New Yorker,* revealed evidence of acute poverty, malnutrition, and even starvation. Robert Kennedy (D., N.Y.) and Joseph Clark (D., Penn.) testified that their personal tour of the Mississippi delta in Louisiana revealed such conditions. But, as Professor Rodgers reports, the most dramatic documentation of U.S. poverty was yet to come:

> In the mid-1960s the Field Foundation and the Citizens' Crusade against Poverty formed the Citizen's Board of Inquiry into Hunger and Malnutrition in the United States. The Citizens Board['s] . . . findings confirmed the worse suspicions of welfare reform advocates. They discovered within the general population of the United States a

---

[22] *Id.* at 594.

[23] Rodgers, *supra* note 13, at 300.

population that might best be described as an underdeveloped nation. They reported "concrete evidence of chronic hunger and malnutrition in every part of the United States where we have held hearings or conducted field trips.[24]

The ghetto riots of the 1960s served to underscore the previous findings. Although many conservatives regarded these incidents as evidence of a moral breakdown in society, most members of Congress agreed that expanding social programs was important to restoring social order. "Thus, with the cities on fire, and media attention focused on the struggles of the black population and the poverty of millions of U.S. citizens, Congress passed a number of civil rights laws and welfare expansions during the 1960s."[25]

Under the framework of John Kennedy's "New Frontier" and Lyndon Johnson's "Great Society," the federal government set out to address what the states had ignored: the plight of the poor who did not qualify for federal assistance under the categorical programs.[26] As Table 12-1 reveals, these new programs constituted a significant increase in spending to assist the poor. Most of the programs listed under "means-tested," except for "Cash-Aid" programs, originated in this period.

d. PERSONAL RESPONSIBILITY AND WORK OPPORTUNITY RECONCILIATION ACT OF 1996

The expansion of support for the poor in the 1960s became the focus of analysis and debate in the following years. Presidents, commissions, and academics urged changes in the social welfare system, although these sources often disagreed concerning the direction that reform should take. In particular, there was an extensive debate concerning whether welfare generated dependency and a culture of poverty. You will read more about these arguments later in the chapter. In his 1994 State of the Union address, President Clinton promised to fulfill his campaign pledge to "end welfare as we know it." In 1994, House Republicans made welfare reform part of their "Contract with America" pledge in that year's election campaign. Congress and the President eventually agreed on a package of reforms. On August 22, 1996, President Clinton signed the Personal Responsibility and Work Opportunity Reconciliation Act (PRWORA).[27]

PRWORA made two fundamental changes in social welfare policy.[28] First, Congress abolished the AFDC program, which previously provided cash assistance to women and children living in poverty, and replaced the program with block grants to the states known as the "Temporary Assistance For Needy Families" (TANF) program. Second, Congress adopted eligibility rules for TANF that were more restrictive than the previous rules for AFDC eligibility. Congress also restricted eligibility for other programs by adopting more

---

[24] *Id.* at 300–01.

[25] *Id.* at 301.

[26] POVERTY AND PUBLIC POLICY, *supra* note 12, at 219.

[27] Pub. L. No. 104-193, 110 Stat. 2279 [hereinafter PRWORA].

[28] The following description is based on Law, *Ending Welfare As We Know It*, 49 STAN. L. REV. 471 (1997); Katz, *After 60 Years, Most Control Is Passing To States*, CONGRESSIONAL QUARTERLY WEEKLY REPORT, August 3, 1996, at 2190–96.

stringent rules for obtaining Food Stamps, by eliminating the eligibility of legal aliens for most types of benefits, and by reducing the number of children eligible for disability assistance.

TANF block grants: When Congress abolished AFDC, it also eliminated the federal government's guarantee of assistance to poor families. Under AFDC, the states determined who was eligible for assistance, but anyone who was qualified was entitled to aid. No matter how many persons became eligible in one year, the federal and state governments would provide cash aid assistance. Since TANF provides a fixed amount of money to each state for support of needy families, it contains no similar entitlement. If a state has more eligible beneficiaries than it has money under TANF, it will have to provide additional funding or ration the money that is available.

Moreover, unlike AFDC, for which the federal government participated in establishing eligibility rules and the amount of benefits, TANF delegates these functions almost exclusively to the states. For example, states are now free to deny assistance to families who conceive a child after beginning welfare, to unwed parents under the age of 18, and to parents under 18 who do not live at home with an adult and attend school. States, however, are subject to a "maintenance of effort" provision. Each state must continue to spend 80 percent of the amount it spent on AFDC for TANF grants and related purposes. Congress also authorized states to also establish lower benefits for persons who have not lived in the state for the previous twelve months, but the Supreme Court declared this provision to be unconstitutional as a violation of the Fourteenth Amendment right to travel.[29]

Stricter eligibility rules: States have discretion under TANF to establish eligibility rules that are stricter than those that were used under AFDC. Congress, however, also established more stringent federal restrictions. First, there is a five-year total limit on the receipt of TANF benefits, regardless of whether the benefits are consecutive. A state can exempt up to 20 percent of its caseload from this cap, but it can also establish a shorter deadline if it wishes. Second, states are obligated to require most recipients of TANF funds to seek and obtain work. A parent or guardian is required to have a job to receive TANF funds after receiving 24 months of benefits, regardless of whether the benefits are consecutive, or as soon as the state determines that the person is ready to work, if this event occurs first.

Congress also established restricted eligibility rules for Food Stamps for recipients between the ages of 18 and 50 who have no dependents. These persons are restricted to three months of Food Stamps out of every three years unless they work twenty hours or more per week or participate in a work program. Such persons, however, are entitled to an additional three months if they have been laid off. Congress also changed how benefits are calculated for persons who remain eligible for assistance.

Finally, PRWORA changed the definitions of when a child is disabled and eligible for SSI benefits. According to the Congressional Budget Office, about 300,000 children, or 22 percent of the total number of children previously eligible for assistance, will lose their benefits under these changes. However,

---

[29] *Saenz v. Roe,* 526 U.S. 489 (1999).

the 1997 budget agreement set aside $24 billion to finance medical care for children without health insurance.[30] It is not clear the extent to which the new program will replace the benefits denied under the 1996 legislation.

e. SOCIAL WELFARE AFTER TANF

Following passage of TANF, there was a dramatic reduction in the number of persons receiving benefits as compared to AFDC.[31] By 1999, there were fewer than 2.5 million families receiving cash assistance from TANF, which is a 51 percent reduction from the caseload of more than five million families receiving AFDC cash assistance in 1994. By December 2001, the caseload had been reduced to 2.1 million families. There were similar, although less drastic, declines in the other programs for which Congress restricted eligibility.

Research indicates that TANF was a significant cause of these reductions, but other factors, particularly a strong economy, also had an effect. Researchers attribute the decline to movement of former recipients into the workforce, departures due to sanctions or time limits, and a reduction in new applicants because they were diverted into other assistance programs or they were reluctant to conform to TANF mandates, particularly work requirements. The decline in the number of persons receiving assistance started in the mid-1990s, shortly before TANF was passed. This decline is attributable to a strong economy and state experimentation with stricter eligibility rules. Welfare reform and a strong economy continued and strengthened this trend, but so did expansion of the earned income tax credit, which reduced the taxes paid by workers with limited incomes. Preliminary evidence indicates, however, that the TANF caseload started to increase with the economic downturn starting in 2001.[32]

The 1996 welfare reform legislation required that many of the key provisions had to be authorized in 2002. Congress, however, was unable to agree on the necessary legislation and it put the matter off until 2003 by enacting a temporary extension. Republicans sought to toughen the work requirements and to fund programs that would promote marriage. Democrats favored additional funding for childcare and elimination of the restrictions on the eligibility of immigrants for welfare benefits.

3. MODELS OF WELFARE POLICY

The material presented thus far indicates that our ideas concerning the extent and structure of social welfare have changed dramatically throughout our history. In the next excerpt, Professor Diller explains that social welfare policy is an attempt to reconcile (in economic and moral terms) a conflict

---

[30] Pear, *$24 Billion Would Be Set Aside For Medical Care For Children*, NEW YORK TIMES, July 30, 1997, at A13.

[31] The information about the impact of welfare reform is based on Blum and Francis, *Welfare Research Perspectives: Past, Present and Future* (2002) (published by the National Center for Children in Poverty, Mailman School of Public Health, Columbia University), *available at* www.researchforum.org/newsletter/RFbrief2.pdf.

[32] *See* Pierre, *When Welfare Reform Stops Working*, WASHINGTON POST, Jan. 9–13, 2002 (national edition).

between relying on markets to distribute wealth and the provision of governmental assistance to the needy. He considers how the public assistance (or "welfare") and social insurance paradigms address this tension, and how each paradigm impacts social welfare policy.

MATTHEW DILLER, ENTITLEMENT AND EXCLUSION: THE ROLE OF DISABILITY IN THE SOCIAL WELFARE SYSTEM, 44 U.C.L.A. LAW REVIEW 361, 370–384 (1996)[*]

In the Anglo-American tradition, the distribution of economic resources is principally a function of the market. Society has tended to view the provision of income assistance to the poor as conflicting with this system of market distribution. Government income support for those who do not work, or those whose labor is not valued highly by the market, is perceived as undermining the system of rewards for skill and hard work conferred by the market, and as vitiating the discipline that the market metes out for poor effort or low productivity. Moreover, this economic structure is reinforced by a moral structure that legitimizes and bolsters distribution of resources based on market principles. Thus, society perceives work as virtuous and nonwork as an individual moral failure.

Despite these perceptions, there is a long tradition of public aid to the needy. The sources of this tradition are open to debate. Aid to the needy could be viewed as a reflection of lingering ambivalence about the operation of the market. Under this view, impulses to provide aid spring from a recognition that some (or most) of those who fare poorly in the market may not be entirely to blame for their circumstances. Others have explained the tradition of assistance as a device to maintain social order while preserving the pool of available labor. Regardless of its source and fluctuations in intensity, the impulse to temper the most extreme negative outcomes of the market economy runs deep.

Social welfare policy is an attempt to reconcile these conflicting principles, both in economic and in moral terms. Moreover, it functions as a public statement of the demands that society places on individuals, and the obligations that society owes in return. Because of this communicative function, welfare policy contains a symbolic content that extends beyond the issue of allocating public funds.

Our society relies on two paradigms for the provision of assistance—public assistance and social insurance. Each of these paradigms seeks to reconcile the tension between the principles of a market economy and the impulses to aid the needy, and communicates a set of expectations and values.

A. The Public Assistance Paradigm

The public assistance paradigm relies on two means of softening the tension between the free market and aid to the needy: the provision of aid based on

---

[*] Originally published in 44 UCLA L. Rev. 361. Copyright 1996, The Regents of the University of California. All Rights Reserved.

categories and the reliance on features that deter potential recipients from
seeking benefits.

1. The Categorical Approach

The absence of any comprehensive program of income support for the needy
is a basic characteristic of the system that grew out of the Elizabethan poor
law and, in important respects, remains with us today. Public assistance
programs sort people into different categories and provide benefits based on
the status of each applicant with respect to these categories. Examples of these
categories include old age, parents and their children, and disability.

The unifying principle behind the categorical system is clear: Each category
represents a reason for being out of the labor market, either temporarily or
permanently, that is to some extent socially acceptable. Individuals who do
not meet the criteria of any of these categories receive only minimal assistance. This categorical system preserves the primacy of market-based distribution of resources by withholding aid to those who do not fit into any of the
established categories. Under this approach, poverty alone does not qualify
an individual for aid. In the absence of a socially acceptable reason for this
poverty, as reflected in the categories, poverty is considered a personal failure
to succeed in the labor market. Individuals with socially acceptable explanations for absence from the work force constitute the "worthy" or "deserving"
poor; individuals without such excuses are deemed to be "unworthy."

Moreover, the system assigns the "worthy" poor moral rankings that reflect
a social judgment about the legitimacy of the need and the relative threat to
the market economy posed by the provision of assistance to each of the
categories. Indeed, our society goes to great lengths to differentiate between
these categories and to create a hierarchy among them. The programs vary
widely in social status, generosity of benefits, security of financing, and
efficiency of administration. The result is a complex pecking order of programs
that serve to exemplify society's moral judgment about each category. As Joel
Handler has written, the different characteristics of the programs reflect
"different social attitudes towards the category of potential beneficiaries."
Where the social consensus about the worthiness of a category is strongest,
the program is the most generous and the most secure. When the social consensus is weaker, the programs tend to be more parsimonious and more
controversial. . . .

2. Deterrent Features of Public Assistance

Although the categories established as bases of eligibility for assistance
represent judgments that in these situations need is, at least to a degree,
legitimate, and that the provision of aid will not undermine the principle of
market distribution, society has also sought to uphold the primacy of the
market by making the terms of relief onerous and unattractive.[31] Thus, to
the extent that society is uncertain about either the establishment of a

---

[31] This tradition descends from the 19th-century approach to public aid for the poor, which
focused on the institution of the poorhouse.

category or its ability to determine who belongs in the category, it can deter all but the most desperate from utilizing an aid program. Although the arsenal of deterrents is extensive,[32] two deterrents that are almost always associated with public assistance are means testing and social stigma.

Means testing ostensibly serves the purpose of determining the degree of need. As implemented by assistance agencies, however, it results in a remarkable intrusion into the recipient's life. All funds that the recipient receives or spends become government business, leading to government oversight of the way the recipient manages his or her life. . . .

Related to this loss of control is the social stigma that accompanies receipt of public assistance. Society views receipt of public assistance as a sign of failure. Thus, even though the recipient may fall into a category that is to some degree excused from the work force, those within that category who turn to the government for aid are still branded.

In sum, under the public assistance paradigm, the principle of market distribution is protected through the restriction of assistance to specified categories of individuals whose needy status can be ascribed to some source other than poor performance in the labor market. As an added protection, aid is provided on onerous terms and in a manner that conveys social failure in order to deter use of these categorical programs. By varying the number and intensity of these deterrent factors, society can fine tune its attitude toward a category.

B. The Social Insurance Paradigm

Social insurance is an intellectual framework, developed in the early twentieth century and promoted in subsequent years, that provides an alternative means of addressing the tension between market distribution and the provision of assistance. It seeks to avoid this tension through reliance on an analogy to insurance as a means of legitimizing payment of benefits. Indeed, in several ways social insurance even reinforces the distribution of rewards and punishment conferred by the market.

Under the insurance analogy, individuals contribute to a fund of pooled resources. These pooled resources are used to create a fund that provides benefits in the event that an individual covered by the program suffers an economic misfortune. Thus, the program is presented as a means of spreading risk among its participants. The image suggests that the government is a passive agent whose only role is to pay out money that has been contributed.

Like public assistance, social insurance is based on a categorical approach. Protection is accorded on the basis of at least two determinations of status—whether an individual is "insured" by the program, and whether he or she has suffered an economic loss that is cognizable under the terms of the

---

[32] Examples of such deterrents include onerous application requirements; administrative "churning," in which cases are continually closed and reopened; work requirements that hold little hope of leading to jobs but consume a great deal of effort; and "suitable home" requirements that police the intimate lives of mothers on public assistance. Although a number of these policies may serve other ends, all of them have a deterrent element.

program. Insured status can be achieved either directly through work in speci-fied types of employment for a specified amount of time, or indirectly through a close family relationship with an insured worker.

In addition, only specified economic risks are "covered" by social insurance programs. The determination of whether an individual has suffered from a loss of income that is protected corresponds to the categorical determination used in public assistance administration. Thus, unemployment insurance covers temporary joblessness not attributed to the fault of the worker. Long-term unemployment due to poor economic conditions is not addressed by any of the major social insurance programs. Like public assistance categories, the determination of which risks will be compensable through social insurance reflects a determination about the social acceptability of an absence from the work force.

Social insurance, however, differs from the traditional public assistance model in that it does not rely on means testing and social stigma to further safeguard the primacy of the market economy. Instead, the principle of market distribution is preserved by tying eligibility to earnings through the use of a payroll tax. Funding through payroll taxes limits participation in the pro-gram to workers or their close relatives. Moreover, the levels of benefits, or as the insurance analogy would term it, the amounts of coverage, depend on the amounts contributed, unmitigated by means testing.

These features are critical to the social insurance model because they tie eligibility for benefits and the amount of benefits to success in the market-place. Individuals who experience long-term failure in the marketplace are excluded from the program, or only eligible for small amounts of benefits. Conversely, success in the market results in greater social insurance pay-ments—the precise opposite of public assistance programs which award benefits in proportion to an individual's economic failure. . . .

Many observers have pointed out the divergences between "real" insurance and Social Security, which is by far the largest "social" insurance program. As Jacobus tenBroek and Floyd Matson have written, the "whole insurance concept . . . [is] only a remote analogy rather than an operative reality." Although benefit levels vary in relation to earnings, they do not reflect any kind of actuarially determined reasonable return on contributions. To the contrary, benefits paid out have tended to far exceed amounts paid in. Additionally, the eligibility of dependents based on the contributions of a wage earner makes the amounts paid out vary with family size as well as with the contributions of wage earners. The disparity between contributions and payments has, until recently, been masked by the use of current contributions to pay current benefits. As long as sufficient contributions rolled in, it did not matter that recipients were taking more out of the trust fund than they had paid in because there was no shortage of funds. Moreover, the benefit calculation formulae are so complex that the lack of parity between contribu-tions and payments is not apparent.

Lastly, individuals acquire no vested contractual rights as a result of their contributions. Congress has the power to alter or eliminate the program unconstrained by any obligation to individuals who have "contributed" but not received any benefits. Stripped of the insurance rhetoric, one could view Social

Security as another categorical public assistance program that adds the parameter of work history to the traditional categories and omits the parameter of means testing. Under such a view, payroll "contributions" are a form of taxation and benefits are simply transfer payments.

Regardless of the ultimate validity of the insurance analogy,[63] the social insurance paradigm has been remarkably successful in creating a system for the delivery of benefits that is viewed by most Americans as distinct from public assistance. Because of the analogy, Social Security appears as a return on an investment, not a government handout. Beneficiaries are viewed as respectable citizens who are receiving a reward for their efforts, rather than malingerers suffering from social pathology. This cognitive separation between social insurance and public assistance has the effect of permitting middle-class Americans to receive public benefits free of social stigma or means testing, while poor Americans are consigned to more traditional public assistance programs that are considered badges of failure.

The insurance analogy serves as a tremendous source of political strength for social insurance programs. Because payment of benefits appears as the return of contributions, any reduction or elimination of benefits can be seen as expropriation. President Roosevelt later explained: "We put those payroll contributions there so as to give the contributors a legal, moral, and political right to collect their pensions. . . . With those taxes in there, no damn politician can ever scrap my social security program."

The insurance analogy, however, also imposes limiting principles on programs based on the social insurance model. First, any expansion of the program must be financed by immediate or eventual increases in payroll taxes. Thus, the cost of any expansion cannot be easily obfuscated. Second, the insurance analogy requires that benefits be limited to those who have some connection, whether directly or indirectly, to the work force. Moreover, the connection must be substantial enough to make the analogy plausible. This link is essential both because of the contributory basis of the program and the notion that the program is a form of insurance against wage loss. If there are no wages, there is no loss to protect against.

NOTES AND QUESTIONS

1. According to Professor Diller, how does the social insurance rationale reconcile the conflict between a market economy and the provision of government assistance to the needy? What is the relationship of the social insurance

---

[63] Supporters of social insurance have argued that despite the differences between "social" insurance and "private" insurance, social insurance programs "are truly 'insurance' in the broad sense of the term [in] that they involve a pooling of risks in a program that is governmentally administered and has definite provisions for the payment of benefits as a right and definite financing therefore."

Of course, welfare programs may also be viewed as a means of pooling the risk of economic misfortune. In this broad sense all of the programs in the Social Security Act of 1935 are part of a scheme of social insurance. . . .

Finally, exposing differences between social insurance and private insurance need not lead to a conclusion that social insurance is illegitimate. Rather, it refocuses the issue on whether social insurance programs reflect sound policy on their own terms. . . .

rationale and the New Deal? How does the public assistance rationale reconcile the conflict between a market economy and government assistance? How is the public assistance rational associated with the English heritage of social welfare in this country?

Since many social security recipients receive more money in benefits than they paid into the system, including the interest obtained by investment of their money, both rationales appear to involve taxing some persons in order to provide assistance to other persons. Is there really a justifiable difference between the rationales?

2. Professors Mamor, Mashaw, and Harvey argue there are two perceptions of public assistance with disagreement concerning its purpose.[33] According to the "behavioralist" conception:

> [S]ocial welfare policy is mainly concerned with the task of inducing the poor to behave in a more socially acceptable manner. The able-bodied should work at whatever jobs are available. Families should assume responsibility for the care of the young, the old, and the disabled. Everyone should look to their own future, providing for both expected and unexpected reductions in earning power. If the poor conformed their behavior to this ideal, social welfare programs could limit their activities to charitable relief for victims of truly exceptional circumstance. Indeed, private charity might reasonably be expected to perform this task without the assistance of the state. The poor are poor—and suffer from a lack of medical care, food, housing, and security—because they do not live as they should. The most basic sense of humaneness requires that such suffering be partially relieved. But generous assistance would reinforce the very behavior patterns that cause the suffering in the first place.

By comparison, the "residualist" conception

> trades on the metaphor of the "safety net." The net of social welfare programs in this view is intended to rescue the victims of capitalism and to give subsistence level relief to those unable to provide for their own needs. This view of purpose also grew out of the English poor law tradition, but it more nearly reflects the legacy of philanthropic humanitarianism in that tradition than the influence of the workhouse disciplinarian. It is found virtually everywhere among capitalist nations, though its popularity varies enormously. In the United States, and in Australia and Canada as well, this residualist conception is the staple not only of business and financial elites, but of large numbers of middle-and lower-income people as well.

How do these conceptions help explain the history of welfare policy in the United States? Do your own beliefs correspond to one of these conceptions? How did you develop your conception, and on what perceptions is it based?

3. Mamor, Mashaw and Harvey also note that there is an "egalitarian populist" theory of welfare states:

---

[33] T. Marmor, J. Mashaw, & P. Harvey, America's Misunderstood Welfare State: Persistent Myths and Enduring Realities 23–26 (1990). Copyright © by Basic Books, Inc. Reprinted by permission of Basic Books, a division of Harper Collins Publishers.

The aim of the egalitarian populist theorist is social change, not guaranteeing insurance payments or providing a safety net for the poor, and certainly not correcting the alleged misbehavior of the poor. The approved means are not ameliorative social programs, but the redistribution of income and power to the less privileged. . . .

The egalitarian populist vision of social transformation has been much less influential in the design of the major transfer programs of the American welfare state than [other perspectives]. But it has not been totally absent. Part of the antipoverty strategy of the 1960s involved efforts to organize the poor to shape the economic and social development of their own communities. There are community development corporations that still aspire to this goal. The financing of legal services for the poor can also be understood as a populist effort to give a measure of "power to the people." Moreover, if we had defined the welfare state more broadly, including, for example, labor relations policy, public education, and progressive taxation, then the influence of egalitarian populist thought would be more evident. In public education particularly, the United States was a leader rather than a laggard in introducing strongly egalitarian principles. . . .[34]

How do you account for the lack of influence of this perspective in the United States? Why has it been more successful in European countries?

4. The federal initiative in the 1960s to eliminate poverty rejected the option of increasing cash payments to the poor. Instead, the government provided in-kind benefits, including medical services (Medicaid), housing, Food Stamps, and legal services. The choice to provide in-kind benefits instead of cash made it necessary to create a bureaucracy to determine eligibility and otherwise administer the programs. It has also created a more chaotic system because poor people had to look to multiple programs for assistance. In response to the additional bureaucracy and coordination problems, some reformers have urged that in-kind programs be replaced with cash payments to the poor, which they could use to purchase medical care, housing, food, and legal services, as needed.[35] Some analysts have attributed the stiff resistance to such proposals in Congress to the lingering effects of English social philosophy.[36] Do you agree?

4. REGULATORY REFORM

The 1996 welfare reforms address three significant issues. First, what is the relationship between welfare and dependency or lack of individual initiative? Second, should welfare standards be set at the federal or state level? Third, should the country offer welfare assistance to immigrants? In this section, you are asked to consider the policy implications of these issues.

---

[34] *Id.* at 28–29.

[35] *E.g.*, Kinsley, *The Ultimate Block Grant*, THE NEW YORKER, May 29, 1995, at 36.

[36] *See* P. MOYNIHAN, THE POLITICS OF A GUARANTEED INCOME (1973).

a. WELFARE AND DEPENDENCY

The concern that "welfare" encourages dependency dates back to the Elizabethan Poor Laws, and as you read earlier, it has long had an influential impact on social welfare policy in this country. The impetus for the work requirements contained in the 1996 welfare reform law, however, can be traced to George Gilder and Charles Murray and other contemporary critics of welfare policy.[37] Some critics argued that increases in benefits in the 1960s caused an increase in welfare dependency and other social ills, and that poverty persists despite massive public aid programs because of such dependency and associated problems.

Gilder argued the "most serious fraud is committed not by members of the welfare culture but by the creators of it, who conceal from the poor, both adults and children, the most fundamental realities of their lives: that to live well and escape poverty they will have to keep their families together at all costs and will have to work harder than the classes above them. In order to succeed, the poor need most of all the spur of their poverty." For that reason, Gilder proposed that "[t]he crucial goal should be to restrict the system as much as possible, by making it unattractive, and even a bit demeaning." To restrict benefits, he recommended:

> Welfare benefits must be allowed to decline steadily in value as inflation proceeds. The Medicaid program, which alone provides a more than adequate reason to remain in poverty, must be amended to require modest payments in all but catastrophic cases. Rents must be paid directly to landlords, who are easier to supervise than hundreds of thousands of welfare clients, most of whom pay their rents only sporadically.

He concluded:

> Such approaches to welfare will win their advocates no plaudits from welfare-rights organizations and few perhaps from politicians who enjoy the power of granting excessive benefits to some and cracking down on others. But a disciplined combination of emergency aid, austere in-kind benefits, and child allowances—all at levels well below the returns of hard work—offers some promise of relieving poverty without creating a welfare culture that perpetuates it. That is the best that any welfare system can hope to achieve.

Charles Murray went one step further. He proposed that thought should be given to "scrapping the entire federal welfare and income-support structure for working-aged persons, including AFDC, Medicaid, Unemployment Insurance, Workers Compensation, subsidized housing, disability insurance, and the rest." Murray suggested that this drastic proposal was the only way to break the culture of dependency that welfare had created: "It would leave the

---

[37] G. GILDER, WEALTH AND POVERTY (1981); C. MURRAY, LOSING GROUND: AMERICA'S SOCIAL POLICY (1950-1980) (1984); *see also* M. BANE & D. ELLWOOD, WELFARE REALITIES: FROM RHETORIC TO REFORM (1994); C. JENCKS, RETHINKING SOCIAL POLICY: RACE, POVERTY, AND THE UNDERCLASS (1992); M. KLAUS, THE END OF EQUALITY (1992); N. GLAZER, THE LIMITS OF SOCIAL POLICY (1988); W.J. WILSON, THE TRULY DISADVANTAGED: THE INNER CITY, THE UNDERCLASS, AND PUBLIC POLICY (1987).

working aged person with no recourse whatsoever except the job market, family members, friends, and public or private locally funded services. It is the Alexandrian solution: cut the knot, for there is no way to untie it."

Murray foresaw that a "large majority" of the population would be unaffected by this proposal, since they go from birth to grave without using any social welfare benefits until they receive Social Security. He noted that three other groups, however, would be affected.

One group is composed of persons who would have to make new arrangements and behave in different ways:

> Sons and daughters who fail to find work continue to live with their parents or relatives or friends. Teenaged mothers have to rely on support from their parents or relatives or friends. People laid off from work have to use their own savings or borrow from others to make do until the next job is found.

As to this group, Murray notes, "I am hypothesizing, with the advantage of powerful collateral evidence, that the lives of large numbers of poor persons would be radically changed for the better."

The second group is composed of those unable to make alternative arrangements such as the teenage mother who has no one to turn to, or those who seek work, which is unavailable because of the economic conditions. Murray suggests that private charity will be the answer for many such persons: "Poor communities in our hypothetical society are still dotted with storefront health clinics, emergency relief agencies, employment services, legal services." Moreover, with the elimination of federal social benefits programs, Murray foresees that tens of billions of dollars will find their way back into the private economy, making it possible for increases in private charity.

Finally, he concedes that it may be necessary to retain unemployment compensation to tide over those who lose their jobs. The final group who is affected is the "hardest of the hard core of the welfare-dependent." They have no jobs, no chance of finding jobs, and no family or friends to help, and assistance is unavailable from local services or private charities. Murray forecasts that few persons will be in this last group. He explains that either persons in this group "will be at the top of the list of services that localities vote for themselves, and at the top of the list of private services, or the person is in a category where help really is not all that essential or desirable." In other words, Murray expects localities and private charities to assist those who are deserving of help (those, for example, who have a disability and cannot work) and not those who are undeserving (those, for example, who are capable of finding a job).

In conclusion, Murray recognized that he cannot be sure that everyone will be taken care of under this proposal. Moreover, he acknowledges that hungry children should be fed. But he counters that "[i]t is no less urgent that children be allowed to grow up in a system free of the forces that encourage them to remain poor and dependent." He asks that those who are dubious consider the following hypothetical:

> Let us suppose that you, a parent, could know that tomorrow your child would be made an orphan. You have a choice. You may put your

child with an extremely poor family, so poor that your children will be badly clothed and will indeed sometimes be hungry. But you also know that the parents have worked hard all their lives, will make sure your child goes to school and studies, and will teach your child that independence is a primary value. Or you may put your child with a family with parents who have never worked, who will be incapable of overseeing your child's education—but who have plenty of food and good clothes, provided by others. If the choice about where one would put one's own child is as clear to you as it is to me, on what grounds does one justify support of a system that, indirectly but without doubt, makes the other choice for other children?

Critics make two types of responses to the Gilder-Murray critique. First, they note that the problem of dependency, to the extent it exists, is limited to public assistance that goes to persons capable of working, but a significant part of social welfare goes to other persons. For example, Professor Mashaw argues:

A basic failing in Murray's argument is [that] . . . [h]is approach is enormously over general. Does he really mean that income transfers and other supports are causing people to get old, to become blind or disabled, to need medical care? Not really. In fact, of the welfare state's major support programs, Murray is really only concerned with "welfare," principally AFDC. And since we know that the major growth areas of the welfare state have been elsewhere, the image that Murray conjures up of massive expenditures on antipoverty efforts to no, or detrimental, effect is just that—image, not reality. Taking "welfare" in its broadest sense of means-tested programs, he could be talking about somewhere between 14 percent and 23 percent of welfare state expenditures.[38]

Second, there is a dispute concerning the extent to which public assistance does cause dependency. Professor Sylvia Law, for example, argues that criticisms like those of Murray and Gilder are based mainly on welfare myths.

SYLVIA LAW, REVIEW ESSAY: ENDING WELFARE AS WE KNOW IT, 49 STANFORD LAW REVIEW 417, 475–483 (1997) *

These stereotypes do not reflect the reality. When the welfare population is examined using monthly data, a different picture is revealed. It is estimated that half of the recipients of AFDC exit the program within one year, and that three-quarters leave within two years, most to take low-wage work. It is true that many women who leave welfare quickly return within the first year. But, even counting multiple enrollments, 30 percent of mothers receive welfare for less than two years and 50 percent of mothers receive welfare for less than four years. Less than 15 percent of mothers stay on welfare continuously for five years. In short, the data reveals, "one group receives welfare for short periods of time and never return. A middle group cycles on and off, some for

---

[38] MARMOR, ET AL., *supra* note 33, at 105–06.

short periods and others for longer periods. . . . And a third, but quite small group stays on welfare for longer periods of time." Finally, individuals who receive welfare spend, on average, a total time of about six years on welfare.

Generational welfare is also a myth. Eighty percent of daughters who grew up in a home that was highly dependent on AFDC never become dependent themselves. Since children of poor women are more likely to be poor themselves, economic class, not welfare receipt, is the best predictor of economic class. Economic class also predicts quality of education. In 1992, more than 40 percent of high school dropouts quit school in order to support their families, care for a family member, or work. "[F]or most recipients, welfare is a safety net rather than a 'way of life.'" For most mothers, welfare is a means to help them through a crisis caused by loss of a job, the departure of a wage earning partner or relative, pregnancy, lack of child care arrangements, a child's illness, or the inability to find steady work.

Despite popular mythology to the contrary, a large number of welfare recipients do look for and find work. Two-thirds of welfare spells end because the woman finds a job or her current wages allow her to leave welfare. However, two-thirds of those who leave the rolls for work find themselves in need of welfare again within the next five years, probably because their wages are so low and jobs so insecure. Only one-third of mothers who leave AFDC earn more than $9000 in the first year after they leave, and 59 percent earn less than $6000 a year. . . .

Harry Holzer . . . found that there is both a shortage of available jobs for unemployed workers in the cities studied, and some difficulty in finding qualified applicants. "The vast majority of jobs available to less-educated workers are in the retail trade and service industries," blue collar jobs are not generally available to this population. "Most jobs available to less-educated workers require the daily performance of one or more cognitive/social tasks, such as dealing with customers, reading and writing, arithmetic calculations, and the use of computers." Many of those jobs are filled through informal referrals and most employers want applicants to have credentials, such as a "high school diploma[], specific experience, references, and/or previous training." Although overall only five to 10 percent of the jobs available for noncollege graduates in central-city areas require few cognitive skills or work credentials, a larger percentage of residents lack the credentials required by employers. About half of the mothers on AFDC have not graduated from high school and a majority score in the bottom quarter on standardized tests of general aptitude and ability. Additionally, about 20 percent of the women receiving aid have a functional disability, another 15 percent are caring for a family member with disabilities, and half have a child under the age of six.

NOTES AND QUESTIONS

1. Murray's analysis and rebuttals of it are supported by additional analysis and statistics too extensive to summarize here. Based on this more limited presentation, do you find Murray's argument (and Gilder's) plausible in light of Mashaw's and Law's rebuttal? Even if Law's statistics are correct, does she establish that there is no welfare dependency? Assuming there is a significant link between welfare assistance and lack of initiative, does this dependency explain why people remain poor, or are there other reasons as well? If dependency is a problem, is the solution to eliminate all benefits for the working poor, or persons who can work, as Murray recommends, or merely to restrict further the benefits, as Gilder suggests?

2. Professor Wax describes TANF as establishing a reciprocity-based welfare system, which she defines as follows:

> The fundamental idea behind a reciprocity-based welfare system is that assistance is owed to those who contribute if they are able and to those who fail to contribute if they are not. Because people differ widely in their capacity for self-sufficiency—and because many low-wage workers earn too little to support themselves—this principle amounts to recognizing the community's duty to make up any shortfall between what persons can command on their own in the market or through private arrangements and an amount sufficient to support a minimally decent standard of living. In effect the government undertakes to act as surety for a basic standard of living on condition the that "insured" make a reasonable effort to contribute to their own self-support through some kind of work or through an alliance with someone who agrees to provide support.[39]

Does the idea of a reciprocal welfare system capture the connection between TANF and the historical distinction between the deserving and undeserving poor? Is the United States committed to making up the "short-fall" between the earnings of the working poor and a basic standard of living?

3. According to a 2002 Columbia University report,[40] numerous studies have documented increased participation in the work force by persons formerly receiving cash assistance, and a reduction in teen birth rates that began before 1996 has continued. At the same time, Census Bureau data indicate that child poverty rates have fallen, including among African-American and Hispanic children. Studies uniformly indicate that most individuals leaving TANF for employment are in low-wage jobs, but nevertheless the majority of low-skilled women appear to have increased their incomes.

Although many former recipients are working, analysts were not certain what had happened to the former recipients who are not working,[41] and little is known about the fate of those persons who have been diverted from aid before they were ever enrolled.[42] Moreover, researchers caution that it is difficult to determine how much of the previous picture reflects changes in welfare policy or how much of it reflects the extraordinary economic boom that occurred in the 1990s. In addition, just when the welfare changes were taking

---

[39] Wax, *A Reciprocal Welfare Program*, 8 VA. J. SOC. POL'Y & L. 477, 485–86 (2001).

[40] Blum & Francis, supra note 31, at 10.

[41] DeParle, *Varied Reasons Found For Welfare Rolls' Drop*, NEW YORK TIMES, May 10, 1997, p. 26; DeParle, *A Sharp Decrease in Welfare Cases Is Gathering Speed*, NEW YORK TIMES, Feb. 2, 1997, at Y1.

[42] *See* Diller, *The Revolution in Welfare Administration: Rules, Discretion and Entrepreneurial Government*, 75 N.Y.U. L. REV. 1121 (2000).

place, poor people were also benefited by increases in the minimum wage and, as mentioned earlier, increases in the earned-income tax credit.[43] Finally, those persons left on the rolls may be the most difficult to move into employment because they have mental health problems, are caring for an infant or disabled child, or lack a high school education.[44]

Does this evidence tend to prove the Murray-Gilder viewpoint or the view point of Professor Law? Or do we not know yet?[45]

4. Murray argues that private charities will play larger roles as government welfare programs are reduced. What role should private charities play in assisting the poor? Do you agree with Murray that if government ends its support, private charities can pick up the gap? An analysis of private charities by the United Way reaches the following conclusions:[46]

> Charities are able to respond to some emergency needs, but cannot meet the everyday basic needs of poor families. It is appropriate for the private sector to provide some emergency and support services, like food banks, child care for working parents, or job preparation training. . . . While the private sector has the ability to fill emergency needs, *local charities do not have the capacity to provide meals to 20 million poor families every day of the week.* On the other hand, the food stamp program is a manageable mechanism to provide daily sustenance to children and poor elderly households that do not have sufficient income for food.

> The private sector can and does provide services efficiently, creatively, and with more flexibility than the government. In fact, a great many public functions are currently being performed by private, charitable organizations as a subcontractor to government. . . .

> Public/private partnerships can reduce overall costs for social welfare programs. However, private charities do not have the capacity to assume responsibility for all programs for the poor. In 1993, United Way of Texas raised $207 million. Federal and state AFDC totaled $513 billion in 1993. There is no way that increased efficiency or increased charitable giving can make up this difference in funding.

> Today, at least 1/3 of charitable organizations' funding comes from the government, which is far greater than private donations to charities. In United Way agencies, 42% of funding is from government sources. This is the same funding that would be reduced under some policy proposals.

5. As briefly mentioned earlier, Republicans are seeking to add promotion of marriage to welfare reform when Congress reauthorizes TANF. The Bush administration is proposing counseling, educational and mentoring activities

---

[43] Bernstein, *Studies Dispute 2 Assumptions About Welfare Overhaul*, N.Y. TIMES, Dec. 12, 2000, at A14.

[44] Brogan, *Tougher Welfare Rules Expected To Get OK*, USA TODAY, Dec. 27, 2002, at A4.

[45] *See Symposium*, Welfore Reform Ends: What's Ahead for Low-Income and No-Income Families, 61 MD. L. REV. 243 (2002).

[46] Waller Memorandum, United Way of America Role of Charities and Welfare (Jan. 1995) (emphasis in original).

that will help married couples stay together. Other reformers seek to promote marriage through advertising and counseling. Finally, some have advocated that states pay a bounty to women who marry a child's biological father, which is what West Virginia currently does. Do you favor any of these initiatives? Is the married status of women the legitimate subject of welfare reform? Why or why not?

b. DEVOLUTION

The 1996 welfare reforms are notable because they shift more decisionmaking power to the states to establish the conditions of eligibility and to determine how much money to spend on aid to poor families. As you read, local and state governments were entirely responsible for aid to the poor until the New Deal. After the Great Depression overwhelmed local resources, Congress adopted the Social Security program, which provided both social insurance and categorical assistance, which is now known as "SSI." Congress utilized joint state-federal administration of SSI until the early 1970s, when the federal government took over all such programs except AFDC. Congress also utilized joint administration for more recent programs, such as Medicaid. The hallmark of joint administration is federal supervision or regulation of state implementation.

The 1996 reforms changed this practice for aid to poor families. TANF delegates almost exclusive authority to the states to establish eligibility rules and the amount of benefits. As noted, the federal government supervised these decisions under the AFDC program that TANF replaced. TANF, however, does establish some mandatory eligibility rules concerning the total amount of time that a person can receive benefits under TANF. The earlier description of TANF has more detail about these restrictions.

This section asks you to consider the advantages and disadvantages of delegating more authority to the states to design and implement public assistance. As a start, the next excerpt discusses the general advantages and disadvantages of state versus federal implementation of public programs.

STEVEN G. CALABRESI, "A GOVERNMENT OF LIMITED AND ENUMERATED POWERS": IN DEFENSE OF *UNITED STATES V. LOPEZ*, 94 MICHIGAN LAW REVIEW 752, 774–784 (1995) [*]

1. The Argument for the States . . .

a. *Responsiveness to Local Tastes and Conditions.* The opening argument for state power is that social tastes and preferences differ, that those differences correlate significantly with geography, and that social utility can be maximized if governmental units are small enough and powerful enough so that local laws can be adapted to local conditions, something the national government, with its uniform lawmaking power, is largely unable to do. . . .

b. *The Tiebout Model and Competition Among Jurisdictions.* The second argument for state power follows ineluctably from the first. If social tastes and preferences differ and if states are allowed to exist and take those differences into account in passing laws, then the states will compete with one another to satisfy their citizens' preferences for public goods. . . . Because it often may be unclear what bundles of public goods are desirable at what cost, competition among jurisdictions holds out the potential for a market mechanism that can provide an empirical answer to the most important questions of governance. . . .

c. *Experimentation*. The possibility of competition among jurisdictions . . . will lead inexorably to experimentation and product differentiation. In a competitive situation, state governments, as competing sellers of bundles of public goods, must strive constantly to improve the desirability of their bundle lest they lose out. The end result is an incentive for state governments to experiment and improve. This is the point of Justice Brandeis's famous statement that:

> To stay experimentation in things social and economic is a grave responsibility. Denial of the right to experiment may be fraught with serious consequences to the Nation. It is one of the happy incidents of the federal system that a single courageous State may, if its citizens choose, serve as a laboratory; and try novel social and economic experiments without risk to the rest of the country.

Competition leads inexorably to innovation and improvement.

d. *Improved Quality of Governmental Decisionmaking and Administration*. Decentralized governments make better decisions than centralized ones for reasons additional to the whip they feel from competition. Decentralization ensures that "those responsible for choosing a given social policy are made aware of the costs of that policy." This helps ensure a more informed weighing of costs and benefits than often occurs at the national level where taxpayers often may be less cognizant of the social costs of particular legislation.

In addition and just as importantly, governmental agency costs often may be lower at the state level than at the national level because monitoring costs may be lower where fewer programs, employees, and amounts of tax revenue are involved. The smaller size of the state governmental jurisdictions thus makes it far easier for citizens to exercise a greater and more effective degree of control over their government officials. For this reason, it often makes sense to lodge dangerous and intrusive police powers over crime and over controversial social issues in the states where government officials may be monitored more easily by the citizenry. . . .

Finally, decentralization improves the quality of governmental decisionmaking by improving the information flow from the populace to the relevant government decisionmakers. Centralized command and control decisionmaking is often economically inefficient beyond a certain point in all social organizations. This point holds true for the military, for corporations that contract out for many goods and services, and for government as well. Large, multilayered bureaucracies cannot process information successfully. Decentralization alleviates this crucial problem by leading to better informed decisionmaking. . . .

2. The Argument for the National Government

Lest we all conclude that the Union should be dissolved forthwith, consider now the very powerful economic and political science arguments for the normative desirability of our national government.

a. *Economies of Scale.* As already mentioned, there are many vital government activities that are characterized by the existence of increasing economies of scale. The provision of nuclear weapons and national defense is an obvious and much-mentioned example, but other such examples abound. Negotiation of trade agreements with foreign nations, ambassadorial and foreign policy apparatuses, large-scale transportation infrastructures, programs of space exploration and basic scientific and medical research, and programs to redistribute social wealth—all of these and more are examples of government-provided public goods that are cheaper when purchased in bulk than when purchased in smaller increments. . . .

b. *Costs of Decentralization.* Second, centralization and uniformity, under some circumstances, can reduce social costs. A single national currency is cheaper to use than would be fifty state currencies. As a result, more exchanges occur causing enormous utility gains. A uniform national gauge for railway tracks similarly may produce general utility gains with minimal losses to the people of any one state. . . .

In theory, of course, state governments always can negotiate over these issues with the goal of producing a uniform law code whenever the savings achieved by uniformity seem as if they would be great. In practice, however, it is costly for fifty state governments to negotiate such codes and costlier still to keep them up to date. . . .

Particularly where government planning and wealth redistribution is involved, centralized government becomes an essential cost saver. State redistribution and planning are frustrated constantly by exit and competition; this is the flip side of the claim that federalism preserves liberty. Thus, critics of federalism complain that it always produces a race to the bottom: the states end up competing with each other to impose the most minimal tax levels possible for the provision of vitally needed public goods. Thus, we are presented with a classic collective action problem. All states would agree to pay for these goods if they could be sure that by doing so they would not impoverish themselves to the benefit of their neighbors, but, because they cannot be sure, they all end up with a suboptimal bundle of public goods. This is precisely the bind the thirteen original states found themselves in under the Articles of Confederation. Absent a central government, public goods were being underprovided because it was too costly for any one state to spend what was needed given the policy choices being made in other states. For this reason, a national role often will be appropriate where redistribution concerns predominate.

c. *Externalities.* The need for a national role in wealth redistribution points to another powerful argument for centralized government: the existence of externalities resulting from state governmental activity. . . . Externalities exist for present purposes whenever a state governmental policy, law, or activity imposes costs or confers benefits on residents of other states. Imposition of costs is a negative externality; conferral of benefits is a positive externality. Absent a national government, the states will overindulge in activities that produce negative externalities and underindulge in activities that produce positive externalities. . . .

. . . The national government can prevent serious negative externalities caused by state governmental action by adopting policies that force the states generating those externalities to pay for the associated costs. Alternatively, in cases in which that is too difficult to do, the national government simply may occupy the field altogether and take over, itself, the provision of the relevant service or activity. Similarly, the national government can subsidize state programs that generate positive externalities to ensure that they are provided at nationally optimal levels. Or it can provide those public goods itself, using national resources. . . .

Nonetheless, it should be noted that not every external effect of state lawmaking can justify national intervention. Otherwise, the competition among states, with all its beneficial effects, would have to come to an end. Competition among states can work only if there are winners and losers, and this in turn means that, in some circumstances, it is legitimate for there to be external effects of one state's policies on other states.

The answer, I think, is to acknowledge a national role in suppressing external effects to further necessary redistributive concerns, to prevent discrimination against minority groups, to prevent damage to the property or environment of other states, and to further distinctively national interests stimulated by foreign policy or uniform law coordination concerns. A national role is not appropriate, however, where the external effects of state laws are the result of the desire of state citizens to have their own social, cultural, and community fabrics or where state citizens seek to maintain a close local hold on local law enforcement functions. A national role also is not appropriate in implementing and administering redistributive programs if the result is to produce a large and unresponsive bureaucracy. In these circumstances, national block grants administered by the states may work much better.

d. *Protection of Minorities.* Lastly, there is the powerful argument that a large and populous national government may protect unpopular minority groups more effectively than will a small homogeneous state government. . . .

This famous argument, made by James Madison in Federalist Ten, . . . for nationalism has proven true, as much as any argument from political science ever can. Indeed, it has proven so true that some reasonably question whether certain undeserving factions and minorities are too well protected at the federal level. In Europe and around the world, we consistently observe international courts and quasi-legislative entities paying more attention to human rights concerns than do national courts and legislatures. The need to protect minority fundamental rights, then, constitutes an important component of the normative case for national power.

One of the disadvantages of state implementation noted by Calabresi is that state implementation can produce a "race to the bottom." A "race to the bottom" occurs when states compete with each other to impose the most minimal tax levels possible for the provisions of public goods. As a result, the level of public goods, such as welfare, declines to "suboptimal" levels. Consider the following example:

> State X is ideologically conservative; it wishes to reduce welfare benefits to a bare minimum and to force many recipients off the welfare rolls altogether. State Y is ideologically liberal; it wishes to maintain welfare programs at current spending levels. Under the most extreme form of devolution, each state will implement its desired program, assuming there are no meaningful federal restrictions. As a result, welfare recipients cut off in state X will have a strong incentive to travel to and establish residence in State Y. State Y will thus experience an influx of additional poor people, not accounted for in its initial budget. State Y's program will have to be scaled back to something more like state X's program. In anticipation of this downward spiral, a rational state . . . will enact a less generous welfare program than it would have otherwise. The race to the bottom occurs despite both state's ideological preferences.[47]

Critics of state implementation argue that citizens will permit their states to lower benefits because:

> taxpayers do not value moral and developmental benefits equally and states must often choose between the two. For a state to maintain high benefit levels in the face of a large influx of new poor, the state would have to funnel public funding away from developmental programs and into redistributive programs. Taxpayers' preferences for the moral benefits conferred by redistributive programs would soon be outweighed by their preferences for the more concrete benefits of developmental programs. These taxpayers would either vote for politicians who would curtail the generous welfare programs, or "vote with their feet" and exit the jurisdiction, leaving such communities without the tax base necessary to support such substantial redistribution.[48]

As Professor Calabresi mentions, the "race to the bottom" is a form of the Prisoner's Dilemma problem studied earlier in the chapter: "All states would agree to pay for these goods if they could be sure that by doing so they would not impoverish themselves to the benefit of their neighbors, but, because they cannot be sure, they all end up with a suboptimal bundle of public goods." In other words, States X and Y in the previous example could avoid a race to the bottom by compromising and implementing middle-ground welfare programs. In the real world, all fifty states would have to reach such an

---

[47] Note, *Devolving Welfare Programs to the States: A Public Choice Perspective*, 109 HARV. L. REV. 1984, 1989 (1996).

[48] *Id.* at 1988.

agreement concerning welfare levels and benefit criteria. The critics maintain that the "transaction costs of reaching such a universal interstate agreement militate in favor of [federalizing] the issue."[49] Yet, as Professor Calabresi points out, there is also benefit to having states compete concerning this and other governmental programs. In particular, he argues that a national role is not appropriate "implementing and administering redistributive programs if the result is to produce a large and unresponsive bureaucracy."

Thus, the answer would seem to be some mixture of federal and state supervision. In the following description of federalism and state discretion, Professor Joel Handler suggests some of the aspects of welfare policy that are best left to the states and others that are best handled by the federal government.

JOEL F. HANDLER, "CONSTRUCTING THE POLITICAL SPECTACLE": THE INTERPRETATION OF ENTITLEMENTS, LEGALIZATION, AND OBLIGATIONS IN SOCIAL WELFARE HISTORY, 56 BROOKLYN LAW REVIEW 899, 941–943 (1990)[*]

The allocation of jurisdictional responsibility has always figured prominently in welfare history. In medieval England, relief of the poor was a local responsibility. Local authorities decided who were "strangers," who was deserving, and how much support to give under what conditions. Settlement and removal were part of the system of labor regulation.

In the United States, the allocation of authority between governments continues to serve important regulatory functions. In general, when issues of industrial discipline and social control are present, programs tend to be administered locally. Conversely, when consensus forms on deserving poor status, programs tend to be federally administered. An expanded federal Social Security system and Old Age Assistance program developed when agreement was reached on a retirement age.

When programs are ambiguous and contradictory, local administrative officials respond to the needs and exigencies of the local economy and the community's definition of morality. State and local political economies vary considerably from each other; some are highly industrialized and unionized resulting in more progressive welfare policies; others are more dependent on agriculture or single industries and suffer more from economic swings than diversified economies. Welfare programs reflect these economic differences. General Relief is different in West Virginia than New York.

State economies also influence patterns of migration and immigration which bear on the supply of low-wage labor. Historically, welfare policies have been used to regulate this flow through residency requirements, benefit levels, and work requirements either to discourage the in-flow of low-wage and potentially dependent populations or to attract industry on the basis of the availability of cheap labor and low taxes. Residency requirements are now illegal, but welfare benefits, work requirements, and low taxes remain important instruments of policy.

---

[49] *Id.* at 1990.

As stated, industrial discipline is never an unambiguous policy. In day-to-day operations, difficult judgments have to be made in individual cases. There are conflicting demands of generosity. Communities differ on the moral assessment of the poor and in their attitudes towards race and gender. Economic and political pluralism allows these conflicts to be fought out at the local level. This is an effective strategy for sharply contested issues. Local elites want to retain control over their labor supply; communities want to retain control over their social victims. At the same time, national leaders find it in their interests to delegate conflicts to low-visibility state and local decision makers. Delegation and diffusion of hot issues serve both levels of government; it is an effective strategy to manage federalism.

NOTES AND QUESTIONS

1. Professor Calabresi refers to the "Tiebout Model" when he discusses the competition between the states to attract residents. Charles Tiebout predicted that competition between states would lead to an efficient match between the demand by citizens for public goods and the public goods supplied by a state. According to Tiebout, "[t]he consumer-voter may be viewed as picking that community which best satisfies his set of preference pattern for public goods. . . . [The consumer-voter] moves to that community whose local government best satisfies his set of preferences."[50] Tiebout recognized that the model works as predicted only under certain assumptions related to the efficient functioning of any market. For example, he assumed that local decisions produced no externalities for other states, that citizen-voters had good information, and that voters were sufficiently mobile to change jurisdictions to indicate their demands.

Is this an accurate description of how citizens choose where to live? Do people move to certain communities because of public goods? If so, which goods? Is such movement likely to match citizens' preferences concerning public goods with a city's supply of such goods?

2. What do Calabresi's "arguments" for state and national government suggest about the advantages and disadvantages of state domination of welfare policy? As an exercise, think through the implications of each "argument" as it would apply to welfare. How do these advantages and disadvantages relate to Professor Handler's perceptions of how authority has been divided in the past?

What is your preferences concerning the division of authority? How would you divide responsibility for setting benefits and establishing eligibility criteria?

3. The 1996 reform legislation permits states an extraordinary degree of discretion:

> Basically, the block grants mean that the states can now do almost anything they want—even provide no cash benefits at all. . . . States may contract out any or all of what they do to charitable, religious, or private organizations, and provide certificates or vouchers to

---

[50] Tiebout, *A Pure Theory of Local Expenditures*, 64 J. Pol. Econ 416, 418 (1956).

> recipients of assistance which can be redeemed with a contract organization if a state so chooses. . . . Or a state could delegate everything to the counties, since the law explicitly says that the program need not be run "in a uniform manner" throughout a state, and the counties could have varying benefit and program frameworks. For good or for ill, the states are in the process of working their way through an enormous—indeed, a bewildering—array of choices. . . .[51]

As you might imagine, private contractors are very interested in being hired to run public assistance programs. The potential for using private contractors to provide public goods, such as medical care, housing, and other government services, is covered in Chapter 13.

Supporters of welfare reform cite state experimentation as one of the keys to reducing poverty:

> Let 50 reforms compete. Basically the law lets states do what they want with welfare. If they want to spend money to provide public jobs and child care (as we both hope they do), the money will most likely be there. If they prefer to keep welfare families on the dole, they will be able to do so, whatever the "absolute" limits and requirements seem to say. The overriding rationale for the law is precisely the freedom it gives the states: With 51 jurisdictions trying various reforms, we will find out soon enough which ones work and which ones don't.[52]

4. There has been little or no evidence of a race to the bottom effect immediately after the 1996 legislation. To the contrary, states increased, not decreased, funding for public assistance for needy families. But most states were spending an infusion of federal funds. Under the 1996 law, states received about $2 billion more than they would have received under AFDC. This windfall resulted from the fact that TANF funding was based on the welfare enrollment of earlier years when the number of eligible recipients was higher.[53]

Critics of the 1996 reforms contend that a race to the bottom will occur because the federal windfall will not last. States will soon receive less money under TANF than they obtained under AFDC because federal funding will remain the same for the next six years, with no adjustments for inflation or population growth. Thus, if a state attracts new recipients because it pays higher benefits, it will receive no additional money from the federal government. In light of this framework, the critics conclude that "[n]o state will want to be a magnet for people from other states by virtue of a relatively generous benefit structure."[54]

Supporters counter that states will recognize their obligation to provide basic levels of housing and food, and that the reforms will reduce the number of persons who need public assistance by forcing persons to make better choices, such as remaining in school, avoiding having children while they are

---

[51] Edelman, *The Worst Thing Bill Clinton Has Done*, ATLANTIC MONTHLY, Mar. 1997, at 49.

[52] Mickey Kaus, *Dispatches & Dialogues: Welfare*, SLATE, Apr. 7, 1996, www.slate.com.

[53] Swarns, *Roll Reversal; Welfare Finds A Few New Friends*, NEW YORK TIMES, July 13, 1997, at p. 4.

[54] *E.g.*, Edelman, *supra* note 51, at 52.

young and unemployed, and so on. In addition, as noted, the 1996 reforms mandate certain levels of performance by the states.

c. AID TO IMMIGRANTS

One of the most controversial aspects of welfare reform was Congress' decision to restrict sharply the eligibility of legal aliens for welfare benefits. PRWORA prohibited legal immigrants from applying for Food Stamps and SSI until they become citizens or until they have lived in the United States for at least five years as legal immigrants. In addition, the law authorized states to deny these persons TANF, nonemergency Medicaid and other benefits. In 1997, however, Congress restored SSI benefits to most immigrants who were already in the country when PRWORA was enacted, and in 1998 it restored food stamp eligibility for immigrant children and for elderly and disabled immigrants who were in the country before 1996. Congress has not, however, restored general eligibility for food stamps. This means that immigrants who were in the country before 1996 are generally eligible for Medicaid, TANF and SSI and immigrants who entered the country after 1996 are not. Only one state (Wyoming) has exercised its authority to deny Medicaid benefits to legal immigrants, and no state has exercised its authority to deny TANF benefits.

Those who support welfare benefits for non-citizens point out that immigrants had wide access to such benefits prior to the 1996 welfare reforms. They contend that immigrants should be eligible for benefits because it supports the principle that non-citizens come to the United States to participate in the full range of American social, economic, and political life and that, with some limited exceptions, they should be treated like other Americans. Moreover, like other Americans, non-citizens pay taxes and unlike non-citizens in many other countries, immigrants can be drafted in times of war.[55]

Those who oppose welfare benefits for immigrants argue that the country has historically always restricted access to welfare. An 1882 federal law, for example, ordered immigration officials to refuse entry to any non-citizen who appeared likely to become a "public charge," and it ordered immigration officials to deport those persons who became public charges, although there is little evidence that such deportations actually took place. They also point to the importance and necessity of saving taxpayer dollars and balancing the budget.[56]

The restrictions have been tested in court and to date the lower federal courts have found no constitutional violations in restricting aid to immigrants. In *City of Chicago v. Sinelnikov*, 189 F.3d 598 (7th Cir. 1999), *cert. denied* 529 U.S. 1036 (2000), for example, the Seventh Circuit upheld the disqualification of legal immigrants from receiving SSI and food stamps.[57] The court

---

[55] *See* Fix & Hakins, *Welfare Benefits for Non-citizens*, Policy Brief No. 15, Brookings Institution, February, 2002.

[56] *Id.*

[57] *See also Lewis v. Thompson*, 252 F.3d 567 (2d Cir. 2001) (holding that the denial of prenatal care to unqualified aliens was constitutional); *Aleman v. Glickman*, 217 F.3d 1191 (9th Cir. 2000) (holding eligibility restrictions concerning food stamps were constitutional).

interpreted a prior Supreme Court opinion, *Mathews v. Diaz*, 426 U.S. 67 (1976), as applying a minimum rational basis level of scrutiny when it upheld a law that restricted certain aliens' eligibility for a medical insurance program. The Supreme Court had said it was appropriate to defer to Congress' plenary authority to regulate the conditions of entry and residence of aliens. The 7th Circuit had little difficulty finding that the SSI and Food Stamp restrictions met a minimum rationale basis test. The opinion noted that Congress had stated three legitimate policy objectives in the legislation: encouraging the self-sufficiency of aliens, ensuring that aliens not depend on public resources to meet their needs, but instead rely on their own capabilities and the resources of their families, their sponsors, and private organizations, and preserving "the public fisc by reducing the rising costs of operating federal benefits programs." The opinion also noted that the Justice Department in defending the statute offered a further justification not found in Congress' statement of policy: the restrictions gave aliens a strong incentive to become naturalized citizens.

NOTES AND QUESTIONS

1. Researchers at the Brookings Institution found the following effects of the restrictions on the eligibility of immigrants for welfare benefits:

> To sum up, welfare reform's immigrant restrictions have led to a rapid decline in TANF and food stamp use among [legally permanent resident] families with children, citizen children in mixed married status families, and refugees. There have also been declines in the use of Medicaid among legal, working-age adult immigrants, but not among poor non-citizen families with children or children themselves. Increased naturalization rates and higher incomes contributed to the declines in benefit receipt by non-citizens, but they fall well short of accounting for the entire decline. We are left to include that the benefit cuts of 1996 directly contributed to the decline in welfare use by non-citizens.[58]

2. Earlier, you read about the justification for public assistance and social insurance programs. Review these justifications and determine the extent to which they apply to legal immigrants. Assuming the previous justifications apply, is there some reason to distinguish legal immigrants from citizens? Or are the restrictions about immigration policy rather than welfare policy?

3. In determining what policy you prefer and why, consider that immigrants need to attain sponsorship from a citizen in order to enter the country. Sponsors must sign an affidavit of support. The 1996 legislation requires this affidavit be executed as a contract, and it makes it legally enforceable against the sponsor. The sponsor is also liable for any means-tested public benefits that the immigrant receives.[59]

4. You may also want to know the following facts: In 2002, about one in nine persons in the United States is an immigrant. One in four low-wage

---

[58] Fix and Haskins, *supra* note 55.
[59] 8 U.S.C. § 1183(a).

workers are foreign born. One in five children in the United States is the child of an immigrant and one in four low-income children in the United States is the child of an immigrant. In 2002, approximately two-thirds of the immigrants in the country entered before 1996, and approximately one-third came after that date.

5. State officials have complained that the impact of the welfare restrictions enacted by Congress has been to shift the cost of welfare support for legal immigrants from the federal government to the states. This has occurred because many states have chosen to use their own dollars to provide assistance to legal immigrants. Does the fact that the states have decided to assist legal immigrants who are barred from federal benefits indicate that the federal restrictions are inappropriate? Should the issue of whether or not immigrants receive welfare support be a matter for the states to decide under the concept of devolution? Does it matter that the federal government takes income tax revenue from legal immigrants, but it does not share that revenue with the states in the form of welfare support for those immigrants?

B. TAX PREFERENCES AND SUBSIDIES

Social welfare programs distribute financial aid to the poor, elderly, disabled, and other needy beneficiaries. Such programs are considered to be a public good because they provide nonexclusive benefits to all citizens to the extent they reduce social ills that poverty creates. Aid to the least well off among us can also be defended on the grounds of fairness and equity. Not all governmental financial assistance, however, is directed to those who are poor, or may become poor without the assistance. Other programs provide financial assistance to the middle-class and even the wealthy. These persons receive financial assistance through tax deductions or abatements, subsidies, or by purchasing public resources at below market prices.

These forms of government assistance raise the same issues of public policy generally discussed in this book. On what grounds is financial assistance to the persons who are not poor justified? Are such programs legitimate public goods, or are they the result of the political power of special interests? And are such policies the best way to achieve a program's goals, or is there a better method to implement such goals?

1. TAX PREFERENCES

The tax system, as you know, is shot full of deductions and abatements that reduce the amount of taxes that some corporations and citizens must pay. The net result is that some persons pay less income tax than other people although they have the same income, or they pay less property tax although they own property of equal value to the property owned by others.

a. FEDERAL INCOME TAX

The federal tax code is full of tax preferences of one type or another. These preferences are:

often referred to as "tax expenditures" to emphasize the extent to which they are functionally equivalent (at least in respect to the net effect on the Treasury) to direct expenditures or outlays. The concept of tax expenditures was first formally introduced to budget analysis by the Treasury Department in 1968. Subsequently recognized by statute, tax expenditures are defined as "those revenue losses attributable to provisions of the Federal tax laws which allow a special exclusion, exemption, or deduction from gross income or which provide a special credit, a preferential rate of tax, or a deferral of tax liability.[60]

The President is required by statute to include an itemization in each annual budget of these deductions in order to alert Congress to the potential revenue consequences. The next table contains a recent estimate of the top fifteen such "expenditures."

Table 12-2

TAX EXPENDITURES IN THE INCOME TAX, RANKED BY TOTAL 2003 REVENUE LOSS (in billions of dollars)	
Total Revenue Loss	2003
Exclusion of employer contribution for medical insurance premiums and medical care	99.2
Deductibility of mortgage interest on owner-occupied homes	66.1
Capital gains (except agriculture, timber, iron ore and coal)	60.2
Net exclusion of pension contributions and earnings: 401(k) plans	59.5
Net exclusion of pension contributions and earnings: employer plans..	53.0
Deductibility of nonbusiness state and local taxes other than on owner occupied homes	48.1
Accelerated depreciation of machinery and equipment	36.5
Deductibility of charitable contributions	32.1
Step-up basis of capital gains at death	28.7
Exclusion of interest on public purpose State and local bonds	24.3
Deductibility of State and local property tax on owner-occupied homes	23.6
Capital gains exclusion on home sales	20.3
Child credit	19.7
Exclusion of interest on life-insurance savings	19.3
Net exclusion of pension contributions and earnings: Individual Retirement Accounts	18.7

Source: Budget of the United States, FY 2003, Analytical Perspectives 107 (2002) (Table 6-3)

The money lost to the Treasury as a result of tax expenditures is significant. For example, compare the tax expenditures (Table 12-2) to the expenditures for means-tested public assistance programs (Table 12-1). The money lost from the first two expenditures (about $165 billion) is more the cost of means-tested

---

[60] S. POLLACK, THE FAILURE OF U.S. TAX POLICY 16 (1996).

spending on medical care for the poor (about $113.8 billion) and more than double the cost of means-tested cash aid for the poor (about $73.8 billion).

We highlight two such expenditures to illustrate the policy issues associated with tax deductions. Try to determine whether these policies—deductions for home ownership and charitable contributions—serve legitimate policy goals. In addition, consider whether there might be a better way to achieve such goals, such as direct subsidies.

Home ownership: One of the most significant "expenditures" concerns home ownership. The federal treasury lost approximately $66.1 billion because home owners deduct interest payment on their mortgages against otherwise taxable income, $23.6 billion home owners deduct state and local property taxes paid on owner-occupied homes, and $20.3 billion because home defer capital gains earned from the sale of a home if another home of equal or greater value is purchased. Thus, tax expenditures concerning home ownership total approximately $110 billion.

What is the rationale of this large investment in promoting and preserving home ownership? Analysts explain:

> First, these deductions are seen as incentives to home ownership which is believed to increase attachment to the community and responsibility. Second, the deduction is thought to help young and moderate-income families to afford homes. These are nonmarket goals of the type that cannot be left to the unguided workings of the economy.[61]

Critics reply that such policies do not achieve their goals:

> The deductions may simply raise the price of land and existing homes, conferring windfalls on owners and not encouraging home ownership. Moreover, the deductions may be poor subsidies to struggling first-time home buyers, because the deductions are worth the most to taxpayers with the most income (therefore in the highest tax brackets); by this standard, it is not the marginal home buyers but the better-off who benefit most from the deductions. For the well-to-do, these deductions can subsidize not starter homes, but luxury and vacation homes.[62]

Reformers have proposed several changes.[63] One would limit the deduction to a person's (or couple's) primary home, but this may not have any significant impact, because wealthy homeowners would likely consolidate their mortgages from multiple homes into larger single mortgages for their primary home. Another change would be to limit the amount of interest that a person (or couple) could deduct, which would limit the subsidy to more basic housing. But it would be difficult to determine at what amount to establish a cap. If the cap is set too high, it would not have much impact, but if it is set too low, it might exclude taxpayers who own relatively modest homes, especially if they lived in areas where the cost of modest housing is high, such as some locations

---

[61] J. Minarik, Making Tax Choices 126 (1985).

[62] *Id.* at 126–27.

[63] *Id.* at 127–28.

in California. A cap might also be unfair because the amount of interest paid by taxpayers varies considerably depending on the cost of housing and the interest rate at the time the purchase is made.

Charitable contributions: Congress permits taxpayers to deduct charitable contributions, which stimulates such gifts because it reduces their cost. The cost of giving is reduced because a person's cost is less than the amount he or she gives to the charity by the amount of the person's tax saving.[64] The federal government makes up the difference through an implicit matching grant, which will cost the treasury $32 billion in 2003.

What goal does this policy serve? If the deduction encourages taxpayers to donate money to assist the poor, such "tax expenditures" serve the same goals as other government efforts to assist the poor. There are, however, many charitable organizations that support other types of activities. Are these also public goods?

Consider promotion of the arts. Contributions to charitable foundations which support museums, symphonies, and theater are tax deductible. These activities, however, can charge those who participate and exclude those who do not. A museum, for example, can charge an admission fee for anyone who wishes to view its collection. Nevertheless, if museums and other cultural attractions had to support themselves entirely through such fees, they would be forced to charge higher fees, which would likely discourage or prevent attendance by many people. Conversely, this tax policy increases the number of persons who are enriched and educated by going to museums, attending concerts, and so on.

The federal government, of course, could support such activities by direct subsidies, but the charitable deduction has widespread public support. One reason may be that it would be "extremely difficult for government to choose which causes to support. Through the deduction, the government gives its matching grants to the causes that the people support." One criticism of this deduction is that it favors causes supported by upper-income people, because their higher tax rate lowers their cost of giving. That is, the government provides a higher matching grant to upper income taxpayers when they give money to charity. Thus, the deduction appears to provide the greatest financial incentive to those who have the least financial need for it. "Or to put the matter another way, for some reason it is felt that a larger incentive is required to induce the high income taxpayer to give the same percentage of his income to charity as his lower-income counterpart."[65] One tax expert proposes that this defect be addressed by adopting a direct federal matching grant program which has equal incentives for taxpayers to make charitable contributions.[66]

---

[64] *Id.* at 131.

[65] Bittker, *The Propriety and Vitality of a Federal Income Tax Deduction for Private Philanthropy*, in TAX IMPACT ON PHILANTHROPY 178 (972).

[66] *Id.* at 192.

NOTES AND QUESTIONS

1. Stanley Surrey, the analyst who originated the concept of tax expenditures, has offered the following technical explanation of why financial losses to the Treasury are the equivalent of a direct expenditure by the government:

> According to the tax expenditure concept, the beneficiary of a tax expenditure has paid the tax due under the normative structure, absent the tax expenditures, and then is paid the amount of the tax reduction effected by special tax provisions. . . . Although the use of tax expenditures short-circuits the direct spending process by involving only one net payment by the taxpayer—the tax actually paid—analysis indicates that in effect there are two transactions involved. One is payment of normative tax liabilities and the other a government appropriation of funds to the taxpayers benefited by the tax expenditure program.[67]

2. Use of the income tax as a policy vehicle is popular with members of both political parties, although Democrats and Republicans tend to favor different policies:

> Democrats have traditionally favored such policies as offering tax credits for low-income earners and for housing the poor, encourage employee stock ownership plans (ESOPS) and retirement plans through tax preferences, limiting executive compensation, and providing preferential tax treatment for employer-provided health insurance and pension plans. Republicans pursue a similarly wide range of social and economic policies through the tax code: income tax cuts, preferential tax treatment for capital gains, tax-favored economic "enterprise zones" as a cure for urban blight, and various tax credits and expenditures aimed at encouraging savings, investment, and the accrual of capital.
>
> . . . In many respects, the most significant difference between the tax policies of congressional Democrats and Republicans lies in the particular policies they choose to write into the tax laws. Both sides of the political spectrum appear equally enamored of the electoral benefits derived from using the tax code to provide nonpartisan constituency service to the home district. The resulting tax policy has left the tax code riddled through and through by a dizzying array of tax credits, preferences, and deductions.[68]

How do you explain the popularity of relying on tax expenditures to affect public policy? Is it because the tax code is a better method of financing the activities favored by the tax preference than some other method, such as direct subsidy? Or is it because such policies are less visible to voters, which makes it harder for voters to hold legislators accountable for these policy decisions?

3. Professor Surrey suggests that political considerations often play a role in the adoption of tax expenditures:

---

[67] S. SURREY & P. MCDANIEL, TAX EXPENDITURES 25 (1985).

[68] POLLACK, *supra* note 60, at 15.

Woven as they are into the myriad provisions of the Internal Revenue Code, tax expenditures are largely invisible. Only the tax expenditure budget acknowledges their existence, and the documents containing the budget are not widely circulated. This mingling of tax expenditure provisions with other tax provisions in turn affects congressional and public perceptions of tax spending: legislators or presidents who do not want to appear to be "big spenders" can comfortably approve tax expenditures without damaging their image of fiscal conservatism.[69]

Surrey offers as an illustration a proposal by President Carter to reduce or eliminate certain expense account entertainment deductions:

Opponents asserted that the proposals would curtail spending in luxury restaurants creating unemployment for workers there, and would also seriously affect theater and sports activities because of their dependence on entertainment ticket purchases. . . . It is unlikely, however, that any of the legislators making these arguments would sponsor a bill giving a direct government grant to a luxury restaurant, with the grant increasing in proportion to the luxury of the restaurant, or a bill giving a direct grant to high-level advertising or other business executives if they promised to continue to eat in luxury restaurants.[70]

4. As you read, upper income taxpayers get greater benefit from deductions for home ownership and charitable contributions. Do tax preferences inherently favor the wealthy over the less wealthy? Consider:

Tax deductions and exclusions in general can offend many tax analysts' perceptions of fairness. If high-income taxpayers are permitted to deduct a dollar of medical expenses or exclude a dollar's worth of employer-paid medical insurance, as two examples, their taxes are reduced by as much as fifty cents. In contrast, the same deduction is worth as little as eleven cents to low-paid workers. In fact, no preference is worth anything at all if the taxpayers do not have enough income to owe tax; and itemized deductions are worthless if taxpayers claim the standard deduction (or zero-bracket amount). If these tax preferences are intended to help people afford medical care, then obviously more of the benefit is directed to the people who need help least. This phenomena of the largest benefit of tax deductions and exclusions going to those with the highest incomes is referred to as an "upside-down subsidy.". . .[71]

Can this upside-down subsidy be justified on policy grounds or does it result from the interest of legislators in rewarding taxpayers who are in a position to make larger campaign donations? Can the upside-down subsidy be defended on the grounds of administrative convenience? As you read, the government could replace tax deductions for charitable contributions with a matching grant program that has equal incentives for taxpayers to make charitable

---

[69] SURREY & MCDONALD, *supra* note 67, at 104.

[70] *Id.* at 105.

[71] MINARIK, *supra* note 61, at 26–27. The financial estimates used by Minarik are based on an earlier version of the tax code.

contributions. Is the current approach preferable because it cost less to administer?

5. The Treasury Department is undertaking a study of tax expenditures after the President Bush's 2002 budget noted: "Because of the breadth of this arbitrary tax base, the Administration believes that the concept of "tax expenditure" is of questionable analytical value."[72] The White House maintains that the budget is "arbitrary" in the sense that it fails to include some aspects of the tax system that should be included in order to offer a more complete picture how the tax code is used for policy purposes. Other critics complain that this failure tilts the tax expenditure budget against those provisions aiding businesses and wealthier taxpayers because it ignores aspects of the tax system, such as the progressive rate structure, which benefit lower-income individuals, and other aspects of the tax system, such as the corporate income tax, that target higher-income individuals. For this reason, they argue the tax expenditure budget incorporates a "liberal agenda."[73]

The White House also contends that the tax expenditure budget is arbitrary because it assumes that a comprehensive income tax—or a system where there are no tax deductions—is the appropriate baseline to measure what constitutes tax expenditures. Thus, the budget treats every tax break as a deviation from proper tax policy, which fails to recognize that many tax breaks have become accepted public policy.[74]

Are these persuasive arguments to eliminate the tax expenditure budget or merely to make it more comprehensive? What is an appropriate baseline for the budget? Should it attempt to measure any departure from a comprehensive tax system?

b. STATE AND LOCAL PROPERTY TAXES

Congress is not alone in providing tax preferences for certain activities. State and local governments engage in the same activity. Because these governmental units depend heavily on property taxes for support, these preferences often involve property tax abatements. A city or state, for example, will offer a prospective business tax abatements if it will stay or relocate in the area. The idea is that the financial benefits gained from the business' activities, such as an increase in local employment, will exceed the lost revenue to the city or state. Critics respond that cities and states often do not recoup the revenues lost through tax abatements. Moreover, even if individual states (or cities) benefit, critics argue that states collectively lose money. This is another "race to the bottom" problem. Finally, critics contend that these tax breaks are unfair because they are unavailable to firms that cannot be moved because of the nature of the business. The following excerpt expands on these concerns and how supporters of property tax incentives respond.

---

[72] Budget of the United States, Fiscal Year 2002, Analytical Perspectives 61 (2001).

[73] Bartlett, *The End of Tax Expenditures As We Know Them*, 92 TAX NOTES 413, 419, 421 (2001).

[74] Budget of the United States, Fiscal Year 2003, Analytical Perspectives 96 (2002).

PETER D. ENRICH, SAVING THE STATES FROM THEMSELVES: COMMERCE CLAUSE CONSTRAINTS ON STATE PROPERTY TAX INCENTIVES FOR BUSINESS, 110 HARVARD LAW REVIEW 377, 397–405 (1996) *

What have been the practical consequences of these intensive efforts by the states to make their tax systems more attractive to businesses? Although the impact on state fiscal conditions, on economic conditions, and on the distribution of tax burdens is significant and complex, one conclusion seems beyond question: the proliferation of tax incentives has not produced the intended effect of expanding economic activity and employment in the competitor states.

The econometric evidence . . . establishes that tax incentives and other reductions in business tax burdens, even when they create significant differentials in tax levels, simply are not large enough to exert substantial influence on business location decisions or on levels of economic activity. Moreover, competitive efforts of other states are likely to cancel out any positive effects that might be achieved by offering tax breaks. . . .

Even if tax incentives can, in special circumstances, strengthen the offering state's economy, they do not provide—and are not meant to provide—a net benefit to the nation as a whole. As many participants and spectators have recognized, the incentives competition is, for the states collectively, at best a zero-sum game. Even when incentive packages do influence location decisions, the business that one state attracts is a business that otherwise would have gone to another state. From the states' collective vantage point, the net effect of the incentive competition is, in fact, far worse than zero-sum. For, although the states can expect to achieve no overall gain in business activity or jobs, they do incur a very substantial loss of tax revenues. Even a tax break that succeeds in attracting a business investment to a state will represent a net loss for the states collectively, as long as that investment (together with all its derivative benefits for the winning state) would have occurred in some state in the absence of the incentive. Moreover, most tax incentives provide tax reductions to a far larger group than the small circle of businesses whose decisions might be influenced by them. . . .

Both the evidence of the recent past and the underlying dynamics of the interstate competition for businesses suggest that these trends may not abate until mobile businesses achieve virtual immunity from state taxation. As long as state decisionmakers perceive footloose businesses as bringing benefits to the state in excess of the costs that the businesses impose, states should be prepared to bid down the tax price on such businesses as low as is necessary to attract them. And, as long as mobile businesses can convince state decisionmakers that comparative tax burdens significantly influence their location choices, the bidding should naturally continue until taxes completely disappear as a location disincentive. In reality, the states are engaged, not in a zero-sum game, but in a race to the bottom. . . .

But where one person sees a destructive race to the bottom, another may see the healthy workings of free market competition. Although interstate competition to attract businesses may look like a vicious cycle from the perspective of the states, some commentators argue that such competition, seen from the vantage point of the national economy, is actually a healthy process that drives down the level of state taxation of mobile capital to its economically optimal level. Capital investment, the argument goes, will be supplied at its most efficient level when it is taxed at a rate that precisely matches the social costs occasioned by the investment. When taxes are higher, capital will be undersupplied; when lower, oversupplied. Likewise, rational state actors engaged in interstate competition for investment should be prepared, as noted above, to reduce tax burdens on capital until—and only until—the resultant tax revenues are in balance with the social costs that the investment imposes on the state. Hence, thanks to the workings of the "invisible hand," interstate competition for capital should yield socially optimal levels of investment, even though states in the process suffer the loss of some revenue that they have previously extracted from business capital. This abstract economic argument has a certain aesthetic, Panglossian appeal. But for several reasons, it is ultimately unconvincing as a defense of unfettered interstate competition over mobile businesses. First, as with so many arguments grounded in economic theory, it attributes to state political actors an unrealistic reservoir of both information and economic rationality. Although it may be economically irrational for a state to offer incentives to a business if the remaining revenues to the state from the business do not cover the attendant net costs, measurement of such net costs is problematic. Indeed, because the economic benefits of new investment are direct and vivid, whereas the costs (such as additional stresses on the state's infrastructure and marginally increased costs of labor and land for other businesses) are often indirect and diffuse, there is an inevitable tendency to underestimate net costs and hence to over-bid. Moreover, because the relevant decisionmakers are accountable to voters, not shareholders, the decisionmakers' calculus is typically more political than economic. The question is not whether the costs of winning the new investment outweigh its benefits, but how the voters, on balance, will view the decision on how aggressively to bid. As seen earlier, a wide range of political considerations is likely to produce incentives for business that are far more generous than economic theory anticipates as rational. . . .

Finally, the fact that only a fraction of businesses are sufficiently mobile to respond to, and to attract, interstate tax competition raises two additional concerns about a competitive process whose benefits flow selectively to those businesses that have the freedom to choose where they operate. The first is a matter of equity. Why should those firms whose businesses dictate their locations pay taxes substantially higher than do those firms that can plausibly threaten to relocate? Although this discrimination is rational from the viewpoint of the states, it is not justified by any differences in the governmental services required by the two classes of business, or by any differences in the benefits that they offer to the states. The only operative distinction is that the members of one class of firms are captives of the states, whereas the members of the other class are in a position to bargain. The second concern raised by the bias in favor of mobile capital is a matter of efficiency. A number of critics of state location incentives complain about the inefficiencies in resource allocation that state subsidies for businesses cause. These critics worry that such incentives will cause businesses to locate in economically suboptimal sites, where the real costs of production are higher than they would be at alternative locations. This type of efficiency concern may be less of a problem than it initially appears, however. Because of the limited efficacy of incentive measures and the competitive tendency of the states to match one another's efforts, the potential for significant distortions of economic decisions about location may not be fully realized. Nonetheless, if the dynamics of interstate competition engender a wide disparity between state taxation of mobile and captive businesses, that disparity may produce a different and more significant kind of allocational inefficiency. The difference in tax burdens results in a higher after-tax rate of return on investments in more mobile businesses, with the result that more capital may flow into such businesses, and less into their immobile competitors, than would occur under neutral conditions. Thus, selective subsidies for mobile capital are likely to shift resources into footloose businesses, even though those resources could have been deployed more productively elsewhere. . . .

NOTES AND QUESTIONS

1. Barnekov and Rich contend, "Civic entrepreneurship turns the free-enterprise system on its head leaving local government in the role of competitor and business as welfare recipient."[75] What is the basis for this claim? Do you agree with this conclusion? Why or why not?

2. If, as the critics contend, property tax abatements and similar tax preferences are poor public policy, why do state and local officials continue to offer them? Professor Enrich offers this answer:

> Why, then, are states so active in developing and deploying tax breaks for businesses? The real answer lies in the politics, not the economics, of location incentives.
>
> In a political atmosphere dominated by concerns about economic viability and jobs, elected officials face intense pressure to engage in the incentive competition. In such an atmosphere, each state strives to match other states' efforts and to make itself more attractive to business than its neighbors and competitors. Failing to do so is perceived as the "equivalent of unilateral disarmament in the face of a first-strike attack."[76]

Moreover, as Enrich explains, "By taking visible steps to encourage economic growth, [state officials] can take credit for subsequent economic successes, whatever their actual causes."[77] Finally, as at the federal level, tax abatements are popular because they are hidden from public view. In addition, because tax abatement reduces public revenues, rather than operates an

---

[75] Barnekov & Rich, *Privatism and the Limits of Local Economic Development Policy*, 25 URB. AFF. Q. 212, 217 (1989).

[76] Enrich, *Saving the States from Themselves: Commerce Clause Constraints on State Property Tax Incentives For Business*, 110 HARV. L. REV. 377, 393 (1996).

[77] *Id.* at 394.

expenditure of public funds, they do not directly compete with other programs demanding scarce state and local resources.

3. Although tax abatements are hidden from the public, they have provoked political opposition.[78] In Cleveland, for example, the teachers union spearheaded a special ballot initiative to decide whether to stop abating future school taxes. The teachers contend that tax abatements cost the schools $21 million a year, which is revenue desperately needed in a school system strapped for financial support. In Texas, the legislature passed a law permitting schools to veto their portion of proposed tax abatements, but schools officials rarely do so because of pressure to go along with efforts to attract new jobs. One study found that Texas schools lost $480 million to abatements from 1985 to 1995.

2. SUBSIDIES

Besides tax preferences, the federal and state governments provide subsidies to some individuals and businesses. For example, the federal governments will spend between $4 and $5.6 billion per year on payments to farmers through the year 2002. As discussed in Chapter 8, most of this money will go middle-class and wealthy farmers, which raises the issue of whether farm subsidies serve a legitimate purpose, or are merely the product of interest group politics.

Other subsidy programs raise the same issue. Consider the merchant marine subsidy.[79] In 1996, the President signed legislation that created a $100 million yearly subsidy for the nation's private merchant marine fleet until 2005. The previous subsidy had been $200 million per year. President Clinton backed the plan as a way to support the nation's dwindling merchant-marine fleet and to insure that the Pentagon can tap civilian cargo ships in times of national emergency. The United States fleet has dwindled to about 320 ships today from about 850 in 1970 and more than 2,000 vessels in the 1940s.

Critics had attacked the bill as "corporate welfare" and pork-barrel politics at its worse.[80] They argued that if the Pentagon needs ships at a time of a national emergency, it would be more efficient to buy the ships and keep them ready, which ensures that the money spent goes to protect national defense. A subsidy, although promoted by supporters as an indirect way of achieving the same purpose, may benefit ships that are not needed for national defense. Indeed, this is a significant possibility because the political system creates an incentive for legislators to give subsidies. Because subsidies create concentrated benefits, it pays shippers to reward legislators with campaign contributions. Consumers are unlikely to be able to stop this activity because subsidies create diffuse costs. The $100 million merchant marine subsidy, for example, has only a limited impact on the millions of individual taxpayers. An individual taxpayer is unlikely to give a political donation to stop the subsidy because

---

[78] Ritter, *Clevelanders' Choice: Business or Schools*, USA TODAY, July 31, 1997, at 11A

[79] *See* Schmitt, *The Senate Clears $1 Billion in Subsidies To Shipping Lines*, NEW YORK TIMES, Sept. 25, 1996, at C1.

[80] *See* Rosenbaum, *Corporate Welfare's New Enemies*, NEW YORK TIMES, Feb. 2, 1997, at 1, § 4; *Suddenly, as the Election Nears, Subsidies Don't Seem So Bad*, NEW YORK TIMES, Oct. 3, 1996, at A1.

the donation would likely cost more money than the taxpayer would save if the subsidy were eliminated.

NOTES AND QUESTIONS

1. Cities spent about $750 million on sports arenas in the 1980s. Since 1992, government has spent more than $1 billion on these facilities, and more than $7 billion is earmarked for future construction.[81] Supporters argue that the new jobs and increased spending attributable to attracting or retaining a professional sports franchise provides real economic benefits. Assuming this is accurate, is a stadium (or the presence of a professional team) a public good? Why or why not?

2. Whether sports arenas are a good investment is controversial. Critics counter that the overall economic impact is close to zero because the amount of money that people have to spend on leisure time activities is inherently limited. As a result, if consumers increase their spending on a professional sport, they will decrease their spending on some other leisure activity, such as attending movies or eating out, by an equivalent amount. Moreover, although professional athletes earn millions of dollars, much of this money is spent outside the local economy because they live in other cities. Arenas do create other jobs, but they are mostly part-time, low-paying positions.

Supporters acknowledge these arguments, but contend that the direct benefits produced, when added to indirect, intangible benefits, such as civic pride, make arenas an overall worthwhile investment. They also note that total dollar value of each citizen's taxes that goes to stadium building is very small and certainly less than individual fans spend willingly for tickets and concessions. Which side of this argument is more convincing and why?

3. Assuming that stadiums may be a dubious investment for a city, are there political reasons that explain why city officials try too hard to keep teams from moving? Moreover, why is it that city officials are not able to negotiate a contract that requires team owners to put up more of the costs of an arena? After all, the less public money a city invests in a stadium, the more likely it is that there will be a net benefit to the public for its investment. Why are owners able to negotiate financing arrangements highly favorable to them by threatening to move to other cities? How does the race to the bottom work in this context? Is there any way to curtail the team owners' leverage over host cities?

4. After having read this chapter, what is the difference between welfare, corporate welfare, tax expenditures, and subsidies? Is the difference between welfare and a subsidy for a sport arena, for example, based on the policy argument that the arena subsidy is an investment in the city? If so, then is welfare an investment in a city's citizens?

---

[81] Barringer, *The New Urban Gamble*, THE AMERICAN PROSPECT, Sept./Oct. 1997, at 28–32; *see also* Burke, *Skyboxed In*, THE AMERICAN PROSPECT, Sept./Oct. 1997, at 30–31

3. REDUCED PRICES

Another way in which government enriches some citizens is to transfer to them valuable public resources at below-market prices. Chapter 12 offered a good example. The owners of radio and television stations use a public resource, the radio spectrum, for free, although the Federal Communications Commission (FCC) auctions off other types of FCC licenses. As you read, Congress has resisted proposals to charge broadcasters for their licenses primarily because of the political opposition of broadcasters. Although the broadcasters are unique, because they have free use of a valuable public resource, they are not the only businesses to benefit from the way in which the government disposes of public resources. Other entrepreneurs are able to purchase resources owned by the public for less money than similar commodities sell for in private markets.

Government grazing rights illustrate such reduced prices. As three well-known analysts note, "The price for leasing public rangeland traditionally has been a political lightening rod with one constant: The fee has always been considerably lower than the going rate for comparable lands in private ownership."[82] Persons seeking to graze cattle on federally owned land must obtain a grazing permit, which permits them to graze so many head of cattle or sheep during specified periods on specific federal tracts. These permits are measured in terms of "animal-unit-months (AUMs)." An AUM is the amount of forage eaten by one cow or five sheep or goats grazing for one month, or approximately 750–800 pounds of grass. The federal government has charged around $2.00 per AUM as compared to a fair market value of between $6–15 per AUM for equivalent grazing on private lands in the western part of the United States. Numerous attempts have been made in Congress to raise grazing fees, but they have failed because of the political power of western ranching interests. In 1995, for example, the Clinton administration abandoned a plan to impose higher grazing fees because of senatorial opposition.[83]

NOTES AND QUESTIONS

1. Besides grazing rights, the government sells timber on public lands for less than market prices. In fact, "it seems clear both that many individual sales [of timber] realize less revenue for the government than the cost of processing the sales, and that the federal Treasury ends up with relatively little to show for the 12 billion or so board feet of federal timber sold annually from the national forests."[84]

2. Professor Coggins notes that ranchers fiercely resist efforts to reduce or end subsidized grazing fees because the subsidy is capitalized into the purchase price and mortgage value of the base ranch.[85] That is, private land

[82] G. COGGINS, C. WILSKINSON, & J. LESHY, FEDERAL PUBLIC LAND AND RESOURCE LAW 702 (3d ed. 1993). The description in the text of grazing fees is based on this source. *Id.* at 702–704.

[83] G. COGGINS, C. WILSKINSON, & J. LESHY, 1996 Case Supplement 125 (1996).

[84] G. COGGINS & R. GLICKSMAN, V. 3 PUBLIC NATURAL RESOURCES LAW § 20.03[4][f], at 20–37 to 20–38 (1997).

[85] Coggins & Lindeberg-Johnson, *The Law of Public Rangeland Management II: The Commons and Taylor Act*, 13 ENVTL. L. 1, 74–75 (1982).

next to national forests and other federal lands is worth more than similar land in other locations because ranchers have the option of grazing their cattle on public lands at subsidized prices. If this policy were to change, the value of such land would drop because accessibility to public lands would not be worth as much. As a result of this change in the market value of their land, ranchers would not be able to sell the land they own for as much money as they paid for it. A new buyer would pay less because the new owner would not be able to graze cattle on public lands at subsidized prices.

Chapter 13

PUBLIC GOODS: EDUCATION ENTITLEMENTS

Welfare programs can be justified as a public good because they create spillover benefits for society as a whole. The purpose of welfare regulation is to ensure that tax revenues are distributed in the manner indicated by social welfare legislation. Like social welfare spending, expenditures for public education can be considered a public good because it also creates spillover benefits for society as a whole. And like public welfare, there are regulatory systems to ensure that tax revenues are distributed in the manner indicated by education legislation.

Social welfare programs and public education are similar in another way. We discussed the public dissatisfaction concerning welfare and linked it with fundamental disagreements about the purpose of social welfare programs in the United States. There is a similar level of discontent and disagreement concerning public education and, as in the case of welfare programs, disagreements affect the design and implementation of regulatory programs.

This chapter starts with a description of the purpose and nature of regulation in public education. The survey considers the justifications for the public financing of universal education and the regulatory structure used in education. The second section asks what methods should be used to improve the quality of K-12 education. The last two sections examine school finance and its racial impact.

Education reforms have occupied the time and attention of federal and state governments and innumerable reformers. In addition, notable private foundations such as The Annie E. Casey Foundation, The Bill and Melinda Gates Foundation, the Ford Foundation and the Annenberg Foundation have invested billions of dollars into school improvement and the challenges remain with little to show for that investment. All reform efforts attempt to improve quality. Needless to say quality is often in the eye of the beholder. Nevertheless, we can identify two large areas of current concern—money and testing.

These two issues are also referred to as standards and school financing. The debate on standards is vigorous and for some time has been carried on in states and local school districts. Today, especially since the passage of The Elementary and Secondary Education Act, also known as the No Child Left Behind Act, signed into law by President Bush on January 8, 2002, the federal government has become significantly involved with school quality issues.

School financing has occupied much litigation over the last quarter century or more and presents deep, perhaps intractable problems. Most importantly, school financing, particularly in urban areas, directly involves questions of race. Indeed, it is the case that our urban schools are more segregated than ever in our history.

The search for quality improvement in our schools has involved any number of efforts ranging from teacher training, scholarships, facilities upgrading, employer-partners, and a wide variety of numerous other initiatives. Two of the more contentious ones involve vouchers and charter schools. Both are contentious for different reasons and, while the evidence of success or failure is mixed, both can be seen as involving a shift away from public and toward private education.

A. PURPOSE AND STRUCTURE OF REGULATION

Our examination of the purpose and structure of education regulation starts with a brief history of public education, followed by an analysis of the justifications for public financing of schools. This section ends with a description of the governmental structure used to regulate public education.

1. HISTORY OF PUBLIC EDUCATION

Public education in the United States started in Massachusetts, where local communities offered free classes beginning in the mid-1600s.[1] In 1642, the Massachusetts General Court required parents and guardians to ensure that children could read and understand religious principles and civil laws. In 1647, the court required towns consisting of fifty families or more to appoint a teacher of reading, and towns consisting of 100 or more families were also required to appoint a Latin teacher. The wages of the teachers were to be paid " 'either by ye parents or masters of such children, or by ye inhabitants in general. . . .' "[2] By 1671, all of the New England colonies except Rhode Island had adopted some form of compulsory education. These developments reflected the residents' interest in using "schooling as a means of preserving their religious, social, and political beliefs by transmitting them to their children."[3]

Prior to the Revolutionary War, children in the Middle Colonies attended private or parochial schools, while children in the South were educated at home. The residents of the Middle Colonies shared the Puritans' commitment to using schooling for purposes of socialization, but Southern states were slow to establish common public schools for several reasons.[4] In the South, "social class distinctions and the often long distances between plantations retarded the development of a formal school system in the southern colonies."[5] Moreover, formal education of slaves was prohibited by law, and plantation owners provided little or no education for them because they regarded it as unnecessary and counterproductive to maintaining slavery. Finally, because wealthy planters used tutors to educate their children, they did not contribute to the education of poor whites and their education was largely informal where it existed.

---

[1] J. RAPP, EDUCATION LAW § 1.01[2][a]–[b] (1989); G. GULEK, EDUCATION AND SCHOOLING IN AMERICA 9–14 (2nd ed. 1988).

[2] GULEK, *supra* note 1, at 10.

[3] *Id.* at 9.

[4] RAPP, *supra* note 1, at § 1.01[2][c]; GULEK, *supra* note 1, at 14–15.

[5] GULEK, *supra* note 1, at 12; *see also* RAPP, *supra* note 1, at § 1.01[2][d].

a. THE COMMON SCHOOL MOVEMENT

After the Revolution, public education was touted as a means of nurturing democratic ideals and spurring economic progress. Leaders such as Benjamin Rush argued that a free and uniform system of education would " 'render the mass of the people more homogenous and thereby fit them more easily for uniform and peaceable government.' "[6] Nonetheless, the "progress from the sporadic and inadequate early general school laws to formal state systems of free public education was a laborious journey with battles over tax support and sectarianism marking the way."[7] It was not until the middle of the 1800s that most of the states had adopted some form of publicly supported education at the elementary level. The public high school did not become a fixture in public education until the end of the 1800s. Moreover, the common school movement took root more slowly in some areas of the country. Public schools did not develop in the South until the post-Civil War Reconstruction Era. And the quality of educational opportunities varied widely. For example, racial segregation in the South and other parts of the country resulted in the creation of a markedly inferior school system for African-Americans.

The common school movement is considered "one of the major events in American cultural, social, and educational history."[8] One reason is that it changed the emphasis within American education away from a religious orientation and toward a cultivation of reverence for the laws and Constitution.[9] Another reason is that the common schools had the effect of "eliminat[-ing] distinctions of wealth, ethnic origin, and religion, and thus promot[ing] the assimilative goals of 'Americanism.' "[10] Finally, the movement ended the monopoly on control of the schools held by local citizens. As states established tax-supported schools and compulsory attendance requirements, local control gradually became complicated by state constitutions and by the actions of state legislatures.[11]

The success of the common school movement is attributable to its cultural role and also to the Industrial Revolution, which created a demand for skilled workers:

> An important argument for common schooling came from political and educational reformers such as James Carter, Horace Mann, and Thaddeus Stevens, who were concerned with the extension of civic education. Democratic processes and procedures required literate voters who were capable of electing public officials. American nationalism was also a motive behind the common school movement. Common schools could encourage shared values and loyalties and cultivate a sense of "Americanness" among people of ethnically, racially, and

[6] K. ALEXANDER & M. ALEXANDER, AMERICAN PUBLIC SCHOOL LAW 22 (2nd ed. 1985).

[7] *Id.* at 23.

[8] GULEK, *supra* note 1, at 23.

[9] Kesler, *Education and Politics: Lessons from American Founding,* 1991 U. CHI. LEGAL F. 101, 112.

[10] McConnell, *Multiculturalism, Majoritarianism, and Educational Choice: What Does Our Constitutional Tradition Say?,* 1991 U. CHI. L. FORUM 123, 135.

[11] RAPP, *supra* note 1, at § 1.01[3][d]; GULEK, *supra* note 1, at 28.

linguistically diverse backgrounds. In addition, the middle classes wanted a more utilitarian education that would prepare skilled workers.[12]

b. RECENT HISTORY

The public school system of today is based on the blueprint established in the 1800s. Public education is considered to be a state responsibility, with the federal government playing a secondary role. Elementary and secondary education are free and compulsory in all states, with only a few minor exceptions. Local school districts exercise day-to-day control over the schools under general state supervision. Finally, schools are supported primarily through state and local taxation.[13]

Although the role of the federal government in educational policy is still secondary, there has been a trend of greater federal involvement as a result of three events. First, the Supreme Court's decision in *Brown v. Board of Education*, 347 U.S. 483 (1954), precipitated an increase in federal control. *Brown* initiated years of litigation concerning the dismantling of state-sanctioned school segregation. The federal government also responded to the physically violent reaction in some communities against school integration (and other civil rights initiatives). The federal government's efforts to promote school integration established a precedent for later civil rights initiatives affecting education, such as the Education for All Handicapped Children Act, which mandated free, appropriate education for disabled children.[14]

Second, the Soviet Union's success in orbiting the Sputnik space satellite in 1957 made many Americans fear that the United States was losing its scientific, technological, and educational superiority to the Soviet Union. In response, Congress enacted the National Defense Education Act in 1958 to improve instruction in mathematics, science, and foreign languages. The Act also provided grants on a matching basis to the states to improve guidance counseling.[15] Until Sputnik, opponents of federal aid had successfully argued that it would unduly interfere with state and local control of schools.[16]

The third major federal intervention is the most recent. The 2002 No Child Left Behind Act imposes standards on the states. A synopsis of the act prepared by the Education Commission of the States says:

> This new law, a potent blend of new requirements, incentives and resources, poses enormous challenges for states. It sets deadlines for them to expand the scope and frequency of student testing, revamp their accountability systems and guarantee that every classroom is staffed by a teacher qualified to teach in his or her subject area. It requires states to make demonstrable progress from year to year in raising the percentage of students proficient in reading and math, and

---

[12] GULEK, *supra* note 1, at 23–24.

[13] RAPP, *supra* note 1, at § 1.01[4][a].

[14] Pub. L. No. 94-142, 89 Stat. 773 (1975) (codified as amended at 20 U.S.C. §§ 1400–1416).

[15] Pub. L. No. 85-864, 72 Stat. 1580 (1958).

[16] GULEK, *supra* note 1, at 90–92.

in narrowing the test-score gap between advantaged and disadvantaged students. And it pushes them to rely more heavily on research-based approaches to improving school quality and student performance.

But the new law also presents states with a range of new resources, tools and opportunities.

Federal spending on ESEA programs will increase significantly. . . . Nearly $1 billion a year will be provided over the next five years to help states and districts strengthen K-3 reading programs, and there will be increased federal support for before-and after-school programs, school libraries, charter schools and "reading readiness" programs for preschoolers in high-poverty neighborhoods. States and school districts will be given added flexibility in several areas, including teacher professional development and education technology, to use federal funds as they see fit. And Title I, the largest ESEA program, has been revised to give school districts with high concentrations of poor children an extra financial boost.[17]

In addition to these efforts, federal officials have sought to stimulate educational change and reform through their activities and through reports and special commissions. In 1976, President Carter created a separate, cabinet level Department of Education to give education issues greater attention and visibility in Washington. Education had been the responsibility of the Department of Health, Education, and Welfare, which became the Department of Health and Human Services. Conservative groups, teachers' organizations, and others opposed the change, because they feared that a separate, more visible department would interfere to a greater extent with state control.[18]

In 1983, the National Commission on Excellence in Education, operating under the auspices of the Department of Education, produced a widely cited report, *A Nation At Risk: The Imperative for Educational Reform.* The report warned:

> . . . [T]he educational foundations of our society are presently being eroded by a rising tide of mediocrity that threatens our very future as a nation and a people.
>
> If an unfriendly foreign power had attempted to impose on America the mediocre educational performance that exists today, we might well have viewed it as an act of war. As it stands, we have allowed this to happen to ourselves. We have squandered the gains in student achievement made in the wake of the Sputnik challenge. Moreover, we have dismantled essential support systems which helped make those gains possible. We have, in effect, committed an act of unthinking, unilateral disarmament.[19]

---

[17] ECS Special Report, No State Left Behind: the Challenges and Opportunities of ESEA 2001 2 (2002).

[18] Gulek, *supra* note 1, at 100.

[19] National Comm'n on Excellence in Educ., A Nation at Risk: the Imperative for Educational Reform 5 (1983).

In 1991, the Department of Education established America 2000, to promote six national education goals by the year 2000, including increasing the high school graduation rate to at least 90 percent.[20] The two most controversial elements of America 2000 relate to school choice plans and voluntary national examinations, which are discussed later in the chapter. In March 1994, President Clinton signed the "Goals 2000: Educate America Act,"[21] which establishes a "national framework" for school reform. The framework contained several goals that were to be accomplished by the year 2000 including the goals: that all children will start school ready to learn; high school graduation rates will increase to at least 90 percent; and all students will leave grades 4, 8, and 12 having demonstrated competency over challenging subject matter, including English, math, science, foreign languages, civics and government, economics, arts, history, and geography. Under each goal, the legislation lists more specific actions to be taken by schools, parents, and states in order to implement or achieve the goal. The Act also establishes a National Education Standards and Improvement Council, which is to identify areas in which voluntary national standards concerning educational achievement need to be developed, certify the voluntary national standards, and forward them to a Goals Panel for approval. The Goals Panel is an eighteen member board, consisting of members of Congress, governors, and state legislators, which is, among other functions, to report on the progress made toward reaching the Act's goals. The Goals 2000 Act, however, did not bind the states to adopt the national standards. President Bush took that step with the No Child Left Behind Act.

2. JUSTIFICATIONS FOR PUBLIC EDUCATION

As the preceding section made clear, compulsory attendance laws and tax-supported public education have a long history in this country. The idea that public education can serve an important socialization function for children dates back to before the Revolution. Although the earliest educational mandate was religious indoctrination, the goal of educating students to be good citizens gradually prevailed. Since the Industrial Revolution, the country has also looked to public schools to provide students with the skills they need in the workplace.

There are two economic justifications for "public" education and mandatory attendance. First, universal education generates external benefits, such as the creation of a law-abiding, productive, informed citizenry sharing some minimum of common values. Because of these spillover benefits, subsidies for education can be justified on the ground that they constitute a "public good." Second, public education can be justified on the ground that individuals will underinvest in their education if schools charge tuition.

a. PUBLIC GOOD

Richard Posner and Michael McConnell draw an analogy between the benefits of public education and the benefit of having all of the citizens in a

---

[20] *See* DEPARTMENT OF EDUC., AMERICA 2000: AN EDUCATION STRATEGY (1991).

[21] Pub. L. No. 103-227, 108 Stat. 125 (1994).

country speak a common language: "The external benefits are similar to those of a language; the fact that others speak our language enlarges our transaction opportunities. Indeed, language—more broadly, a common culture that facilitates social interactions—is one of the most important things that school instills in our children."[22]

These external benefits are a "public good." As you have learned, a public good is one whose benefits can be consumed by more than one person without eliminating the possibility that others can also benefit from the good. Education has this attribute, because all citizens benefit from having a better-educated citizenry.

As in the case of other public goods, there is a free rider problem. Unless government relies on taxes to support the schools, citizens would be tempted to let others pay for the schools. The reason is that individuals would obtain the benefit of the positive spillover effects created by education regardless of whether they paid for those benefits. Those who did pay would have no method by which they could exclude the nonpayers from obtaining these benefits. Of course, this assumes that enough persons would voluntarily pay for education to permit the public schools to exist. The free rider problem is the reason that local school bond levies are so hotly contested most often, but not exclusively, between parents with children in public schools and those without. If, however, most persons chose to be free-riders, there would be insufficient support to have free, public schools. In this case, all parents who wished to educate their children would have to send them to private schools.

If there were no public school system in the United States, the private market would respond. Parents could send their children to private schools that would charge them tuition. Such a system, however, would lead to an underinvestment in education, because the quality of education offered would depend on the parents' ability to pay. Moreover, some parents might opt not to send their children to school at all. Thus, some children would be undereducated in the sense that if they attended school, or attended better schools, they would generate additional, positive benefits for society. The country is able to obtain these benefits by requiring children to attend free public schools.

By educating its children, the country also avoids negative external effects.[23] For example, men and women who have sufficient skills to obtain jobs are less likely to resort to crime or require welfare assistance. The avoidance of these negative effects is therefore also a public good.

b. HUMAN CAPITAL

The second justification for public education is that individuals will underinvest in their education. Posner and McConnell explain that underinvestment occurs because persons other than the student obtain some of the value of that person's education, and because students will have difficulty borrowing money to finance educational purchases:

---

[22] McConnell & Posner, *An Economic Approach to Issues of Religious Freedom,* 56 U. CHI. L. REV. 1, 17 (1989).

[23] *See* Lott, *Juvenile Delinquency and Education: A Comparison of Public and Private Provision,* 7 INT'L REV. L. & ECON. 163, 163 (1987).

Moreover, education contributes to the formation of "human capital," and since it is difficult for the "owner" of that capital to realize the full social return on it, there may be underinvestment in education unless education is subsidized. (For example, an inventor, scientist, or scholar is unlikely to capture his full social product in patent or copyright royalties, salary, or other forms of earning.) Second, even the private benefits of education are not fully self-financing because children cannot borrow easily against their future earnings and cannot always depend on their parents' acting as perfect agents for them. Free public education is the equivalent of a loan to each student, to be repaid by education taxes over the rest of his life.[24]

According to this alternative explanation, there is in theory no public subsidy for education. Instead, each person pays a lifetime worth of taxes for public education and receives that education in advance. In practice, things do not work out this neatly. There is a subsidy from the rich to the poor, from those who live longer to those who do not live as long, and among those who move from one community to another to avoid paying higher taxes or to obtain a better education for their children.

3. REGULATORY STRUCTURE

As you would expect, there is a considerable bureaucracy whose function it is to oversee how public monies for education are spent. It is the responsibility of these federal and state regulators to ensure that local school systems comply with the wishes of the public, expressed in legislation, concerning how tax dollars are to be used.

The authority of the states to regulate the provision of education is drawn from state constitutions. Practically all state constitutions require some form of state system of universal, free public education.[25] These constitutional provisions have been the basis of school funding litigation as described below. Although the constitutional provisions concerning education vary somewhat, most state legislatures have set up a similar system of school governance. All states (except Hawaii, which has a statewide school system) have authorized local school districts to establish and manage public schools within their territorial boundaries.[26] School districts are managed by the members of local school boards, who are almost always elected officials.[27] Boards rely on rulemaking to establish school regulations, and on adjudication to enforce those regulations. Boards also act as the business managers of the school

---

[24] McConnell & Posner, *supra* note 22, at 17; West, *An Economic Analysis of the Law and Politics of Non-Public School Aid,* 19 J.L. & ECON. 79, 81 (1976); *see* Holcome & Holcome, *The Return to the Federal Government From Investment in Higher Education,* 12 PUB. FIN. Q. 365, 365 (1984) ("Federal investment in human capital makes sense from the standpoint of a purely wealth-maximizing government, given that a return on that investment will be earned in the form of high taxes paid by individuals whose incomes have risen as a result of their increased human capital.")

[25] W. VALENTE, EDUCATION LAW: PUBLIC AND PRIVATE § 2.2 (1985).

[26] *Id.* at § 3.7; RAPP, *supra* note 1, at 3.03.

[27] VALENTE, *supra* note 25, at § 3.13; RAPP, *supra* note 1, at 3.04; *see generally* H. HUDGINS, JR. & R. VACCA, LAW & EDUCATION: CONTEMPORARY ISSUES AND COURT DECISIONS ch. 3 (1991).

district, responsible for such functions as contracting and other private law functions. Boards typically appoint a superintendent of schools to administer the school system on a day-to-day basis.

The power and authority of school districts is defined by state legislation. To ensure compliance with that legislation, most states rely on a board of education and a state department of education, although the titles may be different.[28] Board members are usually appointed and have the responsibility of filling in the gaps in state legislation by establishing statewide school policies. For example, legislatures typically authorize state boards to establish minimum curricular requirements for graduation. The department of education has the responsibility for day-to-day implementation of the state rules such as ensuring that school districts comply with curricular requirements. The administrator of most departments is referred to as the state commissioner of education or the secretary of education. This position is an elected one in about one-third of the states.

The constitutional authority for federal regulation is less obvious than for state regulation. The framers did not allocate to the federal government any direct authority to control public education outside of federal enclaves and territories (note that the term "education" is not used in the original Constitution). Despite the Tenth Amendment,[29] the authority for federal involvement has been implied from several constitutional provisions. The federal government's aid to education is justified under the spending powers of the General Welfare Clause[30] and under the power to promote national security and international relations,[31] while efforts to eliminate discrimination and segregation are justified under the Commerce Clause.[32] The Department of Education has been assigned the responsibility for implementation of most of these responsibilities. As noted earlier, it was established during the Carter administration, and has the mandate to coordinate the federal government's participation in education activities.[33] Prior to the creation of the Department of Education, these responsibilities were assigned to the Department of Health, Education, and Welfare.

NOTES AND QUESTIONS

1. What does the history of education in this country reveal about its purposes? Is the purpose to give persons the necessary skills to earn a living, participate in the political system, be a functional member of society, or be happy and content? Has the purpose changed or been expanded over time?

2. Is there societal agreement concerning the purposes of education? The public good and human capital justification are generally accepted as justifying *some* public subsidy for education. This social consensus, however, does

---

[28] Valente, *supra* note 25, at §§ 3.2–3.5.

[29] The Tenth Amendment provides, "The powers not delegated to the United States by the Constitution, nor prohibited by it to the States, are reserved to the States respectively, or to the people." U.S. Const. amend. X.

[30] *Id.* art. I, § 8, cl. 1.

[31] *Id.* art. I, § 8, cl. 1, 3.

[32] *Id.* art. I, § 8, cl. 3.

[33] *See* 20 U.S.C. at § 3401.

not mean that the government regulation of public education is uncontroversial. Indeed, the opposite is true. While everyone accepts the idea of public education, there is considerably less agreement concerning such issues as the size of the subsidy, who should pay for it, who should receive it and what the public should require of educators who are paid the subsidy—what are the goals of education and how do we achieve them?

According to Glen Robinson, there are no easy answers to questions such as these, for two reasons.[34] First, identifying something as a public good does not also tell us what amount of the public good the government should purchase and how that money should be spent. Robinson notes, for example, that "[w]e may know that national defense is a public good and, hence, defense expenditures are, up to a point, in 'the public interest.'" He points out, however, that "recognition of its public status tells us little about the level and character of defense expenditures. . . . [S]hould defense spending exceed, say, $300 billion; should we invest in more bombers or nuclear submarines?" Second, Robinson finds that questions about such tradeoffs are politically controversial, because of their distributional consequences. Again using defense as an example, Robinson explains:

> The classic public goods model fails to tell us very much about how . . . tradeoffs are to be made; neither does it describe how they are made in fact. The political choice between, say, bombers and submarines is influenced less by the contribution each makes to national defense than how much each makes to some particular political constituency. However indivisible national defense may be in some generic sense, the fallout benefits from particular national defense *expenditures* are very divisible in just the way that classic pork barrel is divisible.

3. The recent history of education is dominated by reports and initiatives to address inadequacies, but not everyone agrees that there is a crisis in public education. "[I]n an escalating debate clouded by a blizzard of conflicting statistics and the currents of politics, a vocal core of scholars and educational revisionists has created a stir by arguing that there has been no broad decline in American education and that the notion that schools are failing miserably has as much to do with politics as reality."[35] Revisionists point to the country's economic, scientific, and intellectual accomplishments as proof that the schools are not doing that badly. They concede, however, that the schools could always do better.

Based on your experience, is there a crisis in public education? Does your answer depend on whether you attended an inner-city school or a suburban school, a public school or a private school?

---

[34] G. ROBINSON, AMERICAN BUREAUCRACY: PUBLIC CHOICE AND PUBLIC LAW 25–34 (1991).

[35] Applebome, *Have Schools Failed? Revisionists Use Army of Statistics to Argue No.*, NEW YORK TIMES, Dec. 13, 1995, at A16 (national edition); *see generally* D. BERLINER, THE MANUFACTURED CRISIS—MYTHS, FRAUD, AND THE ATTACK ON AMERICAN'S PUBLIC SCHOOLS (1995); O'Neill, *The History of a Hoax*, NEW YORK TIMES MAGAZINE, Mar. 6, 1994, at 46.

B. SCHOOL REFORM

The issue of school reform has dominated the history of public education since the 1950s. [36] Countless reports, such as those described earlier, bemoan the limited achievements of many students and propose new methods to improve public education. Elected officials, having taken due notice of this dissatisfaction, are ever ready to consider how to improve the performance of our schools. Voters, who pay for the schools, as well as parents, who are dissatisfied with the quality of education received by the children, are likewise interested in what steps government can take, if any, to improve the quality of public education.

This section examines school choice in three forms: vouchers, charters, and private contract. The idea common to each method is the belief that public schools are failing in their essential mission and that competitive pressure is needed to break through public school bureaucracy. Vouchers accomplish this by letting students (and their parents) vote with their feet and move to another, hopefully better, school. Charter schools are deregulated and specialized alternatives to traditional public schools. And there are private entities that promise to deliver a better quality of education than that provided by existing public school systems.

1. ALTERNATIVE SCHOOL CHOICE PLANS

There are several prominent plans that would give parents more choices about which schools their children attended: [37]

Vouchers: There are two approaches to voucher—universal vouchers and low-income vouchers. Under the first form, funds are allocated to schools based entirely on their enrollment. The hope is to establish a complete market system for education. Milwaukee and Cleveland provide vouchers to low-income students to attend private schools. Such programs are seen as a way to test the voucher idea and to give public schools the shock of competition. While voucher programs can be publicly or privately funded, the existing programs are public which raises constitutional issues, discussed later, concerning whether children are allowed to enroll in parochial schools. [38]

Public school choice: This idea dates back to the 1960s when school districts created "magnet" schools in an attempt to enroll a more diverse group of students. Today some school districts permit students to attend any school in the district or even outside the district. [39] Proponents claim that competition between public schools for students will improve educational performance. To prevent segregation by race or class, school districts typically set limits on enrollment and inform lower-income parents of their options.

---

[36] *See* D. Tyack & L. Cuban, Tinkering Toward Utopia: A Century of Public School Reform (1995).

[37] *See* Judis, *Bad Choice,* the New Republic, Sept. 30, 1996; C. Finn, B. Manno & G. Vanourek, Charter Schools in Action: Renewing a Public Education (2000).

[38] D. Peterson & D. Campbell (eds.), Charters, Vouchers & Public Education ch. 1 (2001).

[39] *See* Smith, *Public School Choice and Open Enrollment,* 74 Neb. L. Rev. 255 (1995).

Charter schools: Charter schools have been established in twenty-five states.[40] Although they are public schools, they operate outside of the traditional school district and are exempt from state and local educational regulations. For example, a charter school may be permitted to hire teachers who do not meet traditional hiring requirements, such as graduation from a school of education. Similarly, such schools forego use of traditional grading and use different methods of accountability, including student portfolios, parent satisfaction surveys, student demonstrations of competency, and testing. Charter schools seek to use their exemption from regulation to adopt innovative teaching methods, such as focussing on a theme or emphasizing technology.

Education by contract. This school reform effort involves contracting between public schools and private investor-owned education firms. Christopher Whittle, head of Whittle Communications, grabbed headlines in 1992, when he lured Benno Schmidt away from the presidency of Yale University to head the Edison Project.[41] The central aim of the Edison Project was to open 200 private, for-profit schools by 1996, and 1,000 schools thereafter, as an alternative to public school education. Whittle believes that he can offer a higher quality, more modern, and more comprehensive school than is now being provided by public school systems.

So far the Edison project has not met with great success, but it has met with political controversy and investor skepticism. To date Edison has entered contracts to operate over 100 schools with over 80,000 students.[42] Its largest contract is with the Philadelphia school district, but this contract only occurred after a contentious battle that may have threatened Edison's financial health. Edison and the school district entered a five-year contract. Edison had hoped to operate 45 schools in the Philadelphia district, but it ended up operating 20 schools. It sought more than $1,500 per pupil but settled for $881. Edison has yet to report a profit losing $86 million on $465 revenue the last fiscal year.

2. THE DEBATE ON SCHOOL CHOICE

The previous reforms have generated enormous debate over which approach or approaches are most likely to improve education. The debate centers around whether it is realistic to think that competition between schools to attract and keep students is the best way to spur educators to improve the quality of the education that they offer. The alternative is regulatory—to subject schools to stricter regulation concerning educational outcomes and performance—which we take up later in this chapter.

---

[40] *See* EDUCATION COMMISSION OF THE STATES AND THE CENTER FOR SCHOOL CHANGE, CHARTER SCHOOLS: WHAT ARE THEY UP TO? (1995).

[41] *See, e.g.,* Ferguson, *Whittle's Lesson Plan for Public Schools,* WALL ST. J., June 2, 1992, at A15; Kleinfield, *Plan for High Tech Private Schools Poses Risks and Challenges,* N.Y. TIMES, May 26, 1992, at A4 (national edition); Chira, *Whittle's School Unit Gains Prestige and Pressure,* N.Y. TIMES, May 27, 1992, at B6 (national edition).

[42] Forelle, *Flunked By Investors, Edison Schools Scorns Talk of Failure,* WALL ST. J. October 22, 2002 at B1. *See also,* O'Reilly, *Why Edison Doesn't Work,* FORTUNE 149 (Dec. 9, 2002).

a. JUSTIFICATIONS FOR CHOICE

The proponents for educational choice can be divided into two groups.[43] One group has as its goal greater efficiency, or "more educational bang for the buck."[44] The second group believes that choice will promote greater diversity in education by permitting parents to chose schools that emphasize an ethnic, racial, language, or religious orientation that the parents favor.

Greater efficiency: Criticism of the current system based on its inefficiency can be traced back to Milton Friedman, the University of Chicago economist and Nobel Prize recipient. In a 1962 book, *Capitalism and Freedom,* Friedman contrasted the traditional, quasi-monopolistic nature of public education—in which students are assigned involuntarily to their neighborhood schools—with the benefits that competition brings to private markets. The spur of competition in private markets causes sellers to cut costs and find ways to become more innovative. By comparison, since local schools have no competition, there are no similar incentives to improve public education.[45] As support for this argument, critics claim that private elementary and high schools spend considerably fewer dollars per pupil than do public schools, while providing comparable or better education.[46]

John Chubb and Terry Moe, who teach public administration, have advanced a related argument for choice.[47] Their statistics indicate that students of the same ability and family background show greater improvement on standardized exams between their sophomore and senior years in some high schools than in others. Further, these differences are not explained by a difference in school resources or race if children are compared whose parents are of the same socioeconomic status. These findings confirm the earlier conclusions reached by James Coleman, a University of Chicago sociologist.[48] Coleman and his co-authors also found that if you statistically control for the factors which do influence achievement, students of similar backgrounds learn more in private and parochial high schools than in public high schools. Coleman was uncertain why this was the case. Chubb and Moe claim to have found the answer.

The explanation according to Chubb and Moe is the nature of the environment in which schools operate:

> Understood as open systems, schools are largely explained by the types of environments that surround them. Different types of environments produce different types of schools. . . . [Thus,] when schools turn out to have undesirable characteristics—those conducive to ineffective performance—the most logical culprit ought to be the environment, not the schools themselves.[49]

---

[43] *See* Sugarman, *Using Private Schools to Promote Public Values,* 1991 U. Chi. Legal F. 171, 172.

[44] *Id.*

[45] M. Friedman, Capitalism and Freedom 85–98 (1962).

[46] Sugarman, *supra* note 43, at 173.

[47] J. Chubb & T. Moe, Politics, Markets, and America's Schools (1990).

[48] J. Coleman, T. Hoffer, & S. Kilgore, High School Achievement (1982).

[49] Chubb & Moe, *supra* note 47, at 19.

Chubb and Moe find that public schools are less effective in educating children than private and parochial schools, because they operate in a different environment than private and parochial schools. Public schools operate in a "democratic" environment, whereas private and parochial schools operate in a "market" environment. The problem with the democratic environment is that it relies on a heavily bureaucratic system to ensure accountability. Large-scale management of school systems is practical only by reliance on uniform rules and issuing standard operating procedures. Yet, such a system is "too heavily bureaucratic—too hierarchical, too rule-bound, too formalistic—to allow for the kind of autonomy and professionalism that schools need if they are to perform well."[50] As James Q. Wilson, a Harvard sociologist, explains:

> [T]op-heavy management, which is rational from the point of view of school administrators, is irrational from the point of view of school principals and teachers. Education is a complex, labor intensive, highly discretionary activity, carried on in small, low visibility settings (that is classrooms). If it were a business, no management consultant would dream of suggesting that the performance of such tasks could be improved by putting day-to-day control of the enterprise in the hands of top executives.[51]

Despite the disparity between good teaching and this method of organizing the schools, politics prevents the reform of public education. Groups besides parents have an interest in educational policy, and these constituencies depend on the bureaucratic controls to implement their wishes. The "more insistent" of these constituencies are "taxpayers (who want economy), organized teachers (who want security), civil rights groups (who want integration), educational reform groups (who want specific programs adopted or changed), and politicians (who want power)."[52]

Because private and parochial schools are subject to the discipline of the marketplace, rather than the discipline of the political system, they are less bureaucratic. Professor Wilson explains:

> To the extent that the organization gets its resources from consumers, it must be attentive to their preferences; the alternative is failure. Moreover, if there are no economies of scale—in education, there are probably few—then there is no organized advantage to having a large bureaucracy to manage the school. Under these circumstances, school systems will delegate a great deal of authority to lower-level managers, principals, or headmasters.[53]

For example, the New York public school system has a bureaucracy made up of about 6,000 officials, while the Catholic schools of the New York City archdiocese, which teaches about a quarter as many pupils, has a central administrative staff of only twenty-five persons.[54]

---

[50] *Id.* at 26.

[51] Wilson, *Multiple Choice Test,* NEW REPUBLIC, Oct. 8, 1990, at 40.

[52] *Id.* at 40–41.

[53] *Id.* at 41.

[54] *Id.*

In summary, critics assert that the fundamental difference between the public and private schools is that public schools are not as responsible to parents:

> The fundamental point to be made about parents and students is . . . that . . . the public schools are *not meant* to be theirs to control and are literally *not supposed* to provide them with the kind of education they might want. The schools are agencies for society as a whole, and everyone has a right to participate in their governance. Parents and students have a right to participate too. But they have no right to win. In the end, they have to take what society gives them.[55]

The exact opposite situation exists regarding private and parochial education. These schools have substantial incentives to be responsive to parents, and no incentives to be responsive to persons who do not pay tuition. This difference leads Chubb and Moe to conclude that public schools are unlikely to become more effective until they become more accountable to their customers.

Greater pluralism: Another objective of the choice movement is educational pluralism.[56] Professor Sugarman explains that:

> [t]his position allies itself with free speech values (the "marketplace of ideas" metaphor) and emphasizes the enormous ethnic, racial, language, and religious diversity in America today. It argues that there is no consensus about the range of things young Americans should learn, or about the most effective ways of teaching those core matters that most agree should be learned. In the face of this "indeterminacy," the wiser strategy should be to let a thousand flowers bloom—a strategy made possible through subsidized choice.[57]

For example, Hispanic-American families who want to preserve their cultural roots could select bilingual, bicultural education, while Hispanic-American families who sought assimilation could select other kinds of schools.

James Coleman, whose research was mentioned earlier, offers a related sociological argument for the effectiveness of choice.[58] He argues that over the last two centuries events have undermined the ability of families to perform their traditional child rearing functions. For example, a "major event in the impairment of the family's child rearing capacity was the loss of the woman's labor from the household through her movement into the paid labor force."[59] As a result, society has shifted the child rearing function to the schools, and the organization of the schools has "largely eliminated the parents' choice about the kind of education that their children will receive."[60] Coleman concludes:

> [T]he classical institutional response to the loss of family socialization functions—the public common school—is insufficient to meet the

---

[55] CHUBB & MOE, *supra* note 47, at 32.

[56] J. COONS & S. SUGARMAN, EDUCATION BY CHOICE 89–108 (1978).

[57] Sugarman, *supra* note 43, at 176.

[58] Coleman, *Changes in the Family and Implications for the Common School,* 1991 U. CHI. L. REV. 153.

[59] *Id.* at 156.

[60] *Id.* at 157.

demands created by the loss of family functions being experienced today. . . . The logic of my analysis is diametrically opposed to the notion of a common school, as the common school necessarily restricts the range of socialization functions that can be carried out—a restriction that is particularly harmful to children as families weaken. The analysis favors further increasing the range of parental choice, for this allows consensus on a broader set of socialization functions. It thus constitutes an argument for, among other things, a voucher system—in which parents can choose among schools in both the public and private sectors—precisely because private schools can do what public schools, tied to the state, cannot.[61]

b.   OBJECTIONS TO CHOICE

Critics of choice argue that choice plans are unlikely to work and that they carry a high price in terms of introducing school segregation by class and racial categories.[62] Consider the following criticisms by Professor Liebman.

JAMES LIEBMAN, BOOK REVIEW: VOICE, NOT CHOICE, 101 YALE LAW JOURNAL 259, 275–77, 278–91 (1991)*

[Moe and Chubb] . . . conclude that market discipline resulting from the threat of parental exit, rather than some other attribute of private schools, accounts for those schools' success. [But] the authors' analysis does not rule out an alternative hypothesis—that educational success coincides with the absence, and not with a surfeit, of market constraint. To begin with, suburban schools do relatively well pedagogically, even though the high cost of residential relocation substantially shields those schools from the threat of exit.

Second, private school patrons have less choice—and their schools need worry about less exit—than the authors suggest. Theoretically, exit can take one of two forms. Parents can move from one school to another, or they can move from one sector (say, private) to another (say, public). In fact, intersectoral exit is not realistically available to private school patrons . . . [because] the bulk of educational alternatives (i.e., public schools) simply are not meaningful options for most private school patrons.

Third, the segment of the education market in which exit is most common and least constrained—the urban public schools—is also the segment in which performance is worst. Urban public schools know from long experience that they are constantly at risk of losing their educational-connoisseur patrons, that they alone face flight-encouraging urban blight and school desegregation, that they alone compete with all sectors of the educational market (particularly now that urban open-enrollment programs invite intrasectoral competition), and that, until recently, they faced the persistent threat of FHA-subsidized outmigration to the suburbs by disgruntled patrons (a subsidy explicitly denied intraurban migrants). Yet, as Chubb and Moe document, the

---

[61] *Id.* at 169.

[62] *See, e.g.,* J. HENIG, RETHINKING SCHOOL CHOICE: LIMITS OF THE MARKET METAPHOR (1994).

* Reprinted by permission of The Yale Journal Company and Fred B. Rothman & Company.

result of this surfeit of disciplining choice on the part of patrons of public schools—discipline largely denied the public schools' private and suburban competitors—has been educational decline and even disaster.

. . . The authors' analysis thus provides no credible basis [to conclude] that market driven policies make a difference. . . .

II. What Price Choice . . .

A. *Just So Free, and No More: The Limited Market for a Partially Public Good*

. . . [N]o credible policymaker would be willing to consign educational consumption and expenditures to whatever, and only so much as, the market will bear. Whether to prepare young adults for self-government, to inaugurate them into a pluralistic society, to empower them to make . . . moral choices . . ., to assure the existence of a minimally productive work force, to promote social reproduction in some other way, or just to keep kids off the street part of the time, the state is going to make children attend school. . . .

In a world in which minimum levels of consumption (by some) and purchase (by others) are compelled—a world in which an educated public, if not education itself, is treated as a "public good"—only three market freedoms potentially remain: the consumer's freedom to decide how much (but not how little) to spend on education; the consumer's freedom to decide where to attend school; and the provider's freedom (subject to constitutional antidiscrimination restrictions) to decide which students to enroll. The next three sections explain why it is not possible, using only these three market freedoms, to construct anything resembling a choice-driven educational market at a tolerable social cost.

B. *Just So Free and No Less: Uncapped Vouchers, Tax Credits, and Class Segregation*

Choice proponents seeking to preserve all three market freedoms advocate either uncapped vouchers or tuition tax credits—mechanisms that lack a ceiling on the amount parents can spend on their children's education. . . .

'. . . A key desideratum of such plans is to preserve the supplier's market freedom to decide how much to charge for a particular service and the consumer's market freedom to decide how much to spend on it. Thus, although educationally and politically viable plans probably would have to provide all students with a benefit sufficient to purchase a minimally adequate education, such plans, by assumption, would not restrict private school tuitions to that benefit or to any other amount.

The consequence of such plans would be the segregation of schools, like other consumer markets, on the basis of class. If we assume only that the market works—educational consumers get what they pay for—and that wealthy families can and will pay for more on average than less wealthy families, we can be sure that uncapped plans will distribute learning, beyond some "minimally adequate" amount, on the basis of wealth. At that point, liberal democracy's basic premise of equal educational opportunity is threatened. Similarly, the four-decade-old premise of racial equality and integration is threatened, given . . . that racial stratification follows class stratification. . . .

By my lights, the equity cost just described is too much to pay, even for modest across-the-board gains in educational excellence. . . .

C. Just So Free and a Little Less: Capped Vouchers and Ability Segregation

. . . By becoming state actors, schools subject themselves to the Bill of Rights, the Fourteenth Amendment, and the various statutory burdens of actors on the left side of the public-private divide. Most importantly, participating schools trade in their First Amendment right to religious free exercise for a First Amendment responsibility of religious disestablishment. Hope as the authors do for parochial school participation, they offer no reason to think that even a future Supreme Court would let the Catholic Church run public schools. As was true of uncapped plans, therefore, the authors' capped plan inevitably must exclude the only segment of private schools that even choice-oriented social scientists can agree provides better-than-ordinary schooling.

With the schools' privacy goes most of their independence—what the authors call "autonomy" and loathe giving up. For example, policing the antidiscrimination norms that the authors favor and the Constitution imposes will necessitate administrative and judicial scrutiny—what the authors call "bureaucracy" and loathe giving in to. Additional bureaucracy will accompany enforcement of the due process and free speech restrictions that schools' inclusion in a public system dictates. More also will accompany the auditing procedures that taxpayers presumably will demand in return for the billions they are assessed. . . .

D. Just So Free and a Lot Less: Open Enrollment, Controlled Choice, and Racial Segregation

What's left in the way of choice? The answer given by the Minnesota and Nebraska Legislatures, many urban public high school systems, and several school districts in Massachusetts is open-enrollment or, in Massachusetts parlance, "controlled choice." Under this approach, a good bit more equity arises, as the second to last market freedom falls. Within some geographic boundary—a school district's, a metropolitan area's, or a state's—parents retain the freedom to choose public schools, but schools give up the freedom to choose students.

[Chubb and Moe] criticize open-enrollment plans on excellence grounds, arguing that such plans retain too much bureaucracy and too little market freedom. The open-enrollment experience of New York City's high schools adds an equity objection—stratification on the basis of consumer sophistication. Confirming the results of investigations conducted elsewhere, a recent study concludes that poor and minority families in New York City have continued sending their children to the nearest school at hand, often unaware that alternatives are available. Meanwhile, middle class and white families have used the open-enrollment program to aggregate their children in superior programs both inside and outside their own neighborhoods. Freedom-of-choice plans also can facilitate racial segregation.

c. MORE PARENTAL INVOLVEMENT

If critics like Professor Liebman are correct that choice will not work, what is the solution to making the schools better. Professor Liebman believes that the work of economist Albert Hirschman suggests the answer.[63] Hirschman argued that consumers have two options if they are dissatisfied with a producer: they can exit (and chose another producer), or they can complain. Hirschman proposed that urban schools are poor because those persons most likely to complain have instead chosen the option of exit, and have moved to the suburbs. Urban schools, however, retain a guaranteed pool of customers, consisting of the families who are financially unable to exit. Thus, "[f]ree of the discipline of exit, public schools also are rid of a good bit of the constraint of voice, because the people who care most about education have left."[64] This analysis leads Liebman to conclude that "Chubb and Moe have it backwards. The trick is not to increase exit but to reduce it."[65] If parents who are likely to complain can be kept in urban schools, Liebman believes those schools would be better.

In the following excerpt, Liebman proposes several methods of discouraging exit and keeping parents who are likely to be effective advocates for better education in poor, urban schools.

JAMES LIEBMAN, BOOK REVIEW: VOICE, NOT CHOICE, 101 YALE LAW JOURNAL 259, 299–312 (1991) *

The way to better schools lies via voice, not choice—via the more successful mobilization of existing parental and student tastes for education on behalf of all children. Increased parental voice requires two reforms: First, as a catalyst to greater voice, exit options . . . should be reduced. Second, to assure that parental voices are heard, the proportion of political power over the schools entrusted to parents, as opposed to other interested parties, should be increased. . . .

Most of the exit options that siphon off [students] from urban public schools are suburban, not private, school options. [Parents] prefer to keep as much of the existing public subsidy as they can, while still congregating in higher quality schools. One means of discouraging such escape—long familiar to interdistrict school desegregation advocates—is to break down school district lines. . . .

Increasing the proportion of state, as opposed to local, financing for schools, as Kentucky, Texas, and Wisconsin recently have done, also can make escape

---

[63] *See* A. HIRSCHMAN, EXIT, VOICE, AND LOYALTY: RESPONSES TO DECLINE IN FIRMS, ORGANIZATIONS, AND STATES (1970).

[64] Liebman, *Book Review: Voice, Not Choice*, 101 YALE L.J. 259, 295 (1991).

[65] *Id.* at 298.

* Reprinted by permission of The Yale Law Journal Company and Fred B. Rothman & Company.

to the suburbs more costly, by diverting a greater share of the tax revenues collected there to city districts and forcing suburbanites to pay even higher taxes than before to maintain their schools' quality differential. Municipal payroll taxes then can be used to increase the incentive of suburban commuters to move back to the city to take better advantage of the services their payroll taxes buy, while rising suburban taxes make it harder for urban employers to flee the payroll tax. . . .

Why should suburban and private school parents stand for exit-reduction programs that make them share, pay more for, or even give up their beloved schools? . . . [Such] changes will come, if at all, only when a coalition of urban and rural parents, teachers, and administrators, suburban school patrons and educators feeling the pinch from private school competition, business interests dependent on the public schools for their labor force, disestablishmentarians, and good-government types can defeat the smaller but politically more formidable coalition made up of the remaining suburbanites, private school consumers, and the Catholic and evangelical churches. Happily, the second necessary component of effective voice proposals—a promise of substantially enhanced parental control over the public schools—may expand the former coalition and contract the latter one. Simply by bringing more educationally oriented and vocal parents into the public schools, exit-reduction programs may increase the ratio of parent to outsider (e.g., union, bureaucrat, taxpayer) voice. . . . Additional concentration of parents' political power over the schools is necessary, however, to make sure that parents' voices count. Legislators and educators currently are experimenting with three parent-centered programs that illustrate the capacity of public policy to enlarge the proportion of political control given parents.

The first set of programs undertakes a variety of efforts to enhance parents' involvement in the day-to-day progress of their children's education. Obviously, the more opportunities parents have to interact with principals, teachers, and each other, the more likely they are to voice their concerns. Likewise, the more parents participate in their children's learning, the more informed their suggestions and complaints will be.

A second set of policies capable of concentrating parents' voices and diluting those of their competitors aims to decrease the size of schools and school districts. Parents at smaller schools have fewer peers by whom they can be drowned out. In addition, as the communitarian literature makes clear, voice-inspiring trust and collegiality are easier to achieve in smaller than in larger polities. Most important, a proliferation of smaller districts and schools can impose diseconomies of scale on outsiders—e.g., politicians, central office bureaucrats, textbook publishers, and union officials—who compete with parents to have their policy-steering voices heard.

[The third set of policies] concern (school-level) representative democracy. Using a variety of "school-based management" and "shared decisionmaking" techniques, school districts from Miami to Seattle are experimenting with plans that devolve the power to set educational policy from the state and district to the school level, and from administrators alone to elected committees of parents and teachers. The most radical proposal, recently adopted by the Illinois Legislature, places the governance of every Chicago public school in the hands of a Local School Council composed of six parents elected mainly by parents, two community residents elected by community residents, two teachers elected by the school's staff, and the principal. After completing an intensive training program, council members appoint principals to four-year performance contracts, develop and approve school operating plans, and design and oversee schools' budgets.

NOTES AND QUESTIONS

1. What arguments do the proponents make that vouchers will improve the quality of education? What is the relationship between parental choice and school quality? Assuming private schools are superior to the public schools, is it because the parents have more choice? On what grounds does Liebman argue that the quality of public education is unrelated to choice? Do you agree with him? Do you agree that the problem with school quality is that parents do not exercise the option of "voice" and complain about the quality of their schools? How would you explain the lack of effort by parents whose children attend poor inner-city schools to complain? Do they not complain, or do they lack the political skills to be effective? Or do such schools lack the resources, such as money and managerial ability, to respond?

2. Would vouchers enable more parents to place their children in schools that emphasized values of special importance to the parents? Do you agree that since parents have less time to mentor their children, they should have more choice about the schools their children attend? Does this objective conflict with the "common school movement"? How important is it that children receive a similar socialization? Who is to decide on the nature of this socialization? How is it decided for the public schools? For example, what if parents object to school lessons that teach tolerance concerning sexual orientation? If a majority of parents support such lessons, should the dissenters be able to enroll their children in alternative schools at public expense?

3. Professor Sugarman, a choice proponent, acknowledges that choice may lead to schools segregated along class and racial lines, but he rejects this scenario: "Awareness and acceptance of these apprehensions about inequality make it important to include in a choice plan features that will assure poor families fair access to schools of their choice."[66] Do you share Professor Sugarman's confidence that this potential problem can be overcome? What does Professor Liebman's analysis suggest about the likelihood of such inequality? Could these problems be overcome if some children received larger vouchers to spend? Consider the following analysis offered by the *New York Times*:

> Children from disadvantaged areas or children with learning disabilities would carry larger scholarships, giving schools an incentive to take them. Once schools were chartered and financed, states would basically step out of the picture.
>
> The proposal to attach larger scholarships to poorer children is designed to minimize "creaming." But the big problem remains:

---

[66] Sugarman, *supra* note 43, at 179.

namely, that two powerful constituencies—well-informed parents aggressively seeking the best schools, and schools aggressively seeking the best and brightest students—will combine to segregate promising students from unpromising ones. The result could be a school system that offers little opportunity for students of different abilities to interact with and learn from each other.[67]

4. Assume that a school district adopts vouchers. How is the success of a voucher system measured? Two measurements suggest themselves. First, are parents and students happier or more satisfied with the voucher system than with the regular school system? Second, have scores improved? A discussion of schools evaluation based on testing follows.

5. Milton Friedman not only supports a voucher system, but he recommends that parents be given less than the full cost of private education tuition. He argues that families should be responsible for paying part of the cost of the education of their children.[68] Because this idea would save a large amount of public money, it is supported by adherents of the taxpayer revolt movement. What is the justification for requiring parents to pay a portion of the cost of the education of their children? Recall the policy arguments that justify public support of education. Do these justifications explain why states do not currently charge parents for the public schools?

6. The idea of using vouchers to provide public services is not new. Vouchers are currently used in programs that subsidize food, housing, and medical care.[69] Are there differences that justify the use of vouchers in these other areas, but not in education? For example, how are Food Stamps different than education vouchers?

3. CHOICE IN THE UNITED STATES SUPREME COURT

The viability of a voucher program may depend on whether parents can use their vouchers to send their children to religious schools or whether state support of such schools violates the Establishment Clause, which provides that "Congress shall make no law respecting an establishment of religion. . . ."[70] In *Lemon v. Kurtzman*, 403 U.S. 602, 612–13 (1971), the Court developed a three-prong test for programs in which church and state participate together. In order to pass constitutional muster, a program must have a secular legislative purpose, must neither advance nor inhibit religion, and must not foster "an excessive government entanglement with religion."

Until recently, the Court has declared unconstitutional "virtually all forms of direct state aid" to religious institutions under the *Lemon* test.[71] In *Agostini v. Felton*, 117 S. Ct. 1997 (1997), however, the Court held that a program which sent public school teachers to provide remedial education to disabled

---

[67] *Wrong Surgery for Sick Schools*, N.Y. Times, July 3, 1990, at A14.

[68] Friedman, *supra* note 45, at 94–95.

[69] *See* Rose-Ackerman, *Social Services and the Market*, 83 Colum. L. Rev. 1405 (1983).

[70] U.S. Const. amend. I.

[71] Anderson, *Religious Groups in the Educational Marketplace: Applying the Establishment Clause to School Privatization Programs* 82 Geo. L. J. 1869, 1876 (1994).

children enrolled in parochial schools did not constitute an excessive entanglement of church and state. It overturned a prior decision, (*Aguilar v. Felton*, 473 U.S. 402 (1985), which had reached the opposite result. The Court noted that since deciding *Aguilar*, its interpretation of the *Lemon* test had changed. Justice O'Connor, writing for the Court, expressed this evolution:

> To be sure, the general principles we use to evaluate whether government aid violates the Establishment Clause have not changed. . . . For example we continue to ask whether the government acted with the purpose of advancing or inhibiting religion, and the nature of the inquiry has remained largely unchanged. [Citations omitted.] Likewise, we continue to explore whether the aid has the "effect" of advancing or inhibiting religion. What has changed . . . is our understanding of the criteria used to assess whether aid to religion has an impermissible effect.

Under the Court's new understanding, state aid that "directly aids the educational function of religious schools" is no longer necessarily constitutionally invalid. Nor does a federal program which allows sectarian organizations to compete for federal funds to provide "[a] religious education . . . confer any message of state endorsement of religion." Last Term, the United States Supreme Court heard argument and ruled on a school voucher program in Cleveland, Ohio. The specific challenge was that the Cleveland program violated the Establishment Clause of the First Amendment. In a lengthy and vigorous 5-4 opinion, the Court upheld the voucher program.

ZELMAN v. DORIS SIMMONS-HARRIS
122 S.Ct. 2460 (2002)

CHIEF JUSTICE REHNQUIST delivered the opinion of the Court.

The State of Ohio has established a pilot program designed to provide educational choices to families with children who reside in the Cleveland City School District. The question presented is whether this program offends the Establishment Clause of the United States Constitution. We hold that it does not.

There are more than 75,000 children enrolled in the Cleveland City School District. The majority of these children are from low-income and minority families. Few of these families enjoy the means to send their children to any school other than an inner-city public school. For more than a generation, however, Cleveland's public schools have been among the worst performing public schools in the Nation. In1995, a Federal District Court declared a "crisis of magnitude" and placed the entire Cleveland school district under state control. Shortly thereafter, the state auditor found that Cleveland's public schools were in the midst of a "crisis that is perhaps unprecedented in the history of American education.". . .

It is against this backdrop that Ohio enacted, among other initiatives, its Pilot Project Scholarship Program. The program provides financial assistance to families in any Ohio school district that is or has been "under federal court order requiring supervision and operational management of the district by the state superintendent." Cleveland is the only Ohio school district to fall within that category.

The program provides two basic kinds of assistance to parents of children in a covered district. First, the program provides tuition aid for students in kindergarten through third grade, expanding each year through eighth grade, to attend a participating public or private school of their parent's choosing. Second, the program provides tutorial aid for students who choose to remain enrolled in public school. . . .

The tuition aid portion of the program is designed to provide educational choices to parents who reside in a covered district. Any private school, whether religious or nonreligious, may participate in the program and accept program students so long as the school is located within the boundaries of a covered district and meets statewide educational standards. Participating private schools must agree not to discriminate on the basis of race, religion, or ethnic background, or to "advocate or foster unlawful behavior or teach hatred of any person or group on the basis of race, ethnicity, national origin, or religion." Any public school located in a school district adjacent to the covered district may also participate in the program. . . . All participating schools, whether public or private, are required to accept students in accordance with rules and procedures established by the state superintendent.

Tuition aid is distributed to parents according to financial need. . . .

The Establishment Clause of the First Amendment, applied to the States through the Fourteenth Amendment, prevents a State from enacting laws that have the "purpose" or "effect" of advancing or inhibiting religion. . . . There is no dispute that the program challenged here was enacted for the valid secular purpose of providing educational assistance to poor children in a demonstrably failing public school system. Thus, the question presented is whether the Ohio program nonetheless has the forbidden "effect" of advancing or inhibiting religion.

To answer that question, our decisions have drawn a consistent distinction between government programs that provide aid directly to religious schools, and programs of true private choice, in which government aid reaches religious schools only as a result of the genuine and independent choices of private individuals. . . .

In *Mueller* [*v. Allen*, 463 U.S. 388 (1983)], we rejected an Establishment Clause challenge to a Minnesota program authorizing tax deductions for various educational expenses, including private school tuition costs, even though the great majority of the program's beneficiaries (96%) were parents of children in religious schools. We began by focusing on the class of beneficiaries, finding that because the class included "*all* parents," including parents with "children [who] attend nonsectarian private schools or sectarian private schools," the program was "not readily subject to challenge under the Establishment Clause." Then, viewing the program as a whole, we emphasized the principle of private choice, noting that public funds were made available to religious schools "only as a result of numerous, private choices of individual parents of school-age children." This, we said, ensured that " 'no imprimatur of state approval' can be deemed to have been conferred on any particular religion, or on religion generally." . . .

Mueller. . .thus make[s] clear that where a government aid program is neutral with respect to religion, and provides assistance directly to a broad class of citizens who, in turn, direct government aid to religious schools wholly as a result of their own genuine and independent private choice, the program is not readily subject to challenge under the Establishment Clause. A program that shares these features permits government aid to reach religious institutions only by way of the deliberate choices of numerous individual recipients. The incidental advancement of a religious mission, or the perceived endorsement of a religious message, is reasonably attributable to the individual recipient, not to the government, whose role ends with the disbursement of benefits. . . .

We believe that the program challenged here is a program of true private choice, . . . *and* thus constitutional. . . .[T]he Ohio program is neutral in all respects toward religion. It is part of a general and multifaceted undertaking by the State of Ohio to provide educational opportunities to the children of a failed school district. It confers educational assistance directly to a broad class of individuals defined without reference to religion, *i.e.,* any parent of a school-age child who resides in the Cleveland City School District. The program permits the participation of *all* schools within the district, religious or nonreligious. Adjacent public schools also may participate and have a financial incentive to do so. Program benefits are available to participating families on neutral terms, with no reference to religion. The only preference stated anywhere in the program is a preference for low-income families, who receive greater assistance and are given priority for admission at participating schools. . . .

JUSTICE O'CONNOR concurring.

. . .The Court's opinion in these cases focuses on a narrow question related to the *Lemon* test: how to apply the primary effects prong in indirect aid cases? Specifically, it clarifies the basic inquiry when trying to determine whether a program that distributes aid to beneficiaries, rather than directly to service providers, has the primary effect of advancing or inhibiting religion, or, as I have put it, of "endors[ing] or disapprov[ing] . . . religion." Courts are instructed to consider two factors: first, whether the program administers aid in a neutral fashion, without differentiation based on the religious status of beneficiaries or providers of services; second, and more importantly, whether beneficiaries of indirect aid have a genuine choice among religious and nonreligious organizations when determining the organization to which they will direct that aid. If the answer to either query is "no," the program should be struck down under the Establishment Clause.

JUSTICE THOMAS concurring.

Frederick Douglass once said that "[e]ducation . . . means emancipation. It means light and liberty. It means the uplifting of the soul of man into the glorious light of truth, the light by which men can only be made free." Today many of our inner-city public schools deny emancipation to urban minority students. Despite this Court's observation nearly 50 years ago in *Brown v. Board of Education,* that "it is doubtful that any child may reasonably be expected to succeed in life if he is denied the opportunity of an education," urban children have been forced into a system that continually fails them. These cases present an example of such failures. Besieged by escalating financial problems and declining academic achievement, the Cleveland City

School District was in the midst of an academic emergency when Ohio enacted its scholarship program. . . .

JUSTICE SOUTER, with whom JUSTICE STEVENS, JUSTICE GINSBURG, and JUSTICE BREYER join, dissenting.

The Court's majority holds that the Establishment Clause is no bar to Ohio's payment of tuition at private religious elementary and middle schools under a scheme that systematically provides tax money to support the schools' religious missions. The occasion for the legislation thus upheld is the condition of public education in the city of Cleveland. The record indicates that the schools are failing to serve their objective, and the vouchers in issue here are said to be needed to provide adequate alternatives to them. If there were an excuse for giving short shrift to the Establishment Clause, it would probably apply here. But there is no excuse. Constitutional limitations are placed on government to preserve constitutional values in hard cases, like these. I therefore respectfully dissent.

The applicability of the Establishment Clause to public funding of benefits to religious schools was settled in *Everson v. Board of Ed. of Ewing*, which inaugurated the modern era of establishment doctrine. The Court stated the principle in words from which there was no dissent:

> "No tax in any amount, large or small, can be levied to support any religious activities or institutions, whatever they may be called, or whatever form they may adopt to teach or practice religion."

The Court has never in so many words repudiated this statement, let alone, in so many words, overruled *Everson*.

Today, however, the majority holds that the Establishment Clause is not offended by Ohio's Pilot Project Scholarship Program, under which students may be eligible to receive as much as $2,250 in the form of tuition vouchers transferable to religious schools. In the city of Cleveland the overwhelming proportion of large appropriations for voucher money must be spent on religious schools if it is to be spent at all, and will be spent in amounts that cover almost all of tuition. The money will thus pay for eligible students' instruction not only in secular subjects but in religion as well, in schools that can fairly be characterized as founded to teach religious doctrine and to imbue teaching in all subjects with a religious dimension. Public tax money will pay at a systemic level for teaching the covenant with Israel and Mosaic law in Jewish schools, the primacy of the Apostle Peter and the Papacy in Catholic schools, the truth of reformed Christianity in Protestant schools, and the revelation to the Prophet in Muslim schools, to speak only of major religious groupings in the Republic.

How can a Court consistently leave *Everson* on the books and approve the Ohio vouchers? The answer is that it cannot. . . .

NOTES AND QUESTIONS

1. Since there are tax dollars that are going to the support of religious training, on what basis does the majority conclude that there is no government support of religion in violation of the First Amendment? Why does it make a difference to the majority that the voucher money is given to parents, rather than directly to religious private schools? Do agree that this should make a difference? Or would you read the Establishment Clause in the same absolute manner as the dissenting Justices, which prevents any state support of religious training, whether direct or indirect?[72]

2. Has the Court completely removed any Establish Clause obstacle to the use of vouchers at private religious schools? What is the relevance of the majority's point that there was "crisis of magnitude" in the Cleveland school system? Did the Court approve the use of vouchers in circumstances where the schools are not failing as badly as in Cleveland? Why is it significant for the majority that the voucher program assistance was available to a "broad class of citizens." Does this mean there might be voucher programs that are not constitutional if they are not so broadly available? Why?

4.   STANDARDS AND TESTING

Not all reform proposals concern choice programs. Some reforms look to another form of regulation—standards—as a solution. For example, many states rely on standardized tests as a reform tool: pupils are required to take competency or proficiency tests at certain rungs of the educational ladder. The idea is to provide information to legislators, administrators, and parents concerning how well the schools are doing. In some states, test results are used to allocate remedial funding to local school districts and award "bonuses" to schools based on test score improvements. Other states go further and require students to pass a standardized test to be promoted to another grade.[73] The requirement that students pass a standardized test to be promoted to the next grade indicates that reformers distrust schools to make such judgments on their own.

President Clinton's *Goal 2000* and President Bush's *No Child Left Behind Act* have moved standards center stage in both state and national reform efforts. Below we have excerpted federal and Ohio's state legislation as a brief case study of this issue.

a.   REGULATORY REFORM

Testing, performance standards, and accountability are central to Title I of the No Child Left Behind Act of 2001. The act runs several hundred pages and addresses other issues including teacher quality, national statistics, language instruction and parental choice among other issues. Here we concentrate on standards and accountability and then look at Ohio's state standards program to compare federal and state legislation. The first excerpt is intended to give you a sense of the language of the act. It is followed by a commentary.

---

[72] For a pro voucher look at *Zelman,* see, D. BRENNAN, VICTORY FOR KIDS: THE CLEVELAND SCHOOL VOUCHER CASE (2002).

[73] *See* MAKING SCHOOLS WORK: IMPROVING PERFORMANCE AND CONTROLLING COSTS (E. Hanusek ed. 1994); P. COOKSON, SCHOOL CHOICE (1994); T. TOCH, IN THE NAME OF EXCELLENCE (1991); C. FINN, JR., WE MUST TAKE CHARGE: OUR SCHOOLS AND OUR FUTURE 42–43 (1990); Airasian, *State Mandated Testing and Education Reform: Context and Consequences,* AM. J. EDUC., May, 1987, at 393–94.

NO CHILD LEFT BEHIND ACT

P.L. No. 107-110 (2001)

(a) PLANS REQUIRED. —

    (1)   IN GENERAL. — For any State desiring to receive a grant under this part, the State educational agency shall submit to the Secretary a plan, developed by the State educational agency, in consultation with local educational agencies, teachers, principals, pupil services personnel, administrators (including administrators of programs described in other parts of this title), other staff, and parents, that satisfies the requirements of this section and that is coordinated with other programs under this Act, the Individuals with Disabilities Education Act, the Carl D. Perkins Vocational and Technical Education Act of 1998, the Head Start Act, the Adult Education and Family Literacy Act, and the McKinney-Vento Homeless Assistance Act.

    (2)   CONSOLIDATED PLAN. — A State plan submitted under paragraph (1) may be submitted as part of a consolidated plan under section 9302.

(b) ACADEMIC STANDARDS, ACADEMIC ASSESSMENTS, AND ACCOUNTABILITY. —

    (1)   CHALLENGING ACADEMIC STANDARDS. —

        (A)   IN GENERAL. — Each State plan shall demonstrate that the State has adopted challenging academic content standards and challenging student academic achievement standards that will be used by the State, its local educational agencies, and its schools to carry out this part, except that a State shall not be required to submit such standards to the Secretary.

        (B)   SAME STANDARDS. — The academic standards required by subparagraph (A) shall be the same academic standards that the State applies to all schools and children in the State.

        (C)   SUBJECTS. — The State shall have such academic standards for all public elementary school and secondary school children, including children served under this part, in subjects determined by the State, but including at least mathematics, reading or language arts, and (beginning in the 2005-2006 school year) science, which shall include the same knowledge, skills, and levels of achievement expected of all children.

        (D)   CHALLENGING ACADEMIC STANDARDS. — Standards under this paragraph shall include —

            (i)   challenging academic content standards in academic subjects that —

          (I)   specify what children are expected to know and be able to do;

          (II)   contain coherent and rigorous content; and

          (III)   encourage the teaching of advanced skills; and

    (ii)   challenging student academic achievement standards that —

          (I)   are aligned with the State's academic content standards;

          (II)   describe two levels of high achievement (proficient and advanced) that determine how well children are mastering the material in the State academic content standards; and

          (III)   describe a third level of achievement (basic) to provide complete information about the progress of the lower-achieving children toward mastering the proficient and advanced levels of achievement.

(E)   INFORMATION. — For the subjects in which students will be served under this part, but for which a State is not required by subparagraphs (A), (B), and (C) to develop, and has not otherwise developed, such academic standards, the State plan shall describe a strategy for ensuring that students are taught the same knowledge and skills in such subjects and held to the same expectations as are all children.

(F)   EXISTING STANDARDS. — Nothing in this part shall prohibit a State from revising, consistent with this section, any standard adopted under this part before or after the date of enactment of the No Child Left Behind Act of 2001.

(2)   ACCOUNTABILITY. —

(A)   IN GENERAL. — Each State plan shall demonstrate that the State has developed and is implementing a single, statewide State accountability system that will be effective in ensuring that all local educational agencies, public elementary schools, and public secondary schools make adequate yearly progress as defined under this paragraph. Each State accountability system shall —

    (i)   be based on the academic standards and academic assessments adopted under paragraphs (1) and (3), and other academic indicators consistent with subparagraph (C)(vi) and (vii), and shall take into account the achievement of all public elementary school and secondary school students;

    (ii)   be the same accountability system the State uses for all public elementary schools and secondary schools or all local educational agencies in the State, except that public elementary schools, secondary schools, and local educational agencies not participating under this part are not subject to the requirements of section 1116; and

(iii)   include sanctions and rewards, such as bonuses and recognition, the State will use to hold local educational agencies and public elementary schools and secondary schools accountable for student achievement and for ensuring that they make adequate yearly progress in accordance with the State's definition under subparagraphs (B) and (C).

(B)   ADEQUATE YEARLY PROGRESS. — Each State plan shall demonstrate, based on academic assessments described in paragraph (3), and in accordance with this paragraph, what constitutes adequate yearly progress of the State, and of all public elementary schools, secondary schools, and local educational agencies in the State, toward enabling all public elementary school and secondary school students to meet the State's student academic achievement standards, while working toward the goal of narrowing the achievement gaps in the State, local educational agencies, and schools. . . .

————

LEARNING FIRST ALLIANCE, MAJOR CHANGES TO ESEA IN THE NO CHILD LEFT BEHIND ACT 2–12 (2002) *

Standards

As with the prior law, the new Act requires that states have challenging academic content and achievement standards for all students in at least reading/language arts and mathematics. The new law also requires states to have science standards in place beginning with school year 2005-06. While standards for other subjects are not required, state plans submitted to the U. S. Department of Education must describe strategies for teaching children in Title I schools the same content in the other subjects as other children in the state receive.

Assessments

The new Act builds on prior Title I assessment provisions, adding additional requirements and specificity.

---

* Reprinted by permission.

General Requirements

First, unlike current law, the new Act requires that states administer assessments and that these assessments be administered to all students in all public schools in the state.

Second, beginning with school year 2005-06, states must assess reading/ language arts and mathematics every year from 3rd through 8th grade, as well as one year in the 10th–12th grade span. . . .

Until these new testing requirements go into effect, states must continue to have annual reading/language arts and mathematics assessments in at least one grade in each of the following grade spans: 3–5, 6–9, and 10–12.

Beginning With the 2007-08 school year, states must administer a science assessment annually in at least one grade in each of the following grade spans: 3–5, 6–9, and 10–12.

To ensure that students' performance is measured against state standards, states must report scores in terms of proficiency levels rather than as percentile scores. In addition, the Act requires that at least 95 percent of the children enrolled in the state and at least 95 percent of each major subgroup described below participate in the assessments. . . .

National Assessment of Educational Progress

Beginning with school year 2002-03, every state must participate in the 4th and 8th grade reading and mathematics sections of the National Assessment of Educational Progress (NAEP) to obtain a national comparison of the rigor of state assessments, provided that the federal government pays the cost of participation. Unlike state assessments, NAEP is only given to a random sample of students in the state. . . .

Accountability

While the changes to standards and assessments are substantial, the changes in accountability are more far reaching. Some of these requirements apply to all districts and schools while others apply only to districts and schools receiving funds under Title I.

State Accountability Requirements

Adequate Yearly Progress

First, each state must define what constitutes adequate yearly progress in increasing student achievement toward the goal of all students reaching proficient levels on the state assessments by 2014. The state must establish a starting bar or measuring point for the percentage of students who must be at the proficient level, which may be based upon the lowest achieving schools (schools at the 20th percentile in the state) or lowest achieving demographic subgroup in the state, whichever is higher, or at a higher point. Once the starting bar and target year are set, the state must "raise the bar" in gradual but equal increments to reach 100 percent of students performing at the proficient level by the target year which must be 2014. The first increase in the percentage of students at the proficient level must occur within two years and increase at least every three years thereafter. . . .

Rewards and Sanctions: All Schools and Districts

Each state must also develop its own system of rewards and sanctions to hold all public schools and districts accountable for making adequate yearly progress. This is because the Act's specific accountability requirements for school improvement and corrective actions apply only to schools and districts receiving the Title I funds.

School Improvement and Corrective Action for Schools and Districts receiving Title I Funds

If a school district, receiving Title I funds, fails to make adequate yearly progress two years in a row, the state must identify it as a district in need of improvement, require the district to develop an improvement plan, and provide technical assistance.

The new plan must be implemented in the district in the school year immediately following its identification. If the district is still not making adequate yearly progress two years after identification as a district in need, the state must authorize students to transfer to a higher performing school in another district and provide transportation. It must also take at least one of the following actions below:
- Withhold funds;
- Institute new curricula;
- Replace district personnel relevant to the failure;
- Remove particular schools from the jurisdiction of the district and provide alternative governance arrangements:
- Appoint a trustee or receiver to run the district; or
- Abolish or restructure the district. . . .

[The act also requires similar "adequate yearly progress" reports from local school districts and schools.]

Report Cards

The Act requires that beginning in school year 2002-03, states and districts must issue annual report cards to the public. They may continue to use existing report cards, provided the report cards are modified as necessary to include required information.

State Report Cards

State report cards must contain at least the following information:

- Aggregate information on student achievement at each proficiency level, as well as data disaggregated by race, ethnicity, gender, disability status, English proficiency, and status as economically disadvantaged;
- A comparison between the actual achievement levels of subgroups of students and the state's annual measurable objectives on each academic assessment;
- The percentage of students not tested, disaggregated by subgroups;
- The most recent two-year trend in student achievement for each grade and subject area;
- Aggregate information on other indicators the state uses to determine adequate yearly progress;
- Graduation rates for students, disaggregated by subgroup;
- Information on the performance of local districts in making yearly progress, including the number and names of each school identified for school improvement; and
- The professional qualifications of teachers, the percentage of teachers with emergency or provisional credentials, and the percentage of classes not taught by highly qualified teachers in the aggregate and for schools in the top and bottom quartile of poverty in the state. . . .

The federal No Child Left Behind Act imposes requirements and time-tables on the states. Many states, among them Ohio, had testing and standards requirements already in place. Below are the applicable Ohio statutory provisions followed by commentary and by a comparison of federal and state laws to determine the proper fit.

OHIO REVISED CODE § 3301.0710
STATEWIDE ACHIEVEMENT TESTS

The state board of education shall adopt rules establishing a statewide program to test student achievement. The state board shall ensure that all tests administered under the testing program are aligned with the academic standards and model curricula adopted by the state board and are created with input from Ohio parents, Ohio classroom teachers, Ohio school administrators, and other Ohio school personnel pursuant to section 3301.079 of the Revised Code.

The testing program shall be designed to ensure that students who receive a high school diploma demonstrate at least high school levels of achievement in reading, writing, mathematics, science, and social studies.

(A)(1) The state board shall prescribe all of the following:

    (a) A statewide achievement test designed to measure the level of reading skill expected at the end of third grade;

    (b) Two statewide achievement tests, one each designed to measure the level of writing and mathematics skill expected at the end of fourth grade;

    (c) Two statewide achievement tests, one each designed to measure the level of science and social studies skill expected at the end of fifth grade;

    (d) Three statewide achievement tests, one each designed to measure the level of reading, writing, and mathematics skill expected at the end of seventh grade;

    (e) Two statewide achievement tests, one each designed to measure the level of science and social studies skill expected at the end of eighth grade.

(2) The state board shall determine and designate at least four ranges of scores on each of the achievement tests described in division (A)(1) of this section. Each range of scores shall be deemed to demonstrate a level of achievement so that any student attaining a score within such range has achieved one of the following:

    (a) An advanced level of skill;

    (b) A proficient level of skill;

    (c) A basic level of skill;

    (d) A below basic level of skill.

(B) The tests prescribed under this division shall collectively be known as the Ohio graduation tests. The state board shall prescribe five statewide high school achievement tests, one each designed to measure the level of reading, writing, mathematics, science, and social studies skill expected at the end of tenth grade, and shall determine and designate the score on each such test that shall be deemed to demonstrate that any student attaining such score has achieved at least a proficient level of skill appropriate for tenth grade. . . .

OHIO DEPARTMENT OF EDUCATION, NO CHILD LEFT BEHIND ACT: ELEMENTARY AND SECONDARY EDUCATION ACT (ESEA)– STATE AND DISTRICT REQUIREMENTS

District: must identify schools failing to make yearly progress for two consecutive years or more before the beginning of each school year. If identified, the school must:

- Offer public school choice (giving the priority to the lowest achieving children);

- Require school to develop a school improvement plan to cover a two-year period;

- School to spend not less than 10 percent of Title I funds on professional development;

- Promptly notify parents and explain:

- What the identification means;

- How the school compares in terms of academic achievement to other schools in the district and the state;

- Reasons for the identification and what the school and the district are doing to address the problem of low achievement

- How the parents can become involved;

- An explanation of how the parent's options to transfer the child.

District: Before the beginning of each school year, must identify schools failing to make adequate yearly progress for three consecutive years. If identified he school must:

- Offer public school choice;

- Make supplemental educational services available;

- Continue to implement the school improvement plan;

- Promptly notify parents and explain:

- What the identification means;

- How the school compares in terms of academic achievement to other schools in the district and the state;

- Reasons for the identification and what the school and the district are doing to address the problem of low achievement;

- How the parents can become involved;

- Parent's options to transfer the child to obtain supplemental educational service,

District: Before the beginning of each year, must identify corrective action schools failing to make adequate yearly progress for four consecutive years. If identified the school must:

- Offer public school choice;
- Make supplemental educational services available;
- Promptly notify parents and explain:
  - What the identification means;
  - How the school compares in terms of academic achievement to other schools in the district and the state;
  - Reasons for the identification;
  - What the school and district are doing to address the problem of low achievement;
  - How the parents can become involved;
  - Parents' options to transfer the child or to obtain supplemental educational services.
- Take corrective action by taking at least one of the following measures:
  - Replace school staff relevant to the failure;
  - Institute and implement a new research-based and professionally-developed curriculum;
  - Significantly decrease management authority at the school level;
  - Appoint an outside expert to advise the school in its progress;
  - Extend the school year or school day for the school;
  - Restructure the internal organizational structure of the school.

District: Publish and disseminate information regarding any corrective action taken to the public and to parents of each student enrolled in the corrective action school.

District: At the beginning of the school year, identify any school failing to make adequate yearly progress after one year in corrective action and:

- Offer public school choice;
- Offer supplemental educational services;
- Prepare a plan, to take effect within a year to do one of the following:
  - Reopen the school as a public charter school;
  - Replace all or most of the staff (which may include the principal);
  - Enter into a contract with an entity, such as a private management company, with a demonstrated record of effectiveness to operate the public school;
  - Turn the operation of the school over to the Ohio Department of Education (ODE), if permitted by state law and agreeable to ODE.

b. DO STANDARDS WORK?

The No Child Left Behind Act is the most significant federal intervention into an area traditionally reserved to state and federal government. The carrot, of course, is federal funding, and the sticks are many but most importantly testing and reporting. Proponents of nationalized testing and similar reforms seek greater school accountability "through an outcomes-oriented enterprise whose institutions, employees, and policymakers will be held responsible for their results by the public they serve."[74] A well-known educational policy analyst, Chester Finn, argues that outcomes-oriented accountability "is the only kind of accountability worth having, . . .certainly the only kind that bears any relationship to the premier education problem we seek to solve—namely the weak academic achievement of our children."[75] This section considers the viability of outcomes-oriented accountability.

PETER AIRASIAN, STATE MANDATED TESTING AND EDUCATION REFORM: CONTEXT AND CONSEQUENCES, AMERICAN JOURNAL OF EDUCATION, MAY 1987, AT 405–07 *

. . . As long as educational benefits and resources are perceived to be important for success in our society, and as long as these benefits and resources are comparatively scarce, the mechanism that is used to distribute them will be extremely important to individuals and groups who seek the benefits and resources. In essence, test scores become a medium of exchange to be bartered for educational, social, and economic benefits or rewards.

By making the results of standardized tests important for decisions involving staff reduction, interschool comparisons, funding allotments, high school graduation, grade-to-grade promotion, program evaluation, and the assessment of educational equity, society has made the tests themselves important. As a consequence, testing necessarily has become intertwined with social, economic, and political issues such as equity and control. By making testing important in social, economic, and political ways, a variety of responses to tests is inevitably produced, some reflecting honest concern over the social role of testing and some reflecting self-interest and fear of lost prerogatives.

As a result, three consequences that influence the climate of testing in America have ensued. First, the audiences and consumers of test information are no longer limited to a few professionals and some interested parents. The media have sensed popular interest in test results and report various forms of test results with growing regularity. State and federal legislators seek to understand and use the results of tests to provide evidence and support for legislation regarding education. The judiciary has found it essential to become conversant with an array of technical features of tests in order to decipher courtroom arguments and to render reasonable decisions. Recently, the Council of Chief State School Officers endorsed a plan to provide annual, public, state-by-state achievement comparisons on national standardized achievement tests.

---

[74] FINN, *supra*, note 73, at 149.

[75] *Id.*

* Copyright © 1987 by the University of Chicago. Reprinted by permission.

In most communities and the nation as a whole, moral and financial support for schools is conditioned by the answer to the question, How are our schools doing? The answer often depends on the results of standardized tests, since the majority of the American public perceives that such tests provide the most credible, objective evidence about schools and learning. Whether wisely or not, the public is unable or unwilling to accept testimonials about the status of education from teachers and school administrators, whom they perceive to have a vested interest in that status. The public seeks some external assurance of the quality of teaching and learning, and so it turns, virtually by default, to the one index it believes provides such an objective view, standardized tests. Of late, the evidence has been disheartening, provoking a call for higher standards, more discipline, and a greater school and teacher accountability, which has been translated into more intrusive forms of standardized testing. The breadth of the audiences for testing means that discussion and debate over testing are no longer technical and arcane but encompass political, legal, social, and economic as well as educational issues.

Second, the increasingly tighter link between test results and decision making poses the serious threat of further erosion of local school control. The use of test results to make important determinations such as judging school effectiveness, awarding high school diplomas, assessing teacher competence, and allocating educational funds makes the content of the tests exceedingly important. As tests developed and/or administered by agencies external to the local school district take on heightened importance, control of the curriculum and other school prerogatives shifts from the local school or district level to that of the test developer or administrator, usually the state. . . . State-mandated pupil and teacher certification testing programs represent a move by legislatures and state departments of education to exert greater power and control over local schools. . . .

Third, the new uses of tests and test results have brought into sharp focus the differences in the goals and priorities of varied social groups. For example, there is a constant tension between the goals of quality and equality, between the use of tests to improve educational quality and current definitions of equal educational opportunity. Test results used to carry out policies designed to raise academic standards or certify pupil and teacher competence inevitably clash with other policies aimed at equalizing educational opportunity and integrating racial/ethnic groups in schools and classrooms. Since test results are a common index for the assessment of equality of educational opportunity and also the trigger for bias and discrimination law suits, decisions made on the basis of test results have clear implications for members of majority and minority groups alike. The implications, in turn, are not confined to the educational arena but also are concerned ultimately with the equitable and just distribution of social and economic prerogatives.

WILLIAM BAINBRIDGE, PROFICIENCY TESTS ARE DRAWING FIRE FOR GOOD REASONS (2002) *

Historically, schools have employed testing as a way to measure students' performance and have used test results to inform parents about their children's progress. In recent times, Ohio has become one of many states that have established a "high-stakes" testing program. Ohio's now infamous proficiency tests have become a lightning rod for criticism from parents, educators, and others who believe there is too much testing and that current tests do not measure the right things.

The perception is spreading that teachers are teaching to the test and centering their lessons on the proficiency test itself, at the expense of a more balanced program of study. Teachers have tried hard to make proficiency testing work, but even teachers and their unions formally have protested the tests, after seeing the impact on students.

How are the tests constructed, implemented and interpreted? Are they valid? Well-documented flaws in the tests appear to undermine the entire standards process.

Evidence to support a lack of test validity is mounting. Two years ago, the results of the fourth-grade proficiency test in mathematics indicated four of Ohio's roughly 600 school districts could boast that half of their students passed the test. In school systems in Bexley, Granville and Upper Arlington, where college-entrance examinations historically have placed high-schoolers in the top 2 percent in the country in mathematics, the passing rates were unbelievably low and lacked credibility.

On the Ohio test, more than half of the top academic achievers in the state could not pass muster. The process created animosity between school systems and the state and undermined the self-confidence of some of the state's finest students. It is difficult to believe that the education process in Ohio has become an inverted Lake Wobegon, where the majority of our students are below average. . . .

Every reputable study has found that socioeconomic status accounts for an overwhelming proportion of variance in test scores when different schools, school systems and states are compared. The level of education in the community, number of children living in poverty and income level of residents continue to be the best predictors of differences in cognitive levels of school-age children.

The high-stakes testing in Ohio requires students to pass reading, writing, math, citizenship and science proficiency tests in order to graduate. What are these test results actually worth? What is the basis for comparison? The tests *really* tell what we already know: Disadvantaged children need more resources and time to develop their academic skills. . . .

If we do not abolish the program, Ohio officials need to change the process radically by providing:

---

* Reprinted with permission. William L. Bainbridge is president of School Match, a Westerville-based national educational research, auditing and consulting company. The commentary is available at: schoolmatch.com/articles/CDMAR01.htm.

1. Field testing on all assessment instruments to avoid a recurrence of the fourth-grade mathematics debacle.

2. Cutting-edge teacher-development programs.

3. Resources to assist student groups with low achievement rather than punishment for schools they attend.

4. Multiple and cross-referenced measures of school district and student accountability.

5. Tests that are nationally normed; Ohio is not an island state.

6. Curricula aligned to district and state standards for teaching.

7. Standards that are well-understood by students, teachers, administrators and parents.

8. Instructional material chosen as a result of field studies.

9. Instructional programs that have established validity.

10. Examinations that permit students to give evidence of a wide range of abilities.

11. More reliance on the expertise of nationally known assessment practitioners.

12. An instructional verification system to compare teacher processes with program outcomes.

Additionally, a critical factor is that all students exposed to proficiency tests have school-provided access to instruction on exam-taking skills *before* their performance is measured. If the future of our state's young people is dependent upon promotion and exit examinations, then the test-taking skills of the students and content of the proficiency exams should be pertinent to all and not just those who can relate to the questions being asked. . . .

———

The growing pains in the development process of these tests have created undue stress for students, teachers and parents. Rather than punishing them, proficiency testing should be redesigned to reward students for their efforts. A broader view of the debate on standards follows:

MARC S. TUCKER, THE ROOTS OF BACKLASH, EDUCATION WEEK (JAN. 9, 2002) *

As a new landmark federal legislation increases the emphasis on school standards and accountability, a backlash against the accountability movement is rapidly gaining strength. . . .

What is crucially important to note, however, is that this movement is actually compounded from quite different—and indeed conflicting—premises, experiences, and solutions. Consider four models of standards-driven reform:

---

* Reprinted by permission.

1. *The Business Model*. The globalization of trade in the late 1970s and early 1980s produced enormous competitive pressure on American business to redesign almost every aspect of the way it functioned—simply to stay in business. The prescription that emerged from that trial by fire went something like this: Get your goals clear and communicate them to everyone in the organization. Develop accurate measures of progress toward those goals. Push the decisions as to how to reach those goals as far down toward the people who make the product or render the service as possible. Thin the ranks of those who used to tell the front line what to do and how to do it. Provide as much support for those people as you can (particularly in the form of training, tools, and technical assistance). Then—and only then—hold them accountable for their performance.

Many in the business community and some in government outside the schools believed that this approach to management could and should be applied to public education. While the business model includes the ideas of standards, measures, and accountability, it also includes other equally important ideas: more autonomy and responsibility where it counts, in that part of the organization that actually renders the services to the customers; more training, better tools, and more technical assistance; fewer people around to tell the people on the front line what to do and how to do it.

Based on their experience, business leaders believed that it was unreasonable to hold people accountable if they were not given the authority to make the decisions that determined the outcomes, and they also believed that it was fruitless and unfair to hold people accountable if one did not give them the training, tools, and technical assistance they needed to do the job.

2. *The Education Accountability Model*. This model was imported by Americans who observed that, in many countries, the annual release of school-by-school test scores, often published in the form of "league tables" of schools in rank order by scores, receives an enormous amount of public attention and puts great pressure on the schools to improve their performance.

Many of the American educators who observed these practices were advocates of the sort of "thinking curriculum" that puts a premium on the ability of students to solve complex, multistep problems that often have no single right answer. One of the reasons they were comfortable with this approach was that they noticed that the examinations used in many of these other countries encourage such a thinking curriculum and could accurately assess student progress against the standards associated with such a curriculum. The implicit "theory of action" here is that a system the main elements of which are standards, assessments, and accountability (in the form of publishing school tests scores) will by itself direct student effort to the right goals and provide the incentives that educators need to do what must be done to drive up student performance substantially.

3. *The Ministry of Education Model*. Among the reports that shaped this model were the "America's Choice" report of our Commission on the Skills of the American Workforce and the reports of the Third International Mathematics and Science Study, or TIMSS. The observers in this camp noticed that nations with a consistently strong record of student achievement across the board shared a common strategy with the following elements: high standards

that applied to all students, at least through the age of 14; high-quality assessments (embodying a thinking curriculum) matched to the standards; a curriculum framework that spells out what topics are to be studied at each grade level in the required courses in the curriculum; texts and other instructional materials closely matched to the curriculum framework, standards, and assessments; and a system for training teachers that focuses on the methods and techniques teachers need to successfully teach the agreed curriculum, within the structure of the agreed curriculum framework. In other countries, the ministry of education coordinates all these functions. In our country, they are probably most appropriately coordinated by state government.

But the fact is that, in the United States, no level of government has ever had as its assignment the performance of the full set of roles just described. Among the consequences is the fact that texts and other instructional materials, in the absence of a framework of topics to be taught at each grade level, must be made to suit the infinitely varied personal preferences of countless teachers and other educators across the United States, with the result that American texts are, as the authors of the TIMSS report put it, "a mile wide and an inch deep."

Another consequence is that the training of school faculties is largely unconnected to the standards that the students will be expected to meet. Still another is that teachers looking for instructional materials that will get their students to the standards are not likely to find them. All students suffer from this lack of even the most rudimentary coordination of the instructional system, but the students likely to suffer the most from these failings are those from the least advantaged backgrounds.

4. *The Political Accountability Model.* This model is only a slight variant of the education accountability model, but it is a distinction with a big difference. All during the 1980s and much of the 1990s, people in positions of political leadership were providing ever-increasing funding levels for public education, in anticipation of commensurate improvements in educational achievement. Funding levels went up, but achievement did not, causing their blood pressure to rise. They saw this accountability model as the very formula needed to provide strong incentives to educators to produce results. What was important to them was the design of the incentives. The quality of the standards and the assessments used was not the focus of their interest.

As 2002 begins, this political accountability model is in the ascendancy. What is causing the backlash is the absence in this model of crucial components of the other three models. One is standards and assessments that embody a thinking curriculum, a curriculum that good teachers would be happy to teach (in the same way that they are happy to teach to the Advanced Placement standards and assessments). Another is sound, thoughtful curriculum frameworks, matched to the standards, and internationally benchmarked, that specify a short list of topics to be taught at each grade level in the core courses in the curriculum.

A third missing component is a strong supply of instructional materials that can plausibly be used to get students from many different starting points to the new standards. Another is powerful professional development, training, and technical assistance that will enable school faculties everywhere to succeed at getting their students to the standards. A fifth is the kind of authority that school principals and faculties need if they are to be held responsible for the quality of their work. And, not least important, missing resources are needed by schools to buy the high-quality assessments, instructional materials, technical assistance, and training they will need to do the job. . . .

NOTES AND QUESTIONS

1. The debate about state standards has been quite vigorous for some time and contains several issues including the philosophical and the political. What policy arguments are implicated in this debate? Politically, schools historically have been locally managed. State regulation often has been seen as intrusive. Consequently, federal intrusion simply complicates matters further adding another layer of bureaucracy. Thus, on the one hand, politically, government intervention dilutes historic local controls. On the other hand, state and federal intervention offer the promise of additional resources for local school boards.

Shouldn't local schools, indeed individual teachers and schools, let alone local school boards, have the authority and obligation to test students according to their best judgment? Further, should that test be used to measure an individual student's ability for the purpose of improving that student's education rather than for larger statistical purposes? Then again, how can we measure a school's, or a district's, or a state's or our nation's educational situation without reliable testing data? These philosophical and political arguments just touch the surface of the debate.

2. Testing and standards have generated significant debate in this country for many years as the readings alone indicate. Not surprisingly, language has been critical in these debates. Should the tests be called achievement tests? Proficiency tests? Academic assessments? How do these labels differ?

3. If we correctly characterize the above debate about standards as involving differing philosophical, political and policy views, it is also worth noting that teachers also had distinct views about the substance of standards. As Diane Ravitch, a former Assistant Secretary for education research in the U.S. Department of Education writes the proposed national standards in history, English, mathematics, reading and language were hotly contested over how to properly teach a specific subject, their rigor, the pedagogical theories behind them or their political rather than educational content. Her conclusion clearly indicates her preference:

> In the debates about standards, the concept of knowledge was constantly under attack. Efforts to define which knowledge should be taught and tested opened up schisms among academics, who made their reputation (and living) by arguing whether knowledge was real, valid, particular, universal, relevant, or the privileged property of some elite group. Schools and the writers of state standards avoided such battles by focusing only on skills and bypassing any definition of what knowledge was important for students to master. In the early decades

of the century, progressives had derided the knowledge taught in school as useless or aristocratic; late-twentieth-century critics called it arbitrary or trivial. The counter-argument, however, remains valid: Knowledge is power, and whose who have it control the debate and ultimately control the levers of power in society. A democratic system of education, as Lester Frank Ward wrote a century earlier, disseminates knowledge as broadly as possible throughout society.

In the 1990s, despite the din of ideological combat, most states engaged in setting academic standards, assessing what students knew, and developing strategies to improve learning, especially for those who had fallen behind. Students of all racial backgrounds responded to the new demands by taking more advanced academic courses in subjects such as science and mathematics; the proportion of high school graduates who enrolled in an academic (as opposed to a general or vocational) program grew from 42 percent in 1982 to 69 percent by 1994.[76]

4. Researchers at the Civil Rights Project at Harvard University are critical of high stakes testing for several reasons including a negative racial impact. Their research indicates: high-stakes, high-standards tests do not have a markedly positive effect on teaching and learning in the classroom; high-stakes tests do not motivate the unmotivated; contrary to popular belief, "authentic" forms of high-stakes assessments are not a more equitable way to assess the progress of students who differ by race, culture, native language, or gender; and high-stakes testing programs have been shown to increase high school dropout rates, particularly among minority student populations.[77] Perhaps of even more concern are the findings of a recent study of 29 comprehensive school reforms, which reports that, while promising, only three indicate improvement in student achievement.[78]

5. A December 2002 study by the Education Policy Studies Laboratory of Arizona State University concludes that such testing does not improve achievement. The executive summary states:

> Based on data from 28 states, there is scant evidence to support the proposition that high-stakes tests—including high-stake high school graduation exams—increase student achievement. The effects of state mandated high-stakes tests on student achievement were established by evaluating student performance on tests that assess the same curriculum domains as are covered by a state's own high-stakes tests. These other independent measures of student achievement included the National Assessment of Educational Progress (NAEP), American College Test (ACT), Scholastic Aptitude Test (SAT), and Advanced Placement (AP) assessments.

---

[76] D. RAVITCH, LEFT BACK: A CENTURY OF FAILED SCHOOL REFORMS 450 (2000).

[77] Madaus & Clarke, *The Adverse Impact of High-Stakes Testing on Minority Students* in RAISING STANDARDS OR RAISING BARRIERS? INEQUALITY AND HIGH-STAKES TESTING IN PUBLIC EDUCATION 85, 86 (Madaus & Clarke eds. 2001).

[78] Boorman, Hewes, Overman & Brown, *Comprehensive School Reform and Student Achievement: A Meta-Analysis* (Nov. 2002). This report is published by the Center for Research on the Education of Students Placed at Risk of Johns Hopkins University. The report is available from: www.csos.jhu.edu.

State-by-state analyses of scores and participation rates for the NAEP, ACT, SAT, and AP (see appendix) reveal that after a state implements high-stake tests, nothing much happens on other measures of the same domain. We found that after high-stakes were attached to tests, grade 4 math achievement decreased. Grade 8 math achievement slightly increased and grade 4 reading achievement stayed the same. The states that have used high-stakes tests, in some cases for more than the past decade, have continued to perform much like the rest of the nation after writing high-stakes tests into their testing policies.

The study concludes from the data that the implementation of high school graduation exams results in a decrease in academic achievement. It was found that after high-stakes graduation exams were implemented, ACT, SAT, and AP scores declined. No comment is made here on the appropriateness of these tests as measures of the outcomes of schooling or as predictors of college performance. That is a separate issue. These tests do claim, however, to measure some of the same domain as do high school graduation examinations. Our analyses suggest that high-stakes tests may inhibit the academic achievement of students, not foster their academic growth, on these different and independent measures of student achievement.

Although test scores on state-administered tests usually increase after high-stakes testing policies are implemented, the evidence presented here suggests that students are learning only the content and item forms of the state-administered test. Training in taking state mandated high-stakes tests appear to work, that is, scores on the tests do go up. Such training, however, does not appear to have any meaningful carryover effect when assessment of student learning is made on the independent measures of achievement that we used.[79]

6. Theodore Sizer, who is chairman of the Coalition of Essential Schools at Brown University, objects to nationalized testing because it weakens local control of education. Sizer asks:

Who sets the standards and by what right? Who in this democracy, elected or appointed, shall be qualified to speak for parents, students, and school people? How can we insure that all constituencies are accommodated by a unitary group of "expert" examiners?[80]

Is this a serious problem? What is the basis of local control of schools? Is that basis challenged by a standardized examination, which measures how well a student knows algebra?

7. Are standardized tests a better solution than vouchers? Why or why not? Or are such tests complimentary to a system of vouchers? Will parents be able

---

[79] Amrein and Berliner, The Impact of High-Stakes Tests on Student Academic Performance: An Analysis of NAEP Results in States with High-Stakes Tests and ACT, SAT, and AP Test Results in States with High School Graduation Exams (2002). *See also*, G. Winter, More Schools Rely on Tests, But Big Study Raises Doubts, N.Y. TIMES, December 28, 2003 at A1.

[80] Sizer, *A Test of Democracy*, N.Y. TIMES, Jan. 30, 1992, at A15.

to judge the quality of a school in a choice program without standardized testing information?[81]

C. EQUALITY IN SCHOOL SPENDING

While all states provide free public education, the amount of public support typically differs depending on where students live. The reason is that education is supported by a combination of state and local taxes, and most localities rely on property taxes for local support. The amount of money that a local district can raise by property taxes depends on the wealth of the district. As a result, if state support is the same for every district, the amount spent on each pupil will vary depending on the wealth of the school district. Recognizing this problem, state legislatures have generally given more support to poorer school districts than richer ones. Nevertheless, substantial differences in the amount of money spent per pupil still exist in many states.

The issue of the legality of funding disparities has been litigated in about two-thirds of the states. These lawsuits raise an important issue concerning free public education: What constitutional obligation, if any, does a state have under its constitution to provide educational opportunities for all students? This issue implicates another, related question: Is the quality of a student's educational experience a product of the amount of money a state spends? Put another way, does money matter? This section considers these issues and one more—the fact that the public schools in urban areas remain heavily segregated nearly 50 years after *Brown v. Board of Education*. As will be discussed, this segregation is related to the school finance issue.

1. CONSTITUTIONAL OBLIGATIONS

In *San Antonio Indep. Sch. Dist. v. Rodriguez,* 411 U.S. 1 (1973), the United States Supreme Court held that the unequal financing of public schools in Texas was not a violation of the Equal Protection Clause of the United States Constitution. The basis of the Supreme Court's decision was that education is not among the rights afforded explicit Constitutional protection. By comparison, every state constitution contains an education clause that generally requires the state legislature to establish a system of free public education.[82] A number of state supreme courts have held that their respective state constitutions obligate the state to equalize spending for education. We offer a series of decisions from Ohio to indicate the nature of these decisions and the difficulty of their implementation.

---

[81] *See* Mosle, *The Answer Is National Standards,* THE NEW YORK TIMES MAGAZINE, Oct. 27, 1996, at 47 ("Choice, however, makes no sense without standards, for how can parents choose without a means to compare schools?").

[82] McUsic, *The Use of Education Clauses in School Finance Litigation,* 28 HARV. J. ON LEGIS. 307, 311 (1991).

SAN ANTONIO INDEPENDENT SCHOOL DISTRICT v. RODRIGUEZ

411 U.S. 1 (1973)

MR. JUSTICE POWELL delivered the opinion of the Court.

This suit attacking the Texas system of financing public education was initiated by Mexican-American parents whose children attend the elementary and secondary schools in the Edgewood Independent School District, an urban school district in San Antonio, Texas. . . .

The school district in which appellees reside, the Edgewood Independent School District, has been compared throughout this litigation with the Alamo Heights Independent School District. This comparison between the least and most affluent districts in the San Antonio area serves to illustrate the manner in which the dual system of finance operates and to indicate the extent to which substantial disparities exist despite the State's impressive progress in recent years. Edgewood is one of seven public school districts in the metropolitan area. Approximately 22,000 students are enrolled in its 25 elementary and secondary schools. The district is situated in the core-city sector of San Antonio in a residential neighborhood that has little commercial or industrial property. The residents are predominantly of Mexican-American descent: approximately 90% of the student population is Mexican-American and over 6% is Negro. The average assessed property value per pupil is $5,960—the lowest in the metropolitan area—and the median family income ($4,686) is also the lowest. . . . [The combination of local and state support for each pupil in this district totaled $248.]

Alamo Heights is the most affluent school district in San Antonio. Its six schools, housing approximately 5,000 students, are situated in a residential community quite unlike the Edgewood District. The school population is predominantly "Anglo," having only 18% Mexican-Americans and less than 1% Negroes. The assessed property value per pupil exceeds $49,000, and the median family income is $8,001. . . . [The combination of local and state support in this district totaled $558 per student.] . . .

Texas virtually concedes that its historically rooted dual system of financing education could not withstand the strict judicial scrutiny that this Court has found appropriate in reviewing legislative judgments that interfere with fundamental constitutional rights or that involve suspect classifications. If, as previous decisions have indicated, strict scrutiny means that the State's system is not entitled to the usual presumption of validity, that the State rather than the complainants must carry a "heavy burden of justification," that the State must demonstrate that its educational system has been structured with "precision," and is "tailored" narrowly to serve legitimate objectives and that it has selected the "less drastic means" for effectuating its objectives, the Texas financing system and its counterpart in virtually every other State will not pass muster. . . .

In *Brown v. Board of Education,* 347 U.S. 483 (1954), a unanimous Court recognized that "education is perhaps the most important function of state and local governments.". . . But the importance of a service performed by the

State does not determine whether it must be regarded as fundamental for purposes of examination under the Equal Protection Clause. . . .

. . . [T]he key to discovering whether education is "fundamental" is not to be found in comparisons of the relative societal significance of education as opposed to subsistence or housing. Nor is it to be found by weighing whether education is as important as the right to travel. Rather, the answer lies in assessing whether there is a right to education explicitly or implicitly guaranteed by the Constitution.

Education, of course, is not among the rights afforded explicit protection under our Federal Constitution. Nor do we find any basis for saying it is implicitly so protected. . . .

. . . While it is no doubt true that reliance on local property taxation for school revenues provides less freedom of choice with respect to expenditures for some districts than for others, the existence of "some inequality" in the manner in which the State's rationale is achieved is not alone a sufficient basis for striking down the entire system. It may not be condemned simply because it imperfectly effectuates the State's goals. Nor must the financing system fail because, as appellees suggest, other methods of satisfying the State's interest, which occasion "less drastic" disparities in expenditures, might be conceived. Only where state action impinges on the exercise of fundamental constitutional rights or liberties must it be found to have chosen the least restrictive alternative. . . .

Moreover, if local taxation for local expenditures were an unconstitutional method of providing for education then it might be an equally impermissible means of providing other necessary services customarily financed largely from local property taxes, including local police and fire protection, public health and hospitals, and public utility facilities of various kinds. We perceive no justification for such a severe denigration of local property taxation and control as would follow from appellees' contentions. It has simply never been within the constitutional prerogative of this Court to nullify statewide measures for financing public services merely because the burdens or benefits thereof fall unevenly depending upon the relative wealth of the political subdivisions in which citizens live.

DEROLPH v. STATE OF OHIO (*DEROLPH I*)
78 Ohio St.3d 193 (1997)

FRANCIS E. SWEENEY, SR., JUSTICE. . . .

Ohio's statutory scheme for financing public education is complex. At the heart of the present controversy is the School Foundation Program (R.C. Chapter 3317) for allocation of state basic aid and the manner in which the allocation formula and other school funding factors have caused or permitted to continue vast wealth-based disparities among Ohio's schools, depriving many of Ohio's public school students of high quality educational opportunities.

According to statute, the revenue available to a school district comes from two primary sources: state revenue, most of which is provided through the School Foundation Program, and local revenue, which consists primarily of locally voted school district property tax levies. Federal funds play a minor role in the financing scheme. Ohio relies more on local revenue than state revenue, contrary to the national trend. . . .

In urging this court to strike the statutory provisions relating to Ohio's school financing system, appellants argue that the state has failed in its constitutional responsibility to provide a thorough and efficient system of public schools. We agree. . . .

The dissent believes that we rely too heavily upon anecdotal evidence to support our holding that the current system is unconstitutional. Glaringly absent from the dissenting opinion, however, is any consideration of the massive evidence presented to us. There is one simple reason for this noticeable omission. The facts are fatal to the dissent. . . .

The results of this study were published in the 1990 Ohio Public School Facility Survey. The survey identified a need for $10.2 billion in facility repair and construction.

Among its findings, the survey determined that one-half of Ohio's school buildings were fifty years old or older, and fifteen percent were seventy years old or older. A little over half of these buildings contained satisfactory electrical systems; however, only seventeen percent of the heating systems and thirty-one percent of the roofs were deemed to be satisfactory. Nineteen percent of the windows and twenty-five percent of the plumbing and fixtures were found to be adequate. Only twenty percent of the buildings had satisfactory handicapped access. A scant thirty percent of the school facilities had adequate fire alarm systems and exterior doors. . . . [The opinion continues to catalogue the poor conditions including the hospitalization of students for carbon monoxide poisoning due to a faulty heating system, the failure to remove asbestos from schools, the lack of school cafeterias, band rooms and other specialized rooms, the lack of handicap accessibility, and falling plaster and crawling cockroaches.]

Obviously, state funding of school districts cannot be considered adequate if the districts lack sufficient funds to provide their students a safe and healthy learning environment.

In addition to deteriorating buildings and related conditions, it is clear from the record that many of the school districts throughout the state cannot provide the basic resources necessary to educate our youth. For instance, many of the appellant school districts have insufficient funds to purchase textbooks and must rely on old, outdated books. For some classes, there were no textbooks at all. For example, at Southern Local during the 1992-1993 school year, none of the students in a Spanish I class had a textbook at the beginning of the year. Later, there was a lottery for books. Students who picked the lucky numbers received a book.

The accessibility of everyday supplies is also a problem, forcing schools to ration such necessities as paper, chalk, art supplies, paper clips, and even toilet paper. A system without basic instructional materials and supplies can hardly constitute a thorough and efficient system of common schools throughout the state as mandated by our Constitution.

Additionally, many districts lack sufficient funds to comply with the state law requiring a district-wide average of no more than twenty-five students for each classroom teacher. . . .

The curricula in the appellant school districts are severely limited compared to other school districts and compared to what might be expected of a system designed to educate Ohio's youth and to prepare them for a bright and prosperous future. . . .

None of the appellant school districts is financially able to keep up with the technological training needs of the students in the districts. The districts lack sufficient computers, computer labs, hands-on computer training, software, and related supplies to properly serve the students' needs. In this regard, it does not appear likely that the children in the appellant school districts will be able to compete in the job market against those students with sufficient technological training.

Lack of sufficient funding can also lead to poor academic performance. Proficiency tests are a method of measuring education. The ninth grade proficiency test was designed to measure that body of knowledge pupils are expected to have mastered by the ninth grade. Passage of the ninth grade proficiency test is required before a student may receive a high school diploma. As of the fall of 1993, thirty-two out of ninety-nine seniors at Dawson-Bryant had not passed all parts of the ninth grade proficiency test. This means that nearly one-third of the senior class had not met basic graduation requirements. The district did not have enough money to pay tutors to assist these students. Poor performance on the ninth grade proficiency tests is further evidence that these schools lack sufficient funds with which to educate their students. . . .

All the facts documented in the record lead to one inescapable conclusion— Ohio's elementary and secondary public schools are neither thorough nor efficient. The operation of the appellant school districts conflicts with the historical notion that the education of our youth is of utmost concern and that Ohio children should be educated adequately so that they are able to participate fully in society. Our state Constitution was drafted with the importance of education in mind. In contrast, education under the legislation being reviewed ranks miserably low in the state's priorities. In fact, the formula amount is established after the legislature determines the total dollars to be allocated to primary and secondary education in each biennial budget. Consequently, the present school financing system contravenes the clear wording of our Constitution and the framers' intent. . . .

We recognize that disparities between school districts will always exist. By our decision today, we are not stating that a new financing system must provide equal educational opportunities for all. In a Utopian society, this lofty goal would be realized. We, however, appreciate the limitations imposed upon us. Nor do we advocate a "Robin Hood" approach to school financing reform. We are not suggesting that funds be diverted from wealthy districts and given to the less fortunate. There is no "leveling down" component in our decision today.

Moreover, in no way should our decision be construed as imposing spending ceilings on more affluent school districts. School districts are still free to augment their programs if they choose to do so. However, it is futile to lay the entire blame for the inadequacies of the present system on the taxpayers and the local boards of education. Although some districts have the luxury of deciding where to allocate extra dollars, many others have the burden of deciding which educational programs to cut or what financial institution to contact to obtain yet another emergency loan. Our state Constitution makes the state responsible for educating our youth. Thus, the state should not shirk its obligation by espousing cliches about "local control." . . .

We therefore hold that Ohio's elementary and secondary public school financing system violates Section 2, Article VI of the Ohio Constitution, which mandates a thorough and efficient system of common schools throughout the state. . . .

Although we have found the school financing system to be unconstitutional, we do not instruct the General Assembly as to the specifics of the legislation it should enact. However, we admonish the General Assembly that it must create an entirely new school financing system. In establishing such a system, the General Assembly shall recognize that there is but one system of public education in Ohio: It is a statewide system, expressly created by the state's highest governing document, the Constitution. Thus, the establishment, organization, and maintenance of public education are the state's responsibility. Because of its importance, education should be placed high in the state's budgetary priorities. A thorough and efficient system of common schools includes facilities in good repair and the supplies, materials, and funds necessary to maintain these facilities in a safe manner, in compliance with all local, state, and federal mandates.

We recognize that a new funding system will require time for adequate study, drafting of the appropriate legislation, and transition from the present scheme of financing to one in conformity with this decision. Therefore, we stay the effect of this decision for twelve months.

DEROLPH v. STATE OF OHIO (*DEROLPH II*)
89 Ohio St.3d 1 (2000)

ALICE ROBIE RESNICK, J.

. . . Our decision in *DeRolph I* required the General Assembly to respond to the untenable funding situation that had developed over time. Rather than allowing the *status quo* to continue, we realized that we could not, in good conscience, ignore the overwhelming evidence before us that our statewide system of public schools was simply not a thorough and efficient system. Significant changes had to be made in the way primary and secondary public education is funded, and if it took a judgment of this court to make those changes happen, then so be it.

We fully realize that no miraculous alternatives will suddenly appear and make the General Assembly's task any easier. In order to create a thorough and efficient system of statewide common schools, hard choices must be made. . .

Throughout its history, this case has presented two contradictory features that have made it difficult for all parties involved, including the courts of this state, to define the roles of those charged with solving the system's problems. On the one hand, the courts of this state are entrusted with the authority to determine whether a school-funding scheme complies with the Constitution. However, this court in *DeRolph I* did not require a specific funding scheme and did not instruct the General Assembly as to what legislation should be enacted, leaving it to the General Assembly to determine the specifics of the remedial legislation. . . . However, while it is for the General Assembly to legislate a remedy, courts *do* possess the authority to enforce their orders, since the power to declare a particular law or enactment unconstitutional must include the power to require a revision of that enactment, to ensure that it is then constitutional. If it did not, then the power to find a particular Act unconstitutional would be a nullity. As a result there would be no enforceable remedy. A remedy that is never enforced is truly not a remedy. . . .

II

A substantial amount of legislation has been enacted since *DeRolph I* was decided. . . .

The key initiatives include:

- The Ohio School Facilities Commission (renovations and repairs).
- Adjustments to the basic aid formula.
- Academic Accountability Bill (tests and district report cards).
- School District Fiscal Accountability Act (maintain budget reserves).
- New system for funding education.
- Capital appropriations bill for the biennium ending June 30, 2000.
- The biennial Education Budget Bill for FY00 and FY01 (first time that the state has created an education budget separate from its main operating budget).
- The Biennial Budget Bill for FY00 and FY01 (allocated state budget surplus revenue to SchoolNet Plus and for school facilities)
- Allocation of money received by the state pursuant to the Tobacco Master Settlement Agreement (school construction and repair).
- Ohio Reads initiative. . . .

In *DeRolph I,* this court held that one of the principal factors rendering the school-funding system unworkable was the state's heavy reliance on local property taxes to fund primary and secondary education. Our holding in *DeRolph I* did not say that local property taxes could not be a component of the state's school-funding formula, but rather that local property taxes could no longer be the primary means of providing for a thorough and efficient system of schools. For instance, in FY97, the state contributed approximately 43.8 percent to districts for school funding, excluding federal funds, while the local share was approximately 56.2 percent.

Property taxes are still the single most important source of funding for schools, and seventy percent or more of all property taxes levied are allocated to public schools. Overreliance on local property taxes was one of the factors that rendered the school-funding scheme deficient, yet this aspect of the former system persists in the state's current funding plan, *wholly unchanged*. The system's dependence on local property taxes has resulted in vast disparities among Ohio's six hundred eleven public school districts due to the differences in revenue generated by each. For instance, according to a memorandum prepared by Mike Sobul at the Ohio Department of Taxation for the 1995 fiscal year, a one-mill property tax on Class I real property produced $272.90 per student in the district with the highest property tax base and $13.34 per student in the district with the lowest. A system that places too much reliance on local property taxes puts property-poor districts at a disadvantage because "they must tax at significantly higher rates in order to meet minimum requirements for accreditation; yet their educational programs are typically inferior.". . .

Ohio's system of public education is a "statewide system." The state is responsible for funding an adequate education for all primary and secondary students who attend public schools. In our earlier opinion, this court informed the General Assembly that a school-funding scheme that relies too heavily on local property taxes for revenue would not satisfy the Thorough and Efficient Clause of the Ohio Constitution. Consequently, a revised funding scheme that increases reliance on local property taxes would not be "thorough and efficient." Thus, the General Assembly must avoid compounding the school-funding system's infirmities with new legislation that increases reliance on local property taxes. . . .

In light of the progress that the Governor and General Assembly have made, in some areas, thus far, and unwilling to reject *in toto* the sum of those efforts, we determine that the best course of action at this time is to provide the defendants more time to comply with Section 2, Article VI of the Ohio Constitution. We are confident that, given the additional opportunity presented by this extension of time, the General Assembly and the Governor will continue to deliberate over the many obstacles they face, and will continue to seek solutions to these complex problems. . . .

DEROLPH v. STATE (*DEROLPH III*)
93 Ohio St.3d 309 (2001)

MOYER, C.J.

. . . A climate of legal, financial, and political uncertainty concerning Ohio's school-funding system has prevailed at least since this court accepted jurisdiction of the case. We have concluded that no one is served by continued uncertainty and fractious debate. In that spirit, we have created the consensus that should terminate the role of this court in the dispute. . . .

In April 2000, Governor Taft created the Governor's Commission for Student Success, whose members included parents, educators, community leaders, and legislators. The commission conducted sixteen focus group discussions, polled one thousand Ohioans, and met with twenty-eight constituent groups to better understand Ohioans' thoughts and concerns about public education. In December 2000, the commission issued its report, entitled "Expecting More:

Higher Achievement for Ohio's Students and Schools." The report contained thirty-one recommendations to create a statewide system of academic performance standards, student and school assessments, and school accountability. In January 2001, legislation incorporating recommendations from the report was introduced as Senate Bill No. 1. The bill was enacted and signed into law on June 12, 2001. . . .

This legislative plan just enacted reflects a public policy decision that local school districts and boards of education ultimately are responsible for managing and allocating their financial resources so as not only to achieve the constitutionally mandated, statewide goal of providing all students a basic educational opportunity, but to achieve a second goal as well—the goal of helping individual students take advantage of that opportunity and thereby receive the lifelong benefits of education. . . .

In *DeRolph I,* this court's primary concern with the state's funding system was that it relied too heavily on local property taxes to fund a statewide system. The problem this creates, as articulated in *DeRolph II,* is that a system overly reliant on local property taxes will result in disparities between districts because the same tax effort in two different districts will produce different results. In defining overreliance, we stated that local taxes need not be totally abandoned, because equality is not constitutionally mandated. *DeRolph I.* Rather than completely rejecting property taxes, the majority stated that "property taxes can no longer be the *primary means* of providing the finances for a thorough and efficient system of schools." (Emphasis added.) Thus, some use of local property taxes is constitutionally permissible.

Therefore, disparity caused by a school-funding system that rests on the dual foundations of state support and local property tax revenues is unconstitutional only if the disparity is so dramatic that children in the poorest of our school districts are deprived of a basic educational opportunity, and a thorough and efficient distribution of funds need only ensure that each Ohio school district is financially able to offer an adequate education. . . .

As we recognized in *DeRolph I,* no system of school funding could address every inequality associated with reliance on local property taxes as a basis for school funding. While this court found in *DeRolph II* that the system then in place did not meet this court's prior mandate, we recognize that the General Assembly has made significant changes to the prior structure in order to reduce reliance on local property taxes. Through changes in gap aid, millage caps, changes in base cost formulation, and the parity aid program, for example, the current system established by H.B. 94, when fully implemented in accordance with this opinion, will reduce reliance on local property taxes to a constitutionally acceptable level by providing substantially more state aid to districts less able to generate local revenue. . . .

Despite the extensive efforts of the defendants to produce a plan that meets the requirements announced by this court, changes to the formula are required to make the new plan constitutional. . . . Because we have no reason to doubt defendants' good faith, we have concluded that there is no reason to retain jurisdiction of the matter before us. If the order receives less than full compliance, interested parties have remedies available to them.

DEROLPH v. STATE (*DEROLPH IV*)

97 Ohio St. 3d _____ (2002)

PFEIFER, J.

. . . We are aware of the difficulties that the General Assembly must overcome, and that is why we have been patient. The consensus arrived at in *DeRolph III* was in many ways the result of impatience. We do not regret that decision, because it reflected a genuine effort by the majority to reach a solution to a troubling constitutional issue. However, upon being asked to reconsider that decision, we have changed our collective mind. Despite the many good aspects of *DeRolph III*, we now vacate it. Accordingly, *DeRolph I and II* are the law of the case, and the current school-funding system is unconstitutional.

To date, the principal legislative response to *DeRolph I* and *DeRolph II* has been to increase funding, which has benefited many schoolchildren. However, the General Assembly has not focused on the core constitutional directive of *DeRolph I*: "a complete systematic overhaul' of the school-funding system. Today we reiterate that that is what is needed, not further nibbling at the edges. Accordingly, we direct the General Assembly to enact a school funding scheme that is thorough and efficient, as explained in *DeRolph I*, *DeRolph II*, and the accompanying concurrences.

We are not unmindful of the difficulties facing the state, but those difficulties do not trump the constitution. Section 2, Article VI of the Ohio Constitution states, "The general assembly shall make such provisions, by taxation, or otherwise, as, with the income arising from the school trust fund, will secure a thorough and efficient system of common schools* * *." This language is essentially unchanged from the initial report from the Standing Committee on Education at the Constitutional Convention of 1850–51. . . .

The Constitution of this state is the bedrock of our society. It expressly directs the General Assembly to secure a thorough and efficient system of common schools, and it does so expressly because the legislature of the mid-nineteenth century would not. . . .

We realize that the General Assembly cannot spend money it does not have. Nevertheless, we reiterate that the constitutional mandate must be met. The Constitution protects us whether the state is flush or destitute. The Free Speech Clause of the United States Constitution, the Equal Protection Clause of the United States Constitution, the Thorough and Efficient Clause of the Ohio Constitution, and all other provisions of the Ohio and United States Constitutions protect and guard us at all times. Harman Stidger, a delegate from Stark County, said, "If we should leave every thing to the Legislature, why not adjourn this Convention sine die, at once?" The same could be said of this court and the Ohio Constitution.

NOTES AND QUESTIONS

1. On what grounds does the Court in *Rodriguez* decide that education is not a fundamental interest? Does the Court adequately justify its conclusion that, even if education were such an interest, "that argument provides no basis for finding an interference with fundamental rights where only relative differences in spending levels are involved. . . ."? Did the majority determine that there was a rational basis for differences in expenditures? What is it?

2. School finance litigation has resulted in one of three outcomes in the states. In some states, such as Kentucky, the court has held that the state has no obligation to provide equal funding for the schools.[83] In other states, such as Maryland, the court has held that the state constitution, like the federal constitution, imposes no obligation of equal funding.[84] In other states, like New Jersey, the court has held that the state has an obligation to ensure minimum adequate funding for public schools, and it has ordered the state to increase the amount of spending for the poorest districts to bring them up to this adequate level.[85] Which position did the Ohio Supreme Court adopt?

3. Constitutional support for a "standards" claim, which argues that a state must provide a minimum level of education, is stronger than for an "equity" claim, which argues that a state must spend an equal amount on each pupil. The reason is that all but one state constitution require some minimal quality for public education, while only about one-half of the constitutions contain language that arguably requires equity in financing.[86] Nevertheless, both types of claims face difficulties. While some state constitutions specify an explicit and significant minimum standard for education, other constitutions use terms that refer only to some "bare minimum."[87] The equity claim is strongest in four states where the constitution actually uses the word "equality" in defining the state's obligation. Other state constitutions require either a "uniform" or an "efficient" public school system, which, as *Rose* and *Hornbeck* indicate, may or may not be interpreted as requiring equal financing.

4. In *DeRolph I* the court declared the Ohio system of school finance unconstitutional and directed the Ohio legislature to remedy the problem. The court also stayed its decision. Why? What directions did the court give the legislature? The court in *DeRolph II* criticizes the legislature for not solving the problem but is reluctant to do so itself. Why? Does *DeRolph II* provide any further guidance to the legislature? It appears that *DeRolph III* concluded the court's involvement with the litigation. However, after the opinion, the parties calculated the costs and then decided to attempt to negotiate a settlement. After the settlement conferences failed the litigants were back in court and the court issued *DeRolph IV*. After this opinion, local newspapers reported the governor saying in response "a $14 billion funding fix and a $10 billion school construction plan passed more than a year ago should be considered constitutional until a future court says otherwise."

5. If your supreme court declares the state's existing system of financing to be unconstitutional, how easy will it be for the legislature to come up with

---

[83] See Rose v. Council for Better Education, 790 S.W.2d 186 (Ky. 1989).

[84] See Hornbeck v. Somerset County Board of Education, 458 A.2d 758, 295 Md. 597 (Md. 1983).

[85] *See* Abbott v. Burke, 575 A.2d 359 (N.J. 1990).

[86] McUsic, *supra* note 82, at 319–26.

[87] *Id.* at 334–39.

a new equalization formula? Consider the following hypothetical suggested by Professor Yudof:[88]

> One school district raises $10,000 per child at a tax rate of $1 per $100 of property value. Another district raises only $1,000 at the same rate. If the legislature wishes to equalize spending, it could simply allocate $9,000 per pupil to the poorer school district. But what if the state does not have sufficient revenue to use this solution? What options does it then have?

One option is to "recapture" revenues from the affluent district and reallocate them to the poorer district. According to this plan, the first district may retain only $5,500 per student of what it raises, and the state government will recapture the remaining $4,500. The state will then reallocate the recaptured $4,500 per student to the second district. This allocation will produce a total expenditure of $5,500 ($4,500 + $1,000) per student in the poorer district. Professor Yudof points out that the advantage of this approach is that the "two districts will have equal expenditures at the same tax effort—exactly what would happen if, serendipitously, they had an identical number of students and exactly the same amount of property tax wealth."[89] What political problems is this solution likely to cause? Will these prevent this solution from being passed?

Assuming the legislature adopts the previous plan, it still has one more problem to consider: Will it permit the richer district to raise taxes and spend more money on its schools? For example, will the richer district be permitted to increase its property taxes to offset the loss in revenue to the state for equalization purposes? Would you advise the committee to cap the amount that the richer district can spend?

2. DOES MONEY MATTER?

Underlying the school finance litigation is the assumption that increased educational spending improve the quality of education. Does it? Consider the conclusions of Erik Hanushek, an economist at the University of Rochester:

> Research has demonstrated conclusively that, within the current organization and operation of schools, there is no consistent relationship between resources and student performance. Common policy arguments, used to justify the plea for added resources to school districts, simply are not supported by the evidence. Ignoring the evidence on the lack of relationship between resources and performance is likely to lead to policies that increase the level of inefficiency without increasing student performance. History indicates that while some districts might use the funds effectively, other districts will probably use them ineffectively—leading to little or no aggregate improvement in education quality from increased funding.[90]

---

[88] See Yudof, *School Finance Reform: Don't Worry, Be Happy?*, 10 REV. LITIG. 585 (1991).

[89] *Id.* at 587.

[90] Hanushek, *When School Finance "Reform" May Not Be Good Policy*, 28 HARV. J. ON LEGIS. 423, 454 (1991).

Richard Murnane, a Professor of Education at Harvard, responds that "it is simply indefensible to use the resources of quantitative studies of the relationship between school resources and student achievement as a basis for concluding that additional funds cannot help public school districts."[91] Murnane argues that existing studies do not adequately address serious questions of causation:

> For example, many school districts have relatively high expenditure levels, including state and federal compensatory education funds, *because* they serve students with low achievement levels. The same is true for the allocation of compensatory education funds among schools within a given school district. Given this situation, any comparison of achievement levels across districts with different expenditure levels per pupil, or across schools within the same district, lends little insight into any beneficial impact on student achievement.[92]

Murnane also points out that there is also a lack of positive results when private schools are studied:

> The results show that, just as with public schools, private schools pay for inputs that are not directly related to student performance, such as teaching experience beyond the first five years. The fact that private schools do this even when under strong competitive pressures makes it illogical to conclude that public schools are wasting money when they pay for experience.[93]

Thus, he concludes, "My point is not to argue that all school districts use resources wisely—some do not. . . . Instead, the point is that it is inappropriate to make judgments about whether school districts use resources wisely or not based solely on the results of educational production studies."[94]

Joshua Shenk offers a more mundane observation: "[I]f money doesn't matter, why do suburban schools districts spend ever-more money on schools—sometimes near $20,000 per-pupil-per-year?"[95]

Bradley Joondeph offers the summary of the state of empirical knowledge:

> . . . Despite substantial empirical research on the subject, the link between educational expenditures and student achievement remains tenuous, particularly for poor students. However, all else being equal, greater resources should improve the educational opportunities of disadvantaged students. But all things are obviously not equal, such as socioeconomic status, the educational achievement of one's parents, parental involvement and support, and the social class of one's peers. Research appears to demonstrate that increasing educational expenditures, if directed appropriately, can overcome some of these preexisting barriers to student achievement. Nonetheless, many studies

---

[91] Murnane, *Interpreting the Evidence on "Does Money Matter"?*, 28 HARV. J. ON LEGIS. 456, 456 (1991).

[92] *Id.* at 458.

[93] *Id.* at 459.

[94] *Id.*

[95] Shenk, *The Public School's Last Hurrah?*, THE WASHINGTON MONTHLY, Mar., 1996, at 16.

indicate that increasing a school's resources has little effect on educational outcomes. [96]

Professor Minow of the Harvard Law School recognizes that it is difficult to sort out the statistics concerning whether money matters, but she expresses the "hope that we do not lose sight of just one more frame around the problem. Let me call it sheer fairness." [97] She explains:

> Schools are not just means to ends, but also places where people spend their days. This means such disparities don't just look bad on paper; they feel bad in life. It is true that researchers find it difficult to measure the outputs of education, and even more difficult to correlate those outputs with inputs. However, equality of inputs is something we *can* measure. Equal inputs also actually affect current equality of daily school experiences. The fact that disparities in expenditures continue to disadvantage schools with predominantly minority student enrollments simply underscores the rank unfairness of the system and demonstrates the continuing legacy of racial segregation that inspired the initial school reform litigation. [98]

NOTES AND QUESTIONS

1. In light of the previous discussion, do you believe that money matters? Does the fact that suburban school districts spend more money than poorer, urban districts support the idea that money matters? Is Professor Minow arguing that states should equalize the financing of public education because it is a "fair" thing to do, regardless of whether more money will improve the schools? Or, is she arguing that we should not be overly concerned if analysts cannot prove that more money will lead to better education? Put another way, is the purpose of equalizing support for schools an economic one (maximize positive spillover effects), or a noneconomic one (fairness), or both?

2. There is some evidence that school finance litigation may have reduced the amount of money spent on education. One study found that five states (Arkansas, California, Connecticut, Washington, and Wyoming) narrowed spending gaps between rich and poor districts after school finance litigation, but state educational funding grew at a rate below the national average in four of the five states. [99] The study found three possible reasons why equalization and the growth of overall school funding may be negatively correlated. First, "As more local revenue is redistributed from wealthy to poor districts, the incentive for affluent school districts to maintain their pre-reform level of local taxation to support public education declines. . . ." Second, if reform creates the perception among parents in wealthy communities that the quality of their public schools has declined, more parents will send their children to private schools. Finally, centralizing funding for schools at the state level can reduce funding because, at the state level, education must compete with

---

[96] Joondeph, *The Good, the Bad, and the Ugly: An Empirical Analysis of Litigation-Prompted School Finance Reform*, 35 SANTA CLARA L. REV. 763, 769–70 (1995).

[97] Minow, *School Finance: Does Money Matter?*, 28 HARV. J. ON LEGIS. 395, 398 (1991).

[98] *Id.* at 399.

[99] Joondeph, *supra* note 96, at 773–74.

"several additional pressing social concerns, such as crime prevention, health care, and various other state responsibilities. . . ." In other words, a state may be compelled by budget priorities or a reduction in tax revenues to reduce the amount spent per pupil on education in order to make it easier to equalize expenditures. Moreover, the revenues from the tax sources on which states traditionally rely, income and sales taxes, "vary more widely with the health of the state's economy than does property tax revenue because real estate values are more stable than income or consumption. . . ."[100]

Do you find the previous reasons persuasive? Is it inevitable that school finance reform will lead to a decrease in state support? If school finance reform does lead to a decrease in overall state spending on education, is the effort self-defeating?

3. SCHOOL FINANCE AND RACE

Perhaps the most troubling aspect of school finance involves races. Racial segregation and education have plagued this country since its inception and we have yet to integrate our schools. In fact, it has been argued that our urban schools are more segregated now than in any other time in our history. It is also the case that the structure of school finance has entrenched the problem. To help us analyze this issue we present a brief excerpts from *Brown v. Board of Education* to set the stage for additional readings and commentary.

BROWN v. BOARD OF EDUCATION OF TOPEKA
347 U.S. 483 (1954)

MR. CHIEF JUSTICE WARREN delivered the opinion of the Court.

. . . Today, education is perhaps the most important function of state and local governments. Compulsory school attendance laws and the great expenditures for education both demonstrate our recognition of the importance of education to our democratic society. It is required in the performance of our most basic public responsibilities, even service in the armed forces. It is the very foundation of good citizenship. Today it is a principal instrument in awakening the child to cultural values, in preparing him for later professional training, and in helping him to adjust normally to his environment. In these days, it is doubtful that any child may reasonably be expected to succeed in life if he is denied the opportunity of an education. Such an opportunity, where the state has undertaken to provide it, is a right which must be made available to all on equal terms.

We come then to the question presented: Does segregation of children in public schools solely on the basis of race, even though the physical facilities and other "tangible" factors may be equal, deprive the children of the minority group of equal education opportunities? We believe that it does.

In *Sweatt v. Painter, supra,* in finding that a segregated law school for Negroes could not provide them equal educational opportunities, this Court relied in part on "those qualities which are incapable of objective measurement but which make for greatness in a law school." In *McLaurin v. Oklahoma State*

---

[100] *Id.* at 814–822.

Regents, supra, the Court, in requiring that a Negro admitted to a white graduate school be treated like all other students, again resorted to tangible considerations: ". . . his ability to study, to engage in discussions and exchange views with other students, and, in general, to learn his profession."

Such considerations apply with added force to children in grade and high schools. To separate them from others of similar age and qualifications solely because of their race generates a felling of inferiority as to their status in the community that may affect their hearts and minds in a way unlikely ever to be undone. The effect of this separation on their educational opportunities was well stated by a finding in the Kansas case by a court which nevertheless felt compelled to rule against the Negro plaintiffs:

> "Segregation of white and colored children in public schools has a detrimental effect upon the colored children. The impact is greater when it has the sanction of the law; for the policy of separating the races is usually interpreted as denoting the inferiority of the Negro group. A sense of inferiority affects the motivation of a child to learn. Segregation with the sanction of law, therefore, has a tendency to [retard] the educational and mental development of negro children and to deprive them of some of the benefits they would receive in a racial[ly] integrated school system."

Whatever may have been the extent of psychological knowledge at the time of *Plessy v. Ferguson*, this finding is amply supported by modern authority. Any language in *Plessy v. Ferguson* contrary to this finding is rejected.

We conclude that in the field of public education the doctrine of "separate but equal" has no place. Separate educational facilities are inherently unequal. Therefore, we hold that the plaintiffs and others similarly situated for whom the actions have been brought are, by reason of the segregation complained of, deprived of the equal protection of the laws guaranteed by the Fourteenth Amendment. . . .

———

Has the United States achieved the desegregation goal of *Brown v. Board of Education*? Not according to author Jonathan Kozol whose books are about his observations in primary education schools throughout the country.[101] Among the schools he has visited is The Mott Haven neighborhood of the South Bronx in New York where one teacher told him "I've been in this school for 18 years. . . . This is the first white student I *ever* taught." Kozol also notes that there are 11,000 elementary school students in Mott Haven, 26 of whom are white, for a segregation rate of 99.8% which "leaves two tenths of one percentage point as the distinction between legally enforced apartheid in the South of 50 years ago and socially and economically enforced apartheid in this New York City neighborhood today." Kozol writes about the failure of *Brown*. Indeed, he takes the position that the country has not even lived up to the "false" promise of *Plessy*:

---

[101] J. Kozol, Ordinary Resurrections: Children in the Years of Hope (2002).

In the spring of that year, which was four decades since the landmark court decision in *Brown v. Board of Education*, New York Newsday noted that the city's public schools were "the most segregated in the nation." For most black and Hispanic children in the city, said the paper, the idea of racial integration is "something to read about in history books," not something to be looked for in their daily lives in the New York City schools. . . .

In vast expanses of the South Bronx, in which residential segregation was encouraged and accelerated by the conscious policies of realtors, banks, and city planners starting in the 1950s, and where federal housing subsidies in recent decades have been used to underwrite a set of policies and practices that deepened pre-existing racial isolation, tens of thousands of black and Hispanic children never see white children in their schools or preschools, parks or playgrounds, churches, libraries, or stores. They don't *know* white children. White children don't know *them*. They're strangers to each other.

Unlike the children seen within the photographs of the old South, moreover, children of Mott Haven do not go to school with even a small number of children of the middle class–the children of schoolteachers, ministers, or doctors, for example. Their separation from the nation's mainstream, for this reason, is more absolute; and, as writer and former Clinton administration official Peter Edelman has observed, this form of segregation, while it's not required by law as in the old days in the South, "is even more pernicious."[102]

Complicating matters of race even more are the consequences of current school financing schemes, which are heavily dependent on local property taxes. The connection between race and wealth is direct as the next reading from The Civil Rights Project of Harvard University demonstrates.

GARY ORFIELD & JOHN T. YUN, RESEGREGATION IN AMERICAN SCHOOLS (JUNE, 1999) *

This report focuses primarily upon four important trends. First, the American South is resegregating, after two and a half decades in which civil rights law broke the tradition of apartheid in the region's schools and made it the section of the country with the highest levels of integration in its schools. Second, the data shows continuously increasing segregation for Latino students, who are rapidly becoming our largest minority group and have been more segregated than African Americans for several years. Third, the report shows large and increasing numbers of African American and Latino students enrolled in suburban schools, but serious segregation within these communities, particularly in the nation's large metropolitan areas. Since trends suggest that we will face a vast increase in suburban diversity, this raises challenges for thousands of communities. Fourth, we report a rapid ongoing change in the racial composition of American schools and the emergence of many schools with three or more racial groups. The report shows that all racial groups

---

[102] Id. at 32–33.

* Reprinted by permission.

except whites experience considerable diversity in their schools but whites are remaining in overwhelmingly white schools even in regions with very high non-white enrollments.

Though we usually think of segregation in racial and ethnic terms, it's important to also realize that the spreading segregation has a strong class component. When African-American and Latino students are segregated into schools where the majority of students are non-white, they are very likely to find themselves in schools where poverty is concentrated. This is of course not the case with segregated white students, whose majority-white schools almost always enroll high proportions of students from the middle class. This is a crucial difference, because concentrated poverty is linked to lower educational achievement. School level poverty is related to many variables that effect a school's overall chance at successfully educating students, including parent education levels, availability of advanced courses, teachers with credentials in the subject they are teaching, instability of enrollment, dropouts, untreated health problems, lower college-going rates and many other important factors. The nation's large program of compensatory education, Title I, has had great difficulty achieving gains in schools where poverty is highly concentrated. When school districts return to neighborhood schools, white students tend to sit next to middle class students and black and Latino students are likely to be next to impoverished students.

Therefore, while debates over the exact academic impact of desegregation continue, there is no question that black and Latino students in racially integrated schools are generally in schools with higher levels of average academic achievement than are their counterparts in segregated schools. Desegregation does not assure that students will receive the better opportunities in those schools—that depends on how the interracial school is run—but it does usually put minority students in schools which have better opportunities and better prepared peer groups. In a period in which mandatory state tests for graduation are being imposed, college admissions standards are rising, remedial courses in college are being cut back, and affirmative action has already been abolished in our two largest states, the harmful consequences for students attending less competitive schools are steadily increasing.

We are clearly in a period when many policymakers, courts, and opinion makers assume that desegregation is no longer necessary, or that it will be accomplished somehow without need of any deliberate plan. Polls show that most white Americans believe that equal educational opportunity is being provided. National political leaders have largely ignored the growth of segregation in the 1990s. Thus, knowledge of trends in segregation and its closely related inequalities are even more crucial now. For example, increased testing requirements for high school graduation, for passing from one grade to the next, and college entrance can only be fair if we offer equal preparation to children, regardless of skin color and language. Increasing segregation, however, pushes us in the opposite direction because it creates more unequal schools, particularly for low income minority children, who are the groups which most frequently receive low test scores. Educational policy decisions that do not take these realities into account will end up punishing students in inferior segregated schools, or even sending more children to such schools while simultaneously raising sanctions for those who do not achieve at a sufficiently high level.

In addition to its focus upon the trends of Southern resegregation, Latino student segregation and suburban segregation, this report documents basic national trends in enrollment and segregation for African-American students, Latinos, White and Asian students by region, by state, by community type—allowing comparison across the country. In the final section, we offer recommendations on how to reverse the trend of rising segregation, concluding that there has been very little national leadership on this issue for the past quarter century, recalling the positive steps taken in the 1960s and 1970s, and suggesting a number of steps that would support successful desegregation schools.

Introduction

As this century nears its end, we are a decade into the resegregation of our nation's schools. . . .

As the new century approaches we have become a far more racially and ethnically mixed nation, but in our schools, the color lines of increasing racial and ethnic separation are rising. There have not been any significant political or legal initiative to offset this trend for a quarter century. . . .

It has been 45 years since *Brown v. Board of Education* outlawed intentional segregation in the south, but a series of Supreme Court decisions in the 1990s helped push the country away from *Brown's* celebrated ideals and closer to the old idea of "separate but equal." Separate but equal was a concept articulated in the 1896 *Plessy v. Ferguson* Supreme Court decision that justified laws segregating schools and other institutions. Separate but equal was overturned six decades later by *Brown's* declaration that separate schools were inherently unequal. . . .

Plessy permitted generations of unequal education and prompted decades of legal struggle against it. The resegregation decisions of our present period may well have a similar impact on the next century since there is considerable evidence that the resegregated schools of the nineties are profoundly unequal. . . .

Segregation by Concentrated Poverty

Concentrated poverty is strongly linked to many forms of educational inequality. Black and Latino students, on average, attend schools with more than twice as many poor classmates as white students and Asians and American Indian students are about halfway in-between. . . .Latinos have the highest average percentage of impoverished classmates (46%), compared to 19% for whites. . . .

The 1996 data also show that 47% of the U.S. schools still had between 1–10% black and Latino students and that only one is 14 (7.7%) of those schools had half or more of their children living in poverty. On the other extreme, 8% of schools were intensely segregated with between 90–100% black and Latino Students. Of those schools, 87% of the children were impoverished.

In other words, the students in the segregated minority schools were 11 times more likely to be in schools with concentrated poverty and 92% of white schools did not face this problem. This relationship is absolutely central to explaining the different educational experiences and outcomes of the schools. A great many of the educational characteristics of schools attributed to race are actually related to poverty but the impacts are easily confused since in most metropolitan areas there are few if any concentrated poverty white schools while the vast majority of segregated black or Latino schools experience such poverty and all the educational differences that are associated with it. These issues are often confused, for example, in the statement by minority critics of desegregation who claim, correctly, that there is nothing magic about sitting next to a white child, but sometimes end up advocating policies that put their child in inferior concentrated poverty schools.

NOTES AND QUESTIONS

1. A more recent study by the Harvard Civil Right Project confirms the previous findings.[103]

> The racial trend in the school districts studied is substantial and clear: *virtually all* school districts analyzed are showing lower levels of inter-racial exposure since 1986, suggesting a trend towards resegregation, and in some districts, these declines are sharp. As courts across the country end long-running desegregation plans and, in some states, have forbidden the use of any racially-conscious student assignment plans, the last 10–15 years have seen a steady unraveling of almost 25 years worth of increased integration. From the early 1970s to the late 1980s, districts in the South had the highest levels of black-white desegregation in the nation; from 1986-2000, however, some of the most rapidly resegregating districts for black students' exposure to whites are in the South. Some of these districts maintained a very high level of integration for a quarter century or more until the desegregation policies were reversed.

2. Are voucher programs constitutional if they cause some schools to decline to the point where students do not receive a comparable, or even an adequate, education?[104] If, as the opponents predict, vouchers will result in the decline of the public schools, might vouchers be unconstitutional in those states where the courts have required some measure of educational quality?

3. Questions about race and wealth are deep, persistent and complicated. More troubling is the fact that answers do not seem to be forthcoming. Our focus on education is a bit narrower. Narrower still is the issue of school finance. For Jonathan Kozol equalization of financial contributions is a good start:

> New York City, at the time this book takes place in the late 1990s, spends about $8,000 yearly on each student overall, including special

---

[103] *See* FRAUKENBERG & LEE, RACE IN AMERICAN PUBLIC SCHOOLS: RAPIDLY RESEGREGATING SCHOOL DISTRICTS 4 (Aug. 2002).

[104] *See The Limits of Choice: School Chocie Reform and State Constitutional Guaranties of Educational Quality*, 101 HARV. L. REV. 2002 (1996).

education (which is disproportionately expensive), but considerably less than this—about $5,000—on each boy or girl like Elio or Ariel in ordinary classrooms of the public elementary schools in the South Bronx. The press is inconsistent and gives several different numbers, but this is the figure that was given to me by the Chancellor of Schools in New York City when we met one night at dinner during the same year that I met Elio—"$5,200, to be accurate," he said.

If you had the power to lift up one of these children in your arms and plunk him down within one of the relatively wealthy districts of Westchester County, a suburban area that borders New York City to the north, he would suddenly be granted public education worth at least $12,000 every year and he would also have a teacher who is likely to be paid as much as $20,000 more than what a teacher can be paid in the South Bronx. If you could take a slightly longer ride and bring these children to an upper middle class school district such as Great Neck or Manhassett on Long Island, Elio and Pineapple and Ariel would be in schools where over $18,000 are invested, on the average, in a child's public education every year.[105]

Do you agree or disagree about this impact of money on education and segregation?

4. Orfield & Yun offer a broader list of policy conclusions and recommendations. Some priorities for avoiding massive resegregation and improving interracial schools would include:[106]

1. active discussion and leadership on this issue by the President and Education and Justice Department leaders, who would explain trends and consequences and discuss constitutional issues. Initiatives of this sort by the Reagan Administration, together with a systematic re-staffing of the courts, have produced the current legal changes that exacerbate segregation.

2. leadership by the Justice Department and the Office of Civil Rights in defining standards for "unitary status" which specify how the various legal requirements of desegregation should be factually examines. Also important is the use of educational expertise to help the courts, which are often making quick and superficial judgments of complex issues, related to schools.

3. aggressive defense of remaining court orders.

4. requirements that charter schools receiving federal funds are desegregated in conformity with local and state desegregation plans and policies.

5. incentives in Title I plans that facilitate and encourage the transfer of low income students from concentrated-poverty low-achieving schools to schools that are more diverse. This is logical, since Title I research shows little success of Title I programs in concentrated poverty schools, which are usually segregated minority schools.

---

[105] *Ordinary Resurrections: Children in the Year of Hope* 45 (2000).

[106] G. Orfield & J. Yun, Resegregation in American Schools 33 (June, 1999), available at www.law.havard.edu/groups/segregation99/resegration99.html.

6. a policy of strong support for diverse suburban communities by the Education, HUD, and Justice Departments. This would include research on successful local practices that create integrated communities and vigorous enforcement against housing market and lending practices that spread segregation.

7. proposing a program of aid for human relations, staff training, and educational reform in the nation's thousands of multiracial schools. Such a program existed until the Reagan Administration eliminated it.

8. fill the vacant federal judgeships.

Which of these recommendations would you adopt and why?

Table of Cases

[Principal cases appear in solid capitals; References are to pages.]

[Principal cases appear in solid capitals; References are to pages.]

[Principal cases appear in solid capitals; References are to pages.]

[Principal cases appear in solid capitals; References are to pages.]

Table of Statutes

[References are to page numbers.]

[References are to page numbers.]

P

Public Law

Number

S

Surface Mining Control and Reclamation Act

Section

T

Toxic Substances Control Act of 1976

Section

U

United States Code

Title:Section

[References are to page numbers.]

United States Constitution
Article:Section

CALIFORNIA/CANAL ZONE
California Civil Code
Section

OHIO/OKLAHOMA
Ohio Revised Code
Section

INDEX

[References are to pages.]

[References are to pages.]